MICHELIN
Road Atlas of
Europe

First published 1988 by
The Hamlyn Publishing Group Limited
a division of the Octopus Publishing Group
Michelin House, 81 Fulham Road, London SW3 6RB

All maps © Michelin et Cie Propriétaires-Éditeurs 1988

Creation, graphic arrangement, text pages XII-XVI and Index
© The Hamlyn Publishing Group Limited 1988

First edition 1988
Third impression 1989

Mapping of Great Britain on pages 2-11
based upon Ordnance Survey mapping with the permission of
the Controller of Her Majesty's Stationery Office, Crown copyright
reserved.

Mapping of Northern Ireland on pages 12-13
based upon Ordnance Survey mapping with the permission of
the Controller of Her Majesty's Stationery Office, Crown copyright
reserved. Permit No 223.

Mapping of the Republic of Ireland on pages 12-15
based on Ordnance Survey by permission of the Government of
the Republic of Ireland. Permit No 4990.

In spite of the care taken in the production of this
book, it is possible that a defective copy may have
escaped our attention. If this is so, please return it to
your bookseller, who will exchange it for you, or contact
The Hamlyn Publishing Group Limited.

The representation in this atlas of a road is no evidence
of the existence of a right of way.

ISBN   Hardback 0 600 55642 5
ISBN   Softback 0 600 56020 1
ISBN   Deluxe edition 0 600 56761 3

Printed and bound in Spain by Cayfosa, Barcelona

MICHELIN
Road Atlas of
Europe

MICHELIN
Touring Services

PAUL HAMLYN

MICHELIN tyres and road maps have a reputation unsurpassed throughout Europe for quality and technical excellence in their respective fields.

It is appropriate that, at a time when the twelve member states of the European Economic Community are preparing for a single European market in 1993, Michelin should provide a new Road Atlas of Europe, compiled from their authoritative cartography, designed to meet the needs of the professional driver and holidaymaker alike.

There are over a hundred pages of mapping in this Atlas, showing the road network from North Cape to Gibraltar and from the Atlantic to the Black Sea. A full range of symbols show road categories and widths, towns and cities and places of interest as well as numerous other details, in keeping with Michelin's reputation for accuracy, legibility and up-to-date information.

Seventy town plans are included to help the driver negotiate built-up areas and the 'Driving in Europe' section provides details of national motoring regulations which are useful to know when crossing national frontiers. The comprehensive index locates about 30 000 towns and features.

The map showing 'Climates in Europe' will assist travellers in deciding which is the best season to visit a particular country.

The indispensable road mapping can be used in conjunction with other Michelin publications which provide complementary information on accommodation and sightseeing. The Red Guides, in particular the 'Europe' volume which contains a selection of hotels and restaurants in major European cities, and the Green Guides to the various countries of Europe are ideal companions for this Atlas.

Michelin are always happy to receive suggestions and comments from readers of their publications; taking these into account when preparing new editions can only improve their service to the public.

Thank you in advance and have a good journey!

MICHELIN maps and guides complement one another: use them together!

Contents

Inside front cover
Key to symbols

IV Michelin
VI **Route Planning**
X **Distances in Europe**
XII **Driving in Europe**

1 **Key to symbols**
2 **Western Europe** at a scale of 1: 1 000 000
78 **Greece** at a scale of 1: 700 000
94 **Scandinavia** at a scale of 1: 1 500 000
110 **Eastern Europe** at a scale of 1: 3 000 000

116 **Index of place names**

Inside back cover
Climates in Europe

Plans of cities and principal towns

118 ● Amsterdam
120 ● Antwerpen
86 ● Athina
122 ● Barcelona
123 ● Basel
124 ● Belfast
125 ● Berlin
126 ● Bern
127 ● Birmingham
128 ● Bologna
129 ● Bonn
130 ● Bordeaux
46 ● Bremen
130 ● Brugge
131 ● Bruxelles-Brussel
130 ● Budapest
136 ● Dijon

137 ● Dublin
137 ● Düsseldorf
138 ● Edinburgh
139 ● Essen
140 ● Firenze
141 ● Frankfurt a. M.
143 ● Genève
143 ● Genova
142 ● Gent
144 ● Glasgow
145 ● Göteborg
146 ● Den Haag
46 ● Hamburg
147 ● Hannover
107 ● Helsinki
149 ● Istanbul
152 ● København
153 ● Köln

155 ● Lausanne
156 ● Liège
157 ● Lille
158 ● Lisboa
159 ● Liverpool
160 ● London
163 ● Luxembourg
162 ● Lyon
164 ● Madrid
165 ● Manchester
33 ● Marseille
166 ● Milano
167 ● Monaco
168 ● München
170 ● Nantes
65 ● Napoli
171 ● Nice
172 ● Nürnberg

174 ● Oslo
69 ● Palermo
176 ● Paris
180 ● Porto
62 ● Roma
184 ● Rotterdam
188 ● Salzburg
190 ● Sevilla
192 ● Stockholm
193 ● Strasbourg
194 ● Stuttgart
196 ● Torino
197 ● Toulouse
199 ● Valencia
200 ● Venezia
203 ● Wien
205 ● Zürich

Ísafjörður

Akureyri

IS

REYKJAVÍK

1 765
△
Vatnajökull

Seyðisfjörður

Jan Mayen

CERCLE POLAIRE ARCTIQUE

SEA NORVÈGE

NORWEGIAN DE

MER

Hitra

Kristiansund

Ålesund

2 470
△
Glittertind

N

Bergen

Skien

Stavanger

Kristiansand

OCEAN

ATLANTIQUE

ATLANTIC

OCÉAN

Føroyar

Shetland

Orkney

Hebrides

Thurso

Skye

Inverness
Loch Ness
1 344
△ Ben Nevis

Aberdeen

Dundee

Glasgow

Edinburgh

NORTH SEA

Skagerrak

DK

Jylland

Londonderry

Belfast

Stanraer

Carlisle

Newcastle

MER DU NORD

Esbjerg

Galway

IRL

DUBLIN

Shannon

Man

IRISH SEA

Leeds

York

Liverpool

Manchester

Sheffield

Limerick

GB

Nottingham

St. George's Channel

Birmingham

Coventry

Norwich

Groningen

Ijsselmeer

NL

Bremen

Cork

Cardiff

Oxford

Cambridge

AMSTERDAM

Hannover

Den Haag

Weser

Southampton

LONDON

Thames

Rotterdam

Waal

Essen

Dortmund

Plymouth

Portsmouth

Dover

Brugge

Kassel

Land's End

Calais

Gent

Antwerpen

Düsseldorf

ENGLISH CHANNEL

Lille

Aachen

Köln

BONN

LA MANCHE

BRUSSEL
BRUXELLES

D

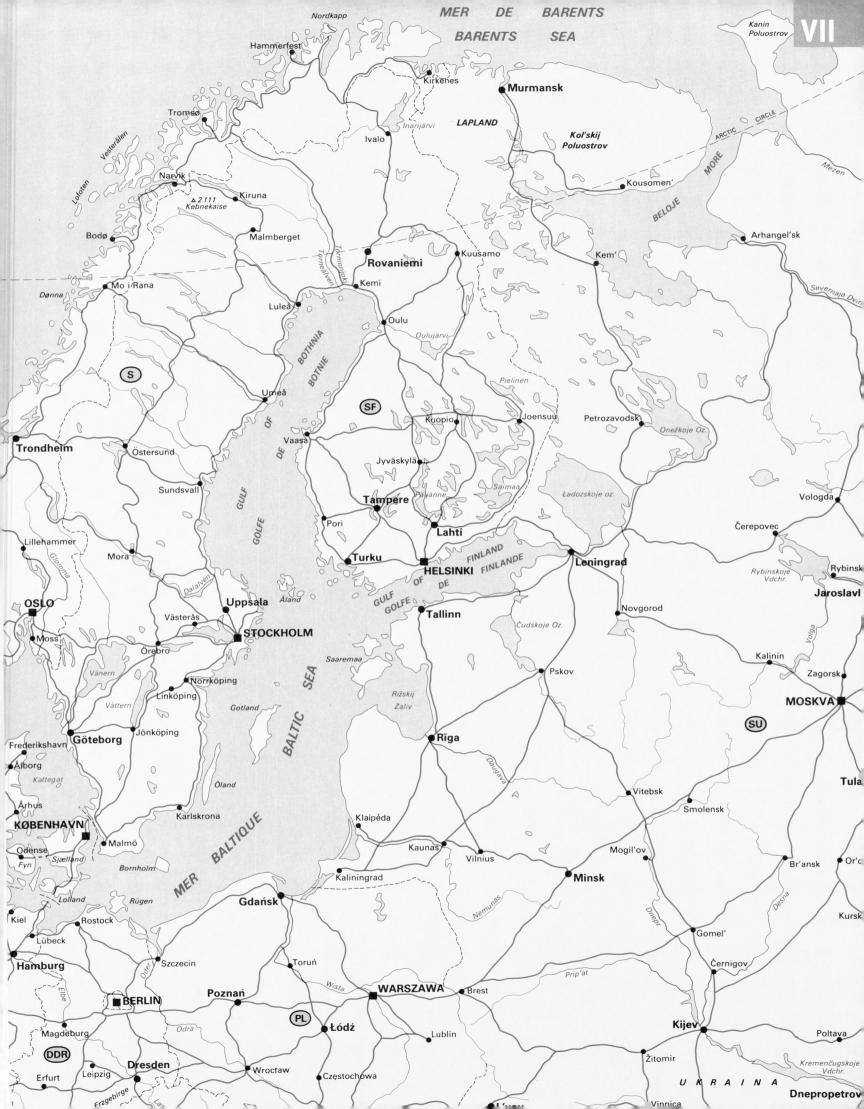

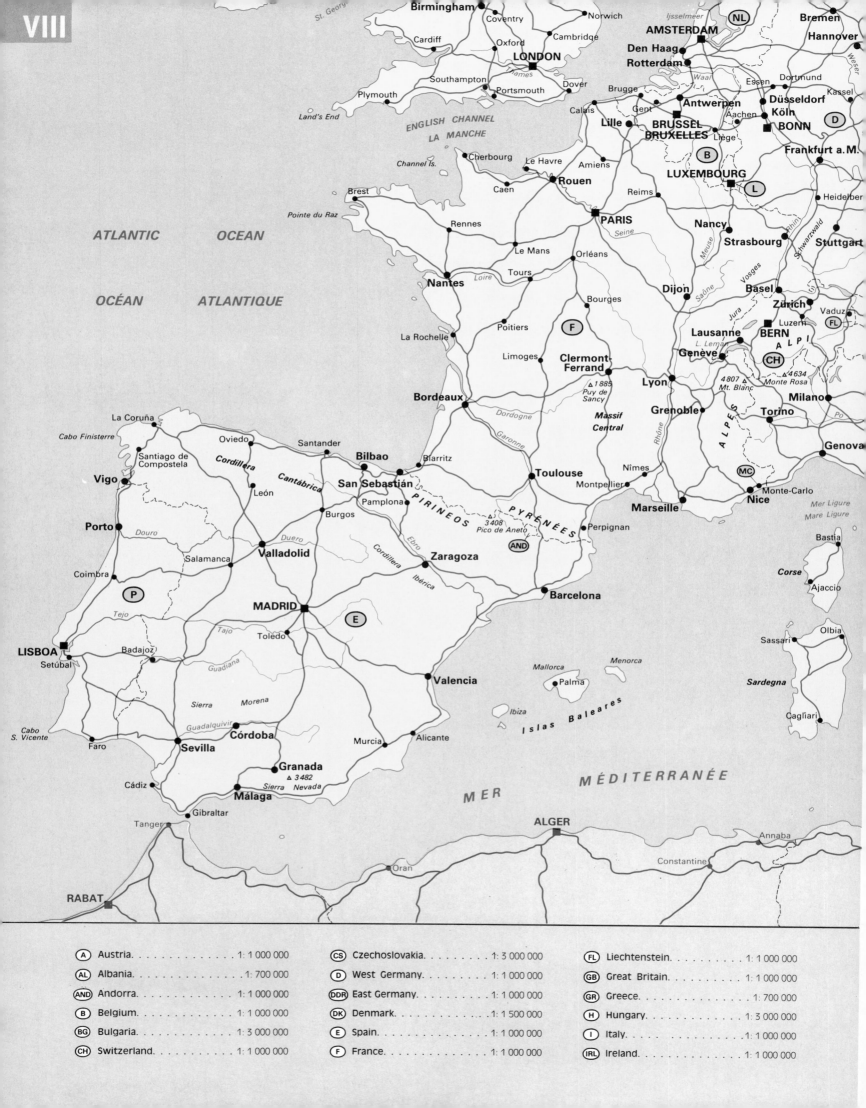

VIII

ATLANTIC   OCEAN

OCÉAN   ATLANTIQUE

ENGLISH CHANNEL
LA MANCHE

MER   MÉDITERRANÉE

MER
LIGURE
Mare Ligure

Ⓐ Austria. 1: 1 000 000	ⒸⓈ Czechoslovakia. 1: 3 000 000	ⒻⓁ Liechtenstein. 1: 1 000 000
ⒶⓁ Albania. 1: 700 000	Ⓓ West Germany. 1: 1 000 000	ⒼⒷ Great Britain. 1: 1 000 000
ⒶⓃⒹ Andorra. 1: 1 000 000	ⒹⒹⓇ East Germany. 1: 1 000 000	ⒼⓇ Greece. 1: 700 000
Ⓑ Belgium. 1: 1 000 000	ⒹⓀ Denmark. 1: 1 500 000	Ⓗ Hungary. 1: 3 000 000
ⒷⒼ Bulgaria. 1: 3 000 000	Ⓔ Spain. 1: 1 000 000	Ⓘ Italy. 1: 1 000 000
ⒸⒽ Switzerland. 1: 1 000 000	Ⓕ France. 1: 1 000 000	ⒾⓇⓁ Ireland. 1: 1 000 000

Map labels (selected):

BERLIN · Poznań · WARSZAWA · Brest · Černigov · Magdeburg · Elbe · Wista · Prip'at · Kijev · Poltava
DDR · Łódź · Lublin · Žitomir · Kremenčugskoje Vdchr.
Erfurt · Leipzig · Dresden · Wrocław · Odra · Częstochowa · UKRAINA · Dnepropetrovsk
Nürnberg · Plzeň · PRAHA · CS · Kraków · L'vov · Vinnica · Krivoj Rog
Regensburg · Brno · KARPATY · Tatry △ 2655 · Černovcy · Dnestr · Dneprr
Main · Donau · Augsburg · Linz · Košice · CARPATII · Iaşi · Kišin'ov · Cherson
München · WIEN · Bratislava · BUDAPEST · Cluj-Napoca · Odessa
Salzburg · Inn · Graz · H · Sibiu · Brašov · CARPATII
Innsbruck · A · ALPEN · △ Großglockner 3797 · Balaton · Duna · Moldoveanu 2543 · R
Bolzano · 2863 △ Triglav · Ljubljana · Pécs · Timişoara · Carpatii Meridionali · BUCUREŞTI · Constanţa
Padova · Trieste · Zagreb · Dráva · Novi Sad · MER NOIRE
Verona · Venezia · Rijeka · Tisza · Sava · Oltr · Dunärea · Ruse · BLACK SEA
Parma · Adige · YU · Drina · BEOGRAD · Dunäv · Varna
Bologna · Ravenna · Sarajevo · Stara Planina · Veliko Tårnovo
Pisa · RSM · Firenze · Dalmatska · Split · Dinara · 2376 △ Botev · Burgas
Siena · Perugia · MER ADRIATIQUE · Kota · Dubrovnik · Titograd · SOFIA · Plovdiv · Edirne · BG
APPENNINI · Gran Sasso 2914 · Pescara · ADRIATIC SEA · Skopje · Rodopi · Istanbul
V · ROMA · I · Bari · Drin · 2764 △ Korab · TR · Marmara Denizi
MER TYRRHÉNIENNE · Napoli · 1277 △ Vesuvio · Taranto · Durrës · TIRANË · Thessaloníki · Bursa
TYRRHENIAN SEA · AL · Ólimbos △ 2917 · Lárissa · AEGEAN SEA · Lésvos
Pindes · Vólos · Izmir
IONIAN SEA · Kérkira · GR · Évia
Palermo · Messina · Reggio di Calabria · Pátra · Kórinthos · ATHÍNA · MER ÉGÉE · Kikládes · Dodekánissa
Etna 3340 △ · Catània · Ionía · Nissiá · Pelopónissos · Ródos
Sicilia · MER IONIENNE · Kríti
TUNIS · Iráklio
Valletta · MEDITERRANEAN SEA
M

Distance chart — European cities (road distances in km). Diagonal labels, top to bottom: Amsterdam, Athina, Barcelona, Bari, Basel, Belfast, Beograd, Bergen, Berlin, Bilbao, Birmingham, Bordeaux, Brest, Brussel/Bruxelles, Bucureşti, Budapest, Clermont-Ferrand, Dublin, Dubrovnik, Edinburgh, Firenze, Frankfurt A. M., Genève, Göteborg, Hamburg, Hannover, Helsinki, Istanbul, Kijev, København, Köln, Leningrad, Lille, Lisboa, Liverpool, London, Luxembourg, Lyon, Madrid, Málaga, Marseille, Milano, Moskva, München, Nantes, Napoli, Nice, Nürnberg, Oslo, Palermo, Paris, Porto, Praha, Roma, Rovaniemi, Salzburg, Sevilla, Sofia, Stockholm, Strasbourg, Stuttgart, Thessaloniki, Torino, Toulouse, Tromsø, Trondheim, Valencia, Venezia, Warszawa, Wien, Zagreb, Zürich.

```
Athina:              2836
Barcelona:           1547 3090
Bari:                1971 2621 1792
Basel:               745 2466 1029 1226
Belfast:             1341 3874 2046 2690 1508
Beograd:             1718 1118 1972 1503 1348 2756
Bergen:              1817 4017 3178 3244 2187 3112 2899
Berlin:              669 2584 1853 1811 862 1906 1466 1463
Bilbao:              1424 3422 607 2124 1174 1755 2304 3196 1990
Birmingham:          782 3316 1487 2131 950 535 2198 2554 1348 1196
Bordeaux:            1081 3240 633 1942 831 1412 2122 2853 1647 334 853
Brest:               1098 3501 1242 2278 1096 1244 2383 2870 1664 965 686 622
Brussel/Bruxelles:   204 2792 1365 1777 551 1150 1674 1969 781 1229 591 886 903
Bucureşti:           2221 1238 2611 2142 1987 3259 639 3200 1711 2943 2701 2761 2886 2177
Budapest:            1393 1510 1952 1482 1073 2431 392 2372 883 2283 1873 2041 2058 1349 828
Clermont-Ferrand:    902 2752 648 1485 477 1337 1634 2636 1311 706 779 371 752 706 2273 1614
Dublin:              1053 3586 1758 2402 1220 165 2468 2824 1618 1467 247 1124 956 862 2971 2143 1049
Dubrovnik:           2024 1265 2049 1580 1425 2892 525 3204 1771 2381 2333 2199 2480 1970 1164 787 1711 2604
Edinburgh:           1289 3823 1994 2638 1457 251 2705 3061 1855 1703 484 1360 1193 1098 3208 2380 1286 416 2840
Firenze:             1391 2115 1075 720 646 2098 997 2664 1231 1407 1539 1225 1686 1197 1636 976 883 1810 1074 2046
Frankfurt A. M.:     446 2396 1318 1553 327 1549 1278 1864 566 1502 991 1159 1176 402 1781 953 776 1261 1583 1498 973
Genève:              885 2446 770 1203 259 1492 1328 2446 1121 1102 934 681 1080 703 1967 1307 310 1204 1405 1441 611 586
Göteborg:            1005 3205 2366 2432 1375 2300 2087 812 651 2384 1742 2041 2058 1157 2388 1560 1824 2012 2392 2249 1852 1052 1634
Hamburg:             441 2780 1802 2007 811 1736 1662 1384 289 1820 1178 1477 1494 593 2026 1198 1260 1448 1967 1685 1427 488 1070 572
Hannover:            386 2637 1659 1864 668 1623 1519 1527 288 1707 1065 1364 1381 498 2022 1194 1117 1335 1824 1572 1284 345 927 715 151
Helsinki:            1204 2640 2348 1397 2441 1422 1186 505 2525 1883 2182 2199 1316 1858 1030 1846 2153 1893 2390 1766 1101 1656 662 776 823
Istanbul:            2665 1171 2919 2450 2295 3703 947 3846 2413 3251 3145 3069 3330 2621 692 1339 2581 3415 1326 3652 1944 2225 2275 3034 2609 2466 2369
Kijev:               2017 2311 3114 2644 2187 3254 1336 2844 1383 3338 2696 2995 3012 2129 1073 1162 2636 2966 1861 3203 2138 1914 2339 2032 1670 1636 1146 489
København:           738 2938 2099 2165 1108 2033 1820 1079 384 2117 1475 1774 1791 890 2121 1293 1557 1745 2125 1982 1585 785 1367 267 305 448 795 2767 1765
Köln:                264 2579 1342 1714 488 1361 1461 1802 575 1440 803 1097 1114 211 1964 1136 802 1073 1766 1310 1134 189 747 990 426 292 1110 2408 1923 723
Leningrad:           1637 2973 2821 2779 1830 2874 1855 1619 938 2958 2316 2615 2632 1749 2625 1463 2279 2586 2326 2823 2199 1534 2089 1095 1209 1256 433 2041 1552 1228 1543
Lille:               283 2910 1308 1836 610 1046 1792 2055 849 1139 487 796 813 116 2295 1467 617 758 2088 994 1256 520 668 1243 679 566 1384 2739 2197 976 329 1817
Lisboa:              2322 4320 1285 3022 2072 2653 3202 4094 2888 907 2094 1232 1863 2127 3841 3181 1604 2365 3279 2601 2305 2400 2000 3282 2718 2605 3423 4149 4236 3015 2338 3856 2037
Liverpool:           971 3504 1676 2320 1138 416 2386 2742 1536 1385 165 1042 874 780 2889 2061 967 167 2522 365 1728 1179 1122 1930 1366 1253 2071 3333 2884 1663 991 2504 676 2283
London:              719 3252 1424 2068 886 722 2134 2490 1284 1133 196 790 622 528 2637 1809 715 434 2270 612 1476 927 870 1678 1114 1001 1819 3081 2632 1411 739 2252 424 2031
Luxembourg:          391 2637 1148 1560 334 1338 1519 1994 767 1290 779 947 964 218 1993 1165 608 1050 1758 1286 980 248 486 1182 618 484 1302 2466 2115 915 193 1735 334 2188
Lyon:                917 2559 630 1292 400 1415 1441 2548 1223 962 857 549 1003 735 2080 1421 178 1127 1518 1364 690 688 141 1736 1172 1029 1758 2388 2548 1469 711 2191 678 1860
Madrid:              1812 3760 686 2462 1562 2143 2642 3584 2378 397 1584 722 1353 1617 3281 2622 1094 1855 2719 2091 1745 1890 1440 2772 2208 2095 2913 3589 3726 2505 1828 3346 1527 658
Málaga:              2360 4086 1012 2788 2025 2691 2968 4132 2849 945 2132 1270 1901 2165 3607 2948 1644 2403 3045 2639 2071 2314 1766 3320 2756 2643 3384 3915 4110 3053 2376 3817 2075 634
Marseille:           1228 2621 493 1323 710 1727 1503 2859 1534 825 1168 643 1315 1046 2142 1483 454 1439 1580 1675 606 999 451 2047 1483 1340 2069 2450 2645 1780 1023 2502 989 1723
Milano:              1088 2128 973 878 343 1810 1010 2493 1040 1305 1251 1123 1398 894 1649 989 629 1522 1087 1758 298 670 323 1681 1117 974 1575 1957 2151 1414 831 2008 953 2203
Moskva:              2463 3169 3630 3306 2639 3700 2194 2313 1829 3784 3142 3441 3458 2575 1931 1918 3088 3412 2705 3649 2800 2360 2898 1789 2116 2082 1127 1347 858 2211 2369 694 2643 4682
München:             837 2063 1370 1224 399 1794 945 2018 585 1615 1236 1272 1421 769 1506 678 918 1506 1184 1743 644 397 599 1206 781 638 1120 1892 1744 939 580 1553 887 2513
Nantes:              887 3290 945 1923 847 1168 2172 2659 1453 669 609 326 296 692 2675 1847 452 880 2125 1116 1331 965 726 1847 1283 1170 1988 3119 2801 1580 903 2421 602 1567
Napoli:              1878 2602 1562 261 1133 2585 1484 3151 1718 1894 2026 1712 2173 1684 2123 1463 1370 2297 1561 2533 490 1460 1098 2339 1914 1771 2253 2431 2625 2072 1621 2686 1743 2792
Nice:                1387 2434 656 1136 658 1886 1316 2808 1355 988 1327 806 1474 1205 1955 1295 613 1598 1393 1834 419 985 472 1996 1432 1289 1890 2263 2457 1729 1146 2323 1148 1886
Nürnberg:            666 2171 1427 1391 436 1715 1053 1867 434 1668 1157 1325 1342 622 1556 728 885 1427 1351 1664 811 226 695 1055 610 467 969 2000 1759 788 409 1402 740 2566
Oslo:                1321 3521 2682 2748 1691 2616 2403 496 967 2700 2058 2357 2374 1473 2704 1876 2140 2328 2708 2565 2168 1368 1950 316 888 1031 690 3350 2348 583 1306 1123 1559 3598
Palermo:             2599 3322 2283 691 1853 3305 2204 3872 2439 2614 2747 2432 2893 2404 2843 2184 2091 3017 2281 3060 2635 2492 2974 3151 3346 2793 2341 3407 2464 3512
Paris:               504 2912 1091 1735 553 965 1794 2275 1069 922 407 579 596 308 2297 1469 399 677 1937 914 1143 587 521 1463 899 786 1604 2741 2417 1196 520 2037 219 1820
Porto:               2143 4141 1167 2843 1893 2474 3023 3915 2709 728 1915 1053 1684 1948 3662 3002 1425 2186 3100 2422 2126 2221 1821 3103 2539 2426 3244 3970 4057 2836 2159 3677 1858 314
Praha:               950 2154 1711 1596 720 1999 1036 1839 350 1952 1441 1609 1626 906 1361 533 1169 1711 1261 1948 1016 510 979 1027 665 603 859 1983 1389 760 693 1292 1024 2850
Roma:                1665 2389 1349 449 920 2372 1271 2938 1505 1681 1813 1499 1960 1471 1910 1250 1157 2084 1348 2320 277 1247 885 2126 1701 1558 2040 2218 2412 1859 1408 2473 1530 2579
Rovaniemi:           2483 4683 3844 3910 2853 3778 3565 2824 2129 3862 3220 3519 3536 2635 3866 3038 3302 3490 3870 3727 3330 2530 3112 1528 2050 2193 837 4512 2557 1745 3288 1005 2721 4760
Salzburg:            980 1932 1539 1172 536 1952 814 2161 728 1772 1393 1429 1578 927 1363 535 1076 1664 1052 1900 660 540 736 1349 924 781 1263 1761 1601 1082 723 1696 1045 2670
Sevilla:             2295 4117 1043 2819 2056 2626 2899 4067 2880 880 2067 1205 1836 2100 3638 2979 1577 2338 3076 2574 2102 2345 1797 3255 2691 2578 3415 3946 4141 2988 2311 3848 2010 417
Sofia:               2104 818 2358 1889 1734 3142 386 3285 1852 2690 2584 2508 2769 2060 420 778 2020 2854 765 3091 1383 1664 1714 2473 2048 1905 1808 561 1493 2206 1847 2241 2178 3588
Stockholm:           1368 3568 2729 2795 1738 2663 2450 1021 1014 2747 2105 2404 2421 1520 2751 1923 2187 2375 2755 2612 2215 1415 1997 497 935 1078 165 3397 2395 630 1353 598 1606 3645
Strasbourg:          634 2438 1110 1371 145 1450 1320 2076 751 1264 892 921 1077 439 1881 1053 568 1162 1559 1399 791 216 404 1264 700 557 1286 2267 2076 997 377 1719 545 2162
Stuttgart:           622 2302 1258 1404 267 1592 1184 2046 631 1413 1034 1070 1219 558 1745 917 716 1304 1423 1541 824 204 526 1234 670 527 1166 2131 1956 967 365 1599 676 2311
Thessaloniki:        2350 511 2604 2135 1980 3388 632 3531 2098 2936 2830 2754 3015 2306 727 1024 2266 3100 779 3337 1629 1910 1960 2719 2294 2151 2054 660 1800 2452 2093 2487 2424 3834
Torino:              1154 2263 779 997 409 1699 1145 2596 1157 1110 1140 864 1287 905 1784 1124 492 1411 1222 1647 395 736 252 1784 1220 1077 1692 2092 2286 1517 897 2125 961 2008
Toulouse:            1199 2994 388 1696 933 1611 1876 3082 1757 447 1053 245 853 1003 2515 1856 397 1323 1953 1560 979 1222 674 2270 1706 1563 2292 2823 3018 2003 1246 2725 914 1345
Tromsø:              3041 5241 4402 4468 3411 4336 4123 1893 2687 4420 3778 4077 4094 3193 4424 3596 3860 4048 4428 4285 3888 3088 3670 2570 2608 2751 1367 5070 3087 2303 3026 1535 3279 5318
Trondheim:           1865 4065 3226 3292 2235 3160 2947 717 1511 3244 2602 2901 2918 2017 3248 2420 2684 2872 3252 3109 2712 1912 2494 1394 1432 1575 949 3894 2892 1127 1850 1382 2103 4142
Valencia:            1892 3435 361 2137 1374 2391 2317 3523 2198 606 1832 771 1402 1710 2956 2297 993 2103 2394 2339 1420 1663 1115 2711 2147 2004 2733 3264 3459 2444 1687 3166 1653 924
Venezia:             1283 1878 1229 760 605 2072 760 2512 1079 1561 1513 1379 1660 1156 1399 739 891 1784 837 2020 254 891 585 1700 1275 1132 1614 1707 1901 1433 1026 2047 1215 2459
Warszawa:            1223 2188 2390 2066 1399 2460 1070 2050 589 2544 1902 2201 2218 1335 1506 678 1848 2172 1465 2409 1560 1120 1658 1238 876 842 352 2017 794 971 1129 785 1403 3442
Wien:                1150 1862 1833 1341 830 2188 744 2131 642 2141 1630 1798 1815 1106 1071 243 1370 1900 969 2137 835 710 1030 1319 957 951 924 1691 1309 1052 893 1357 1224 3039
Zagreb:              1337 1499 1591 1122 967 2375 381 2518 1085 1923 1817 1741 2002 1293 1020 350 1253 2087 618 2324 616 897 947 1706 1281 1138 1287 1328 1512 1439 1080 1720 1411 2821
Zürich:              831 2416 1058 1176 86 1594 1298 2267 852 1260 1036 917 1182 637 1816 988 597 1306 1375 1543 596 412 287 1455 891 748 1387 2245 2054 1188 573 1820 696 2158
```

Distances in Europe

Distances are calculated from centres and along the best roads from a motoring point of view - not necessarily the shortest

Example: **Luxembourg – Warszawa** 1321 km

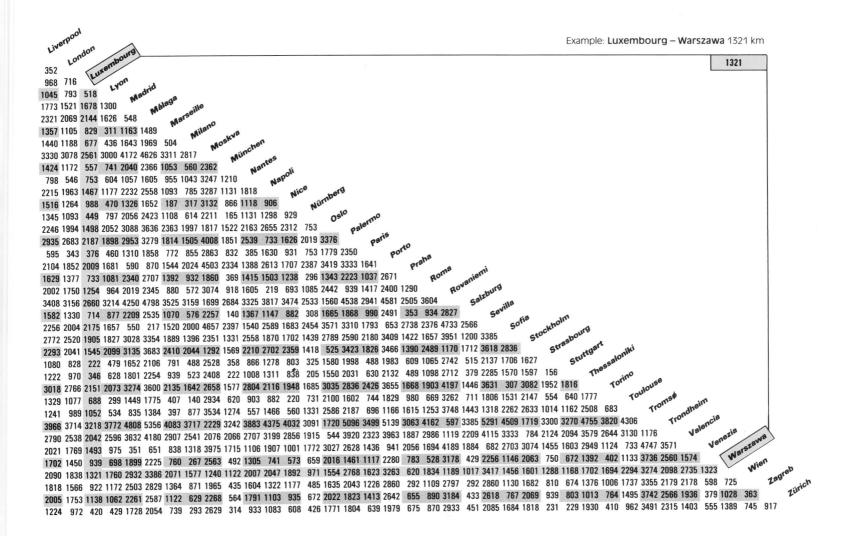

Driving in Europe

Introduction

The information panels which follow give the principal motoring regulations for all the countries included in this atlas; an explanation of the symbols is given below, together with some additional notes.

🔧 The name, address and telephone number of the national motoring organisation or organisations; the initials FIA and AIT indicate membership of the international touring associations, the Fédération Internationale de l'Automobile and the Alliance Internationale de Tourisme

◠ Speed restrictions in kilometres per hour applying to:

  �ōmotorways
  🔼 dual carriageways
  🔺 single carriageways
  🏙 urban areas

Where restrictions for 'trailers' or 'towing' are given, it may be assumed that these apply to both trailers and caravans

🍷 The maximum permitted level of alcohol in the bloodstream. This should not be taken as an acceptable level; it is NEVER sensible to drink and drive

🔖 Whether the wearing of seat belts is compulsory

🧒 Restrictions applying to children

△ Whether a warning triangle must be carried

✚ Whether a first aid kit must be carried

💡 Whether a spare bulb kit must be carried

⭕ Whether crash helmets are compulsory for motorcyclists

🚏 Whether tolls are payable on motorways and/or other parts of the road network

⛽ Whether petrol concessions or restrictions apply

⊖ The minimum age for drivers

🪪 Documentation required; note that while insurance for driving at home usually provides the legally required minimum third party cover abroad, it will not provide cover against damage, fire, theft or personal accident; for this reason, an International Motoring Certificate (Green Card) is recommended for all countries and essential where 'Green Card required' is given

★ In this section are given any other regulations not falling into the categories above

Andorra

🔧 **Automobil Club d'Andorra**, FIA, Babet Camp 4, Andorra-la-Vella   Tel: 20-8-90

	🚎	🔼	🔺	🏙
◠		70	70	40 km/h

🍷 0.08%

🔖 Compulsory if fitted for drivers and front seat passengers

🧒 Children under 10 years of age not allowed in front seats

△ Not compulsory unless vehicle exceeds 3000 kg, but advised

✚ Recommended

💡 Compulsory

⭕ Compulsory for motorcyclists and passengers

🚏

⛽

⊖ 18

🪪 Valid driving licence; Vehicle registration document or Vehicle on hire certificate; Green Card recommended; National vehicle identification plate

Austria

🔧 **Österreicher Automobil-, Motorrad- und Touring Club (ÖAMTC)**, FIA & AIT, Schubertring 1-3, 1010 Wien 1   Tel: (01) 9276510

	🚎	🔼	🔺	🏙
◠	130	100	100	50 km/h
	70	60	60	50 km/h
			if towing trailer over 14.5 cwt	
	100	100	100	50 km/h
			if towing trailer under 14.5 cwt	

🍷 0.08%

🔖 Compulsory if fitted for driver and front and rear seat passengers

🧒 Children under 12 years of age not allowed in front seats

△ Compulsory

✚ Compulsory

💡

⭕ Compulsory for motorcyclists and passengers

🚎 Tolls payable on most motorways and some roads (especially Austrian trans-Alpine routes)

⛽

⊖ 18

🪪 Valid driving licence; Vehicle registration document or Vehicle on hire certificate; Green Card recommended; National vehicle identification plate

Belgium

🔧 **Royal Automobile Club de Belgique (RACB)**, FIA, 53 rue d' Arlon, 1040 Bruxelles Tel: (02) 2300810

Touring Club Royal de Belgique (TCB), AIT, 44 rue de la Loi, 1040 Bruxelles Tel: (02) 2332211

Vlaamse Automobilistenbond, Sint Jakobsmarkt 45, 2000 Antwerpen Tel: (03) 2203211

	🚎	🔼	🔺	🏙
◠	120	90	90	60 km/h

🍷 0.08%

🔖 Compulsory if fitted for drivers and front seat passengers

🧒 Children under 12 years of age not allowed in front seats unless there is no room in back seats

△ Compulsory

✚ Recommended

💡

⭕ Compulsory for motorcyclists

🚎 None at present

⛽

⊖ 18

🪪 Valid driving licence; Vehicle registration document or Vehicle on hire certificate; Green Card recommended; National vehicle identification plate

Bulgaria

🔧 **Union of Bulgarian Motorists (SBA)**, FIA & AIT, 6 Sveta Sofia St., Sofia C Tel: (02) 87 88 01/87 88 02

	🚎	🔼	🔺	🏙
◠	120	80	80	60 km/h

🍷 0.03%

🔖 Compulsory if fitted for drivers and front seat passengers

🧒 Children under 10 years of age not allowed in front seats

△ Compulsory

✚ Compulsory

💡

⭕ Compulsory for motorcyclists

🚎

⛽ Foreign motorists must buy fuel with coupons available in unlimited quantities at border posts and within Bulgaria

⊖ 18

🪪 Valid driving licence plus authorized translation into Bulgarian or International Driving Permit; Vehicle registration document or Vehicle on hire certificate; Green Card required; National vehicle identification plate

Czechoslovakia

🔧 **Ustředni Automotoklub ČSSR**, FIA & AIT, Na Strži 9, 14000 Praha 4   Tel: (02) 432 987

🚗	🛣️	🅰️	🏙️
🔄 110	90	90	60 km/h

🍷 0.0%   any amount of alcohol found in the blood may result in prosecution

🔖 Compulsory if fitted for drivers and front seat passengers

👤 Children under 12 years of age not allowed in front seats

△ Compulsory

➕ Compulsory

🔦

⭕ Crash helmets and goggles compulsory for drivers of motorcycles over 50cc; crash helmets only for passengers

🚗

⛽ Tuzex petrol coupons can be purchased with foreign currency at frontier posts, Tuzex shops and banks; also from Czech Tourist Bureau Cedok (London) Ltd

🚫 18

📋 Valid driving licence; Vehicle registration document or Vehicle on hire certificate; Green Card recommended; National vehicle identification plate

Denmark

🔧 **Forenede Danske Motorejere (FDM)**, AIT, FDM-Huset, Blegdamsvej 124, 2100 København Ø Tel: (31) 38 21 12

🚗	🛣️	🅰️	🏙️
🔄 100	80	80	50 km/h
70	70	70	50 km/h if towing

🍷 0.08%

🔖 Compulsory if fitted for drivers and front seat passengers over 15 years

👤

△ Compulsory

➕ Recommended

🔦

⭕ Compulsory for motorcyclists and passengers

🚗

⛽

🚫 17

📋 Valid driving licence; Vehicle registration document or Vehicle on hire certificate; Green Card recommended; National vehicle identification plate

Finland

🔧 **Autoliitto (Automobile and Touring Club of Finland) (ATCF)**, FIA & AIT, Kansakoulukatu 10, 00101 Helsinki 10   Tel: (90) 6940022

🚗	🛣️	🅰️	🏙️
🔄 120	60-100	60-100	50 km/h
80	60-80	60-80	50 km/h towing if trailer has brakes
50	50	50	50 km/h towing if trailer unbraked

🍷 0.05%

🔖 Compulsory if fitted for drivers and front and rear seat passengers

👤

△ Recommended

➕ Recommended

🔦

⭕ Compulsory for motorcyclists and passengers

🚗

⛽

🚫 18

📋 Valid driving licence; International Driving Permit required for car hire or after 3 months; Vehicle registration document or Vehicle on hire certificate; Green Card recommended; National vehicle identification plate

★ Compulsory use of headlights at all times outside built-up areas

France

🔧 **Automobile Club de France**, FIA, 6-8 Place de la Concorde, 75008 Paris   Tel: (01) 42 65 08 26 **Association Française des Automobiles-Clubs (AFA)**, FIA & AIT, 9 rue Anatole de la Forge, 75017 Paris   Tel: (01) 42 27 82 00

🚗	🛣️	🅰️	🏙️
🔄 110-130	110	90	60 km/h
100-110	100	80	60 km/h if wet

🍷 0.08%

🔖 Compulsory if fitted for drivers and front seat passengers

👤 Children under 10 years of age not allowed in front seats

△ Compulsory unless hazard warning lights are fitted

➕ Recommended

🔦 Compulsory

⭕ Compulsory for motorcyclists and passengers

🚗 Tolls payable on most motorways although short urban sections of motorway around Paris and some other major cities are free; tolls also payable on some major bridges and in some tunnels

⛽

🚫 18

📋 Valid driving licence; Vehicle registration document or Vehicle on hire certificate; Green Card recommended; National vehicle identification plate

FDR (West Germany)

🔧 **Allgemeiner Deutscher Automobil-Club (ADAC)**, FIA & AIT, Am Westpark 8, 8000 München 70   Tel: (089) 76760 **Automobil-Club von Deutschland (AvD)**, FIA, Lyonerstraße 16, 6000 Frankfurt am Main 71 Tel: (069) 66060

🚗	🛣️	🅰️	🏙️
🔄 130*	130*	100	50 km/h
80	80	80	50 km/h if towing

*recommended

🍷 0.08%

🔖 Compulsory if fitted for drivers and front and rear seat passengers

👤 Children under 12 years of age not allowed in front seats

△ Compulsory

➕ Compulsory

🔦

⭕ Compulsory for motorcyclists and passengers

🚗

⛽

🚫 18

📋 Valid driving licence; Vehicle registration document or Vehicle on hire certificate; Green Card recommended; National vehicle identification plate

DDR (East Germany)

🔧 **Allgemeiner Deutscher Motorsport Verband der DDR**, FIA, 60 Charlottenstraße, 108 Berlin (Ost)   Tel: (02) 2071931/2071932

🚗	🛣️	🅰️	🏙️
🔄 100	80	80	50 km/h
80	80	80	50 km/h if towing

🍷 0.0%   any amount of alcohol found in the blood may result in prosecution

🔖 Compulsory if fitted for drivers and front seat passengers

👤 Children under 7 years of age not allowed in front seats

△ Compulsory

➕ Compulsory

🔦 Compulsory

⭕ Compulsory for motorcyclists; smoking not allowed whilst driving

🚗 Tolls levied on private cars depending on distance travelled; may be paid in Marks obtained by currency exchange; information available at frontier posts

⛽ Reduced price petrol coupons available at main frontier posts; indefinite validity but cannot be returned

🚫 18

📋 Valid driving licence; Vehicle registration document or Vehicle on hire certificate; Green Card recommended; National vehicle identification plate

Great Britain

🔧 **Automobile Association (AA)**, FIA & AIT, Fanum House, Basingstoke, Hampshire RG21 2EA Tel: (0256) 20123
Royal Automobile Club (RAC), FIA & AIT, Lansdowne Road, Croydon CR9 2JA Tel: (01) 686 2525

🏛	⚠	🅰	🏭
🔊 112	96	96	48 km/h
96	96	80	48 km/h if towing

🍷 0.08%

🔧 Compulsory if fitted for drivers and front seat passengers; compulsory if fitted in back seats for children under 14

✊

△

➕ Recommended

♀

💼 Compulsory for motorcyclists and passengers

🏛

⛽

🚫 17

📖 Valid driving licence; Vehicle registration document or Vehicle on hire certificate; Green Card recommended; National vehicle identification plate

★ Drive on the left!

Hungary

🔧 **Magyar Autóklub (MAK)**, FIA & AIT, Römer Flóris utca 4a, Budapest 11   Tel: (01) 152 040

🏛	⚠	🅰	🏭
🔊 120	80-100	80-100	60 km/h
80	70	70	50 km/h if towing

🍷 0.0%   if the alcohol test changes colour, the driver is taken to a hospital for a blood test and his driving licence confiscated

🔧 Compulsory if fitted for drivers and front seat passengers

✊ Children under 6 years of age not allowed in front seats

△ Compulsory

➕ Recommended

♀ Compulsory

💼 Compulsory for motorcyclists and passengers

🏛

⛽ IBUSZ vouchers available (no price reduction); diesel for foreign vehicles must be bought with coupons paid for in foreign currency from exchange offices and travel agencies; unused coupons not refundable

🚫 18

📖 Valid driving licence; Vehicle registration document or Vehicle on hire certificate; Green Card strongly recommended; National vehicle identification plate

Ireland

🔧 **Automobile Association (AA)**, FIA & AIT, 23 Suffolk Street, Dublin 2   Tel: (01) 779481
Royal Automobile Club (RAC), FIA & AIT, 34 Dawson Street, Dublin 2   Tel: (01) 775141

🏛	⚠	🅰	🏭
🔊	88	64-88	48 km/h
	56	56	48 km/h if towing

🍷 0.10%

🔧 Compulsory if fitted for drivers and front seat passengers

✊

△ Recommended

➕ Recommended

♀

💼 Compulsory for motorcyclists and passengers

🏛 Toll payable on one bridge over River Liffey

⛽ Contact Irish Tourist Board for current information

🚫 17

📖 Valid driving licence; Vehicle registration document or Vehicle on hire certificate; Green Card recommended; National vehicle identification plate

★ Drive on the left!

Greece

🔧 **The Automobile and Touring Club of Greece (ELPA)**, FIA & AIT, 2-4 Messogion, 115 27 Athina   Tel: (01) 779 1615
Hellenic Touring Club, AIT, 12 Politechniou, 104 33 Athina   Tel: (01) 524 0854

🏛	⚠	🅰	🏭
🔊 100	80	80	50 km/h

🍷 0.05%

🔧 Compulsory if fitted for drivers and front seat passengers

✊ Children under 10 years of age not allowed in front seats

△ Compulsory

➕ Compulsory

♀

💼 Compulsory for motorcyclists and passengers

🏛 Tolls payable on most 'national' roads

⛽

🚫 17

📖 Valid driving licence; Vehicle registration document or Vehicle on hire certificate; Green Card required; National vehicle identification plate

★ Fire extinguisher compulsory

Iceland

🔧 **Felag Islenskra Bifreidaeigenda (FIB)**, FIA & AIT, Borgatun 33, 105 Reykjavik Tel: (01) 29999

🏛	⚠	🅰	🏭
🔊	70	70	50 km/h

🍷 0.05%

🔧 Compulsory for drivers and front seat passengers; rear seat belts recommended

✊

△ Recommended

➕ Recommended

♀ Recommended

💼 Compulsory for motorcyclists and passengers

🏛

⛽

🚫 17

📖 Driver's passport; Valid driving licence; Vehicle registration document or Vehicle on hire certificate; Green Card required; Temporary importation permit; National vehicle identification plate

★ Vehicle mud flaps are compulsory; headlights must be used at all times

Italy

🔧 **Automobile Club d'Italia (ACI)**, FIA & AIT, Via Marsala 8, 00185 Roma   Tel: (06) 49981
Touring Club Italiano (TCI), AIT, Corso Italia 10, 20122 Milano   Tel: (02) 85261

🏛	⚠	🅰	🏭
🔊 110*-130	110*-130	90	50 km/h
110*-130	110*-130	90	50 km/h if towing

as at 1989
* for vehicles up to 1100 cc

🍷 Severe penalties for drinking and driving

🔧 Compulsory if fitted

✊

△ Compulsory

➕ Recommended

♀

💼 Compulsory for motorcyclists and passengers

🏛 Tolls payable on most motorways

⛽ Coupons at a discount available at RAC, AA, and Port Offices and frontier Automobile Clubs to personal callers; must be paid for in foreign currency

🚫 18; visitors under 21 years of age may not drive a private car capable of exceeding 180 km/h

📖 Valid driving licence; Vehicle registration document or Vehicle on hire certificate; Green Card recommended; Temporary importation document; National vehicle identification plate

Luxembourg

�* **Automobile Club du Grand Duché de Luxembourg (ACL)**, FIA & AIT, 13 rue de Longwy, 8007 Bertrange Tel: (012) 45 00 45

🚗	🚙	🅰	🚛
🕐 90	75	75	60 km/h

🍷 0.08%

🎗 Compulsory if fitted for drivers and front seat passengers

👶 Children under 10 years of age not allowed in front seats

△ Compulsory

✚ Recommended

💡

⬜ Compulsory

🚗

⛽

⊖ 18

📇 Valid driving licence; Vehicle registration document or Vehicle on hire certificate; Green Card recommended; National vehicle identification plate

Netherlands

⚙ **Koninklijke Nederlandsche Automobiel Club (KNAC)**, FIA, Westvlietweg 118, Leidschendam   Tel: (070) 99 74 51
Koninklijke Nederlandsche Toeristenbond (ANWB), AIT, Wassenaarseweg 220, Den Haag Tel: (070) 26 44 26

🚗	🚙	🅰	🚛
🕐 100-120	80	80	50 km/h
80	80	80	50 km/h if towing

🍷 0.05%

🎗 Compulsory if fitted for drivers and front seat passengers

👶 Children under 12 years of age not allowed in front seats unless using child's safety seat and under 4 years of age

△ Compulsory

✚ Recommended

💡

⬜ Compulsory for motorcyclists and passengers

🚗 Tolls payable on: Zeeland Brug, Kiltunnel (from Dordrecht – Hoekse Waard), Waal Brug, Prins Willem Alexander Brug

⛽

⊖ 18

📇 Valid driving licence; Vehicle registration document or Vehicle on hire certificate; Green Card recommended; National vehicle identification plate

Norway

⚙ **Kongelig Norsk Automobilklub (KNA)**, FIA, Parkveien 68, Oslo 2   Tel: (02) 562690
Norges Automobil-Forbund (NAF), AIT, Storgata 2, Oslo 1   Tel: (02) 429400

🚗	🚙	🅰	🚛
🕐 80-90	80-90	80-90	50 km/h
80	80	80	50 km/h
			if towing trailer with braking system
60	60	60	50 km/h
			if towing trailer without braking system

🍷 0.05%

🎗 Compulsory if fitted for drivers and front and rear seat passengers

👶 Children under 12 years of age not allowed in front seats

△ Compulsory

✚ Recommended

💡

⬜ Compulsory for motorcyclists and passengers

🚗 Tolls payable on most new major roads

⛽

⊖ 17 for temporarily imported vehicle; 18 to hire or borrow local vehicle

📇 Valid driving licence; Vehicle registration document or Vehicle on hire certificate; Green Card recommended; National vehicle identification plate

★ Dipped headlights compulsory at all times

Poland

⚙ **Polski Zwiazek Motorowy (PZM)**, FIA & AIT, Kazimierzowska 66, 02-518 Warszawa Tel: (022) 499361/499212
Auto Assistance, Krucza 6-14, 00-537 Warszawa   Tel: (022) 293541/210467

🚗	🚙	🅰	🚛
🕐 110	90	90	60 km/h
70	70	70	60 km/h if towing

🍷 0.02%

🎗 Compulsory if fitted for drivers and front seat passengers

👶 Children under 10 years of age not allowed in front seats

△ Compulsory

✚ Recommended

💡

⬜ Compulsory for motorcyclists and passengers

🚗

⛽ Coupons available at frontier offices or branches of Polish Tourist Office (ORBIS) in Poland; also from Fregata Travel Ltd, 100 Dean Street, London; unused coupons refundable

⊖ 18

📇 Valid driving licence; International Driving Permit after 3 months; Vehicle registration document or Vehicle on hire certificate; Green Card required; National vehicle identification plate

Portugal

⚙ **Automóvel Club de Portugal (ACP)**, FIA & AIT, Rua Rosa Araújo 24-26, 1200 Lisboa Tel: (01) 563931

🚗	🚙	🅰	🚛
🕐 120	90	90	60 km/h
100	70	70	50 km/h if towing

🍷 0.05%

🎗 Compulsory if fitted for drivers and front seat passengers outside built-up areas

👶

△ Compulsory

✚ Recommended

💡

⬜ Compulsory for motorcyclists

🚗 Tolls payable in certain directions on some motorways and bridges

⛽

⊖ 17

📇 Valid driving licence; Vehicle registration document or Vehicle on hire certificate; Green Card required; National vehicle identification plate

Romania

⚙ In the event of breakdown or accident contact the National Tourist Office Carpați-București, Bd Magheru 7, București   Tel: (00) 145160

🚗	🚙	🅰	🚛
🕐 70-90*	60-90*	60-90*	60 km/h

*according to cylinder capacity

🍷 0.0%   any alcohol found in the bloodstream may result in immediate imprisonment

🎗 Recommended if fitted

👶 Children under 12 years of age not allowed in front seats

△ Compulsory

✚ Recommended

💡

⬜ Compulsory for motorcyclists and passengers

🚗

⛽ Coupons compulsory; obtainable with convertible currency only at frontier posts, tourist offices and some hotels; for use at PECO filling stations

⊖ 17

📇 Valid driving licence; Vehicle registration document or Vehicle on hire certificate; Green Card required; National vehicle identification plate

Spain

🔧 **Real Automóvil Club de España (RACE)**, FIA & AIT, José Abascal 10, 28003 Madrid
Tel: (91) 447 3200

🚗	🛣️	🅰️	🏭
120	90-100	90-100	60 km/h
80	70	70	60 km/h if towing

these limits are increased by 20 km/h for overtaking

🍷 0.08%
🔖 Compulsory if fitted for drivers and front seat passengers outside built-up areas
● Children in front seats not recommended
△ Two are compulsory for vehicles with 9 or more seats; recommended for other vehicles
➕ Recommended
💡 Compulsory
🪖 Compulsory for motorcycles but not for mopeds
🚧 Tolls payable on most motorways and Cadí tunnel
⛽
⊖ 18
📖 International Driving Permit required if 'pink' EEC licence not held; Vehicle registration document or Vehicle on hire certificate; Green Card required; Bail Bond strongly recommended; National vehicle identification plate

Sweden

🔧 **Motormännens Riksförbund (M)**, AIT, Sturegatan 32, Stockholm   Tel: (08) 7 82 38 00

🚗	🛣️	🅰️	🏭
110	70-110	70-110	50 km/h
70	70	70	50 km/h if towing with braking device
40	40	40	40 km/h if towing with no braking device

🍷 0.05%
🔖 Compulsory if fitted for drivers and front and rear seat passengers
●
△ Recommended
➕ Recommended
💡
🪖 Compulsory for motorcyclists and passengers
🚧
⛽
⊖ 18
📖 Valid driving licence; Vehicle registration document or Vehicle on hire certificate; Green Card recommended; National vehicle identification plate
★ Dipped headlights compulsory at all times

Switzerland

🔧 **Automobile Club de Suisse (ACS)**, FIA, Wasserwerkgasse 39, 3000 Bern 13
Tel: (031) 22 47 22
Touring Club Suisse (TCS), AIT, 9 rue Pierre-Fatio, 1211 Genève 3   Tel: (022) 37 12 12

🚗	🛣️	🅰️	🏭
120	80	80	50 km/h
80	80	80	50 km/h if towing – up to 20 cwt trailer
60	60	60	50 km/h if towing – over 20 cwt trailer

🍷 0.08%
🔖 Compulsory if fitted for drivers and front seat passengers
● Children under 12 years of age not allowed in front seats
△ Compulsory
➕ Compulsory
💡
🪖 Compulsory for motorcyclists and passengers
🚧 Vignette compulsory: obtainable from frontier posts, post offices, garages, motoring organisations or Swiss National Tourist Office (London); separate vignette required for trailer or caravan
⛽
⊖ 18
📖 Valid driving licence; Vehicle registration document or Vehicle on hire certificate; Green Card recommended; National vehicle identification plate

Turkey

🔧 **Turkiye Turing ve Otomobil Kurumu (TTOK)**, FIA & AIT, Halaskargazi Cad. 364, 80222 Sisli, Istanbul   Tel: (01) 1314631/6

🚗	🛣️	🅰️	🏭
130	90	90	50 km/h
110	70	70	40 km/h if towing

🍷 0.0%
🔖 Compulsory if fitted for drivers and front and rear seat passengers
● Children in front seats not recommended
△ Two must be carried – one to place in front of the vehicle, one behind
➕ Recommended
💡
🪖 Compulsory for motorcyclists
🚧
⛽
⊖ Normally 18, but drivers holding a valid foreign driving licence who are not yet 18 are allowed to drive foreign registered vehicles
📖 Valid driving licence; International Driving Permit advised and compulsory if driving Turkish vehicle; Vehicle registration document or Vehicle on hire certificate; Green Card compulsory – must cover European & Asian regions; National vehicle identification plate

USSR

🔧 In the event of breakdown or accident contact officer of State Automobile Inspection (Militia) or nearest office of Intourist (obliged to give tourists assistance)

🚗	🛣️	🅰️	🏭
90	90	90	60 km/h

🍷 0.0%
🔖 Compulsory if fitted for drivers and front seat passengers
● Children under 12 years of age not allowed in front seats
△ Compulsory
➕ Compulsory
💡 Recommended
🪖 Not applicable; motorcycles may not be hired
🚧 Road tax payable on entry to USSR though some foreign cars exempt
⛽ Petrol coupons compulsory; obtainable at border posts
⊖ 18
📖 Valid driving licence meeting requirements of International Convention on Road Traffic; Vehicle registration document or Vehicle on hire certificate; Car insurance obtainable on entry to USSR at Ingosstrakh offices; Itinerary card, service coupons and motor routes map issued by Intourist; Customs obligation to take the car out of the country on departure; National vehicle identification plate
★ Fire extinguisher must be carried

Yugoslavia

🔧 **Auto-Moto Savez Jugoslavija (AMSJ)**, FIA & AIT, Ruzveltova 18, 11001 Beograd
Tel: (011) 401699

🚗	🛣️	🅰️	🏭
120	80-100	80-100	60 km/h
80	80	80	60 km/h if towing

🍷 0.05%
🔖 Compulsory if fitted for drivers and front and rear seat passengers
● Children under 12 years of age not allowed in front seats
△ Compulsory – two are necessary if towing trailer or caravan
➕ Compulsory
💡 Compulsory
🪖 Compulsory for motorcyclists and passengers
🚧 Tolls payable on several major roads, Tito Bridge and Ucka tunnel
⛽ Concessionary petrol coupons available at frontier posts for purchase with convertible currency; unused coupons refundable
⊖ 18
📖 Valid driving licence; Vehicle registration document or Vehicle on hire certificate; Green Card required; National vehicle identification plate

Signos convencionales

Para más información ver el interior de la cubierta anterior

Importancia de los itinerarios

- Autopista con calzadas separadas
- con calzada única
- Autovía con calzadas separadas
- Número de acceso
- Accesos: completo – medio acceso
- parcial – sin precisión

Carretera de comunicación internacional o nacional asfaltada:
- calzadas separadas
- 4 carriles – 3 carriles
- 2 carriles anchos – 2 carriles

Carretera de comunicación interregional asfaltada:
- calzadas separadas
- 2 carriles o más – 2 carriles estrechos
- Sin asfaltar: transitable, con macadán

- Otra carretera asfaltada – sin asfaltar
- Pista o camino forestal, sendero
- Carretera en construcción
- 10-1992 Fecha prevista de entrada en servicio

Distancias en kilómetros (totales o parciales)
- 12 en autopista:
- tramo de peaje
- 12 tramo libre
- 12 en carretera

Transporte
- Línea férrea – Tren-coche
- Barcaza – Barcaza (DK, N, S, SF)
- Enlace marítimo: permanente – de temporada
- Aeropuerto

Zeichenerklärung

Vollständige Zeichenerklärung siehe Umschlaginnenseite

Verkehrsbedeutung der Straßen

- Autobahn mit getrennten Fahrbahnen
- mit nur einer Fahrbahn
- Schnellstraße mit getrennten Fahrbahnen
- Nummer der Anschlußstelle
- Anschlußstellen: Autobahnein- und/oder
- -ausfahrt – ohne Angabe

Internationale bzw. nationale Hauptverkehrsstraße mit Belag:
- getrennte Fahrbahnen
- 4 Fahrspuren – 3 Fahrspuren
- 2 breite Fahrspuren – 2 Fahrspuren

Überregionale Verbindungsstraße mit Belag:
- getrennte Fahrbahnen
- 2 u. mehr Fahrspuren – 2 schmale Fahrspuren
- Ohne Belag: befahrbar, mit Makadam

- Sonstige Straßen: mit Belag, ohne Belag
- Wirtschaftsweg – Weg, Pfad
- Straße im Bau
- 10-1992 Voraussichtliches Datum der Verkehrsfreigabe

Entfernungsangaben in Kilometern (Gesamt- und Teilentfernungen)
- 12 auf der Autobahn:
- gebührenpflichtiger Abschnitt
- 12 gebührenfreier Abschnitt
- 12 auf anderen Straßen

Transport
- Bahnlinie – Autoreisezug
- Fähre – Fähre (DK, N, S, SF)
- Schiffsverbindung: ganzjährig – während der Saison
- Flughafen

Légende

Voir la légende complète à l'intérieure de la couverture

Importance des itinéraires

- Autoroute à chaussées séparées
- à une seule chaussée
- Double chaussée de type autoroutier
- Numéro d'échangeur
- Échangeurs: complet – demi-échangeur
- partiel – sans precision

Route de liaison internationale ou nationale revêtue:
- chaussées séparées
- 4 voies – 3 voies
- 2 voies larges – 2 voies

Route de liaison interrégionale revêtue:
- chaussées séparées
- 2 voies et plus – 2 voies étroites
- Non revêtue: carrossable, en macadam

- Autre route revêtue – non revêtue
- Chemin d'exploitation, sentier
- Route en construction
- 10-1992 Date de mise en service prévue

Distances en kilomètres (totalisées et partielles)
- 12 sur autoroute:
- section à péage
- 12 section libre
- 12 sur route

Transport
- Voie ferrée – Train-auto
- Bac – Bac (DK, N, S, SF)
- Liaison maritime: permanente – saisonnière
- Aéroport

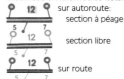

Segni convenzionali

Vedere la legenda completa all'interno della copertina

Importanza degli itinerari

- Autostrada a carreggiate separate
- a carreggiata unica
- Doppia carreggiata di tipo autostradale
- Numero dello svincolo
- Svincoli: completo – semi-svincolo
- parziale – non precisato

Strada di comunicazione internazionale o nazionale rivestita:
- a carreggiate separate
- a 4 corsie – a 3 corsie
- a 2 corsie larghe – a 2 corsie

Strada di comunicazione interregionale rivestita:
- a carreggiate separate
- a 2 corsie e più – a 2 corsie strette
- Non rivestita: carrozzabile, in macadam

- Altre strade con rivestimento – senza rivestimento
- Strada per carri, sentiero
- Strada in costruzione
- 10-1992 Apertura prevista

Distanze in chilometri (totali e parziali)
- 12 su autostrada:
- tratto a pedaggio
- 12 tratto esente da pedaggio
- 12 su strada

Trasporti
- Ferrovia – trasporto automobili per ferrovia
- Su chiatta – su chiatta (DK, N, S, SF)
- Collegamento via-traghetto: tutto l'anno – stagionale
- Aeroporto

Verklaring der tekens

Zie voor de volledige verklaring der tekens de binnenzijde van het omslag

Belang van het wegennet

- Autosnelweg met gescheiden rijbanen
- met één rijbaan
- Dubbele rijbaan van het type autosnelweg
- Nummer knooppunt/aansluiting
- Knooppunten/aansluitingen : volledig – half
- gedeeltelijk – niet nader aangegeven

Internationale of nationale verharde verbindingsweg:
- gescheiden rijbanen
- 4 rijstroken – 3 rijstroken
- 2 brede rijstroken – 2 rijstroken

Regionale verharde verbindingsweg:
- gescheiden rijbanen
- 2 of meer rijstroken – 2 smalle rijstroken
- Onverhard: berijdbaar, macadamweg

- Andere weg: verhard – onverhard
- Bedrijfsweg, pad
- Weg in aanleg
- 10-1992 Vermoedelijke datum ingebruikneming

Afstanden in kilometers (totaal en gedeeltelijk)
- 12 op de autosnelweg:
- gedeelte met tol
- 12 tolvrij gedeelte
- 12 op de weg

Vervoer
- Spoorweg – Autotrein
- Veerpont – Veerpont (DK, N, S, SF)
- Scheepvaartverbinding : permanent – alleen in het seizoen
- Luchthaven

Key to symbols

A full key to symbols appears inside the front cover

Road classification

- Motorway: dual carriageway
- single carriageway
- Dual carriageway with motorway characteristics
- Interchange number
- Interchange: complete – half
- limited – unspecified

International and national surfaced road network:
- dual carriageway
- four lanes – three lanes
- two wide lanes – two lanes

Interregional surfaced road network:
- dual carriageway
- two lanes or more – two narrow lanes
- Unsurfaced: suitable for vehicles, macadam

- Other surfaced road – unsurfaced
- Service road or cart track, footpath
- Road under construction
- 10-1992 Scheduled opening date

Distances in kilometres (total and intermediate)
- 12 on motorway:
- toll section
- 12 free section
- 12 on other roads

Transportation
- Railway – Motorail
- Ferry – Ferry (DK, N, S, SF)
- Car ferry: all the year – seasonal
- Airport

1

2

3

4

A   B   C

Cape Wrath

Butt of Lewis
Port of Ness
A 857
16
LEWIS
Barvas
A 858
Carloway
292   12   A 857
34   Stornoway
Garynahine   Broad
A 858   Bay   Portnaguran
A 859   12   A 866   Tiumpan Head
574   Eye Peninsula

Whiten Head
Durness
Kinlochbervie   A 838   20   Loch Eriboll
908 △ Foinaven   A 838
31   Tongue
927 △
Scourie   A 894   Ben Hope
A 838   Laxford Bridge
Eddrachillis   A 838   34
Bay   Kylestrome   Altnaharra
Ben Klib
19   A 884   961
A 837   Inchnadamph   39   40
Lochinver   998 △   A 838
Ben More Assynt
Rubha Cóigeach   849 △   Ledmore   Loch Shin
Coigach   18   Lairg
743   A 835   A 837
Loch Broom   27   A 839
31
A 837

Flannan I.

H E B R I D E S

W E S T E R N

THE MINCH

Hushinish   A 859   Kebock Head
B 887   Clisham
799 △   572
Tarbert

West Loch Tarbert

Toe Head   24
A 859   Harris
A 859   Leverburgh
Rodel
Renish Point

I S L E S

Rubha Réidh   Laide
Gruinard   Ullapool
Bay
Dundonnell   29   12
1062 △   15   Bonar Bridge
1084 △
A 832   Beinn Dearg
Gairloch   Loch Maree   Sgurr Mór   A 835   57   E a s t e r
1110   19   92   Ben Wyvis
20   A 832   1046
Wester   Ross   Garve   Dingwall
Liathach   Kinlochewe   15   A 832   3
Torridon   1054 △   10   A 896   9   Achnasheen   Contin   19   Fc
Shieldaig   A 832   Muir of Ord   A 831   Tore
19   Glen Carron   A 890   1083 △
896 △   A 896   24   Glen Carron
Lochcarron   A 831   A 832
Stromeferry   15   Cannich   A 831   Drumnadrochit
Kyle of   A 890   Carn Eige   H I G H L A
Lochalsh   Dornie   1183 △   Glen   More
Broadford   A 850   Eilean Donan Castle   A 82
Kyleakin   Shiel Bridge   Invermoriston   Foyers
Kylerhea   A' Chràlaig   A 887   69   White Bridge
Glenelg   1120 △   32   33   43   7
50   16   Fort Augustus
80   13   7
Sgurr na Ciche   Invergarry   Glen   Carn Ban
1040 △   Monadhliath
25   942 △
15   40   Newtonmore
Spean Bridge   Creag Meagaidh   Laggan
882   76   Glenfinnan   30   1130 △   Dalwhinnie
46   A 861   27   Caledonian   Canal
Fort William   Loch Laggan
Ben Nevis   Ben Alder   1148
1344 △   △ 1148

North Uist
Tigharry   A 865
25   A 865
13 △ 347
Balivanich   A 865
Benbecula
Creagorry

Waternish
Point
Loch
Snizort   Staffin
Uig   34
A 855   Rona
The Storr   Inner Sound
719   Sound of Raasay
Dunvegan   22   16
Head   A 855   A 850
Dunvegan   A 850   Portree
Bracadale   Raasay
21   444 △
Sligachan   B
17   Sconser   Scalpay
SKYE   Kyle of Lochalsh
The Cuillins   Broadford
993   14   Kyleakin
A 851   Kylerhea
Elgol   Isleornsay
17   Sleat
Ardvasar

The Little Minch

Dunvegan
Head

Loch Torridon

SEA OF
THE HEBRIDES
South Uist
22
620 △
Daliburgh   Lochboisdale

Sound of Barra
Barra   A 888
583 △
Castlebay   Bayhirivagh
9

Mingulay
Barra Head

Canna
Rhum
812 △
Eigg

Muck

Cuillin Sound

Mallaig   Loch Nevis
Arisaig   19   Loch Morar
Glenfinnan
Loch Shiel   A 861   A 830
33   888
Kilchoan   528   Salen   Strontian
B 8007   A 861   13
Corran   S C
Inchree   Onich
Ballachulish   Glen   Coe
Kentallen   1141 △   Bidean nam Bian   Loch Rannoch
Kinloch Rannoch
Schiehalli

Coll
Arinagour
Tiree   Tobermory   B 8013
Dervaig   A 848
A   B

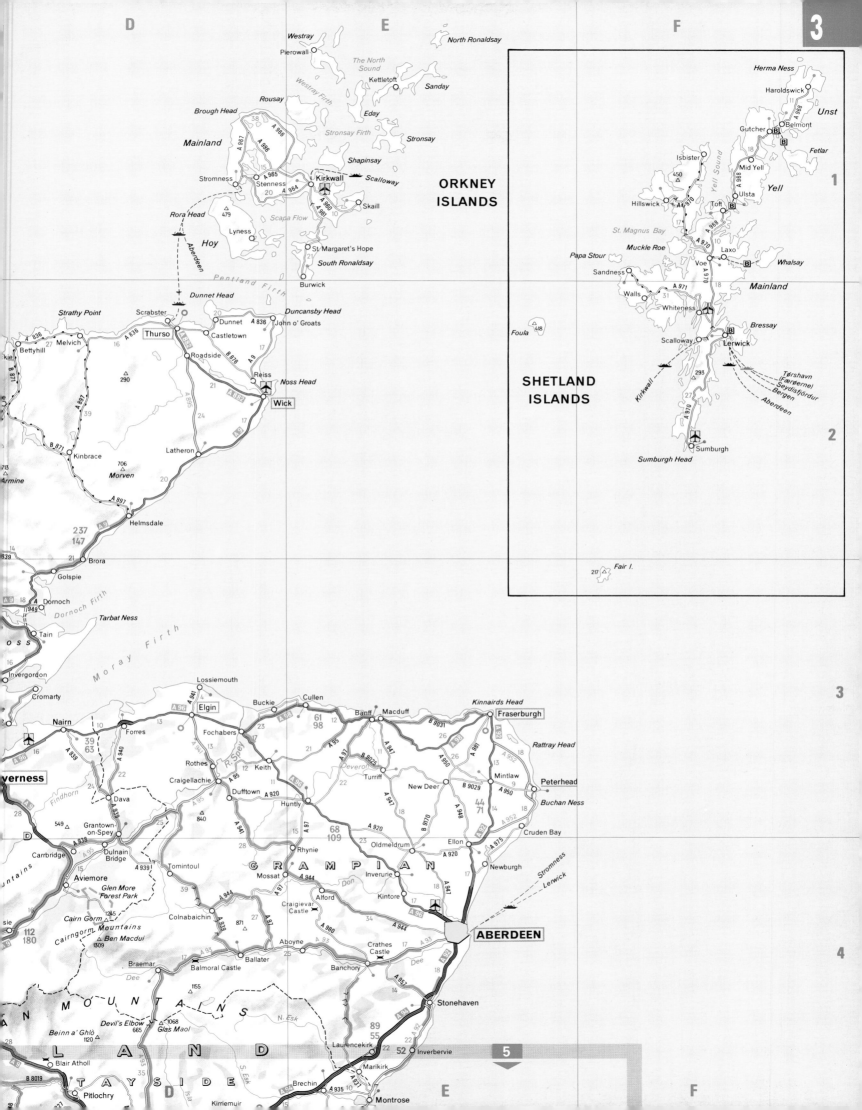

ORKNEY ISLANDS

SHETLAND ISLANDS

Westray
Pierowall
North Ronaldsay
The North Sound
Kettletoft
Sanday
Rousay
Brough Head
Eday
Mainland
Stronsay Firth
Stronsay
Westray Firth
A 967
A 966
38
Shapinsay
Stromness
Stenness
15
A 965
Kirkwall
Scalloway
20
A 964
A 960
Skaill
Rora Head
479
10
A 961
Hoy
Lyness
21
St Margaret's Hope
Scapa Flow
South Ronaldsay
Pentland Firth
Burwick
Aberdeen

Herma Ness
Haroldswick
11
A 968
Unst
Gutcher
Belmont
Fetlar
Isbister
18
Mid Yell
Yell
Hillswick
450
A 970
Ulsta
A 4 970
17
Toft
St Magnus Bay
A 968
Papa Stour
Muckle Roe
Laxo
Sandness
Voe
A 970
Whalsay
Walls
A 971
Mainland
31
18
Foula
418
Whiteness
Scalloway
Bressay
Lerwick
293
Tørshavn (Færøerne)
Seydisfjordur
Bergen
A 970
27
Aberdeen
Sumburgh Head
Sumburgh

Fair I.
217

Strathy Point
Scrabster
Dunnet Head
A 836
Thurso
20
Duncansby Head
Dunnet
A 836
John o' Groats
A 897
Bettyhill
Melvich
16
Castletown
A 882
27
Roadside
B 876
A 9
A 836
Reiss
Noss Head
290
Kinbrace
39
21
Wick
B 871
24
A 885
17
Latheron
Morven
706
20
A 9
A 897
Helmsdale
237
147
Brora
21
Golspie
839
14
Dornoch
A 9
18
A 949
Dornoch Firth
Tarbat Ness
Tain
Moray Firth
ROSS
Invergordon
16
Cromarty

Lossiemouth
Cullen
Kinnairds Head
A 941
4
Elgin
Buckie
Banff
Macduff
Fraserburgh
Nairn
A 96
13
Fochabers
B 9031
26
Rattray Head
39
63
Forres
23
A 98
61
98
12
A 941
17
A 95
A 98
A 92
Inverness
A 939
A 340
Rothes
12
Keith
B 9025
11
A 947
A 981
18
Deveron
A 950
Peterhead
22
Craigellachie
A 95
11
Turriff
New Deer
B 9029
A 950
9
Buchan Ness
Dava
Dufftown
A 920
22
B 9170
A 948
44
71
14
840
15
A 97
68
109
A 920
18
A 952
Cruden Bay
549
Grantown-on-Spey
28
23
Oldmeldrum
A 975
Carrbridge
A 938
Rhynie
Ellon
A 920
Dulnain Bridge
25
GRAMPIAN
Inverurie
Newburgh
A 939
Tomintoul
Mossat
A 944
17
A 947
Aviemore
Glen More Forest Park
39
A 944
Alford
Kintore
Stromness
Cairn Gorm
1245
Colnabaichin
A 939
871
A 97
34
A 96
Lerwick
Cairngorm Mountains
A 980
Craigievar Castle
ABERDEEN
112
180
Ben Macdui
1309
Aboyne
A 93
Crathes Castle
A 957
Braemar
Balmoral Castle
Ballater
25
Banchory
Dee
18
MOUNTAINS
Dee
N. Esk
A 92
1155
89
55
Devil's Elbow
1068
Glas Maol
665
Laurencekirk
52
Inverbervie
Beinn a' Ghlò
1120
A 94
22
LAND
S. Esk
Marikirk
Blair Atholl
TAYSIDE
Brechin
A 935
10
B 8019
Pitlochry
Kirriemuir
Montrose

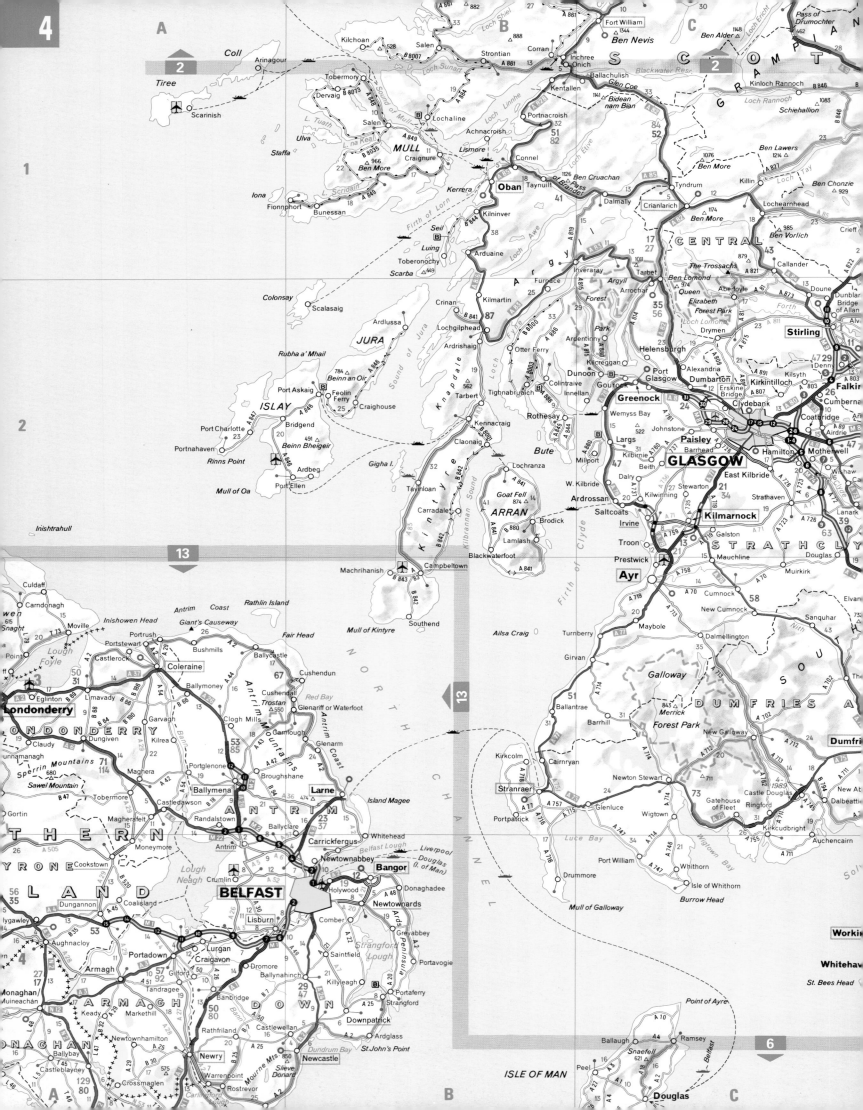

A

B

C

1

2

Coll

Tiree

Arinagour

Scarinish

Kilchoan

Salen

Strontian

Corran

Inchree

Onich

Ballachulish

Glen Coe

Kentallen

Portnacroish

Ben Nevis

Fort William

Ben Alder

Pass of Drumochter

Kinloch Rannoch

Loch Rannoch

Schiehallion

GRAMPIAN

Tobermory

Dervaig

L. Tuath

Ulva

Staffa

MULL

Ben More

Iona

Fionnphort

Bunessan

Lochaline

Achnacroish

Lismore

Craignure

Kerrera

Oban

Taynuilt

Connel

Ben Cruachan

Bidean nam Bian

Ben Lawers

Ben More

Killin

Loch Tay

Ben Chonzie

Crieff

Glenorchy

Dalmally

Tyndrum

Crianlarich

Lochearnhead

Ben More

Ben Vorlich

Callander

Doune

CENTRAL

Kilninver

Arduaine

Seil

Luing

Toberonochy

Scarba

Colonsay

Scalasaig

Ardlussa

JURA

Rubha a' Mhail

Beinn an Oir

Port Askaig

Feolin Ferry

Craighouse

ISLAY

Bridgend

Beinn Bheigeir

Port Charlotte

Portnahaven

Rinns Point

Ardbeg

Mull of Oa

Port Ellen

Gigha I.

Tayinloan

Carradale

Blackwaterfoot

ARRAN

Goat Fell

Brodick

Lamlash

Kilmartin

Crinan

Lochgilphead

Ardrishaig

Otter Ferry

Knapdale

Tarbert

Kennacraig

Claonaig

Kilmichael

Furnace

Inveraray

Argyll Forest

Arrochar

Ben Lomond

Loch Lomond

The Trossachs

Aberfoyle

Drymen

Stirling

Tarbet

Dunoon

Kilcreggan

Port Glasgow

Helensburgh

Alexandria

Dumbarton

Kirkintilloch

Kilsyth

Denny

Falkirk

Cumbernauld

Greenock

Gourock

Clydebank

Erskine Bridge

Coatbridge

Airdrie

Colintraive

Innellan

Tighnabruaich

Rothesay

Bute

Wemyss Bay

Johnstone

Paisley

Barrhead

GLASGOW

Hamilton

Motherwell

Wishaw

Lanark

STRATHCLYDE

Largs

Millport

Kilbirnie

Beith

W. Kilbride

Dalry

Lochranza

Ardrossan

Saltcoats

Irvine

Kilwinning

Stewarton

East Kilbride

Strathaven

Troon

Prestwick

Ayr

Mauchline

Douglas

Machrihanish

Campbeltown

Southend

Mull of Kintyre

Kintyre

Kilbrannan Sound

Firth of Clyde

Ailsa Craig

Turnberry

Maybole

Dalmellington

New Cumnock

Cumnock

Muirkirk

Sanquhar

Culdaff

Carndonagh

Moville

Inishowen Head

Giant's Causeway

Antrim Coast

Rathlin Island

Fair Head

Girvan

Ballantrae

Barrhill

Galloway Forest Park

Merrick

New Galloway

DUMFRIES

Portrush

Portstewart

Bushmills

Ballycastle

Cushendun

Coleraine

Ballymoney

Cushendall

Trostan

Glenariff or Waterfoot

Red Bay

Antrim Mountains

Londonderry

Eglinton

Limavady

Castlerock

Lough Foyle

LONDONDERRY

Garvagh

Kilrea

Clogh Mills

Dungiven

Claudy

Maghera

Portglenone

Camlough

Glenarm

Antrim Glens

Antrim Coast

Kirkcolm

Cairnryan

Newton Stewart

Stranraer

Glenluce

Portpatrick

Wigtown

Luce Bay

Port William

Whithorn

Isle of Whithorn

Burrow Head

Mull of Galloway

Castle Douglas

Gatehouse of Fleet

Ringford

Kirkcudbright

Auchencairn

Dalbeattie

Dumfries

Sperrin Mountains

Sawel Mountain

Tobermore

Castledawson

Ballymena

Broughshane

Magherafelt

Gortin

Moneymore

Larne

Island Magee

Whitehead

Carrickfergus

Randalstown

Antrim

Ballyclare

Cookstown

Lough Neagh

Crumlin

Newtownabbey

Holywood

Bangor

Newtownards

Liverpool

Douglas (I. of Man)

Belfast Lough

NORTH CHANNEL

Dungannon

Coalisland

BELFAST

Lisburn

Comber

Greyabbey

Portavogie

Aughnacloy

Armagh

Portadown

Craigavon

Lurgan

Dromore

Ballynahinch

Killyleagh

Portaferry

Strangford

Strangford Lough

Ards Peninsula

Saintfield

Monaghan

Muineachán

ARMAGH

DOWN

Keady

Markethill

Gilford

Banbridge

Castlewellan

Downpatrick

Ardglass

St John's Point

Dundrum Bay

Ballybay

Newtownhamilton

Rathfriland

Mourne Mts

Slieve Donard

Newcastle

Crossmaglen

Newry

Keady

Warrenpoint

Rostrevor

Carlingford

Ramsey

Ballaugh

Point of Ayre

Snaefell

Peel

ISLE OF MAN

Douglas

Workington

Whitehaven

St. Bees Head

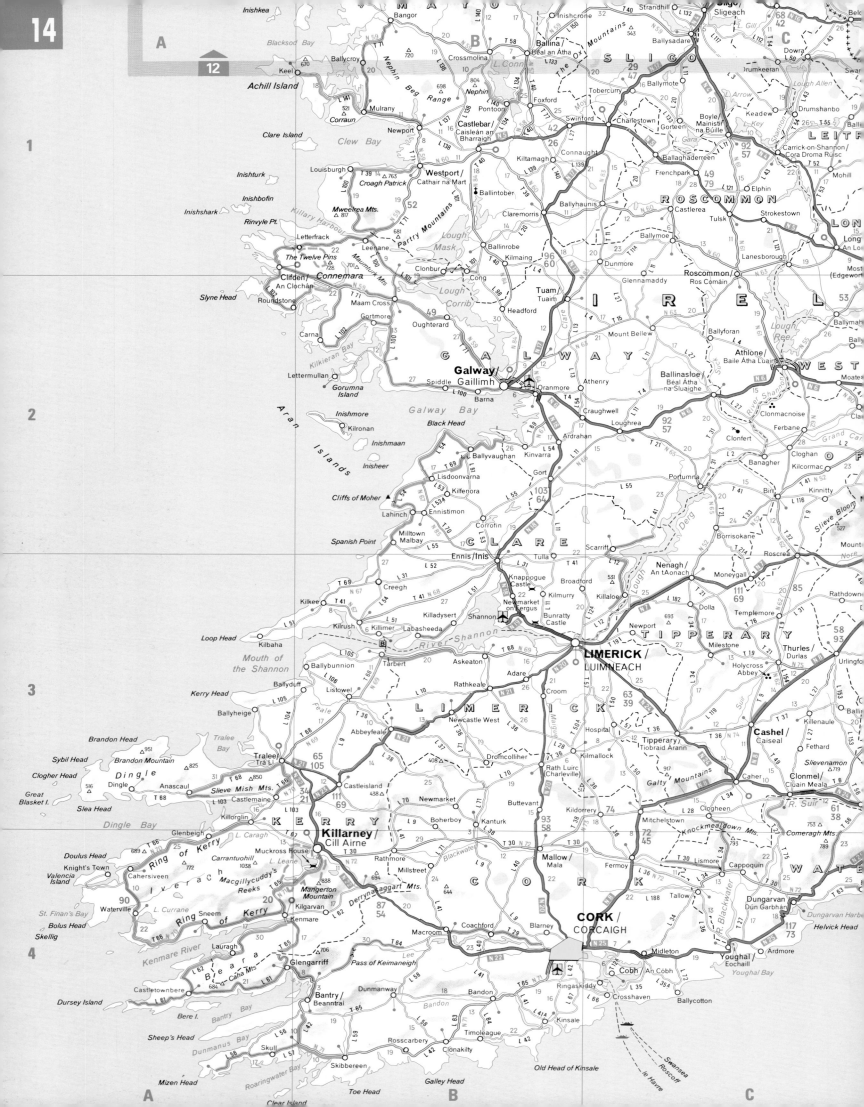

Alençon · Chartres · Étampes · Fontainebleau · Montereau

Nogent-le-Rotrou · Mamers · Bellême · Nemours · Montargis

Châteaudun · Orléans · Bellegarde

Vendôme · Beaugency · Sully · Gien · Briare

Château-du-Loir · Montoire · Blois · Chambord · Lamotte-Beuvron · Châtillon-s.-L.

Tours · Amboise · Chaumont · Bracieux · Aubigny · Cosne

Langeais · Montbazon · Chenonceaux · Romorantin · Salbris · Sancerre · Pouilly

Chinon · Ste Maure-de-T. · St Aignan · Chabris · Vierzon · Mehun

Richelieu · Loches · Valençay · Graçay · Bourges · Baugy

Châtellerault · Châtillon-s.-I. · Levroux · Issoudun · St Florent · Dun-s-Auron · Sancoins

la Roche-Posay · Buzançais · Châteauroux · Lignières · St Amand-Montrond · Meillant

Poitiers · Chauvigny · le Blanc · St Gaultier · Argenton-s.-C. · la Châtre · Châteaumeillant · Culan · Bourbon-l'Archambault

St Savin · Bélâbre · Gargilesse · Neuvy-St Sépulchre · Cérilly

Montmorillon · Crozan · Dun-le-Palestel · Aigurande · Huriel · Montluçon · Commentry

Magnac-Laval · la Souterraine · St Vaury · Bonnat · Boussac · Néris-les-B.

Châteauponsac · le Dorat · Grand-Bourg · Guéret · Evaux-les-B. · Montaigut

Bellac · Bessines · Laurière · Bénévent-l'Abbaye · Ahun · Bellegarde-en-Marche · Pionsat

Confolens · Nantiat · Bourganeuf · Aubusson · Felletin · Pontaumur · Chambon-s-V.

Limoges · St Junien · Rochechouart · St Léonard-de-Noblat · Royère-de-Vassivière · Gentioux · Châtelguyon

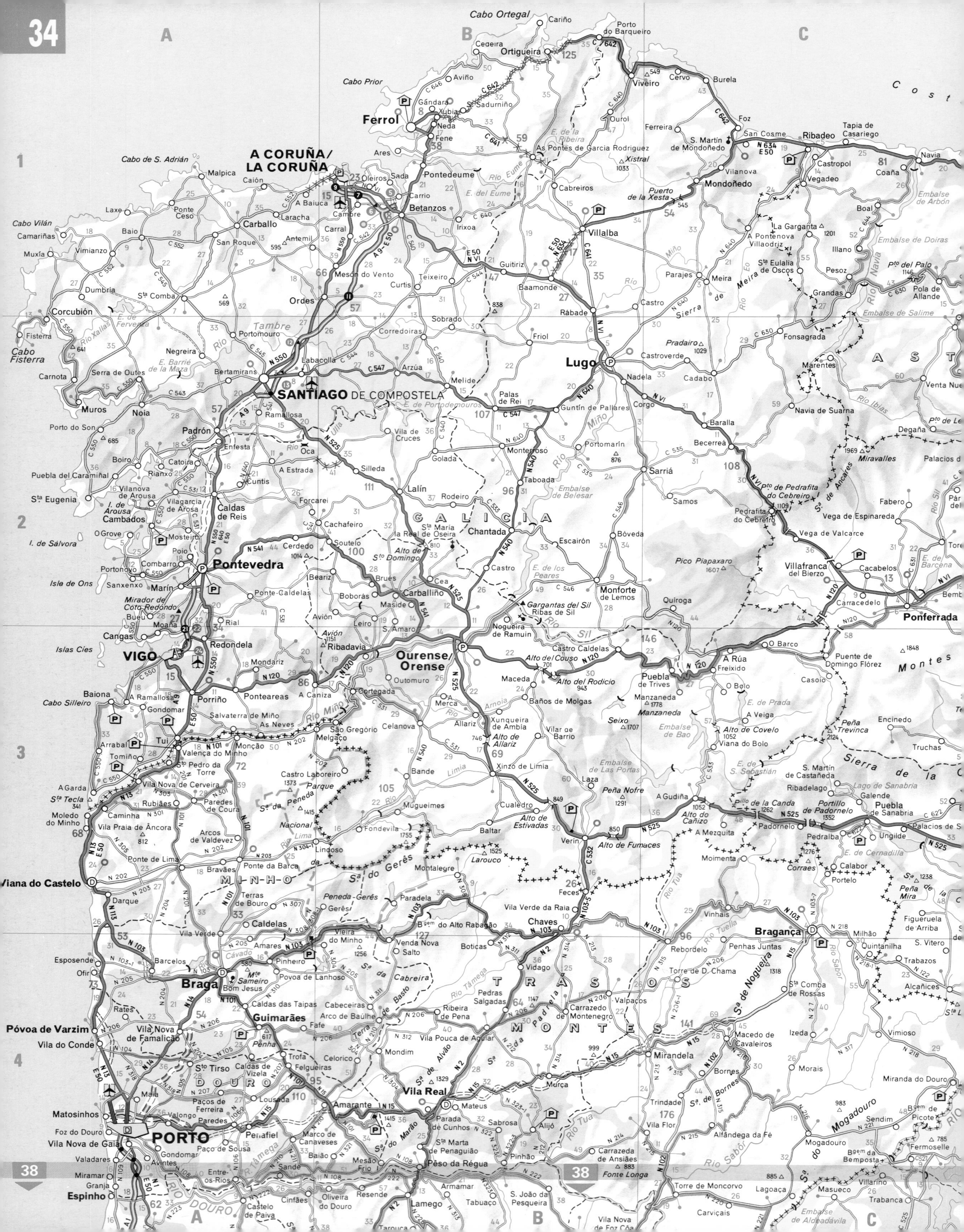

A
B
C
1
2
3
4
Cabo Ortegal
Cariño
Porto do Barqueiro
Cedeira
Ortigueira
Viveiro
Cervo
Burela
Costa
Cabo Prior
Aviño
Gándara
Xubia
S. Sadurniño
Ferrol
Neda
Fene
Ares
E. de la Ribeira
As Pontes de García Rodríguez
Xistral
Ourol
Ferreira
S. Martín de Mondoñedo
Foz
San Cosme
Ribadeo
Tapia de Casariego
Navia
Cabo de S. Adrián
A CORUÑA/ LA CORUÑA
Malpica
Caión
Oleiros
Sada
Pontedeume
Cabreiros
Puerto de la Xesta
Mondoñedo
Vilanova
Castropol
Vegadeo
Coaña
Embalse de Arbón
Laxe
Ponte Ceso
A Baiuca
Carrio
Betanzos
E. del Eume
Río Eume
Cabo Vilán
Camariñas
Laracha
Cambre
Irixoa
Villalba
A Pontenova
Villaodriz
La Garganta
Boal
Baio
Carballo
Carral
Embalse de Doiras
Muxía
Vimianzo
San Roque
Antemil
Illano
Sta Eulalia de Oscos
Pesoz
Pto del Palo
Pola de Allande
Guitiriz
Parajes
Meira
Sierra de Meira
Mesón do Vento
Teixeiro
Curtis
Baamonde
Grandas
Embalse de Salime
Dumbría
Sta Comba
Ordes
Corcubión
E. de Fervenza
Río Xallas
Fisterra
Cabo Fisterra
Tambre
Río Tambre
Portomouro
Corredoiras
Sobrado
Friol
Rábade
Castro
Pradairo
Fonsagrada
Negreira
E. Barrié de la Maza
Labacolla
Arzúa
Lugo
Castroverde
Carnota
Serra de Outes
Bertamirans
SANTIAGO DE COMPOSTELA
Melide
Nadela
Cadabo
Marentes
ASTURIAS
Venta Nueva
Muros
Noia
E. de Portodemouros
Palas de Rei
Guntín de Pallares
Corgo
Navia de Suarna
Río Ibias
Porto do Son
Padrón
Ramallosa
Ulla
Vila de Cruces
Baralla
Pto de Lei
Degaña
Enfesta
Oca
Monterroso
Portomarín
Becerreá
Miravalles
Palacios del Sil
Boiro
Catoira
Rianxo
A Estrada
Silleda
Golada
Sarriá
Puebla del Caramiñal
Cuntis
Taboada
Embalse de Belesar
Pto de Pedrafita do Cebreiro
Sa de Ancares
Vilanova de Arousa
Vilagarcía de Arosa
Lalín
Rodeiro
Samos
Fabero
Sta Eugenia
I. de Arousa
Cambados
Caldas de Reis
Forcarei
GALICIA
Pedrafita do Cebreiro
Vega de Espinareda
O Grove
Mosteiro
Cachafeiro
Sta María la Real de Oseira
Chantada
Bóveda
Vega de Valcarce
I. de Sálvora
Poio
Cerdedo
Soutelo
Alto de Sto Domingo
Escairón
Pontevedra
Combarro
Portonovo
Sanxenxo
Isla de Ons
Beariz
Brués
Cea
Castro
E. de los Peares
Monforte de Lemos
Pico Piapaxaro
Villafranca del Bierzo
Cacabelos
E. de Bárcena
Marín
Mirador de Coto Redondo
Bueu
Ponte-Caldelas
Boborás
Carballiño
Maside
Gargantas del Sil
Ribas de Sil
Quiroga
Carracedelo
Ponferrada
Moaña
Cangas
Rial
Avión
Leiro
S. Amaro
Ribadavia
Nogueira de Ramuín
Río Sil
Islas Cíes
VIGO
Redondela
Mondariz
Ourense/ Orense
Castro Caldelas
Alto del Couso
O Barco
A Rúa
Puente de Domingo Flórez
Montes
Baiona
Cabo Silleiro
A Ramallosa
Gondomar
Porriño
Ponteareas
A Cañiza
Cortegada
Outomuro
Maceda
Alto del Rodicio
Puebla de Trives
Freixido
Casoio
O Bolo
Salvaterra de Miño
As Neves
Río Miño
São Gregório
Melgaço
Celanova
A Merca
Allariz
Xunqueira de Ambía
Baños de Molgas
Manzaneda
Seixo
E. de Prada
A Veiga
Peña Trevinca
Encinedo
Arrabal
Tui
Tomiño
Valença do Minho
Monção
Alto de Allariz
Vilar de Barrio
Embalse de Bao
Alto de Covelo
Viana do Bolo
Truchas
Sierra de la Cabrera
Sto Pedro da Torre
Castro Laboreiro
Bande
Limia
Xinzo de Limia
Embalse de Las Portas
E. de S. Sebastián
S. Martín de Castañeda
A Garda
Sta Tecla
Vila Nova de Cerveira
Parque Nacional
Sa da Peneda
Laza
Peña Nofre
Ribadelago
Lago de Sanabria
Galende
Moledo do Minho
Caminha
Rubiães
Paredes de Coura
Mugueimes
Cualedro
A Gudiña
Alto do Cañizo
Pllo de la Canda
Portillo de Padornelo
Puebla de Sanabria
Vila Praia de Âncora
Arcos de Valdevez
Lima
Fondevila
Alto de Estivadas
Baltar
Verín
Alto de Fumaces
A Mezquita
Padornelo
Pedralba
Ungilde
Palacios de Sanabria
Lindoso
Larouco
Montalegre
Moimenta
E. de Cernadilla
Ponte de Lima
Bravães
Ponte da Barca
MINHO
Sa do Gerês
Calabor
Corrales
Portelo
Viana do Castelo
Darque
Terras de Bouro
Peneda-Gerês
Gerês
Paradela
Feces
Vila Verde da Raia
Vinhais
Sa de Mira
Peña de Mira
Figueruela de Arriba
Caldelas
Vieira do Minho
Bgem do Alto Rabagão
Chaves
Bragança
Milhão
Vila Verde
Amares
Venda Nova
Salto
Boticas
Rebordelo
Penhas Juntas
Quintanilha
S. Vitero
Esposende
Ofir
Barcelos
Pinheiro
Cávado
Povoa de Lanhoso
Sa da Cabreira
Vidago
Torre de D. Chama
Sa de Nogueira
Trabazos
Alcañices
Braga
Mte Sameiro
Bom Jesus
TRÁS-OS-MONTES
Sta Comba de Rossas
Rates
Caldas das Taipas
Cabeceiras
Arco de Baúlhe
Terra de Basto
Ribeira de Pena
Pedras Salgadas
Carrazedo de Montenegro
Sa da Padrela
Valpaços
Póvoa de Varzim
Vila Nova de Famalicão
Guimarães
Fafe
Vila Pouca de Aguiar
Macedo de Cavaleiros
Izeda
Vimioso
Vila do Conde
Penha
Trofa
Celorico
Mondim
Mirandela
Morais
Sto Tirso
Caldas de Vizela
Felgueiras
Sa de Alvão
Bornes
Sa de Bornes
Miranda do Douro
DOURO
Maia
Paços de Ferreira
Lousada
Amarante
Vila Real
Mateus
Murça
Trindade
Matosinhos
Valongo
Paredes
Parada de Cunhos
Sabrosa
Alijó
Vila Flor
Sendim
Bgem de Picote
Foz do Douro
PORTO
Penafiel
Marco de Canaveses
Sa do Marão
Sta Marta de Penaguião
Alfândega da Fé
Mogadouro
Vila Nova de Gaia
Gondomar
Paço de Sousa
Baião
Carrazeda de Ansiães
Pinhão
Bgem da Bemposta
Fermoselle
Valadares
Avintes
Sande
Mesão Frio
Peso da Régua
Rio Sabor
Rio Tua
Río Tâmega
Miramar
Entre-os-Rios
Fonte Longa
Torre de Moncorvo
Villarino
Granja
Espinho
Cinfães
Oliveira do Douro
Resende
Armamar
Lamego
Tabuaço
S. João da Pesqueira
Lagoaça
Masueco
Trabanca
Castelo de Paiva
Vila Nova de Foz Côa
Carviçais
Embalse de Aldeadávila
Tarouca
RIO DOURO
38

Espinho
Miramar
Granja
Entre-os-Rios
Sande
Frio
N 108
S. João da Pesqueira
Tabuaço
Armamar
Lamego
Resende
Oliveira do Douro
Cinfães
Castelo de Paiva
RIO DOURO
N 222
N 2
Penedono
Moimenta da Beira
Sernancelhe
Vila Nova de Paiva
S. João de Tarouca
Tarouca
Castro Daire
S. Pedro do Sul
Arouca
S. João de Madeira
Stª Maria da Feira
Furadouro
Ovar
Vale de Cambra
Sever do Vouga
Aguiar da Beira
Trancoso
Vila Franca das Nav
Penalva do Castelo
Sátão
Fornos de Algodres
Celorico da Beira
Viseu
Mangualde
Nelas
Oliveira do Bairro
Anadia
Vouzela
Oliveira de Frades
Albergaria-a-Velha
Aveiro
S. Jacinto
Praia da Barra
Ilhavo
Vagos
Águeda
Caramulo
Campo de Beisteros
Tondela
Canas de Senhorim
Guarda
Vale de Estrela
Gouveia
Seia
Manteigas
Valhelhas
Belmonte
Penhas da Saúde
Loriga
Unhais da Serra
S. Romão
Oliveira do Hospital
Tábua
Mortágua
Buçaco
Luso
Mealhada
Curia
Praia de Mira
Mira
Mamarrosa
Praia de Tocha
Cantanhede
Tocha
Arazede
Pampilhosa
COIMBRA
Penacova
Vila Nova de Poiares
Arganil
S. Pedro de Açor
Góis
SERRA DA ESTRELA
Covilhã
Tortosendo
Paúl
Teixoso
Caria
Sto Estêvão
Meimoa
Penar
Figueira da Foz
Cabo Mondego
Buarcos
Montemor-o-Velho
Condeixa-a-Nova
Soure
Miranda do Corvo
Lousã
Castanheira de Pêra
Pampilhosa da Serra
Fundão
Silvares
Vale de Prazeres
Alpedrinha
S. Vicente da Beira
Orvalho
Cambas
Foz Giraldo
Medelim
Idanha a Nova
Zebreira
Pedrógão
Praia da Vieira
Monte Redondo
Vieira
Monte Real
Degracias
Penela
Ansião
Pombal
Sicó
Pontão
Pedrógão Grande
Figueiró dos Vinhos
Bgem do Cabril
Oleiros
Alvelos
Salgueiro do Campo
Alcains
Escalos de Cima
S. Pedro de Moel
Marinha Grande
Leiria
Alvaiázere
Barqueiro
Cernache de Bonjardim
Sertã
Sobreira Formosa
Sarzedas
Castelo Branco
Ladoeiro
Rosmaninhal
Martingança
Batalha
Cruz da Légua
Vila Nova de Ourém
Ferreira do Zêzere
Vila de Rei
Proença-a-Nova
Vila Velha de Ródão
Bgem de Cedillo
Malpica
Nazaré
Alcobaça
S. Martinho do Porto
Alfeizerão
Cova da Iria
Porto de Mós
Mira de Aire
Fátima
Serra de Aire
Tomar
Sardoal
Mação
Gavião
Nisa
Cedillo
Fratel
Montalvão
Herrera de Alcántara
Santiago de Alcántara
Foz do Arelho
Cabo Carvoeiro
Baleal
Peniche
Ilha Berlenga
Atouguia da Baleia
Óbidos
Caldas da Rainha
Alcanede
Alcanena
Torres Novas
Entroncamento
Castelo de Bode
Constância
Abrantes
Rossio
Tramagal
Vila Nova da Barquinha
Almourol
Arez
Tolosa
Alpalhão
Castelo de Vide
Marvão
Valencia de Alcántara
Galegos
S. Vicente de Alcántara
Lourinhã
Bombarral
Cadaval
Rio Maior
Golegã
Chamusca
Bemposta
Crato
Flor da Rosa
Portalegre
La Codosera
Praia de Stª Cruz
Cercal
Santarém
Alpiarça
Chouto
Ponte de Sor
Alter do Chão
Arronches
Pto de los Conejeros
Torres Vedras
Atalaia
Cartaxo
Almeirim
Muge
Galveias
Cabeço de Vide
Monforte
Campo Maior
Ericeira
Sapataria
Alenquer
Sobral de Mte Agraço
Arruda dos Vinhos
Carregado
RIO TEJO
São José da Lamarosa
Bgem de Montargil
Montargil
Bgem do Maranhão
Avis
Fronteira
Veiros
Elvas
Caya
Mafra
Malveira
Lousa
Bucelas
Vila Franca de Xira
Alverca do Ribatejo
Samora Correia
Benavente
Salvaterra de Magos
Coruche
Mora
Pavia
Casa Branca
Sousel
Estremoz
Vila Boim
Vila Fernando
Sintra
Colares
Amadora
Loures
Sacavém
Sto Estêvão
Couço
Brotas
Arraiolos
Évoramonte
Borba
Vila Viçosa
Juromenha
Cabo da Roca
Queluz
Oeiras
LISBOA
Alcochete
Montijo
Canha
Lavre
Vimieiro
Estremoz
Vila Fernando
Estoril
Cascais
Cabo Raso
Trafaria
Almada
Barreiro
Seixal
Moita
Pinhal Novo
Tajpadas
Vendas Novas
Arraiolos
Évoramonte
Borba
Azaruja
Redondo
Terena
Alandroal
Olivenza
Costa da Caparica
Cova
Palmela
Maratreca
Montemor-o-Novo
S. Miguel de Machede
Évora
Vila Fresca de Azeitão
Santana
Arrábida
Setúbal
Cruzamento de Pegões
Montoito
Cabo Espichel
Sesimbra
Península de Tróia
Santiago do Escoural
S. Cristóvão
Alcácer do Sal
Alcáçovas
Bgem de Pego do Altar
Comporta
S. Manços
Alconchel
Monsaraz

BEIRA LITORAL
BEIRA ALTA
BEIRA BAIXA
ESTREMADURA
RIBATEJO
ALENTEJO
P O R T U G A L
RIO TEJO
RIO MONDEGO
RIO ZÊZERE
RIO SADO
GUADIANA

44

Caracuel · Almagro · Bolaños de Calatrava · Villanueva de Franco · Alhambra · Ossa de Montiel · Los Barreros · Lezuza · Albacete · Sta. Ana · N 322 · Chinchilla de Monte

A · B · C · 40 · N 301

Puertollano · C 424 · C 410 · Aldea del Rey · Calzada de Calatrava · Moral de Calatrava · S. Carlos del Valle · Valdepeñas · C 415 · Villahermosa · Villanueva de la Fuente · Viveros · S. Pedro · Pozuelo · El Salobral · Pozo Cañada · Balazote

Convento de Calatrava · Villanueva de S. Carlos · Atalaya de la Calzada · Sta Cruz de Mudela · Torrenueva · Villanueva de los Infantes · Montiel · Villanueva de la Fuente · Alcaraz · Peñascosa · Peñas de S. Pedro · Pozohondo · Robledo · Roble 1257 · 1070

Mestanza · Viso del Marqués · Castellar de Santiago · Villamanrique · Albaladejo · 1151 · Sa de Alcaraz · Bogarra · Ayna · Liétor · Tobarra

S. Lorenzo de Calatrava · Estrella 1300 · Desfiladero de Despeñaperros · Torre de Juan Abad · 1001 · Almenaras 1798 · Fábricas de Riópar · Molinicos · C 415 · Elche de la Sierra · Hellín

El Centenillo · Sta Elena · Puente de Génave · C 321 · Siles · Yeste · E. del Cenajo · Las Minas

La Carolina · Santisteban del Puerto · Arroyo del Ojanco · La Puerta de Segura · Orcera · Arguellite · Segura de la Sierra · Socovos · Letur

Baños de la Encina · Vilches · Guarromán · Navas de S. Juan · Castellar de Santisteban · Beas de Segura · Cortijos Nuevos · Yelmo · 1809 · Segura de la Sierra · Casicas del Río Segura · Moratalla · Calasparra

Las Viñas · Virgen de la Cabeza · Bailén · Linares · Arquillos · Villanueva del Arzobispo · Garganta · Hornos · Santiago de la Espada · Nerpio · Caravaca de la Cruz · Cehegín

Andújar · Sabiote · Villacarrillo · Blanquilla 1830 · E. del Tranco · Pontones · M U R C

Villanueva de la Reina · Mengíbar · Baeza · Torreperogil · Mogón · Sa de Cazorla · 1964 · Puebla de Don Fadrique · El Moral · Bárranda · Bullas

Higuera de Arjona · Arjona · Fuerte del Rey · Úbeda · Sto Tomé · Peal de Becerro · Pto de las Palomas 1290 · Sa de la Sagra 2381 · La Losa · Santiago de la Espada · El Moral

Torredonjimeno · Torre del Campo · Jaén · Jimena · Bedmar · Jódar · Cazorla · Quesada · Pto de Tiscar 1183 · Cabañas · Huesa · Castril · Huéscar · La Paca

Martos · Mancha Real · Pegalajar · Mágina 2167 · Cabra del Sto Cristo · Hinojares · Castilléjar · Galera · María · Baños de la Fuensanta

La Guardia de Jaén · Cambil · Huelma · Alicún de Ortega · Pozo Alcón · Cortes de Baza · Orce · Vélez Blanco · Vélez Rubio · Lorca

Los Villares · Fuensanta de Martos · Valdepeñas de Jaén · Campillo de Arenas · Montejícar · Guadahortuna · Villanueva de las Torres · Cuevas del Campo · Benamaurel · Cúllar Baza · Chirivel · Las Vertientes · Puerto Lumbreras

Alcalá la Real · Pto del Castillo 940 · Fráiles · Benalúa de las Villas · Moreda · Mencal 1447 · Zújar · Baza · Lúcar 1722 · Oria · Sta María de Nieva · Pozo Higuera · Pulpí

Montefrío · Moclín · Iznalloz · Huélago · Behalúa de Guadix · Caniles · Sta Bárbara 2271 · Tíjola · Olula del Río · Albox · Huércal-Overa

Illora · Parapanda 1601 · Colomera · Diezma · Purullena · Sta Cruz · Serón · Purchena · Cantoria · Macael · Cuevas del Amanzora · Los Lobos · S. Juan de

Pinos Puente · Pto de la Mora 1390 · Río Fardes · Guadix · Alcudia de Guadix · Sierra de Baza · Tetica 2080 · Albánchez · Antas · Villaricos

Atarfe · Albolote · Huétor-Santillán · Lacalahorra · Fiñana · 2168 · Sierra de los Filabres · Lubrín · Los Gallardos · Vera

Santa Fe · GRANADA · Armilla · Escúllar · Doña María Ocaña · Calar Alto · Tahal · Uleila del Campo · Sorbas · Turre · Mojácar

Moraleda de Zafayona · Gabia la Grande · Pto del Suspiro del Moro 860 · Horcajo de Trevélez 3182 · Abla · Gérgal · Tabernas · Lucainena de las Torres · 139

Ventas de Huelma · Padul · Solynieve · Pico Veleta 3398 · Mulhacén 3482 · Pto de la Ragua 2609 · Ohanes · Abrucena · Alhamilla 1387 · Carboneras

Dúrcal · Lanjarón · Trevélez · Laroles · Canjáyar · Alboloduy · Gádor · Níjar · La Mesa Roldán

Béznar · Capileira · Cádiar · Uglijar · Laujar de Andarax · Illar · Benahadux · S. Isidro · Las Negras

SIERRA NEVADA · Las Alpujarras · Órgiva · Pto Camacho 1219 · Morrón 2236 · Sierra de Gádor · Alhama de Almería · ALMERÍA · Punta del Río

Cómpeta · Navachica 1832 · Frigiliana · Cueva de Nerja · Vélez de Benaudalla · Contraviesa · Berja · Dalías · El Ejido · Aguadulce · El Alquián · Cabo de Gata

Algarrobo · Torrox · Nerja · La Herradura · Almuñécar · Salobreña · Motril · Albuñol · Adra · Balanegra · Roquetas de Mar · Almerimar · Golfo de Almería · Costa del Sol

Sa de Almíjara · Sa de Tejeda 2065 · Otívar · Cabo Sacratif · Castell de Ferro · Calahonda · La Rábita · Balerma · Guardias Viejas · Almerimar · Pta de la Polacra · Cabo de Gata · S. José

C O S T A · d e l · S O L

43

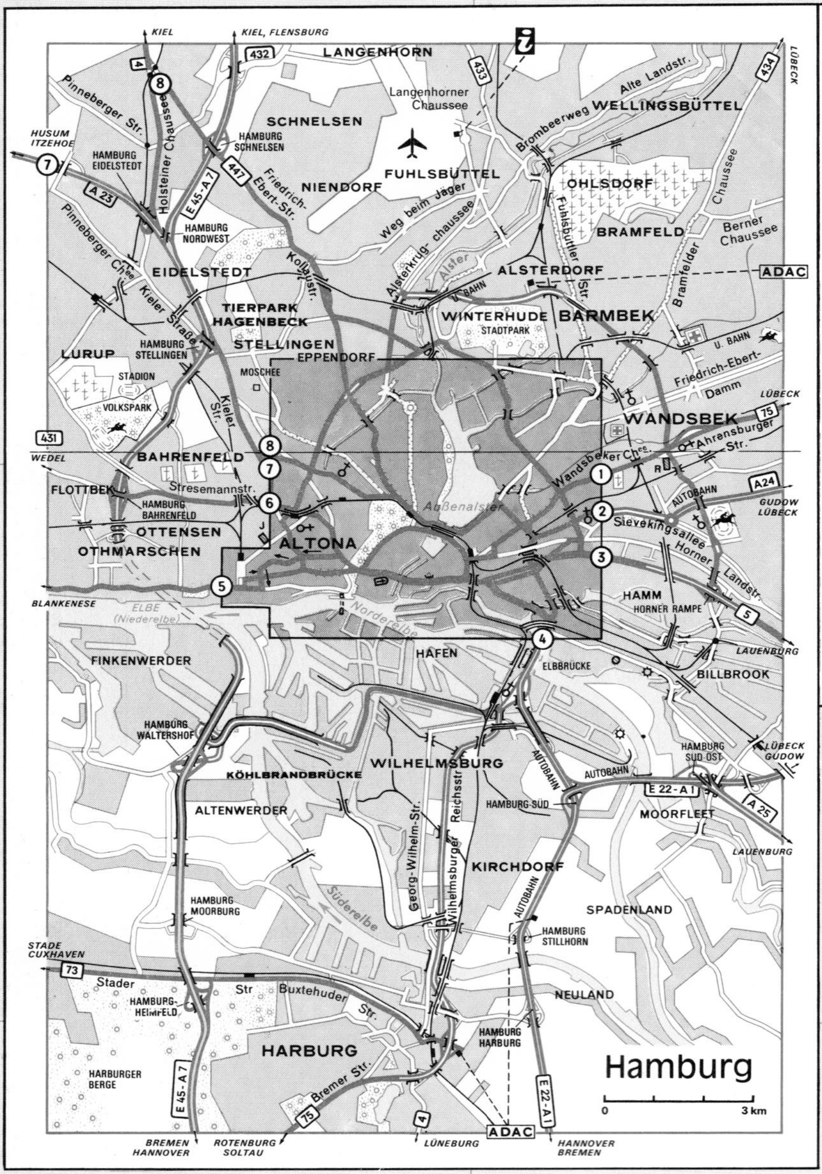

Hamburg

LANGENHORN
KIEL, FLENSBURG
KIEL
432
433
HAMBURG SCHNELSEN
SCHNELSEN
Alte Landstr.
Brombeerweg WELLINGSBÜTTEL
LÜBECK
A 23
HUSUM ITZEHOE
7
HAMBURG EIDELSTEDT
Langenhorner Chaussee
FUHLSBÜTTEL
Weg beim Jäger
Friedrich-Ebert-Str.
NIENDORF
OHLSDORF
Fuhlsbütteler Chaussee
Berner Chaussee
8
Pinneberger Str.
Holsteiner Chaussee
447
A 45·A 7
HAMBURG NORDWEST
Koll-str.
Alsterkrug chaussee
Alster
BRAMFELD
Bramfelder Str.
ADAC
EIDELSTEDT
Kieler Str.
ALSTERDORF
Pinneberger Chr.
TIERPARK HAGENBECK
STELLINGEN
EPPENDORF
WINTERHUDE BARMBEK STADTPARK
U. BAHN
Friedrich-Ebert-Damm
LÜBECK
LURUP
STADION VOLKSPARK
HAMBURG STELLINGEN
Moschee
WANDSBEK
A 24
WEDEL
431
BAHRENFELD
8
7
Außenalster
Wandsbeker Ch.
Wandsbeker Chaussee
Ahrensburger Str.
GUDOW LÜBECK
FLOTTBEK
Stresemannstr.
6
1
R
AUTOBAHN
OTTENSEN
HAMBURG BAHRENFELD
ALTONA
2
Sievekingsallee
Horner
Landstr.
OTHMARSCHEN
5
3
HAMM HORNER RAMPE
BLANKENESE
ELBE (Niederelbe)
Norderelbe
HAFEN
ELBBRÜCKE
4
LAUENBURG
5
FINKENWERDER
BILLBROOK
HAMBURG SÜD OST
LÜBECK GUDOW
KÖHLBRANDBRÜCKE
WILHELMSBURG
Reichsstr.
AUTOBAHN
HAMBURG SÜD
E 22·A 1
A 25
ALTENWERDER
Georg-Wilhelm-Str.
Wilhelmsburger
MOORFLEET
LAUENBURG
HAMBURG MOORBURG
Süderelbe
KIRCHDORF
SPADENLAND
HAMBURG STILLHORN
STADE CUXHAVEN
73
Stader Str.
Buxtehuder Str.
NEULAND
E 45·A 7
HAMBURG HEIMFELD
HAMBURG HARBURG
HARBURG
HARBURGER BERGE
Bremer Str.
75
E 22·A 1
ADAC
BREMEN HANNOVER
ROTENBURG SOLTAU
LÜNEBURG
HANNOVER BREMEN
4

0   3 km

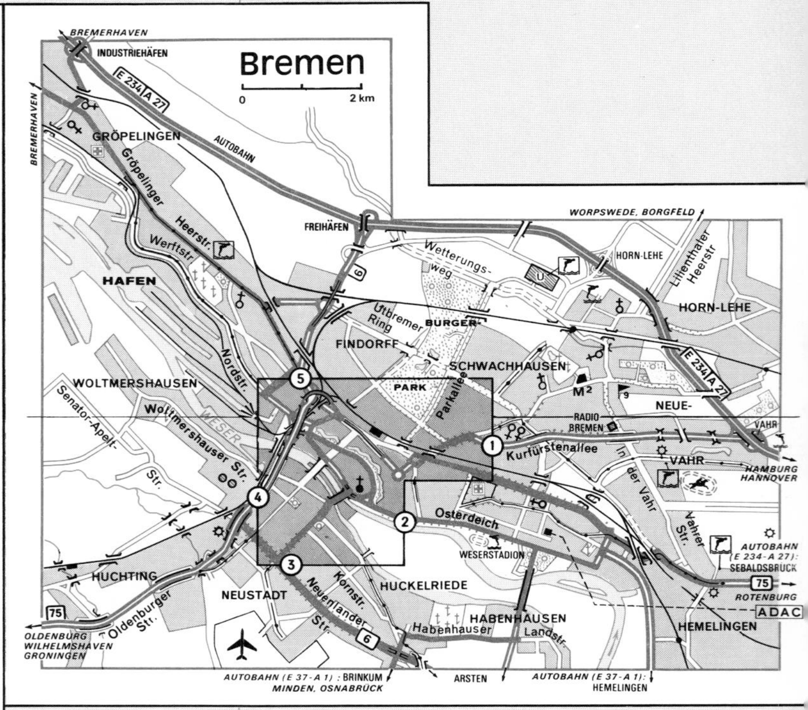

Bremen

BREMERHAVEN
INDUSTRIEHÄFEN
E 234·A 27
0   2 km
BREMERHAVEN
AUTOBAHN
GRÖPELINGEN
Heerstr.
Werftstr.
Gröpelinger Str.
WORPSWEDE BORGFELD
FREIHÄFEN
Wetterungsweg
HORN-LEHE
HAFEN
Nordstr.
BURGER
HORN-LEHE
Lilienthaler Heerstr.
WOLTMERSHAUSEN
Uhlemer Ring
FINDORFF
SCHWACHHAUSEN
E 234·A 27
5
WESER
Woltmershauser Str.
PARK
Parallelw.
RADIO BREMEN
NEUE-
M
Senator-Apelt-Str.
Kurfürstenallee
1
VAHR
4
HAMBURG HANNOVER
HUCHTING
Oldenburger Str.
2
Osterdeich
den Vahr
VAHR
Vahrer Str.
AUTOBAHN (E 234·A 27) SEBALDSBRÜCK
3
Kornstr.
NEUSTADT
Neuenlander Str.
WESERSTADION
ROTENBURG
75
6
HUCKELRIEDE
HABENHAUSEN
Habenhauser Landstr.
HEMELINGEN
OLDENBURG WILHELMSHAVEN GRONINGEN
ADAC
AUTOBAHN (E 37·A 1): BRINKUM MINDEN, OSNABRÜCK
ARSTEN
AUTOBAHN (E 37·A 1): HEMELINGEN

NOORDZEE
NOORD DUNEN
Waddeneilanden
Amelar Nes
Hollum
Oosterend
West-Terschelling
Terschelling
Oost-Vlieland
Vlielan
Leeuwarden
A 31
Harlingen
N 31
34
Francker
N 359
De Koog
Texel
FRI
Den Burg
Bolsward
12
A 7·E 22
Snee
Den Helder
Den Oever
Afsluitdijk
54
Workum
Staveren
Sloten
Lemmer
NOORD-
Schagen
Medemblik
Enkhuizen
Urk
Emmeloord
NEDER
HOLLAND
Bergen
Bergen aan Zee
Alkmaar
Hoorn
Edam
Egmond aan Zee
Markermeer
A 9
102
Purmerend
Lelystad
Dronten

Major cities: BRNO, BRATISLAVA, WIEN, LINZ, GRAZ, České Budějovice

Vyškov, Bučovice, Kyjov, Dubňany, Čejč, Hodonín, Holíč, Kúty, Stupava, Malacky, Břeclav, Mikulov, Poštorná, Bernhardsthal, Hohenau, Angern, Marchegg, Gänserndorf, Drnholec, Hrušovany, Hevlin, Drasenhofen, Poysdorf, Wilfersdorf, Zistersdorf, Mistelbach, Dürnkrut, Deutsch-Wagram, Großenzersdorf, Leopoldsdorf, Wolkersdorf, Korneuburg, Stockerau, Klosterneuburg

Jihlava, Velké Meziříčí, Velká Bíteš, Křižanov, Tišnov, Kuřim, Blansko, Pernštejn, Macocha

Pelhřimov, Pacov, Mladá Vožice, Tábor, Sezimovo-Ústí, Bernartice, Milevsko, Soběslav, Veselí, Jindřichuv Hradec, Kamenice, Telč, Třešť, Třebíč, Náměšť, Rosice, Ivančice, Židlochovice, Pohořelice, Moravský Krumlov, Moravské Budějovice, Jaroměřice, Jemnice, Dačice, Slavonice, Nová Bystřice, Gramatten, Litschau, Heidenreichstein, Dobersberg, Waidhofen, Gr.-Siegharts, Raabs, Geras, Retz, Pulkau, Hardegg, Drosendorf Stadt, Znojmo, Hatě, Kleinhaugsdorf, Laa an der Thaya, Hollabrunn, Eggenburg, Horn, Maissau, Ziersdorf, Göllersdorf, Ernstbrunn

Třeboň, Chlum u Třeboně, Schrems, Gmünd, České Velenice, Neunagelberg, Halámky, Trhové Sviny, Weitra, Allentsteig, Neupölla, Zwettl, Rastenfeld, Gföhl, Langenlois, Kirchberg, Hadersdorf

Hluboká, Bezdrev, Lišov, Kaplice, Dolní Dvořiště, Wullowitz, Vyšší Brod, Lipno, Freistadt, Bad Leonfelden, Gallneukirchen, Unterweißenbach, Königswiesen, Arbesbach, Groß Gerungs, Mönchdorf, Laimbach, Pöggstall, Aggsbach-Markt, Spitz, Weißenkirchen, Dürnstein, Krems, Stein, Traismauer, Herzogenburg, Tulln, Judenau, Purkersdorf, Pressbaum, Schönbrunn, Mödling, Schwechat

Urfahr, Pregarten, Perg, Mauthausen, Enns, St. Florian, St. Valentin, Strengberg, Ybbs, Persenbeug, Pöchlarn, Melk, Loosdorf, Maria Taferl, Mank, Obergrafendorf, Wilhelmsburg, St. Pölten, Neulengbach, St. Christophen, Altlengbach, Alland, Mayerling, Baden, Bad Vöslau, Berndorf, Pottenstein, Leobersdorf, Sollenau, Ebenfurth, Wiener-Neudorf, Eisenstadt, Rust, Mörbisch, Purbach, Neusiedl, Mannersdorf, Bruck, Pärndorf, Hegyeshalom, Kittsee, Hainburg, Berg, Bad Deutsch-Altenburg, Fischamend Markt

Traun, Neuhofen an der Krems, Kremsmünster, Bad Hall, Grünburg, Steyr, Sierninghofen, Haag, St. Peter in der Au, Aschbach Markt, Amstetten, Euratsfeld, Waidhofen, Wieselburg, Purgstall, Scheibbs, Gaming, Lunz, Göstling, Mariazell, Annaberg, Türnitz, Hohenberg, Lilienfeld, Traisen, Hainfeld, Kirchberg a.d. Pielach, Gutenstein, Puchberg, Pernitz, Wöllersdorf, Wiener Neustadt, Mattersburg, Ebenfurth, Klingenbach, Sopron, Deutschkreutz, Nagycenk

Kirchdorf, Micheldorf, Großraming, Weyer-Markt, Altenmünster, Windischgarsten, Hinterstoder, St. Gallen, Wildalpen, Seewiesen, Mürzsteg, Semmering, Mürzzuschlag, Langenwang, Krieglach, Kindberg, Mönichkirchen, Aspang, Kirchschlag, Wiesmath, Lockenhaus, Bernstein, Köszeg, Bük, Lövö

Liezen, Irdning, Tauplitz, Admont, Rottenmann, Trieben, Hohentauern, Eisenerz, Vordernberg, Trofaiach, Leoben, Bruck an der Mur, Kapfenberg, Donawitz, St. Michael, Frohnleiten, Birkfeld, Pöllau, Hartberg, Friedberg, Pinkafeld, Oberwart, Vorau, Ratten, Weiz, Gleisdorf, Anger, Kaindorf, Großpetersdorf, Fürstenfeld, Güssing, Moschendorf, Szombathely

Tamsweg, Murau, Neumarkt, St. Lambrecht, Scheifling, Judenburg, Weißkirchen, Knittelfeld, Zeltweg, Fohnsdorf, Oberwölz, Seckau, Gaaldorf, Oberzeiring, Gleinalmtunnel, Gratkorn, GRAZ, Voitsberg, Köflach, Piber, Stainz, Deutschlandsberg, Wildon, Kalsdorf, Feldbach, Fehring, Bad Gleichenberg, Riegersburg, Heiligenkreuz, Rábafüzes, Körmend, Szentgotthárd

Bad St. Leonhard, Twimberg, Klippitztörl, Wolfsberg, Metnitz, Friesach, Hüttenberg, Strassburg, Flattnitz, Deutschlandsberg, Leibnitz, Mureck, Bad Radkersburg, Gornji Petrovci, Mačkovci, Szilvágy, Zalabaksa, Lenti

Road numbers and features (selection): E15, E7, E55, E60, E58, E59, E461, E49, E84, A1, A2, A3, A4, A21, DONAU, Thaya, March, Mur, Enns, Ybbs, Raab, Leitha, Neusiedler See, Wienerwald, Gesäuse, Hochschwab, Schneeberg, Rax, Semmering-P., Pyhrnpaß, Hengstpaß, Schoberpaß, Präbichl, Erzberg, Packsattel, Obdacher Sattel, Gaberl-Sattel, Sölkerpaß

Gr. Priel △2515, Hochtor △2369, Gr. Bösenstein △2449, Hochreichart 2416, Speikkogel 1988, Gr. Ötscher 1893, Schneeberg 2076, Heukuppe 2007, Schöckl 1445

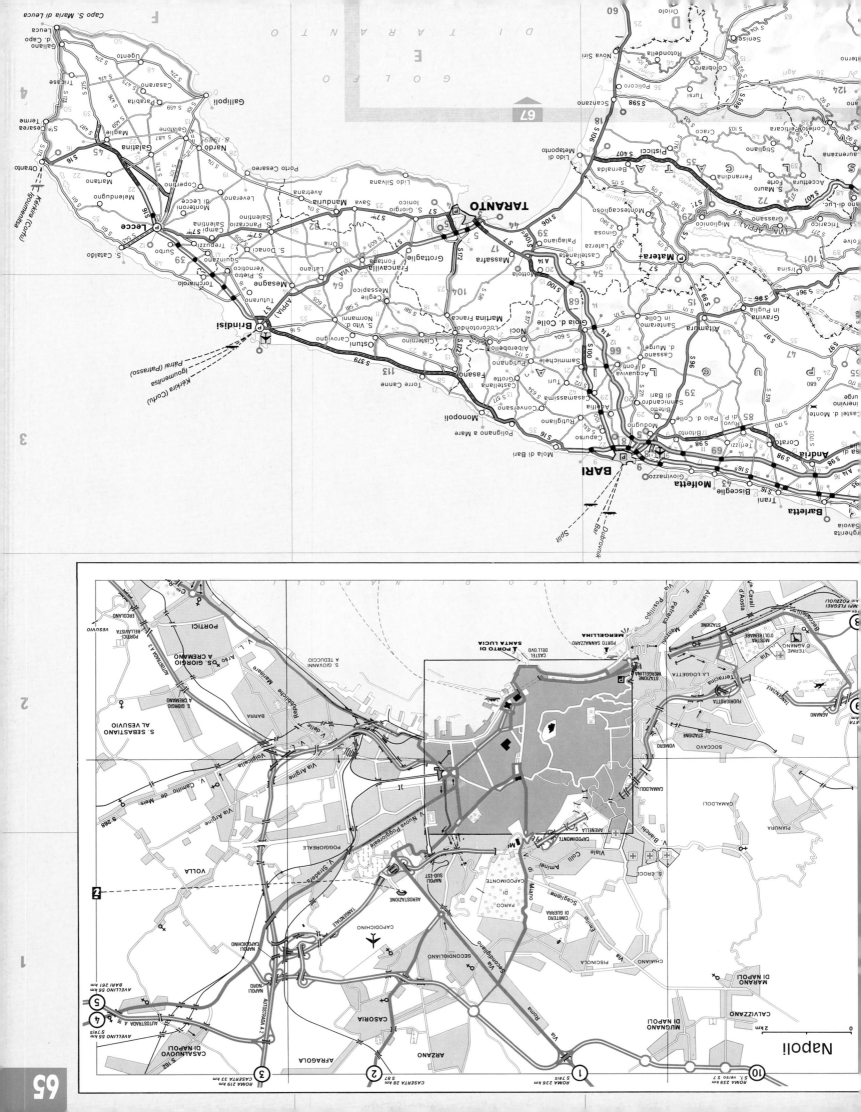

Napoli

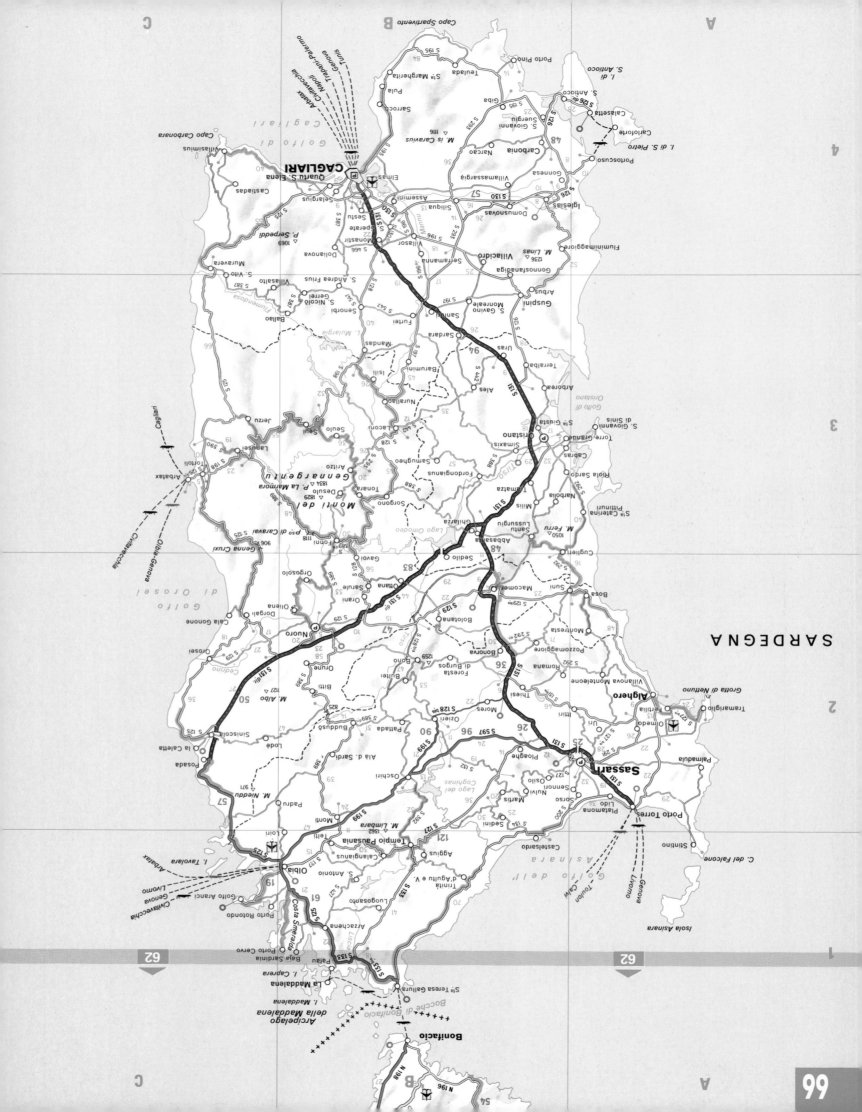

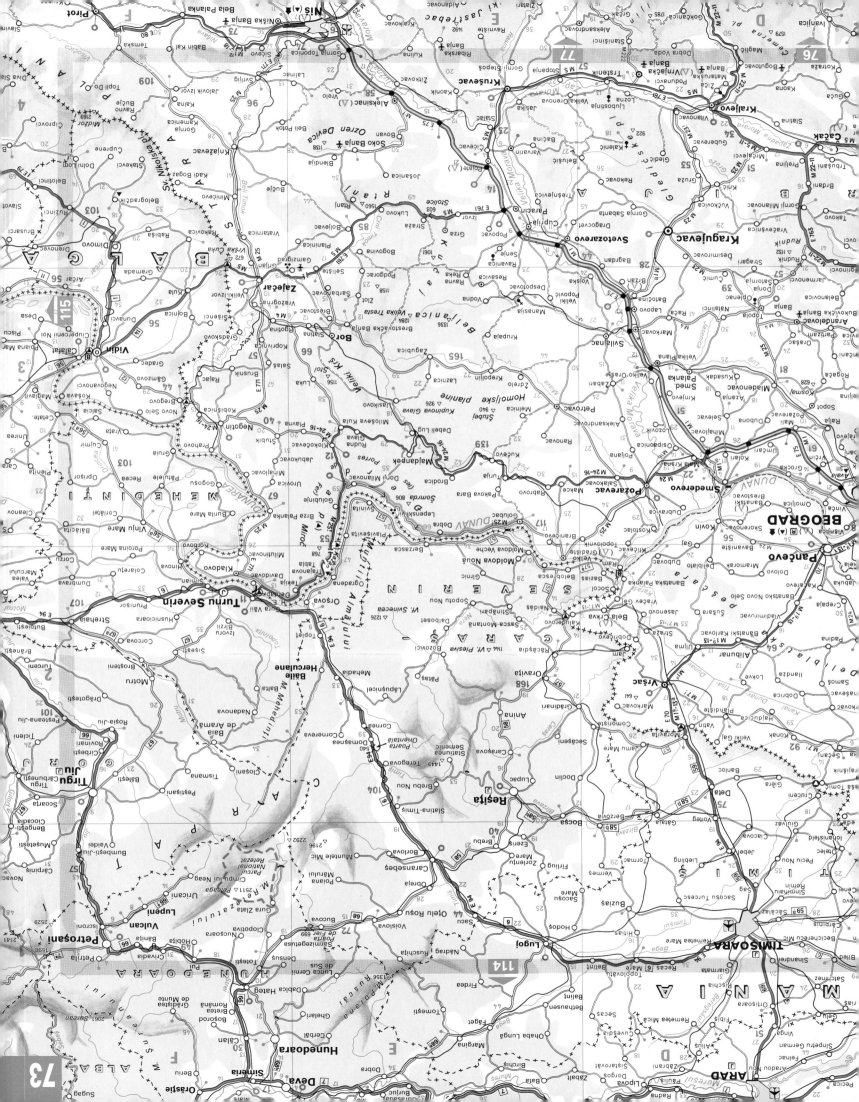

SOFIA
SKOPJE
Niš
Priština
Prizren
Tetovo
Gostivar
Kičevo
Debar
Struga
Ohrid
Bitola
Prilep
Titov Veles
Štip
Strumica
Kumanovo
Vranje
Leskovac
Prokuplje
Pirot
Dimitrovgrad
Pernik
Kjustendil
Blagoevgrad
Kriva Palanka
Kočani
Delčevo
Berovo
Gevgelija
Kavadarci
Titova Mitrovica
Podujevo
Kuršumlija
Surdulica
Flórina
Édessa
Pogradec
Prespansko ezero
Ohridsko ezero
Dojransko ezero
Suva planina
Veliki Jastrebac
Radan
Kukavica
Vardenik
Osogovske planine
Plačkovica
Jakupica
Babuna
Baba
Šar planina
Korab
Vitoša
Kožuf
Óros Vóras
M A K E D O N I J A
H E L L Á S
Thessaloniki 20
Thessaloniki 32
Sandanski 65
Petrič 55
Plovdiv
Samokov
Varna 468
Vraca 116
Burgas 382
Plovdiv 156
73
78
79
115

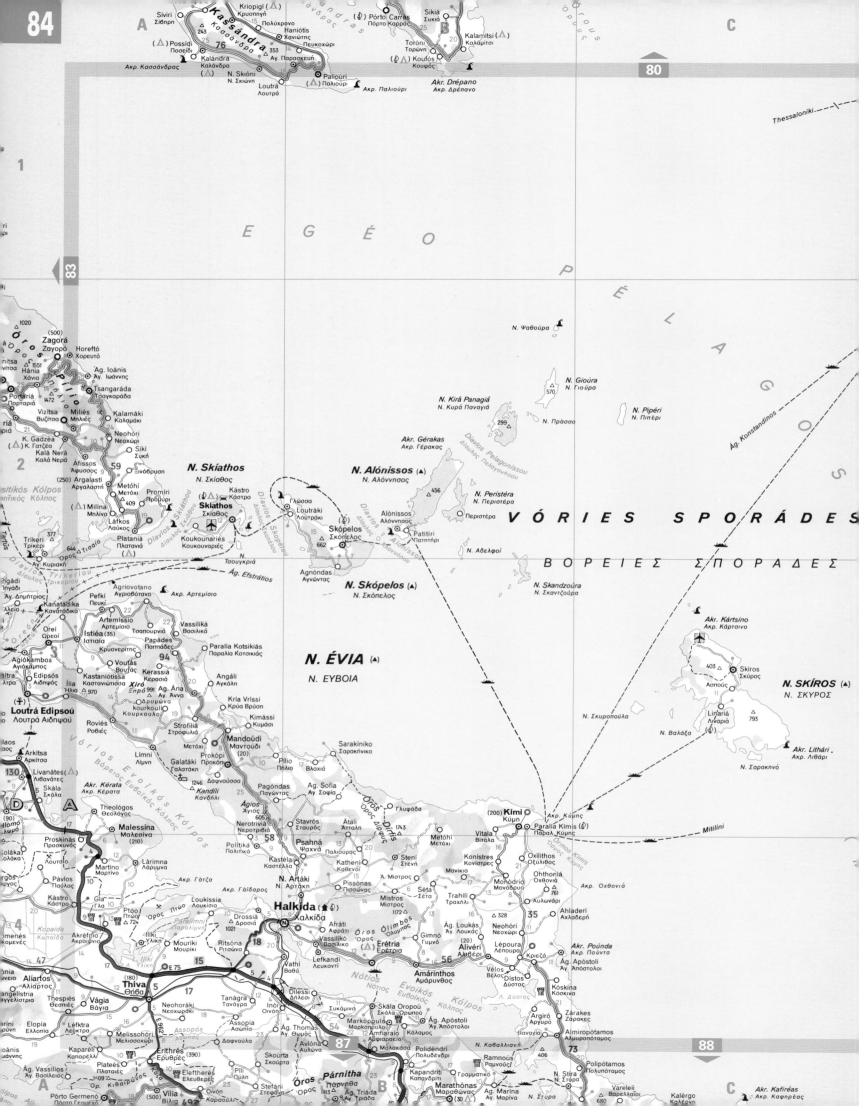

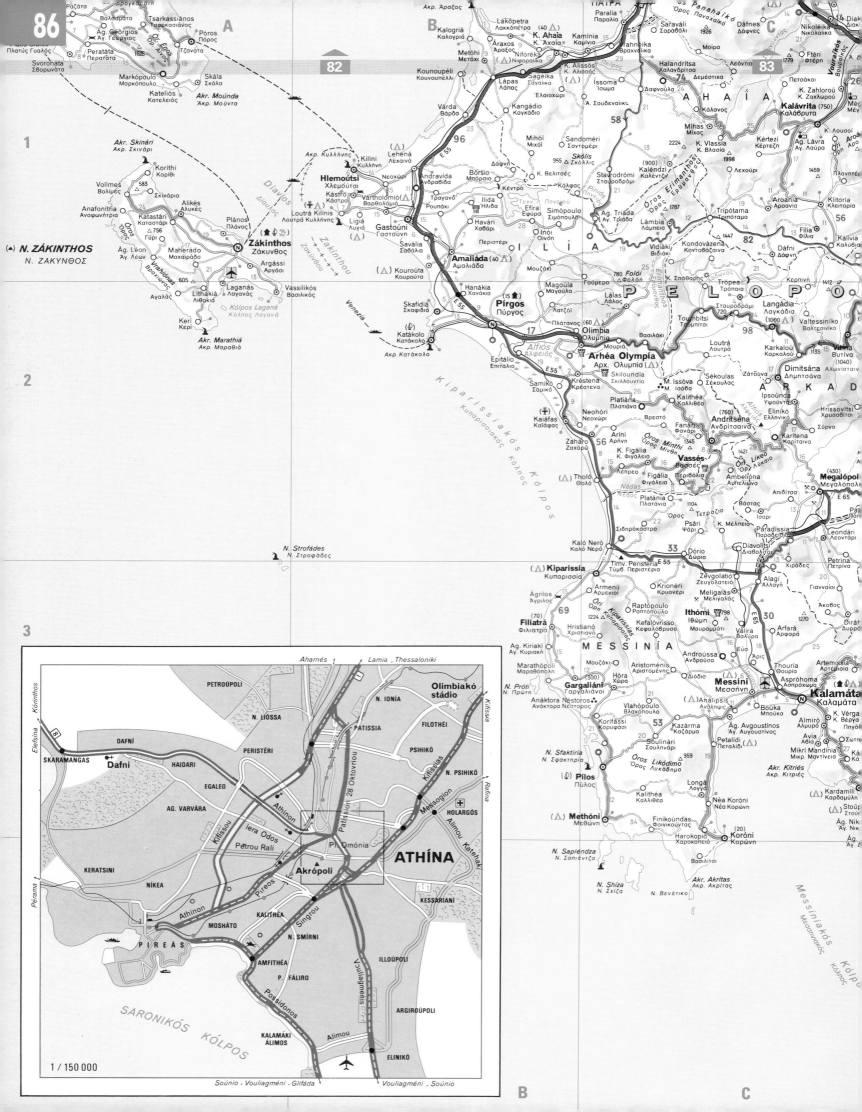

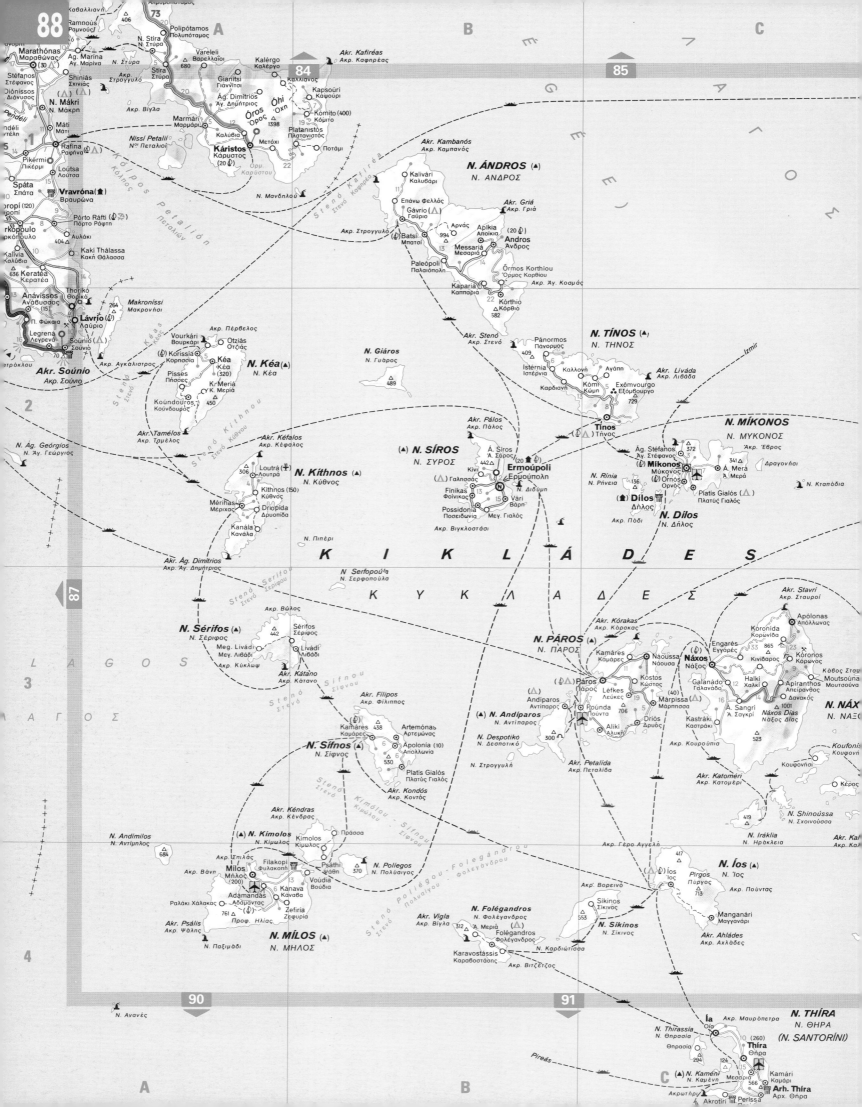

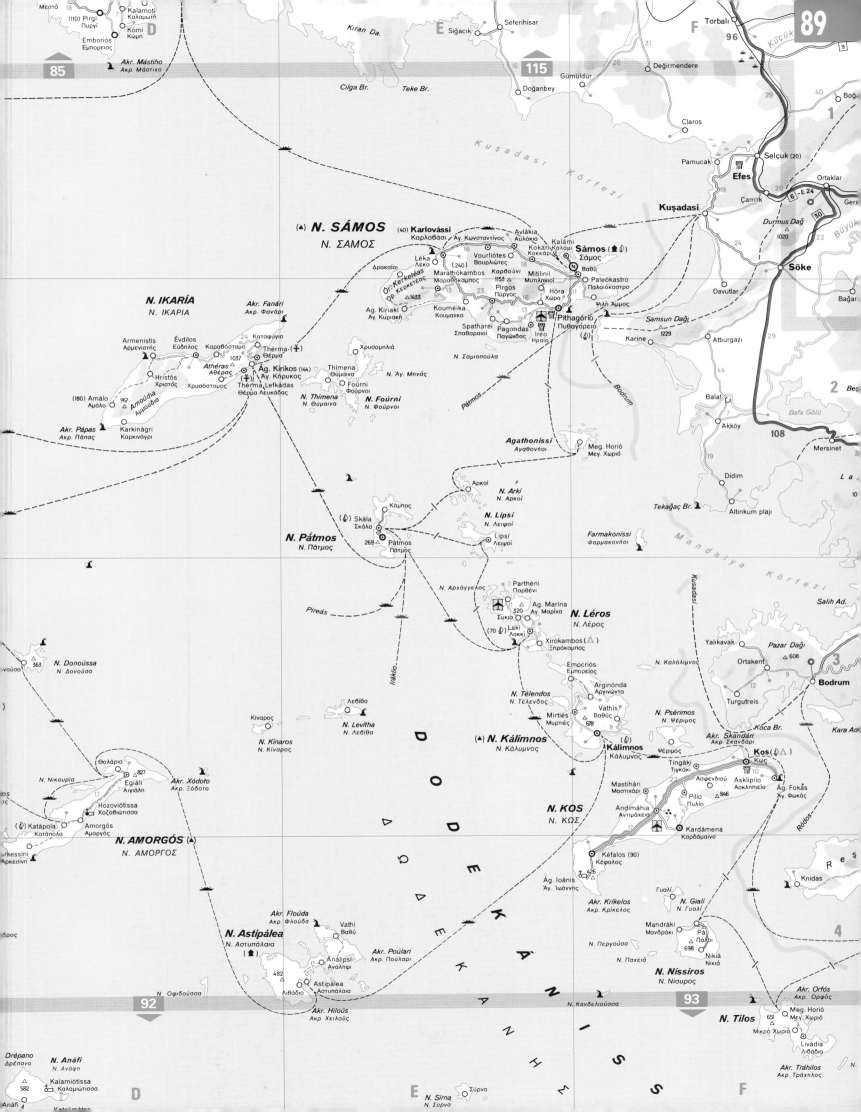

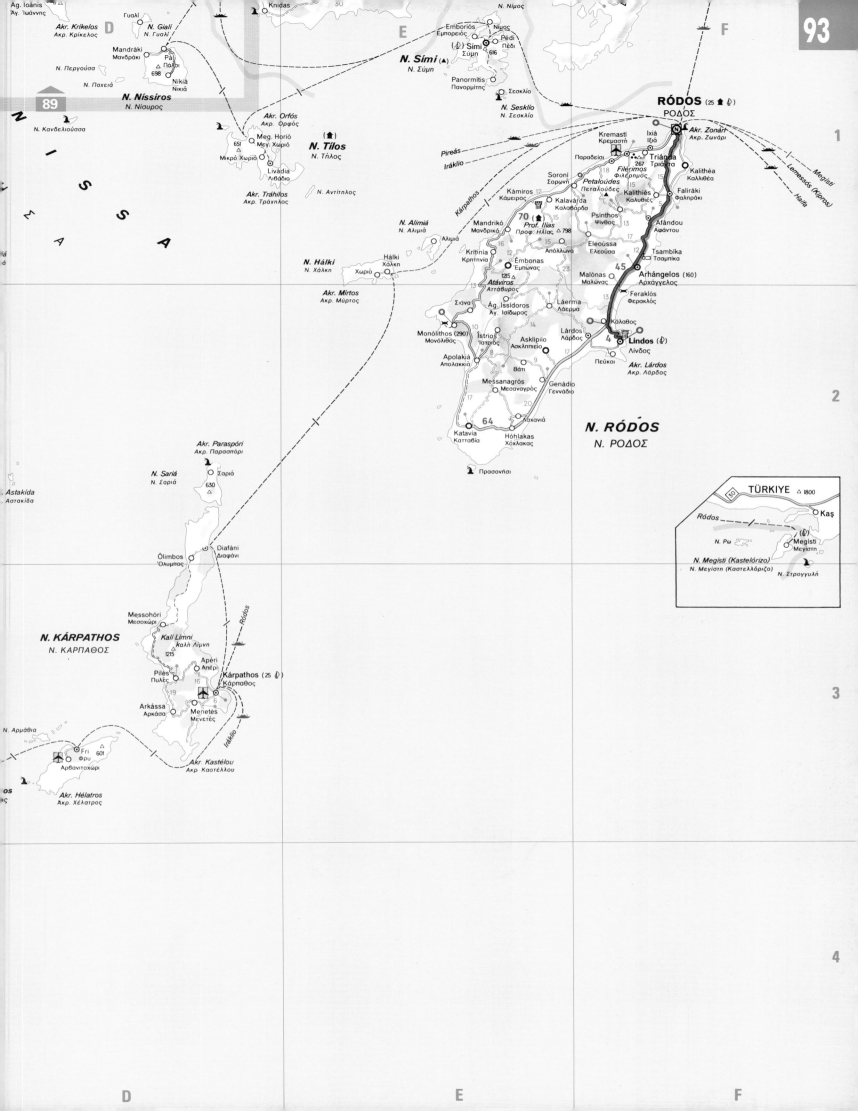

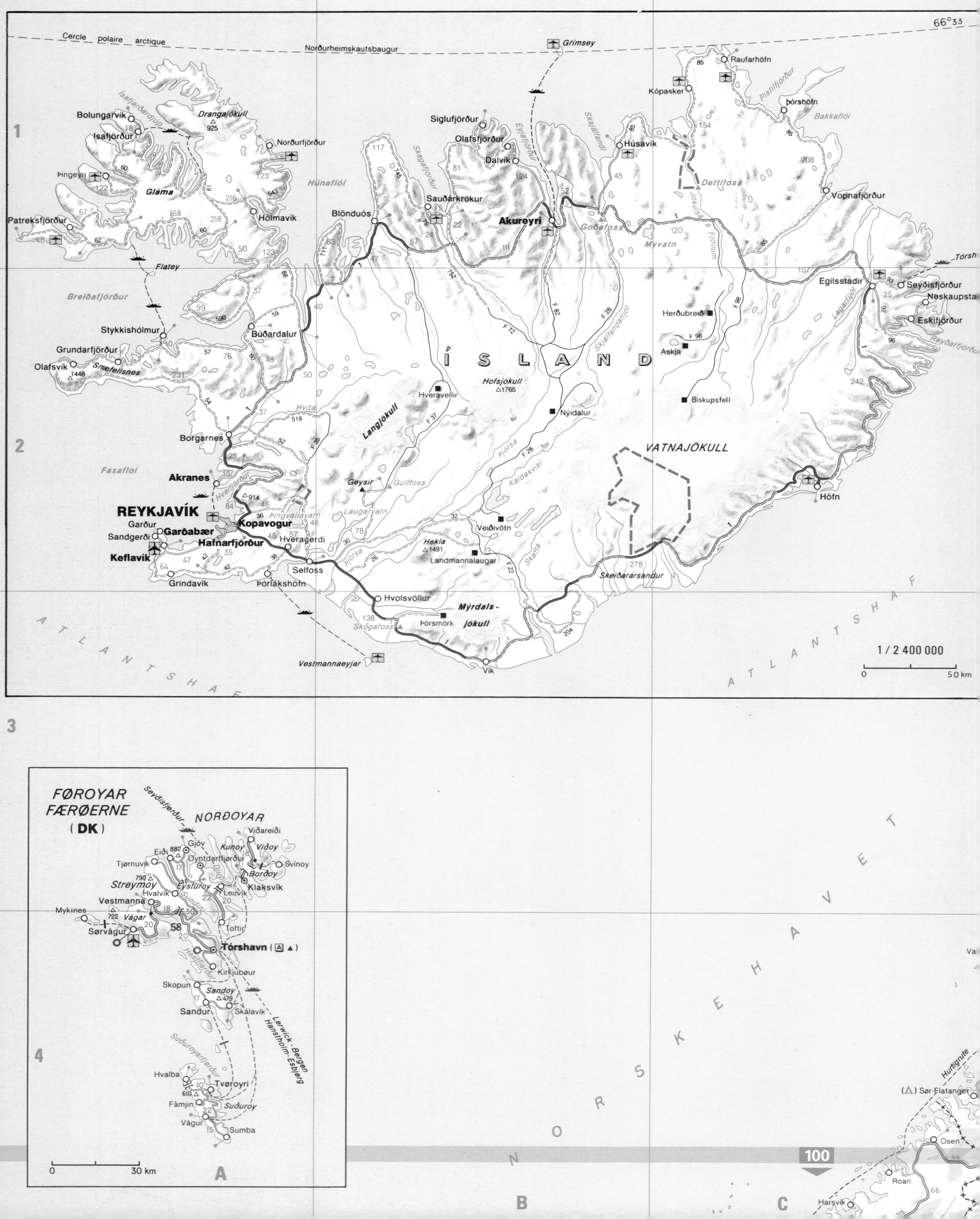

A B C

Cercle polaire arctique
Norðurheimskautsbaugur
66°33

Grímsey

Raufarhöfn
85
Kópasker
Þórshöfn
Bakkaflói
154

Bolungarvík
Ísafjörður
18
Drangajökull
925
Norðurfjörður
117
Siglufjörður
Olafsfjörður
Dalvík
Húsavík
81
124
45
208

Þingeyri
60
122
Gláma
643
216
61
Húnaflói
145
Skagafjörður
Akureyri
Dettifoss

Patreksfjörður
48
62
67
168
218
Hólmavík
60
50
123
83
Blönduós
Sauðárkrókur
76
22
24
111
52
120
85
107
Vopnafjörður

Flatey
99
57
711
57
47
752
F 72
F 28
Egilsstaðir
93
Seyðisfjörður
Neskaupsta
Breiðafjörður
590
Herðubreið
F 98
25
26
Eskifjörður

Stykkishólmur
59
40
7
ÍSLAND
Askja
F 98
96
Reyðarfjörður

Grundarfjörður
57
Búðardalur
43
Hofsjökull
1765
Biskupsfell
242

Olafsvík
1448
231
46
50
37
Hveravellir
Nýidalur

Snæfellsnes
37
Hvítá
519
Langjökull
F 37
Þjórsá
F 28
VATNAJÖKULL

Borgarnes
52
23
Geysir
Gullfoss
Kaldakvísl

Akranes
151
914
36
Laugarvatn
32
Veiðivötn
Höfn

REYKJAVÍK
84
46
Þingvallavatn
46
78
Skaftá

Garður
Kopavogur
57
Hekla
Landmannalaugar
F 22
278

Sandgerði
Garðabær
Hafnarfjörður
Hveragerði
30
1491
Skeiðarársandur

Keflavík
47
42
35
26
Þjórsá

Grindavík
64
42
Þorlákshöfn
Selfoss

138
Hvolsvöllur
Myrdals-
jökull

ATLANTSHAF
Skógafoss
Þórsmörk
1
204

Vestmannaeyjar
Vík
ATLANTSHAF

1 / 2 400 000
0   50 km

FØROYAR
FÆRØERNE
(DK)

NORÐOYAR
Viðareiði
Seyðisfjörður

Gjógv
Kunoy
Viðoy
Eiði
882
Øyndarfjørður
Tjørnuvík
17
Borðoy
Svínoy
Streymoy
790
Eysturoy
Klaksvík
Vestmanna
Hvalvík
18
Leirvík
Mykines
722
Vágar
20
58
20

Sørvágur
Toftir

Tórshavn (A ▲)

Kirkjubøur

Skopun
Sandoy
479

Sandur
Skálavík

Hvalba
10
Tvøroyri
610
Suðuroy
Fámjin
22
Vágur
15
Sumba

0   30 km
A

NORSKEHAVET

100

(▲) Sør-Flatanget

Osen
66
Roan
Harsvík
C

B

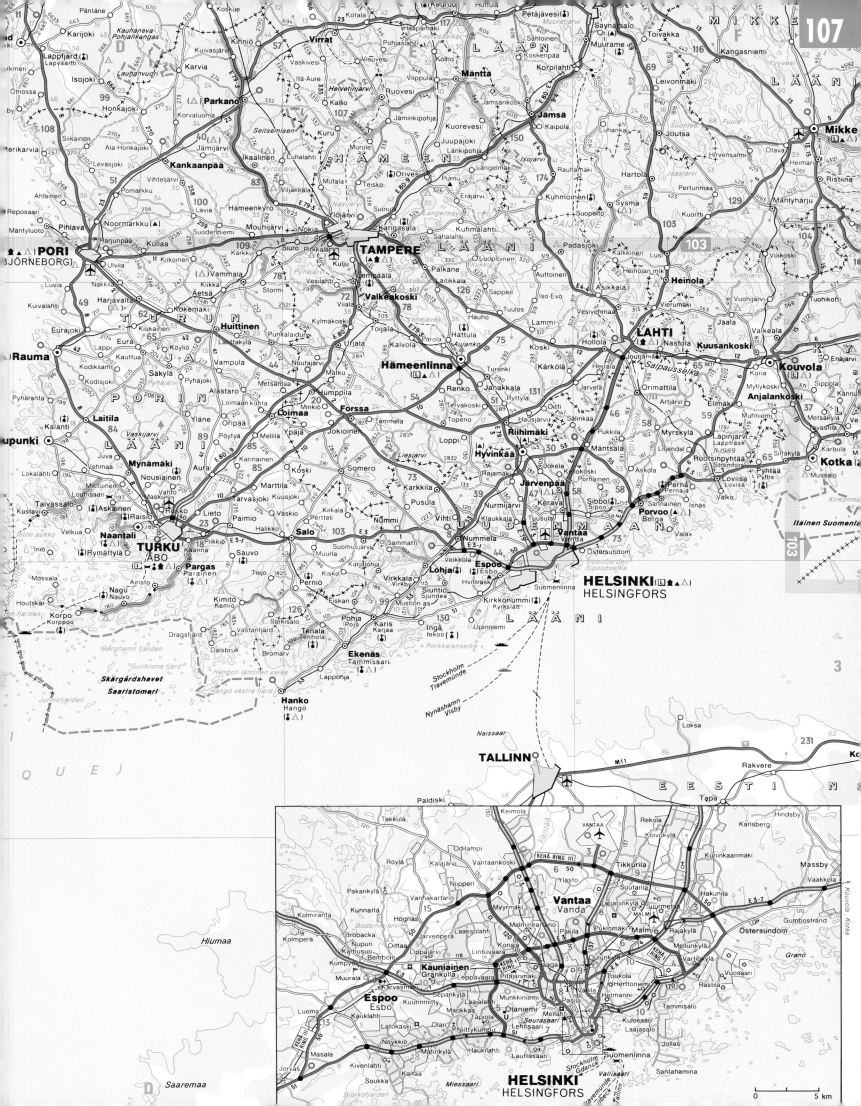

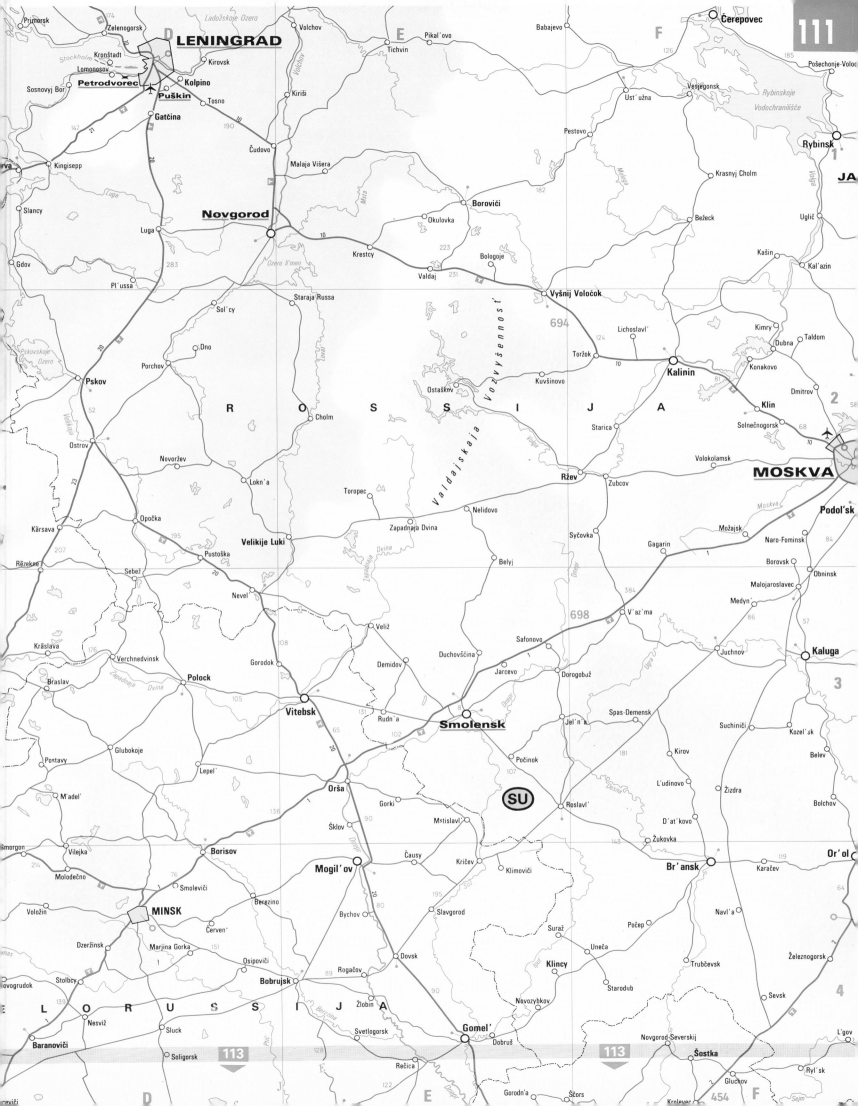

(**F**) Lorsqu'un nom figure plusieurs fois dans l'index, une précision est ajoutée entre parenthèses pour permettre de l'identifier plus facilement: pays, région ou ville la plus proche, élément géographique d'après les abréviations ci-dessous.

(**GB**) Where there are two or more identical place names, the name of the distinguishing country or region or nearest large town is given in brackets; geographical features are indicated by the abbreviations below.

(**D**) Tritt ein Name mehrfach im Register auf, wird er durch eine in Klammern gesetzte nähere Bestimmung genauer definiert. Sie finden folgende Zusätze: Land, Region oder nächstgelegene Stadt, geographische Gegebenheiten, ggf. abgekürzt.

(**NL**) Bij namen die meermalen in het register voorkomen, staat tussen haakjes een aanduiding ter verklaring: het land, de streek, de dichtstbijgelegen stad of een geografisch gegeven (zie de afkortingen hieronder).

(**E**) Cuando un mismo nombre figura varias veces en el índice, para poder localizarlo con facilidad, se añade entre paréntesis el país, la región o la ciudad más cercana; los accidentes geográficos se indican con las abreviaturas siguientes.

(**I**) Quando un nome figura più volte nell'indice, una precisazione viene aggiunta tra parentesi per permettere d'identificarlo più facilmente: nazione, regione o città la più vicina, elemento geografico come da abbreviazioni qui di seguito.

Ákr	Ákra, Akrotírion	Liq	Liquen	Pk	Park
B	Bay, Baie, Bucht, Bahia, Baía, Bukt(en), Bugt, Bukhta	Meg	Mëga, Megál, -a, -i, -o	Pl	Planina
		Mikr.	Mikr-í, -ón	Pque	Parque
Bgem	Barragem	Mgne(s)	Montagne(s)	Prov	Province
C	Cape, Cap, Cabo, Capo	M, Mte(s)	Maj, Maj'e, Monte(s)	Pso	Passo
Co	County	Mt(s), *Mt(s)*	Mount(s), Mountain(s), Mont(s)	Pt(e)	Point(e)
Ch	Chaîne			Rib	Ribeirão
Chan	Channel	Mti	Monti, Muntii	R, *R*	River, Rivière, Rio, Ria, Rijeka
Dépt	Département	Nac	Nacional(e)	Reg	Region, Région
Emb	Embalse	Nat	National	Res	Reservoir, Reservoire
Ez	Ezero	Naz	Nazionale	Sa	Sierra, Serra
G	Gulf, Golfe, Golfo	N	Nissí, Nissos	Sd	Sound, Sund
Gges	Gorges	Ni	Nissiá, Nissi	St	Saint, Sankt, Sint
I(s), *I(s)*	Isles(s), Island(s), Ile(s), Ilha(s), Isla(s), Isola(e)	Os	Ostrov(a)	Ste(s)	Sainte(s)
		Ot	Otok(i), Otoci	Teh L	Tehnití Límni
Jez	Jezoro, Jezioro	Oz	Ozero(a)	V	Valley, Vale, Vallée, Val, Valle, Vall
K	Kanal, Kanaal	P	Pass		
L, *L*	Lake, Loch, Lough, Llyn, Lac, Laguna, Lago, Límni	Pal	Paleós, á, ó		
		Pen	Peninsula, Penisola		

Acehuche	39	D3		Afjord	100	C1			
Acerno	64	B4		Åfjorden	104	A1			
Acerra	64	B4		Aflenzer					
Aceuchal	39	D4		Seeberg	57	E3			
Ache	59	E1		Aflenz Kurort	57	E3			
Achenkirch	59	D1		Afráti	84	B4			
Achenpaß	56	A4		Afsluitdijk	16	C1			
Achensee	59	D1		A Garda	34	A3			
Achern	54	C3		Agathonissi	89	E2			
Acheux	19	F2		Agay	31	E4			
Achill I	12	A2		Agazzano	60	B2			
Achim	17	F1		Agde	30	A4			
Achnacroish	4	B1		Agdenes	100	C1			
Achnasheen	2	C3		Agen	28	C3			
A'Chràlaig	2	C4		Åger	37	F3			
Aci Castello	69	D3		Ager	56	C3			
Acipayam	115	F4		Ageranós	87	D4			
Acireale	69	D3		Agerbæk	108	A3			
Aci Trezza	69	D3		Agger	17	E4			
Acle	7	F3		Aggius	66	B1			
A Coruña	34	B1		Aggsbach-Dorf	57	E2			
Acqualagna	61	E4		Aggsbach-Markt	57	E2			
Acquapendente	63	D1		Agiá	83	F1			
Acquasanta				Agiá, Akr	83	F4			
Terme	63	F1		Agía Ána (Évia)	84	A3			
Acquasparta	63	E1		Agía Ána					
Acquaviva dei				(Viotía)	83	F4			
Fonti	65	D3		Agía Efimía	82	B4			
Acqui-Terme	60	A2		Agía Efthimía	83	E4			
Acri	67	E2		Agía Ekateríni, Akr	82	A1			
Ada	72	C1		Agía Fotiá	91	F4			
Adaja, R	39	F2		Agía Galíni	91	D4			
Adak	98	A3		Agía Kiriakí					
Ådalsel	104	C2		(Makedonía)	78	C3			
Adamandás	88	A4		Agía Kiriakí					
Adamclisi	115	E1		(Pelopónissos)	86	B3			
Adamello	58	C3		Agía Kiriakí					
Adamello Brenta,				(Sámos)	89	E2			
Parco Naturale	58	C3		Agía Lávra	86	C1			
Adamello, Mont'	58	C3		Agía Marína					
Adamuz	43	F2		(Égina)	87	F2			
Adanero	39	F1		Agía Marína (Kríti)	90	B3			
Adapazarı	115	F3		Agía Marína (Léros)	89	E3			
Adare	14	B3		Agía Marína					
Adaševci	72	B3		(Stereá Eláda)	83	E3			
Adda	60	B2		Agía Marína					
Adelboden	27	E3		(Stereá Eláda)	88	A1			
Adelfia	65	D3		Agía Paraskeví					
Adelsheim	55	D1		(Lésvos)	85	F2			
Ademuz	41	D3		Agía Paraskeví					
Adenau	51	E4		(Makedonía)	80	C2			
Ádendro	79	F3		Agía Paraskiés	91	E4			
Adéres, Óros	87	E2		Agía Pelagía					
Adiça, Sa da	42	C1		(Kíthira)	90	A1			
Adige	61	D1		Agía Pelagía (Kríti)	91	D3			
Adjud	113	E4		Agía Rouméli	90	B4			
Admont	57	D3		Agiásma	80	C2			
Adolfström	97	F3		Agiásmata	85	E4			
Adorf	53	D3		Agía Sofía (Évia)	84	B3			
Adour	28	B4		Agía Sofía					
Adra	44	B4		(Pelopónissos)	87	D2			
Adradas	36	B4		Agía Sotíra	87	E1			
Adrall	32	A3		Agiássos	85	F2			
Adrano	69	D3		Agía Triáda (Kríti)	91	D4			
Adria	61	D2		Agía Triáda					
Adriatic Sea	114	A3		(Makedonía)	79	F3			
Adzaneta	41	E3		Agía Triáda					
Aenona	74	C1		(Pelopónissos)	86	C1			
Aerinó	83	F2		Agía Triáda					
Ærø	108	B4		(Stereá Eláda)	87	F1			
Ærøskøbing	108	B4		Agía Varvára	91	D4			
A Estrada	34	A2		Agiófilo	83	D1			
Aetópetra	82	B1		Agiókambos					
Aetós (Kefaloniá)	82	B4		(Évia)	83	F3			
Aetós				Agiókambos					
(Makedonía)	79	D3		(Thessalía)	83	F1			
Aetós				Agionóri	87	E2			
(Stereá Eláda)	82	C3		Ágio Óros	80	C4			
Äetsä	107	D2		Agiopigí	83	D2			
Afándou	93	F1		Ágios	84	A3			
Áfarnes	100	B3		Ágios Anárgiri					
Aféa	87	F2		(Pelopónissos)	87	D3			
Affi	60	C1		Ágios Anárgiri					
Afiónas	82	A1		(Thessalía)	83	E2			
Afissós	83	F2		Ágios Andónios	80	A3			
Áfitos	80	B4		Ágios Andréas					
				(Arkadía)	87	D2			

A

			Abanilla	45	D2	Abcoude	16	C2	Aberhonddu	8	C1	Aboyne	3	E4			
			Abano Terme	61	D1	Abejar	36	B3	Aberlady	5	D2	Abrantes	38	B3			
Aachen	51	D3	Abbadia			Abejuela	41	E3	Aberpennar	8	C2	Abreschviller	21	E4		
Aalen	55	E2	San Salvatore	63	D1	Abela	42	A1	Aberporth	8	B1	Abrets, les	30	C1		
Aalsmeer	16	C2	Abbasanta	66	B3	Abelvær	97	D4	Abersoch	6	A3	Abriès	31	E2		
Aalst	50	B3	Abbazia di			Abenberg	55	E2	Abertawe	8	C2	Abruzzo	63	F2		
Aalten	17	D3	Casamari	63	F3	Abenójar	39	F4	Aberteifi	8	B1	Abruzzo, Parco				
Aalter	50	B3	Abbazia di			Abenrå	108	A4	Abertillery	9	D2	Nazionale d'	64	A2		
Äänekoski	103	D2	Fossanova	63	F3	Abensberg	55	F2	Aber-Wrac'h, l'	22	A2	Abstadt-				
Aapajärvi	95	F4	Abbazia di			Aberaeron	8	C1	Aberystwyth	8	C1	Tailfingen	55	D3		
Aarau	27	F2	Montecassino	64	A3	Aberdâr	8	C2	Abetone	60	C3	Abtenau	59	E1		
Aarberg	27	E2	Abbazia San Clemente			Aberdare	8	C2	Abiego	37	E3	Åby	105	F4		
Aarburg	27	F2	a Casauria	64	A2	Aberdaron	6	A3	Abingdon	9	E2	Åbybro	108	B2		
Aare	58	A3	Abbeville	19	E2	Aberdaugleddau	8	B2	Abington	5	D3	A Caniza	34	A3		
Aargau	27	F2	Abbeyfeale	14	B3	Aberdeen	3	E4	Abisko	94	B3	Acceglio	31	E2		
Aarlen	21	D2	Abbeyleix	12	C4	Aberdovey	6	A3	Abisko (Nat park)	94	B4	Accettura	65	D4		
Aarschot	50	C3	Abbey Town	5	D4	Aberfeldy	4	C1	Abla	44	B3	Acciaroli	67	D4		
Aavasaksa	98	C2	Abbiategrasso	60	A1	Aberfoyle	4	C2	Ablis	19	E4	Accous	37	D1		
Abades	40	A1	Abborrträsk	98	B3	Abergavenny	9	D2	Åbo	107	D2	Accrington	6	C2		
Abadiño	36	B1	Abbots Bromley	6	C3	Abergele	6	B2	Abondance	27	E3	Acebo	39	D2		
A Baiuca	34	A1	Abbotsbury	9	D3	Abergwaun	8	B1	Abony	112	B4	Acedo	36	B2		

Ágios Andréas (Lakonía) 87 E4
Ágios Apóstoli (Évia) 84 B4
Ágios Apóstoli (Pelopónissos) 87 E4
Ágios Apóstoli (Stereá Eláda) 84 B4
Ágios Athanássios (Dráma) 80 C2
Ágios Athanássios (Péla) 79 D2
Ágios Avgoustínos 86 C3
Ágios Déka 91 D4
Ágios Dimítrios, Akr 88 A3
Ágios Dimítrios (Évia) 88 A1
Ágios Dimítrios (Lakonía) 87 D3
Ágios Dimítrios (Makedonía) 79 E4
Ágios Dimítrios (Messinía) 87 D4
Ágios Dimítrios (Stereá Eláda) 83 D3
Ágios Dioníssios 79 E4
Ágios Efstrátios, N 85 D2
Ágios Fokás 89 F3
Ágios Fokás, Akr 85 F3
Ágios Geórgios (Évia) 83 F3
Ágios Geórgios, N 87 F2
Ágios Geórgios (Stereá Eláda) 83 D3
Ágios Geórgios (Zákinthos) 86 A1
Ágios Georgíou, Órmos 87 E3
Ágios Germanós 79 D2
Ágios Górdis 82 A1
Ágios Harálambos 81 E2
Ágios Ioánis, Akr 91 F3
Ágios Ioánis (Dodekánissa) 89 F4
Ágios Ioánis (Pelopónissos) 87 E2
Ágios Ioánis (Stereá Eláda) 83 F4
Ágios Ioánis (Thessalía) 83 F3
Ágios Ioánis (Thessalía) 83 F2
Ágios Irínis, Akr 85 D1
Ágios Issídoros 93 E2
Ágios Kírikos 89 D2
Ágios Konstandínos (Stereá Eláda) 83 F3
Ágios Konstandínos (Thessalía) 83 E2
Ágios Kosmás (Grevená) 79 D4
Ágios Kosmás (Kavála) 80 C2
Ágios Léon 86 A1
Ágios Loukás 84 B4
Ágios Mámas 80 A4
Ágios Márkos 80 A2
Ágios Mathéos 82 A2
Ágios Míronas 91 D4
Ágios Nikítas 82 B3
Ágios Nikólaos (Etolía-Akarnanía) 82 B3
Ágios Nikólaos (Fokída) 83 E4
Ágios Nikólaos (Fthiótida) 83 F3
Ágios Nikólaos (Hers.Methánon) 87 E2
Ágios Nikólaos (Ípiros) 82 B1
Ágios Nikólaos (Kríti) 91 E4
Ágios Nikólaos (Lakonía) 87 D3
Ágios Nikólaos (Makedonía) 80 B4
Ágios Nikólaos (Messinía) 86 C3
Ágios Pandeleímonos 79 D3
Ágios Pángalos, Akr 83 E4

Ágios Paraskeví (Ípiros) 78 C4
Ágios Paraskeví (Makedonía) 79 F2
Ágios Pávlos 80 A3
Ágios Pétros 87 D2
Ágios Pnévma 80 B2
Ágios Pródromos 80 A3
Ágios Sóstis 83 E3
Ágios Stéfanos (Kikládes) 88 C2
Ágios Stéfanos (Stereá Eláda) 87 F1
Ágios Theódori (Makedonía) 79 D4
Ágios Theódori (Pelopónissos) 87 E1
Ágios Theódori (Thessalía) 83 F3
Ágios Thomás (Kríti) 91 D4
Ágios Thomás (Stereá Eláda) 84 B4
Ágios Vassílios (Makedonía) 80 A3
Ágios Vassílios (Stereá Eláda) 84 A4
Ágios Vissários 83 E2
Agíou Órous, Kólpos 80 C4
Agira 68 C3
Agly 32 B2
Ágnanda 82 C2
Agnanderó 83 D2
Ágnandi 83 F3
Agnóndas 84 B3
Agnone 64 B2
Agnoúnda 87 E2
Agorá 80 C2
Agordo 59 D3
Agost 45 E1
Agout 29 D4
Agrafiótis 83 D2
Agramunt 37 F3
Agrate Br. 60 A1
Agreda 36 C3
Agreliá 83 D1
Agri 65 D4
Agriá 83 F2
Agrigento 68 B4
Agriliá 82 C4
Agriliá, Akr 85 F3
Ágrilos 86 B3
Agrínio 82 C3
Agriovótano 83 F3
Agrópoli 64 B4
Agskaret 97 E2
Aguadulce (Almería) 44 B4
Aguadulce (Sevilla) 43 E3
Aguas Vivas, R 37 D4
Aguaviva 41 E2
A Gudiña 34 C3
Agudo 39 F4
Agueda 38 B1
Agueda, R 39 D2
Aguiar 42 B1
Aguiar da Beira 38 C1
Aguilafuente 40 A1
Aguilar 43 F2
Aguilar de Campóo 35 F2
Aguilar del Alfambra 41 E2
Aguilar, Emb de 35 F2
Águilas 44 C3
Ahaía 86 C1
Aharnés 87 F1
Ahaus 17 E3
Åheim 100 A3
Ahelóos 82 C4
Ahendriás 91 E4
Ahérondas 82 B2
Ahigal 39 D2
Ahílio (Kérkira) 82 A1
Ahílio (Thessalía) 83 E2
Ahinós 80 B2
Ahjärvi 103 F3
Ahladerí 84 B4
Ahládes, Akr 88 C4
Ahladohóri 80 B1
Ahlainen 102 B3
Ahlbeck 49 E2

Ahlen 17 E3
Ahlhorn 17 F1
Ahrensbok 48 B2
Ahrensburg 48 B2
Ahrweiler 51 E4
Ähtäri 102 C2
Ähtärinjärvi 102 C2
Ähtävänjoki 102 C2
Ahtopol 115 D2
Ahun 25 E4
Åhus 109 D3
Ahvenanmaa 106 C3
Ahvenselkä 99 E1
Aichach 55 F3
Aidenbach 56 B2
Aidone 68 C3
Aigen 56 C2
Aigle 27 E3
Aigle, Bge de l' 29 E1
Aigle, l' 19 D4
Aignan 28 C4
Aignay-le-Duc 26 C2
Aigoual, Mt 29 F3
Aigre 24 C4
Aigrefeuille-d'Aunis 24 B4
Aigrefeuille-sur-Maine 24 B3
Aiguablava 32 C3
Aiguebelette 30 C1
Aiguebelle 31 D1
Aigueperse 26 A4
Aigues 30 C3
Aigues-Mortes 30 B4
Aigües Tortes, Parque Nac de 37 F2
Aiguilles 31 E2
Aiguillon 28 C3
Aiguillon, l' 24 B4
Aigurande 25 E4
Ailefroide 31 D2
Aillant 26 A1
Ailly-le-Haut-locher 19 E2
Ailly-sur-Noye 19 F2
Ailsa Craig 4 B3
Aimargues 30 B4
Aime 31 D1
Ain 27 D3
Ain (Dépt) 26 C4
Ainhoa 28 A4
Ainsa 37 E2
Ainsdale 6 B2
Ainzón 36 C3
Airaines 19 E2
Airasca 31 E2
Airdrie 4 C2
Aire 19 F1
Aire, I del 45 F2
Aire, Sa de 38 B3
Aire-sur-l'Adour 28 B4
Airisto 107 D3
Airolo 58 A3
Airvault 24 C3
Aisne 20 A3
Aisne (Dépt) 20 A2
Aitana 45 E1
Aiterhofen 56 B2
Aitrach 55 E3
Aitzgorri 36 B1
Aiud 112 C4
Aix-d'Angillon, les 26 A2
Aixe 29 D1
Aix-en-Othe 26 B1
Aix-en-Provence 30 C4
Aix, I d' 24 B4
Aix-les-Bains 27 D4
Aizenay 24 B3
Ajaccio 33 E4
Ajaureforsen 97 F3
Ajdanovac 77 D1
Ajdovščina 70 A2
Ajka 112 A4
Ajo 35 F1
Ajo, C de 36 A1
Ajos 99 D3
Ajtos 115 E2
Akarnaniká, Óri 82 C3
Äkäsjokisuu 95 D4
Äkäskero 95 D4
Äkäslompolo 95 D4
Akçakoca 115 F3
Aken 53 D1

Åkersberga 106 B3
Akershus 105 D3
Åkers styckebruk 106 B4
Akhisar 115 F4
Akhirkeby 109 D4
Akkajaure 94 B4
Akkerhaugen 104 C3
Akku 95 E3
Akranes 96 A2
Akráta 87 D1
Ákrathos, Akr 80 C4
Akréfnio 83 F4
Åkrehamn 104 A3
Akrestrømmen 100 C3
Akrítas 79 D2
Akrítas, Akr 86 C4
Akrogiáli 80 B3
Akropótamos 80 B3
Akrotíri 91 E1
Akrovoúni 80 C2
Aktí Apólona 87 F2
Akujärvi 95 F3
Akureyri 96 B1
Ál 104 C2
Ala 60 C1
Ala di Stura 31 E1
Alà d. Sardi 66 B2
Alaejos 35 E4
Alagí 86 C3
Alagna Valsesia 27 F4
Alagnon 29 F2
Alagón 37 D3
Alagón, R 39 D2
Alagonía 86 C3
Alahärmä 102 C2
Ala-Honkajoki 102 B3
Alaior 45 F2
Alajärvi 102 C2
Alakylä 99 D1
Alalkomenés 83 F4
Alameda 43 F3
Alamillo 43 F1
Alanäs 101 F1
Aland 48 C3
Åland 106 C3
Alandroal 38 C4
Alange 39 D4
Alange, Emb de 39 D4
Alanis 43 E2
Alapitkä 103 E2
Alaraz 39 E1
Alarcón 40 C3
Alarcón, Emb de 40 C3
Alar del Rey 35 F3
Alaşehir 115 F4
Alassio 31 F3
Alastaro 107 D2
Alatoz 41 D4
Alatri 63 F3
Alavieska 102 C1
Ala-Vuokki 99 F4
Alavus 102 C2
Alba 31 F2
Alba Adriatica 64 A1
Albacete 40 C4
Albacken 101 F2
Alba de Tormes 39 E1
Ålbæk 108 B1
Albaida 45 E1
Albaida, Pto de 45 E1
Alba Iulia 114 C1
Albaladejo 44 B1
Albalate de Cinca 37 E3
Albalate del Arzobispo 37 D4
Albalate de las Nogueras 40 C2
Alban 29 E3
Albánchez 44 C3
Albano di Lucania 65 D4
Albano Laziale 63 E3
Albarca 37 F4
Albarella, I 61 D1
Albarracin 41 D2
Albarracin, Sa de 41 D2
Albares 35 D2
Albatana 45 D1
Albatera 45 D2
Albena 115 E2
Albenga 31 F3
Albens 27 D4
Alberche, R 39 F2
Alberga 105 F4

Albergaria-a-Velha 38 B1
Alberique 41 E4
Albernoa 42 B1
Alberobello 65 E3
Albersdorf 48 A2
Albert 19 F2
Albert Kanaal 50 C3
Albertville 27 D4
Albestroff 21 E3
Albi 29 E3
Albiano 31 F1
Albinia 63 D2
Albino 58 B4
Albisola Marina 60 A3
Albocácer 41 F2
Albolodúy 44 B3
Albolote 44 A3
Albo, M 66 C2
Alborea 41 D4
Ålborg 108 B2
Ålborg Bugt 108 B2
Albox 44 C3
Albstadt-Ebingen 55 D3
Albufeira 42 A3
Albujón 45 D2
Albulapass 58 B3
Albuñol 44 A4
Alburno, Mte 64 C4
Alburquerque 38 C3
Alby (F) 27 D4
Alby (S) 101 E3
Alcácer do Sál 42 A1
Alcáçovas 42 B1
Alcadozo 44 C1
Alcafozes 38 C2
Alcains 38 C2
Alcalá de Chivert 41 F2
Alcalá de Guadaira 43 D3
Alcalá de Henares 40 B2
Alcalá de la Selva 41 E2
Alcalá del Júcar 41 D4
Alcalá de los Gazules 43 D4
Alcalá del Río 43 D2
Alcalá la Real 44 A3
Alcamo 68 B3
Alcanadre, R 37 E3
Alcanar 41 E4
Alcanede 38 A3
Alcanena 38 B3
Alcanhões 38 B3
Alcañices 34 C4
Alcañiz 37 E4
Alcántara 39 D3
Alcántara, Emb de 39 D3
Alcantarilha 42 A2
Alcantarilla 45 D2
Alcaracejos 43 E1
Alcaraz 44 B1
Alcaraz, Sa de 44 C1
Alcaria do Cume 42 B2
Alcaria Ruiva 42 B2
Alcarràs 37 E4
Alcaudete 43 F3
Alcaudete de la Jara 39 F3
Alcázar de San Juan 40 B4
Alceda 35 F2
Alcester 9 E1
Alcoba 39 F4
Alcobaça 38 A3
Alcoba de los Montes 39 F4
Alcobendas 40 B2
Alcoceber 41 F3
Alcochete 38 A4
Alcolea 43 F2
Alcolea de Cinca 37 E3
Alcolea del Pinar 36 B4
Alcolea del Río 43 E2
Alconchel 42 C1
Alcora 41 E3
Alcorisa 41 E2
Alcorlo, Emb de 40 B1
Alcoutim 42 B2
Alcover 37 F4
Alcoy 45 E1
Alcubierre 37 D3
Alcubierre, Sa de 37 D3

Alcubilla de Avellaneda 36 A3
Alcublas 41 E3
Alcudia 45 F2
Alcudia de Crespins 41 E4
Alcudia de Guadix 44 B3
Alcuéscar 39 D4
Aldeacentenera 39 E3
Aldeadávila, Emb de 34 C4
Aldea del Cano 39 D3
Aldea del Fresno 40 A2
Aldea del Rey 44 A1
Aldeanueva de Ebro 36 C3
Aldeanueva de la Vera 39 E2
Aldeanueva del Camino 39 E2
Aldeburgh 11 E1
Aldeia da Ponte 39 D2
Aldeia Nova de São Bento 42 C1
Alderney 18 A3
Aldershot 9 F3
Aldinci 77 E3
Aldocer 40 C2
Aledo 44 C2
Aleksandrija 113 F2
Aleksandrovac (Srbija) 73 D3
Aleksandrovac (Srbija) 77 D1
Aleksa Šantić 72 B1
Aleksinac 73 E4
Alençon 23 F3
Alenquer 38 A3
Alentejo 42 B1
Alepohóri (Pelopónissos) 87 D2
Alepohóri (Stereá Eláda) 87 E1
Aléria 33 F3
Alès 30 B3
Ales 66 B3
Aleşd 112 C4
Alessandria 60 A2
Alessandria d. Rocca 68 B3
Ålestrup 108 A2
Ålesund 100 A2
Aletschhorn 27 F3
Alexandria (GB) 4 C2
Alexándria (GR) 79 F3
Alexandria (RO) 115 D2
Alexandroúpoli 81 E2
Alf 51 E4
Alfajarín 37 D3
Alfambra (E) 41 D2
Alfambra (P) 42 A2
Alfambra, R 41 E2
Alfândega da Fé 34 C4
Alfaro 36 C3
Alfarrás 37 E3
Alfaz del Pi 45 E1
Alfedena 64 A2
Alfeizerão 38 A3
Alfeld (Bayern) 55 F1
Alfeld (Niedersachsen) 52 B1
Alfiós 86 B2
Alfonsine 61 D2
Alfonso XIII, Emb de 44 C2
Alford (Grampian) 3 E4
Alford (Lincs) 7 E3
Alfreton 7 D3
Alfta 101 F4
Algar 43 D4
Ålgård 104 A4
Algaida 45 F3
Algar de Palancia 41 E3
Algarinejo 43 F3
Algarrobo 42 B2
Algarve 42 B2
Algatocin 43 E4
Algeciras 43 D4
Algemesí 41 E4
Alghero 66 A2
Alginet 41 E4
Algodonales 43 E3
Algodor, R 40 A3
Algora 40 C1

Algorta 36 B1
Algoz 42 A2
Alhama de Almería 44 B3
Alhama de Aragón 36 C4
Alhama de Granada 43 F3
Alhama de Murcia 45 D2
Alhambra 44 B1
Alhamilla, Sa 44 B3
Alhaurin el Grande 43 E4
Alhóndiga 40 B2
Alía (E) 39 E3
Alia (I) 68 C3
Aliaga 41 E2
Aliaguilla 41 D3
Aliákmona, L 79 E4
Aliákmonas 79 D4
Alíartos 83 F4
Alibunar 73 D2
Alicante 45 E2
Alicudi, I 68 C2
Alicún de Ortega 44 B2
Alife 64 B3
Alijó 34 B4
Alikés 86 A1
Alikianós 90 B3
Alikí (Kikládes) 88 C3
Alikí (Thássos) 81 D3
Alimiá, N 93 E1
Alingsås 108 C1
Alinyà 32 A3
Aliseda 39 D3
Alise-Ste-Reine 26 B2
Aliste, R 35 D4
Alistráti 80 B2
Ali Terme 69 D2
Alivéri 84 B4
Aljezur 42 A2
Aljibe 43 D4
Aljucén 39 D4
Aljustrel 42 B1
Alkionídon, Kólpos 87 E1
Alkmaar 16 C2
Allaire 22 C4
Allaman, M 76 C4
Allanche 29 E2
Alland 57 E3
Allariz 34 B3
Alleen 104 B4
Alleghe 59 D3
Allègre 29 F2
Allen, L 12 C2
Allensbach 55 D4
Allentsteig 57 E2
Allepuz 41 E2
Aller 48 A4
Allersberg 55 F1
Allershausen 55 F3
Alleuze 29 F2
Allevard 31 D1
Allier (Dépt) 26 A3
Allier R 26 A3
Allinge-Sandvig 109 D4
Allo 36 C2
Alloa 5 D2
Allonnes 23 F4
Allos 31 D3
Allos, Col d' 31 D3
Alloza 41 E1
Allstedt 52 C2
Almacelles 37 E3
Almáchar 43 F3
Almada 38 A4
Almadén 39 F4
Almadén de la Plata 43 D2
Almadenejos 43 F1
Almagro 40 A4
Almajano 36 B3
Almansa 45 D1
Almansil 42 B3
Almanza 35 E2
Almanzora, R 44 B3
Almanzor, Pico 39 E2
Almaraz 39 E3
Almargen 43 E3
Almarza 36 B3
Almazán 36 B3
Almazora 41 E3
Almedinilla 43 F3
Almeida (E) 35 D4
Almeida (P) 39 D1
Almeirim 38 B3

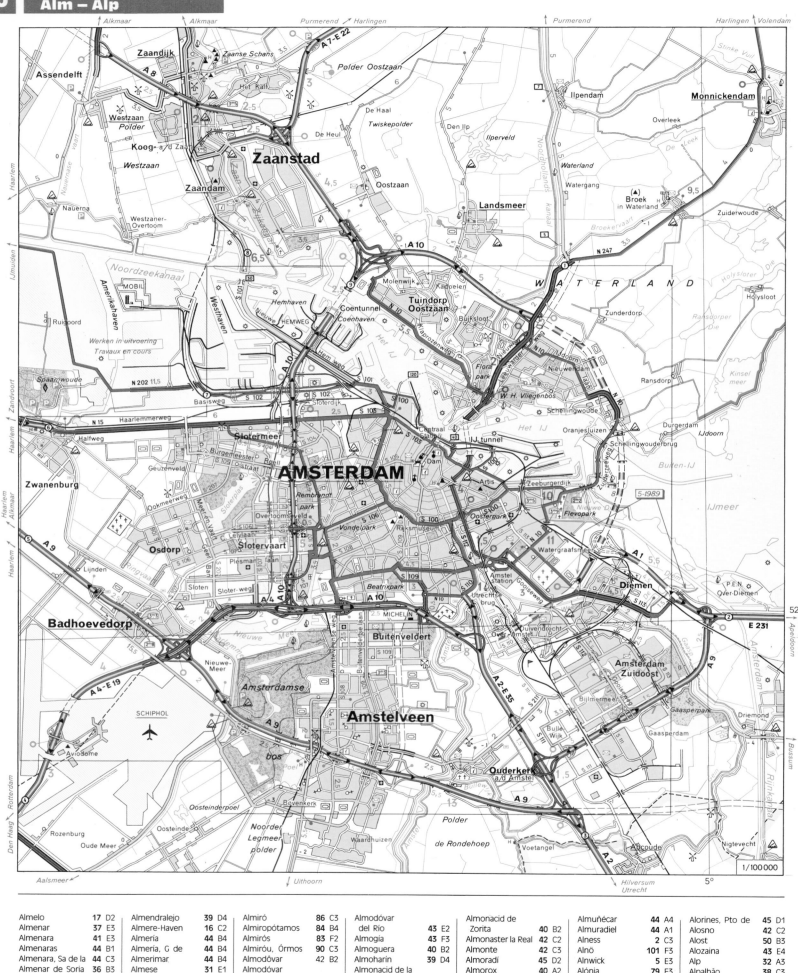

Almelo	17 D2	Almendralejo	39 D4	Almiró	86 C3	Almodóvar		Almonacid de		Almuñécar	44 A4	Alorines, Pto de	45 D1
Almenar	37 E3	Almere-Haven	16 C2	Almiropótamos	84 B4	del Rio	43 E2	Zorita	40 B2	Almuradiel	44 A1	Alosno	42 C2
Almenara	41 E3	Almería	44 B4	Almirós	83 F2	Almogía	43 F3	Almonaster la Real	42 C2	Alness	2 C3	Alost	50 B3
Almenaras	44 B1	Almería, G de	44 B4	Almiróu, Órmos	90 C3	Almoguera	40 B2	Almonte	42 C3	Alnö	101 F3	Alozaina	43 E4
Almenara, Sa de la	44 C3	Almerimar	44 B4	Almodóvar	42 B2	Almoharin	39 D4	Almoradí	45 D2	Alnwick	5 E3	Alp	32 A3
Almenar de Soria	36 B3	Almese	31 E1	Almodóvar		Almonacid de la		Almorox	40 A2	Alónia	79 F3	Alpalhão	38 C3
Almendra,		Älmhult	109 D2	del Campo	43 F1	Sierra	36 C4	Almourol	38 B3	Alónissos	84 B2	Alpbach	59 D1
Emb de	35 D4	Almijara, Sa de	44 A3	Almodóvar del		Almonacid de		Almsee	56 C3	Alónissos, N	84 B2	Alpe-d'Huez, l'	31 D1
Almendral	38 C4	Almiri	87 E1	Pinar	40 C3	Toledo	40 A3	Almudébar	37 D3	Alora	43 E3	Alpedrinha	38 C2

Alpera 41 D4
Alpes-de-Haute-Provence 31 D3
Alpes-Maritimes 31 E3
Alpe Veglia 58 A3
Alphen aan den Rijn 16 C3
Alpi Apuane 60 B3
Alpiarça 38 B3
Alpignano 31 E1
Alpi Orobie 58 B3
Alpirsbach 54 C3
Alpua 99 D4
Alqueva 42 B1
Alqueva, Bgem de 42 B1
Alquézar 37 E3
Als 108 B2
Als (Reg) 108 B4
Alsasua 36 B2
Alsdorf 17 D4
Alsen 101 E2
Alsfeld 52 A3
Alstahaug 97 D3
Alston 5 E4
Alta 95 D2
Altaelva 95 D2
Altafjorden 95 D2
Altamura 65 D3
Alta, Sa 41 D2
Altastenberg 17 F4
Altaussee 56 C3
Altavilla 68 B3
Altdöbern 53 E1
Altdorf (CH) 58 A2
Altdorf (D) 55 F1
Altea 45 E1
Altedo 61 D2
Altena 17 E4
Altenahr 51 E4
Altenau 52 B2
Altenberg 53 E3
Altenberge 17 E3
Altenburg 53 D3
Altenholz 48 A1
Altenhundem 17 F4
Altenkirchen (D) 51 E3
Altenkirchen (DDR) 49 D1
Altenmarkt (D) 56 B3
Altenmarkt (Salzburg) 59 F1
Altenmarkt (Steiermark) 57 D3
Altenstadt 55 E3
Altensteig 54 C3
Altentreptow 49 D2
Altenwalde 47 F2
Alte Oder 49 E3
Alter do Chão 38 C3
Altglashütten 54 C4
Altheim 56 C3
Althofen 70 B1
Altkirch 27 E1
Altlandsberg 49 E4
Altlengbach 57 E2
Altmühl 55 F2
Altmühlsee 55 E2
Altmünster 56 C3
Altnaharra 2 C2
Alto Campó 35 F2
Alto Cruz 36 C4
Alto de Allariz 34 B3
Alto de Barazar 36 B1
Alto de Covelo 34 C3
Alto de Estividas 34 B3
Alto de Fumaces 34 B3
Alto del Couso 34 B3
Alto del Portalé 37 E4
Alto del Rodicio 34 B3
Alto de Santo Domingo 34 B2
Alto do Cañizo 34 C3
Alto Laza 37 D2
Altomira 40 B2
Alton 9 F3
Altopascio 60 C3
Alto Rabagão, Bgem do 34 B3
Altorricon 37 E3
Altotero 36 A2
Altötting 56 B3
Altrincham 6 C2
Alt Ruppin 49 D3
Altshausen 55 D4
Altstätten 58 B2
Altura 41 E3
Altweilnau 51 F4
Alustante 41 D2
Alva 4 C2
Alvaiázere 38 B2
Alvalade 42 A1
Alvão, Sa de 34 B4
Alva, R 38 B2
Alvdal 100 C3
Älvdalen 101 E4
Alvelos, Sa de 38 B2
Alverca do Ribatejo 38 A4
Alvesta 109 D2
Alvignac 29 D2
Ålvik 104 B2
Alvito 42 B1
Alvito, Bgem do 42 B1
Älvkarleby 106 B2
Alvor 42 A2
Älvros 101 E3
Älvsborgs Län 108 C1
Älvsbyn 98 B3
Alyth 5 D1
Alytus 110 C4
Alz 56 B3
Alzenau 52 A4
Alzey 54 C1
Alzira 41 E4
Alzola 36 B1
Alzon 29 F3
Alzonne 32 B1
Amadora 38 A4
Åmål 105 E4
Amalfi 64 B4
Amaliáda 86 B1
Amaliápoli 83 F2
Amálo 89 D2
Amance 27 D1
Amancey 27 D2
Amandola 61 F4
Amantea 67 E3
Amárandos (Ípiros) 78 C4
Amárandos (Thessalía) 83 D2
Amarante 34 B4
Amareleja 42 C1
Amares 34 A4
Amárinthos 84 B4
Amatrice 63 F1
Amay 50 C4
Amaya 35 F3
Ambarès-et-Lagrave 28 B2
Ambasaguas 35 E2
Ambazac 25 E4
Ambelákia (Thessalía) 83 E1
Ambelákia (Thráki) 81 F1
Ambelía 83 E2
Ambelikó 85 F3
Ambelióna 86 C2
Ambelónas 83 E1
Amberg 55 F1
Ambérieu-en-Bugey 26 C4
Ambert 29 F1
Ambès 28 B2
Ambierle 26 B4
Amble 5 E3
Ambleside 5 D4
Amblève 51 D4
Amboise 25 D2
Ambra 61 D4
Ambrières-les-Vallées 18 C4
Ameixial 42 B2
Ameland 16 C1
Amelia 63 E2
Amélie-les-Bains-Palalda 32 B3
Amelinghausen 48 B3
Amer 32 B3
A Merca 34 B3
Amerongen 16 C3
Amersfoort 16 C3
Amersham 9 F2
Amesbury 9 E3
A Mezquita 34 C3
Amfiaraío 84 B4
Amfiklia 83 E3
Amfilohía 82 C3
Amfipoli 80 B2
Ámfissa 83 E4
Amiata, Mont' 63 D1
Amiens 19 F2
Amigdaleónas 80 C2
Amigdaliá 83 E4
Amindeo 79 D3
Åmli 104 B4
Amlwch 6 A2
Ammanford 8 C2
Ämmänsaari 99 E3
Ammarfjället 97 F3
Ammarnäs 97 F3
Ammel 56 A4
Ammersattel 55 F4
Ammersee 56 A3
Amohóri 79 D3
Amolianí 80 B4
Amorbach 55 D1
Amorebieta 36 B1
Amorgós 89 D3
Amorgós, N 89 D3
Amório 81 F1
Åmot (Buskerud) 104 C3
Åmot (S) 105 F2
Åmot (Telemark) 104 B3
Åmotfors 105 D3
Amótopos 82 C2
Amou 28 B4
Amoudára 91 D3
Amoudára 91 E4
Amoúdia 89 D2
Ampezzo 59 E3
Ampfing 56 B3
Amphion 27 D3
Amplepuis 26 B4
Amposta 41 F2
Ampthill 9 F2
Ampudia 35 E4
Ampuero 36 A1
Amriswil 58 B1
Amrum 47 F1
Amsele 98 B4
Amstelveen 16 C2
Amsterdam 16 C2
Amstetten 57 D3
Amungen 101 E4
Amurrio 36 B1
Amusco 35 F3
Amvrakía, L 82 C3
Amvrakikós Kólpos 82 C3
Anadia 38 B1
Anáfi 91 E1
Anáfi, N 91 F1
Anafonítria 86 A1
Anagni 63 F3
Anáktora Néstoros 86 B3
Análipsi 83 F4
Análipsi 92 C1
Análipsis 86 C3
Ananjev 113 E3
Anaráhi 79 D3
Anárgiri 79 D3
Änarjohka 95 E2
Anascaul 14 A3
Ånaset 102 B1
Åna Sira 104 A4
Anatolí (Ípiros) 82 C1
Anatolí (Kríti) 91 E4
Anatolí (Thessalía) 83 F1
Anatolikí Rodópi 81 D2
Anatolikó 79 D3
Änättijärvi 99 F4
Anávatos 85 E4
Anávissos 87 F2
Anávra (Karditsa) 83 E2
Anávra (Magnissía) 83 E3
An Cabhán 13 D3
Ancares, Sa de 34 C2
Ancenis 23 D4
Ancerville 20 C4
Anchuras 39 F3
An Clochán 12 A3
An Cóbh 14 C4
Ancona 61 F3
Ancy-le-Franc 26 B1
Anda 100 A3
Andalo 58 C3
Åndalsnes 100 B2
Andalucía 43 E2
Andarax, R 44 B3
Andartikó 79 D2
Andebu 104 C3
Andelot 26 C1
Andelys, les 19 E3
Andenes 94 A3
Andenne 50 C4
Anderlues 50 B4
Andermatt 58 A3
Andernach 51 E4
Andernos 28 A2
Anderstorp 109 D2
Andfjorden 94 B3
Andigonos 79 D3
Andikíra 83 E4
Andikíras, Kólpos 83 E4
Andikíthira, N 90 A2
Andimáhia 89 F3
Andimilos, N 88 A4
Andinitsa 83 E3
Andiparos 88 B3
Andíparos, N 88 B3
Andípaxi, N 82 B2
Andípsara, N 85 E4
Andirio 83 D4
Ándissa 85 E2
Andoain 36 C1
Andorno Micca 31 F1
Andorra 41 E1
Andorra la Vella 32 A2
Andosilla 36 C2
Andover 9 E3
Andøya 94 A3
Andratx 45 E3
Andravida 86 B1
Andretta 64 C3
Andrézieux-Bouthéon 30 B1
Andria 65 D3
Andrijevica 76 C2
Andritsena 86 C2
Andros 88 B1
Ándros, N 88 B1
Androússa 86 C3
Andselv 94 B3
Andújar 43 F2
Anduze 30 B3
Aneby 109 D1
Ånes 100 B2
Anet 19 E4
Aneto, Pico de 37 E2
Angáli 84 A3
Ånge (Jämtlands Län) 101 E2
Ånge (Västernorrlands Län) 101 E3
Angeja 38 B1
Ängelholm 108 C3
Angeli 95 E3
Angelohóri 79 E3
Angelókastro (Pelopónissos) 87 E2
Angelókastro (Stereá Eláda) 82 C4
Anger 57 E4
Angera 58 A4
Ångermanälven 101 F2
Angermünde 49 E3
Angern 57 F2
Angers 23 E4
Angerville 25 E1
Ängesån 98 C2
Anghiari 61 D4
Angístis, Stathmós 80 B2
Angístri 87 E2
Angístri, N 87 E2
Ángistro 80 B1
Angitis 80 B2
Angles 25 D3
Anglès (E) 32 B3
Anglès (F) 32 B1
Anglesey, I of 6 A2
Anglesola 37 F3
Anglet 28 A4
Anglure 20 B4
Angoulême 28 C1
Angri 64 B4
Ängsö 106 C3
Angüés 37 E3
Anguiano 36 B2
Anguillara Veneta 61 D1
Angvik 100 B2
Anholt 108 C2
Aniane 30 A4
Aniche 20 A1
Aniene 63 F2
Ánixi 79 D4
Anizy-le-Château 20 A3
Anjalankoski 107 F2
Anjum 47 D3
Ankaran 70 A3
Ankarsrum 109 E1
Anklam 49 E2
Ankogel 59 E2
An Longfort 12 C3
An Muileann gCearr 13 D3
Ånn 101 D2
Ånn L 101 D2
Annaberg 57 E3
Annaberg-Buchholz 53 E3
Annaburg 53 E1
Annan 5 D3
Annan R 5 D3
Anndalsvågen 97 D3
Annecy 27 D4
Annemasse 27 D4
Annevoie-Rouillon 50 C4
Annonay 30 B1
Annone Veneto 59 E4
Annot 31 D3
Annweiler 54 C2
Áno Drossiní 81 E2
Anógia 87 D3
Anógia 91 D3
Áno Hóra 83 D4
Anoia, R 32 A4
Áno Kalendíni 82 C2
Áno Kaliniki 79 D2
Áno Kómi 79 E4
Áno Lefkími 82 A2
Áno Melás 79 D3
Áno Merá 88 C2
Anópoli 90 C4
Áno Polidéndri 83 F1
Áno Poróïa 80 A2
Áno Rodákino 90 C4
Áno Sangrí 88 C3
Áno Síros 88 B2
Añover de Tajo 40 A3
Áno Viános 91 E4
Áno Vrondoú 80 B2
Áno Zervohóri 79 E3
Ansbach 55 E1
Anse 26 C4
Ansedonia 63 D2
Ansião 38 B2
Ansnes 100 C1
Ansó 37 D2
Anstruther 5 D2
An tAonach 12 C4
Antas 44 C3
Antegnate 60 B1
Antemil 34 A1
Antequera 43 F3
Anterselva 59 D2
Ánthia 81 E2
Anthili 83 E3
Anthis 80 B2
Antholz 59 D2
Anthótopos 83 E2
Antibes 31 E4
Antifer, Cap d' 19 D3
An tInbhear Mór 15 E3
Antnäs 98 C3
Antraigues 30 B2
Antrain 18 B4
Antrim 13 E2
Antrim (Co) 13 E2
Antrim Coast 13 E1
Antrim Mts 13 E1
Antrodoco 63 F2
Anttola 103 E3
Antwerpen 50 B3
Antwerpen (Prov) 50 C3
An Uaimh 13 D3
Anvers 50 B3
Anzano di Puglia 64 C3
Anzio 63 E3
Anzola d'Ossola 58 A4
Anzy-le-Duc 26 B4
Aoiz 36 C2
Aóos 78 C4
Aosta 27 E4
Aoste 27 E4
Apatin 72 B2
Apatovac 71 D2
Apecchio 61 E4
Apeldoorn 17 D2
Apen 47 E3
Apéri 93 D3
Aphrodisias 115 F4
Apidiá 87 D3
Apíkia 88 B1
Apíranthos 88 C3
Apolakiá 93 E2
Apolda 52 C3
Apolitáres, Akr 90 A2
Apólonas 88 C3
Apolonía (Kiklådes) 88 B3
Apolonía (Makedonía) 80 B3
A Pontenova Villaodriz 34 C1
Apóstoli 90 C4
Äppelbo 105 E2
Appenweier 54 C3
Appenzell 58 B2
Appiano 59 D3
Appingedam 47 D3
Appleby 5 D4
Aprica 58 C3
Apricena 64 C2
Aprilia 63 E3
Ápsalos 79 E2
Apt 30 C3
Áptera 90 C3
Aquileia 59 F3
Aquitaine, L' 25 E2
Arabba 59 D3
Aracena 42 C2
Aracena, Emb de 43 D2
Aracena, Sa de 42 C2
Aračinovo 77 E3
Arad 112 C4
Åradalsfjorden 104 B1
Arada, Sa de 38 B1
Aragón 37 D3
Aragona 68 B4
Aragón, R 36 C2
Arahnéo, Óros 87 E2
Aráhova (Etolía-Akarnanía) 83 D3
Aráhova (Viotía) 83 E4
Arákinthos, Óros 83 D4
A Ramallosa 34 A3
Aramits 37 D1
Aranda de Duero 36 A3
Aranđelovac 73 D3
Aran I 12 C1
Aran Is 12 A4
Aranjuez 40 B3
Arantzazu 36 B1
Aran, Vall d' 37 F2
Araquil, R 36 C2
Ara, R 37 E2
Aras de Alpuente 41 D3
Arasluokta 97 F1
Aráhthos 82 C2
Áratos 81 E2
Aravaca 40 A2
Aravis, Col des 27 D4
Aravissós 79 E2
Araxos 86 B1
Áraxos, Akr 86 B1
Arazede 38 B2
Arba, R 36 C3
Arbatax 66 C3
Arbeca 37 F4
Arbesbach 57 D2
Arboga 105 F3
Arbois 27 D3
Arbon 58 B1
Arbón, Emb de 34 C1
Arborea 66 B3
Arborio 31 F1
Arbrå 101 F4
Arbroath 5 E1
Arbresle, l' 26 B4
Arbúcies 32 B4
Arbus 66 B3
Arc 31 D1
Arcachon 28 A2
Arce 64 A3
Arcen 17 D3
Arc-en-Barrois 26 C1
Arceniega 36 A1
Arcevia 61 E4
Archena 45 D2
Arches 27 D1
Archiac 28 B1
Archidona 43 F3
Arcidosso 63 D1
Arcipelago Toscano 62 B1
Arcis 20 B4
Arciz 113 E4
Arco 58 C4
Arco de Baúlhe 34 B4
Arcos 35 F3
Arcos de Jalón 36 B4
Arcos de la Frontera 43 D3
Arcos de Valdevez 34 A3
Arcouest, Pte de l' 22 C2
Arcs, les (Savoie) 31 D1
Arcs, les (Var) 31 D4
Arcusa 37 E2
Arda 115 E3
Ardales 43 E3
Årdalstangen 104 B1
Ardánio 81 F2
Ardara 12 C1
Árdas 81 F1
Ardbeg 4 B2
Ardèche (Dépt) 30 B2
Ardèche R 30 B2
Ardèche, Gges de l' 30 B3
Ardee 13 D3
Ardennes (Dépt) 20 B3
Ardennes, Canal des 20 C3
Ardentes 25 E3
Ardentinny 4 C2
Ardes 29 F1
Ardez 58 B2
Ardglass 13 E2
Ardila, R 42 C1
Ardila, Rib de 42 C1
Ardisa 37 D3
Ardlussa 4 B2
Ardmore 14 C4
Ardrahan 12 B4
Ardres 19 E1
Ardrishaig 4 B2
Ardrossan 4 C2
Ards Pen 13 E2
Arduaine 4 B1
Ardvasar 2 B4
Åre 101 D2
Arenas de Cabrales 35 E2
Arenas de Iguña 35 F2
Arenas de San Juan 40 B4
Arenas de San Pedro 39 F2
Arendal 104 C4
Arendonk 50 C3
Arendsee 48 C3
Arenos, Emb de 41 E3
Arenys de Mar 32 B4
Arenzano 60 A3
Areópoli 87 D4
Arès 28 A2
Ares (Galicia) 34 B1
Ares (Valencia) 41 E2
Ares, Col des 37 F2
Ares, Pto de 32 B3
Åreskutan 101 D2
Aréthoussa 80 B3
Areti 80 A3
Arévalo 39 F1
Arez 38 C3
Arezzo 61 D4
Arfará 86 C3
Argalasti 83 F2
Argamasilla de Alba 40 B4
Argamasilla de Calatrava 44 A1
Arganda 40 B2
Arganil 38 B2
Arga, R 36 C2
Argássi 86 A2
Argelès 32 B2
Argelès-Gazost 37 E1
Argens 31 D4
Argent 25 F2
Argenta 61 D2
Argentan 19 D4
Argentario, Mte 63 D2

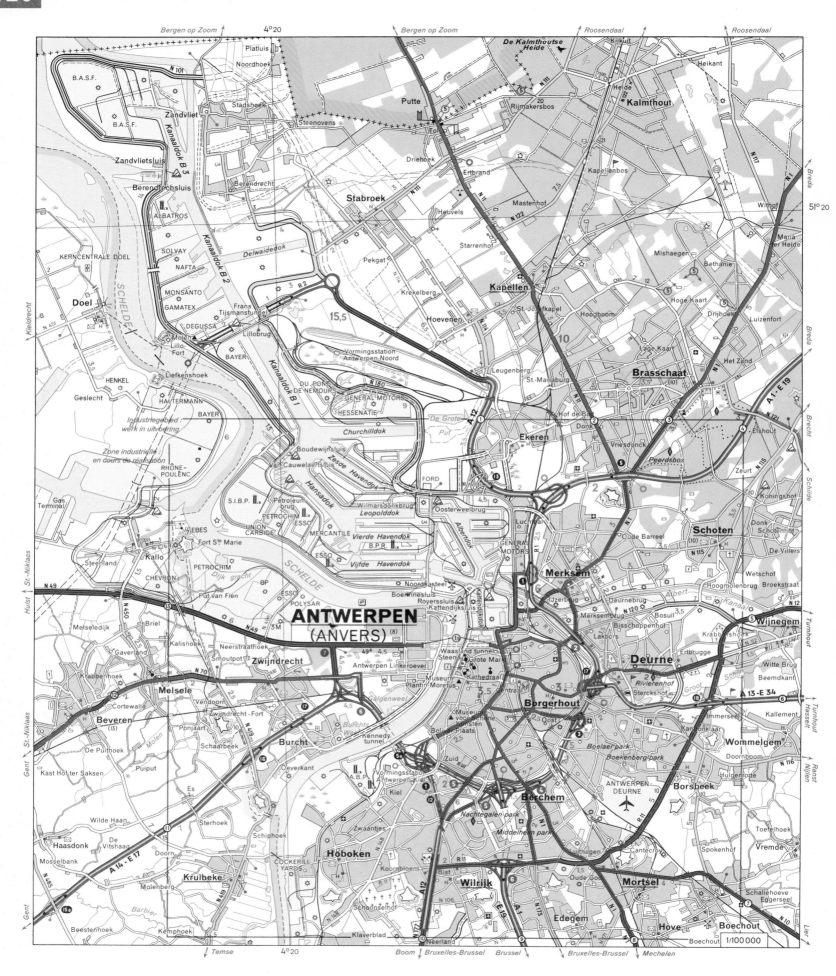

ANTWERPEN
(ANVERS) (8)

1/100 000

Argentat 29 D2
Argente 41 D2
Argentera 31 E3
Argentière 27 E4
Argentière-la-Bessée, l' 31 D2
Argentona 32 B4
Argenton-Château 24 C3
Argenton-sur-Creuse 25 E3
Argentré-du-Plessis 23 E3
Arginónda 89 F3
Argirádes 82 A2
Argiró 84 B4
Argiropoúlio 83 E1
Argiroúpoli 90 C3
Argithéa 83 D2
Argolida 87 E2
Argolikós Kólpos 87 E2
Árgos 87 D2
Árgos Orestikó 79 D3
Argos, R 44 C2
Argostóli 82 B4
Arguedas 36 C3
Argueil 19 E3
Arguellite 44 B1
Arguis 37 D2
Argyll 4 B1
Argyll Forest Park 4 C2
Arhánes 91 D4
Arhángelos (Makedonía) 79 E2
Arhángelos (Ródos) 93 F1
Arhéa Epídavros 87 E2
Arhéa Kleonés 87 D1
Arhéa Kórinthos 87 E1
Arhéa Neméa 87 D1
Arhéa Olympía 86 C2
Arhéa Thíra 91 E1
Árhus 108 B3
Arianá 81 E2
Ariano Irpino 64 B3
Ariano nel Polesine 61 D2
Aridéa 79 E2
Ariège (Dépt) 32 A2
Ariège R 32 A2
Arija 35 F2
Arild 108 C3
Arilje 72 C4
Arinagour 2 B4
Arini 86 C2
Ariño 37 D4
Arinthod 27 D3
Arisaig 2 B4
Arisaig, Sd of 2 B4
Arísti 78 C4
Aristoménis 86 C3
Arísvi 81 E2
Aritzo 66 B3
Arive 36 C2
Ariza 36 B4
Årjäng 105 D3
Arjeplog 98 A3
Arjona 44 A2
Arkádi 91 D3
Arkadía 86 C2
Arkaig, L 2 C4
Arkalohóri 91 E4
Arkássa 93 D3
Arkessíni 89 D3
Arki, N 89 E2
Arkítsa 83 F3
Arklow 15 E3
Arkona, Kap 49 D1
Arkoúdi, N 82 B4
Arlaban, Pto de 36 B1
Arlanc 29 F1
Arlanda 106 B3
Arlanza, R 36 A3
Arlanzón 36 A2
Arlanzón, R 35 F3
Arlbergpaß 58 B2

Arlberg-Straßentunnel 58 B2
Arlempdes 30 A2
Arles (Bouches-du-Rhône) 30 B4
Arles (Pyrénées-Orientales) 32 B3
Arlesheim 27 E2
Arlon 21 D2
Arlsleben 52 C2
Armação de Pêra 42 A3
Armadale 5 D2
Arma di Taggia 31 F3
Armagh 13 D2
Armagh (Co) 13 D2
Armamar 34 B4
Arméni 90 C3
Armenii 86 C3
Armenistís 89 D2
Armentières 19 F1
Armilla 44 A3
Armólia 85 E4
Armunia 35 D3
Árna 87 D3
Arnac-Pompadour 29 D1
Arnay-le-Duc 26 B2
Arnéa 80 B3
Arneburg 48 C4
Arnedillo 36 B3
Arnedo 36 C3
Arnes 41 F2
Árnes 105 D3
Arnhem 17 D3
Arni 60 B3
Árnissa 79 E2
Arno 60 C4
Arnoldstein 59 F2
Arnon 25 F3
Arnøy 94 C2
Arnsberg 17 F3
Arnstadt 52 C3
Arnstein 52 B4
Aroania, Óri 86 C1
Aroche 42 C2
Aroche Mt 42 C1
Arogí 81 D2
Arolsen 52 A2
Arona 58 A4
Aroniádika 90 A1
Aronkylä 102 B3
Åros 104 C3
Arosa 58 B2
Arouca 38 B1
Arousa, I de 34 A2
Årøysund 104 C3
Arpajon 19 F4
Arpela 99 D3
Arquata del Tronto 63 F1
Arques (Pas-de-Calais) 19 F1
Arques (Seine-Maritime) 19 E2
Arquillos 44 A2
Arrabal 34 A3
Arrábida, Sa da 38 A4
Arracourt 21 D4
Arraiolos 38 B4
Arran 4 B2
Arras 19 F2
Arrasate-Mondragon 36 B1
Arreau 37 E2
Arrecife 42 C4
Arredondo 36 A1
Arrée, Mts d' 22 B2
Arrens 37 E2
Arrifana 38 C1
Arrigorriaga 36 B1
Arriondas 35 E1
Arrochar 4 C2
Arromanches 18 C3
Arronches 38 C4
Arroux 26 B3

Arrow, L 12 C2
Arroyo de la Luz 39 D3
Arroyo del Ojanco 44 B1
Arroyo de San Serván 39 D4
Arroyomolinos de León 43 D1
Arroyomolinos de Montánchez 39 D4
Arruda dos Vinhos 38 A3
Års 108 A2
Ars (Charente-Maritime) 24 B4
Ars (Moselle) 21 D3
Arsiè 59 D3
Arsiero 59 D4
Arsunda 106 B2
Arsy 19 F3
Artà 45 F2
Árta 82 C2
Artajona 36 C2
Arta Terme 59 E3
Arteaga, G de 36 B1
Artemíssia 86 C3
Artemíssio (Évia) 83 F3
Artemíssio (Pelopónissos) 87 D2
Artemónas 88 B3
Artena 63 F3
Artenay 25 E1
Artern 52 C2
Artesa de Segre 37 F3
Artessianó 83 D2
Artfjället 97 E3
Arth (CH) 58 A2
Arth (D) 56 B2
Arthurstown 15 D4
Arties 37 F2
Artjärvi 107 F2
Artotína 83 D3
Artruix, C de 45 F2
A Rúa 34 C3
Arucas 42 B4
Arudy 37 D1
Arundel 9 F3
Arve 27 E4
Árvi 91 E4
Arvidsjaur 98 A3
Årvik 100 A2
Arvika 105 E3
Årviksand 94 C2
Arzachena 66 B1
Arzacq-Arraziguet 28 B4
Arzano 22 B3
Aržano 75 E1
Arzberg 53 D4
Arzignano 60 C1
Árzos 81 F1
Arzúa 34 B2
As 50 C3
Aš 53 D4
Åsa 108 C2
Asamati 77 D4
Åsarna 101 E2
Åsarp 109 D1
Ascain 28 A4
Ascha 56 B2
Aschach 56 C2
Aschaffenburg 52 A4
Aschau 56 B3
Aschbach Markt 57 D3
Ascheberg (Nordrhein-Westfalen) 17 E3
Ascheberg (Schleswig-Holstein) 48 B2
Aschendorf 17 E1
Aschersleben 52 C2
Asciano 61 D4
Ascione, Colle d' 67 F3
Asco 33 F3
Ascó 37 E4
Ascoli Piceno 63 F1
Ascoli Satriano 64 C3
Ascona 58 A3
Ascot 9 F2

Åse 94 A3
Åseda 109 E2
Åsele 101 F1
Åsen 101 D1
Asenovgrad 115 D3
Åseral 104 B4
Asfáka 82 B1
Asfeld 20 B3
Åsgårdstrand 104 C3
Ashbourne (GB) 6 C3
Ashbourne (IRL) 13 D3
Ashburton 8 C4
Ashby de la Zouch 6 C3
Ashford 11 D3
Ashington 5 E3
Ashton-under-Lyne 6 C2
Asiago 59 D4
Asikkala 107 F2
Asín 37 D3
Asinara, G dell' 66 B1
Asinara, I 66 A1
Ask 105 D3
Askainen 107 D2
Askeaton 14 B3
Askersund 105 F4
Askifou 90 C3
Askim 105 D3
Askja 96 C2
Asklipío (Dodekánissa) 89 F3
Asklipío (Ródos) 93 E2
Askola 107 F2
Askós 80 A3
Askøy 104 A2
Askvoll 104 A1
Asmunti 99 D3
Asnæs 108 B3
Asnen 109 D2
As Neves 34 A3
Asola 60 B1
Asolo 59 D4
Aspang 57 F3
Aspatria 5 D4
Aspe 45 D2
Aspe, Gave d' 37 D1
Asperg 55 D2
Aspet 37 F2
Aspin, Col d' 37 E2
As Ponte de Garcia Rodriguez 34 B1
Áspra Spítia 83 E4
Aspres 30 C2
Áspro 79 E3
Aspróhoma 86 C3
Aspromonte 67 E4
Asprópirgos 87 F1
Asproválta 80 B3
Asse 50 B3
Assemini 66 B4
Assen 17 D1
Assens 108 B3
Assergi 63 F2
Assíni 87 E2
Assisi 63 E1
Aßmannshausen 51 F4
Assomáton 91 D3
Assopía 84 A4
Assopós (Korinthía) 87 D1
Assopós (Lakonía) 87 E4
Assopós R 87 E1
Ássos (Ípiros) 82 B2
Ássos (Kefaloniá) 82 B4
Astaffort 28 C3
Astakída, N 93 D2
Astakós 82 C4
Asten 57 D3
Asti 31 F2
Astipálea 92 C1
Astipálea, N 92 C1
Astorga 35 D3

Åstorp 108 C3
Ástros 87 D2
Astudillo 35 F3
Asturias 34 C2
Asvestádes 81 F1
Asvestohóri 82 B1
Asvestópetra 79 D3
Ataláia 38 A3
Atalándi 83 F3
Atalaya de la Calzada 44 A1
Atalayassa 45 D4
Átali 84 B3
Ataquines 39 F1
Atarfe 44 A3
Atáviros 93 E2
Ateca 36 C4
Atella 64 C3
Atessa 64 B2
Ath 50 B4
Athamánon, Óri 82 C2
Athánio 82 B3
Athéras 89 D2
Athéras, Akr 82 B4
Athenry 12 B3
Athína 87 F1
Áthira 79 F2
Athlone 12 C3
Áthos 80 C4
Athy 13 D4
Atienza 36 B4
Atiki-Piréas 87 F1
Atina 64 A3
Átokos, N 82 C4
Atouguia da Baleia 38 A3
Átran 108 C2
Átran R 108 C2
Atri 64 A1
Atsikí 85 D1
Attendorn 17 F4
Attersee 56 C3
Attersee L 56 C3
Attigny 20 B3
Attleborough 11 D1
Attnang 56 C3
Åtvidaberg 109 E1
Au 55 F2
Aub 55 E1
Aubagne 30 C4
Aubange 21 D2
Aube 20 B4
Aube (Dépt) 20 B4
Aubenas 30 B2
Aubenton 20 B2
Auberive 26 C1
Aubeterre 26 C1
Aubigny (Cher) 25 F2
Aubigny (Pas-de-Calais) 19 F2
Aubin 29 E3
Aubisque, Col d' 37 E1
Aubonne 27 D3
Aubrac, Mts d' 29 F2
Aubusson 25 F4
Auch 28 C4
Auchencairn 4 C3
Auchterarder 5 D1
Auchtermuchty 5 D1
Aude (Dépt) 32 B2
Aude R 32 B1
Audenge 28 A2
Audeux 27 D2
Audierne 22 A3
Audincourt 27 E2
Audlem 6 C3
Audruicq 19 F1
Audun-le-Roman 21 D3
Audun-le-Tiche 21 D3
Aue R 48 A4
Aue 53 D3
Auer 59 D3
Auerbach (D) 55 F1

Auerbach (DDR) 53 D3
Auffach 59 D1
Aughnacloy 13 D2
Aughrim 13 D4
Augusta 69 D4
Augsburg 55 F3
Augustenborg 108 B4
Augustów 110 C4
Augustusburg 53 E3
Aukan 100 B2
Aukra 100 B2
Aulanko 107 E2
Auletta 64 C4
Aulla 60 B3
Aullène 33 F4
Aulnay 24 C4
Aulne 22 B3
Aulnoye-Aymeries 20 B2
Ault 19 E2
Aulus-les-Bains 37 F2
Auma 53 D3
Aumale 19 E2
Aumetz 21 D3
Aumont-Aubrac 29 F2
Aunay-sur-Odon 18 C3
Auneau 19 E4
Auneuil 19 E3
Auning 108 B2
Aups 31 D4
Aura 107 D2
Aurajoki 107 D2
Aurdal 104 C2
Aure 100 B2
Aure R 18 C3
Aurich 47 E3
Aurignac 37 F1
Aurillac 29 E2
Aurland 104 B2
Auron 31 E3
Auron R 25 F3
Auronzo di Cadore 59 E2
Auros 28 B3
Aursjøen 100 B3
Aursuden 101 D2
Ausonia 64 A3
Außernbrünst 56 C2
Ausso Corno 59 F3
Aust-Agder 104 B4
Austbygd 104 C3
Austvågøy 94 A3
Auterive 37 F1
Authie 19 F2
Autol 36 C3
Autrans 30 C1
Autrey 26 C2
Auttoinen 107 E1
Autun 26 B3
Auvézère 28 C2
Auvillar 28 C3
Auxerre 26 A1
Auxi-le-Château 19 E2
Auxonne 26 C2
Auzances 25 F4
Auzon 29 F1
Availles-Limouzine 25 D4
Avala 73 D3
Avaldsnes 104 A3
Avallon 26 B3
Avaloirs, Mt des 23 E3
Åvas 81 E2
Avaviken 98 A3
Ávdira 81 D2
A Veiga 34 C3
Avebury 9 F2
Aveiras de Cima 38 A3
Aveiro 38 B1
Aveiro, R de 38 B1
Avellino 64 B4
Aven Armand 29 F3
Aven d'Orgnac 30 B3
Averøya 100 B2
Aversa 64 B4
Avesnes 20 B2
Avesnes-le-Comte 19 F2

Avesta 105 F3
Avetrana 65 E4
Aveyron 29 D3
Aveyron (Dépt) 29 E3
Avezzano 63 F2
Avgerinós 79 D4
Avgó 82 C2
Avía 86 C3
Aviano 59 E3
Aviémonas 90 C3
Aviemore 3 D4
Aviés 79 E4
Avigliana 31 E1
Avigliano 64 C4
Avignon 30 B3
Ávila 39 F2
Ávila, Sa de 39 F2
Avilés 35 D1
Aviño 34 B1
Avintes 34 A4
Avión 34 B2
Avioth 20 C3
Avis 38 B4
Avisio 59 D3
Avize 20 B3
Avlákia 89 E1
Avli 80 C2
Avliótes 82 A1
Avlóna 84 B4
Avlum 108 A2
Avola 69 D4
Avon (Co) 9 D2
Avon R (Hants) 9 E1
Avon R (Warw) 9 E3
Avonmouth 9 D2
Avord 25 F3
Avoriaz 27 E4
Avranches 18 B4
Avre 19 E3
Avtovac 76 A2
Awe, L 4 B1
Axams 59 D2
Axat 32 B2
Axiohóri 79 F2
Axiós 79 F3
Axioúpoli 79 F2
Ax-les-Thermes 32 A2
Axminster 9 D3
Axós 91 D3
Ay 20 B3
Ayamonte 42 B2
Aydın 115 F4
Ayedo 36 B3
Ayerbe 37 D3
Aylesbury 9 F2
Ayllón 36 A4
Ayllón, Sa de 36 A4
Aylsham 7 F3
Ayna 44 C1
Ayora 41 D4
Ayr 4 C3
Ayre, Pt of 6 A1
Ayvacık 115 E4
Ayvalık 115 E4
Aywaille 51 D4
Azáceta, Pto de 36 B2
Azaila 37 D4
Azambuja 38 A3
Azanja 73 D3
Azaruja 38 B4
Azay-le-Ferron 25 E3
Azay-le-Rideau 25 D2
Azinheira dos Barros 42 A1
Azkoitia 36 B1
Aznalcázar 43 D3
Aznalcóllar 43 D3
Azpeitia 36 B1
Azuaga 43 E1
Azuara 37 D4
Azuer, R 40 A4
Azuqueca de Henares 40 B2
Azután, Emb de 39 F3
Azzano Decimo 59 E3

B

Baad	58 B2	Bačko Petrovo Selo	72 C1	Bad Friedrichshall	55 D2
Baal	17 D4	Bačkovo	115 D3	Bad Gandersheim	52 B1
Baamonde	34 B1	Bacoli	64 A4	Badgastein	59 E2
Baarle-Nassau	16 C4	Bacqueville	19 D2	Bad Gleichenberg	57 F4
Baarn	16 C2	Baczyna	49 F3	Bad Godesberg	51 E3
Baba	77 E4	Bad Aibling	56 B3	Bad Goisern	56 C2
Babadag	113 E4	Badajoz	38 C4	Bad Gottleuba	53 D3
Babajevo	111 E1	Badalona	32 B4	Bad Griesbach	56 C2
Babelsberg	49 D4	Bad Aussee	56 C3	Bad Grund	52 B2
Babenhausen (Bayern)	55 E3	Bad Bentheim	17 E2	Bad Hall	57 D3
Babenhausen (Hessen)	52 A4	Bad Bergzabern	54 C2	Bad Harzburg	52 B1
Babina Greda	71 F3	Bad Berka	52 C3	Bad Herrenalb	54 C2
Babin Kal	73 F4	Bad Berleburg	17 F4	Bad Hersfeld	52 B3
Babin Most	77 D2	Bad Berneck	53 D4	Bad Hofgastein	56 C3
Babino Polje	75 F2	Bad Bertrich	51 E4	Bad Homburg	51 F4
Babin Potok	70 C4	Bad Bevensen	48 B3	Bad Honnef	51 E3
Babljak	76 B2	Bad Bibra	52 C2	Bad Honnigen	51 E4
Babuna	77 E3	Bad Blankenburg	52 C3	Badia Polesine	61 D2
Babušnica	77 E1	Bad Brambach	53 D4	Badia Tedalda	61 D3
Bač	72 B2	Bad Bramstedt	48 A2	Bad Iburg	17 F2
Bački Breg	72 B1	Bad Brückenau	52 B4	Badija	75 E2
Bacau	113 D4	Bad Buchau	55 D3	Bad Ischl	56 C3
Baccarat	21 E4	Bad Camberg	51 F4	Bad Karlshafen	52 A2
Bæccegæhal'di	94 C2	Bad Deutsch Altenburg	57 F2	Bad Kissingen	52 B4
Baceno	58 A3	Bad Doberan	48 C2	Bad Kleinen	48 C2
Bacharach	51 E4	Bad Driburg	52 A2	Bad Kleinkirchheim	59 F2
Bächistock	58 A2	Bad Düben	53 D2	Bad König	55 D1
Bachmač	113 F1	Bad Dürkheim	54 C1	Bad Königshofen	52 B4
Bačina	73 E4	Bad Dürrenberg	53 D2	Bad Kösen	52 C2
Bačka Palanka	72 B2	Bad Durrheim	54 C3	Bad Kreuznach	54 B1
Bäckaskog	109 D3	Bad Elster	53 D4	Bad Krozingen	54 C3
Bačka Topola	72 B1	Bad Ems	51 E4	Bad Laasphe	17 F4
Backe	101 F1	Baden (A)	57 F3	Bad Langensalza	52 B3
Bäckebo	109 E2	Baden (CH)	27 F2	Bad Lauchstädt	53 D2
Bäckefors	105 D4	Baden-Baden	54 C2	Bad Lausick	53 D2
Bački Breg	71 F1	Bad Endorf	56 B3	Bad Lauterberg	52 B2
Bački Brestovac	72 B2	Badenweiler	54 C4	Bad Leonfelden	57 D2
Bački Monoštor	72 B2	Baden-Württemberg	55 D3	Bad Liebenstein	52 B3
Bački Petrovac	72 B2	Baderna	70 A3	Bad Liebenwerda	53 E2
Backnang	55 D2	Bad Essen	17 F2	Bad Liebenzell	54 C2
Bačko Gradište	72 C2	Bad Frankenhausen	52 C2	Bad Lippspringe	17 F3
Bačko Novo Selo	72 B2	Bad Freienwalde	49 E3	Badljevina	71 E2
				Bad Meinberg	52 A2
				Bad Mergentheim	55 D1
				Bad Mitterndorf	56 C4

Bad Münder	52 A1	Bad Sachsa	52 B2	Bad Urach	55 D3
Bad Münster am Stein-Ebernburg	54 B1	Bad Säckingen	54 C4	Bad Vilbel	52 A4
Bad Münstereifel	51 E4	Bad St Leonhard	57 D4	Bad Vöslau	57 F3
Bad Muskau	53 F1	Bad Salzdetfurth	52 B1	Bad Waldsee	55 D4
Bad Nauheim	52 A3	Bad Salzschlirf	52 B3	Bad Wiessee	56 A4
Bad Nenndorf	52 A1	Bad Salzuflen	17 F2	Bad Wildungen	52 A3
Bad Neuenahr-Ahrweiler	51 E4	Bad Salzungen	52 B3	Bad Wilsnack	48 C3
Bad Neustadt	52 B4	Bad Schallerbach	56 C3	Bad Wimpfen	55 D2
Bad Oeynhausen	17 F2	Bad Schandau	53 F2	Bad Windsheim	55 E1
Bad Oldesloe	48 B2	Bad Schmiedeberg	53 D1	Bad Wörishofen	55 E3
Badolato	67 F3	Bad Schönborn	54 C2	Bad Wurzach	55 E4
Badolatosa	43 F3	Bad Schussenried	55 D3	Bad Zwischenahn	47 E3
Badonviller	21 E4	Bad Schwälbach	51 F4	Bae Colwyn	6 B2
Bad Orb	52 A4	Bad Schwartau	48 B2	Baena	43 F2
Badovinci	72 B3	Bad Segeberg	48 B2	Baeza	44 A2
Bad Peterstal-Griesbach	54 C3	Bad Soden	51 F4	Bagà	32 A3
Bad Pyrmont	52 A1	Bad Soden-Salmünster	52 A4	Bâgé-le-Châtel	26 C4
Bad Radkersburg	70 C1	Bad Sooden-Allendorf	52 B2	Bagenalstown	15 D3
Bad Ragaz	58 B2	Bad Sulza	52 C2	Bagenkop	108 B4
Bad Rappenau	55 D2	Bad Sülze	49 D2	Bagheria	68 B3
Bad Reichenhall	56 B3	Bad Tatzmannsdorf	57 F4	Bagnacavallo	61 D2
Bad Rippoldsau-Schapbach	54 C3	Bad Tennstedt	52 C2	Bagnara Calabra	67 E4
Bad Rothenfelde	17 F2	Bad Tölz	56 A4	Bagnères-de-Bigorre	37 E1
Bad Saarow-Pieskow	49 E4	Badules	36 C4	Bagnères-de-Luchon	37 E2
				Bagni del Masino	58 B3
				Bagni di Lucca	60 C3
				Bagno a Ripoli	61 D3

Bagno di Romagna	61 D3
Bagnoles-de-l'Orne	18 C4
Bagnoli del Trigno	64 B2
Bagnolo Mella	60 B1
Bagnols-les-Bains	29 F3
Bagnols-sur-Cèze	30 B3
Bagnoregio	63 E1
Bagolino	58 C4
Bagrationovsk	110 B4
Bagrdan	73 E4
Baia Mare	112 C3
Baiano	64 B4
Baião	34 B4
Baiersbronn	54 C3
Baignes-Ste-Radegonde	28 B1
Baigneux-les-Juifs	26 C2
Baile Átha Cliath	13 E4
Baile Átha Luain	12 C3
Bǎile Herculane	114 C1
Bailén	44 A2
Bǎile Tuşnad	113 D4
Bailieborough	13 D3
Bailleul	19 F1
Bain-de-Bretagne	23 D3

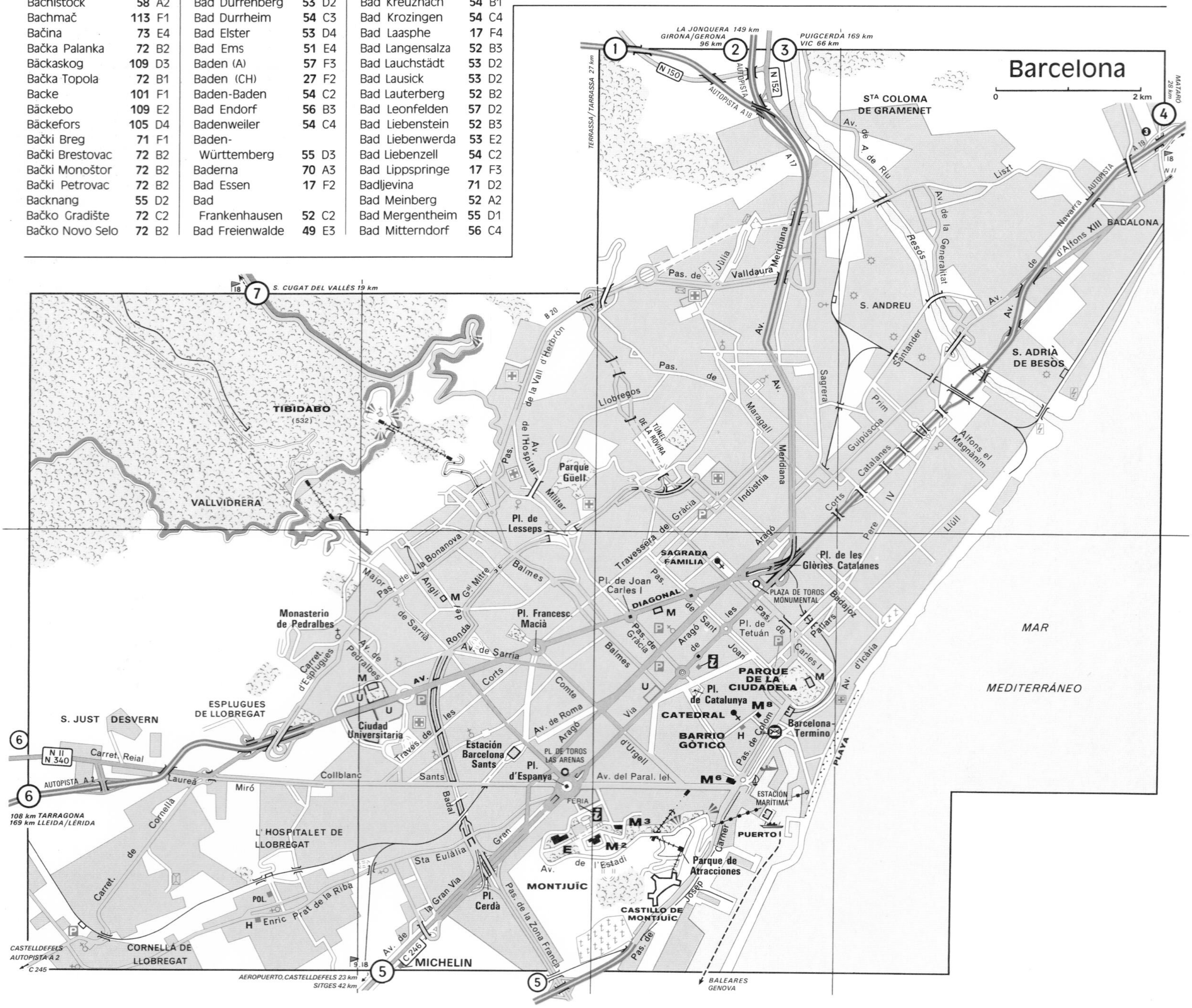

Barcelona

0 ———— 2 km

LA JONQUERA 149 km — GIRONA/GERONA 96 km — PUIGCERDA 169 km — VIC 66 km — MATARÓ 28 km — TERRASSA/TARRASSA 27 km — S. CUGAT DEL VALLÉS 19 km

N 150 · N 152 · A 17 · A 18 · AUTOPISTA A 18 · N II

Sᵀᴬ COLOMA DE GRAMENET · S. ANDREU · S. ADRIÀ DE BESÓS · BADALONA

Av. Meridiana · Pas. de Valldaura · Av. de la Generalitat · Resós · Av. d'Alfons XIII · Alfons el Magnànim · Guipúscoa · Pere IV · Bac de Roda · Meridiana · Indústria · Aragó · Sagrera

TIBIDABO (532) · VALLVIDRERA · Parque Güell · Pl. de Lesseps · Travessera de Gràcia · SAGRADA FAMILIA · Pl. de les Glòries Catalanes · Pl. de Joan Carles I · DIAGONAL · Pl. de Tetuán · PLAZA DE TOROS MONUMENTAL · PARQUE DE LA CIUDADELA · Pl. de Catalunya · CATEDRAL · BARRIO GÓTICO · Barcelona-Termino

Monasterio de Pedralbes · Pl. Francesc Macià · Pas. de la Bonanova · Balmes · Ronda · Av. de Sarrià · Pas. de Gràcia · Gran Via · Via

ESPLUGUES DE LLOBREGAT · S. JUST DESVERN · Ciudad Universitaria · Estación Barcelona Sants · Pl. d'Espanya · Pl. de Toros Las Arenas · L'HOSPITALET DE LLOBREGAT · CORNELLÀ DE LLOBREGAT

Av. de Roma · Av. d'Urgell · Av. del Paral.lel · Collblanc · Sants · Sta Eulàlia · Carret. Reial · Laureà Miró · Badal · FERIA

MONTJUÏC · CASTILLO DE MONTJUÏC · Parque de Atracciones · ESTACIÓN MARÍTIMA · PUERTO · Av. de l'Estadi

MAR · MEDITERRÁNEO · MAR MEDITERRÁNEO

MICHELIN

AEROPUERTO, CASTELLDEFELS 23 km — SITGES 42 km · BALEARES GENOVA · 108 km TARRAGONA — 169 km LLEIDA/LÉRIDA · CASTELLDEFELS AUTOPISTA A 2 · C 245 · N II · N 340 · AUTOPISTA A 2

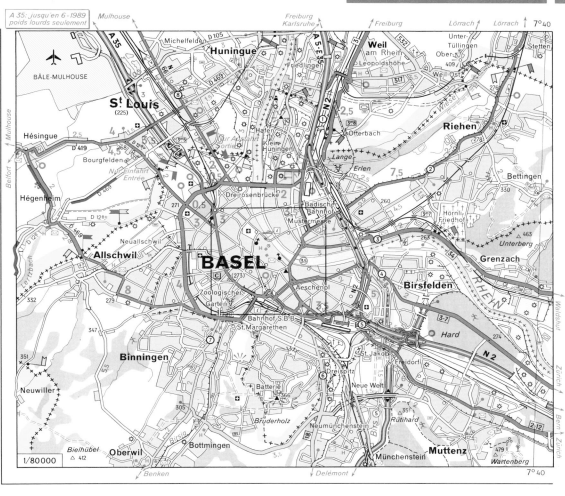

Bains-les-Bains	27 D1	Balneario de Panticosa	37 E2
Baio	34 A1	Balsareny	32 A3
Baiono	34 A3	Balsfjorden	94 B2
Bais	23 E3	Balsicas	45 D2
Baïse	28 C3	Balsorano	63 F2
Baïse-Darré	37 E1	Bålsta	106 B3
Baja	114 B1	Balsthal	27 E2
Baja Sardinia	66 B1	Balta	113 E3
Bajgora	77 D1	Baltanás	35 F4
Bajina Bašta	72 C4	Baltar	34 B3
Bajmok	72 B1	Baltic Sea	110 B2
Bajram Curri	76 C2	Baltijsk	110 B4
Bajša	72 B1	Baltinglass	13 D4
Bajzë	76 B3	Baltrum	47 E3
Bakar	70 B3	Bambalió	82 C3
Bakarac	70 B3	Bamberg	52 C4
Bakewell	6 C3	Bambini	82 C3
Bakio	36 B1	Bamburgh	5 E3
Bakkaflói	96 C1	Bampton	8 C3
Bakony	112 A4	Banagher	12 C4
Bakvattnet	101 E1	Banat	114 C1
Bala	6 B3	Banatska Palanka	73 D2
Balaguer	37 F3	Banatska Topola	72 C1
Balanegra	44 B4	Banatski Brestovac	73 D3
Balaruc	30 A4	Banatski Dvor	72 C2
Balassagyarmat	112 B3	Banatski Karlovac	73 D2
Balaton	112 A4	Banatsko Aranđelovo	72 C1
Balatonfüred	112 B4	Banatsko Karađorđevo	72 C2
Balatonkeresztúr	112 A4	Banatsko Novo Selo	73 D2
Balazote	40 C4	Banbridge	13 E2
Balbigny	26 B4	Banbury	9 E1
Balbriggan	13 E3	Banchory	3 E4
Balčik	115 E2	Bande	34 B3
Balderschwang	55 E4	Bandak	104 B2
Baldock	9 F2	Bandırma	115 E3
Baldo, Mte	58 C4	Bandol	30 C4
Bale	70 A4	Bandon	14 B4
Baleal	38 A3	Bandon R	14 B4
Baleizão	42 B1	Bañeres	45 E1
Balerma	44 B4	Banff	3 E3
Balestrand	100 A3	Bangor (IRL)	12 B2
Balí	91 D3	Bangor (N Ire)	13 E2
Balikesir	115 E4	Bangor (Wales)	6 A2
Bälinge	106 B3	Bangsund	97 D4
Balingen	55 D3	Banie	49 E3
Balivanich	2 A3	Banja (Srbija)	73 D3
Ballachulish	2 C4	Banja (Srbija)	76 B1
Ballaghaderreen	12 C3	Banja Koviljača	72 B3
Ballangen	94 B3	Banja Luka	71 E3
Ballantrae	4 B3	Banjani	72 C3
Ballao	66 B3	Banja Vrućica	71 F3
Ballater	3 D4	Banjska	76 C1
Ballaugh	6 A1	Bankeryd	109 D1
Ballenstedt	52 C2	Bann (N Ire)	13 D1
Balleroy	18 C3	Bann (Wexford)	15 D3
Ballerup	108 C3	Bannalec	22 B3
Ballina	12 B2	Banon	30 C3
Ballinamore	12 C3	Bañon	41 D2
Ballinasloe	12 C3	Baños de Cerrato	35 F4
Ballingarry	14 C3	Baños de la Encina	44 A2
Ballinrobe	12 B3	Baños de la Fuensanta	44 C2
Ballintober	12 B3	Baños de Molgas	34 B3
Ballobar	37 E4	Baños de Montemayor	39 E2
Ballon	23 F3	Baños de Fuensanta	35 E1
Ballon d'Alsace	27 E1	Banova Jaruga	71 D2
Ballstad	97 E1	Banovići	71 F4
Ballybay	13 D2	Banque de Fraiture	51 D4
Ballybofey	12 C1	Banque Michel	51 D4
Ballybunnion	12 A4	Bansin	49 E2
Ballycastle	12 B2	Banská-Bystrica	112 B3
Ballyclare	13 E1	Banská-Štiavnica	112 B3
Ballyconnell	12 C2	Bansko	77 F3
Ballycotton	14 C4	Bantry	14 B4
Ballycroy	12 B2	Bantry B	14 A4
Ballyduff	14 B3	Bañuela	43 F1
Ballyforan	12 C3	Banyalbufar	45 E2
Ballygawley	13 D2	Banyoles	32 B3
Ballyhaunis	12 B3	Banyuls	32 C3
Ballyheige	14 A3	Bao, Emb de	34 C3
Ballyjamesduff	13 D3	Bapaume	19 F2
Ballymahon	12 C3	Bar (SU)	113 D3
Ballymena	13 E2	Bar (YU)	76 B3
Ballymoe	12 C3	Baracaldo	36 B1
Ballymoney	13 E1	Baraći	71 E4
Ballymote	12 C2	Baradla	112 B3
Ballynahinch	13 E2		
Ballysadare	12 C2		
Ballyshannon	12 C2		
Ballyvaughan	12 B4		
Balmaseda	36 A1		
Balme	31 E1		
Balmoral Castle	3 D4		

Barahona	36 B4	Bare	76 B1	Barre-des-Cévennes	29 F3	Bassano del Grappa	59 D4	Baux, les	30 B3
Barajas	40 B2	Barèges	37 E2	Barreiro	38 A4	Bassée, la	19 F1	Bavanište	73 D2
Barajas de Melo	40 B3	Barentin	19 D3	Barrême	31 D3	Bassella	37 F3	Bavay	20 B1
Barajevo	73 D3	Barenton	18 C4	Barrhead	4 C2	Bassens	28 B2	Bavella, Col de	33 F4
Baralla	34 C2	Bares, Estaca de	34 B 1	Barrhill	4 C3	Bassum	17 F1	Båven	106 B4
Barane	76 C2	Barfleur	18 B2	Barri	9 D2	Båstad	108 C3	Baveno	58 A4
Baranovici	111 D4	Barfleur, Pte de	18 B2	Barrow	13 D4	Bastasi	71 D4	Bawtry	7 D2
Baraqueville	29 E3	Bargas	40 A3	Barrow-in-Furness	6 B1	Bastelica	33 F3	Bayard, Col	31 D2
Barasona, Emb de	37 E3	Bargoed	9 D2	Barrow, R	15 D3	Bas'tevarri	95 D3	Bayerisch Eisenstein	56 C1
Barbadillo del Mercado	36 A3	Bargteheide	48 B2	Barruecopardo	39 D1	Bastia	33 F2	Bayerischer Wald	56 B2
Barban	70 A3	Bari	65 D3	Barruelo de Santullán	35 F2	Bastide-de-Sérou, la	37 F2	Bayern	55 F2
Barbarano Vicentino	61 D1	Barić Draga	70 C4	Barry	9 D2	Bastogne	20 C2	Bayeux	18 C3
Barbarušince	77 E2	Barisciano	63 F2	Barsinghausen	52 A1	Bastunäsfjället	97 E4	Bayhirivagh	2 A4
Barbastro	37 E3	Barjac	30 B3	Bar-sur-Aube	26 B1	Bastuträsk	98 B3	Bayındır	115 F4
Barbat	70 B4	Barjols	31 D4	Bar-sur-Seine	26 B1	Bataille, Col de la	30 C2	Bayon	21 D4
Barbate de Franco	43 D4	Barlby	7 D2	Barth	49 D1	Batajnica	72 C3	Bayonne	28 A4
Barbate, Emb de	43 D4	Bar, le	31 E3	Barthe-de-Neste, la	37 E1	Batak	115 D3	Bayreuth	52 C4
Barbazan	37 F2	Bar-le-Duc	20 C4	Barton-upon-Humber	7 D2	Batalha	38 B3	Bayrischzell	56 B4
Barberino di Mugello	60 C3	Barletta	65 D3	Baruth	53 E1	Batea	41 F1	Baza	44 B3
Barbezieux	28 B1	Barlinek	49 F3	Barumini	66 B3	Bath	9 D2	Bazas	28 B3
Barbizon	19 F4	Barlovento	42 A4	Barvas	2 B2	Bathgate	5 D2	Baza, Sa de	44 B3
Barbotan	28 B3	Barmouth	6 A3	Barycz	112 A2	Bâtie-Neuve, la	31 D2	Bazoches-sur-Hoëne	19 D4
Barby	52 C1	Barmstedt	48 A2	Barzio	58 B4	Batina	72 B1	Bazzano	60 C2
Barca de Alva	39 D1	Barna	12 B3	Bašaid	72 C1	Batlava	77 D1	Beachy Head	10 C3
Barca, Emb de la	35 D1	Barnard Castle	5 E4	Bàscara	32 B3	Batočina	73 D3	Beaconsfield	9 F2
Barcarrota	42 C1	Bärnau	53 D4	Baschi	63 E1	Båtsfjord	95 F1	Béal an Átha	12 B2
Barcellona Pozzo di Gotto	69 D2	Barneveld	16 C3	Basconcillos del Tozo	35 F2	Batsí	88 B3	Béal Átha na Sluaighe	12 C3
Barcelona	32 B4	Barneville	18 B3	Basel	27 E2	Battaglia Terme	61 D1	Beaminster	9 D3
Barcelonnette	31 D2	Barnsley	7 D2	Baselga di Pinè	59 D3	Battenberg	17 F4	Beanntraí	14 B4
Barcelos	34 A4	Barnstaple	8 C3	Bas-en-Basset	30 B1	Battice	51 D3	Beara	14 A4
Barcena, Emb de	34 C2	Barnstorf	17 F1	Basento	65 D4	Battipaglia	64 B4	Beariz	34 B2
Barchfeld	52 B3	Barntrup	52 A1	Basildon	11 D2	Battle	11 D3	Beas	42 C2
Barcis	59 E3	Barovo	77 E3	Basilicata	65 D4	Batz (Finistère)	22 B2	Beasain	36 C1
Barcones	36 B4	Barquero	38 B2	Basingstoke	9 E3	Batz (Loire-Atlantique)	24 A2	Beas de Segura	44 B2
Barcs	114 A1	Barr	21 E4	Baška	70 B3	Baud	22 C3	Beattock	5 D3
Bardal	101 D1	Barra	2 A4	Baška Voda	75 E2	Baugé	23 E4	Beaucaire	30 B3
Bardejov	112 C3	Barracas	41 E3	Baške Oštarije	70 C4	Baugy	26 A2	Beaufort (Jura)	26 C3
Bardi	60 B2	Barrachina	36 B4	Baslow	6 C3	Baule, la	24 A2	Beaufort (Savoie)	27 E4
Bardineto	31 F3	Barraco	39 F2	Basovizza	59 F4	Baume, Cirque de	27 D3	Beaufort-en-Vallée	23 E4
Bardolino	60 C1	Barrafranca	68 C4	Bas-Rhin	21 E4	Baume-les-Dames	27 D2	Beaugency	25 E2
Bardonecchia	31 D1	Barra Head	2 A4			Baumholder	54 B1	Beaujeu	26 C4
Bardu	94 B3	Barrancos	42 C1			Bauska	110 C3	Beaulieu (Alpes-Maritime)	31 E3
Bardufoss	94 B3	Barranco Velho	42 B2			Bautzen	53 F2		
		Barranda	44 C2						
		Barra, Sd of	2 A4						
		Barrax	40 C4						
		Barrea	64 A2						

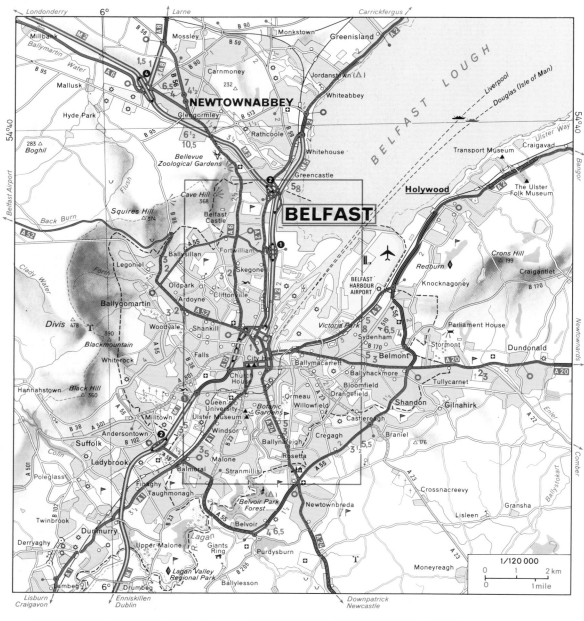

Name	Ref		Name	Ref
Bellême	23 F3		Benifaió	41 E4
Bellencombre	19 E2		Beninar, Emb de	44 B3
Bellerive	26 A4		Benissa	45 E1
Belleville	26 C4		Benitses	82 A1
Belley	27 D4		Ben Klibreck	2 C2
Bellinzona	58 A3		Benkovac	74 C1
Bell-lloc d'Urgell	37 F3		Ben Lawers	4 C1
Bello	41 D1		Ben Lomond	4 C1
Bellpuig	37 F4		Ben Macdui	3 D4
Belluno	59 E3		Ben More (Grampian)	4 C1
Bellver	45 E3		Ben More (Mull)	4 B1
Bellver de Cerdanya	32 A3		Ben More Assynt	2 C2
Bélmez	43 E1		Benneckenstein	52 B2
Belmont (F)	26 B4		Ben Nevis	2 C4
Belmont (GB)	3 F1		Bénodet	22 B3
Belmonte (Asturias)	35 D1		Benquerencia de la Serena	43 E1
Belmonte (Castilla-la-Mancha)	40 C3		Bensberg	17 E4
Belmonte (P)	38 C2		Bensersiel	47 E3
Belmonte-sur-Rance	32 B1		Bensheim	54 C1
Belmullet	12 A2		Bentley	7 D2
Belo Brdo	76 C1		Ben Vorlich	4 C1
Belo jez	72 C2		Ben Wyvis	2 C3
Beloljin	77 D1		Bény-Bocage, le	18 C3
Beloœil	50 B4		Beočin	72 C2
Belo Polje	76 C2		Beograd	73 D3
Belopolje	113 F1		Bérarde, la	31 D2
Belorado	36 A2		Berat	114 C3
Belorussija	111 D4		Berbegal	37 E3
Belpech	32 A2		Berberana	36 B1
Belper	6 C3		Berbería, C de	45 D3
Belsay	5 E3		Berceto	60 B3
Belsh	76 C4		Berching	55 F2
Beltinci	70 C1		Berchtesgaden	56 C4
Belturbet	13 D2		Berck-Plage	19 E1
Belušić	73 E4		Berdičev	113 E2
Belvedere Marittimo	67 E2		Beregovo	112 C3
Belver	37 E3		Bereguardo	60 A2
Belvès	28 C2		Bere I	14 A4
Belvis de la Jara	39 F3		Berek	71 D2
Belyj	111 E2		Bere Regis	9 D3
Belz	22 C4		Beret	37 F2
Belzig	53 D1		Berettyóújfalu	112 C4
Bembézar, Emb de	43 E2		Berezina	111 E4
Bembézar, R	43 E2		Berezino	111 D4
Bembibre	35 D2		Berg (A)	57 F2
Bemposta	38 B3		Berg (Nordland)	97 D3
Bemposta, Bgem da	34 C4		Berg (S)	101 E2
Benabarre	37 E3		Berg (Troms)	94 B2
Benaguacil	41 E3		Berga (DDR)	52 C2
Benahadux	44 B3		Berga (E)	32 A3
Ben Alder	2 C4		Bergama	115 E4
Benalmádena	43 F4		Bergamo	60 B1
Benalúa de las Villas	44 A3		Bergara	36 B1
Benamargosa	43 F3		Bergby	106 B2
Benamaurel	44 B2		Bergedorf	48 B3
Benamejí	43 F3		Bergen (B)	50 B4
Benamocarra	43 F4		Bergen (DDR)	49 D1
Benaoján	43 E4		Bergen (N)	104 A2
Ben Armine	3 D2		Bergen (Niedersachsen)	48 A4
Benasal	41 E2		Bergen (Niedersachsen)	48 B3
Benasque	37 E2		Bergen (NL)	16 C2
Benavente (E)	35 D3		Bergen aan Zee	16 C2
Benavente (P)	38 A4		Bergen op Zoom	16 B4
Benavides	35 D3		Bergerac	28 C2
Benbecula	2 A3		Berggießhübel	53 F2
Ben Chonzie	4 C1		Berghamn fjärden	107 D3
Ben Cruachan	4 B1		Bergheim	17 D4
Bendery	113 E4		Bergisch Gladbach	17 E4
Bendorf	51 E4		Bergnäset	98 C3
Benediktbeuern	56 A4		Bergneustadt	17 E4
Benešov (Severočeský)	53 F3		Bergö	102 B2
Benešov (Středočeský)	53 F4		Berg-Rudolphstein	53 D3
Bénévent-l'Abbaye	25 E4		Bergsjö	101 E2
Benevento	64 B3		Bergsviken	98 B3
Benfeld	21 E4		Bergum	47 D3
Benfleet	11 D2		Bergün	58 B3
Bengtsfors	105 D2		Beringel	42 B1
Ben Hope	2 C2		Beringen	50 C3
Beničanci	71 E2		Berja	44 B4
Benicarló	41 F2		Berka	52 B3
Benicasim	41 F3		Berkåk	100 C2
Benidorm	45 E1		Berkel	17 D2
			Berkhamsted	9 F2
			Berkheim	55 E3
			Berkhof	48 A4
			Berkovica	114 C2
			Berkovići	75 F2

Name	Ref		Name	Ref		Name	Ref		Name	Ref		Name	Ref
Beaulieu (Corrèze)	29 D2		Bebington	6 B2		Beerfelden	55 D1		Béjar, Pto de	39 E2		Belforte all'Isauro	61 E3
Beaulieu (GB)	9 E3		Bebra	52 B3		Beeskow	49 E4		Békés	112 C4		Belgern	53 E2
Beaumaris	6 A2		Beccles	11 E1		Beetzendorf	48 B4		Békéscsaba	112 C4		België	16 B3
Beaumesnil	19 D3		Becedas	39 E2		Bégard	22 C2		Bel	41 F2		Belgique	50 B3
Beaumetz-lès-Loges	19 F2		Beceite	41 F2		Begejci	72 C2		Bělá	56 B1		Belgodère	33 F3
Beaumont (B)	50 B4		Bečej	72 C2		Begejski kanal	72 C2		Bélâbre	25 E3		Belgorod-Dnestrovskij	113 F4
Beaumont (Dordogne)	28 C2		Becerreá	34 C2		Beg-Meil	22 B3		Bela Crkva (Srbija)	72 C3		Belianes	37 F4
Beaumont (Manche)	18 B2		Bec-Hellouin, le	19 D3		Begna	104 C2		Bela Crkva (Vojvodina)	73 D2		Belice	68 B3
Beaumont (Val d'Oise)	19 F3		Bécherel	23 D3		Begov Han	71 F4		Belaja Cerkov'	113 E2		Beli Drim	76 C2
Beaumont-de-Lomagne	28 C3		Bechet	115 D2		Bégude-de-Mazenc, la	30 C2		Belalcázar	43 E1		Beli Manastir	71 F2
Beaumont-le-Roger	19 D3		Bechhofen	55 E3		Begues	32 A4		Belanovce	77 E2		Belin-Béliet	28 B3
Beaumont-sur-Sarthe	23 F3		Bečići	76 B3		Begur	32 C3		Belanovica	73 D3		Beli Potok	73 F4
Beaune	26 C2		Becilla de Valderaduey	35 E3		Behalúa de Guadix	44 B3		Bela Palanka	77 E1		Belišće	71 F2
Beaune-la-Rolande	25 F1		Beckenried	58 A2		Behobia	28 A4		Belasica	77 E2		Beli Timok	73 F4
Beaupréau	24 C2		Beckington	9 D3		Behringersmühle	52 C4		Belcaire	32 A2		Beljakovce	77 E2
Beauraing	50 C4		Beckum	17 F3		Beiarn	97 E2		Belchen	54 C4		Beljanica	73 E3
Beaurepaire	30 C1		Bečov	53 E4		Beilen	17 D1		Belchite	37 D4		Beljina	73 D3
Beaurepaire-en-Bresse	26 C3		Bedale	6 C1		Beilngries	55 F2		Belčište	77 D4		Bellac	25 D4
Beausset, le	31 D4		Bédarieux	30 A4		Beinn a'Ghlò	3 D4		Belcoo	12 C2		Bellagio	58 B4
Beauvais	19 E3		Beddgelert	6 A3		Beinn an Oir	4 A3		Bel'cy	113 E3		Bellano	58 B4
Beauvoir (Deux-Sèvres)	24 C4		Bederkesa	47 F3		Beinn Bheigeir	4 B2		Belec	70 C2		Bellaria	61 E3
Beauvoir (Vendée)	24 A3		Bedford	9 F1		Beinn Dearg	2 C3		Belecke	17 F3		Bellcaire d'Urgell	37 F3
			Bedfordshire	9 F1		Beira Alta	38 B1		Belegiš	72 C2		Belledonne, Chaîne de	31 D1
			Bedlington	5 E3		Beira Baixa	38 C2		Belej	70 B4		Belleek	12 C2
			Bedmar	44 A2		Beira Litoral	38 B1		Beleña, Emb de	40 B1		Bellegarde (Ain)	27 D4
			Bednja	70 C1		Beisfjord	94 B3		Belesar, Emb de	34 B2		Bellegarde (Gard)	30 B3
			Bedonia	60 B3		Beith	4 C1		Belev	111 F3		Bellegarde (Loiret)	25 F1
			Bedum	47 D3		Beitostølen	104 C1		Bele Vode	76 C1		Bellegarde-en-Marche	25 F4
			Bedwas	9 D2		Beitstadfjorden	101 D1		Belfast	13 E2		Belle-Ile	22 B4
			Bedworth	9 E1		Beiuş	112 C4		Belfast L	13 E2		Belle-Isle-en-Terre	22 B2
			Beeford	7 E2		Beja	42 B1		Belford	5 E3			
			Beelitz	49 D4		Béjar	39 E2		Belfort	27 E2			

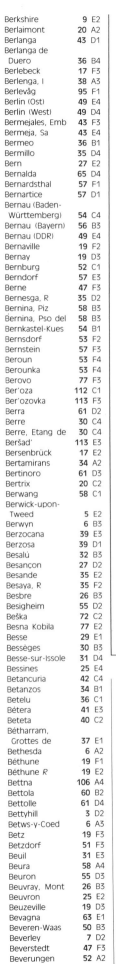

Berkshire	9	E2
Berlaimont	20	A2
Berlanga	43	D1
Berlanga de Duero	36	B4
Berlebeck	17	F3
Berlenga, I	38	A3
Berlevåg	95	F1
Berlin (Ost)	49	E4
Berlin (West)	49	D4
Bermejales, Emb	43	F3
Bermeja, Sa	43	E4
Bermeo	36	B1
Bermillo	35	D4
Bern	27	E2
Bernalda	65	D4
Bernardsthal	57	F1
Bernartice	57	D1
Bernau (Baden-Württemberg)	54	C4
Bernau (Bayern)	56	B3
Bernau (DDR)	49	E4
Bernaville	19	F2
Bernay	19	D3
Bernburg	52	C1
Berndorf	57	E3
Berne	47	F3
Bernesga, R	35	D2
Bernina, Piz	58	B3
Bernina, Pso del	58	B3
Bernkastel-Kues	54	B1
Bernsdorf	53	F2
Bernstein	57	F3
Beroun	53	F4
Berounka	53	F4
Berovo	77	F3
Ber'oza	112	C1
Ber'ozovka	113	F3
Berra	61	D2
Berre	30	C4
Berre, Etang de	30	C4
Beršad'	113	E3
Bersenbrück	17	E2
Bertamirans	34	A2
Bertinoro	61	D3
Bertrix	20	C2
Berwang	58	C1
Berwick-upon-Tweed	5	E2
Berwyn	6	B3
Berzocana	39	E3
Berzosa	39	D1
Besalú	32	B3
Besançon	27	D2
Besande	35	E2
Besaya, R	35	F2
Besbre	26	B3
Besigheim	55	D2
Beška	72	C2
Besna Kobila	77	E2
Besse	29	E1
Bessèges	30	B3
Besse-sur-Issole	31	D4
Bessines	25	E4
Betancuria	42	C4
Betanzos	34	B1
Betelu	36	C1
Bétera	41	E3
Beteta	40	C2
Bétharram, Grottes de	37	E1
Bethesda	6	A2
Béthune	19	F1
Béthune R	19	E2
Bettna	106	A4
Bettola	60	B2
Bettole	61	D4
Bettyhill	3	D2
Betws-y-Coed	6	A3
Betz	19	F3
Betzdorf	51	F3
Beuil	31	E3
Beura	58	A4
Beuron	55	D3
Beuvray, Mont	26	B3
Beuvron	25	E2
Beuzeville	19	D3
Bevagna	63	E1
Beveren-Waas	50	B3
Beverley	7	D2
Beverstedt	47	F3
Beverungen	52	A2
Beverwijk	16	C2
Bewdley	9	D1

Bex	27	E3
Bexhill	11	D3
Beynac	29	D2
Beynat	29	D2
Bežanija	72	C3
Bézards, les	26	A1
Bezas	41	D2
Bezdan	72	B1
Bezdrep	57	D1
Bežeck	111	F1
Béziers	30	A4
Bezmisht	77	D4
Béznar	44	A3
Biała Podlaska	112	C1
Białowieska	112	C1
Białystok	112	C1
Biancavilla	69	D3
Bianco	67	E4
Bianco, M	27	E4
Biandrate	31	E1
Biar	45	D1
Biarritz	28	A4
Biasca	58	A3
Bibbiena	61	D4
Biberach	54	C3
Biberach an der Riß	55	E3
Bibinje	74	C1
Bibione	59	F4
Bibury	9	E2

Bicaj	76	C3
Bicaz	113	D4
Bicester	9	E2
Bichl	56	A4
Bidache	28	A4
Bidart	28	A4
Bidasoa, R	36	C1
Biddendon	11	D3
Bidean nam Bian	4	C1
Bideford	8	C3
Biebelried	55	E1
Biedenkopf	17	F4
Biel	27	E2
Bielefeld	17	F2
Bielerhöhe	58	B2
Biella	31	F1
Bielsa	37	E2
Bielsa, Tunnel de	37	E2
Bielsko-Biała	112	B3
Bielsk Podlaski	112	C1
Bienne R	27	D3
Bienne	27	E2
Bientina	60	C4
Bienvenida	43	D1
Bierné	23	E4
Bierre	26	B2
Biesbosch	16	C3
Biescas	37	D2
Biese	48	C4

Biesenthal	49	E3
Bietigheim-Bissingen	55	D2
Biferno	64	B2
Biga	115	D3
Biggar	5	D2
Biggleswade	9	F1
Bignasco	58	A3
Bihać	70	C3
Bihorului, M	112	C4
Bijele Poljane	76	B2
Bijeljani	75	F2
Bijeljina	72	B3
Bijelo Brdo	71	F2
Bijelolasica	70	B3
Bijelo Polje	76	B2
Bilbao	36	B1
Bileća	76	A2
Bilecik	115	F3
Bilećko jez	76	A2
Biłgoraj	112	C2
Bilina	53	E3
Biljača	77	E2
Biljanovac	76	C1
Bilje	71	F2
Billerbeck	17	E3
Billericay	11	D2
Billingham	5	E4
Billingshurst	10	C3
Billom	29	F1

Billund	108	A3
Bilo	77	E1
Bilogora	71	D2
Bilto	94	C2
Bilzen	50	C3
Binaced	37	E3
Binačka Morava	77	D2
Binasco	60	A1
Binche	50	B4
Binéfar	37	E3
Bingen	51	F4
Bingham	7	D3
Bingley	6	C2
Bingsjö	101	E4
Binic	22	C2
Binz	49	D1
Bioča	76	C1
Bioče	76	B2
Biograd	74	C1
Biogradsko, nac park	76	B2
Biokovo	75	D2
Bionaz	27	E4
Biot, le	27	E3
Birchington	11	D2
Birgi	68	A3
Biri	105	D2
Birkebeiner veien	104	C1
Birkeland	104	B4

Birkenfeld	54	B1
Birkenhead	6	B2
Birkenwerder	49	D4
Birkerød	108	C3
Birkfeld	57	E4
Birmingham	9	E1
Birnau	55	D4
Birr	12	C4
Biržai	110	C3
Bîrlad	113	E4
Birzebugga	68	B4
Bisaccia	64	C3
Biscarrosse	28	A3
Biscarrosse-Plage	28	A3
Bisceglie	65	D3
Bischofsgrün	53	D4
Bischofsheim	52	B4
Bischofshofen	59	E1
Bischofswerda	53	F2
Bischofswiesen	56	C4
Bischofszell	58	A1
Bischwiller	21	F4
Bisenti	63	F1
Biševo	75	D2
Bishop Auckland	5	E4
Bishop's Castle	9	D1
Bishop's Stortford	10	C2
Bisignano	67	E2
Bisko	75	D1
Biskupfell	96	C2

Bismark	48	C4
Bismo	100	B3
Bispgården	101	F2
Bispingen	48	A3
Bistar	77	E2
Bistra pl	77	D3
Bistrica (Crna Gora)	76	B2
Bistrica (Srbija)	76	B1
Bistrica ob S.	70	C2
Bistričak	71	E4
Bistrica	113	D4
Bistrița R	113	D4
Bitburg	54	A1
Bitche	21	E3
Bitetto	65	D3
Bitola	77	E4
Bitonto	65	D3
Bitovnja	75	F1
Bitterfeld	53	D2
Bitti	66	B2
Bizàkos	82	C3
Bizau	58	B2
Bizovac	71	F2
Bjala	115	D2
Bjarkøy	94	B3
Bjästa	102	A2
Bjelašnica	75	F1
Bjelašnica	76	A2
Bjelovar	71	D2

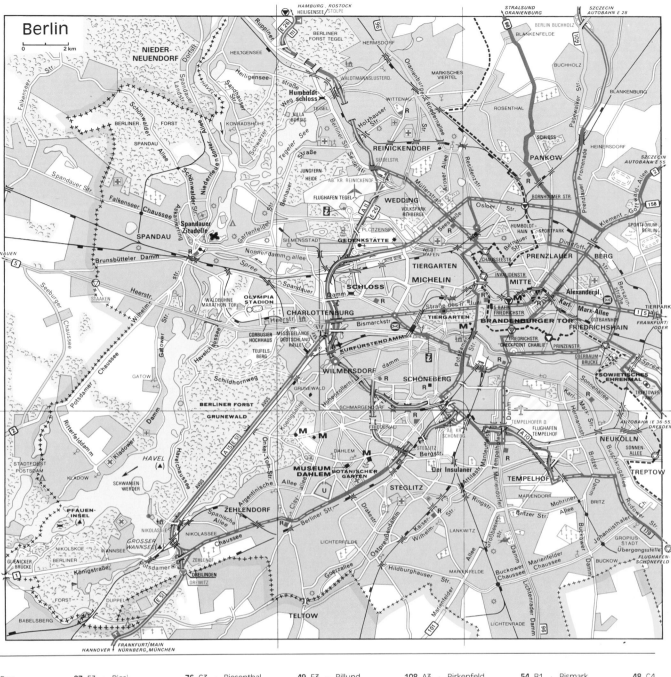

Berlin

0 — 2 km

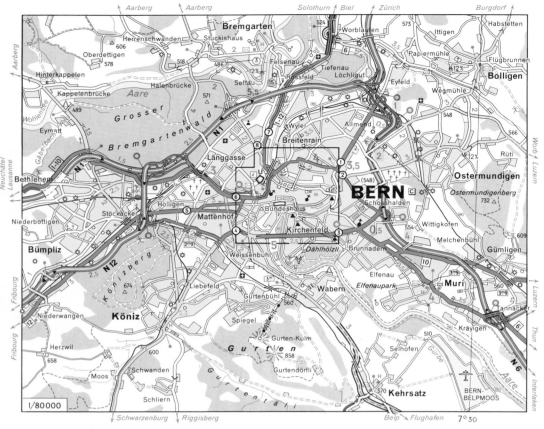

Name	Pg	Grid
Bjerkreim	104	A4
Bjerkvik	94	B3
Bjerringbro	108	B2
Bjørkelangen	105	D3
Björketorp	109	E3
Bjorkfjället	97	F3
Björkliden	94	B3
Björklinge	106	B3
Björköby	102	B2
Björksele	98	A4
Bjorli	100	B3
Björna	102	A2
Bjørnafjorden	104	A3
Bjørneborg	107	D1
Bjørnevatn	95	F2
Bjørntoppen	97	F1
Björsäter	109	E1
Bjurholm	102	A1
Bjursås	101	E4
Bjuv	108	C3
Blace	77	D1
Blackburn	6	C2
Black Head	12	B4
Black Isle	2	C3
Black Mt	8	C2
Black Mts	9	D2
Blackpool	6	B2
Black Sea	115	F2
Blacksod B	12	A2
Blackstairs Mts	15	D3
Blackwater	15	D3
Blackwaterfoot	4	B2
Blackwater, R	14	C4
Blackwater Res	2	C4
Blaenau Ffestiniog	6	A3
Blaenavon	9	D2
Blåfjellhatten	101	E1
Blagaj	75	F2
Blagnac	29	D4
Blagoevgrad	115	D3
Blåhammaren	101	D2
Blåhø	100	C2
Blain	23	D4
Blainville	21	D4
Blair Atholl	3	D4
Blairgowrie	5	D1
Blå Jungfrun	109	E2
Blakeney	7	F3
Blakstad	104	B4
Blåmannsisen	97	F2
Blåmont	21	E4

Name	Pg	Grid
Blanca	45	D2
Blanc, C	45	E3
Blanc, le	25	D3
Blanc, Mont	27	E4
Blanco, R	43	E3
Blandford Forum	9	D3
Blanes	32	B4
Blangy	19	E2
Blangy-le-Château	19	D3
Blankenberge	50	A3
Blankenburg	52	C2
Blankenheim	51	D4
Blankenhain	52	C3
Blanquefort	28	B2
Blanquilla	44	B2
Blansko	57	F1
Blanzac	28	C1
Blanzy	26	B3
Blåøret	100	C2
Blarney	14	B4
Blatná	56	C1
Blatnica	71	E4
Blato	75	E1
Blattniksele	98	A3
Blaubeuren	55	D3
Blauen	54	C4
Blaufelden	55	E2
Blaustein	55	E3
Blavet	22	C3
Blaye	28	B2
Bleckede	48	B3
Bled	70	A2
Blefjell	104	C3
Bleiburg	70	B1
Bleicherode	52	B2
Bleik	94	A3
Bleiloch-Talsperre	53	D3
Blekinge Län	109	D3
Blendija	73	E4
Bléneau	26	A2
Blenheim Palace	9	E2
Blénod	21	D3
Bléone	31	D3
Blérancourt	19	F3
Bléré	25	D2
Blesle	29	F1
Bletchley	9	F2
Bletterans	26	C3
Blexen	47	F3

Name	Pg	Grid
Bleymard, le	29	F3
Blidinje jez	75	E1
Blieskastel	54	B2
Bligny	26	C2
Blinisht	76	C3
Blinja	71	D3
Bloemendaal	16	B2
Blois	25	E2
Blokhus	108	B2
Blomberg	52	A1
Blönduós	96	B1
Blonville	19	D3
Bloody Foreland Head	12	C1
Blosenberg	53	D3
Bloška Polica	70	B2
Blovice	56	C1
Bludenz	58	B2
Blue Stack Mts	12	C2
Blumberg (D)	54	C4
Blumberg (DDR)	49	E4
Blyth	5	E3
Bø (Telemark)	104	C3
Bø (Vesterålen)	94	A3
Boadella, Emb de	32	B3
Boal	34	C1
Boan	76	B2
Boara Pisani	61	D1
Bobbio	60	A2
Boborás	34	B2
Bobova	72	C4
Bóbr	53	F1
Bobrinec	113	F3
Bobrovica	113	E2
Bobrujsk	111	E4
Bočac	71	E4
Bocairent	45	E1
Bocca di Bonifacio	33	F4
Bocco, Pso del	60	B3
Boceguillas	36	A4
Bocholt	17	D3
Bochov	53	E4
Bochum	17	E3
Bockel	48	A3
Bockenem	52	B1

Name	Pg	Grid
Böckstein	59	E2
Bockum-Hövel	17	E3
Bocognano	33	F3
Boda	101	E4
Böda	109	F2
Bodafors	109	D2
Bodďani	72	B2
Bode	52	C1
Bodegraven	16	C3
Boden	98	B3
Bodenmais	56	B1
Bodensee	58	B1
Bodenteich	48	B4
Bodenwerder	52	A1
Bodenwöhr	56	B1
Bodman-Radolfzell	55	D4
Bodmin	8	B4
Bodø	97	E1
Boecillo	35	E4
Boëge	27	D4
Boën	26	B4
Boeza	35	D2
Boffalora	60	A1
Bogarra	44	C1
Bogatić	72	C3
Bogdanci	77	F3
Bogdaniec	49	F3
Bogë	76	C2
Bogen (D)	56	B2
Bogen (N)	94	B3
Bogense	108	B3
Bogetići	76	B2
Boglárlelle	112	B4
Bognanco	72	C4
Bognes	94	A4
Bognor Regis	9	F3
Bogodol	75	F1
Bogojevo	72	B2
Bogomila	77	E3
Bogomolje	75	E2
Bogorodika	77	F4
Bogovina	73	E4
Bogøy	97	E1
Boguslav	113	E2
Bogutovac	73	D4
Bohain-en-Vermandois	20	A2
Boherboy	14	B3
Bohinjska Bistrica	70	A2
Bohinjsko jez	70	A2

Name	Pg	Grid
Böhlen	53	D2
Böhme	48	A4
Böhmenkirch	55	E2
Böhmer Wald	56	B1
Bohmte	17	F2
Böhönye	114	A1
Boiano	64	B3
Boiro	34	A2
Bois-d'Amont	27	D3
Boitzenburg	49	E3
Bóixols	37	F3
Boizenburg	48	B3
Bojana	76	B3
Bøjden	108	B4
Bojnik	77	D1
Boka Kotorska	76	A3
Bøkfjorden	95	F2
Bokn	104	A3
Boknafjorden	104	A3
Bol	75	E2
Bøla	101	D1
Bøle	26	B4
Bolbec	19	D3
Bolchov	111	F3
Bolera, Emb de la	44	B2
Bolesławiec	112	A2
Boleszkowice	49	E3
Bolgrad	113	E4
Boliden	98	B4
Boliqueime	42	A2
Boljanići	76	B1
Boljevac	73	E4
Boljevci	72	C3
Boljkovci	73	D4
Boljuni	75	F2
Bolkesjø	104	C3
Bollebygd	108	C1
Bollène	30	B3
Bollnäs	101	F4
Bollstabruk	101	F2
Bollullos de la Mitación	43	D2
Bollullos par del Condado	42	C2
Bolmen	109	D2
Bolnãos de Calatrava	40	A4
Bologna	60	C2
Bologne	26	C1
Bologoje	111	E1
Bolos	40	B4
Bolotana	66	B2

Name	Pg	Grid
Bolsena	63	D1
Bolsena, L di	63	D2
Bolsward	16	C1
Boltaña	37	E2
Boltenhagen	48	B2
Bolton	6	C2
Bolungarvík	96	A1
Bolus Head	14	A4
Bolzano	59	D3
Bombarral	38	A3
Bomenzien	48	C3
Bom Jesus	34	A4
Bømlo	104	A3
Bonaigua, Pto de la	37	F2
Boñar	35	E2
Bonar Bridge	2	C3
Bonares	42	C2
Bonassola	60	B3
Bondeno	60	C2
Bondone, Mte	58	C3
Bonefro	64	B2
Bo'-Ness	5	D2
Bonete	45	D1
Bonette, Col de la	31	D3
Bonhomme, Col du	27	E1
Bonifacio	33	F4
Bonn	51	E3
Bonnåsjøen	97	F1
Bonnat	25	E4
Bonndorf	54	C4
Bonnétable	23	F3
Bonneuil-Matours	25	D3
Bonneval (Eure-et-Loir)	25	E1
Bonneval (Savoie)	31	E1
Bonneville	27	D4
Bonneville, la	19	E4
Bonnières	19	E3
Bonnieux	30	C3
Bono	66	B2
Bonorva	66	B2
Bønsnes	104	C3
Boo	106	B4
Boom	50	B3
Boos	19	E3
Bootle	6	B2
Bopfingen	55	E2
Boppard	51	E4
Bor (CS)	53	E4
Bor (YU)	73	E3
Boračko jez	75	F1
Borås	108	C1
Borba	38	C4
Borbollón, Emb de	39	D2
Borbona	63	F1
Borča	72	C3
Borci	75	F1
Bordeaux	28	B2
Bordeira	42	A2
Bordères-Louron	37	E2
Border Forest Park, The	5	D3
Borders Region	5	D3
Bordesholm	48	A2
Bordighera	31	E3
Bordøy	96	A3
Bore	60	B2
Borello	61	D3
Borensberg	105	F4
Boréon, le	31	E3
Borga	107	F2
Borgafjäll	97	E4
Borga-fjällen	97	E4
Borgarnes	96	A2
Børgefjell	97	E3
Børgefjellet	97	E3
Borger	17	D1
Börger	17	E1
Borghetto	63	E2
Borghetto S.S.	31	F3
Borgholm	109	E2
Borgholzhausen	17	F2
Borghorst	17	E2
Borgia	67	F3
Borgomanero	58	A4
Borgone	31	E1
Borgonovo Val Tidone	60	B2
Borgorose	63	F2

Name	Pg	Grid
Borgo San Dalmazzo	31	E2
Borgo San Lorenzo	61	D3
Borgosesia	58	A4
Borgo Tufico	61	E4
Borgo Val di Taro	60	B3
Borgo Valsugana	59	D3
Borgsjö	101	F3
Borgund	104	B1
Borgvattnet	101	F2
Boričje	76	B2
Borisov	111	D4
Borispol'	113	E2
Borja (E)	36	C3
Borja (YU)	71	E4
Borken	17	E3
Borkenes	94	A3
Børkop	108	B3
Borkum	47	D3
Borlänge	105	F2
Bormes-les-Mimosas	31	D4
Bormida	60	A2
Bormio	58	C3
Born	48	C1
Borna	53	D2
Bornes	34	C4
Bornes, Sa de	34	C4
Bornholm	109	D4
Bornhöved	48	B2
Börnicke	49	D4
Bornos	43	D3
Bornos, Emb de	43	D3
Boroughbridge	7	D1
Borovec	115	D3
Boroviči	111	E1
Borovnica	70	B2
Borovo	72	B2
Borovsk	111	F2
Borre	104	C3
Borriol	41	E3
Borris	15	D3
Borrisokane	12	C4
Borşa	113	D3
Børselv	95	E1
Børselva	95	E2
Børsélvfjellet	95	E2
Bórsio	86	B1
Bort-les-Orgues	29	E1
Börtnan	101	E3
Borzna	113	F1
Borzonasca	60	A3
Bosa	66	A2
Bosanci	70	C3
Bosanska Dubica	71	D3
Bosanska Gradiška	71	E3
Bosanska Kostajnica	71	D3
Bosanska Krupa	71	D3
Bosanska Rača	72	B3
Bosanski Brod	71	E3
Bosanski Kobaš	71	E3
Bosanski Novi	71	D3
Bosanski Petrovac	71	D4
Bosanski Šamac	71	F3
Bosansko Grahovo	71	D4
Bosansko Petrovo Selo	71	F3
Bosco	61	E4
Bosco Chiesanuova	59	D4
Bosilegrad	77	E2
Bosiljevo	70	C3
Bosjökloster	109	D3
Boskoop	16	C3
Bosna	71	F4
Bosna i Hercegovina	71	E4
Bošnjace	77	E1
Bošnjaci	72	B3
Bossòst	37	F2
Bostan	75	E2
Boštanj	70	B2
Boston	7	E3
Bosut	72	B2
Botev	115	D2
Botevgrad	115	D2
Boticas	34	B4
Botley	9	E3
Botngård	100	C

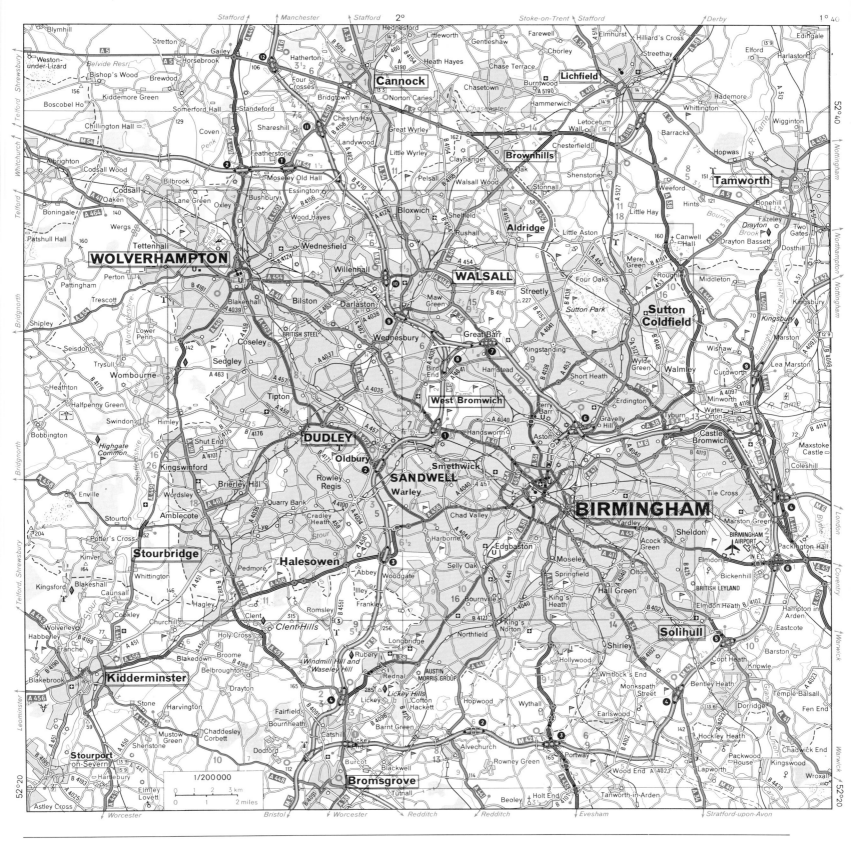

Botnie, G de	102 A3	Bouaye	24 B2	Boulogne		Bourboule, la	29 E1	Bourg-en-Bresse	26 C4	Bourgueil	25 D2	Bouxwiller	21 E3
Botoš	72 C2	Boucau	28 A4	(Pas-de-Calais)	19 E1	Bourbourg	19 F1	Bourges	25 F3	Bourmont	26 C1	Bouzonville	21 D3
Botoşani	113 D3	Bouchain	20 A2	Boulogne R	24 B3	Bourbriac	22 C2	Bourget, le	30 C1	Bourne	7 D3	Bov	108 A4
Botrange	51 D4	Bouches-		Bouloire	23 F3	Bourdeaux	30 C2	Bourg-Lastic	29 E1	Bourne,		Bovalino Marina	67 F4
Botsmark	102 A1	du-Rhône	30 B4	Boulou, le	32 B2	Bourdeilles	28 C1	Bourg-Madame	32 A3	Gges de la	30 C2	Bova Marina	67 F4
Botte Donato,		Boudry	27 E2	Boumort	37 F3	Bourg	28 B2	Bourgneuf		Bournemouth	9 E3	Bovan	73 E4
Mte	67 F2	Bouillon	20 C2	Bourbon-		Bourg-Achard	19 D3	-en-Retz	24 B3	Bourniá, Akr	87 E3	Bovec	70 A2
Bottenhavet	102 A3	Bouilly	26 B1	Lancy	26 B3	Bourganeuf	25 E4	Bourgogne	26 C2	Bousquet-d'Orb,		Bóveda	34 B2
Bottniska Viken		Bouka	86 C3	Bourbon-		Bourg-Argental	30 B1	Bourgoin-Jallieu	30 C1	le	30 A4	Bøverdal	100 B3
Pohjanlahti	102 A3	Boulay-Moselle	21 D3	l'Archambault	26 A3	Bourg-de-Péage	30 C2	Bourg-St-Andéol	30 B3	Boussac	25 F4	Boves	19 F2
Bottrop	17 E3	Boulogne		Bourbonne-		Bourg-de-Visa	28 C3	Bourg-St-Maurice	31 D1	Boussens	37 F1	Boves	31 E3
Botun	77 D4	(Haute-Garonne)	37 F1	les-Bains	27 D1	Bourg-d'Oisans, le	31 D2	Bourgtheroulde	19 D3	Boutonne	24 C4	Bovey Tracy	8 C3

Bologna

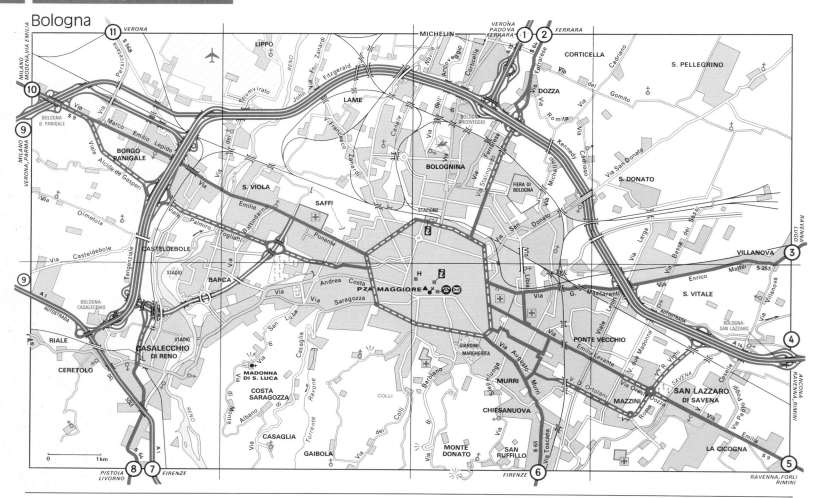

Bovolone	60 C1	Brǎila	113 E4	Braunschweig	52 B1	Bremen	47 F3	Brezovica	77 D2	Brisighella	61 D3	Bronchales	41 D2
Bowes	5 E4	Braine	20 A3	Braunton	8 C3	Bremerhaven	47 F3	Brezovo Polje (Bosna		Brissac-Quincé	24 C2	Brønderslev	108 B2
Bowness	6 B1	Braine-le-Comte	50 B4	Braus, Col de	31 E3	Bremervörde	47 F3	i Hercegovina)	72 B3	Brissago	58 A3	Broni	60 A2
Bowness-		Braintree	11 D2	Bravães	34 A3	Bremsnes	100 B2	Brezovo Polje		Bristol	9 D2	Brønnøysund	97 D3
on-Solway	5 D3	Brake	47 F3	Bravuogn	58 B3	Breña, Emb de la	43 E2	(Hrvatska)	71 E2	Bristol Chan	8 C2	Brøns	108 A3
Boxholm	109 E1	Brakel	52 A2	Bray (IRL)	13 E4	Brenes	43 D2	Briançon	31 D2	Brive-la-Gaillarde	29 D2	Bronte	69 D3
Boxmeer	17 D3	Bräkne-Hoby	109 D3	Bray		Brenna	53 D2	Briare	26 A2	Briviesca	36 A2	Bronzani Majdan	71 D3
Boxtel	16 C3	Brallo		(Seine-et-Marne)	20 A4	Brenner	59 D2	Bribirske Mostine	75 D1	Brixen	59 D2	Broom, L	2 C2
Boyle	12 C2	di Pregola	60 A2	Bray (Somme)	19 F2	Brennilis	22 B3	Bricquebec	18 B3	Brixham	8 C4	Broons	22 C3
Boyne	13 D3	Brálos	83 E3	Bray-Dunes	19 F1	Breno	58 C4	Brides	31 D1	Brixlegg	59 D1	Brora	3 D3
Božaj	76 B3	Bramming	108 A3	Brazatortas	43 F1	Brénod	26 C4	Bridgend		Brka	72 B3	Brösarp	109 D3
Božava	74 C1	Brampton	5 D3	Brbinj	74 C1	Brentwood	10 C2	(Scotland)	4 A2	Brna	75 E2	Brossac	28 B1
Bozdoğan	115 F4	Bramsche	17 E2	Brčko	72 B3	Brescia	60 B1	Bridgend (Wales)	8 C2	Brnaze	75 D1	Brøstadbotn	94 B3
Bozel	31 D1	Brancaleone	67 E4	Brda	110 A4	Breskens	16 B1	Bridge of Allan	4 C2	Brno	57 F1	Brotas	38 B4
Bozen	59 D3	Brancion	26 C3	Brđani	73 D4	Bresle	19 E2	Bridgnorth	9 D1	Bro (Gotlands		Broto	37 E2
Božica	77 E2	Brand	58 B2	Brea	36 C4	Bresles	19 F3	Bridgwater	9 D3	Län)	109 F4	Brotton	5 F4
Boži Dar	53 E3	Brandbu	105 D2	Brécey	18 B4	Bressanone	59 D2	Bridlington	7 E1	Bro (Stockholms		Brøttum	105 D2
Bozouls	29 E3	Brande	108 A3	Brechin	3 E4	Bressay	3 F2	Bridport	9 D3	Län)	106 B3	Brou (Ain)	26 C4
Bozüyük	115 F3	Brandenburg	49 D4	Brecht	50 C3	Bresse, la	27 E1	Briec	22 B3	Broad B	2 B2	Brou
Bozzolo	60 C2	Brand-Erbisdorf	53 E3	Břeclav	57 F1	Bressuire	24 C3	Brie-Comte-		Broadford (GB)	2 B3	(Eure-et-Loir)	25 E1
Bra	31 F2	Brander, Pass of	4 B1	Brecon	8 C1	Brest (F)	22 A2	Robert	19 F4	Broadford (IRL)	12 B4	Brouage	24 B4
Brabant	50 B3	Brandis	53 D2	Brecon Beacons		Brest (SU)	112 C1	Brielle	16 B3	Broad Haven	12 B2	Brough	5 E4
Brač	75 E2	Brändö	107 D2	Nat Pk	8 C2	Brest R	23 D4	Brienne-		Broad Law	5 D3	Brough Head	3 D1
Bracadale	2 B3	Brandon	11 D1	Breda (E)	32 B4	Brestanica	70 C2	le-Château	20 B4	Broadstairs	11 D3	Broughshane	13 E1
Bracadale, L	2 B3	Brandon Head	14 A3	Breda (NL)	16 C3	Brestova	70 B3	Brienon	26 A1	Broadway	9 E1	Broughton-
Bracciano	63 E2	Brandon Mt	14 A3	Bredbyn	102 A2	Brestovac		Brienz	27 F3	Broager	108 A4	in-Furness	6 B1
Bracciano, L di	63 E2	Brandýs Stará		Bredelar	17 F3	(Hrvatska)	71 E2	Brienza	64 C4	Broby	109 D3	Brouis, Col de	31 E3
Bracco, Pso del	60 B3	Boleslav	53 F3	Bredstedt	47 F1	Brestovac (Srbija)	73 E3	Briey	21 D3	Brocken	52 B2	Brovst	108 B2
Bračevci	71 F2	Braničevo	73 E3	Bree	50 C3	Brestovac (Srbija)	77 D1	Brig	27 F3	Brod (Bosna i		Brownhills	9 E1
Bracieux	25 E2	Braniewo	110 B4	Bregalnica	77 F3	Brestovac (Srbija)	77 E1	Brigg	7 D2	Hercegovina)	76 A1	Brozas	39 D3
Bräcke	101 E2	Branne	28 B2	Breganze	59 D4	Brestovačka		Brighouse	6 C2	Brod (Makedonija)	77 D3	Bruay-en-Artois	19 F1
Brackenheim	55 D2	Braño Caballo	35 D2	Bregenz	58 B1	Banja	73 E3	Brightlingsea	11 D2	Brodarevo	76 B1	Bruay-sur-l'Escaut	20 A1
Brackley	9 E2	Brañosera	35 F2	Bréhal	18 B4	Bretenoux	29 D2	Brighton	10 C3	Brodica	73 E3	Bruchsal	54 C2
Brackwede	17 F3	Br'ansk	111 E4	Bréhat, I de	22 C2	Breteuil (Eure)	19 D4	Brignogan	22 A2	Brodick	4 B2	Brück	53 D1
Brad	112 C4	Brantôme	28 C1	Breiðafjörður	96 A2	Breteuil (Oise)	19 F3	Brignoles	31 D4	Brod na Kupi	70 B3	Bruck (D)	56 B1
Bradano	65 D4	Braskereidfoss	105 D2	Breil-sur-Roya	31 E3	Bretten	54 C2	Brihuega	40 B2	Brodnica	112 B1	Bruck
Bradashesh	76 C4	Braslav	111 D3	Breisach	54 B4	Breuil-Cervinia	27 F4	Brijuni	70 A4	Brody (PL)	53 F1	(Niederösterreich)	57 F2
Bradford	6 C2	Brašov	113 D3	Breitengüßbach	52 C4	Brevik	104 C4	Briksdal	100 B3	Brody (SU)	113 D2	Bruck (Salzburg)	59 E1
Bradford-on-Avon	9 D2	Brasschaat	50 B3	Breitungen	52 B3	Breza	71 F4	Brilon	17 F3	Broglie	19 D3	Bruck an der Mur	57 E4
Bradina	75 F1	Bratislava	112 A3	Breivikbotn	95 D1	Brežđe	72 C4	Brimnes	104 B2	Brohl-Lützing	51 E4	Brückl	70 B1
Brading	9 E3	Brattvåg	100 A2	Breivikeidet	94 C2	Brežice	70 C2	Brinches	42 B1	Brolo	69 D2	Bruckmühl	56 B3
Bradwell-on-Sea	11 D2	Bratunac	72 B4	Brekke	104 A1	Breznica	70 C2	Brindisi	65 F3	Bromarv	107 D2	Brüel	48 C2
Braemar	3 D4	Braubach	51 E4	Brekken	101 D2	Breznica		Brinon	26 A2	Brombachsee	55 E2	Brués	34 B2
Braga	34 A4	Braunau	56 C3	Brekkvassel	97 D4	Đakovačka	71 F2	Brionne	19 D3	Brome	48 B4	Bruges	50 A3
Bragança	34 C3	Braunfels	51 F4	Brekstad	100 C1	Březnice	56 C1	Brioude	29 F1	Bromölla	109 D3	Brugg	27 F2
Braguia, Pto de	35 F2	Braunlage	52 B2	Bremanger		Brezno	112 B3	Brioux	24 C4	Bromsgrove	9 E1	Brügge	17 E4
Braies, L di	59 D2	Braunsbedra	53 D2	Landet	100 A3	Brezolles	19 E4	Briouze	18 C4	Bromyard	9 D1	Brugge	50 A3

Bonn

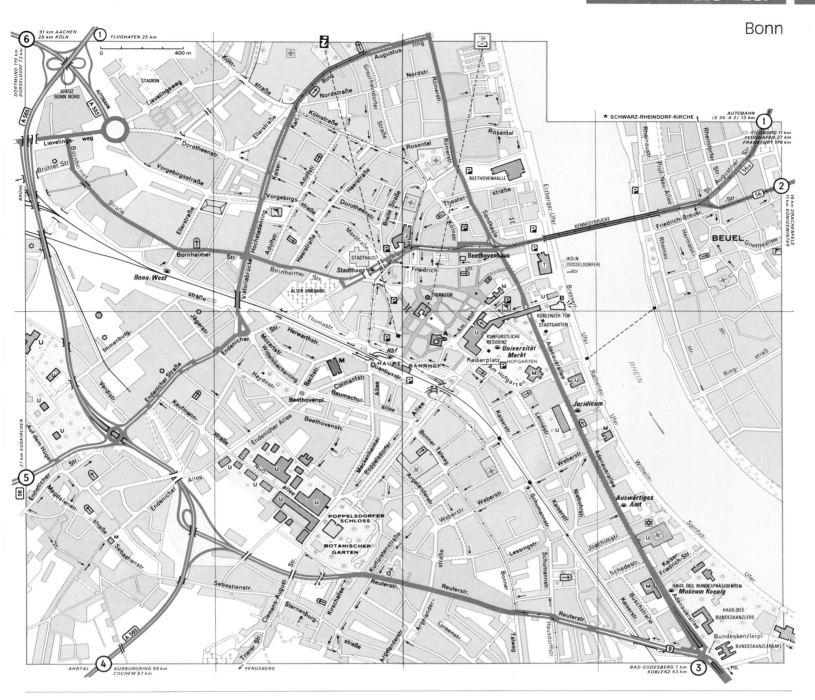

Brühl	17 E4	Bruton	9 D3	Bucine	61 D4	Budrio	61 D2	Bujaraloz	37 E4	Buñol	41 E4	Burgess Hill	10 C3
Brújula, Pto de la	36 A2	Bruvno	70 C4	Bučje	73 F4	Budva	76 B3	Buje	70 A3	Bunratty Castle	12 B4	Burggrub	52 C4
Bruksvallarna	101 D2	Bruxelles	50 B3	Bückeburg	52 A1	Budyně nad		Bujeo, Pto del	43 D4	Buntingford	9 F2	Burghasungen	52 A2
Brülon	23 E3	Bruyères	27 D1	Buckfastleigh	8 C4	Ohře	53 F3	Bukinje	71 F3	Buñuel	36 C3	Burghausen	56 B3
Brumath	21 E4	Brvenik	76 C1	Buckhaven	5 D2	Buenache		Bukova Gora	75 E1	Buonabitacolo	67 D1	Burgjoß	52 B4
Brummen	17 D3	Bryne	104 A4	Buckie	3 D3	de Alarcón	40 C3	Bukovi	72 C4	Buonalbergo	64 B3	Burgkunstadt	52 C4
Brumunddal	105 D2	Brynmawr	9 D2	Buckingham	9 F2	Buen Amor	39 E1	Bukovo	77 D4	Buonconvento	61 D4	Burglengenfeld	55 F1
Bruneck	59 D2	Brzan	73 D3	Buckinghamshire	9 F2	Buenavista		Bülach	58 A1	Buonfornello	68 C3	Burgohondo	39 F2
Brunete	40 A2	Brza Palanka	73 F3	Buckovička		de Valdavia	35 E3	Buldan	115 F4	Burbach	51 F3	Burgos	35 F3
Brunflo	101 E2	Brzeće	77 D1	Banja	73 D3	Buendía	40 C2	Bulgnéville	27 D1	Burbáguena	41 D1	Burgsinn	52 B4
Brunico	59 D2	Brzeg	112 A2	Buckow	49 E4	Buendía, Emb de	40 C2	Bullas	44 C2	Búrdalo, R	39 E4	Burgstädt	53 E3
Brünigpass	27 F3	Buarcos	38 B2	Bückwitz	49 D3	Buet, Mt	27 E4	Bulle	27 E3	Bure	7 F3	Burg Stargard	49 D2
Bruniquel	29 D3	Buavåg	104 A3	Bučovice	57 F1	Bueu	34 A2	Büllingen	51 D4	Bureå	98 B4	Burgsvik	109 F4
Brunkeberg	104 B3	Bubry	22 C3	Bucovina	113 D3	Bug	112 C1	Bully	19 F1	Burela	34 C1	Burgsviken	109 F4
Brunnen	58 A2	Bučač	113 D3	București	115 D1	Bugeat	29 D1	Bultei	66 B2	Büren	17 F3	Burguete	36 C1
Brunsbüttel	47 F2	Buçaco	38 B2	Bud	100 B2	Bugojno	71 E4	Buna	75 F2	Buren	47 D3	Burgui	37 D2
Brunssum	17 D4	Buccheri	69 D4	Budapest	112 B4	Bugøynes	95 F2	Bunclody	15 D3	Burfjord	95 D2	Burguillo,
Bruntál	112 A3	Bucchianico	64 A2	Buðardalur	96 A2	Bugue, le	28 C2	Buncrana	13 D1	Burford	9 E2	Emb de	39 F2
Bruravik	104 B2	Bucelas	38 A4	Buddon Ness	5 D1	Bühl	54 C3	Bünde	17 F2	Burg (D)	48 B1	Burguillos
Brus	77 D1	Buchan Ness	3 E1	Buddusò	66 B2	Builth Wells	9 D1	Bunde	47 E3	Burg (DDR)	48 C4	del Cerro	43 D1
Brusand	104 A4	Büchen	48 B3	Bude	8 B3	Buin, Piz	58 B2	Bun Dobhráin	12 C2	Burgas	115 E2	Burhaniye	115 E4
Brušane	70 C4	Buchen	55 D1	Büdelsdorf	48 A2	Buis-les-		Bundoran	12 C2	Burgau	55 E3	Burhave	47 F3
Brusasco	31 F1	Buchenwald	52 C3	Büdingen	52 A4	Baronnies	30 C3	Bunë	76 B3	Burgbernheim	55 E1	Burie	28 B1
Brusnik	73 F3	Buchholz	48 A3	Budimlić Japra	71 D3	Buitrago		Bunessan	4 B1	Burgdorf (CH)	27 E2	Burjassot	41 E4
Brussel	50 B3	Buchloe	55 E3	Budinščina	70 C2	del Lozoya	40 B1	Bungay	11 D1	Burgdorf (D)	48 B4	Burk	53 F2
Brusson	27 F4	Buchs	58 B2	Budleigh		Bujalance	43 F2	Bunić	70 C4	Bürgel	52 C3	Burkau	53 F2
Brüssow	49 E2	Buchy	19 E3	Salterton	8 C3	Bujanovac	77 E2	Bunmahon	14 C4	Burgenland	57 F4	Burnham	9 D3

Bordeaux

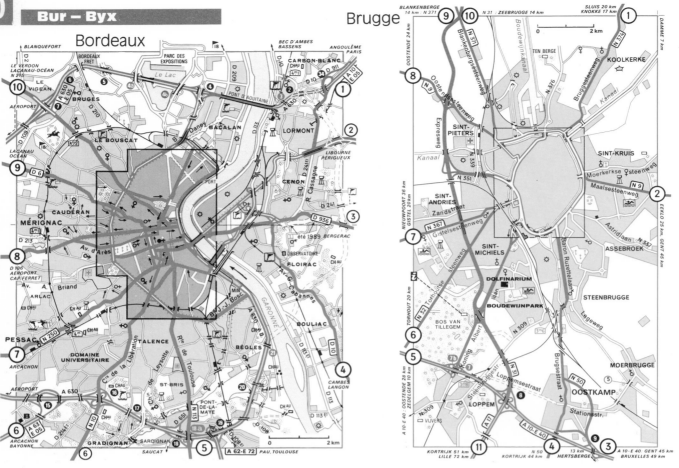

Brugge

Burnham-on-Crouch	11	D2
Burnley	6	C2
Burntisland	5	D2
Buronzo	31	F1
Burrel	76	C3
Burriana	41	E3
Burrow Head	4	C4
Burry Port	8	C2
Bursa	115	F3
Burscheid	17	E4
Bürstadt	54	C1
Burton-upon-Trent	6	C3
Burträsk	98	B4
Burwick	3	E1
Bury	6	C2
Buryn'	113	F1
Bury St Edmunds	11	D1
Busalla	60	A3
Busambra, Rca	68	B3
Busca	31	E2
Buševa pl	77	D3
Buševec	70	C2
Bushat	76	C3
Bushmills	13	E1
Buskerud	104	C2
Buško Blato	75	E1
Busko-Zdrój	112	B2
Busovača	71	F4
Bussang	27	E1
Busseto	60	B2
Bussière-Badil	28	C1
Bussolengo	60	C1
Bussum	16	C2
Busto Arsizio	60	A1
Busto de Bureba	36	A2
Büsum	47	F2
Bute	4	B2
Butera	68	C4
Buthrotum	114	C4
Buttermere	5	D4
Buttevant	14	B3
Butt of Lewis	2	B2
Buttstädt	52	C2
Butzbach	51	F4
Bützow	48	C2
Buxtehude	48	A3
Buxton	6	C3
Buxy	26	C3
Buzançais	25	E3
Buzancy	20	C3
Buzău	113	E4
Buzău R	113	E4
Buzet	70	A3
Bužim	70	C3
Bychov	111	E4
Bydgoszcz	112	A1
Bygdeå	102	B1
Bygdin	100	B3
Bygdin L	100	B3
Bygdsiljum	102	B1
Bygland	104	B4
Byglandsfjord	104	B4
Byglandsfjord L	104	B4
Bykle	104	B3
Bykleheiene	104	B3
Byrkjelo	100	A3
Byske	98	B4
Byskeälven	98	B3
Bytom	112	B2
Bytów	110	A4
Byxelkrok	109	E2

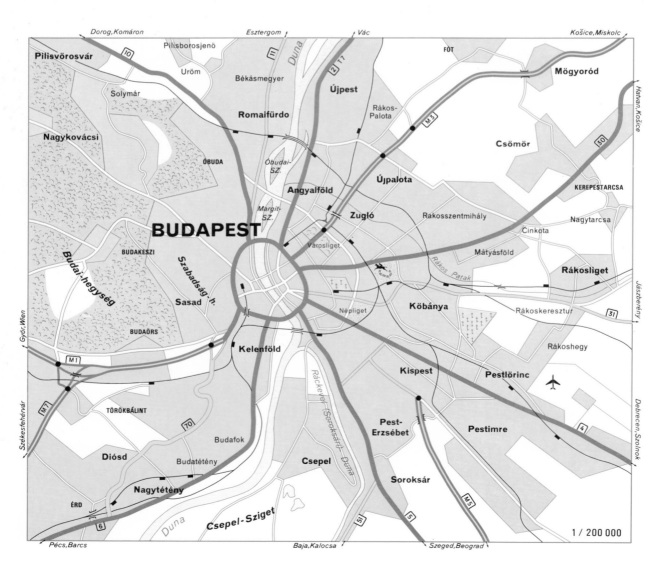

1 / 200 000

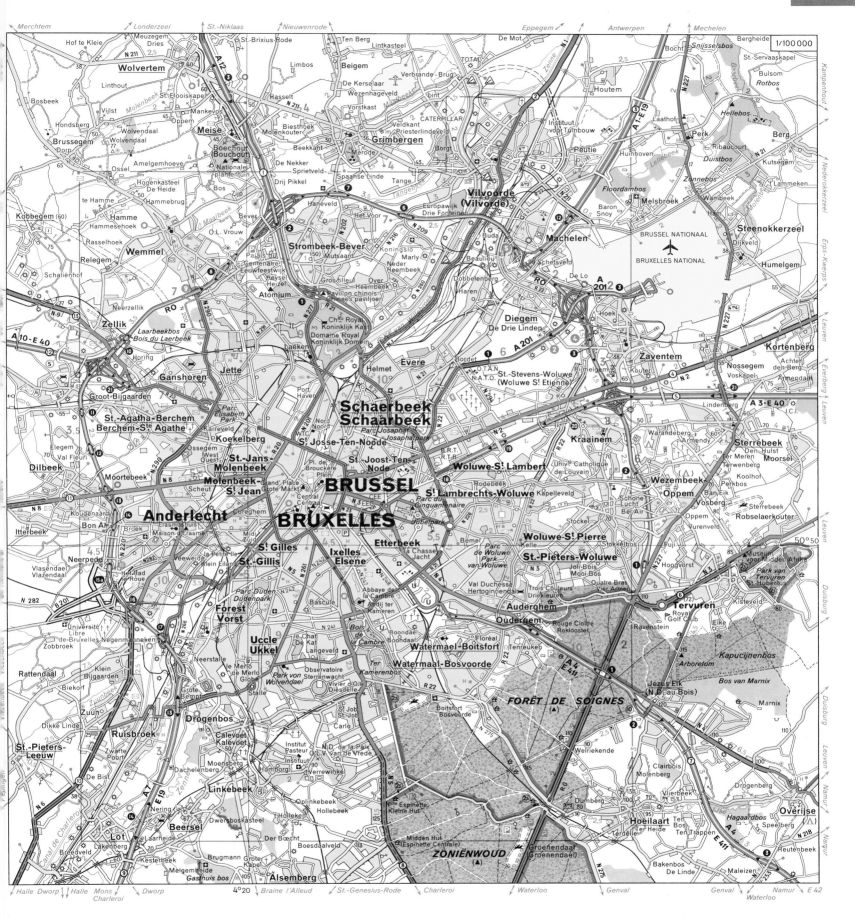

C

Cabañaquinta 35 D2
Cabañas 44 B2
Cabanes 41 F3
Cabannes, les 32 A2
Čabar 70 B3
Cabeceiras 34 B4
Cabeço de Vide 38 C3
Cabella Ligure 60 A2
Cabeza del Buey 39 E4
Cabezas Rubias 42 C2
Cabezo Gordo 42 C2
Cabezón 35 E4
Cabezón de la Sal 35 F2
Cabezuela del Valle 39 E2
Cabo de Gata 44 C4
Cabourg 18 C3
Cabra 43 F2
Cabra del Santo Cristo 44 A2
Cabras 66 A3
Cabre, Col de 30 C2
Cabreira, Sa da 34 B4
Cabreiros 34 B1
Cabrejas, Pto de 40 C3
Cabrejas, Sa de 36 A3
Cabréra 36 C4
Cabrera, I de 45 F3
Cabrera, Sa de la 34 C3
Cabrerets 29 D3
Cabriel, R 41 D3
Cabril, Bgem do 38 B2
Cabrillas 39 E1
Cabrito, Pto del 43 D4
Cabuérniga 35 F2
Čabulja 75 E1
Cacabelos 34 C2
Čačak 73 D4
Caccamo 68 B3
Cacela 42 B3
Cáceres 39 D3
Cachafeiro 34 A2
Cachopo 42 B2
Čačinci 71 E2
Cadabo 34 C2
Cadalso de los Vidrios 40 A2
Cadaqués 32 C3
Cadarache 30 C3
Cadaval 38 A3
Čađavica 71 E4
Čadca 112 B3
Cadelbosco di Sopra 60 C2
Cadenabbia 58 B4
Cadena, Pto de la 45 D2
Cadenberge 47 F2
Cadenet 30 C3
Cader Idris 6 A3
Cádiar 44 A3
Cadillac 28 B2
Cadipietra 59 D2
Cadi, Serra del 32 A3
Cádiz 43 D4
Cádiz, B de 43 D4
Cádiz, G de 42 C3
Cadouin 28 C2
Čadyr-Lunga 113 E4
Caen 18 C3
Caerdydd 9 D2
Caerfyrddin 8 C2
Caergybi 6 A2
Caernarfon 6 A3
Caernarfon B 6 A3
Caerphilly 9 D2
Caersws 9 D1
Cafasan 77 D4
Cagli 61 E4
Cagliari 66 B4
Cagliari, G di 66 B4
Čaglin 71 E2
Cagnano Varano 64 C2
Cagnes 31 E3
Caha Mts 14 A4
Caher 14 C3
Cahersiveen 14 A4
Cahore Pt 15 E3
Cahors 29 D3
Caia, Bgem do 38 C4
Caianello 64 A3
Caión 34 A1
Cairn Gorm 3 D4
Cairngorm Mts 3 D4
Cairnryan 4 B3
Cairo Montenotte 31 F2
Caiseal 14 C3
Caisleán an Bharraigh 12 B3
Caistor 7 D2
Caivano 64 B4
Cajarc 29 D3
Čajetina 72 C4
Čajniče 76 B1
Čakor 76 C2
Čakovec 70 C1
Cakovice 53 F3
Çal 115 F4
Calabor 34 C3
Calabria 67 E2
Calaceite 41 F1
Calacuccia 33 F3
Cala d'Or 45 F3
Cala, Emb de la 43 D2
Calaf 37 F3
Calafat 114 C2
Calafell 37 F4
Calafort Ros Láir 15 D4
Cala Gonone 66 C2
Calahonda 44 A4
Calahorra 36 C2
Calais 19 E1
Calamocha 41 D1
Calañas 42 C2
Calanche, les 33 E3
Calanda 41 E1
Calanda, Emb de 41 E2
Calangianus 66 B1
Cala'n Porter 45 F2
Calar Alto 44 B3
Călărași 115 E1
Cala Ratjada 45 F2
Calasetta 66 A4
Calasparra 44 C2
Calatafimi 68 B3
Calatañazor 36 B3
Calatayud 36 C4
Calatorao 36 C4
Calau 53 E1
Calazzo 64 B3
Calbe 52 C1
Calcena 36 C3
Caldaro 59 D3
Caldarola 61 F4
Caldas da Rainha 38 A3
Caldas das Taipas 34 A4
Caldas de Reis 34 A2
Caldas de Vizela 34 A4
Caldeirão, Sa do 42 B2
Caldelas 34 A3
Caldera de Taburiente, Pque Nac de la 42 A4
Calderina 40 A4
Caldes de Boí 37 F2
Caldes de Malavella 32 B3
Caldes de Montbui 32 A4
Caldirola 60 A2
Caledonian Canal 2 C4
Calella (Palamós) 32 C3
Calella (Pinedo de Mar) 32 B4
Calenzana 33 F3
Calera de León 43 D1
Calera y Chozas 39 F3
Caleruega 36 A3
Caletta, la 66 C2
Càlig 41 F2
Călimănești 115 D1
Călimani, M 113 D4
Calitri 64 C3
Calizzano 31 F3
Callac 22 B3
Callan 15 D3
Callander 4 C1
Calla, Pso della 61 D3
Callington 8 C4
Callosa de Ensarriá 45 E1
Callosa de Segura 45 D2
Calmazzo 61 E3
Calmbach 54 C2
Calne 9 E2
Calolziocorte 58 B4
Calonge 32 B3
Calpe 45 E1
Caltabellotta 68 B3
Caltagirone 69 D4
Caltanissetta 68 C3
Caltavuturo 68 C3
Caluso 31 E1
Calvados 18 C3
Calvi 33 E3
Calvitero 39 E2
Calvörde 48 C4
Calw 54 C2
Calzada de Calatrava 44 A1
Calzada de Valdunciel 39 E1
Cam 9 F1
Camacho, Pto 44 A3
Camaiore 60 C3
Camaldoli 61 D3
Camaleño 35 E2
Camarasa 37 F3
Camarasa, Emb de 37 F3
Camarat, Cap 31 D4
Camarena 40 A2
Camarès 32 B1
Camaret 22 A3
Camarillas 41 E2
Camarillas, Emb de 44 C1
Camariñas 34 A1
Camarzana 35 D3
Camas 43 D2
Cambados 34 A2
Cambas 38 C2
Camberley 9 F2
Cambil 44 A2
Cambo-les-Bains 28 A4
Camborne 8 B4
Cambrai 20 A2
Cambre 34 B1
Cambremer 19 D3
Cambrian Mts 8 C1
Cambridge 10 C1
Cambridgeshire 10 C1
Cambrils de Mar 37 F4
Camburg 52 C3
Camelford 8 B3
Camerino 61 E4
Camigliatello Silano 67 E2
Caminha 34 A3
Caminomorisco 39 D2
Caminreal 41 D2
Camogli 60 A3
Campagna 64 C4
Campagne-lès-Hesdin 19 E2
Campan 37 E1
Campana 67 F2
Campanario 39 E4
Campania 64 B4
Campaspero 35 F4
Campbeltown 4 B3
Campello 45 E1
Campi Bisenzio 60 C3
Campiglia Marittima 62 C1
Campilhas, Bgem de 42 A1
Campillo de Altobuey 41 D3
Campillo de Aragón 36 C4
Campillo de Arenas 44 A2
Campillo de Llerena 43 D1
Campillos 43 E3
Campione 58 A4
Campi Salentina 65 F4
Campitello M 64 B3
Campli 63 F1
Campo 37 E2
Campobasso 64 B3
Campobello di Licata 68 C4
Campobello di Mazara 68 A3
Campo Carlo Magno 58 C3
Campo de Beisteros 38 B1
Campo de Caso 35 E2
Campo de Criptana 40 B4
Campo di Fiori 58 A4
Campo di Giove 64 A2
Campodonico 61 E4
Campoformido 59 F3
Campogalliano 60 C2
Campo Imperatore 63 F1
Campo Ligure 60 A3
Campo Maior 38 C4
Campomanes 35 D2
Campomarino 64 B2
Campora San Giovanni 67 E3
Camporredondo, Emb de 35 E2
Camporrobles 41 D3
Campos 45 F3
Camposampiero 59 D4
Campos, Canal de 35 E4
Campotosto, L di 63 F1
Campo Tures 59 D2
Camprodon 32 B3
Camucia 61 D4
Camuñas 40 B3
Cañada de Benatanduz 41 E2
Cañadas, Pto 43 D1
Çanakkale 115 E3
Çanakkale Boğazı 115 E3
Canal du Nord 19 F2
Canal du Rhône au Rhin 27 E2
Canales de la Sierra 36 A3
Canals 41 E4
Canal San Bovo 59 D3
Cañamero 39 E3
Canarias, Is 42 B4
Canas de Senhorim 38 C1
Cañaveral 39 D3
Cañaveral de León 43 D2
Cañaveras 40 C2
Canazei 59 D3
Cancale 18 B4
Cancárix 45 D1
Canche 19 E1
Cancon 28 C2
Candanchu 37 D2
Candas 35 D1
Candasnos 37 E4
Candé 23 E4
Candeeiros, Sa dos 38 A3
Candela 64 C3
Candelaria, Sa 39 E2
Candelario 39 E2
Candelaro 64 C2
Candeleda 39 F2
Candes 25 D2
Canelles, Emb de 37 F3
Canelli 31 F2
Canero 35 D1
Canet de Mar 32 B4
Cañete 41 D3
Cañete de las Torres 43 F2
Cañete la Real 43 E3
Canet-Plage 32 B2
Canfranc-Estación 37 D2
Cangas 34 A3
Cangas de Narcea 34 C2
Cangas de Onís 35 E1
Canha 38 B4
Canicattì 68 C4
Canicattini Bagni 69 D4
Canigou, Pic du 32 B2
Cañigral 41 D3
Caniles 44 B3
Canin, M 59 F3
Canino 63 D2
Canis 18 B3
Cañizál 39 E1
Canjáyar 44 B3
Canna 2 B4
Cannero Riviera 58 A4
Cannes 31 E4
Canneto 60 C4
Cannich 2 C3
Cannobio 58 A4
Cannock 9 E1
Canonbie 5 D3
Canosa di Puglia 64 C3
Canourgue, la 29 F3
Cansano 64 A2
Cansiglio 59 E3
Cantabria 35 F2
Cantal (Dépt) 29 E2
Cantal, Mts du 29 E2
Cantalapiedra 39 F1
Cantalejo 40 A1
Cantalpino 39 E1
Cantanhede 38 B2
Cantavieja 41 E2
Čantavir 72 B1
Canterbury 11 D3
Cantillana 43 D2
Cantoira 31 E1
Cantoral 35 E2
Cantoria 44 C3
Cantù 60 A1
Canvey I 11 D2
Cany-Barville 19 D2
Caorle 59 E4
Caorso 60 B2
Capaccio 64 C4
Capaci 68 B3
Capalbio 63 D2
Capannelle, Pso delle 63 F1
Caparde 72 B4
Caparroso 36 C2
Capbreton 28 A4
Cap Corse 33 F2
Cap-d'Agde, le 30 A4
Cap d'Antibes 31 E4
Capdenac-Gare 29 E2
Capel Curig 6 A3
Capelle, la 20 B2
Capendu 32 B2
Capestang 30 A4
Capestrano 64 A2
Capileira 44 A3
Capistrello 63 F2
Čapljina 75 F2
Capmany 32 B3
Cappelle sul Tavo 64 A1
Cappoquin 14 C4
Capracotta 64 A2
Capraia, I di 62 B1
Caprera, I 66 B1
Capri 64 B4
Capriati a Volturno 64 A3
Capri,I di 64 B4
Captieux 28 B3
Capua 64 B3
Capurso 65 D3
Capvern 37 E1
Caracal 115 D2
Caracuel 40 A4
Caragh, L 14 A4
Caraman 29 D4
Caramanico Terme 64 A2
Caramulo 38 B1
Caramulo, Sa do 38 B1
Caransebeș 114 C1
Carantec 22 B2
Caravaca de la Cruz 44 C2
Caravai, Pso di 66 B3
Caravius, M. is 66 B4
Carbajales de Alba 35 D4
Carballiño 34 B2
Carballo 34 A1
Carbayo 35 D2
Carbonara, C 66 C4
Carbonara, Pzo 68 C3
Carbon-Blanc 28 B2
Carboneras 44 C3
Carboneras de Guadazaón 41 D3
Carbonero el Mayor 40 A1
Carbonia 66 B4
Carbonin 59 E2
Carbonne 37 F1
Carcaboso 39 D2
Carcabuey 43 F3
Carcaixent 41 E4
Carcans 28 A2
Carcans-Plage 28 A2
Carcare 31 F2
Carcassonne 32 B1
Carcastillo 36 C2
Carcès 31 D4
Carche 45 D1
Čardak 71 F4
Çardak 115 F4
Cardedeu 32 B4
Cardeña 43 F1
Cardener, R 32 A4
Cardenete 41 D3
Cardiff 9 D2
Cardigan 8 B1
Cardigan B 8 B1
Cardona 32 A3
Carei 112 C3
Carentan 18 B3
Cares, R 35 E2
Carevdar 71 D2
Carev Dvor 77 D4
Cargèse 33 E3
Carhaix-Plouguer 22 B3
Caria 38 C2
Cariati 67 F2
Caričin Grad 77 D1
Carignan 20 C2
Carignano 31 E2
Carina 77 D4
Cariñena 36 C4
Carini 68 B3
Cariño 34 B1
Carinola 64 A3
Carisio 31 F1
Carlet 41 E4
Carling 21 D3
Carlingford 13 E3
Carlingford L 13 E3
Carlisle 5 D3
Carlit, Pic 32 A2
Carloforte 66 A4
Carlow 13 D4
Carlow (Co) 13 D4
Carloway 2 B2
Carluke 4 C2
Carmagnola 31 E2
Carmarthen 8 C2
Carmarthen B 8 B2
Carmaux 29 E3
Carmona 43 E2
Carna 12 A3
Carnac 22 C4
Carnaio, Pso del 61 D3
Carn Ban 2 C4
Carndonagh 13 D1
Carnedd Llewelyn 6 A3
Carn Eige 2 C3
Carneros, Pto de los 39 F4
Carnew 15 D3
Carnforth 6 B1
Carnia 59 F3
Carnia (Reg) 59 E3
Carnlough 13 E1
Carnon 30 B4
Carnota 34 A2
Carnoustie 5 D1
Carnsore Pt 15 D4
Carnwath 5 D2
Caroch 41 D4
Carolles 18 B4
Carovigno 65 E3
Carpaneto Piacentino 60 B2
Carpații Meridionali 114 C1
Carpenedolo 60 B1
Carpentras 30 C3
Carpi 60 C2
Carpignano Sesia 58 A4
Carpineti 60 C3
Carpineto Romano 63 F3
Carpinone 64 A3
Carquefou 24 B2
Carqueiranne 31 D4
Carracedelo 34 C2
Carradale 4 B2
Carraig na Siúire 14 C3
Carral 34 B1
Carrantuohill 14 A4
Carranza 36 A1
Carrara 60 B3
Carrascal 41 E2
Carrascosa del Campo 40 C3
Carrascoy 45 D2
Carrasqueta, Pto de la 45 E1
Carrazeda de Ansiães 34 B4
Carrazedo de Montenegro 34 B4
Carrbridge 3 D4
Carregado 38 A3
Carregal do Sal 38 B2
Carreña de Cabrales 35 E1
Carrickfergus 13 E2
Carrickmacross 13 D3
Carrick-on-Shannon 12 C3
Carrick-on-Suir 14 C3
Carrigart 12 C1
Carrio 34 B1
Carrión de Calatrava 40 A4
Carrión de los Condes 35 E3
Carrión, R 35 E3
Carrizo de la Ribera 35 D2
Carro 30 C4
Carrouges 18 C4
Carrù 31 F2
Carry-le-Rouet 30 C4
Carsoli 63 F2
Cartagena 45 D3
Cártama 43 F4
Cartaxo 38 A3
Cartaya 42 C2
Carter Bar 5 D3
Carteret 18 B3
Carvajal 43 F4
Carviçais 39 D1
Carvin 19 F1
Carvoeira 42 A3
Carvoeiro, C 38 A3
Casabermeja 43 F3
Casa Branca (Alentejo) 42 A1
Casa Branca (Ribatejo) 38 B4
Casacalenda 64 B2
Casalárreina 36 B2
Casalbordino 64 B2
Casalbuttano 60 B1
Casal di Principe 64 A4
Casalecchio di Reno 60 C2
Casale Monferrato 31 F1
Casale sul Sile 59 E4
Casalmaggiore 60 B2
Casalpusterlengo 60 B2
Casamassima 65 D3
Casamicciola Terme 64 A4
Casa Nuevas 44 C2
Casarabonela 43 E3
Casarano 65 F4
Casar de Cáceres 39 D3
Casares 43 E4
Casares de las Hurdes 39 D2
Casariche 43 E3
Casarsa 59 E3
Casas de Don Pedro 39 E4
Casas de Fernando Alonso 40 C4
Casas de Juan Núñez 41 D4
Casas del Puerto 45 D1
Casas de Luján 40 B3
Casas de Miravete 39 E3
Casas Ibáñez 41 D4
Casasimarro 40 C4
Casatejada 39 E3
Casavieja 39 F2
Cascais 38 A4
Cascante 36 C3
Cascia 63 E1
Casciana Terme 60 C4
Cascina 60 C4
Casei Gerola 60 A2
Caselle in Pittari 67 D1
Caselle Torinese 31 E1
Caserío del Puente 35 D3
Caserta 64 B3

Casetas 37 D3
Cas-gwent 9 D2
Cashel 14 C3
Casicas del Río Segura 44 B2
Casillas 39 D2
Casina 60 C2
Casinos 41 E3
Casneywdd 9 D2
Casoio 34 C3
Casola in Lunigiana 60 B3
Casoli 64 A2
Casoria 64 B4
Caspe 37 E4
Cassà de la Selva 32 B3
Cassagnes-Begonhès 29 E3
Cassano allo Ionio 67 E2
Cassano delle Murge 65 D3
Cassel 19 F1
Cassino 64 A3
Cassis 30 C4
Castalla 45 D1
Castanet-Tolosan 29 D4
Castanheira de Pêra 38 B2
Castaños, Pto de los 39 D3
Castasegna 58 B3
Casteggio 60 A2
Castejón 36 C3
Castejón de Monègros 37 E4
Castejón de Sos 37 E2
Castejón de Valdejasa 37 D3
Castelbuono 68 C3
Casteldaccia 68 B3
Casteldelfino 31 E2
Castel del Monte (Abruzzo) 63 F2
Castel del Monte (Puglia) 65 D3
Castel del Rio 61 D3
Castel di Sangro 64 A2
Castelfidardo 61 F4
Castelfiorentino 60 C4
Castelfranco Emilia 60 C2
Castelfranco in Miscano 64 B3
Castelfranco Veneto 59 D4
Castel Gandolfo 63 E3
Casteljaloux 28 B3
Castellabate 67 D1
Castellamare di Stabbia 64 B4
Castellammare d. Golfo 48 B3
Castellammare, G di 68 B3
Castellamonte 31 E1
Castellana Grotte 65 E3
Castellane 31 D3
Castellaneta 65 E4
Castellar de la Muela 41 D2
Castellar del Vallès 32 A4
Castellar de Santiago 44 B1
Castellar de Santisteban 44 B2
Castell' Arquato 60 B2
Castelldans 37 F4
Castelldefels 32 A4
Castell de Ferro 44 A4
Castelleone 60 B1
Castellfollit de la Roca 32 B3
Castellina in Chianti 61 D4
Castell-nedd 8 C2
Castelló de la Plana 41 F3
Castello del Lago 64 B3
Castelló d'Empúries 32 B3
Castelloli 32 A4
Castellón de la Plana 41 F3

Castellón de Rugat 45 E1
Castellote 41 E2
Castello Tesino 59 D3
Castellterçol 32 A4
Castelluccio 63 F1
Castel Madama 63 F2
Castelmassa 60 C2
Castelmauro 64 B2
Castelmoron 28 C3
Castelnaudary 32 A1
Castelnau-de-Médoc 28 B2
Castelnau-de-Montmiral 29 D3
Castelnau-Magnoac 37 E1
Castelnau-Montratier 29 D3
Castelnau-Rivière-Basse 28 B4
Castelnovo ne' Monti 60 B3
Castelnuovo Berardenga 61 D4
Castelnuovo Bocca d'Adda 60 B2
Castelnuovo della Daunia 64 B3
Castelnuovo di Garfagnana 60 C3
Castelnuovo di Porto 63 E2
Castelnuovo Scrivia 60 A2
Castelo Branco 38 C2
Castelo de Bode, Bgem do 38 B3
Castelo de Paiva 34 A4
Castelo de Vide 38 C2
Castelraimondo 61 E4
Castelrotto 59 D3
Castel San Giovanni 60 A2
Castel San Lorenzo 64 C4
Castel San Pietro Terme 61 D3
Castelsardo 66 B1
Castelsarrasin 29 D3
Castelserás 41 E1
Casteltermini 68 B3
Castelvecchio Subequo 63 F2
Castelvetrano 68 A3
Castel Volturno 64 A4
Castets 28 A3
Castiadas 66 C4
Castiglioncello 60 C4
Castiglione d'Adda 60 B2
Castiglione dei Pepoli 60 C3
Castiglione del Lago 61 D4
Castiglione della Pescaia 62 C1
Castiglione delle Stiviere 60 C1
Castiglione in Teverina 63 E1
Castiglione Messer Marino 64 B2
Castiglione Olona 60 A1
Castiglion Fiorentino 61 D4
Castilblanco 39 F4
Castilblanco de los Arroyos 43 D2
Castilla, Canal de 35 E4
Castilla-La Mancha 40 A4
Castilla-León 35 F4
Castilla, Mar de 40 C2
Castilleja del Campo 43 D2
Castilléjar 44 B2
Castillejo 39 E1
Castillejo de Martín Viejo 39 D1
Castillo de Loarre 37 D2
Castillo de Locubín 43 F2
Castillo, Bge de 31 D3
Castillon-en-Couserans 37 F2

Castillon-la-Bataille 28 B2
Castillonnès 28 C2
Castillo, Pto del 44 A3
Castillo y Elejabeitia 36 B1
Castilruiz 36 C3
Castions di Strada 59 F3
Castlebar 12 B3
Castlebay 2 A4
Castlebellingham 13 D3
Castleblayney 13 D3
Castlecomer 13 D4
Castledawson 13 D2
Castlederg 13 D2
Castledermot 13 D4
Castle Douglas 4 C3
Castleford 7 D2
Castleisland 14 B3
Castlemaine 14 A3
Castlepollard 13 D3
Castlerea 12 C3
Castlerock 13 D1
Castleton 6 C2
Castletownbere 14 A4
Castletown (I of Man) 6 A1
Castletown (Scotland) 3 D2
Castlewellan 13 E2
Castocalbón 35 D3
Castrejón 39 F1
Castrejón, Emb de 40 A3
Castres 32 B1
Castries 30 B4
Castríl 44 B2
Castrillo de la Reina 36 A3
Castrillo de Villavega 35 F3
Castro 34 B2
Castro Caldelas 34 B3
Castrocaro Terme 61 D3
Castrocontrigo 35 D3
Castro Daire 38 C1
Castro del Río 43 F2
Castrogeriz 35 F3
Castro Laboreiro 34 B3
Castro Marim 42 B2
Castromonte 35 E4
Castronuevo 35 D4
Castronuño 35 E4
Castropol 34 C1
Castrop-Rauxel 17 E3
Castroreale 69 D2
Castroreale Terme 69 D2
Castrotierra 35 E3
Castro Urdiales 36 A1
Castroverde 34 C2
Castro Verde 42 B2
Castroverde de Campos 35 E3
Castrovillari 67 E2
Castuera 39 E4
Cataluña 32 A3
Catalunya 37 F3
Catania 69 D3
Catania, G di 69 D3
Catanzaro 67 F3
Catanzaro Lido 67 F3
Catarroja 41 E4
Cateau, le 20 A2
Catelet, le 20 A2
Catenanuova 69 D3
Catez 70 C2
Cathair na Mart 12 B3
Catici 71 F4
Catignano 64 A2
Catoira 34 A2
Catoute 35 D2
Catral 45 D2
Catria, Mte 61 E4
Cattenom 21 D3
Cattolica 61 E3
Catus 29 D2
Caudebec 19 D3
Caudete 45 D1
Caudiel 41 E3
Caudry 20 A2
Caulnes 23 D3
Caulonia 67 F4
Caumont-l'Eventé 18 C3
Caunes 32 B1

Caussade 29 D3
Causy 111 E4
Cauterets 37 E2
Cava de' Tirreni 64 B4
Cávado, R 34 A4
Cavaglià 31 F1
Cavaillon 30 C3
Cavalaire 31 D4
Cavalerie, la 29 F3
Cavalese 59 D3
Cavalière 31 D4
Cavan 13 D3
Cavan (Co) 13 D3
Cavarzere 61 D1
Cavazzo 59 E3
Çavdarhisar 115 F4
Cavero, Pto de 36 C4
Cavezzo 60 C2
Cavo 62 C1
Cavo, Mte 63 E3
Cavour 31 E2
Cavtat 76 A3
Caya 38 C4
Cayeux 19 E2
Caylar, le 29 F3
Caylus 29 D3
Cayolle, Col de la 31 E3
Cayres 29 F2
Cazalla de la Sierra 43 D2
Cazals 29 D2
Cazaubon 28 B3
Cazaux 28 A2
Cazères 37 F1
Cazin 70 C3
Cazma 71 D2
Cazorla 44 B2
Cazorla, Sa de 44 B2
Cea 34 B2
Ceanannus Mor 13 D3
Cea, R 35 E3
Ceatharlach 13 D4
Cebolla 39 F3
Cebollera 36 B3
Cebreros 40 A2
Ceccano 63 F3
Cece 112 B4
Cechy 53 F3
Cecina 60 C4
Cecina R 60 C4
Cecita, L di 67 F2
Ceclavín 39 D3
Cedeira 34 B1
Cedillo, Bgem de 38 C3
Cedrillas 41 E2
Cedrino 66 C2
Cedynia 49 E3
Cefalù 68 C3
Cega, R 40 A1
Cegléd 112 B4
Ceglie Messapico 65 E3
Cegrane 77 D3
Cehegín 44 C2
Cehotina 76 A1
Ceira, R 38 C2
Çejč 57 F1
Celákovice 53 F3
Celano 63 F2
Celanova 34 B3
Celavevo 72 B2
Čelebić 75 D1
Čelebići 76 B1
Celemín, Emb de 43 D4
Čelić 72 B3
Čelinac Donji 71 E3
Celje 70 B2
Cella 41 D2
Celle 48 B4
Celle Ligure 60 A3
Celles 24 C4
Čelopeci 77 D3
Celorico 34 B4
Celorico da Beira 38 C1
Čemerna pl 73 D4
Čemernica 71 E4
Čemerno 76 A2
Cenajo, Emb del 44 C1
Cencenighe 59 D3
Cenicero 36 B2
Čenta 72 C2
Centelles 32 B4
Cento 60 C2
Cento Croci, Pso 60 B3
Central Region 4 C1
Centre, Canal du 26 B3

Centuripe 69 D3
Cepagatti 64 A2
Cepedosa 39 E2
Cepin 71 F2
Ceppo 63 F1
Ceprano 63 F3
Cer 72 C3
Čeralije 71 E2
Cerbère 32 C3
Cercal (Alentejo) 42 A1
Cercal (Estremadura) 38 A3
Cercedilla 40 A2
Cerchiara di Calabria 67 E2
Cerchov 56 B1
Cerdedo 34 A2
Cerdeira 39 D2
Cère 29 E2
Cerea 60 C1
Cereda, Pso di 59 D3
Ceres 31 E1
Ceresole Reale 31 E1
Cerezo de Abajo 36 A4
Cerezo de Riotirón 36 A2
Cerignola 64 C3
Cerílly 26 A3
Cerisiers 26 A1
Cerisy-la-Salle 18 B3
Cerizay 24 C3
Čerkassy 113 F2
Cerknica 70 B2
Cerkniško jez 70 B2
Cerkno 70 A2
Cerler 37 E2
Cerná 56 C2
Cerna 71 F2
Cernache de Bonjardim 38 B2
Čern'achovsk 110 B4
Cernadilla, Emb de 34 C3
Cernavodă 115 E1
Cernay 27 E1
Černigov 113 E1
Cernik 71 E3
Cernobbio 58 B4
Černobyl' 113 E1
Cernomorskoje 113 F4
Černovcy 113 D3
Cerreto, Pso del 60 B3
Cerreto Sannita 64 B3
Cerrigydrudion 6 B3
Cèrrik 76 C4
Certaldo 60 C4
Certosa di Pavia 60 A2
Cervales 39 E3
Cervaro 64 C3
Cervati, Mte 67 D1
Cervatos 35 F2
Cervatos de la Cueza 35 E3
Červen 111 D4
Cervera 37 F3
Cervera de la Cañada 36 C4
Cervera del Río Alhama 36 C3
Cervera de Pisuerga 35 F2
Cerveteri 63 E2
Cervia 61 E3
Cervialto, Mte 64 C4
Cervignano del Friuli 59 F3
Cervinara 64 B3
Cervino 27 E4
Cervione 33 F3
Cervo 34 C1
Červonograd 112 C2
Cesana Torinese 31 D2
Cesarica 70 C4
Cesarò 69 D3
Cesena 61 D3
Cesenatico 61 E3
Cēsis 110 C2
Česka Kamenice 53 F2
Česká Lípa 53 F3
České Budějovice 57 D1
České Velenice 57 D1
Český Krumlov 57 D1
Chard 9 D3

Çeşme 115 E4
Cespedosa 39 E2
Cessalto 59 E4
Cetina (E) 36 C4
Cetina R (YU) 75 D1
Cetinje 76 B3
Cetraro 67 E2
Cevedale, Mte 58 C3
Cévennes, Parc Nat des 29 F3
Cevico de la Torre 35 F4
Cevo 76 B2
Ceyrat 29 F1
Ceyzériat 26 C4
Cèze 30 B3
Chabanais 25 D4
Chabeuil 30 C2
Chablis 26 B1
Chabris 25 E2
Chagny 26 C3
Chailland 23 E3
Chaillé 25 D3
Chaise-Dieu, la 29 F1
Chalabre 32 A2
Chalais 28 C1
Chalamont 26 C4
Chalampé 27 E1
Chalindrey 26 C1
Challans 24 B3
Challes 31 D1
Chalon ne' 24 C2
Châlons-sur-Marne 20 B3
Chalon-sur-Saône 26 C3
Châlus 28 C1
Cham 56 B1
Chambéry 31 D1
Chambley 21 D3
Chambly 19 F3
Chambon, Bge du 31 D2
Chambon-Feugerol-les, le 30 B1
Chambon-sur-Lac 29 E1
Chambon-sur-Lignon, le 30 B2
Chambon-sur-Voueize 25 F4
Chambord 25 E2
Chambre, la 31 D1
Chamonix 27 E4
Champagnac-de-Belair 28 C1
Champagne-Mouton 25 D4
Champagnole 27 D3
Champdeniers 24 C3
Champeaux 23 D3
Champéry 27 E4
Champex 27 E4
Champlitte 26 C2
Champlon, Bre.de 50 C4
Champoluc 27 F4
Champorcher 31 E1
Champs-sur-Tarentaine 29 E1
Champtoceaux 24 B2
Chamrousse 31 D1
Chamusca 38 B3
Chanac 29 F3
Chanas 30 B1
Chança, R 42 C2
Chantada 34 B2
Chantelle 26 A4
Chantemerle 31 D2
Chantilly 19 F3
Chantonnay 24 B3
Chanza, Emb del 42 B2
Chaource 26 B1
Chapel-en-le-Frith 6 C2
Chapelle-d'Angillon, la 25 F2
Chapelle-de-Guinchay, la 26 C4
Chapelle-en-Valgaudemar, la 31 D2
Chapelle-en-Vercors, la 30 C2
Chapinería 40 A2
Charbonnières 26 C4
Charco Redondo, Emb de 43 D4

Charente 28 B1
Charente (Dépt) 28 C1
Charente-Maritime 24 B4
Charenton-du-Cher 25 F3
Charité, la 26 A2
Charleroi 50 B4
Charlestown 12 B3
Charleville 14 C3
Charleville-Mézières 20 C2
Charlieu 26 B4
Charlottenberg 105 D3
Charly 20 A3
Charmes 21 D4
Chârost 25 E3
Charquemont 27 E2
Charroux 25 D4
Chartre, la 23 F4
Chartres 19 E4
Chàs 38 B1
Chasseneuil 28 C1
Chasseral la Neuveville 27 E2
Chasseron, le 27 D3
Châtaigneraie, la 24 C3
Château-Arnoux 31 D3
Châteaubourg 23 D3
Châteaubriant 23 D4
Château-Chinon 26 B2
Château-de-Bonaguil 29 D2
Château de Ventadour 29 E1
Château d'Oex 27 E3
Château-du-Loir 23 F4
Châteaudun 25 E1
Châteaugiron 23 D3
Château-Gontier 23 E4
Château-Landon 25 F1
Château-la-Vallière 25 D2
Château, le 24 B4
Châteaulin 22 B3
Châteaumeillant 25 F3
Châteauneuf (Charente) 28 B1
Châteauneuf (Ille-et-Vilaine) 18 B4
Châteauneuf-de-Randon 29 F2
Châteauneuf-du-Faou 22 B3
Châteauneuf-du-Pape 30 B3
Châteauneuf-en-Thymerais 19 E4
Châteauneuf-la-Forêt 29 D1
Châteauneuf-les-Bains 26 A4
Châteauneuf-sur-Cher 25 F3
Châteauneuf-sur-Loire 25 F1
Châteauneuf-sur-Sarthe 23 E4
Châteauponsac 25 E4
Château-Porcien 20 B3
Château-Queyras 31 D2
Château-Regnault 20 C2
Châteaurenard (Loiret) 25 F1
Châteaurenard (Vaucluse) 30 B3
Château-Renault 25 D2
Châteauroux 25 E3
Château-Salins 21 D4
Château-Thierry 20 A3
Châteauvillain 26 C1
Châtel 27 E3
Châtelaillon-Plage 24 B4
Châtelard, le 27 D4
Châtelaudren 22 C2
Châteldon 26 A4
Châtelet 50 C4
Châtelet, le (Cher) 25 F3
Châtelet, le (Seine-et-Marne) 19 F4
Châtelguyon 26 A4

Châtellerault	25	D3
Châtel-Montagne	26	B4
Châtel-St-Denis	27	E3
Châtel-sur-Moselle	21	D4
Châtelus-Malvaleix	25	E4
Châtenois	27	D1
Chatham	11	D2
Châtillon	27	F4
Châtillon-Coligny	26	A1
Châtillon-en-Bazois	26	B2
Châtillon-en-Diois	30	C2
Châtillon-sur-Chalaronne	26	C4
Châtillon-sur-Indre	25	E3
Châtillon-sur-Loire	26	A2
Châtillon-sur-Marne	20	B3
Châtillon-sur-Seine	26	B1
Châtre, la	25	E3
Chatsworth House	6	C3
Chatteris	9	F1
Chaudes-Aigues	29	F2
Chauffailles	26	B4
Chaufour	19	E4
Chaulnes	19	F2
Chaumergy	26	C3
Chaumont-en-Vexin	19	E3
Chaumont (Haute-Marne)	26	C1
Chaumont (Loir-et-Cher)	25	E2
Chauny	20	A2
Chausey, I	18	B4
Chaussin	26	C3
Chauvigny	25	D3
Chaux-de Fonds, la	27	E2
Chaves	34	B3
Chazelles	30	B1
Cheb	53	D4
Cheddar Gorge	9	D3
Chef-Boutonne	24	C4
Cheles	42	C1
Chełm	112	C2
Chełmno	112	A1
Chelmsford	11	D2
Cheltenham	9	E2
Chelva	41	D3
Chemillé	24	C2
Chemin	26	C3
Chénérailles	25	F4
Chenonceaux	25	E2
Chepstow	9	D2
Cher	25	F3
Cher (Dépt)	25	F2
Chera	41	D3
Cherbourg	18	B2
Chéroy	26	A1
Cherson	113	F3
Chert	41	F2
Cheshire	6	C2
Cheshunt	9	F2
Chesne, le	20	C3
Cheste	41	E4
Chester	6	B3
Chesterfield	7	D3
Chester-le-Street	5	E4
Chevagnes	26	A3
Chevillon	20	C4
Cheviot Hills, The	5	E3
Cheviot, The	5	E3
Chèvre, Cap de la	22	A3
Chevreuse	19	E4
Cheylard, le	30	B2
Chèze, la	22	C3
Chiampo	59	D4
Chianciano Terme	63	D1
Chianti	61	D4
Chiaramonte Gulfi	69	D4
Chiaravalle	61	F3
Chiaravalle Centrale	67	F3
Chiari	60	B1
Chiasso	58	A4
Chiavari	60	A3
Chiavenna	58	B3
Chichester	9	F3
Chiclana de la Frontera	43	D4
Chieming	56	B3
Chiemsee	56	B3
Chieri	31	E1
Chiers	20	C3
Chiesa in Valmalenco	58	B3
Chiesina Uzz	60	C3
Chieti	64	A1
Chiltern Hills	9	F2
Chimay	50	B4
Chimorra	43	E1
Chinchilla de Monte Aragón	41	D4
Chinchón	40	B2
Chinon	25	D2
Chioggia	61	D1
Chioula, Col de	32	A2
Chipiona	42	C3
Chippenham	9	E2
Chipping Campden	9	E1
Chipping Norton	9	E2
Chipping Sodbury	9	D2
Chirivel	44	C2
Chişineu-Criş	112	C4
Chisone	31	E2
Chiusa	59	D2
Chiusa di Pesio	31	E2
Chiusa Sclafani	68	B3
Chiusaforte	59	F3
Chiusi	63	D1
Chiva	41	E4
Chivasso	31	F1
Chlum u Třeboně	57	D1
Chmel'nickij	113	D2
Chmel'nik	113	E2
Chociwel	49	F2
Chodov	53	E4
Chojna	49	E3
Chojnice	110	A4
Chojniki	113	E1
Cholet	24	C3
Chollerford	5	E3
Cholm	111	E2
Chomutov	53	E3
Chorges	31	D2
Chorley	6	C2
Chorol	113	F2
Choszczno	49	F3
Chotin	113	D3
Chouto	38	B3
Chrastava	53	F2
Christchurch	9	E3
Christiansfeld	108	A3
Christiansø	109	D4
Chur	58	B2
Church Stretton	9	D1
Chust	112	C3
Ciamarella	31	E1
Cians, Gorges du	31	E3
Çićarija	70	A3
Čičavica	77	D2
Cicciano	64	B4
Ćićevac	73	E4
Čičevo	76	A2
Cidacos, R	36	B3
Cidade Nova de Santo André	42	A1
Cidones	36	B3
Ciechanów	112	B1
Ciechocinek	112	B1
Ciempozuelos	40	B2
Cíes, Is	34	A3
Cieszyn	112	B3
Cieza	45	D2
Cifuentes	40	C2
Cigliano	31	F1
Cigüela R	40	B3
Cijara, Emb de	39	F4
Cijevna	76	B3
Čilipi	76	A3
Cill Airne	14	B4
Cillas	36	C4
Cill Chainnigh	15	D3
Cilleros	39	D2
Cilleruelo de Bezana	35	F2
Cill Mhantáin	13	E4
Cima Brenta	58	C3
Cima d'Asta	59	D3
Cimadolmo	59	E4
Cima Presanella	58	C3
Čimišlija	113	E4
Cimone, Mte	60	C3
Cîmpeni	112	C4
Cîmpina	115	D1
Cîmpulung	115	D1
Cîmpulung Moldovenesc	113	D3
Cinca, R	37	E3
Cincar	75	E1
Cinctorres	41	E2
Ciney	50	C4
Cinfães	34	A4
Cingoli	61	F4
Cinigiano	63	D1
Cinisi	68	B3
Cinovec	53	E3
Cinque Terre	60	B3
Cintegabelle	32	A1
Cinto, M	33	F3
Cintruénigo	36	C3
Ciórraga	36	B1
Ciotat, la	30	C4
Čiovo	75	D2
Cirencester	9	E2
Cirey	21	E4
Ciria	36	C3
Ciriè	31	E1
Cirò	67	F2
Cirò Marina	67	F2
Čírpan	115	D2
Cisa, Pso della	60	B3
Cisneros	35	E3
Čista	74	C1
Cista Provo	75	E1
Cisterna di Latina	63	F3
Cisternino	65	E3
Cistierna	35	E2
Čitluk (Mostar)	75	F2
Čitluk (Posušje)	75	E1
Cittadella	59	D4
Città del Pieve	63	D1
Città di Castello	61	E4
Cittaducale	63	F2
Cittanova	67	E4
Cittareale	63	F1
Città Sant' Angelo	64	A1
Ciudad Encantada	40	C3
Ciudad Real	40	A4
Ciudad Rodrigo	39	D1
Ciutadela de Menorca	45	F1
Cividale del Friuli	59	F3
Civita Castellana	63	E2
Civitanova Marche	61	F4
Civitavecchia	63	D2
Civitella del Tronto	63	F1
Civitella Roveto	63	F2
Civray	25	D4
Çivril	115	F4
Clacton-on-Sea	11	D2
Clain	25	D4
Clairvaux-les-Lacs	27	D3
Clamecy	26	A2
Claonaig	4	B2
Clapham	6	C1
Clara	12	C4
Clare	11	D1
Clare	12	B3
Clare (Co)	12	B4
Clare I	12	A3
Claremorris	12	B3
Claudy	13	D1
Clausthal-Zellerfeld	52	B2
Claut	59	E3
Claviere	31	D2
Clavin, Pto de	39	D3
Clay Cross	6	C3
Claye-Souilly	19	F4
Clayette, la	26	B4
Clear I	14	A4
Clécy	18	C4
Clefmont	26	C1
Cléguérec	22	C3
Clelles	30	C2
Clères	19	E3
Clermont	19	F3
Clermont-en-Argonne	20	C3
Clermont-Ferrand	29	F1
Clermont-l'Hérault	30	A4
Clervaux	21	D2
Cléry	25	E2
Cles	58	C3
Clevedon	9	D2
Cleveland Hills	7	D1
Cleveleys	6	B2
Clew B	12	B3
Clifden	12	A3
Clisham	2	B2
Clisson	24	B2
Clitheroe	6	C2
Cloghan	12	C4
Clogheen	14	C3
Clogherhead	13	E3
Clogher Head	14	A3
Clogh Mills	13	E1
Clonakilty	14	B4
Clonbur	12	B3
Clondalkin	13	D4
Clones	13	D2
Clonfert	12	C4
Clonmacnoise	12	C4
Clonmel	14	C3
Cloppenburg	17	E1
Clovelly	8	B3
Cloyes	25	E1
Cluain Meala	14	C3
Cluj-Napoca	112	C4
Clun	9	D1
Cluny	26	C3
Clusaz, la	27	D4
Cluse de Pontarlier	27	D3
Cluses	27	E4
Clusone	58	B4
Clwyd	6	B3
Clyde	4	C2
Clydebank	4	C2
Clyde, Firth of	4	B2
Coachford	14	B4
Coalisland	13	D2
Coalville	9	E1
Coaña	34	C1
Côa, R	39	D2
Coatbridge	4	C2
Cobeña	40	B2
Cobh	14	C4
Coburg	52	C4
Coca	40	A1
Coca, Pso di	58	B3
Cocentaina	45	E1
Cochem	51	E4
Cockburnspath	5	E2
Cockermouth	5	D4
Codevigo	61	D1
Codigoro	61	D2
Codogno	60	B2
Codos	36	C4
Codroipo	59	E3
Coesfeld	17	E3
Coevorden	17	D2
Cofrentes	41	D4
Coghinas, L del	66	B2
Cognac	28	B1
Cogne	31	E1
Cogolin	31	D4
Cogolludo	40	B1
Coigach	2	C2
Coimbra	38	B2
Coín	43	E4
Coina	38	A4
Čoka	72	C1
Col	70	A2
Colares	38	A4
Cölbe	17	F4
Colchester	11	D2
Coldbackie	2	C2
Colditz	53	D2
Coldstream	5	E2
Coleford	9	D2
Coleraine	13	D1
Colfiorito	63	E1
Colico	58	B3
Coligny	26	C3
Colindres	36	A1
Colintraive	4	B2
Coll	2	A4
Collado Bajo	41	D2
Coll de Nargó	37	F3
Colle di Val d'Elsa	60	C4
Collecchio	60	C2
Colle Isarco	59	D2
Colle Salvetti	60	C4
Colle Sannita	64	B3
Collesano	68	C3
Colli a Volturno	64	A3
Collina, Pso della	60	C3
Collinée	22	C3
Colline Metallifere	60	C4
Collio	58	C4
Collioure	32	B2
Collobrières	31	D4
Collodi	60	C3
Collonges	27	D4
Collonges-la-Rouge	29	D2
Colmar	27	E1
Colmars	31	D3
Colmenar	43	F3
Colmenar de Oreja	40	B3
Colmenar Viejo	40	A2
Colnabaichin	3	D4
Colne	6	C2
Colobraro	65	D4
Cologna Veneta	60	C1
Cologne	28	C4
Colombey-les-Belles	21	D4
Colombey-les-Deux-Eglises	26	C1
Colombière, Col de la	27	D4
Colombres	35	F1
Colomera	44	A3
Colonsay	4	A2
Colorno	60	B2
Colosimi	67	F3
Columbretes, I	41	F3
Colunga	35	E1
Colwyn Bay	6	B2
Comacchio	61	D2
Comăneşti	113	D4
Coma-ruga	37	F4
Combarro	34	A2
Combeaufontaine	27	D1
Combe Laval	30	C2
Combe Martin	8	C3
Comber	13	E2
Combloux	27	E4
Combourg	18	B4
Combronde	26	A4
Comeglians	59	E2
Comercy	20	C4
Comines	19	F1
Comino	68	B4
Comiso	69	D4
Commentry	26	A4
Commercy	20	C4
Como	58	B4
Como, L di	58	B3
Cómpeta	43	F3
Compiègne	19	F3
Comporta	38	A4
Comps-sur-Artuby	31	D3
Comunanza	63	F1
Concarneau	22	B3
Conches	19	D4
Concordia sulla Secchia	60	C2
Condat	29	E1
Condé	20	A1
Conde, Emb del	43	E3
Condé-en-Brie	20	A3
Condeixa-a-Nova	38	B2
Condé-sur-Noireau	18	C4
Condom	28	C3
Condrieu	30	B1
Conegliano	59	E3
Conejeros, Pto de los	38	C4
Conflans	21	D3
Confolens	25	D4
Cong	12	B3
Congleton	6	C3
Congost de Tresponts	32	A3
Congosto de Valdavia	35	E2
Congresbury	9	D2
Conil de la Frontera	43	D4
Conisbrough	7	D2
Coniston	5	D4
Conlie	23	F3
Conliège	26	C3
Connaught	12	B3
Connel	4	B1
Connemara	12	A3
Connerré	23	F3
Conn, L	12	B2
Čonoplja	72	B1
Conques	29	E2
Conquet, le	22	A2
Conquista	43	F1
Conselice	61	D2
Conselve	61	D1
Consett	5	E4
Constância	38	B3
Constanţa	115	E1
Constantina	43	E2
Consuegra	40	A3
Consuma	61	D3
Contamines, les	27	E4
Contarina	61	D2
Conthey	27	E3
Contigliano	63	E2
Contin	2	C3
Contrasto, C del	68	C3
Contraviesa, Sa de la	44	B4
Contreras, Emb de	41	D3
Contres	25	E2
Contrexéville	27	D1
Conty	19	F2
Convento de Calatrava	44	A1
Conversano	65	E3
Conwy	6	A2
Cookstown	13	D2
Cootehill	13	D3
Čop	112	C3
Cope	45	D3
Cope, C	45	D3
Copertino	65	F4
Copparo	61	D2
Corabia	115	D2
Cora Droma Rúisc	12	C3
Corato	65	D3
Coray	22	B3
Corbeil-Essonnes	19	F4
Corbie	19	F2
Corbigny	26	B2
Corbola	61	D2
Corbones, R	43	E2
Corbridge	5	E3
Corby	9	F1
Corcaigh	14	B4
Corcieux	27	E1
Córcoles, R	40	C4
Corconte	35	F2
Corcubión	34	A1
Cordes	29	D3
Córdoba	43	F2
Cordobilla de Lácara	39	D4
Cordobilla, Emb de	43	F3
Corduente	40	C2
Corella	36	C3
Coreses	35	D4
Corfe Castle	9	E3
Corgo	34	B2
Cori	63	F3
Coria	39	D2
Coria del Río	43	D3
Corias	34	C2
Corigliano Calabro	67	F2
Corinaldo	61	E3
Coripe	43	E3
Cork	14	B4
Cork (Co)	14	B4
Corlay	22	C3
Corleone	68	B3
Corleto Perticara	65	D4
Çorlu	115	E3
Cormatin	26	C3
Cormeilles	19	D3
Cormery	25	D2
Cormons	59	F3
Cornago	36	C3
Cornellana	35	D1
Corniche des Cévennes	29	F3
Corniglio	60	B3
Cornimont	27	E1
Cornuda	59	D4
Cornus	29	F3
Cornwall	8	B4
Corps	31	D2
Corraes	34	C3
Corral de Almaguer	40	B3
Corral de Cantos	39	F3
Corralejo	42	C4
Corrales	35	D4
Corran	2	C4
Corraun	12	B2
Corredoiras	34	B2
Correggio	60	C2
Corrèze	29	D1
Corrèze (Dépt)	29	D1
Corrèze R	29	D1
Corrib, L	12	B3
Corridonia	61	F4
Corrofin	12	B4
Corse	33	E2
Corse-du-Sud	33	F3
Corsham	9	D2
Čortanovci	72	C2
Corte	33	F3
Corte de Peleas	39	D4
Cortegada	34	B3
Cortegana	42	C2
Cortemaggiore	60	B2
Cortemilia	31	F2
Corteolona	60	A2
Cortes de Aragón	41	E1
Cortes de Baza	44	B2
Cortes de la Frontera	43	E4
Cortijos Nuevos	44	B2
Cortina d'Ampezzo	59	E3
Čortkov	113	D3
Cortona	61	D4
Coruche	38	B4
Corvara in Badia	59	D3
Corvera	45	D2
Corvera Toranzo	35	F2
Corwen	6	B3
Cosenza	67	E2
Cosham	9	E3
Cosne	26	A2
Cosne-d'Allier	26	A3
Cossato	31	F1
Cossé-le-Vivien	23	E3
Cosson	25	E2
Cossonay	27	D3
Costa Blanca	45	E2
Costa Brava	32	C3
Costa da Caparica	38	A4
Costa del Sol	44	A4
Costa de Santo André	42	A1
Costalunga, Pso di	59	D3
Costa Smeralda	66	B1
Costa Vasca	36	B1
Costa Verde	35	D1
Costigliole d'Asti	31	F2
Coswig (Dresden)	53	E2
Coswig (Halle)	53	D1
Côte-d'Or (Dépt)	26	C2
Côtes-du-Nord	22	C3
Côte-St-André, la	30	C1
Cotignac	31	D4
Cottbus	53	F1
Coubet, Collado de	32	B3
Coubre, Pointe de la	28	A1
Couches	26	B3
Couço	38	B4
Coucy-le-Château-Auffrique	20	A3
Couesnon	23	D3
Couhé	25	D4
Couilly	19	F4
Couiza	32	B2
Coulanges	26	A2
Coulanges-la-Vineuse	26	A2
Coulommiers	19	F4
Coulon	24	C4
Coulonges	24	C3
Coupar Angus	5	D1
Couptrain	18	C4
Courchevel	31	D1
Cour-Cheverny	25	E2
Courçon	24	C4

Courmayeur	27 E4	Crailsheim	55 E2	Creuse (Dépt) 25 E4
Couronne, la	28 C1	Craiova	115 D2	Creußen 53 D4
Courpière	29 F1	Cranborne	9 E3	Creusot, le 26 B3
Cours	26 B4	Crans	27 E3	Creutzwald 21 D3
Coursan	32 B1	Craon	23 E3	Creuzburg 52 B3
Coursegoules	31 E3	Craonne	20 B3	Crevacuore 58 A4
Courseulles	18 C3	Craponne	29 F1	Crevalcore 60 C2
Courson-les-		Crathes Castle	3 E4	Crèvecœur-
Carrières	26 A2	Crati	67 E2	le-Grand 19 E3
Courtenay	26 A1	Crato	38 C3	Crevillente 45 D2
Courthézon	30 C3	Craughwell	12 B4	Crewe 6 C3
Courtine, la	29 E1	Crau, la	31 D4	Crewkerne 9 D3
Courtomer	19 D4	Craven Arms	9 D1	Crianlarich 4 C1
Courtown	15 E3	Crawinkel	52 C3	Criccieth 6 A3
Courtrai	50 A3	Crawley	10 C3	Crickhowell 9 D2
Courville	19 E4	Creag Meagaidh	2 C4	Cricklade 9 E2
Cousin	26 B2	Creagorry	2 A3	Crieff 4 C1
Coussey	20 C4	Crécy	20 A2	Criel 19 E2
Coutainville	18 B3	Crécy-en-		Crikvenica 70 B3
Coutances	18 B3	Ponthieu	19 E3	Crimmitschau 53 D3
Coutras	28 B2	Crécy-la-Chapelle	19 F4	Crinan 4 B2
Couvertoirade, la	29 F3	Crediton	8 C3	Criquetot-
Couvin	50 C4	Creegh	12 B4	l'Esneval 19 D3
Couze	25 E4	Creeslough	12 C1	Crissolo 31 E2
Cova da Iria	38 B3	Creglingen	55 E2	Crişu Alb 112 C4
Covadonga	35 E1	Creil	19 F3	Crişu Negru 112 C4
Covadonga, Pque		Crema	60 B1	Crişu Repede 112 C4
Nac de la Sa de	35 E2	Crémieu	26 C4	Crivitz 48 C2
Covarrubias	36 A3	Cremona	60 B1	Crkvice 76 A2
Coventry	9 E1	Créon	28 B2	Crmljan 76 C2
Covilhã	38 C2	Crepaja	73 D2	Črmošnjice 70 B2
Cowbridge	8 C2	Crépy-en-Valois	19 F3	Črna 70 B1
Cowdenbeath	5 D2	Cres	70 B4	Crna Bara (Srbija) 72 B3
Cowes	9 E3	Cres /	70 B4	Crna Bara
Cowfold	10 C3	Crescentino	31 F1	(Vojvodina) 72 C1
Cozes	28 B1	Crespino	61 D2	Crnac (Hrvatska) 71 E2
Craco	65 D4	Crest	30 C2	Crnac (Srbija) 76 C1
Craigavon	13 E2	Cresta	58 B3	Crna Gora 76 B2
Craigellachie	3 D3	Cresta del Gallo	45 D2	Crna gora 77 E2
Craighouse	4 B2	Créteil	19 F4	Crna reka 77 E4
Craigievar Castle	3 E4	Crêtes, Route des	27 E1	Crna Trava 77 E1
Craignure	4 B1	Creully	18 C3	Crnča 72 B4
Crail	5 D2	Creuse	25 E4	Crni Drim 77 D4

Crni Guber 72 C4	Crotoy, le 19 E2	Cueva de Nerja 44 A4	Cumbres Mayores 42 C1
Crni Lug (Bosna i	Crowborough 10 C3	Cueva Foradada, Emb	Cumbria 5 D4
Hercegovina) 75 D1	Crowland 9 F1	de 41 E1	Cumbrian Mts 5 D4
Crni Lug (Hrvatska) 70 B3	Crowle 7 D2	Cueva, Sa do 35 E1	Cumiana 31 E2
Crni Timok 73 E4	Croyde 8 C3	Cuevas de	Čumić 73 D3
Crni vrh Mt (Bosna	Croydon 9 F2	Altamira 35 F1	Cumnock 4 C3
i Hercegovina) 71 D4	Crozant 25 E4	Cuevas de Artà 45 F3	Cunault 24 C2
Črni vrh Mt	Crozon 22 A3	Cuevas del	Cuneo 31 E2
(Slovenija) 70 B1	Cruden Bay 3 E3	Amanzora 44 C3	Cunlhat 29 F1
Crni vrh Mt	Crudgington 6 C3	Cuevas del	Čunski 70 B4
(Srbija) 76 B1	Crumlin 13 E2	Becerro 43 E3	Cuorgné 31 E1
Črni vrh	Cruseilles 27 D4	Cuevas del Campo 44 B2	Cupar 5 D1
(Slovenija) 70 A2	Crussol 30 B2	Cuevas del Drac 45 F3	Cupello 64 B2
Crnivec 70 B2	Cruz 40 B3	Cuevas del Valle 39 F2	Cupramontana 61 E4
Crnjelovo Donje 72 B3	Cruzamento de	Cuevas de	Čuprija 73 E4
Črnkovci 71 F2	Pegões 38 A4	San Clemente 35 F3	Cure 26 B2
Crno jez 76 B2	Cruz da Légua 38 A3	Cuevas de	Cure, la 27 D3
Črnomelj 70 B3	Cruz de Tejeda 42 B4	San Marcos 43 F3	Curia 38 B1
Croagh Patrick 12 B3	Crven Grm 75 E2	Cuevas de	Currane, L 14 A4
Croce dello Scrivano,	Crvenka 72 B2	Valporquero 35 D2	Curtea de Argeş 115 D1
Pso 64 C4	Crymmych 8 B1	Cuevas de	Curtis 34 B1
Croce Domini,	Csongrád 112 B4	Vinromá 41 F2	Čurug 72 C2
Pso di 58 C4	Csorna 112 A4	Cuglieri 66 A3	C'urupinsk 113 F3
Crocello, Pso di 64 C4	Cuacos 39 E2	Cuijk 17 D3	Cusano Mutri 64 B3
Crocq 25 F4	Cualedro 34 B3	Cuillin Sd 2 B4	Cushendall 13 E1
Croisic, le 24 A2	Cuba 42 B1	Cuillins, The 2 B3	Cushendun 13 E1
Croisière, la 25 E4	Cubel 36 C4	Cuiseaux 26 C3	Cusna, Mte 60 C3
Croix de Fer,	Cucalón, Sa de 41 D1	Cuisery 26 C3	Cusset 26 A4
Col de la 31 D1	Cuckfield 10 C3	Culan 25 F3	Cutro 67 F3
Croix Haute,	Cudillero 35 D1	Culdaff 13 D1	Cuxhaven 47 F2
Col de la 30 C2	Čudovo 111 D1	Culebra, Sa de la 34 C3	Cvikov 53 F3
Croix-Valmer, la 31 D4	Čudskoje Ozero 110 C1	Culemborg 16 C3	Cvrsnica 75 E1
Crolly 12 C1	Cuéllar 35 F4	Cúllar Baza 44 B2	Čvrstec 71 D2
Cromarty 3 D3	Cuenca 40 C3	Cullen 3 E3	Cwmbrân 9 D2
Cromer 7 F3	Cuenca, Serr de 40 C2	Cullera 41 E4	Cybinka 49 F4
Crook 5 E4	Cuenca, Serr de 40 C3	Cullompton 8 C3	Cysoing 20 A1
Croom 14 B3	Cuerda 41 D3	Culoz 27 D4	Czarnków 112 A1
Cross Fell 5 D4	Cuerda del Pozo,	Culross 5 D2	Czersk 110 A4
Cross Hands 8 C2	Emb de la 36 B3		Częstochowa 112 B2
Crosshaven 14 C4	Cuers 31 D4	Cumbernauld 4 C2	Człuchów 112 A1
Crossmaglen 13 D3	Cuerva 40 A3	Cumbre Alta 39 F3	
Crossmolina 12 B2	Cueva de la Pileta 43 E4		
Crotone 67 F3	Cueva de la Vieja 41 D4		

D

Dabar 70 C3	Daimuz 41 E4	Damgan 22 C4	Dasburg 51 D4
Dąbie 49 E2	Dajt, Mal i 76 C4	Damianó 79 F2	Dasing 55 F3
Dabie, Jez 49 E2	Đakovica 76 C2	Dammartin-en-	Dassel 52 B2
Dabilje 77 F3	Đakovo 71 F2	Goële 19 F3	Dassohóri 81 D2
Dabo 21 E4	Đala 72 C1	Damme 17 F2	Dassow 48 B2
Dachau 55 F3	Dalälven 106 A3	Damnjane 76 C2	D'at'kovo 111 F3
Dachsteingruppe 59 F1	Dalane 104 A4	Dampierre 27 D2	Datteln 17 E3
Dačice 57 E1	Dalbeattie 4 C3	Dampierre-sur-	Daugava 110 C3
Dadiá 81 F2	Dalbosjön 105 E4	Salon 27 D2	Daugavpils 110 C3
Dáfnes 86 C1	Dalby 109 D3	Damville 19 E4	Daun 51 E4
Dáfni (Límnos) 85 D1	Dale (Hordaland) 104 A2	Damvillers 20 C3	Dava 3 D3
Dáfni (Makedonía) 80 C4	Dale (Sogn og	Dangé 25 D3	Davat 77 D4
Dáfni	Fjordane) 104 A1	Danilovgrad 76 B2	Davia 87 D2
(Pelopónissos) 86 C1	Dalen 104 B3	Dannemarie 27 E2	Davidovac 73 F2
Dáfni (Stereá	Dalhem 109 F4	Dannenberg 48 B3	Dávlia 83 F4
Eláda) 83 D4	Dalías 44 B4	Dão, R 38 C1	Davor 71 E3
Dafní (Stereá	Daliburgh 2 A3	Daoulas 22 B3	Davos 58 B2
Eláda) 87 F1	Dalj 72 B2	Darda 71 F2	Dawlish 8 C3
Dáfnio 87 D3	Dalkeith 5 D2	Dardesheim 52 C1	Dax 28 A4
Dafnónas	Dalkey 13 E4	Darfo Boario	Deãdnu 95 E2
(Stereá Eláda) 83 D3	Dalmally 4 C1	Terme 58 C4	Deal 11 D3
Dafnónas (Thráki) 80 C2	Dalmellington 4 C3	Dargilan,	Deauville 19 D3
Dafnotí 82 C2	Dalmine 60 B1	Grotte de 29 F3	Deba 36 B1
Dafnoúdi, Akr 82 B4	Dalry 4 C2	Dargun 49 D2	Debar 77 D3
Dagali 104 C2	Dalsbruk 107 D3	Darlington 5 E4	Debarska Banja
Dagebüll 47 F1	Dalsfjorden 104 A1	Darłowo 110 A4	Banjišta 77 D3
Dagenham 10 C2	Dalsjöfors 109 D1	Darmstadt 54 C1	Debeli Lug 73 E3
Dahlen 53 E2	Dals Långed 105 D4	Darney 27 D1	Debeli vrh 70 B2
Dahlenburg 48 B3	Dalton 6 B1	Daroca 36 C4	Debeljača 72 C2
Dahme (D) 48 B2	Daluis, Gorges de 31 E3	Darque 34 A3	Dębica 112 B2
Dahme (DDR) 53 E1	Dalvík 96 B1	Darß 48 C1	De Bilt 16 C3
Dahme R 53 E1	Dalwhinnie 2 C4	Dartford 10 C2	Dęblin 112 C2
Dahn 54 B2	Damaskiniá 79 D3	Dartmoor Nat Pk 8 C3	Dębno 49 F3
Daimiel 40 A4	Damássi 83 E1	Dartmouth 8 C4	Debrc 72 C3
	Damazan 28 C3	Daruvar 71 E2	Debrecen 112 C4
	Damelevières 21 D4	Darwen 6 C2	

Dečani 76 C2	Delianuova 67 E4	Denizli 115 F4
Decazeville 29 E2	Deliblato 73 D2	Denkendorf 55 F2
Děčín 53 F3	Deliblatska	Dennington 11 D1
Decize 26 A3	Peščara 73 D2	Denny 4 C2
Dedemsvaart 17 D2	Deliceto 64 C3	Den Oever 16 C1
Dee (Scotland) 3 D4	Delimedde 76 C1	Dent de Vaulion 27 D3
Dee (Wales/Eng) 6 B3	Delitzsch 53 D2	De Panne 50 A3
Degaña 34 C2	Delle 27 E2	Đeravica 76 C2
Degebe, R 38 B4	Dellen, N 101 F3	Derby 6 C3
Degerfjärden 102 A2	Dellen, S 101 F3	Derbyshire 6 C3
Degerfors 105 E4	Delme 21 D3	Der Chantecoq,
Degerndorf 56 B4	Delmenhorst 47 F3	L du 20 C4
Deggendorf 56 B2	Delnice 70 B3	Đerdap, H.E. 73 F2
Degracias 38 B2	Delsbo 101 F3	Đerdap, Klisura 73 E3
Dego 31 F2	Delta Dunării 113 E4	Derekoy 115 E2
Deià 45 E2	Delvin 13 D3	Derenburg 52 C1
Deidesheim 54 C1	Delvináki 82 B1	Derg, L (Clare) 12 C4
Deinze 50 B3	Demanda, Sa de la 36 B2	Derg, L (Donegal) 12 C2
Deiva Marina 60 B3	Demer 50 C3	Der Grabow 49 D1
Dej 112 C4	Demidov 111 E3	Dermatás, Akr 83 F1
Deje 105 E3	Demirci 115 F4	Dermbach 52 B3
Dejë, Mal 76 C3	Demir Kapija 77 E3	Derneburg 52 B1
De Koog 16 C1	Demmin 49 D2	Derravaragh, L 13 D3
Delčevo 77 F2	Demoiselles,	Derrynasaggart
Delden 17 D2	Grotte des 29 F3	Mts 14 B4
Deleitosa 39 E3	Demonía 87 E4	Derryveagh Mts 12 C1
Delémont 27 E2	Denain 20 A1	Deruta 63 E1
Deléria 83 E1	Denbigh 6 B3	Dervaig 4 B1
Delet Teili 106 C3	Den Burg 16 C1	Derval 23 D4
Delfi 83 E4	Dendermonde 50 B3	Dervéni 87 D1
Delft 16 B3	Dendre 50 B4	Derventa 71 E3
Delfzijl 47 D3	Dendrohóri 79 D3	Derviziana 82 B2
Delia 68 C4	Denekamp 17 E2	Derwent (Derbys) 6 C3
	Denia 45 E1	Derwent (Durham) 5 E4
		Derwent (Yorks) 7 D1
		Derwent Water 5 D4

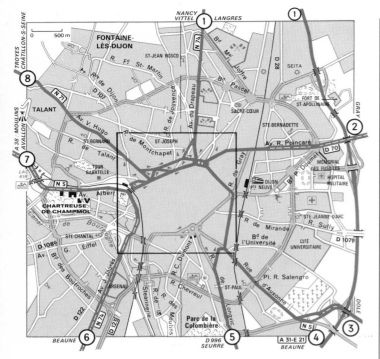

Dijon

Name	Page	Grid
Desborough	9	F1
Descartes	25	D3
Desenzano	60	B1
Desertas	42	A3
Desfiladero de Despeñaperros	44	A1
Desfiladero de la Hermida	35	F2
Desfiladero de los Beyos	35	E2
Desfiladero del Teverga	35	D2
Desfina	83	E4
Desimirovac	73	D4
Desio	60	A1
Deskáti	83	D1
Desna	111	F3
Despotikó, N	88	B3
Despotovac	73	E3
Despotovo	72	B2
Dessau	53	D1
Destriana	35	D3
Desulo	66	B3
Desvres	19	E1
Deta	114	C1
Detinja	72	C4
Detmold	52	A1
Dettelbach	55	E1
Dettifoss	96	C1
Deurne	17	D3
Deutsche Alpenstraße	55	E4
Deutsche Bucht	47	E2
Deutschkreutz	57	F3
Deutschlandsberg	70	B1
Deutsch-Wagram	57	F2
Deux-Alpes, les	31	D2
Deux-Sèvres	24	C3
Deva	114	C1
Deve Bair	77	E2
Deventer	17	D2
Deveron	3	E3
Devetak	72	B4
Devil's Bridge	8	C1
Devil's Elbow	3	D2
Devizes	9	E2
Devnja	115	E2
Dewsbury	6	C2
Deza	36	C4
Diablerets, les	27	E3
Diablerets, les Mt	27	E3
Diafáni	93	D2
Diakoftó	86	C1
Diamante	67	E2
Día, N	91	E3
Diano Marina	31	F3
Diápora Nissiá	87	E1
Diavatá	79	F3
Díavlos Aloníssou	84	B2
Díavlos Oreón	83	F3
Díavlos Pelagoníssou	84	B2
Díavlos Skiáthou	84	A2
Díavlos Skopélou	84	A2
Díavlos Trikeríou	83	F3
Díavlos Zákinthou	86	A1
Diavolítsi	86	C3
Diavolo, Pso del	64	A2
Diavolórema	81	E2
Dibbersen	48	A3
Dicmo	75	D1
Dicomano	61	D3
Dídima	87	E2
Dídimo, Óros	87	E2
Didimótiho	81	F1
Die	30	C2
Dieburg	52	A4
Diedorf	52	B2
Diego Alvaro	39	E2
Diekirch	21	D2
Diemel	52	A2
Diemelstadt	52	A2
Dieppe	19	E2
Dierdorf	51	E4
Dieren	17	D3
Diesdorf	48	B4
Dießen	56	A3
Diest	50	C3
Dietenheim	55	E3
Dietfurt	55	F2
Dietikon	27	F2
Dietmannsried	55	E4
Dieulefit	30	C2
Dieulouard	21	D4
Dieuze	21	D4
Diez	51	F4
Diezma	44	A3
Differdange	21	D3
Digerkampen	100	B3
Digermulen	94	A4
Dignano	59	E3
Digne	31	D3
Digoin	26	B3
Dijle	50	C3
Dijon	26	C2
Dikanäs	97	F3
Díkea	81	F1
Dikela	81	E2
Diksmuide	50	A3
Diktéo Ándro	91	E4
Diktinéon	90	B3
Díkti, Óros	91	E4
Dílessi	84	B4
Dilináta	82	B4
Dilj	71	E2
Dillenburg	51	F3
Dillingen (Bayern)	55	E2
Dillingen (Saarland)	54	A2
Dílofos	81	F1
Dílos	88	C2
Dílos, N	88	C2
Dímena	87	E2
Dímitra	83	E1
Dimitrítsi	80	B2
Dimitrovgrad (BG)	115	D3
Dimitrovgrad (YU)	77	F1
Dimitsána	86	C2
Dinami	67	E4
Dinan	18	B4
Dinant	50	C4
Dinar	115	F4
Dinara Mt	75	D1
Dinara (Reg)	75	D1
Dinard	18	B4
Dinbych	6	B3
Dinbych-y-pysgod	8	B2
Dingelstädt	52	B2
Dingle	14	A3
Dingle	105	D4
Dingle (Reg)	14	A3
Dingle B	14	A3
Dingli	68	B4
Dinglingen	54	C3
Dingolfing	56	B2
Dingwall	2	C3
Dinjiška	70	C4
Dinkelsbühl	55	E2
Dinklage	17	F2
Dinslaken	17	D3
Diónissos	87	F1
Dióriga Korínthou	87	E1
Dipótama	80	C1
Dippoldiswalde	53	E2
Diráhio	86	C3
Dírfis, Óros	84	B3
Disentis	58	A3
Díe, la	27	D3
Disgrazia, Mte	58	B3
Dispílio	79	D3
Diss	11	D1
Dissen	17	F2
Dístomo	83	E4
Dístos	84	B4
Ditikí Rodópi	80	C1
Dittaino	69	D3
Ditzingen	55	D2
Divača	70	A3
Divaráta	82	B4
Divčibare	72	C4
Dives	18	C3
Dives R	18	C3
Divič	72	B4
Divjakë	76	C4
Divljana	77	E1
Divonne	27	D3
Divor, Bgem do	38	B4
Divor, Rib de	38	B4
Divoúnia, Ni	92	C2
Divri	83	E1
Divuša	71	D3
Djupini	96	A3
Djupvik	94	C2
Djurås	105	F2
Djursland	108	B2
Dmitrov	111	F2
Dnepr	111	E3
Dneprodzeržinskoje Vodochranilišče	113	F2
Dneprovskij Liman	113	F3
Dnestr	112	C3
Dnestrovskij Liman	113	F4
Dno	111	D2
Dobanovci	72	C3
Dobbiaco	59	E2
Dobel	54	C2
Dobele	110	C3
Döbeln	53	E2
Doberlug-Kirchhain	53	E1
Döbern	53	E1
Dobersberg	57	E1
Dobieszczyn	49	E2
Doboj	71	F3
Dobošnica	71	F3
Dobra (PL)	49	F2
Dobra (YU)	73	E3
Dobra R	70	C3
Dobra Voda	73	D4
Dobra Voda Mt	77	D3
Dobrašinci	77	F3
Dobratsch	59	F2
Dobrčane	77	D2
Döbriach	59	F2
Dobrica	73	D2
Dobričevo	73	D2
Dobri Do	77	D1
Dobrinj	70	B3
Dobříš	53	F4
Dobrljin	71	D3
Dobrna	70	B1
Dobromani	75	F2
Dobro Polje	76	A1
Dobrovnik	70	C1
Dobrun	72	C4
Dobruš	111	E4
Dobruševo	77	E4
Dobrzany	49	F2
Dobšiná	112	B3
Docksta	102	A2
Doc Penfro	8	B2
Dodekánissa	89	E3
Dodóni	82	B1
Doesburg	17	D3
Doetinchem	17	D3
Doganović	77	D2
Dogliani	31	F2
Doïráni	79	F2
Doïránis, L	79	F2
Doiras, Emb de	34	C1
Dojransko Ez	77	F3
Dokanj	72	B3
Dokka	104	C2
Dokkum	47	D3
Dokós, N	87	E3
Doksy	53	F3
Dolac	76	C2
Dol-de-Bretagne	18	B4
Dole	26	C2
Dôle, la	27	D3
Dolenci	77	D4
Dolenja Vas	70	B2
Dolenjske Toplice	70	B2
Dolga Vas	71	D1
Dolgellau	6	A3
Doliana	78	C4
Dolianova	66	B4
Dolíhi	79	E4
Dolina	112	C3
Doljani	71	D4
Ðorđe Petrov	77	D3
Doljevac	77	D1
Dolla	12	C4
Döllach	59	E2
Dollar	5	D2
Dolle	48	C4
Dolní Dvořiště	57	D2
Dolno Kosovrasti	77	D3
Dolo	61	D1
Dolomiti	59	D3
Dolores	45	D2
Dolovo	73	D2
Dol Poustevna	53	E2
Domaševo	75	F2
Domažlice	56	B1
Dombås	100	B3
Dombóvár	114	B1
Dombasle	21	D4
Domburg	16	B3
Domène	30	C1
Doméniko	83	E1
Domèvre-en-Haye	21	D4
Domfront	18	C4
Dömitz	48	C3
Domme	29	D2
Dommltzsch	53	D2
Domnísta	83	D3
Domodossola	58	A4
Domokós	83	E2
Dompaire	27	D1
Dompierre	26	B3
Domrémy	20	C4
Domusnovas	66	B4
Domžale	70	B2
Don (England)	7	D2
Don (Scotland)	3	E3
Donaghadee	13	E2
Doña María Ocaña	44	B3
Doña Mencía	43	F2
Doñana, Parque Nac de	43	D3
Donau	56	C2
Donaueschingen	54	C4
Donauwörth	55	E2
Donawitz	57	E4
Don Benito	39	E4
Doncaster	7	D2
Donegal	12	C2
Donegal B	12	C2
Donegal (Co)	12	C1
Dongen	16	C3
Donges	23	D4
Donington	7	E3
Donja Bebrina	71	F3
Donja Brela	75	E2
Donja Brezna	76	B2
Donja Bukovica	76	B2
Donja Kamenica	72	C3
Donja Šatornja	73	D3
Donje Crniljevo	72	C3
Donje Dragovlje	77	E1
Donje Ljupče	77	D2
Donji Andrijevci	71	F3
Donji Barbeš	77	E1
Donji Kanzanci	75	D1
Donji Lapac	71	D4
Donji Malovan	75	E1
Donji Miholjac	71	E2
Donji Milanovac	73	E3
Donji Ruzani	75	D1
Donji Seget	75	D2
Donji Vakuf	71	E3
Donji Vijačani	71	E3
Donji Zemunik	74	C1
Donjon, le	26	B3
Donnemarie-Dontilly	20	A4
Donnersbachwald	57	D4
Dønnes	97	D2
Donon	21	E4
Donon, Col du	21	E4
Donostia-San Sebastián	36	C1
Donoússa, N	89	D3
Donzenac	29	D2
Donzère	30	B2
Donzy	26	A2
Doorn	16	C3
Doornik	50	A4
Dora Baltéa	27	E4
Dora Riparia	31	E1
Dorat, le	25	D4
Dordives	25	F1
Dordogne	29	E1
Dordogne (Dépt)	28	C2
Dordogne R	28	B2
Dordrecht	16	C3
Dore	29	F1
Dorfen	56	B3
Dorfmark	48	A4
Dorgali	66	C2
Dória	86	C3
Dório	86	C3
Dorkáda	80	B2
Dorking	10	C3
Dormagen	17	E4
Dormans	20	A3
Dornbirn	58	B2
Dornburg	52	C3
Dorndorf	52	B3
Dornes	26	A3
Dornie	2	B3
Dornoch	3	D3
Dornoch Firth	3	D3
Dornstetten	54	C3
Dornum	47	E3
Dorog	112	B4
Dorogobuž	111	E3
Dorohoi	113	D3
Dorotea	101	F1
Dörpstedt	48	A1
Dorset	9	D3
Dorsten	17	E3
Dortan	27	D3
Dortmund	17	E3
Dortmund-Ems-Kanal	17	E2
Dorum	47	F3
Dörzbach	55	D1
Dosbarrios	40	B3
Dos Hermanas	43	D3
Dosse	49	D3
Douai	19	F2
Douarnenez	22	A3
Doubs	26	C3
Doubs (Dépt)	27	D2
Doucier	27	D2
Doudeville	19	D2
Doué	24	C2
Douglas (I of Man)	6	A1
Douglas (Scotland)	4	C2
Doukáto, Akr	82	B3
Doulaincourt	20	C4
Doullens	19	F2
Doulus Head	14	A4
Doune	4	C2
Doupov	53	E3
Dourdan	19	E4
Dourgne	32	A1
Douro	34	A4
Douro, R	34	A4
Douvaine	27	D3
Douve	18	B3
Douvres	18	C3
Dover	11	D3
Dover, Str of	11	D3
Dovre	100	C3
Dovrefjell	100	C3
Dovsk	111	E4
Down	13	E2
Downham Market	10	C1
Downpatrick	13	E2
Dowra	12	C2
Doxarás	83	E2
Doxáto	80	C2
Dozulé	19	D3
Drac	30	C2
Dračevo	77	E3
Drachten	17	D1
Drag	94	A4
Dragalovci	71	E3
Dragaš	77	D3
Drăgăşani	115	D1
Dragaši	76	B1
Draginac	72	C3
Draginje	72	C3
Dragocvet	73	D4
Dragoevo	77	E3
Dragoman	114	C2
Dragonera, I	45	E3
Dragoni	64	B3
Dragør	108	C3
Dragoš	77	E4
Dragotiná	82	A2
Dragović	71	E2
Dragovića Polje	76	B2
Dragozetići	70	B3
Dragsfjärd	107	D3
Dragsvik	100	A3
Draguignan	31	D4
Dráma	80	C2
Dráma (Nomos)	80	C1
Drammen	104	C3
Drammen selva	104	C3
Drangajökull	96	A1
Drangedal	104	C3
Dranske	49	D1
Drápano, Akr	90	C3
Drasenhofen	57	F1
Drau	59	F2
Dráva	71	E2
Dravograd	70	B1
Drawno	49	F2
Drawsko Pomorskie	112	A1
Draženov	56	B1
Draževac	72	C3
Drebkau	53	F1
Drenewydd	9	D1
Drenovac	77	E1
Drenovci	72	B3
Drenovo	77	E3
Drenthe	17	D1
Drépano (Makedonía)	79	E3
Drépano (Pelopónnisos)	87	E2
Drépano, Akr (Anáfi)	91	E1
Drépano, Akr (Makedonía)	80	B4
Dresden	53	E2
Dreux	19	E4
Drežnik-Grad	70	C3
Driebergen	16	C3
Driebes	40	B2
Driméa	83	E3
Drimós	79	F3
Drin	76	C3
Drina	76	A1
Drini i Zi	77	D3
Drinit, Gjiri i	76	B3
Drinjača	72	B4
Drinjača R	72	B4
Drinovci	75	E2
Driopída	88	A2
Driós	88	C3
Drisht	76	C3
Driva	100	B2
Drlače	72	C4
Drnholec	57	F1
Drniš	75	D1
Drnje	71	D1
Drnovo	70	C2
Drøbak	105	D3
Drobeta-Turnu Severin	114	C1
Drochtersen	48	A2
Drogheda	13	D3
Drogobyč	112	C3
Droichead Átha	13	D3
Droichead Nua	13	D3
Droitwich	9	E1
Drokija	113	E3
Dromcolliher	14	B3
Dromore (Down)	13	E2
Dromore (Tyrone)	13	D2
Drôme (Dépt)	30	C2
Drôme R	30	C2
Dronero	31	E2
Dronfield	7	D2
Drongaráti	82	B4
Dronne	28	C1
Dronninglund	108	B2
Dronten	16	C2
Drosendorf Stadt	57	E1
Drossáto	79	F2
Drosseró	79	E2
Drossiá	84	A4
Drossohóri	84	E4
Drossopigí (Árta)	82	C2
Drossopigí (Ioánina)	78	C4
Drossopigí (Makedonía)	79	D3
Drottningholm	106	B4
Droué	25	E1
Drulingen	21	E3

Map: **DUBLIN / BAILE ÁTHA CLIATH**

Scale 1/120 000

Drumkeeran	12 C2	Dubrave Donje	72 B3	Dulovo	115 E2
Drummore	4 B4	Dubravica	73 D3	Dumbarton	4 C2
Drumnadrochit	2 C3	Dubrovnik	76 A2	Dumbria	34 A1
Drumochter,		Ducey	18 B4	Dumfries	4 C3
Pass of	2 C4	Ducherow	49 E2	Dumfries and	
Drumshanbo	12 C2	Duchkov	53 E3	Galloway	4 C3
Drusenheim	21 F4	Duchovščina	111 E3	Dun	20 C3
Druskininkai	110 C4	Duclair	19 D3	Dunaföldvár	112 B4
Druten	16 C3	Dudelange	21 D3	Dunajevcy	113 D3
Drvenik (Hrvatska)	75 D2	Duderstadt	52 B2	Dunárea	113 E4
Drvenik (Hrvatska)	75 E2	Dudley	9 E1	Dunaújváros	112 B4
Dryburgh	5 D3	Dudweiler	54 B2	Dunav	72 B2
Drymen	4 C2	Dueñas	35 E4	Dunav	114 D2
Duben	53 E1	Duero, R	35 D4	Dunbar	5 E2
Dubí	53 E3	Duesund	104 A1	Dunblane	4 C2
Dubica	71 D3	Dufftown	3 D3	Duncansby Head	3 E2
Dublin	13 E4	Duga Poljana	76 C1	Dundalk	13 D3
Dublin (Co)	13 D4	Duga Resa	70 C3	Dundalk B	13 E3
Dubna	111 F2	Dugi Otok	74 C1	Dun Dealgan	13 D3
Dubňany	57 F1	Dugi Rat	75 D2	Dundee	5 D1
Dubno	113 D2	Dugo Selo	70 C2	Dundonnell	2 C3
Dubona	73 D3	Duingt	27 D4	Dundrum B	13 E2
Dubossary	113 E3	Duino	59 F3	Dunfanaghy	12 C1
Duboštica	71 F4	Duisburg	17 D3	Dunfermline	5 D2
Dubovac	73 D2	Dukagjin	76 C2	Dungannon	13 D2
Dubovsko	71 D4	Dukat	77 E2	Dún Garbhán	14 C4
Dubrava		Duleek	13 D3	Dungarvan	14 C4
(Hrvatska)	71 D2	Dulje	77 D2	Dungarvan	
Dubrava (Pelješac)	75 F2	Dülken	17 D4	Harbour	14 C4
Dubrava Stara	71 E3	Dülmen	17 E3	Dungeness	11 D3
Dubrave	71 F3	Dulnain Bridge	3 D4	Dungiven	13 D1

Map: **Düsseldorf**

Dunglow 12 C1
Dunje 77 E4
Dunkeld 5 D1
Dunkerque 19 F1
Dún Laoghaire 13 E4
Dun-le-Palestel 25 E4
Dunmanus B 14 A4
Dunmanway 14 B4
Dunmore 12 B3
Dunmore East 15 D4
Dunnamanagh 13 D1

Dún na nGall 12 C2
Dunnet 3 D2
Dunnet Head 3 D2
Dunoon 4 C2
Duns 5 E2
Dunshaughlin 13 D3
Dunstable 9 F4
Dunster 8 C3
Dun-sur-Auron 25 F3
Dunvegan 2 B3
Dunvegan Head 2 B3

Duolbbadasgai'sa 95 E1
Đurakovac 76 C4
Durance 30 C3
Durango 36 B1
Duran, Pso 59 D3
Duras 28 C2
Duratón, R 40 A1
Durban-Corbières 32 B2
Durbuy 50 C4
Dúrcal 44 A3
Đurđevac 71 D2

Đurđevića Tara 76 B1
Durdevik 72 B4
Düren 51 D3
Durham 5 E4
Durham (Co) 5 E4
Durlach 54 C2
Durlas 14 C3
Durmanec 70 C2
Durmitor 76 B2
Durness 2 C2
Dürnkrut 57 F2

Dürnstein 57 E2
Durrës 76 C4
Durrësit, Gjiri i 76 C4
Durrow 12 C4
Dursey I 14 A4
Dursley 9 D2
Durtal 23 E4
Duruelo de la
  Sierra 36 B3
Dusina 75 F1
Düsseldorf 17 E4

Duved 101 D2
Duvno 75 E1
Duži (Bosna
  i Hercegovina) 75 F2
Duži (Bosna
  i Hercegovina) 76 A2
Dverberg 94 A3
Dvor 71 D3
Dyfed 8 C1
Dyje 57 E1
Dyrnes 100 B1

Dyrøya 94 B3
Džami tepe 77 F3
Džaniči 75 F1
Džep 77 E1
Dzermiádo 91 E4
Dzeržinsk 111 E4
Dzierżoniów 112 A3
Dziwnów 49 F1
Džumajlija 77 E1
Dźwirzyno 49 F1

E

Eaglescliffe 5 E4
Eaní 79 D4
Earith 10 C1
Earlston 5 D2
Earn 5 D1
Easingwold 7 D1
Easky 12 B2
Eastbourne 10 C3
East Dereham 7 F3
Easter Ross 2 C3
East Grinstead 10 C3
East Kilbride 4 C2
Eastleigh 9 E3
East Linton 5 D2
East Retford 7 D2
East Sussex 10 C3
Eaux-Bonnes 37 D2
Eauze 28 B3
Ebbw Vale 9 D2
Ebeleben 52 C2
Ebeltoft 108 B3
Eben 59 F1
Ebenfurth 57 F3
Ebensee 56 C3

Eberbach 55 D1
Ebermannstadt 52 C4
Ebern 52 C4
Eberndorf 70 B1
Ebersbach 53 F2
Ebersberg 56 B3
Eberstein 70 B1
Eberswalde 49 E3
Ebmath 53 D3
Eboli 64 C4
Ebrach 52 C4
Ebreichsdorf 57 F3
Ebreuil 26 A4
Ebro, Emb del 35 F2
Ebro, R 37 D4
Ebstorf 48 B3
Eceabat 115 E3
Echallens 27 D3
Echarmeaux, les 26 B4
Echarri-Aranaz 36 C2
Echegárate,
  Pto de 36 B1
Echelles, les 30 C1
Echt 17 D4
Echte 52 B2

Echternach 21 D2
Écija 43 E2
Ečka 72 C2
Eckartsberga 52 C2
Eckernförde 48 A1
Eckerö 106 C3
Ecommoy 23 F4
Ecos 19 E3
Ecouché 18 C4
Ecrins, les 31 D2
Ecrins, Massif des 31 D2
Ecrins,
  Parc Nat des 31 D2
Ecueillé 25 E3
Ed 105 D4
Eda glasbruk 105 D3
Edam 16 C2
Edane 105 E3
Eday 3 E1
Eddrachillis B 2 C1
Ede 16 C3
Edelény 112 B3
Edelweißspitze 59 E2
Eden 5 D4
Edenderry 13 D4
Edenkoben 54 C2

Eder 52 A3
Eder-Stausee 52 A3
Édessa 79 E3
Edewecht 47 E3
Edgeworthstown 12 C3
Edinburgh 5 D2
Edipsós 83 F3
Edirne 115 E3
Edland 104 B3
Edolo 58 C3
Edremit 115 E4
Edsåsdalen 101 D2
Edsbro 106 B3
Edsbyn 101 E4
Edsele 101 F2
Eeklo 50 B3
Eelde 47 D3
Eemshaven 47 D3
Eferding 56 C2
Efes 115 E4
Efira 86 B1
Efkarpía
  (Makedonía) 79 F2
Efkarpía
  (Makedonía) 80 B2
Eforie 115 E1

Efxinoúpoli 83 F2
Egadi, Is 68 A3
Ega, R 36 C2
Egeln 52 C1
Egéo Pélagos 84 A1
Eger 112 B3
Egersund 104 A4
Egeskov 108 B4
Egestorf 48 A3
Egg 58 B1
Eggenburg 57 E2
Eggenfelden 56 B2
Eggesin 49 E2
Eggum 94 A3
Eghezée 50 C4
Egiáli 89 D3
Egie 87 D4
Egilsstadir 96 C2
Égina 87 E2
Égina, N 87 F2
Eginio 79 F3
Égio 83 E4
Égira 87 D1
Egletons 29 D1
Eglinton 13 D1
Egloffstein 55 F1
Egmond aan Zee 16 C2
Egósthena 87 E1
Egremont 5 D4
Egtved 108 A3
Egués 36 C2
Eguzon 25 E3
Ehinádes Nissiá 82 C4
Ehingen 55 D3
Ehinos 81 D2
Ehra-Lessien 48 B4
Ehrang-Pfalzel 54 A1
Ehrenberg 52 B3
Ehrenhausen 70 C1
Ehrwald 58 C1
Eibar 36 B1
Eibenstock 53 D3
Eibiswald 70 B1
Eichstätt 55 F2
Eide 100 B2
Eider 48 A2
Eidfjord 104 B2
Eidfjorden 104 B2
Eidi 96 A3
Eidkjosen 94 B2
Eidsborg 104 B3
Eidsbugarden 100 B3
Eidsdal 100 B2
Eidsfjorden 94 A3
Eidsfoss 104 C3
Eidsvåg 100 B2
Eidsvoll 105 D2
Eigg 2 B4
Eikelandsosen 104 A2
Eikeren 104 B4
Eikeren 104 C3
Eikesdal 100 B2
Eilean Donan Castle 2 B3
Eilenburg 53 D2
Eilsleben 52 C1
Einbeck 52 B2
Eindhoven 16 C4
Einsiedeln 58 A2
Eisenach 52 B3
Eisenberg 53 D3
Eisenerz 57 D3
Eisenerzer Alpen 57 D4

Eisenhüttenstadt 49 F4
Eisenkappel 70 A1
Eisenstadt 57 F3
Eisfeld 52 C3
Eisleben 52 C2
Eislingen 55 D2
Eisriesenwelt-
  Höhle 59 E1
Eitorf 51 E3
Eivissa 45 D4
Ejea de los
  Caballeros 37 D3
Ejulve 41 E2
Ekára 83 E2
Ekenäs 107 E3
Ekshärad 105 E3
Eksjö 109 D1
Elafohóri 81 F1
Elafónissi 87 E4
Élafos 82 B2
El Algar 45 D2
El Almendro 42 C2
El Aquián 44 B4
El Arahal 43 E3
El Arenal 45 E3
Elassóna 83 E1
El Atazar, Emb de 40 B1
Eláti (Makedonía) 79 E4
Eláti (Thessalía) 83 D2
Eláti Mt 82 B3
Elátia 83 F3
Elatohóri 79 E3
Elatoú 83 D4
Elatóvrissi 83 D3
Elba, Isola d' 62 C2
El Barco de Ávila 39 E2
Elbasan 76 C4
Elbe-Lübeck-Kanal 48 B2
El Berrón 35 D1
Elbe-Seitenkanal 48 B4
Elbeuf 19 D3
Elbigenalp 58 C2
Elbingerode 52 C2
Elblag 110 B4
El Bodón 39 D2
El Bonillo 40 C4
El Bosque 43 E3
Elburg 17 D2
El Burgo 43 E3
El Burgo de Osma 36 A3
El Burgo Ranero 35 E3
El Cabaco 39 D2
El Caló 45 D4
El Campo de
  Peñaranda 39 F1
El Carpio 43 F2
El Carpio de Tajo 39 F3
El Casar de
  Talamanca 40 B2
El Castillo de las
  Guardas 43 D2
El Centenillo 44 A1
El Cerro de
  Andévalo 42 C2
Elche 45 D2
Elche de la Sierra 44 C2
El Coronil 43 D3
El Cubillo 41 D3
El Cubo de
  Don Sancho 39 D1

El Cubo de Tierra del
  Vino 39 E1
El Cuervo 43 D3
Elda 45 D1
Elde 48 C3
Eldena 48 C3
Elefsína 87 F1
Eleftherés
  (Makedonía) 80 C2
Eleftherés
  (Stereá Eláda) 87 E1
Eleftherés
  (Thessalía) 83 E1
Eléftheró 78 C4
Eleftheróhori 79 D4
Eleftheroúpoli 80 C2
El Ejido 44 B4
Elemir 72 C2
Elena 115 D2
Eleófito 82 C3
Eleohóri 80 C3
Eleohória 80 A3
Eleónas 83 E4
Eleoússa 93 F1
El Escorial 40 A2
El Espinar 40 A2
El Figueró 32 B4
El Formigal 37 D2
Elgå 100 D3
Elgin 3 D3
Elgóibar 36 B1
Elgol 2 B4
El Grado 37 E3
El Grado, Emb de 37 E3
El Grao 41 E4
El Grau 41 F3
Elhovo 115 E2
El Hoyo de Pinares 40 A2
Eliá 87 D4
Elie 5 D2
Elikónas, Óros 83 F4
Elimäki 107 F2
Eliniko 86 C2
Elinohóri 81 F1
Elizondo 36 C1
Ełk 110 C4
Ellesmere 6 B3
Ellesmere Port 6 B2
Ellingen 55 E2
Ellon 3 E4
Ellös 108 C1
Ellrich 52 B2
Ellwangen 55 E2
El Madroño 42 C2
El Maestrazgo 41 E2
Elmas 66 B4
El Masnou 32 B4
El Molar 40 B2
El Molinillo 40 A3
El Moral 44 C2
Elmshorn 48 A2
Elne 32 B2
Elnesvågen 100 B2
Elóna 87 D3
Elopía 83 F4
Elorn 22 B3
Élos (Kríti) 90 B3
Élos
  (Pelopónissos) 87 D4
Eloúnda 91 E3
Eloyes 27 D1
El Pardo 40 A2

El Paular	40	A1	Ems-Jade-Kanal	47	E3	Eppingen	55	D2	
El Pedernoso	40	B3	Emskirchen	55	E1	Epsom	10	C3	
El Pedroso	43	D2	Enafors	101	D2	Eptahóri	78	C4	
El Perelló (Catalunya)	41	F2	Enäjärvi	103	E4	Eptálofos	83	E3	
El Perelló (Valencia)	41	E4	Enånger	101	F4	Epte	19	E3	
Elphin	12	C3	Encamp	32	A2	Epworth	7	D2	
El Picazo	40	C4	Encausse	37	E1	Eraclea	59	E4	
El Pinell de Brai	41	F1	Encinas de Abajo	39	E1	Eraclea-Mare	59	E4	
El Pobo de Dueñas	41	D2	Encinasola	42	C1	Eräjärvi	103	D3	
El Pont d'Armentera	37	F4	Encinedo	34	C3	Erásmio, N.	81	D2	
El Portal	43	D4	Endelave	108	B3	Eratiní	83	E4	
El Port de la Selva	32	C3	Endrinal	39	E2	Eratinó	80	C2	
El Port de Llança	32	B3	Enego	59	D3	Erátira	79	D3	
El Prat de Llobregat	32	A4	Enfesta	34	A2	Erba	58	B4	
El Puente	36	A1	Eng	59	D1	Erbach	55	D1	
El Puente del Arzobispo	39	F3	Engadin	58	B3	Erbalunga	33	F2	
El Puerto de Sagunto	41	E3	Engarés	88	C3	Erbendorf	53	D4	
El Puerto de Santa María	43	D4	Engelberg	27	F3	Ercina, L de la	35	E2	
El Real de la Jara	43	D2	Engelhartszell	56	C2	Ercolano	64	B4	
El Real de San Vicente	39	F2	Engeln	97	E1	Érd	112	B4	
El Remolcador, Pto	41	E3	Engelsdorf	53	D2	Erdek	115	E3	
El Robledo	39	F4	Engelskirchen	17	E4	Erdevik	72	B2	
El Rocío	42	C3	Engen	58	A1	Erding	56	A3	
El Romeral	40	B3	Enger	17	F2	Erdut	72	B2	
El Rompido	42	C3	Engerdal	101	D3	Eresma, R	40	A1	
El Ronquillo	43	D2	Enghien	50	B3	Eressós	85	E2	
El Royo	36	B3	England	9	F1	Erétria	84	B4	
El Rubio	43	E3	English Channel	10	A4	Erezée	50	C4	
Elsa	60	C4	Engstingen	55	D3	Erfde	48	A2	
El Saler	41	E4	Enguera	41	E4	Erft	17	D4	
El Salobral	40	C4	Enguidanos	41	D3	Erftstadt	51	E3	
El Saucejo	43	E3	Enhammarsfjärden	101	F4	Erfurt	52	C3	
Elsdorf	17	D4	Enipéas	83	E2	Erges, R	39	D2	
Elserdorf	55	F2	Enkhuizen	16	C2	Ergolsbach	56	B2	
El Serrat	32	A2	Enköping	106	B3	Eriboll, L	2	C2	
Elsfleth	47	F3	Enna	68	C3	Erice	68	A3	
Elsterberg	53	D3	Enneberg	59	D2	Ericeira	38	A3	
Elsterwerda	53	E2	Ennell, L	12	C3	Ericht, L	2	C4	
El Tiemblo	40	A2	Ennepetal	17	E4	Erikoússa, N	78	A4	
Eltisley	9	F1	Ennezat	26	A4	Eriksberg	106	A4	
Eltmann	52	C4	Ennis	12	B4	Eriksmåle	109	E2	
El Toboso	40	B3	Enniscorthy	15	D3	Erillas	43	E1	
El Torcal	43	F3	Enniskerry	13	D4	Erimanthos	86	C2	
Eltz	51	E4	Enniskillen	13	D2	Erímanthos, Óros	86	C1	
El Vado, Emb de	40	B1	Ennistimon	12	B4	Eripol, Pto del	37	E3	
Elvanfoot	4	C3	Enns	57	D3	Erithrés	87	E1	
Elvas	38	C4	Enns R	57	D3	Erkelenz	17	D4	
Elvekrok	100	B3	Eno	103	F2	Erkner	49	E4	
El Vellón, Emb de	40	A2	Enol, L	35	E2	Erla	37	D3	
Elven	22	C4	Enonkoski	103	F3	Erlangen	55	F1	
El Vendrell	37	E4	Enontekiö	95	D3	Erlsbach	59	E2	
Elverum	105	D2	Énos, Óros	86	A1	Ermenonville	19	F3	
El Vicario, Emb de	40	A4	Enschede	17	E2	Ermidas-Aldeia	42	A1	
El Villar de Arnedo	36	C2	Ensisheim	27	E1	Ermióni	87	E2	
El Viso	43	E1	Entlebuch	27	F2	Ermoúpoli	88	B2	
El Viso del Alcor	43	D2	Entraygues-sur-Truyère	29	E2	Ermsleben	52	C2	
Elx	45	D2	Entredichos	40	C3	Erndtebrück	17	F4	
Ely	10	C1	Entre-os-Rios	34	A4	Erne	13	D3	
Elygsfors	109	E2	Entrepeñas, Emb de	40	C2	Ernée	23	E3	
Elzach	54	C3	Entrevaux	31	E3	Erne, R	12	C3	
Elze	52	B1	Entrèves	27	E4	Ernestinovo	71	F2	
Emån	109	E2	Entroncamento	38	B3	Ernstbrunn	57	F2	
Embessós	82	C3	Envalira, Pto de	32	A2	Erquy	22	C2	
Embid	41	D1	Envermeu	19	E2	Errazu	36	C1	
Embid de Ariza	36	C4	Enviken	101	E4	Errigal Mt	12	C1	
Émbonas	93	E1	Enz	54	C2	Erris Head	12	A2	
Emboriós (Híos)	89	D1	Enza	60	B2	Erskine Bridge	4	C2	
Emboriós (Sími)	93	E1	Enzklösterle	54	C2	Erstein	21	E4	
Embrun	31	D2	Eochaill	14	C4	Ervenik	75	D1	
Emden	47	E3	Eolie o Lipari, Is	69	D2	Ervidel	42	B1	
Emet	115	F4	Eo, R	34	C1	Ervy	26	B1	
Emilia-Romagna	60	C3	Epanomí	79	F3	Erwitte	17	F3	
Emlichheim	17	E2	Epe	17	D2	Erzberg	57	D3	
Emmaboda	109	E2	Epernay	20	B3	Erzen	76	C4	
Emmeloord	16	C2	Epernon	19	E4	Erzgebirge	53	E2	
Emmen	17	E1	Epidávrou, Kólpos	87	E2	Esbjerg	108	A3	
Emmendingen	54	C3	Epidávrou Limirás, Kólpos	87	E4	Esblada	37	F4	
Emmerich	17	D3	Épila	36	C3	Esbo	107	E3	
Emocriós	89	F3	Epinac	26	B3	Escabas, R	40	C2	
Em. Papás	80	B2	Epinal	27	D1	Escairón	34	B2	
Empoli	60	C4	Epine, l'	20	B3	Escalada	35	F2	
Empúries	32	C3	Episkopí (Kríti)	90	C3	Escalante	36	A1	
Ems	17	E1	Episkopí (Kríti)	91	E3	Escaldes, les	32	A2	
Emsdetten	17	E2	Episkopí (Makedonía)	79	E3	Escalona	40	A2	
			Episkopí (Pelopónnissos)	87	E3	Escalonilla	40	A3	
			Epitálio	86	B2	Escalos de Cima	38	C2	
			Eppan	59	D3	Escandón, Pto de	41	D2	
			Epping	10	C2	Esca, R	37	D2	
						Escarène, l'	31	E3	
						Escároz	37	D2	
						Escatrón	37	D4	
						Escaut (B)	50	B3	
						Escaut (F)	20	A2	

Essen

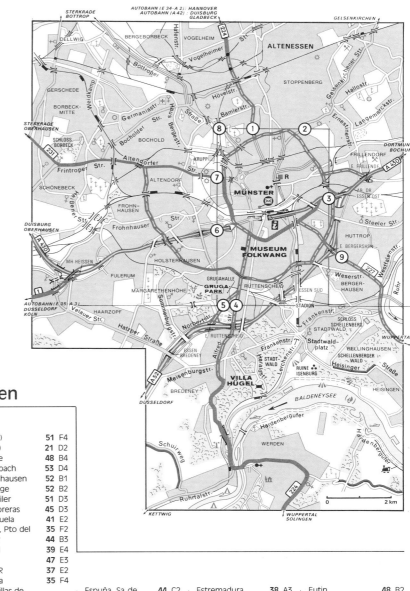

Esch (D)	51	F4	Esguevillas de Esgueva	35	F4
Esch (L)	21	D2	Esher	9	F2
Eschede	48	B4	Esino	61	E4
Eschenbach	53	D4	Esk	5	D3
Eschershausen	52	B1	Eskifjörður	96	C2
Eschwege	52	B2	Eskilstuna	106	A4
Eschweiler	51	D3	Eskisehir	115	E3
Escombreras	45	D3	Eskoriatza	36	B1
Escorihuela	41	E2	Esla, R	35	D4
Escudo, Pto del	35	F2	Eslarn	56	B1
Escúllar	44	B3	Eslohe	17	F4
Escurial	39	E4	Eslöv	109	D3
Esens	47	E3	Espa	105	D2
Esera, R	37	E2	Espadañedo	34	C3
Esgueva	35	F4	Espadán, Sa de	41	E3
			Espalion	29	E3
			Esparreguera	32	A4
			Espedal	100	C3
			Espejo	43	F2
			Espelette	28	A4
			Espelkamp	17	F2
			Espenschied	51	F4
			Espera	43	D3
			Esperó, Pta	45	F2
			Espichel, C	38	A4
			Espiel	43	E1
			Espigüete	35	E2
			Espinama	35	E2
			Espinosa de Cerrato	35	F4
			Espinosa de los Monteros	36	A1
			Espoo	107	E3
			Esporles	45	E3
			Esposende	34	A4
			Espot	37	F2

Espuña, Sa de	44	C2	Estremadura	38	A3	Eutin	48	B2			
Esquedas	37	D3	Estremoz	38	C4	Evangelismós	83	E1			
Esquivias	40	A2	Estret de Collegats	37	F3	Evangelístria	83	E4			
Esher	9	F2	Estrées-St-Denis	19	F3	Evaux-les-Bains	25	F4			
Esino	61	E4	Esztergom	112	B4	Évdilos	89	D2			
Esk	5	D3	Etables	22	C2	Evendorf	48	B3			
Esse	102	C1	Etain	20	C3	Evenes	94	B3			
Essen (Niedersachsen)	17	E2	Etampes	19	F4	Evenskjær	94	B3			
Essen (Nordrhein-Westfalen)	17	E3	Etaples	19	E1	Evergem	50	B3			
Essenbach	56	B2	Etel	22	B4	Everöd	109	D3			
Essex	11	D2	Etelhem	109	F4	Evertsberg	101	E4			
Essími	81	E2	Etive, L	4	B1	Evesham	9	E1			
Esslingen	55	D2	Etna, M	69	D3	Evian	27	D3			
Essonne	25	F1	Etne	104	A3	Évia, N	84	B3			
Essoyes	26	B1	Etolia-Akarnanía	82	C3	Evijärvi	102	C2			
Est, Canal de l'	27	D1	Etolikó	82	C4	Evinohóri	83	D4			
Estaca, Pto de la	42	A4	Etrépagny	19	E3	Évinos	83	D3			
Estacas de Trueba, Pto de las	35	F2	Etretat	19	D2	Evisa	33	F3			
Estadilla	37	E3	Ettelbruck	21	D2	Evje	104	B4			
Estagel	32	B2	Etten	16	C3	Évlalo	81	D2			
Estaires	19	F1	Ettenheim	54	C3	Evolène	27	E4			
Estarreja	38	B1	Ettington	9	E1	Évora	38	B4			
Estats, Pic d'	37	F2	Ettlingen	54	C2	Évoramonte	38	B4			
Estavayer	27	E3	Eugénie-les-Bains	28	B4	Evran	18	B4			
Este	61	D1	Eume, Emb del	34	B1	Evrecy	18	C3			
Estella	36	C2	Eume, R	34	B1	Evreux	19	E3			
Estepa	43	E3	Eupen	51	D4	Evritania	82	C3			
Estepona	43	E4	Eura	107	D2	Evron	23	E3			
Esteras de Medina	36	B4	Eurajoki	107	D2	Evropós	79	F2			
Esterel	31	E4	Euratsfeld	57	D3	Évros R	81	F2			
Esternay	20	A4	Eure	19	E4	Evrostina	87	D1			
Esterri d'Àneu	37	F2	Eure (Dépt)	19	E3	Evrótas	87	D3			
Estissac	26	B1	Eure-et-Loir	25	E1	Évzoni	79	F2			
Estói	42	B3	Europabrücke	59	D2	Exaplátanos	79	E2			
Estonija	110	C2	Europoort	16	B3	Éxarhos	83	E4			
Estoril	38	A4	Eußenhausen	52	B3	Excideuil	29	D1			
Estrela, Sa da	38	C2	Euskadi	36	B2	Exe	8	C3			
Estrella	44	A1	Euskirchen	51	E3						

Exeter	8 C3	Exohí (Ípiros)	78 C4	Exter	17 F2	Eyemouth	5 E2	Eygurande	29 E1	Eyre	28 B3	Ezcaray	36 B2
Exmes	19 D4	Exohí (Makedonía)	79 E3	Extremadura	39 E4	Eye Pen	2 B2	Eyjafjördur	96 A1	Eyrieux	30 B2	Eze	31 E3
Exmoor Nat Pk	8 C3	Exohí (Makedonía)	80 B1	Eydehavn	104 E4	Eygues	30 C2	Eymet	28 C2	Eysturoy	96 A3	Ezine	115 E4
Exmouth	8 C3	Exómvourgo	88 C2	Eye	9 F1	Eyguières	30 C4	Eymoutiers	29 D1	Eyzies, les	29 D2		

F

Faak	59 F2	Falces	36 C2	Fanári, Akr	89 D2	Fårösund	109 F3
Fabara	37 E4	Falconara Marittima	61 F3	Fanefjord	108 C4	Farra d'Alpago	59 E3
Fåberg	105 D2	Falcone	69 D2	Fani i Madh	76 C3	Fársala	83 E2
Fabero	34 C2	Falcone, C del	66 A1	Fani i Vogël	76 C3	Farsø	108 A2
Fåborg	108 B4	Falerna	67 E3	Fanjeaux	32 A1	Farsund	104 A4
Fabriano	61 E4	Faliráki	93 F1	Fannich, L	2 C3	Farum	108 C3
Fábricas de Riópar	44 C1	Falkefjellet	95 F1	Fano	61 E3	Fasano	65 E3
Fabro	63 D1	Falkenberg (D)	53 E2	Fanø	108 A3	Fašku Vaskojoki	95 E3
Facinas	43 D4	Falkenberg (S)	108 C2	Fanø Bugt	108 A3	Fastov	113 E2
Facture	28 A2	Falkensee	49 D4	Fanós	79 F2	Fátima	38 B3
Faenza	61 D3	Falkenstein	53 D3	Faouët, le	22 B3	Fatmomakke	97 E4
Færøerne	96 A3	Falkirk	4 C2	Faou, le	22 B3	Faucille, Col de la	27 D3
Faeto	64 B3	Falkland	5 D2	Farángi Samariás	90 B4	Faucogney	27 D1
Fafe	34 A4	Falkonéra, N	87 F3	Farángi Víkou	78 C4	Faulquemont	21 D3
Fågåras	113 D4	Falköping	109 D1	Fara Novarese	58 A4	Fauquembergues	19 E1
Fågårasului, M	113 D4	Fallersleben	48 B4	Fårbo	109 E2	Fauske	97 F2
Fågelfors	109 E2	Fällfors	98 B4	Fardes, R	44 A3	Fauville	19 D3
Fagernes (Oppland)	104 C2	Fallingbostel	48 A4	Fareham	9 E3	Favara	68 C4
Fagernes (Troms)	94 C2	Falmouth	8 B4	Fårevejle	108 B3	Favareta	41 E4
Fagersta	105 F3	Falset	37 F4	Färgelanda	105 D4	Faverges	27 D4
Fairford	9 E2	Falster	108 C4	Färila	101 F3	Faverney	27 D1
Fair Head	13 E1	Falterona Mte	61 D3	Faringdon	9 E2	Faversham	11 D3
Fair I	3 F3	Fålticeni	113 D3	Farini d'Olmo	60 B2	Favignana, I	68 A3
Fakenham	7 E3	Falun	105 F2	Färjestaden	109 E2	Fawley	9 E3
Fakovići	72 C4	Falzarego, Pso	59 D3	Farkadóna	83 E1	Faxaflói	96 A2
Fakse	108 C4	Fámjin	96 A4	Farkaždin	72 C2	Fayence	31 D4
Fakse Ladeplads	108 C4	Fanad Head	13 D1	Farlete	37 D3	Fayl-Billot	26 C1
Falaise	18 C4	Fanári (Pelopónissos)	87 E2	Farmakoníssi	89 F2	Fayón	37 E4
Falakró, Óros	80 C1	Fanári (Pelopónissos)	86 C2	Farnborough	9 F3	Fay-sur-Lignon	30 B2
Falássarna	90 B3	Fanári (Thessalía)	83 D2	Farnese	63 D2	Fažana	70 A4
Falcade	59 D3	Fanári (Thráki)	81 D2	Farnham	9 F3	Feale	14 B3
				Faro	42 B3	Fécamp	19 D2
				Fårö	109 F3	Féclaz, la	31 D1

Feda	104 B4	Fervenza, Emb de	34 A1	Finnøy	104 A3
Feggesund	108 A2	Festós	91 D4	Finnsnes	94 B3
Fehmarn	48 B1	Festre, Col du	30 C2	Finow	49 E3
Fehmarnbelt	48 B1	Festvåg	97 E1	Finowfurt	49 E3
Fehmarnsund	48 B1	Fethard	14 C3	Finskij Zaliv	110 C1
Fehrbellin	49 D3	Fetlar	3 F1	Finspång	105 F4
Fehring	57 F4	Fetsund	105 D3	Finsteraarhorn	27 F3
Fejø	108 B4	Feucht	55 F1	Finsterau	56 C2
Feketić	72 B2	Feuchtwangen	55 E2	Finsterwalde	53 E1
Felanitx	45 F3	Feunte Dé	35 E2	Finström	106 C3
Felbertauern-tunnel	59 E2	Feurs	26 B4	Fintona	13 D2
Feld	59 F2	Feyzin	30 B1	Fintown	12 C1
Feldafing	56 A3	Ffestiniog	6 A3	Fionnphort	4 A1
Feldbach	57 F4	Fflint	6 B2	Fiorenzuola d'Arda	60 B2
Feldberg (D)	54 C4	Fiano R.	63 E2	Firenze	60 C3
Feldberg (DDR)	49 D3	Fiastra	61 F4	Firenzuola	61 D3
Feldkirch	58 B2	Ficarolo	60 C2	Firminy	30 B1
Feldkirchen	59 F2	Fichtel-gebirge	53 D4	Firmo	67 E2
Felgueiras	34 A4	Fidenza	60 B2	Fischamend Markt	57 F2
Felixstowe	11 D2	Fieberbrunn	59 E1	Fischbach	55 F1
Fellbach	55 D2	Fier	114 B3	Fischbeck	48 C4
Felletin	25 F4	Fiera di Primiero	59 D3	Fischen	55 E4
Fellingsbro	105 F3	Fierzës, Liq i	76 C3	Fishbourne	9 E3
Felton	5 E3	Fiesole	61 D3	Fishguard	8 B1
Feltre	59 D3	Fife	5 D2	Fiskárdo	82 B4
Femer Bælt	108 B4	Fife Ness	5 D1	Fiskari	107 E3
Femundsmarka	101 D3	Figália	86 B3	Fiskebøl	94 A3
Fene	34 B1	Figeac	29 E2	Fismes	20 A3
Fener	59 D3	Figline Valdarno	61 D4	Fissíni	85 D1
Fenestrelle	31 E1	Figueira da Foz	38 B2	Fisterra	34 A2
Fénétrange	21 E3	Figueira de Castelo Rodrigo	39 D1	Fitero	36 C3
Feolin Ferry	4 B2	Figueiró dos Vinhos	38 B2	Fities	82 C3
Fer à Cheval, Cirque du	27 E4	Figueras	32 B3	Fitjar	104 A2
Feraklós	93 F2	Figueres	32 B3	Fiuggi	63 F3
Ferbane	12 C4	Figueruela de Arriba	34 C3	Fiumicino	63 E3
Ferdinandovac	71 D1	Fíhtio	87 D2	Fivemiletown	13 D2
Ferdinandshof	49 E2	Filabres, Sa de los	44 B3	Fivizzano	60 B3
Fère-Champenoise	20 B4	Filadélfi	80 B3	Fjällåsen	94 C4
Fère-en-Tardenois	20 A3	Filadelfia	67 F3	Fjällbacka	105 D4
Fère, la	20 A2	Filáki	83 E2	Fjällnäs	101 D2
Ferentino	63 F3	Filákio	81 F1	Fjärdhundra	106 B3
Féres	81 F2	Filakopí	88 A4	Fjærland	100 A3
Feria	43 D1	Filérimos	93 F1	Fjätervålen	101 D3
Feričanci	71 E2	Filey	7 E1	Fjelie	108 C3
Ferlach	70 A1	Filfola	68 B4	Fjellerup	108 B2
Fermanagh	12 C2	Fili	87 F1	Fjerritslev	108 A2
Fermo	61 F4	Fília (Lésvos)	85 F2	Fjerze	76 C3
Fermoselle	34 C4	Fília (Pelopónissos)	86 C1	Flå	104 C2
Fermoy	14 C4	Filiátes	82 B1	Fladså	108 A3
Fernancaballero	40 A4	Filiatrá	86 B3	Fladungen	52 B3
Fernán Núñez	43 F2	Filicudi, I	68 C2	Flaine	27 E4
Ferney-Voltaire	27 D4	Filiourí	81 E2	Flakk	100 C2
Fernpaß	58 C1	Filipi	80 C2	Flåm	104 B2
Ferrandina	65 D4	Filipiáda	82 C2	Flamborough Head	7 E1
Ferrara	61 D2	Filipjakov	74 C1	Flambourári	82 C1
Ferreira	34 C1	Filipos, Akr	88 B3	Flámbouro (Makedonía)	79 D3
Ferreira do Alentejo	42 B1	Filipstad	105 E3	Flámbouro (Makedonía)	80 B2
Ferreira do Zêzere	38 B3	Fílira	81 E2	Flamignano	63 F2
Ferreiras	42 A3	Fillan	100 C1	Flamouriá	79 E3
Ferreras de Abajo	35 D3	Fille-fjell	104 B1	Flannan I	2 A2
Ferreries	45 F2	Filo	83 E2	Flåsjön	101 F1
Ferreruela de Huerva	41 D1	Filótas	79 D3	Flåten	94 C2
Ferret, Cap	28 A2	Filottrano	61 F4	Flatey	96 A1
Ferrette	27 E2	Finale Emilia	60 C2	Flatråker	104 A2
Ferriere	60 B2	Finale Ligure	31 F3	Flattnitz	59 F2
Ferrières	25 F1	Fiñana	44 B3	Flatval	100 C1
Ferrol	34 B1	Finca de la Concepción	43 F3	Flèche, la	23 E4
Ferru, M	66 B3	Finchingfield	11 D2	Fleetwood	6 B1
Ferté-Alais, la	19 f4	Findhorn	3 D3	Flekkefjord	104 A4
Ferté-Bernard, la	23 F3	Fínikas	88 B2	Flen	106 A4
Ferté-Frênel, la	19 D4	Finikoúndas	86 C4	Flensborg Fjord	108 A3
Ferté-Gaucher, la	20 A4	Finistère	22 B3	Flensburg	48 A1
Ferté-Macé, la	18 C4	Finisterre, Emb de	40 A3	Flers	18 C4
Ferté-Milon, la	20 A3	Finja	109 D3	Flesberg	104 C3
Ferté-St-Aubin, la	25 E2	Finn	13 D1	Flesnes	94 A3
Ferté-sous-Jouarre, la	20 A3	Finneidfjord	97 E2	Fleurance	28 C4
Ferté-Vidame, la	19 D4	Finnentrop	17 F4	Fleurier	27 D3
Fertilia	66 A2	Finnmark	95 D2	Fleurus	50 C4
		Finnmark	95 E1	Fleury	19 F4
		Finnmarksvidda	95 D3	Fleury-sur-Andelle	19 E3
				Fléves, N	87 F2

FIRENZE
PIANTA D'INSIEME

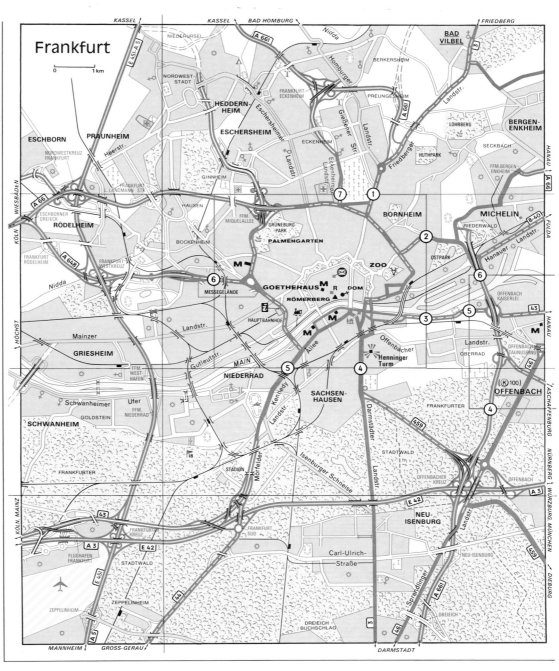

Frankfurt

Flevoland	16 C2	Fonollosa	32 A4		
Flexenpaß	58 B2	Fonsagrada	34 C2		
Flims Waldhaus	58 B2	Fontaine	27 E1		
Flint	6 B2	Fontainebleau	19 F4		
Flisa	105 D2	Fontaine-de-Vaucluse	30 C3		
Flix	37 E4	Fontaine-Française	26 C2		
Flixecourt	19 F2	Fontaine-Henry	18 C3		
Flize	20 C2	Fontaine-le-Dun	19 D2		
Floda	105 F2	Fontanigorda	60 A3		
Flogny	26 B1	Fonte Longa	34 B4		
Flöha	53 E3	Fontenay	26 B2		
Flomohóri	87 D4	Fontenay-le-Comte	24 C3		
Flora	77 F3	Fontenay-Trésigny	19 F4		
Florac	29 F3	Fontevraud-l'Abbaye	25 D2		
Flor da Rosa	38 C3	Fontfroide, Abbaye de	32 B2		
Florennes	50 C4	Fontgombault	25 D3		
Florensac	30 A4	Fontibre	35 F2		
Florenville	20 C2	Fontiveros	39 F1		
Florešty	113 E3	Fontoy	21 D3		
Floriáda	82 C2	Font-Romeu	32 A2		
Floridia	69 D4	Fontvieille	30 B4		
Flórina	79 D2	Fonz	37 E3		
Flórina (Nomos)	79 D3	Fonzaso	59 D3		
Florø	104 A1	Foppolo	58 B3		
Flörsheim-Dalsheim	54 C1	Forata, Emb de	41 E4		
Flötningen	101 D3	Forbach	21 E3		
Floúda, Akr	92 C1	Forca Canapine	63 F1		
Floúnda	91 E3	Forca Caruso	64 A2		
Flüelapass	58 B2	Forca d'Acero	64 A2		
Flüelen	58 A2	Forcall	41 E2		
Flühli	27 F3	Forcalquier	30 C3		
Flumendosa	66 C3	Forcarei	34 A2		
Flumen, R	37 D3	Forchheim	55 F1		
Flumet	27 D4	Forclaz, Col de la	27 E4		
Fluminimaggiore	66 A4	Forcola di Mte Rest	59 E3		
Flums	58 B2	Førde	100 A3		
Fluvià, R	32 B3	Førdefjorden	104 A1		
Foča	76 A1	Förderstedt	52 C1		
Foça	115 E4	Fordingbridge	9 E3		
Foce Verde	63 F3	Fordongianus	66 B3		
Fochabers	3 D3	Foreland	9 F3		
Fockbek	48 A2	Forenza	64 C3		
Focşani	113 E4	Foresta di Burgos	66 B2		
Fódele	91 D3	Føresvik	104 A3		
Foggia	64 C3	Forêt d'Orient, Lac de la	26 B1		
Föglö	106 C3	Forez, Monts du	29 F1		
Fohnsdorf	57 D4	Forfar	5 D1		
Föhr	47 F1	Forges-les-Eaux	19 E3		
Foiano della Chiana	61 D4	Forggensee	55 F4		
Foinaven	2 C2	Forio	64 A4		
Foix	32 A2	Forli	61 D3		
Fojnica (Bosna i Hercegovina)	75 F1	Forli del Sannio	64 A2		
Fojnica (Bosna i Hercegovina)	75 F2	Forlimpopoli	61 D3		
Foki	83 E4	Formazza	58 A3		
Fokstuhø	100 C3	Formby	6 B2		
Folda	97 E1	Formentera	45 D4		
Foldereid	97 D4	Formentor, C	45 F2		
Foldfjorden	97 D4	Formerie	19 E3		
Foleá	80 C2	Formia	64 A3		
Folégandros	91 D1	Formigine	60 C2		
Folégandros, N	91 D1	Fornaci di Barga	60 C3		
Følen	104 A3	Fornells	45 F1		
Folgaria	59 D4	Forni Avoltri	59 E2		
Folgefonna	104 B2	Forni di Sopra	59 E3		
Folgoët, le	22 A2	Forno di Zoldo	59 E3		
Folgoso de la Ribera	35 D2	Fornos de Algodres	38 C1		
Foligno	63 E1	Fornovo di Taro	60 B2		
Folkestad	100 A3	Forøy	97 E2		
Folkestone	11 D3	Forøyar	96 A3		
Follafoss	101 D1	Forres	3 D3		
Folldal	100 C3	Forsa	101 F3		
Follebu	104 C1	Forserum	109 D1		
Follina	59 E3	Forshaga	105 E3		
Föllinge	101 E1	Forsnes	100 B1		
Follonica	62 C1	Forssa	107 E2		
Folmava	56 B1	Forst	53 F1		
Folói	86 C2	Fort Augustus	2 C4		
Fombellida	35 F4	Forte dei Marmi	60 B3		
Fond-de-France, le	31 D1	Forth	55 F1		
Fondevila	34 B3	Forth R	4 C2		
Fondi	63 F3	Forth Bridges	5 D2		
Fondo	59 D3	Forth, Firth of	5 D2		
Fonfría (Aragón)	37 D4	Fort-Mahon	19 E2		
Fonfría (Castilla-León)	35 D4	Fortore	64 B2		
Fongen	101 D2	Fortrose	3 D3		
Fonn	100 A3				
Fonni	66 B3				

Fortuna	45 D2	Fourmies	20 B2	Frammersbach	52 B4	Fränk Rezat	55 E2	Fregene	63 E3		
Fortuneswell	9 D4	Fourná	83 D3	Fræna	100 B2	Fränk Saale	52 B4	Fréhel, Cap	22 C2		
Fort William	2 C4	Fournels	29 F2	Francavilla al Mare	64 A1	Františkovy Lázně	53 D4	Frei	100 B2		
Forvik	97 D3	Fournés	90 B3	Francavilla di Sicilia	69 D3	Franzburg	49 D1	Freiberg	53 E3		
Fos (Ariège)	37 F2	Foúrni (Dodekánissa)	89 E2	Francavilla Fontana	65 E4	Franz-Josephs-Höhe	59 E2	Freiberger Mulde	53 D2		
Fos (Bouches-du-Rhône)	30 C4	Fourní (Kríti)	91 E3	Francavilla in Sinni	65 D4	Frascati	63 E3	Freiburg (Baden-Württemberg)	54 C4		
Foscagno, Pso di	58 C3	Foúrni (Pelopónissos)	87 E2	Francker	16 C1	Frascineto	67 E2	Freiburg (Niedersachsen)	48 A2		
Fosnavåg	100 A2	Fourniá, Akr	85 E2	Francofonte	69 D4	Frasdorf	56 B3	Freienhufen	53 E1		
Fossacesia	64 B2	Foúrni, N	89 E2	Francolí, R	37 F4	Fraserburgh	3 E3	Freilassing	56 C3		
Fossano	31 E2	Fours	26 B3	Francorchamps	51 D4	Frasno, Pto del	36 C4	Freilingen	51 F4		
Fossat, le	37 F1	Fousseret, le	37 F1	Frändefors	105 D4	Fratel	38 C3	Freising	55 F3		
Fossbakken	94 B3	Foústani	79 E2	Frangádes	82 C1	Fratta Polesine	61 D2	Freistadt	57 D2		
Fosses	50 C4	Fowey	8 B4	Frangísta	83 D3	Frauenfeld	58 A1	Freital	53 E2		
Fossli	104 B2	Foxford	12 B3	Frangokástelo	90 B3	Frauenkirchen	57 F3	Freiwalde	53 E1		
Fossombrone	61 E3	Foyers	2 C4	Frangy	27 D4	Frauenstein	53 E3	Freixedas	38 C1		
Fotiná	79 E4	Foyle, L	13 D1	Frankenberg (D)	52 A3	Frechen	17 E4	Freixido	34 C3		
Fotolivos	80 B2	Foyle, R	13 D1	Frankenberg (DDR)	53 E3	Frechilla	35 E3	Freixo de Espada à Cinta	39 D1		
Fouesnant	22 B3	Foz	34 C1	Frankenburg	56 C3	Freckenhorst	17 F3	Fréjus	31 D4		
Foug	21 D4	Foz do Arelho	38 A3	Frankenmarkt	56 C3	Fredensborg	108 C3	Fréjus, Tunnel du	31 D1		
Fougères	23 D3	Foz do Douro	34 A4	Frankenstein	54 C1	Fredericia	108 B3	Frêne, Col du	31 D1		
Fougerolles	27 D1	Foz Giraldo	38 C2	Frankenthal	54 C1	Frederikshavn	108 B1	Freren	17 E2		
Foula	3 E2	Frabosa Soprana	31 F3	Frankfurt am Main	52 A4	Frederikssund	108 C3	Freshford	12 C4		
Foulness Pt	11 D2	Fraddon	8 B4	Frankfurt an der Oder	49 F4	Frederiksværk	108 C3	Freshwater	9 E3		
Fountains Abbey	6 C1	Fraga	37 E4			Fredrika	102 A1	Fresnay-sur-Sarthe	23 F3		
Fouras	24 B4	Frailes	44 A3			Fredrikshamn	105 E3				
Fourchamboult	26 A2	Fraize	27 E1			Fredrikstad	105 D3				
Fourfourás	91 D4	Fram	70 C1	Frankfurt an der Oder	49 F4	Fregenal de la Sierra	42 C1				
Foúrka	83 E3										

Fresne-St-Mamès 27 D2
Fresnes-en-Woëvre 20 C3
Fresno Alhándiga 39 E1
Fresvikbreen 104 B1
Freudenberg (Baden-Württemberg) 55 D1
Freudenberg (Nord-rhein-Westfalen) 17 F4
Freudenstadt 54 C3
Frévent 19 F2
Freyburg 52 C2
Freyenstein 48 C3
Freyung 56 C2
Frí 93 D3
Frias 36 A2
Frías de Albarracín 41 D2
Fribourg 27 E3
Fridingen 55 D3
Friedberg (A) 57 F3
Friedberg (Bayern) 55 F3
Friedberg (Hessen) 52 A4
Friedeburg 47 E3
Friedersdorf 49 E4
Friedland (D) 52 B2
Friedland (DDR) 49 D2
Friedrichroda 52 B3
Friedrichshafen 55 D4
Friedrichskoog 47 F2
Friedrichsort 48 A1
Friedrichstadt 47 F1
Friedrichsthal 54 B2
Friesach 57 D4
Friesack 49 D4
Friesland 16 C1
Friesoythe 17 E1
Frigiliana 44 A4
Frihetsli 94 c3
Friis veien 100 C3
Frikes 82 B4
Frilingiánika 90 A1
Frinton-on-Sea 11 D2
Friol 34 B2
Fristad 109 D1
Fritsla 108 C1
Fritzlar 52 A3
Friuli-Venezia Giulia 59 E3
Frizington 5 D4
Frodsham 6 B2
Frogner 105 D3
Frohavet 100 C1
Frohburg 53 D2
Frohnleiten 57 E4
Froissy 19 F3
Froitzheim 51 D3
Frome 9 D3
Fromentine 24 A3
Frómista 35 F3
Fronteira 38 C4
Frontenay-Rohan-Rohan 24 C4
Frontenhausen 56 B2
Frontera 42 A4
Frontignan 30 A4
Fronton 29 D3
Frosinone 63 F3
Frosolone 64 B3
Frösön 101 E2
Frosta 100 C1
Frostavallen 109 D3
Frøstrup 108 A2
Frouard 21 D4
Froússa 82 C2
Frövi 105 F3
Frøya 100 B1
Frøyfjorden 100 B1
Frøysjøen 100 A3
Fruges 19 F1
Fruška 72 b2
Frutigen 27 E3
Frýdek-Místek 112 B3
Fteliá 80 C2
Ftéri (Makedonía) 79 E4
Ftéri (Pelopónissos) 86 C1
Fthiótida 83 E3
Fucecchio 60 C4
Fuencaliente (Castilla-la-Mancha) 43 F1
Fuencaliente (Is Canarias) 42 A4
Fuendejalón 36 C3
Fuendetodos 37 D4
Fuengirola 43 F4
Fuenlabrada 40 A2
Fuenlabrada de los Montes 39 F4
Fuenmayor 36 B2
Fuensalida 40 A3
Fuensanta de Martos 43 F2
Fuensanta, Emb de la 44 C1
Fuente-Alamo 45 D1
Fuente Alamo 45 D2
Fuentecén 35 F4
Fuente de Cantos 43 D1
Fuente del Maestre 43 D1
Fuente de Pedro Naharro 40 B3
Fuente de Piedra 43 E3
Fuente el Fresno 40 A4
Fuenteguinaldo 39 D2
Fuente la Higuera 45 D1
Fuentelapeña 39 E1
Fuente Obéjuna 43 E1
Fuente Palmera 43 E2
Fuentepinilla 36 B3
Fuentesauco 39 E1
Fuentes de Andalucía 43 E2
Fuentes de Ayódar 41 E3
Fuentes de Ebro 37 D4
Fuentes de León 43 D1
Fuentes de Nava 35 E3
Fuentes de Oñoro 39 D1
Fuentes de Ropel 35 D3
Fuentes de Valdepero 35 F3
Fuentidueña 35 F4
Fuentidueña de Tajo 40 B3
Fuerte del Rey 44 A2
Fuerteventura 42 C4
Fügen 59 D1
Fuglebjerg 108 B4
Fugløysundet 94 C2
Fulda 52 B3
Fulda R 52 B3
Fulgatore 68 A3
Fulpmes 59 D2
Fulufjället 101 D4
Fumay 20 B2
Fumel 28 C3
Funäsdalen 101 D2
Funchal 42 A3
Fundão 38 C2
Funes 59 D2
Fuorn, Pso dal 58 C3
Furadouro 38 B1
Furci 64 B2
Furkapass 58 A3
Furnace 4 B2
Furnás 45 D3
Fürstenau 17 E2
Fürstenberg 49 D3
Fürstenfeld 57 F4
Fürstenfeldbruck 55 F3
Fürstenlager 54 C1
Fürstenwalde 49 E4
Fürstenwerder 49 E3
Fürstenzell 56 C2
Furtei 66 B3
Fürth 55 E1
Furth 56 B1
Furtwangen 54 C3
Furudal 101 E4
Furuflaten 94 C2
Fuscaldo 67 E2
Fusch 59 E1
Fuschl 56 C3
Fuseta 42 B3
Fushë Arrez 76 C3
Fushë Muhur 76 C3
Fusignano 61 D2
Füssen 55 E4
Fustiñana 36 C3
Futa, Pso della 60 C3
Futog 72 C2
Futrikelv 94 B2
Fyn 108 B4
Fyne, L 4 B2
Fynshav 108 B4
Fyresdal 104 B3
Fyresvatn 104 B3
Fyrkat 108 B2

G

Gaaldorf 57 D4
Gabarret 28 B3
Gabela 75 F2
Gaberl-Sattel 57 E4
Gabia la Grande 44 A3
Gabicce Mare 61 E3
Gabriel y Galán, Emb de 39 E2
Gabrovka 70 B2
Gabrovo 115 D2
Gacé 19 D4
Gacilly, la 23 D4
Gacko 76 A2
Gad'ač 113 F1
Gäddede 97 E4
Gadebusch 48 B2
Gádor 44 B3
Gádor, Sa de 44 B3

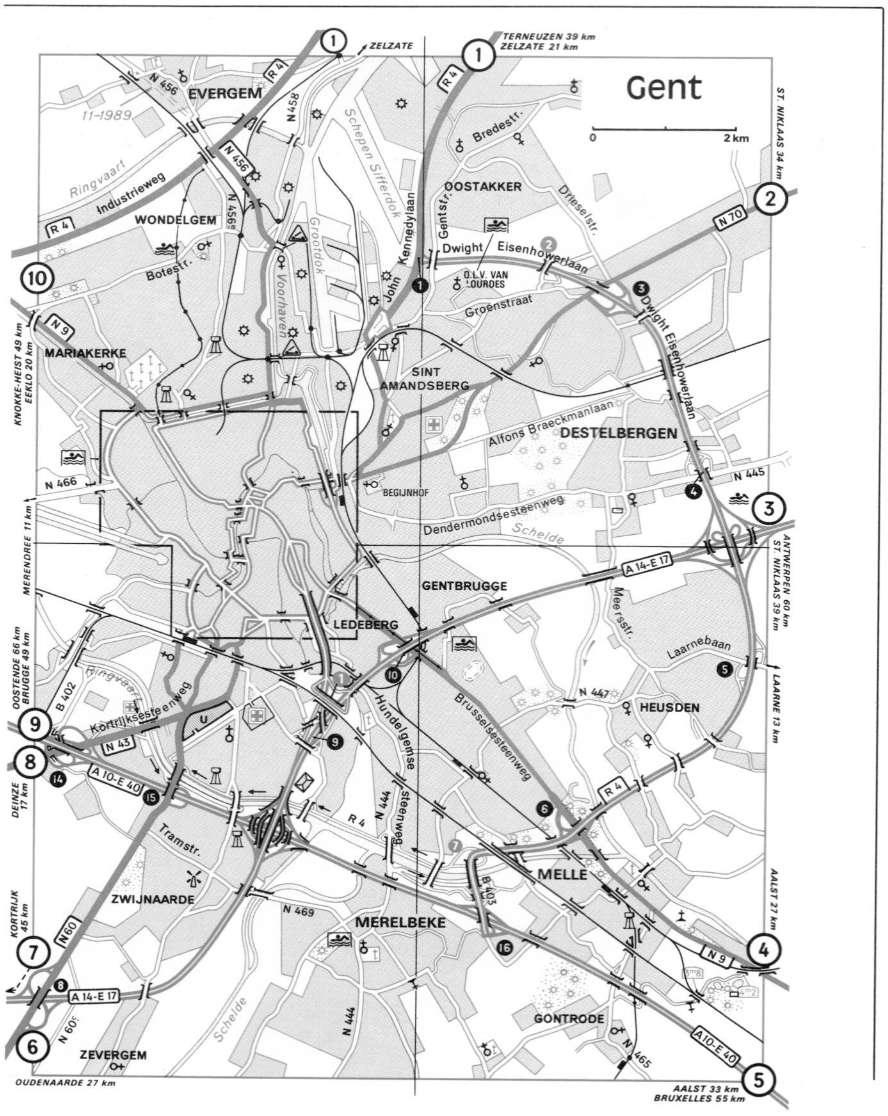

Gent
0
2 km
11-1989
ZELZATE
TERNEUZEN 39 km
ZELZATE 21 km
ST. NIKLAAS 34 km
EVERGEM
WONDELGEM
MARIAKERKE
OOSTAKKER
SINT AMANDSBERG
DESTELBERGEN
BEGIJNHOF
GENTBRUGGE
LEDEBERG
HEUSDEN
MELLE
MERELBEKE
ZWIJNAARDE
GONTRODE
ZEVERGEM
Ringvaart
Industrieweg
Botestr.
Voorhaven
Grootdok
Kennedylaan
Gentstr.
Bredestr.
Drieselstr.
Dwight Eisenhowerlaan
Groenstraat
O.L.V. VAN LOURDES
Alfons Braeckmanlaan
Dendermondsesteenweg
Schelde
Meersstr.
Laarnebaan
Brusselsesteenweg
Hundelgemsesteenweg
Kortrijksesteenweg
Tramstr.
KNOKKE-HEIST 49 km
EEKLO 20 km
MERENDREE 11 km
OOSTENDE 66 km
BRUGGE 49 km
DEINZE 17 km
KORTRIJK 45 km
OUDENAARDE 27 km
ANTWERPEN 60 km
ST. NIKLAAS 39 km
LAARNE 13 km
AALST 27 km
AALST 33 km
BRUXELLES 55 km

Gadžin Han 77 E1
Găești 115 D1
Gaeta 64 A3
Gaeta, Golfo di 64 A3
Gagarin 111 F2
Gaggenau 54 C2
Gagnef 105 F2
Gail 59 E2
Gailbergsattel 59 E2
Gaildorf 55 D2
Gailey 9 E1
Gaillac 29 D3
Gaillimh 12 B3
Gaillon 19 E3
Gainsborough 7 D2
Gairloch 2 B3
Gaj 73 D2
Gajdobra 72 B2
Gajsin 113 E3
Gajvoron 113 E3
Gakovo 72 B1
Galan 37 E1
Galanádo 88 C3
Galanianá 90 A2
Galanta 112 A3
Galapagar 40 A2
Galarinós 80 A3
Galaroza 42 C2
Galashiels 5 D2
Galatádes 79 E3
Galatáki 84 A3
Galatás (Argolída) 87 E2
Galatás (Korinthía) 87 D1
Galați 113 E4
Galatina 65 F4
Galatiní 79 D3
Galátista 80 A3
Galatone 65 F4
Galaxídi 83 E4
Galdakao 36 B1
Galdhøpiggen 100 B3
Galeata 61 D3
Galegos 38 C3
Galende 34 C3
Galera 44 B2
Galiano del Capo 65 F4
Galibier, Col du 31 D1
Galicia 34 B2
Galičica 77 D4
Galičnik 77 D3
Galikós 79 F3
Galipsós 80 B2
Galisteo 39 D2
Galiz, Pto de 43 D4
Gallarate 60 A1
Gallardon 19 E4
Gallargues 30 B3
Gállego, R 37 D3
Galley Head 14 B4
Galliate 60 A1
Gallipoli 65 F4
Gällivare 98 B2
Gallneukirchen 57 D2
Gällö 101 E2
Gallo, C 68 B2
Gallocanta, L de 41 D1
Gallo, R 41 D2
Galloway Forest Park 4 C3
Gallspach 56 C3
Gallur 36 C3
Gälöfjärden 106 B4
Galston 4 C2
Galten 108 B3
Galtür 58 C2
Galty Mts 14 C3
Galveias 38 B3
Gálvez 40 A3
Galway 12 B3
Galway (Co) 12 B3
Galway B 12 B4
Gamaches 19 E2
Gambarie d'Aspromonte 67 E4
Gaming 57 D3
Gamleby 109 E1
Gammelstaden 98 C3
Gammertingen 55 D3
Gampenjoch 58 C3
Gams 58 B2
Gamvik 95 E1
Gamzigrad 73 E4
Ganacker 56 B2
Gand 50 B3
Gándara 34 B1
Ganderkesee 17 F1
Gandesa 41 F1
Gandía 41 E4
Gandino 58 B4
Gandria 58 A4
Gangáles 91 D4
Ganges 29 F3
Gangi 68 C3
Gangkofen 56 B2
Gannat 26 A4
Gänserndorf 57 F2
Gañuelas 45 D2
Gap 31 D2
Garabit, Viaduc de 29 F2
Garajonay 42 A4
Garajonay (Parque Nac) 42 A4
Gara, L 12 C3
Garching 56 B3
Garcia 37 E4
Garcia de Sola, Emb de 39 F4
Garciaz 39 E3
Gard (Dépt) 30 B3
Gard R 30 B3
Garda 60 C1
Garda, L di 58 C4
Garðabær 96 A2
Gardanne 30 C4
Gårdby 109 E2
Garde 109 F4
Garde-Freinet, la 31 D4
Gardelegen 48 C4
Gardermoen 105 D3
Gardiken 97 F3
Gardíki 83 D3
Garding 47 F2
Gardjönäs 97 F3
Gärdnäs 101 E1
Gardone Riviera 60 C1
Gardone Val Trompia 60 B1
Gärdslösa 109 E2
Gardunha, Sa da 38 C2
Garður 96 A2
Garešnica 71 D2
Garessio 31 F3
Garforth 7 D2
Gargaliáni 86 B3
Gargano, Promontorio del 64 C2
Garganta 44 B2
Garganta del Chorro 43 E3
Garganta del Escalar 37 E2
Garganta la Olla 39 E2
Gargantas 40 C2
Gargantas del Sil 34 B2
Gargellen 58 B2
Gargilesse 25 E3
Gargnano 58 C4
Gargnäs 98 A3
Garigliano 64 A3
Gariglione, Mte 67 F3
Garlasco 60 A2
Garlin 28 B4
Garlstorf 48 B3
Garmisch-Partenkirchen 55 F4
Garona, R 37 F2
Garonne 28 B2
Garpenberg 105 F3
Garphyttan 105 F4
Garraf 32 A4
Garrafe de Torio 35 D2
Garray 36 B3
Garrel 17 E1
Garrovillas 39 D3

Garrucha	44 C3	Gebesee	52 C2		
Gars	57 E2	Gebze	115 F3		
Gartempe	25 E4	Gedern	52 A4		
Gartow	48 C3	Gediz	115 F4		
Gartz	49 E3	Gediz R	115 E4		
Garvagh	13 C1	Gedser	108 C4		
Garvão	42 A2	Geel	50 C3		
Garve	2 C3	Geertruidenberg	16 C3		
Garynahine	2 B2	Geesthacht	48 B3		
Garz	49 D1	Gefell	53 D3		
Gaschurn	58 B2	Géfira	79 F3		
Gassino Torinese	31 E1	Gefíria	83 E2		
Gastoúni	86 B1	Gefrees	53 D4		
Gata		Gehren	52 C3		
(Extremadura)	39 D2	Geilenkirchen	17 D4		
Gata (Valencia)	45 E1	Geilo	104 C2		
Gata, C de	44 C4	Geiranger	100 B3		
Gata, Sa de	39 D2	Geirangerfjorden			
Gatčina	111 D1		100 B3		
Gatehouse of Fleet	4 C3	Geisa	52 B3		
Gateshead	5 E3	Geiselhöring	56 B2		
Gattinara	31 F1	Geisenfeld	55 F2		
Gattorna	60 A3	Geisenhausen	56 B2		
Gatwick Airport	10 C3	Geising	53 E3		
Gaucín	43 E4	Geisingen	54 C4		
Gauja	110 C2	Geislingen	55 E2		
Gaula	100 C2	Geismar	52 B2		
Gauldalen	100 C2	Geisnes	97 D4		
Gaulstad	101 D1	Geithain	53 D2		
Gauting	56 A3	Gela	68 C4		
Gavà	32 A4	Gelderland	17 D2		
Gavardo	60 B1	Geldern	17 D3		
Gavarnie	37 E2	Geldrop	16 C4		
Gavarnie,		Geleen	17 D4		
Cirque de	37 E2	Gelibolu	115 E3		
Gavdopoúla, N	90 B4	Gelnhausen	52 A4		
Gávdos, N	90 C4	Gelsa	37 D4		
Gave d'Oloron	28 A4	Gelsdorf	51 E4		
Gavi	60 A2	Gelsenkirchen	17 E3		
Gavião	38 B3	Gelting	48 A1		
Gavia, Pso di	58 C3	Gembloux	50 C4		
Gavirate	58 A4	Gemeaux	26 C2		
Gävle	106 B2	Gémenos	30 C4		
Gävleborgs Län	101 E3	Gemert	17 D3		
Gävlebukten	106 B2	Gemlik	115 F3		
Gavoi	66 B2	Gemona del			
Gavray	18 B4	Friuli	59 F3		
Gâvrio	88 B1	Gémozac	28 B1		
Gâvsta	106 B3	Gemünd	51 D4		
Gåxsjö	101 E1	Gemünden			
Gazzuolo	60 C2	(Bayern)	52 B4		
Gdańsk	110 A4	Gemünden			
Gdov	111 D1	(Hessen)	52 A3		
Gdynia	110 A4	Gemünden			
Geaune	28 B4	(Rheinland-Pfalz)	54 B1		

Genádio	93 E2	Generalísimo		Generalski Stol	70 C3
Gençay	25 D4	Emb del	41 D3	General-Toševo	115 E2
		Generoso, Mte	58 A4	Genova	60 A3
		Genève	27 D4	Genova, Golfo di	60 A4
		Genil, R	43 E2	Genova, Val di	58 C3
		Genisséa	81 D2	Gent	50 B3
		Génissiat,		Genthin	49 D4
		Barrage de	27 D4	Gentioux	29 D1
		Genk	50 C3	Genzano di	
		Genlis	26 C2	Lucania	64 C3
		Genna Cruxi	66 C3	Genzano di Roma	63 E3
		Gennargentu,		Georgiani	79 E3
		Mti del	66 B3	Georgioúpoli	90 C3
		Gennep	17 D3	Georgitsi	87 D3
		Gennes	24 C2	Gera	53 D3
				Geraardsbergen	50 B3

Génolhac	29 F3	Gerabronn	55 E2
Genova	60 A3	Gerace	67 F4
Genova, Golfo di	60 A4	Gerakári (Kríti)	90 C4
Genova, Val di	58 C3	Gerakári	
Gent	50 B3	(Makedonía)	79 F2
Genthin	49 D4	Gerakaroú	80 A3
Gentioux	29 D1	Gerakás	87 E4
Genzano di		Gérakas, Akr	84 B2
Lucania	64 C3	Geráki	87 D3
Genzano di Roma	63 E3	Gerakini	80 B4
Georgiani	79 E3	Gerakovoúni	83 F3
Georgioúpoli	90 C3	G>	
Georgitsi	87 D3	Geránia	87 E1
Gera	53 D3	Gérardmer	27 E1
Geraardsbergen	50 B3	Geras	57 E2
		Gerbeviller	21 D4

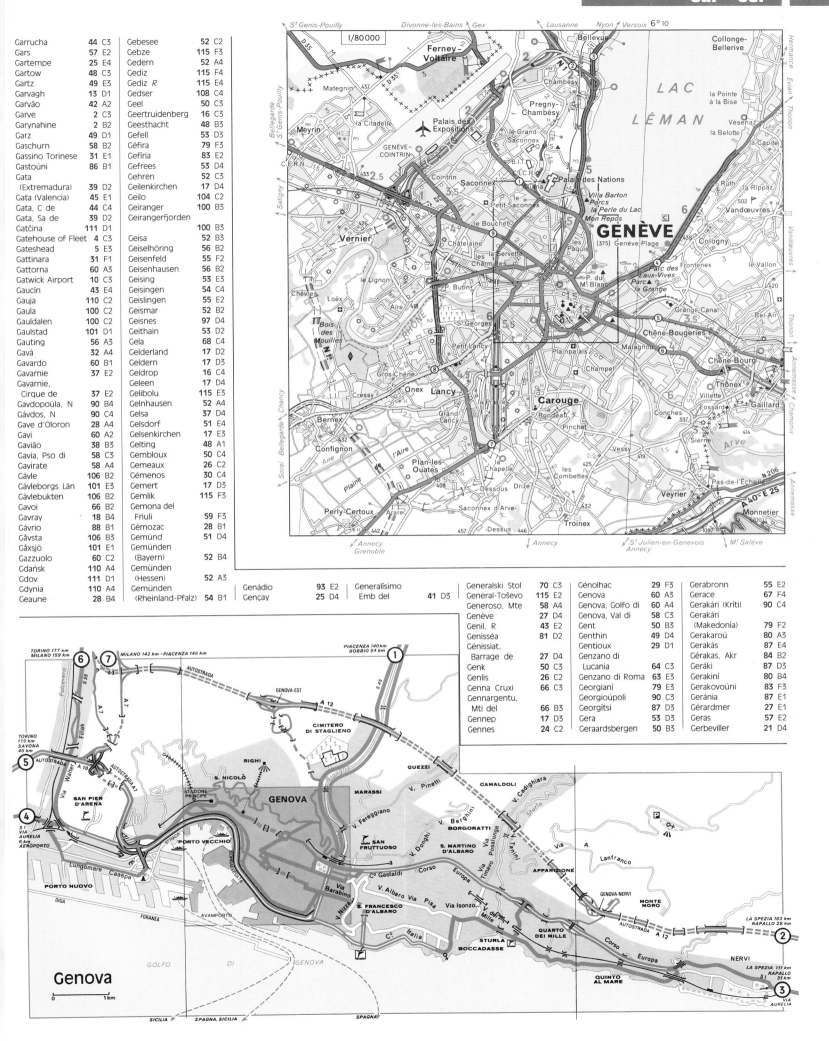

Genova

Name	Pg	Grid
Gerbier de Jonc	30	B2
Gerbini	69	D3
Gerbstedt	52	C2
Gerena	43	D2
Gerês	34	B3
Gerês, Sa do	34	B3
Geretsried	56	A3
Gérgal	44	B3
Geringswalde	53	E2
Gerlitzen	59	F2
Gerlos	59	D2
Gerlospaß	59	D1
Gérmas	79	D3
Germering	55	F3
Germersheim	54	C2
Gernika-Lumo	36	B1
Gernrode	52	C2
Gernsbach	54	C2
Gernsheim	54	C1
Gerola Alta	58	B3
Geroliménas	87	D4
Gerolstein	51	D4
Gerolzhofen	52	B4
Gerona	32	B3
Geroplátanos	80	B3
Gerovo	70	B3
Gerri de la Sal	37	F3
Gers	28	C3
Gers (Dépt)	28	C4
Gersau	58	A2
Gersfeld	52	B4
Gerstetten	55	E2
Gersthofen	55	E3
Gerswalde	49	E3
Gesäuse	57	D3
Gescher	17	E3
Geseke	17	E3
Gesualdo	64	B3
Geta	106	C2
Getafe	40	A2
Gets, les	27	E4
Gettorf	48	A1
Gevelsberg	17	E4
Gevgelija	77	F4
Gevrey-Chambertin	26	C2
Gex	27	D3
Geysir	96	B2
Geyve	115	F3
Gföhl	57	E2
Ghedi	60	B1
Gheorghe Gheorghiu-Dej	113	D4
Gheorgheni	113	D4
Ghilarza	66	B3
Ghisonaccia	33	F3
Ghisoni	33	F3
Giali, N	89	F4
Giáltra	83	F3
Gianitsá	79	E3
Gianitsi	84	C4
Giannádes	82	A1
Giannutri I di	63	D2
Gianoúli	81	F2
Giant's Causeway	13	E1
Giardini	69	D3
Giáros, N	88	B2
Giarratana	69	D4
Giarre	69	D3
Giat	29	E1
Giaveno	31	E1
Giba	65	D3
Gibostad	94	B2
Gibraleón	42	C2
Gibraltar	43	E4
Gideå	102	A2
Gideälven	102	A2
Gieboldehausen	52	B2
Gien	26	A2
Giengen	55	E2
Giens	31	D4
Giethoorn	17	D2
Gifhorn	48	B4
Gigha I	4	B2
Giglio, I del	62	C2
Giglio Porto	62	C2
Gignac	30	A4
Gilching	56	A3
Gilford	13	E2
Giljevo	76	C1
Gilleje	108	C3
Gillhov	101	E2
Gillingham (Dorset)	9	D3
Gillingham (Kent)	11	D2
Gill, L	12	C2
Gilze	16	C3
Gimenells	37	E3
Gimnó	84	B4
Gimo	106	B3
Gimont	28	C4
Gingst	49	D1
Ginosa	65	D4
Ginzling	59	D2
Giogo di Scarperia	61	D3
Gioia del Colle	65	E3
Gioia Tauro	67	E4
Gióna, Óros	83	E3
Gioúhtas	91	D4
Gioúra, N	84	B2
Giovinazzo	65	D3
Giovi, Pso dei	60	A3
Girifalco	67	F3
Giromagny	27	E1
Girona	32	B3
Gironde	28	B1
Gironde (Dépt)	28	B2
Gironella	32	A3
Girvan	4	C3
Gisburn	6	C2
Gislaved	109	D2
Gisors	19	E3
Gissi	64	B2
Gistel	50	A3
Githio	87	D4
Gittun	98	A2
Giugliano in Campo	64	B4
Giulianova	64	A1
Giurgiu	115	D2
Give	108	A3
Givors	30	B1
Givry	26	C3
Givry-en-Argonne	20	C3
Gizéla	81	D2
Giżycko	110	B4
Gjalicë, M	77	D3
Gjendesheim	100	B3
Gjermundshavn	104	A2
Gjesvær	95	D1
Gjøra	100	C2
Gjøvik	105	D2
Gjuhezës, Kepi i	114	B4
Gla	83	F4
Gladbeck	17	E3
Gladenbach	17	F4
Gladstad	97	D3
Glafsfjorden	105	E3
Gláma	96	A1
Glamis	5	D1
Glamis Castle	5	D1
Glamoč	71	E4
Glamorgan	8	C2
Glamsbjerg	108	B3
Glan	54	B1
Glandon, Col du	31	D1
Glandorf	17	F2
Glan-Münchweiler	54	B1
Glanshammar	105	F4
Glarus	58	A2
Glasgow	4	C2
Glas Maol	3	D4
Glastonbury	9	D3
Glauchau	53	D3
Glava	105	D3
Glavatičevo	75	F1
Glavičice	72	B3
Glavnik	77	D1
Gledić	73	D4
Gledićske pl	73	D4
Gleinalmtunnel	57	E4
Gleisdorf	57	E4
Glen Albyn	2	C4
Glenamoy	12	B2
Glénan, I de	22	B4
Glenariff	13	E1
Glenarm	13	E1
Glenbeigh	14	A4
Glen Carron	2	C3
Glen Coe	4	C1
Glencolumbkille	12	C1
Glendalough	13	D4
Glenelg	2	B4
Glenfinnan	2	B4
Glengarriff	14	A4
Glenluce	4	C3
Glen More	2	C4
Glen More Forest Park	3	D4
Glennamaddy	12	C3
Glenrothes	5	D2
Glenties	12	C1
Glifa	83	F3
Glifáda (Atikí-Piréas)	87	F1
Glifáda (Fokída)	83	D4
Glikí	82	B2
Glikóvrissi	87	D4
Glina	70	C3
Glittertind	100	B3
Gliwice	112	B2
Globino	113	F2
Globočica	77	D2
Gloggnitz	57	E3
Głogów	112	A2
Glomfjord	97	E2
Glomma	105	D3
Glommersträsk	98	B3
Gloppet	102	B2
Glossop	6	C2
Gloucester	9	D2
Gloucestershire	9	D2
Gložan	72	B2
Głubczyce	112	A2
Glubokoje	111	D3
Głuchołazy	112	A2
Gluchov	113	F1
Glücksburg	48	A1
Glückstadt	48	A2
Glumsø	108	C4
Glušci	72	C3
Glyn Ebwy	9	D2
Gmund (D)	56	A4
Gmünd (Kärnten)	59	F2
Gmünd (Nieder-österreich)	57	D2
Gmunden	56	C3
Gnarp	101	E3
Gnesta	106	B4
Gniezno	112	A1
Gnjilane	77	D2
Gnoien	49	D2
Gnosjö	109	D2
Goat Fell	4	B2
Goce Delčev	115	D3
Goch	17	D3
Godafoss	96	B1
Godalming	9	F3
Godby	106	C3
Godelheim	52	A2
Goderville	19	D3
Godmanchester	9	F1
Gödöllő	112	B4
Godovič	70	A2
Goduš	72	B3
Goeree	16	B3
Goes	16	B3
Göggingen	55	F3
Göhren	49	D1
Goirle	16	C3
Góis	38	B2
Goito	60	C1
Gökčanica	73	D4
Gökçe	115	E3
Gol	104	C2
Gola	71	D1
Golada	34	B2
Golaja Pristan'	113	F3
Golczewo	49	F2
Goldbach	52	A4
Goldberg	48	C2
Goldenstedt	17	F1
Golegã	38	B3
Golema reka	77	D3
Golemo Selo	77	E2
Goleniów	49	F2
Goleš	77	E2
Golfe-Juan	31	E4
Golfo Aranci	66	C1
Goli	70	B4
Golija (Crna Gora)	76	A2
Golija (Srbija)	76	C1
Goljak	77	D2
Goljaki, M.	70	A2

Goljam Perelik 115 D3
Göllersdorf 57 E2
Golling 59 E1
Golo 33 F3
Golpejas 39 E1
Golßen 53 E1
Golspie 3 D3
Golubac 73 E3
Golubovci 76 B3
Golubovec 70 C2
Golzow 49 D4
Gómara 36 B3
Gomáti 80 B3
Gombrèn 32 A3
Gomecello 39 E1
Gomel' 111 E4
Gomera 42 A4
Gómfi 83 D2
Gommern 52 C1
Goncelin 31 D1
Gondomar 34 A4
Gondomar (E) 34 A3
Gondrecourt 20 C4
Gönen 115 E3
Góni 83 E1
Goniá 90 B3
Goniés 91 B3
Gonnesa 66 B4
Gonnosfanadiga 66 B4
Goole 7 D2
Goor 17 D2
Goppenstein 27 F3
Göppingen 55 D2
Gora 70 C3
Goražde 76 A1
Gördalen 101 D3
Gordes 30 C3
Gorenja Vas 70 A2
Gorey (GB) 18 B3
Gorey (IRL) 15 D3
Gorgona, I di 60 B4
Gorgonzola 60 A1
Gorgopótamos 78 C4
Gorica (Bosna i Hercegovina) 75 E2
Gorica (Makedonija) 77 D4
Goričan 71 D1
Gorice 70 B3
Gorinchem 16 C3
Goritsá 87 D3
Gorizia 59 F3
Gorjanci 70 C2
Gorki 111 E3
Gorleston-on-Sea 7 F4
Gorlice 112 B3
Görlitz 53 F2
Gorna Orjahovica 115 D2
Gornja Dobrinja 72 C4
Gornja Grabovica 75 F1
Gornja Kamenica 73 F4
Gornja Klina 77 D2
Gornja Ljubovidđa 72 C4
Gornja Ljuta 75 F1
Gornja Ploča 70 C4
Gornja Radgona 70 C1
Gornja Sabanta 73 D4
Gornja Sanica 71 D4
Gornja Slatina 71 F3
Gornja Toplica 72 C4
Gornja Toponica 73 E4
Gornja Tuzla 72 B3
Gornje Dubočke 76 A2
Gornje Ratkovo 71 E4
Gornje Selo 75 D2
Gornji Grad 70 B2
Gornji Kokoti 76 B3
Gornji Kosinj 70 C4
Gornji Lapac 71 D4
Gornji Lukavac 76 A2
Gornji Milanovac 73 D4
Gornji Petrovci 70 C1
Gornji Podgradci 71 D3
Gornji Rajić 71 E3
Gornji Stepoš 73 E4
Gornji Vakuf 75 E1
Gornji Zabar 71 F3
Gorno Orizari 77 E3
Goro 61 D2
Gorodišče 113 F2
Gorodn'a 111 E4
Gorodok (Belorussija) 111 D3

Gorodok (Ukraina) 112 C2
Gorredijk 17 D1
Gorron 23 E3
Gort 12 B4
Gorteen 12 C3
Gortin 13 D2
Górtis 91 D4
Gortmore 12 B3
Gorumna I 12 B3
Goryn' 113 D2
Góry Świętokrzyskie 112 B2
Görzke 53 D1
Gorzów Wielkopolski 49 F3
Gosaldo 59 D3
Gosau 59 F1
Gosausee 59 F1
Göschenen 58 A3
Gościno 49 F1
Gosforth 5 D4
Gößl 56 C3
Goslar 52 B1
Gößnitz 53 D3
Gospić 70 C4
Gospodđinci 72 C2
Gosport 9 E3
Gossau 58 B2
Gosselies 50 B4
Gossensass 59 D2
Gössweinstein 52 C4
Gostivar 77 D3
Göstling 57 D3
Gostyń 112 A2
Götaälv 108 C1
Göta Kanal 105 E4
Göteborg 108 C1
Göteborgs och Bohus Län 108 C1
Götene 105 E4
Gotha 52 C3
Gothem 109 F4
Gotland 109 F4
Gotlands Län 109 F4
Gotska Sandön 106 C4
Göttingen 52 B2
Gottwaldov 112 A3
Götzis 58 B2
Gouarec 22 C3
Gouda 16 C3
Gouménissa 79 F2
Goumois 27 E2
Goúra 87 D1
Gourdon 29 D2
Gourin 22 B3
Gournay-en-Bray 19 E3
Goúrnes 91 E3
Gourniá 91 E4
Gourock 4 C2
Gouveja 38 C2
Goúves 91 E3
Gouviá 82 A1
Gouzon 25 F4
Goveddari 75 E2
Goverla 113 D3
Gowienica 49 F2
Göynük 115 F3
Gozd 70 A1
Gozo 68 B4
Gozzano 58 A4
Graal-Müritz 48 C1
Graben-Neudorf 54 C2
Grabenstätt 56 B3
Grabovac 75 E2
Grabovci 72 C3
Grabow 48 C3
Gračac 70 C4
Gračanica (Bosna i Hercegovina) 71 F3
Gračanica (Crna Gora) 76 B2
Gračanica (Kosovo) 77 D2
Gračanica (Srbija) 72 C4
Gracay 25 E2
Grächen 27 F4
Gradac (Crna Gora) 76 B1
Gradac (Hrvatska) 75 E2
Gradac (Srbija) 76 C1
Gradara 61 E2
Gradče, Ez 77 E2
Gradec 71 D2

Gradefes 35 E2
Gradeška pl 77 F3
Gradina 77 F1
Gradisca d'Isonzo 59 F3
Gradište (Hrvatska) 71 E2
Gradište (Makedonija) 77 E2
Grado (E) 35 D1
Grado (I) 59 F4
Gradsko 77 E3
Gradskovo 73 F3
Grafelfing 56 A3
Grafenau 56 C2
Gräfenberg 55 F1
Gräfenhainichen 53 D1
Grafenwöhr 55 F1
Grafing 56 B3
Gragnano 64 B4
Grahovo (Bosna i Hercegovina) 76 A2
Grahovo (Slovenija) 70 A2
Graiguenamanagh 15 D3
Grain 11 D2
Grainau 55 F4
Grajewo 110 C4
Gram 108 A3
Gramat 29 D2
Gramatikó 83 E2
Gramatikoú 83 D3
Graméni 80 B2
Graméno 82 B1
G3Gr metten 57 D1
Grammichele 69 D4
Grámos, Óros 78 C3
Grampian 3 E4
Grampian Mts 4 C1
Gramsh 77 D4
Gramzow 49 E3
Gran 105 D2
Granada 44 A3
Granadella 37 E4
Granadilla de Abona 42 B4
Granard 12 C3
Gran Canaria 42 B4
Grancey-le-Château 26 C2
Grandas 34 C1
Grand Ballon 27 E1
Grand Bois, Col du 30 B1
Grand-Bornand, le 27 D4
Grand-Bourg 25 E4
Grandcamp-Maisy 18 C3
Grand Canal d'Alsace 27 E1
Grand Canyon du Verdon 31 D3
Grand-Champ 22 C4
Grand-Colombier 27 D4
Grand-Combe, la 30 B3
Grand Combin 27 E4
Grand-Couronne 19 D3
Grand-Croix 30 B1
Grande Casse 31 D1
Grande de Europa, Punta 43 E4
Grande Dixence, Bge de la 27 E4
Grande-Motte, la 30 B4
Grande Sassière 31 E1
Grandes Rousses 31 D1
Grand-Fougeray 23 D4
Grand-Lemps, le 30 C1
Grand Lieu, L de 24 B3
Grand-Lucé, le 23 F4
Grand Morin 20 A4
Grândola 42 A1
Grandpré 20 C3
Grand-Pressigny, le 25 D3
Grand Rhône 30 B4
Grandrieu 29 F2
Grand-Serre, le 30 C1
Grands Goulets 30 C2
Grandval, Bge de 29 F2
Grandvilliers 19 E3
Grañen 37 D3
Grangärde 105 F3
Grangemouth 5 D2
Grange-Over-Sands 6 B1
Grängesberg 105 F3

Granges-sur-Vologne 27 E1
Granier, Col du 30 C1
Granítis 80 B1
Granítsa 83 D2
Granja (Alentejo) 42 C1
Granja (Douro) 34 A4
Granja de Torrehermosa 43 E1
Granja, Pto de la 43 D1
Gränna 109 D1
Granollers 32 A4
Granön 102 A1
Gran Paradiso 31 E1
Gran San Bernardo, Colle del 27 E4
Gran San Bernardo, Traforo del 27 E4
Gran Sasso d'Italia 63 F1
Gransee 49 D3
Gran Tarajal 42 C4
Grantham 7 D3
Grantown-on-Spey 3 D3
Granville 18 B4
Granvin 104 B2
Grappa, Mte 59 D3
Grasleben 52 C1
Grasmere 5 D4
Grassano 65 D4
Grasse 31 E3
Gråsten 108 A4
Grästorp 108 C1
Gratangen 94 B3
Gratiní 81 E2
Gratkorn 57 E4
Graubünden 58 B2
Grau-du-Roi, le 30 B4
Graulhet 29 D4
Graus 37 E3
Gravalos 36 C3
Gravdal 97 E1
Grave 17 D3
Grave, la 31 D1
Gravedona 58 B3
Gravelines 19 F1
Gravellona-Toce 58 A4
Grave, Pointe de 28 A1
Gravesend 11 D2
Graviá 83 E3
Gravina in Puglia 65 D3
Gravona 33 F3
Gravoúna 80 C2
Gray 26 C2
Grays Thurrock 10 C2
Graz 57 E4
Grazalema 43 E3
Grazzanise 64 A3

Grdelica 77 E1
Great Blasket I. 14 A3
Great Driffield 7 D1
Great Dunmow 11 D2
Great Grimsby 7 E2
Great Malvern 9 D1
Great Ormes Head 6 A2
Great Ouse 7 E3
Great Torrington 8 C3
Great Yarmouth 7 F4
Grebbestad 105 D4
Greccio 63 E2
Greding 55 F2
Gredos, Sa de 39 F2
Greenhead 5 D3
Greenlaw 5 E2
Greenock 4 C2
Greenodd 6 B1
Greggio 31 F1
Gregolímano 83 F3
Greifenburg 59 E2
Greiffenberg 49 E3
Greifswald 49 D1
Greifswalder Bodden 49 D1
Grein 57 D2
Greiz 53 D3
Grenå 108 B2
Grenade (Haute-Garonne) 29 D3
Grenade (Landes) 28 B4
Grenchen 27 E2
Grenoble 30 C1
Grense Jakobselv 95 F2
Gréoux-les-Bains 31 D3
Gressåmoen 101 E1
Gresse 30 C2
Gressoney-la-Trinite 27 F4
Gressoney-St-Jean 27 F4
Gresten 57 D3
Greußen 52 C2
Greve 61 D4
Greven 17 E2
Grevená 79 D4
Grevená (Nomos) 79 D4
Grevenbroich 17 D4
Grevenbrück 17 E3
Grevenítio 82 C1
Grevesmühlen 48 B2
Greve Strand 108 C3
Greyabbey 13 E2

Greystones 13 E4
Grez-en-Bouère 23 E3
Grezzana 60 C1
Grgur 70 B4
Griá, Akr 88 B3
Grianan of Aileach 13 D1
Griebenow 49 D2
Gries 59 D2
Gries im Sellrain 58 C2
Grieskirchen 56 C3
Griffen 70 B1
Grignan 30 B2
Grigno 59 D3
Grignols 28 B3
Grimaldi 67 E3
Grimaud 31 D4
Grimma 53 D2
Grimmen 49 D2
Grimone, Col de 30 C2
Grimsbu 100 C3
Grimselpass 27 F3
Grímsey 96 B1
Grimstad 104 B4
Grindaheim 104 C2
Grindavík 96 A2
Grindelwald 27 F3
Grindsted 108 A3
Griñón 40 A2
Grintavec 70 B2
Gripsholm 106 B4
Grisignano 61 D1
Gris Nez, Cap 19 E1
Grisolles 29 D4
Grisslehamn 106 B3
Griva 79 E2
Grizáno 83 D1
Grk 71 E3
Grljan 73 F3
Grmec 71 D4
Grøa 100 B2
Gröbming 59 F1
Grocka 73 D3
Gröditz 53 E2
Grodno 110 C4
Groenlo 17 D3
Grøer Arber 56 B1
Groitzsch 53 D2
Groix 22 B4
Groix, I de 22 B4
Grömitz 48 B2
Gronau 17 E2
Grong 97 D4
Grönhögen 109 E3
Groningen 47 D3
Groningen (Prov) 47 D3
Gröningen 52 C1

Grönskåra 109 E2
Grønsund 108 C4
Gropello Cairoli 60 A2
Grgur 70 B4
Großbreitenbach 52 C3
Großburgwedel 48 A4
Groscavallo 31 E1
Großenbrode 48 B1
Großenhain 53 E2
Großenzersdorf 57 E2
Groß Gerungs 57 D2
Großglockner 59 E2
Großglockner Hochalpenstraße 59 E2
Großhabersdorf 55 E1
Grosio 58 C3
Grosne 26 C3
Groß Ötscher 57 E3
Großpetersdorf 57 F4
Großraming 57 D3
Großräschen 53 E1
Groß Reken 17 E3
Großröhrsdorf 53 F2
Groß Rosennock 59 F2
Gross Beerberg 52 C3
Gross Bösenstein 57 D4
Groß-Schönebeck 49 D3
Grosse Pierre 27 E1
Grosse Röder 53 E2
Grosser Plöner See 48 B2
Grosseto 62 C1
Gross Feldberg 51 F4
Gross-Gerau 54 C1
Groß Siegharts 57 E2
Gross Priel 57 D3
Gross Rachel 56 C2
Grossschönau 53 F2
Gross-Umstadt 55 D1
Grostenquin 21 D3
Grosuplje 70 B2
Großvenediger 59 E2
Großweil 56 A4
Grötlingbo 109 F4
Grøtsundet 94 C2
Grotta di Nettuno 66 A2
Grottaglie 65 E4
Grottaminarda 64 B3
Grottammare 61 F4
Grotte di Pertosa 64 C4
Grotteria 67 F4
Grouin, Pte du 18 B4
Grove 34 A2
Grövelsjön 101 D3
Grovfjord 94 B3
Grubišno Polje 71 D2
Gruda 76 A3

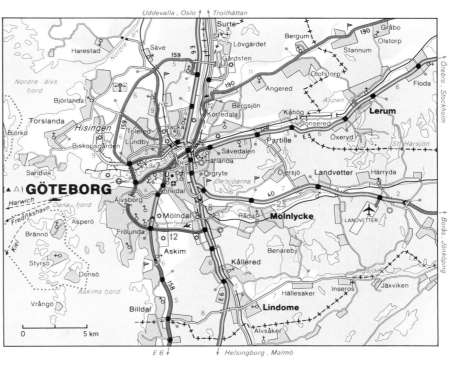

Grude	75 E2	Gstadt	56 B3	Guadal, R	44 B2	Guardiagrele	64 A2	Guérande	22 C4	Guingamp	22 C2	Gurk	70 A1
Grudziądz	112 B1	Guadahortuna	44 A2	Guadalteba-Guadalhorce,		Guardia		Guerche-de-		Guipavas	22 A2	Gurk R	59 F2
Gruinard B	2 C3	Guadaira, R	43 E3	Emb del	43 E3	Sanframondi	64 B3	Bretagne, la	23 D3	Guisborough	5 F4	Gurrea de Gállego	37 D3
Gruissan	32 B2	Guadajira, R	39 D4	Guadalupe	39 E3	Guardias Viejas	44 B4	Guerche, la	26 A3	Guiscard	19 F3	Gusev	110 B4
Grums	105 E3	Guadajoz, R	43 F2	Guadalupe, Sa de	39 E3	Guardo	35 E2	Guéret	25 E4	Guise	20 A2	Gusinje	76 C2
Grünau	56 C3	Guadalajara	40 B2	Guadarrama	40 A2	Guareña	39 D4	Guérigny	26 A2	Guissona	37 F3	Guspini	66 B3
Grünberg	52 A3	Guadalaviar	41 D2	Guadarrama,		Guarrizas, R	44 A1	Guerlédan, L de	22 C3	Guist	7 F3	Güssing	57 F4
Grünburg	57 D3	Guadalaviar, R	41 D2	Pto de	40 A2	Guarromán	44 A2	Guernsey	18 A3	Guitiriz	34 B1	Güsten	52 C1
Grundarfjörður	96 A2	Guadalcacin,		Guadarrama, R	40 A2	Guastalla	60 C2	Guéthary	28 A4	Guitres	28 B2	Güstrow	48 C1
Grundforsen	101 D4	Emb de	43 D3	Guadarrama,		Gubbio	61 E4	Gueugnon	26 B3	Gujan-Mestras	28 A2	Gutcher	3 F1
Grundlsee	56 C3	Guadalcanal	43 D1	Sa de	40 A1	Guben	53 F1	Güglingen	55 D2	Gulbene	110 C2	Gutenstein	57 E3
Grundlsee L	56 C3	Guadalén, Emb de	44 A1	Guadarranque,		Guberevac	73 D4	Guglionesi	64 B2	Guldborg Sund	108 C4	Gütersloh	17 F3
Grundsund	108 C1	Guadalén, R	44 B1	Emb del	43 E4	Gubin	53 F1	Guía	42 B4	Gullesfjorden	94 A3	Gutulia	100 D3
Grundtjärn	101 F2	Guadalest	45 E1	Guadasuar	41 E4	Guča	73 D4	Guía de Isora	42 A4	Gullfoss	96 B2	Gützkow	49 D2
Grünstadt	54 C1	Guadalete, R	43 D4	Guadazaón, R	40 C3	Guca Gora	71 E4	Guichen	23 D3	Gullkrona fjärd	107 D3	Guyhirn	10 C1
Grünwald	56 A3	Guadalfeo, R	44 A4	Guadiamar, R	43 D3	Gúdar, Sa de	41 E2	Guidonia	63 E2	Gullspång	105 E4	Gvardejsk	110 B4
Grupčin	77 D3	Guadalhorce, R	43 E4	Guadiana Menor, R	44 B2	Gudavac	71 D3	Guignes	19 F4	Gumiel de Hizán	36 A3	Gvarv	104 C3
Gruyères	27 E3	Guadalimar, R		Guadiana, R	39 F4	Gudbrandsdalen	100 C3	Guijo de Granadilla	39 D2	Gummersbach	17 E4	Gvozd	76 B2
Gruža	73 D4	(Andalucia)	43 D3	Guadiaro	43 E4	Guderup	108 A4	Guijuelo	39 E2	Gundelfingen	55 E3	Gweebarra B	12 C1
Gruža R	73 D4	Guadalimar, R		Guadiaro, R	43 E4	Gudhjem	109 D4	Guildford	9 F3	Gundelsheim	55 D2	Gwent	9 D2
Grycksbo	105 F2	(Andalucia)	44 B2	Guadiato, R	43 E2	Gudingen	109 E1	Guillaumes	31 E3	Gunnarn	97 F4	Gwynedd	6 A3
Gryfice	49 F2	Guadalmellato,		Guadiela, R	40 C2	Gudow	48 B3	Guillena	43 D2	Gunnarsbyn	98 B3	Gy	27 D2
Gryfino	49 E3	Emb de	43 F2	Guadix	44 B3	Gudvangen	104 B2	Guillestre	31 D2	Gunnarsfjärden	98 B4	Gyöngyös	112 B4
Gryllefjord	94 B2	Guadalmena,		Guajaraz, Emb de	40 A3	Guebwiller	27 E1	Guillon	26 B2	Gunnarskog	105 E3	Györ	112 A4
Grythyttan	105 E3	Emb de	44 B1	Gualdo Tadino	61 E4	Guémené	22 B3	Guilvinec	22 A3	Gunten	27 F3	Gysinge	106 A3
Grytøya	94 B3	Guadalmena, R	44 B1	Guara, Sa de	37 E3	Guémené-		Güimar	42 B4	Günterode	52 B2	Gyula	112 C4
Grza	73 E4	Guadalmez, R	43 F1	Guarda	38 C1	Penfao	23 D4	Guimarães	34 A4	Guntín de Pallares	34 B2	
Gschütt, Paß	59 F1	Guadalope, R	41 E2	Guardamar del		Güeñes	36 B1	Guimiliau	22 B2	Günzburg	55 E3	
Gstaad	27 E3	Guadalquivir, R	43 D3	Segura	45 D2	Guer	23 D3	Guînes	19 E1	Gunzenhausen	55 E2	

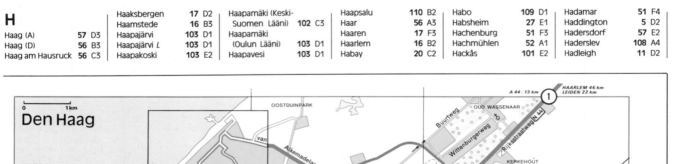

H

		Haaksbergen	17 D2	Haapamäki (Keski-		Haapsalu	110 B2	Habo	109 D1	Hadamar	51 F4	Hadmersleben	52 C1
		Haamstede	16 B3	Suomen Lääni)	102 C3	Haar	56 A3	Habsheim	27 E1	Haddington	5 D2	Hadrian's Wall	5 E3
Haag (A)	57 D3	Haapajärvi	103 D1	Haapamäki		Haaren	17 F3	Hachenburg	51 F3	Hadersdorf	57 E2	Hadselfjorden	94 A3
Haag (D)	56 B3	Haapajärvi L	103 D1	(Oulun Lääni)	103 D1	Haarlem	16 B2	Hachmühlen	52 A1	Haderslev	108 A4	Hadsten	108 B2
Haag am Hausruck	56 C3	Haapakoski	103 E2	Haapavesi	103 D1	Habay	20 C2	Hackås	101 E2	Hadleigh	11 D2	Hadsund	108 B2

Hadžići	75 F1
Hafnarfjörður	96 A2
Haganj	71 D2
Hægebostad	104 B4
Hagen (Niedersachsen)	47 F3
Hagen (Nordrhein-Westfalen)	17 E4
Hagenow	48 B3
Hagetmau	28 B4
Hagfors	105 E3
Häggdånger	101 F3
Haggenås	101 E2
Hagondange	21 D3
Hague, Cap de la	18 B2
Haguenau	21 E3
Hahn	47 F3
Hahnbach	55 F1
Haigerloch	55 D3
Hailsham	10 C3
Hailuoto	99 D4
Hainaut	50 B4
Hainburg	57 F2
Hainfeld	57 E3
Hainichen	53 E2
Hajdúböszörmény	112 C4
Hajdučica	73 D2
Hajdúszoboszló	112 C4
Hajla	76 C2
Hajnówka	112 C1
Hakarp	109 D1
Hakkas	98 B2
Häkkilä	103 D2
Halámky	57 D2
Halandritsa	86 C1
Halbe	53 E1
Halberstadt	52 C1
Halden	105 D4
Haldensleben	48 C4
Halesowen	9 E1
Halesworth	11 E1
Halhjem	104 A2
Halifax	6 C2
Halikko	107 E2
Halju	95 D4
Halkeró	80 C2
Hálki (Dodekánissa)	93 E1

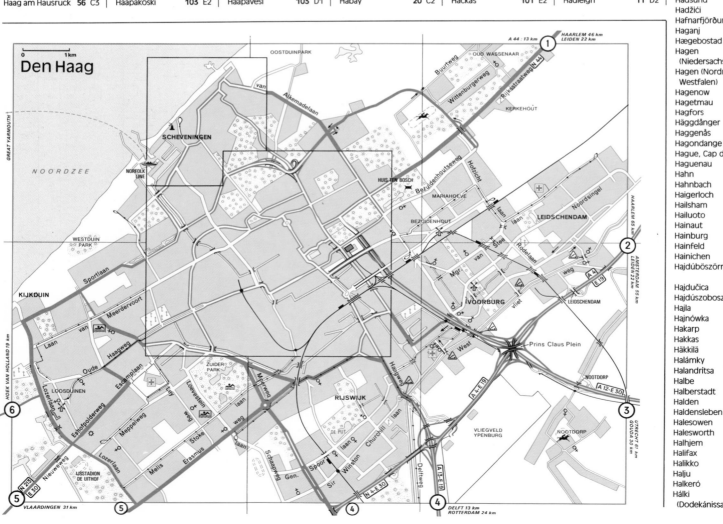

Den Haag

Place	Ref		Place	Ref		Place	Ref
Halki (Kikládes)	88 C3		Haniá (Nomos)	90 B3		Hasle	109 D4
Hálki (Thessalía)	83 E1		Hánia (Thessalía)	83 F2		Haslemere	9 F3
Halkiádes	83 E2		Hani i Hotit	76 B3		Haslev	108 C4
Halkida	84 B4		Hanión, Kólpos	90 B3		Hasparren	28 A4
Halkidikí	80 B3		Haniótis	80 B4		Hassela	101 F3
Hálki, N	93 E1		Hankamäki	103 E1		Hasselfelde	52 C2
Halkidóna	79 F3		Hankasalmen as	103 D3		Hasselt	50 C3
Halkió	85 F4		Hankasalmi	103 D3		Hássia, Óri	83 D1
Halkío	87 D1		Hankensbüttel	48 B4		Hässleholm	109 D3
Halkodóni, Óros	83 E2		Hanko	107 E3		Hastière	50 C4
Hallands Län	108 C2		Hannover	48 A4		Hastings	11 D3
Halle (B)	50 B3		Hannut	50 C4		Hasvik	95 D1
Halle (D)	17 F2		Hanöbukten	109 D3		Hațeg	114 C1
Halle (DDR)	53 D2		Han Pijesak	72 B4		Hatfield	9 F2
Hällefors	105 E3		Hansnes	94 C2		Hatherleigh	8 C3
Hälleforsnäs	105 E4		Han-sur-Lesse	50 C4		Hattem	17 D2
Hallein	56 C3		Hanstedt	48 A3		Hattfjelldal	97 E3
Hällekis	105 E4		Hanstholm	108 A2		Hattingen	17 E3
Hallenberg	17 F4		Haparanda	98 C3		Hattula	107 E2
Hallencourt	19 E2		Harads	98 B3		Hattuvaara (Lieksa)	103 F1
Halle-Neustadt	53 D2		Harafjärden	98 C3		Hattuvaara (Ilomantsi)	103 F2
Hällesjö	101 F2		Haraldshaugen	104 A3		Hatvan	112 B4
Hällevadsholm	105 D4		Haranes	97 D4		Hatvik	104 A2
Halligen	47 F1		Haravgí	79 E3		Hatzí	82 C2
Hallingdal	104 C2		Harburg (Bayern)	55 E2		Haubourdin	19 F1
Hallingskarvet	104 B2		Harburg (Hamburg)	48 A3		Hauge	104 A4
Hall in Tirol	59 D1		Hårby	108 B4		Haugesund	104 A3
Hällnäs	102 A1		Hardangerfjorden	104 A2		Hauho	107 E2
Hallsberg	105 F4		Hardangerjøkulen	104 B2		Haukelifjell	104 B2
Hallstadt	52 C4		Hardangervidda	104 B2		Haukeligrend	104 B3
Hallstahammar	105 F3		Hardbakke	104 A1		Haukipudas	99 D3
Hallstatt	59 F1		Hardegg	57 E1		Haukivesi	103 E3
Hallstavik	106 B3		Hardegsen	52 B2		Haukivuori	103 E3
Halluin	19 F1		Hardelot	19 E1		Haunstetten	55 F3
Halmstad	108 C2		Hardenberg	17 D2		Haus	59 F1
Hals	108 B2		Harderwijk	16 C2		Hausach	54 C3
Halsa	100 B2		Hardheim	55 D1		Hausham	56 A4
Halsafjorden	100 B2		Hardwick Hall	7 D3		Hausjärvi	107 E2
Hälsingtuna	101 F3		Hareid	100 A2		Hautajärvi	99 E2
Halsskov	108 B3		Harelbeke	50 A3		Hautecombe	27 D4
Halstead	11 D2		Haren (D)	17 E1		Haute-Corse	33 F3
Halsteren	16 B3		Haren (NL)	47 D3		Hautefort	29 D1
Halsua	102 C2		Harewood	6 C2		Haute-Garonne	29 D4
Haltdålen	101 D2		Haria	42 C3		Haute-Loire	29 F2
Haltern	17 E3		Haringvlietdam	16 B3			
Halti-Haldi	94 C3		Haritoméni	80 B2			
Halver	17 E4		Härjångsfjällen	101 D2			
Ham	19 F2		Harjavalta	107 D2			
Hamar	105 D2		Harjunpää	107 D1			
Hamarøy	94 A4		Hårkan	101 E2			
Hamburg	48 A3		Härkmeri	102 B3			
Hambye	18 B4		Harlech	6 A3			
Hamdorf	48 A2		Harlesiel	47 E3			
Hämeenkyrö	102 C3		Harleston	11 D1			
Hämeen Lääni	102 C3		Harlingen	16 C1			
Hämeenlinna	107 E2		Harlow	10 C2			
Hämelerwald	52 B1		Harmånger	101 F3			
Hameln	52 A1		Harmanli	115 D3			
Hamersleben	52 C1		Härnösand	101 F3			
Hamili, N	92 C2		Haro	36 B2			
Hamilton	4 C2		Harokopió	86 C4			
Hamina	103 F4		Haroldswick	3 F1			
Hamm	17 E3		Haroué	21 D4			
Hammarland	106 C3		Harpenden	9 F2			
Hammarstrand	101 F2		Harplinge	108 C2			
Hammaslahti	103 F2		Harpstedt	17 F1			
Hammel	108 B3		Harris	2 A2			
Hammelburg	52 B4		Harrislee	47 F1			
Hammerdal	101 E2		Harrogate	6 C1			
Hammerfest	95 D1		Härryda	108 C1			
Hammershus	109 D4		Harsefeld	48 A3			
Hamneidet	94 C2		Harsprånget	98 B2			
Hamningberg	95 F1		Harstad	94 B3			
Hamoir	50 C4		Harsvik	96 C4			
Hampshire	9 E3		Hartberg	57 F4			
Hamra	101 E3		Hårteigen	104 B2			
Hamra (Reg)	101 E3		Hartha	53 E2			
Hamre	104 B4		Hartkjölen	101 E1			
Hamzali	77 F3		Hartland Pt	8 B3			
Hamzići	75 F2		Hartlepool	5 F4			
Hanákia	86 B2		Hartmannsdorf	53 E3			
Hanau	52 A4		Hartola	103 D3			
Handrás	91 F4		Harwich	11 D2			
Hanerau-Hademarschen	48 A2		Harz	52 B2			
Hangö	107 E3		Harzgerode	52 C2			
Hangon läntinenselkä	107 D3		Hase	17 E2			
Hangö västra fjärd	107 D3		Haselünne	17 E2			
Haniá (Haniá)	90 B3		Haßfurt	52 C4			
Hánia (Lakonía)	87 D3		Haskovo	115 D3			
			Haslach (A)	56 C2			
			Haslach (D)	54 C3			

Place	Ref		Place	Ref		Place	Ref
Haute-Marne	26 C1		Hedal	104 C2		Hekla	96 B2
Hautes-Alpes	31 D2		Heddal	104 C3		Hekuravë, Maj'e	76 C2
Haute-Saône	27 D1		Hédé	23 D3		Helagsfjället	101 D2
Haute-Savoie	27 D4		Hede	101 E3		Hélatros, Akr	93 D3
Haute-Vienne (Dépt)	29 D1		Hedemora	105 F3		Heldburg	52 C4
Hauteville-Lompnes	27 D4		Hedenäset	98 C2		Heldrungen	52 C2
Haut-Rhin (Dept)	27 D1		Hedensted	108 B3		Helechal	43 E1
Hautmont	20 B2		Hedesundafjärdarna	106 B3		Helensburgh	4 C2
Havant	9 F3		Hedeviken	101 E3		Helgå (N)	101 D2
Havári	86 B1		Hedmark	104 C1		Helgaå (S)	109 D2
Havdalsfjellet	97 E4		Hedon	7 E2		Helgasjön	109 D2
Havdáta	82 B4		Heemstede	16 C3		Helgoland	47 E2
Havel	49 D4		Heerde	17 D2		Hella	104 B1
Havelange	50 C4		Heerenveen	17 D1		Hellemofjorden	97 F1
Havelberg	48 C4		Heerlen	51 D3		Hellendoorn	17 D2
Haverfordwest	8 B2		Heeze	16 C4		Hellesylt	100 A3
Haverhill	11 D1		Hegge	104 C1		Hellevoetsluis	16 B3
Haverö	101 E3		Hegra	101 D2		Hellin	44 C1
Havneby	108 A4		Heia	94 C3		Hellvik	104 A4
Havøysund	95 D1		Heide	47 F2		Helmbrechts	53 D4
Havraň	53 E3		Heidelberg	54 C1		Helme	52 C2
Havre, Le	19 D3		Heidenheim	55 E2		Helmond	17 D3
Hawes	6 C1		Heidenreichstein	57 D1		Helmsdale	3 D2
Hawick	5 D3		Heikendorf	48 A1		Helmsley	7 D1
Hawkhurst	11 D3		Heikkila	99 F2		Helmstadt	55 D1
Hayange	21 D3		Heilbronn	55 D2		Helmstedt	52 C1
Haye-du-Puits, la	18 B3		Heiligenberg	55 D4		Helpter Berge	49 E2
Haye-Pesnel, la	18 B4		Heiligenblut	59 E2		Helsa	52 B2
Hayle	8 A4		Heiligenhafen	48 B1		Helsingborg	108 C3
Hay-on-Wye	9 D1		Heiligenkirchen	17 F3		Helsinge	108 C3
Haywards Heath	10 C3		Heiligenkreuz	57 F4		Helsingfors	107 F3
Hazebrouck	19 F1		Heiligenstadt	52 B2		Helsingør	108 C3
Headford	12 B3		Heilsbronn	55 E1		Helsinki	107 F3
Heanor	7 D3		Heimari	103 E3		Helston	8 B4
Héas	37 E2		Heimdal	100 C2		Helvetinjärvi	102 C3
Heathfield	10 C3		Heimertingen	55 E3		Helvick Head	14 C4
Heathrow Airport	9 F2		Heinävaara	103 F2		Hemau	55 F2
Hebrides, Outer	2 A2		Heinävesi	103 E2		Hemavan	97 E3
Hebrides, Sea of the	2 A3		Heinola	107 F1		Hemel Hempstead	9 F2
Heby	106 B3		Heinolan mlk	107 F1		Hemer	17 E3
Hechingen	55 D3		Heinsberg	17 D4		Hemme	100 C2
Hecho	37 D2		Heist	50 A3		Hemmoor	48 A2
Hechtel	50 C3		Heist-op-den-Berg	50 C3		Hemnefjorden	100 C1
Hecklingen	52 C1		Hejde	109 F4		Hemnes	105 D3
						Hemnesberget	97 E2
						Hemsedal	104 C2
						Hemsedal V	104 C2

Place	Ref
Henares, R	40 B2
Hendaye	28 A4
Hengelo	17 D2
Hengersberg	56 B2
Hengstpaß	57 D3
Hénin-Beaumont	19 F1
Henley	9 E1
Henley-on-Thames	9 F2
Henneberg	52 B3
Hennebont	22 B3
Hennef	51 E3
Hennigsdorf	49 D4
Henrichemont	25 F2
Henstedt-Ulzburg	48 A2
Henstridge	9 D3
Hepoköngäs	99 E4
Heppenheim	54 C1
Heraclea	77 E4
Hérault	29 F4
Hérault (Dépt)	30 A4
Herbault	25 E2
Herbertingen	55 D3
Herbiers, les	24 B3
Herbignac	22 C4
Herbolzheim	54 C3
Herborn	51 F3
Herbrechtingen	55 E2
Herbstein	52 A3
Herceg Novi	76 A3
Hercegovac	71 D2
Hercegov Goleša	76 B1
Herðubreið	96 C2
Hereford	9 D1
Hereford and Worcester	9 D1
Herencia	40 B4
Herentals	50 C3
Herford	17 F2
Héricourt	27 E2
Heringsdorf	49 E2
Herisau	58 B2
Hérisson	26 A3
Hérisson, Cascades du	27 D3
Herk	50 C3
Herleshausen	52 B3
Hermagor	59 F2

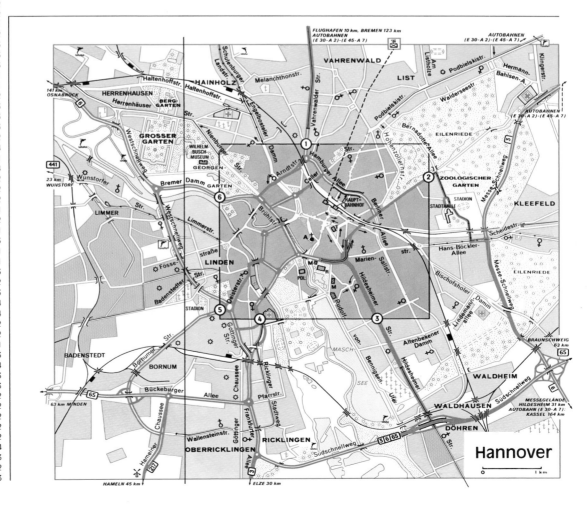

Hannover

0 ____ 1 km

Herma Ness 3 F1
Hermannsburg 48 B4
Hermansverk 104 B1
Hermenault, l' 24 C3
Herment 29 E1
Hermeskeil 54 B1
Hermigua 42 A4
Hermsdorf 53 D3
Hernani 36 C1
Hernansancho 39 F1
Herne 17 E3
Herne Bay 11 D3
Herning 108 A3
Heroldsberg 55 F1
Herónia 83 F4
Herøy 100 A2
Herrala 107 F2
Herre 104 C3
Herrenberg 55 D3
Herrenchiemsee 56 B3
Herrera (Andalucía) 43 E3
Herrera (Aragón) 37 D4
Herrera *Mt* 37 D4
Herrera de Alcántara 38 C3
Herrera del Duque 39 F4
Herrera de Pisuerga 35 F3
Herrera, Pto de 36 B2
Herreruela 39 D3
Herrestad 108 C1
Herrieden 55 E2
Herrljunga 109 D1
Herrnburg 48 B2
Herrnhut 53 F2
Herrsching 56 A3
Herrskog 102 A2
Hersbruck 55 F1
Herselt 50 C3
Hérso 79 F2
Hersónissos Akrotíri 90 C3
Hersónissos Methánon 87 E2
Hersónissos Spinalónga 91 E3
Herstal 51 D3
Herten 17 E3
Hertford 9 F2
Hertfordshire 9 F2
Hervás 39 E2
Herzberg (D) 52 B2
Herzberg (DDR) 53 E1
Herzogenaurach 55 E1
Herzogenburg 57 E2
Herzsprung 49 D3
Hesdin 19 E2
Hesel 47 E3
Hessen 52 A3
Hesseng 95 F2
Hessisch-Lichtenau 52 B2
Hessisch Oldendorf 52 A1
Hestfjørður 96 A4
Hetekylä 99 E3
Hetin 72 C1
Hettange 21 D3
Hettstedt 52 C2
Heubach 55 E2
Heuchin 19 F1
Heukuppe 57 E3
Hevlin 57 F1
Hexham 5 E3
Heyrieux 30 C1
Heysham 6 B1
Hiddensee 49 D1
Hieflau 57 D3
Hiekkasarkät 102 C1
Hierbas 41 E3
Hierro 42 A4
Hiersac 28 C1
Hietaniemi 95 F4
Higham Ferrers 9 F1
Highland 2 C3
High Peak 6 C2
High Willhays 8 C3
High Wycombe 9 F2
Higuera de Arjona 44 A2
Higuera de la Serena 43 E1
Higuera de la Sierra 43 D2
Higuera de Vargas 42 C1
Higuera la Real 42 C1
Higueruela 41 D4
Hiidenportti 103 E1
Hiiumaa 110 B1
Híjar 37 D4
Hilchenbach 17 F4
Hildburghausen 52 C3
Hilden 17 E4
Hilders 52 B3
Hildesheim 52 B1
Hiliomódi 87 E1
Hillegom 16 B2
Hillerød 108 C3
Hillesøy 94 B2
Hillswick 3 F1
Hiloús, Akr 92 C1
Hilpoltstein 55 F2
Hiltula 103 E3
Hilvarenbeek 16 C4
Hilversum 16 C2
Himanka 102 C1
Hímaros 80 A2
Himmerland 108 B2
Hinckley 9 E1
Hindelang 55 E4
Hindhead 9 F3
Hindsholm 108 B3
Hinnøya 94 A3
Hinodejo 36 B3
Hinojares 44 B2
Hinojosa de Duero 39 D1
Hinojosa del Duque 43 E1
Hinterrhein 58 B3
Hintersee (D) 56 B4
Hintersee (DDR) 49 E2
Hinterstoder 57 D3
Hintertux 59 D2
Hinterweidenthal 54 B2
Híos 85 F4
Híos, N 85 E4
Hirschau 55 F1
Hirschberg 53 D3
Hirschegg 58 B2
Hirsingue 27 E2
Hirson 20 B2
Hirşova 115 E1
Hirtshals 108 B1
Hirvasvaara 99 E2
Hirvensalmi 103 E3
Hirvilahti 103 E2
Hirwaun 8 C2
Hisarja 115 D2
Histria 115 E1
Hitchin 9 F2
Hitra 100 C1
Hitzacker 48 B3
Hjälmaren 105 F4
Hjartdal 104 C3
Hjellestad 104 A2
Hjelmeland 104 A3
Hjelmsøya 95 D1
Hjo 109 D1
Hjørring 108 B1
Hjørundfjorden 100 A2
Hlebine 71 D1
Hlemoútsi 86 B1
Hlomó, Óros 83 F3
Hluboká 57 D1
Hobro 108 B2
Höchberg 55 D1
Hochdorf 27 F2
Hochfeiler 59 D2
Hochfelden 21 E4
Hochgolling 59 F1
Hochgrabe 59 E2
Hochosterwitz 70 B1
Hochreichart 57 D4
Hochschober 59 E2
Hochschwab 57 D3
Hochspeyer 54 C1
Höchst 55 D1
Höchstadt 55 E1
Höchstädt 55 E2
Hochtannbergpaß 58 B2
Hochtor (Osttirol) 59 E2
Hochtor (Steiermark) 57 D3
Hockenheim 54 C2
Hoddesdon 9 F2
Hodenhagen 48 A4
Hœdic 22 C4
Hódmezővásárhely 114 B1
Hodnet 6 B3
Hodonín 57 F1
Hodoš 70 C1
Hodovo 75 F2
Hoedekenskerke 16 B4
Hoek van Holland 16 B3
Hoemsbu 100 B2
Hof 53 D4
Hofgeismar 52 A2
Hofheim 52 B4
Hofles 97 D4
Höfn 96 C2
Hofolding 56 A3
Hofors 105 F2
Hofsjökull 96 B2
Höganäs 108 C3
Høgebru 100 A3
Höglekardalen 101 E2
Högsäter 105 D4
Högsby 109 E2
Høgset 100 B2
Hohe Acht 51 E4
Hohenau 57 F2
Hohenberg 57 E3
Hohenems 58 B2
Hohengandern 52 B2
Hohenlimburg 17 E4
Hohenlinden 56 B3
Hohenlockstedt 48 A2
Hohenmölsen 53 D2
Hohenpeißenberg 56 A4
Hohenseeden 48 C4
Hohenstein 53 D3
Hohentauern 57 D4
Hohenwestedt 48 A2
Hohenzollern 55 D3
Hoher Zinken 56 C3
Hohe Tauern 59 E2
Hohe Tauern, Nat Pk 59 E2
Hóhlakas 93 E2
Hohneck 27 E1
Hohwachter Bucht 48 B1
Hohwald, le 21 E4
Højer 108 A4
Hokksund 104 C3
Hol 104 C2
Holbæk 108 C3
Holbeach 7 E3
Holdorf 17 F2
Holič 57 F1
Höljäkkä 103 E1
Höljes 101 D4
Hollabrunn 57 E2
Høllen 104 B4
Hollenstedt 48 A3
Höllental 57 E3
Holles 97 D4
Hollfeld 52 C4
Hollingsholm 100 B2
Hollola 107 F2
Hollum 16 C1
Hollywood 13 D4
Holm (N) 97 D3
Holm (S) 101 F2
Hólmavík 96 A1
Holmec 70 B1
Holmen 105 D2
Holmestrand 104 C3
Holmfirth 6 C2
Holmön 102 B1
Holmsjön 101 E3
Holmslands Klit 108 A3
Holmsund 102 B1
Holomóndas, Óros 80 B3
Holstebro 108 A2
Holsted 108 A3
Holsworthy 8 C3
Holt 7 F3
Holwerd 47 D3
Holycross Abbey 14 C3
Holyhead 6 A2
Holy I (Anglesey) 6 A2
Holy I (Northumberland) 5 E2
Holywell 6 B2
Holywood 13 E2
Holzappel 51 F4
Holzgau 58 C2
Holzkirchen 56 A3
Holzleitner Sattel 58 C2
Holzminden 52 A2
Homberg (Hessen) 52 A3
Homberg (Nordrhein-Westfalen) 17 D3
Homburg 54 B2
Hommelstø 97 D3
Hommelvik 100 C2
Hommersåk 104 A3
Homoljske planine 73 E3
Hondarribia Fuenterrabia 36 C1
Hondón de las Nieves 45 D2
Hönebach 52 B3
Hønefoss 104 C3
Honfleur 19 D3
Høng 108 B3
Hónikas 87 D2
Honiton 9 D3
Honkajoki 102 B3
Honningsvåg 95 E1
Honrubia 40 C3
Honrubia de la Cuesta 36 A3
Hontalbilla 40 A1
Hontoria del Pinar 36 A3
Hooge 47 F1
Hoogeveen 17 D2
Hoogezand 47 D3
Hoogstraten 50 C2
Hook Head 15 D4
Höör 109 D3
Hoorn 16 C2
Hopetoun House 5 D2
Hopfgarten 59 D1
Hopperstad 104 B1
Hóra (Dodekánissa) 89 E2
Hóra (Pelopónissos) 86 C3
Hora Svatého Šebestiána 53 E3
Horažďovice 56 C1
Horb 54 C3
Hörby 109 D3
Horcajo de los Montes 39 F4
Horcajo de Santiago 40 B3
Horcajo de Trevélez 44 A3
Horcajo-Medianero 39 E2
Horche 40 B2
Hordaland 104 B2
Horden 5 E4
Horeftó 83 F2
Horezu 115 D1
Horgen 58 A2
Horgoš 72 C1
Horley 10 C3
Horn (A) 57 E2
Horn (Baden-Württemberg) 55 D4
Horn (N) 97 D3
Horn (Nordrhein-Westfalen) 52 A2
Hornachos 43 D1
Hornachuelos 43 E2
Hornavan 98 A2
Hornberg 54 C3
Hornburg 52 B1
Horncastle 7 E3
Horndal 106 A3
Horneburg 48 A3
Hörnefors 102 A2
Hörnerkirchen 48 A2
Hornet 100 C2
Hornindal 100 A3
Hornindalsvatn 100 A3
Hørning 108 B3
Horni Počernice 53 F3
Hornisgrinde 54 C3
Horni Slavkov 53 E4
Hornos 44 B2
Hornoy 19 E2
Hornsea 7 E2
Hörnum 47 F1
Hořovice 53 F4
Horsens 108 B3
Horsham 10 C3
Hørsholm 108 C3
Horšovský Týn 56 B1
Horst 48 B3
Horstmar 17 E2
Hortafjorden 97 D3
Horten 104 C3
Hortezuela 36 B4
Hortiátis 80 A3
Hospental 58 A3
Hospital 14 C3
Hospital de Orbigo 35 D3
Hossa 99 F3
Hossegor 28 A4
Hostalric 32 B4
Hotagen 101 E1
Hotagen *L* 101 E1
Hotton 50 C4
Houat 22 C4
Houches, les 27 E4
Houdain 19 F1
Houdan 19 E4
Houeillès 28 B3
Houffalize 51 D4
Houghton-le-Spring 5 E4
Houlgate 18 C3
Houmnikó 80 B2
Hoúni 83 D3
Hourtin 28 A2
Houtskär 107 D3
Hov 108 B3
Hovärken 101 D3
Hovden 104 B3
Hove 10 C3
Hovet 104 B2
Hovmantorp 109 E2
Høvringen 100 C3
Howden 7 D2
Howth 13 E4
Höxter 52 A2
Hoy 3 D1
Hoya 17 F1
Høyanger 100 A3
Hoyerswerda 53 F2
Hoylake 6 B2
Høylandet 97 D4
Hoym 52 C1
Hoyos 39 D2
Höytiäinen 103 F2
Hoz de Beteta 40 C2
Hozoviótissa 89 D3
Hracholuská přehr nádrž 53 E4
Hradec-Králove 112 A2
Hrádek 57 E1
Hrádek nad Nisou 53 F2
Hranice (Severomoravský) 112 A3
Hranice (Západočeský) 53 D4
Hrasnica 75 F1
Hrastnik 70 B2
Hrastovlje 70 A3
Hřensko 53 F2
Hrissafa 87 D3
Hrissí, N 91 E4
Hrissó 80 B2
Hrissoskalítissa 90 B3
Hrissoúpoli 80 C2
Hrissovítsi 86 C2
Hristianí, N 91 D1
Hristianó 86 C3
Hristós 89 D2
Hrómio 79 D4
Hrtkovci 72 C3
Hrušovany 57 F1
Hrvace 75 D1
Hrvatska 70 C2
Hückeswagen 17 E4
Hucknall 7 D3
Hucqueliers 19 E1
Huddersfield 6 C2
Hude 47 F3
Hudiksvall 101 F3
Huebra, R 39 E1
Huedin 112 C4
Huélago 44 A3
Huélamo 40 C2
Huelgoat 22 B3
Huelma 44 A2
Huelva 42 C2
Huelva, Riv. de 43 D2
Huércal-Overa 44 C3
Huérguina 41 D3
Huerta del Rey 36 A3
Huerta de Valdecarábanos 40 A3
Huertahernando 40 C2
Huerto 37 E3
Huerva, R 37 D4
Huesa 44 B2
Huesca 37 D3
Huéscar 44 B2
Huesna, Emb de 43 D2
Huete 40 B3
Huétor-Santillán 44 A3
Huétor-Tájar 43 F3
Hüfingen 54 C4
Huftarøy 104 A2
Huisne 23 F3
Huittinen 107 D2
Huizen 16 C2
Hulst 16 B4
Hultsfred 109 E2
Humada 35 F3
Humanes 40 B1
Humber Bridge 7 D2
Humber, R 7 E2
Humberside 7 D2
Humberside (Airport) 7 D2
Humenné 112 C3
Humppila 107 E2
Hundested 108 C3
Hundorp 100 C3
Hunedoara 114 C1
Hünfeld 52 B3
Hungerford 9 E2
Hunnebostrand 105 D4
Húnsflói 96 A1
Hunspach 21 F3
Hunsrück 54 B1
Hunstanton 7 E3
Hunte 17 F1
Huntingdon 9 F1
Huntly 3 E3
Hurdal 105 D2
Huriel 25 F4
Hurones, Emb de los 43 D3
Hurskaala 103 E3
Hürth 17 E4
Hurum 104 C1
Hurup 108 A2
Húsavík 96 B1
Husavik 104 A2
Husbands Bosworth 9 F1
Hushinish 2 A2
Huşi 113 E4
Huskvarna 109 D1
Husnes 104 A2
Hustadvika 100 B2
Hustopeče 57 F1
Husum (D) 47 F1
Husum (S) 102 A2
Hutovo 75 F2
Hutovo Blato 75 F2
Hüttenberg 57 D4
Hüttschlag 59 E1
Huttula 103 D3
Huttwil 27 F2
Huy 50 C4
Hvalba 96 A4
Hvalfjörður 96 A2
Hvalpsund 108 A2
Hvalvik 96 A3
Hvar 75 D2
Hvar *I* 75 E2
Hvarski kan 75 D2
Hveragerði 96 A2
Hveravellir 96 B2
Hvidbjerg 108 A2
Hvide Sande 108 A3
Hvitá 96 A2
Hvittingfoss 104 C3
Hvitträsk 107 E3
Hvolsvöllur 96 B3
Hwlffordd 8 B2
Hyde 6 C2
Hyen 100 A3
Hyères 31 D4
Hyères, Iles d' 31 D4
Hylsfjorden 104 A3
Hyltebruk 108 C2
Hyrynsalmi 99 E4
Hythe 11 D3
Hyvinkää 107 E2
Hyypiö 99 D2

I

Ia 91 E1
Ialomiţa 115 E1
Iaşi 113 E3
Íasmos 81 D2
Ibañeta, Pto 36 C1
Ibar 73 D4
Ibbenbüren 17 E2
Ibestad 94 B3
Ibi 45 E1
Ibias, R 34 C2
Ibiza 45 D4
Ibiza I 45 D3
Iblei, Mti 69 D4
Ičn'a 113 F1
Icod de los Vinos 42 A4
Idanha a Nova 38 C2
Idar-Oberstein 54 B1
Idéo Ándro 91 D4
Ídi, Óros 91 D4
Idoméni 79 F2
Iddoš 72 C1
Ídra 87 F2
Ídra, N 87 F3
Ídras, Kólpos 87 E2
Idre 101 D3
Idrigill Pt 2 B3
Idrija 70 A2
Idrijca 70 A2
Idro 58 C4
Idstein 51 F4
Ielsi 64 B3
Ieper 50 A3
Ierápetra 91 E4
Ierissós 80 B3
Ieropigi 78 C3
If, Château d' 30 C4
Ifestía 85 D1
Ifjord 95 E1
Ifjordfjellet 95 E1
Igalo 76 A3
Iga Vas 70 B2
Iggesund 101 F3
Iglesias 66 B4
Igls 59 D2
Igoumenítsa 82 B2
Igrane 75 E2
Igualada 37 F4
Ihtiman 115 D2
Ii 99 D3
Iijarvi 95 E2
Iijoki 99 D3
Iisalmi 103 E1
Iisvesi 103 E2
IJmuiden 16 B2
IJssel 17 D3
IJsselmeer 16 C2
IJsselmuiden 17 D2
IJzendijke 16 B4
IJzer 50 A3
Ikaalinen 102 C3
Ikaría, N 89 D2
Ikast 108 A3
Ilandža 73 D2
Ilanz 58 B3
Ilche 37 E3
Ilchester 9 D3
Ile-Bouchard, l' 25 D3
Ile-Rousse, l' 33 F2
Ilfracombe 8 C3
Ílhavo 38 B1
Ília 83 F3
Ília 86 B1
Il'ičevsk 113 F4
Ílida 86 B1
Ilidza 75 F1
Ilijas 71 F4
Ilíki 84 A4
Ilíki, L 84 A4
Iliókastro 87 E2
Ilirska Bistrica 70 B3
Ilkeston 7 D3
Ilkley 6 C2
Illana 40 B2
Illano 34 C1

Illar 44 B3
Ille 23 D3
Ille et Rance, Canal d' 23 D3
Ille-et-Vilaine 23 D3
Iller 55 E4
Illertissen 55 E3
Illescas 40 A2
Illingen 55 D2
Illmitz 57 F3
Illora 44 A3
Illueca 36 C4
Ilm 52 C3
Ilmajoki 102 C2
Ilmenau (D) 48 B3
Ilmenau (DDR) 52 C3
Il'men, Ozero 111 D1
Ilminster 9 D3
Ilok 72 B2
Ilomantsi 103 F2
Ilova 71 D2
Ilovik 70 B4
Ilsenburg 52 B1
Ilsfeld 55 D2
Imathía 79 E3
Imatra 103 F4
Ímeros 81 E2
Imitós 87 F1
Immenstaad 55 D4
Immenstadt 55 E4
Immingham 7 E2
Immingham Dock 7 E2
Imola 61 D3
Imotski 75 E1
Imperia 31 F3
Imphy 26 A3
Impruneta 61 D4
Imst 58 C2
Ina 49 F3
Inari 95 E3
Inarijärvi 95 E3
Inarijoki 95 E3
Inca 45 F2
Inchnadamph 2 C2
Inchtree 2 C4
Incisa in Val d'Arno 61 D4
Incudine, M 33 F4
Indal 101 F3
Indalsälven 101 E2
Indija 72 C2
Indre 25 D2
Indre (Dépt) 25 E3
Indre-et-Loire 25 D2
Infiesto 35 E1
Ingå 107 E3
Ingelmunster 50 A3
Ingleton 6 C1
Ingolstadt 55 F2
Ingrandes 23 E4
Ingul 113 F3
Ingulec 113 F3
Ingulec R 113 F3
Ingwiller 21 E3
Iniesta 41 D4
Iniö 107 D2
Iniön aukko 107 D2
Inis 12 B4
Inis Córthaidh 15 D3
Inishbofin 12 A3
Inishcrone 12 B2
Inisheer 12 B4
Inishkea 12 A2
Inishmaan 12 B4
Inishmore 12 B4
Inishmurray 12 C2
Inishowen 13 D1
Inishowen Head 13 D1
Inishshark 12 A3
Inishtrahull 13 D1
Inishturk 12 A3
Inkee 99 E3
Inkoo 107 E3

Inn (CH) 58 B3
Inn (D) 56 B3
Innbygda 104 C1
Inndyr 97 E2
Innellan 4 B2
Innerleithen 5 D2
Inner Sd 2 B3
Innfield 13 D3
Innhavet 97 F1
Innichen 59 E2
Inning 56 A3
Innsbruck 59 D2
Innset 94 B3
Innvik 100 A3
Inói (Pelopónissos) 86 B1
Inói (Stereá Eláda) 84 A4
Inoússes 85 F4
Inoússes, N 85 F4
Inowrocław 112 A1
Ins 27 E2
Ínsko 49 F2
Interlaken 27 F3
Întorsura Buzăuli 113 D4
Inveraray 4 B1
Inverbervie 3 E4
Invergarry 2 C4
Invergordon 3 D3
Inverkeithing 5 D2
Invermoriston 2 C4
Inverness 2 C3
Inverurie 3 E4
Inzell 56 B3
Ioánina 82 C1
Ioánina (Nomos) 82 B1
Ioanínon, L 82 C1
Iona 4 A1
Iónia Nissiá 82 A2
Íos 88 C4
Íos, N 88 C4
Ipáti 83 E3
Ipéria 83 E2
Iphofen 55 E1
Ípiros 82 B2
Ipsilí Ráhi 80 C2
Ípsos 82 A1
Ipsoúnda 86 C2
Ipswich 11 D2
Iput' 111 E4
Irákila (Makedonía) 80 A2
Irákila (Stereá Eláda) 83 E3
Irákila, N 88 C3
Iráklio 91 D3
Iráklio (Nomos) 91 D4
Irati, R 36 C2
Irbes Šaurums 110 B2
Irdning 57 D4
Iregua, R 36 C2
Iréo (Argolída) 87 D2
Iréo (Dodekánissa) 89 E2
Iréo (Korinthía) 87 E1
Iréo, Akr 87 E1
Íria 87 E2
Irig 72 C2
Irish Sea 13 F3
Iriški venac 72 C2
Irixoa 34 B1
Irnijärvi 99 E3
Iron-Bridge 9 D1
Irschenberg 56 B3
Irsina 65 D4
Irún 36 C1
Irurzun 36 C2
Irvine 4 C2
Irvinestow 12 C2
Irxleben 52 C1
Isaba 37 D2
Isaccea 113 E4
Ísafjarðardjúp 96 A1
Ísafjörður 96 A1
Ísala 115 E3
Isane 100 A3

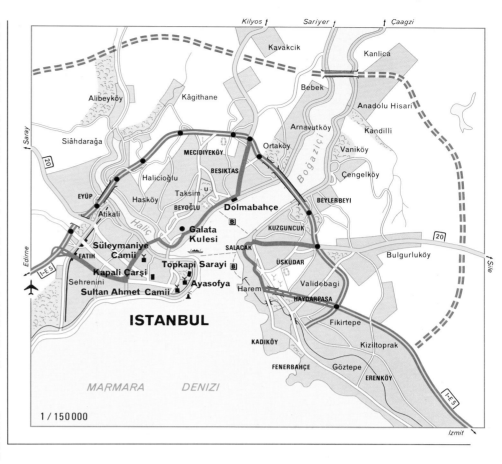

Isar 56 B2
Isarco 59 D2
Isbister 3 F1
Iscar 35 E4
Ischgl 58 C2
Ischia 64 A4
Ischia, I d' 64 A4
Ise 105 D3
Isefjord 108 C3
Iselle 58 A3
Iselsberg 59 E2
Iseo 60 B1
Iseo, L d' 58 B4
Iseran, Col de l' 31 E1
Isère (Dépt) 30 C1
Isère (R) 30 C1
Iserlohn 17 E3
Isernia 64 A3
Isfjellet 94 C2
Isfjorden 100 B2
Ishavsleden 94 C3
Ishëm 76 C4
Ishëm R 76 C4
Isigny 18 C3
Isili 66 B3
Is'kuras 95 E2
Iskår 115 D2
Isla 3 D4
Isla 36 A1
Isla Cristina 42 C3
Isla Mayor 43 D3
Island Magee 13 E2
Islay 4 A2
Isle 28 C2
Isle-Adam, l' 19 F3
Isle-de-Noé, l' 28 C4
Isle-en-Dodon, l' 37 F1
Isle-Jourdain, l' (Gers) 28 C4
Isle-Jourdain, l' (Vienne) 25 D4
Isle of Man 6 A1

Isle of Portland 9 D4
Isle of Whithorn 4 C4
Isle of Wight 9 E4
Isleornsay 2 B4
Isles of Scilly 8 A4
Isle-sur-la-Sorgue,l' 30 C3
Isle-sur-le-Doubs, l' 27 D2
Isle-sur-Serein, l' 26 B2
Ismaning 55 F3
Isnäs 107 F2
Isny 55 E4
Iso-Evo 107 E2
Isojärvi 103 D3
Isojoki 102 B3
Isokylä 99 E2
Isokyrö 102 B2
Isola del Gran Sasso d'Italia 63 F1
Isola della Scala 60 C1
Isola del Liri 64 A3
Isola di Capo Rizzuto 67 F3
Isona 37 F3
Isonzo 59 F3
Isorella 60 B1
Iso-Syöte 99 E3
Ispica 69 D4
Issambres, les 31 D4
Issel 17 D3
Issigeac 28 C2
Issoire 29 F1
Issóva, M. 86 C2
Íssoma 86 C1
Issoudun 25 E3
Is-sur-Tille 26 C2
Issy-l'Evêque 26 B3
Ist 74 B1
Istán 43 E4
İstanbul 115 F3

Istarske Toplice 70 A3
Istérnia 88 B2
Istha 52 A2
Isthmía 87 E1
Istibanja 77 F2
Istiéa 83 F3
Istindan 94 B3
Istok 76 C2
Istres 30 C4
Ístrios 93 E2
Isturits et d'Oxocelhaya, Grottes d' 28 A4
Itä-Aure 102 C3
Itaïnen Suomenlahti 107 F2
Itanós 91 F3
Itéa (Flórina) 79 D2
Itéa (Grevená) 79 D2
Itéa (Stereá Eláda) 83 E4
Itéa (Thessalía) 83 E2
Itéas, Kólpos 83 E4
Itháki 82 B4
Itháki, N 82 B4
Ithómi 86 C3
Iti 83 E3
Ítilo 87 D4
Íti, Óros 83 E3
Iton 19 E3
Itri 64 A3
Itta 52 B3
Ittiri 66 A2
Itz 52 C4
Itzehoe 48 A2
Ivacevici 112 C1
Ivajlovgrad 115 E3
Ivalo 95 E3
Ivalojoki Ävvil 95 E3
Ivančice 57 F1
Ivančići 71 F4
Ivančna Gorica 70 B2
Ivanec 70 C1

Ivangrad 76 C2
Ivanić Grad 71 D2
Ivanjica 73 D4
Ivanjska 71 E3
Ivankovo 71 F2
Ivano-Frankovsk 113 D3
Ivanščica 70 C2
Ivan Sedlo 75 F1
Ivanska 71 D2
Iveland 104 B4
Iveragh 14 A4
Ívira 80 B2
Iviron 80 C4
Ivrea 31 F1
Ivry-la-Bataille 19 E4
Ixiá 93 F1
Ixworth 11 D1
Iž 74 C1
Izeda 34 C4
Izegem 50 A3
Izlake 70 B2
Izmail 113 E4
İzmir 115 E4
İzmit 115 F3
Iznájar 43 F3
Iznájar, Emb de 43 F3
Iznallos 44 A3
İznik 115 F3
İznik Gölü 115 F3
Izoard, Col d' 31 D2
Izola 70 A3
Iz Veli 74 C1
Izvor (Makedonija) 77 D4
Izvor (Makedonija) 77 E3
Izvor (Srbija) 73 E4

J

Jaala 107 F2
Jääsjärvi 103 D3
Jabalón, R 44 A1
Jabbeke 50 A3
Jablanac 70 B4
Jablan Do 76 A2
Jablanica 75 F1
Jablanica (Reg) 77 D4
Jablanica *R* 77 D1
Jablaničko jez 75 F1
Jablonec nad Nisou 112 A2
Jablonné v Podještědí 53 F3
Jabugo 42 C2
Jabuka (Bosna i Hercegovina) 76 A1
Jabuka (Srbija) 76 B1
Jabuka (Vojvodina) 73 D2
Jabuka, I 74 C2
Jabukovac (Hrvatska) 71 D3
Jabukovac (Srbija) 73 F3
Jabukovik 77 E1
Jaca 37 D2
Jáchymov 53 E3
Jadar (Bosna i Hercegovina) 72 C4
Jadar (Srbija) 72 B3
Jäder 106 A3
Jaderberg 47 F3
Jadovik 76 B1
Jadovnik 71 D4
Jadranska Lešnica 72 B3
Jadransko More 74 B2
Jadraque 40 B1
Jaén 44 A2
Jagodnjac 71 F2
Jagotin 113 F2
Jagst 55 E2
Jagsthausen 55 D2
Jahorina 76 A1
Jahorina (Reg) 76 A1
Jajce 71 E4
Jäkkvik 97 F2
Jakobselv 95 F2
Jakobstad 102 C1
Jakšić 71 E2
Jakupica 77 E3
Jalasjärvi 102 C3
Jaligny 26 A3
Jalón, R 36 C3
Jalovik Izvor 73 F4
Jambol 115 E2
Jamena 72 B3
Jämijärvi 102 C3
Jäminkipohja 102 C3
Jämjö 109 E3
Jammerbugten 108 A2
Jamnička Kiselica 70 C2
Jämsä 103 D3
Jämsänkoski 103 D3
Jämtlands Län 101 E2
Janakkala 107 E2
Janče 77 D3
Jandía, Pta de 42 C4
Jándula, Emb del 44 A1
Jándula, R 44 A1
Jänisselkä 103 F2
Janja 72 B3
Janjevo 77 D2
Janjina 75 E2
Jankov kamen 76 C1
Jañona 39 D2
Jantra 115 D2
Janville 25 E1
Janzé 23 D3
Japetić 70 C2
Jäppilä 103 E2
Jaraba 36 C4
Jarafuel 41 D4
Jaraicejo 39 E3
Jaráiz 39 E2
Jarak 72 C3
Jarama, R 40 B2
Jarandilla de la Vera 39 E2
Järbo 106 A2
Jarcevo 111 E3
Jard 24 B3
Jæren 104 A4
Jaren 105 D2
Jargeau 25 E1
Jarkovac 73 D2
Jarmen 49 D2
Jarmenovci 73 D3
Jarnac 28 B1
Jarnages 25 E4
Järna (Kopparbergs Län) 105 E2
Järna (Stockholms Län) 106 B4
Jarny 21 D3
Jarocin 112 A2
Jaroměřice 57 E1
Jarosław 112 C2
Järpen 101 E2
Jarrow 5 E3
Jarvelä 107 F2
Järvenpää 107 E2
Järvsö 101 F3
Jaša Tomić 73 D2
Jasenak 70 B3
Jasenica (Bosna i Hercegovina) 71 D3
Jasenica (Srbija) 73 D3
Jasenovac 71 D3
Jasenovo (Crna Gora) 76 B2
Jasenovo (Srbija) 76 B1
Jasenovo (Vojvodina) 73 D2
Jasień 53 F1
Jasika 73 E4
Jasikovo 73 E3
Jasło 112 C3
Jasmund 49 D1
Jastrebarsko 70 C2
Jastrowie 112 A1
Jászberény 112 B4
Jau, Col de 32 B2
Jaufenpass 59 D2
Jaunay-Clan 25 D3
Jaunpass 27 E3
Jausiers 31 D2
Javalambre 41 D3
Javalambre, Sa de 41 E3
Javalón 41 D2
Javea 45 E1
Jävenitz 48 C4
Javie, la 31 D3
Javor 76 C1
Javořice 57 D1
Javornjača 71 D4
Javorov 112 C2
Jävre 98 B4
Javron 23 E3
Jedburgh 5 D3
Jedincy 113 D3
Jędrzejów 112 B2
Jeesiö 95 E4
Jeetze 48 B3
Jegun 28 C4
Jegunovce 77 D3
Jēkabpils 110 C3
Jektevik 104 A2
Jelah 71 E3
Jelašca 76 A1
Jelenia Góra 112 A2
Jelenje 70 B3
Jelgava 110 C3
Jelling 108 A3
Jel'n'a 111 E3
Jelsa (N) 104 A3
Jelsa (YU) 75 E2
Jemnice 57 E1
Jena 52 C3
Jenbach 59 D1
Jengejetneme 97 E4
Jennersdorf 57 F4
Jeppo 102 C2
Jerez de la Frontera 43 D3
Jerez de los Caballeros 42 C1
Jérica 41 E3
Jerichow 49 D4
Jerisjärvi 95 D4
Jerpoint Abbey 15 D3
Jersey 18 A3
Jerte 39 E2
Jerte, R 39 E2
Jerxheim 52 B1
Jerzu 66 C3
Jesenice (CS) 53 E4
Jesenice (YU) 70 A1
Jeseník 112 A2
Jesi 61 F4
Jeßnitz 53 D2
Jesolo 59 E4
Jessen 53 D1
Jessheim 105 D3
Jetzelsdorf 57 E2
Jeumont 20 B1
Jevenstedt 48 A2
Jever 47 E3
Jevišovice 57 E1
Jevnaker 105 D2
Jezerane 70 C3
Jezerce 77 D2
Jezercë, M 76 C2
Jezero 71 E4
Jezero Šćit 75 E1
Jezersko 70 B1
Ježevica 72 C4
Jičín 112 A2
Jiekkevarre 94 C2
Jihlava 57 E1
Jihlava *R* 57 E1
Jijona 45 E1
Jiloca, R 41 D2
Jílové u Prahy 53 F4
Jimbolia 114 C1
Jimena 44 A2
Jimena de la Frontera 43 E4
Jindřichovice 53 D3
Jindřichuv Hradec 57 D1
Jirkov 53 E3
Jiu 115 D2
Jizera 53 F3
Joachimsthal 49 E3
Jockfall 98 C2
Jódar 44 A2
Jodoigne 50 C3
Joensuu 103 F2
Jõgeva 110 C1
Johanngeorgenstadt 53 D3
John o'Groats 3 D2
Johnstone 4 C2
Johovac 71 F3
Joigny 26 A1
Joinville 20 C4
Jokela 107 E2
Jokijärvi 99 E3
Jokikylä 99 E4
Jokioinen 107 E2
Jokkmokk 98 B2
Jökulsá-á Fjöllum 96 C1
Joloskylä 99 D3
Jølstravatnet 100 A3
Jomala 106 C3
Jönåker 106 A4
Jondal 104 B2
Jongunjärvi 99 E3
Joniškis 110 C3
Jönköping 109 D1
Jönköpings Län 109 D2
Jonzac 28 B1
Jordbro 106 B4
Jordbruksveien 95 D2
Jormlien 97 E4
Jörn 98 B4
Joroinen 103 E3
Jørpeland 104 A3
Jørstadmoen 105 D2
Jošanica 73 E4
Jošanička Banja 76 C1
Jošavka 71 E3
Josenfjorden 104 A3
Jošipdol 70 C3
Josipovac 71 F2
Josselin 22 C3
Jostedalsbreen 100 A3
Jotunheimen 100 B3
Jou, Coll de 32 A3
Joué 25 D2
Jougne 27 D3
Joutjärvi 107 F2
Joutsa 103 D3
Joutseno 103 E4
Joutsijärvi 99 E2
Joyeuse 30 B2
Juankoski 103 E2
Juan-les-Pins 31 E4
Júcar, R 41 E4
Jüchen 17 D4
Juchnov 111 F3
Judaberg 104 A3
Judenau 57 E2
Judenburg 57 D4
Judio 43 F1
Juelsminde 108 B3
Jugenheim 54 C1
Jugon 22 C3
Jugorje 70 B2
Juillac 29 D1
Juist 47 E3
Jukkasjärvi 94 C4
Jülich 17 D4
Julierpass 58 B3
Jullouville 18 B4
Jumaliskylä 99 F4
Jumeaux 29 F1
Jumièges 19 D3
Jumilhac-le-Grand 29 D1
Jumilla 45 D1
Jumilla, Pto de 45 D1
Juminen 103 E1
Jumisko 99 E2
Juneda 37 F4
Jungfrau 27 F3
Junik 76 C2
Juniville 20 B3
Junkeren 97 E2
Junosuando 95 D4
Junsele 101 F2
Juntusranta 99 F3
Juojärvi 103 E2
Juoksenki 98 C2
Juorkuna 99 E4
Jura 4 B2
Jura (Canton) 27 E2
Jura (Dépt) 27 D3
Jura, Sd of 4 B2
Jurbarkas 110 C3
Jurjevo 70 B4
Jūrmala 110 C2
Jurmofjärden 107 D3
Jurmu 99 E3
Juromenha 38 C4
Jurva 102 B2
Jussey 27 D1
Justel 34 D3
Jüterbog 53 E1
Juuka 103 E2
Juupajoki 103 D3
Juurusvesi 103 E2
Juva (Mikkelin Lääni) 103 E3
Juva (Turun ja Porin Lääni) 107 D2
Juvigny-le-Tertre 18 C4
Juvigny-sous-Andaine 18 C4
Juvola 103 E3
Juzennecourt 26 C1
Južna Morava 73 E4
Južnyj Bug 113 E2
Jyderup 108 B3
Jylland 108 A3
Jyrkkä 103 E1
Jyväskylä 103 D3

K

Kaamanen 95 E3
Kaamaskoki 95 E2
Kaaresuvanto 95 D3
Kaarina 107 D2
Kaatsheuvel 16 C3
Kaavi 103 E2
Kaavinjärvi 103 E2
Kåbdalis 98 B3
Kablart 72 C4
Kać 72 C2
Kačanik 77 D2
Kačarevo 73 D2
Kačikol 77 D2
Kadaň 53 E3
Kadi Bogaz 73 F4
Kadrifakovo 77 E3
Kafiréas, Akr 84 C4
Kafiréa, Stenó 88 B1
Kåfjord 95 E1
Kåfjorden 94 C2
Kaga 106 A4
Kagarlyk 113 E2
Kagul 113 E4
Kahla 52 C3
Kaiáfas 86 B2
Kailbach 55 D1
Kaïmaktsalán 79 E2
Kainasto 102 B3
Kaindorf 57 E4
Kaipola 103 D3
Kairala 95 F4
Kaisergebirge 59 D1
Kaiserslautern 54 B1
Kaisheim 55 E2
Kaitumälven 94 C4
Kaiuđerovo 73 E2
Kajaani 99 E4
Kakan 74 C1
Kakanj 71 F4
Kakí Thálassa 88 A1
Kakí Vígla 87 F1
Kakslauttanen 95 E3
Kalajoki 102 C1
Kalajoki *R* 102 C1
Kalak 95 E1
Kalamáki (Lárissa) 83 F2
Kalamáki (Magnissía) 84 A2
Kalamáki, Akr 85 D2
Kalamáta 86 C3
Kalambáka 83 D1
Kalambáki 80 C2
Kalámi 89 E1
Kalamiótissa 91 F1
Kalamítsi (Makedonía) 80 B4
Kalamítsi (Stereá Eláda) 82 B3
Kálamos, N 82 C3
Kalamotí 85 F4
Kalamotó 80 A3
Kalándra 80 A4
Kalá Nerá 83 F2
Kalá Nissiá 87 E1
Kalanti 107 D2
Kalapódi 83 F3
Kalaraš 113 E3
Kälarne 101 F2
Kalavárda 93 E1
Kalávrita 86 C1
Kal'azin 111 F1
Kalbe 48 C4
Kalce 70 A2
Kaldakvísl 96 B2
Kaléndzi (Ípiros) 82 C2
Kaléndzi (Pelopónissos) 86 C1
Kalenić 73 D4
Kalérgo 84 C4
Kalesija 72 B3
Kali 74 C1
Kaliakoúda 83 D3
Kaliáni 87 D1
Kalidromo, Óros 83 E3
Kalífitos 80 C2
Kalí Liménes 91 D4
Kalí Límni 93 D3
Kalimassiá 85 F4
Kalimenci, Ez 77 F2
Kálimnos 89 F3
Kálimnos, N 89 E3
Kalinin 111 F2
Kaliningrad 110 B4
Kalinkoviči 113 E1
Kalinovik 75 F1
Kalipéfki 79 E4
Kalirráhi 79 D4
Kalithéa (Dodekánissa) 93 F1
Kalithéa (Ilía) 86 C2
Kalithéa (Makedonía) 80 B2
Kalithéa (Messinía) 86 C3
Kalithéa (Stereá Eláda) 83 D3
Kalithéa (Thessalía) 80 B4
Kalithiés 93 F1
Kalíthiro 83 D2
Kalivári 88 B1
Kalíves (Kríti) 90 C3
Kalíves (Thássos) 80 C3
Kalívia (Ahaïa) 86 C1
Kalívia (Atikí-Piréas) 87 F1
Kalívia (Etolía-Akarnanía) 82 C3
Kalívia (Korinthía) 87 D1
Kalívia Varikoú 79 F4
Kalix 98 C3
Kalixälven 98 C2
Kaljord 94 A3
Kalkar 17 D3
Kalkkinen 107 F1
Kall 101 D2
Kallaktjäkkå 94 B4
Kallavesi 103 E2
Kållby 102 C1
Källby 105 E4
Kallinge 109 E3
Kallio 102 C3
Kalliojoki 99 F4
Kallislahti 103 E3
Kallmünz 55 F2
Kallsjön 101 D1
Kalmar 109 E2
Kalmar Län 109 E2
Kalmar sund 109 E2
Kalmit 54 C2
Kalna 73 F4
Kalnik 71 D2
Kalnik *Mt* 71 D2
Kalocsa 112 B4
Kalogerikoú 87 D2
Kalogriá 86 B1
Kalohóri 83 D1
Kaló•Horió 91 E4
Kalókastro 80 A2
Kaló Neró 86 C3
Kaloni (Lésvos) 85 F2
Kaloní (Pelopónissos) 87 E2
Kalonís, Kólpos 85 F2
Kaloskopí 83 E3
Kalotássi, Akr 89 D4
Kalø Vig 108 B3
Kalpáki 78 C4
Kals 59 E2
Kalsdorf 57 E4
Kaltbrunn 58 A2
Kaltenkirchen 48 A2
Kaltennordheim 52 B3
Kaltern 59 D3
Kaltezés 87 D2
Kaluga 111 F3
Kalundborg 108 B3
Kaluš 112 C3
Kalvåg 104 A1
Kalvehave 108 C4
Kälviä 102 C1
Kalvola 107 E2
Kalvträsk 98 B4
Kamáres (Kríti) 91 D4
Kamarés (Páros) 88 C3
Kamáres (Pelopónissos) 83 D4
Kamáres (Sífnos) 88 B3
Kamári 91 E1
Kamariótissa 81 E3
Kambanós, Akr 88 B1
Kambiá 85 E4
Kámbos (Kríti) 90 B3
Kámbos (Pelopónissos) 86 C3
Kámbos (Stereá Eláda) 83 D4
Kamčija 115 E2
Kamen 17 E3
Kamenari 76 A3
Kaména Voúria 83 F3
Kamenec-Podol'skij 113 D3
Kamenica 77 F2
Kamenice 57 D1
Kaméni, N 91 E1
Kamenjak, Rt 70 A4
Kamenka 113 F2
Kamensko (Hrvatska) 71 E2
Kamensko (Hrvatska) 75 E1
Kamenz 53 F2
Kamień Pomorski 49 E2
Kamieński, Zalew 49 E2
Kamilári 91 D4
Kamínia 86 B1
Kámiros 93 E1
Kamnik 70 B2
Kamp 57 E2
Kamp-Bornhofen 51 E4
Kampen (D) 47 F1
Kampen (NL) 17 D2
Kamp-Lintfort 17 D3
Kanal 70 A2
Kanála 88 A2
Kanal Dunav-Tisa-Dunav 73 D2
Kanália 55 D4
Kanatádika 83 F3
Kánava 88 A4
Kándanos 90 B3
Kandel 54 C2
Kandel *Mt* 54 C3
Kandern 54 C4
Kandersteg 27 F3
Kándia 87 E2
Kandíla (Pelopónissos) 87 D2
Kandíla (Stereá Eláda) 82 C3
Kandíli 84 A3
Kandıra 115 F3
Kandrše 70 B2
Kanestraum 100 B2
Kanev 113 F2
Kanfanar 70 A3
Kangádio 86 B1
Kangasala 107 E1
Kangaslampi 103 E2
Kangasniemi 103 D3
Kangosjärvi 95 D4
Kanjiža 72 C1
Kankaanpää 102 C3
Kannonkoski 103 D2
Kannus 102 C1
Kannusjärvi 103 E4

Kanturk 14 B3
Kaona 73 D4
Kaonik (Bosna i Hercegovina) 71 F4
Kaonik (Srbija) 73 E4
Kapandriti 87 F1
Kaparéli 83 F4
Kapariá 88 B2
Kapele, Vrh 70 C3
Kapellskär 106 C3
Kapélo, Akr 90 A2
Kapfenberg 57 E3
Kaplice 57 D2
Kaposvár 114 B1
Kapp 105 D2
Kappel 51 E4
Kappeln 48 A1
Kappelshamnsviken 109 F3
Kaprije 74 C1
Kaprun 59 E1
Kapsáli 90 A2
Kápsas 87 D2
Kapsoúri 88 B1
Kapsukas 110 C4
Kapuvár 112 A4
Karabiga 115 E3
Karaburun 115 E4
Karačev 111 F4
Karadeniz Boğazı 115 F3
Karan 72 C4
Karasjåkka 95 E2
Karasjok 95 E2
Karasu 115 F3
Karats 98 A2
Karavás 90 A1
Karavómilos 83 F3
Karavónissia 92 C2
Karavostássis 91 D1
Kårböle 101 E3
Karcag 112 B4
Kardámena 89 F3
Kardámila 85 E4
Kardamíli 86 C3
Kardeljevo 75 E2
Kärdla 110 B1
Karditsa 55 D4
Karditsa (Nomos) 55 D4
Kărdžali 115 D3
Karerpass 59 D3
Karesuando 95 D3
Karfás 85 F4
Karhukangas 99 D4
Karhula 103 F4
Karhunkierros 99 F2
Karhutunturi 95 F4
Kariá (Pelopónissos) 87 D2
Kariá (Stereá Eláda) 83 F3
Kariés (Makedonía) 80 C4
Kariés (Pelopónissos) 87 D3
Karigasniemi 95 E2
Karijoki 102 B3
Karinainen 107 D2
Kariótisa 79 E3
Karis 107 E3
Káristos 88 A1
Karítena 86 C2
Karjaa 107 E3
Karjalohja 107 E3
Karkaloú 86 C2
Karkinágri 89 D2
Karkku 107 D1
Kärkölä 107 E2
Karleby 102 C1
Karlevi 109 E3
Karlino 49 F1
Karl-Marx-Stadt 53 E3
Karlobag 70 C4
Karlovac 70 C3
Karlovássi 89 E1
Karlovo 115 D2
Karlovy Vary 53 E4
Karlsborg 105 E4
Karlsburg 49 D2
Karlsfeld 55 F3
Karlshamn 109 D3
Karlshuld 55 F2
Karlskoga 105 E4
Karlskrona 109 E3
Karlsøy 94 C2
Karlsruhe 54 C2
Karlstad 105 E3
Karlstadt 52 B4
Karlštejn 53 F4
Karlstift 57 D2
Karmøy 104 A3
Karnezéika 87 E2
Karnobat 115 E2
Kärnten 59 F2
Karolinerleden 101 E2
Karow 48 C2
Kärpänkylä 99 F2
Kárpathos 93 D3
Kárpathos, N 93 D3
Karpeníssi 83 D3
Karperí 80 A2
Karperó 79 D4
Kärsämäki 103 D1
Kårsatjåkka 94 B4
Kārsava 111 D2
Karstädt 48 C3
Karstula 103 D2
Kartal 115 F3
Kartéri (Ípiros) 82 B2
Kartéri (Pelopónissos) 87 D1
Karterós 91 D3
Kártsino, Akr 84 C3
Karttula 103 E2
Kartuzy 110 A4
Karungi 98 C3
Karunki 98 C3
Karup 108 A2
Karvala 102 C2
Kärväskylä 103 D2
Karvia 102 C3
Karviná 112 B3
Karvoskylä 103 D1
Karvounári 82 B2
Karwendelgebirge 59 D1
Kašalj 76 C1
Kašin 111 F1
Kašina 70 C2
Kaskinen 102 B3
Kasko 102 B3
Káspakas 85 D1
Kašperské Hory 56 C1
Kassándra 80 B4
Kassándras, Kólpos 80 B4
Kassándria 80 A4
Kassel 52 A2
Kassiópi 82 A1
Kassópi 82 B2
Kássos, N 93 D3
Kastaniá (Makedonía) 79 E3
Kastaniá (Pelopónissos) 87 D1
Kastaniá (Thessalía) 82 C1
Kastaniá (Thessalía) 83 D2
Kastaniés 81 F1
Kastaniótissa 83 F3
Kastéla 84 B4
Kastelhoms 106 C3
Kastéli (Kríti) 90 B3
Kastéli (Kríti) 91 E4
Kastellaun 51 E4
Kastelórizo 93 F2
Kastélou, Akr 93 D3
Kastelruth 59 D3
Kaštel Stari 75 D1
Kaštel Žegarski 75 D1
Kasterlee 50 C3
Kastl 55 F1
Kastorf 48 B2
Kastóri 87 D3
Kastoriá 79 D3
Kastoriá (Nomos) 78 C3
Kastoriás, L 79 D3
Kastós, N 82 C4
Kastráki (Kikládes) 88 C3
Kastráki (Stereá Eláda) 82 C3
Kastráki (Thessalía) 83 D1
Kastrakíou, Teh L 82 C3
Kastrí (Pelopónissos) 87 D2
Kastrí (Stereá Eláda) 83 E3
Kastrí (Thessalía) 83 F1
Kástro (Pelopónissos) 86 B1
Kástro (Skíathos) 84 A2
Kástro (Stereá Eláda) 83 F4
Kastrossikiá 82 B2
Katafígio 79 E4
Katáfito 80 B1
Katáfourko 82 C3
Katahás 79 F3
Katákolo 86 B2
Katálako 85 D1
Katáno, Akr 88 A3
Katápola 89 D3
Katára 82 C1
Katastári 86 A1
Katavía 93 E2
Katelimátsa 91 F1
Kateliós 86 A1
Kateríni 79 F4
Katerloch 57 E4
Katharó 91 E4
Katheni 84 B4
Katići 76 C1
Kätkäsuvanto 95 D4
Katlanovo 77 E3
Katlanovska Banja 77 E3
Katlenburg-Duhm 52 B2
Káto Ahaïa 86 B1
Káto Alissós 86 B1
Káto Asséa 87 D2
Káto Dolianá 87 D2
Káto Figália 86 C2
Káto Gadzéa 83 F2
Katohí 82 C4
Káto Kamíla 80 B2
Káto Klinés 79 D2
Káto Makrinoú 83 D4
Katoméri, Akr 88 C3
Káto Moussounítsa 83 E3
Káto Nevrokópi 80 B1
Káto Ólimbos 83 E1
Káto Tithoréa 83 E4
Katoúna (Lefkáda) 82 B3
Katoúna (Stereá Eláda) 82 C3
Káto Vassilikí 83 D4
Káto Vérga 86 C3
Káto Vérmio 79 E3
Káto Vlassía 86 C1
Katowice 112 B2
Káto Zahloroú 86 C1
Káto Zákros 91 F4
Katrineholm 106 A4
Katschberg 59 F2
Katschberg-Tunnel 59 F2
Kattegat 108 C2
Katwijk aan Zee 16 B2
Kaub 51 F4
Kaufbeuren 55 E3
Kauhajärvi 102 C2
Kauhajoki 102 B3
Kauhaneva-Pohjankangas 102 C3
Kauhava 102 C2
Kaukonen 95 E4
Kaunas 110 C3
Kaupanger 104 B1
Kaušany 113 E4
Kaustinen 102 C2
Kautokeino 95 D3
Kautokeinoelva 95 D3
Kauttua 107 D2
Kavadarci 77 E3
Kavajë 76 C4
Kavála 80 C2
Kavála (Nomos) 80 C2
Kavála, Kólpos 80 C2
Kavarna 115 E2
Kavíli 81 F1
Kävlinge 108 C3
Kávos 82 A2
Kavoússi 91 F4
Käylä 99 E2
Kaysersberg 27 E1
Kazan 73 E2
Kažani 77 E4
Kazanlăk 115 D2
Kazárma 86 C3
Kazatin 113 E2
Kazimierz Dolny 112 C2
Kazincbarcika 112 B3
Kdyně 56 B1
Kéa 88 A2
Keadew 12 C2
Keady 13 D2
Keähkkiljohka 95 D3
Keal, L na 4 B1
Kéa Meriá 88 A2
Kéa, N 88 A2
Kéas, Stenó 88 A2
Kebnekaise 94 B4
Kebnekaise *Mt* 94 B4
Kebock Head 2 B2
Kecskemét 112 B4
Kėdainiai 110 C3
Kédros 83 D2
Kędzierzyn-Koźle 112 B2
Keel 12 A2
Keerbergen 50 C3
Kefalári 87 D2
Kefálas, Akr 80 C3
Kefáli, Akr 90 A2
Kefaloniá, N 82 B4
Kéfalos 89 F4
Kéfalos, Akr 88 A2
Kefalóvrisso (Ípiros) 78 C4
Kefalóvrisso (Pelopónissos) 86 C3
Kefalóvrisso (Stereá Eláda) 82 C4
Kefalóvrisso (Thessalía) 83 D1
Keflavík 96 A2
Kehl 54 C3
Kehlstein 56 C4
Kehrókambos 80 C2
Kéhros 81 E2
Keighley 6 C2
Keimaneigh, Pass of 14 B4
Keitele 103 D2
Keitele *L* 103 D2
Keith 3 D3
Kéla 79 D2
Kelankylä 99 E3
Kelberg 51 E4
Kelbra 52 C2
Këlcyrë 114 C4
Kelebija 72 B1
Kelefá 87 D4
Kelheim 55 F2
Kellinghusen 48 A2
Kellojärvi 99 F4
Kellokoski 107 E2
Kells 13 D3
Kelso 5 E2
Kelujärvi 95 E4
Kemberg 53 D1
Kembs 27 E1
Kemi 99 D3
Kemihaara 95 F4
Kemijärvi 99 E2
Kemijärvi *L* 99 E2
Kemijoki 99 D2
Keminmaa 99 D3
Kemiö 107 D3
Kemnath 53 D4
Kempele 99 D4
Kempen 17 D4
Kempenich 51 E4
Kempten 55 E4
Kendal 6 B1
Kéndras, Akr 88 B3
Kendrikó 79 F2
Kenilworth 9 E1
Kenmare 14 A4
Kenmare River 14 A4
Kennacraig 4 B2
Kenoúrgio 83 D3
Kent 11 D3
Kentallen 4 B1
Kenzingen 54 C3
Keramía 85 F2
Keramídi 83 F2
Keramitsa 82 B1
Kéramos 85 E4
Keramotí 81 D2
Kerassiá (Évia) 84 A3
Kerassiá (Thessalía) 83 F2
Kerassiés 79 E2
Kerassohóri 83 D3
Kerassóna 82 C2
Kérata, Akr 83 F3
Keratéa 87 F2
Kerava 107 E2
Kerdília, N. 80 B3
Kërës 72 C1
Kerí 86 A2
Kerimäki 103 F3
Kerken 17 D3
Kerketéas, Óros 89 E1
Kerkétio, Óri 83 D2
Kerkíni, Óros 80 A1
Kerkínis, L 80 A2
Kérkira 82 A1
Kérkira, N 82 A1
Kerkonkoski 103 D2
Kerkrade 51 D3
Kernascléden 22 B3
Kéros, N 88 C3
Kerpen 17 D4
Kerrera 4 B1
Kerry 14 B3
Kerry Head 14 A3
Kerteminde 108 B3
Kértezi 86 C1
Kerzers 27 E2
Kesälahti 103 F3
Keşan 115 E3
Kesch, Piz 58 B3
Kesh 12 C2
Keski-Suomen Lääni 103 D2
Kessariani 87 F1
Kestilä 99 D4
Keswick 5 D4
Keszthely 112 A4
Kętrzyn 110 B4
Kettering 9 F1
Kettletoft 3 E1
Kettwig 17 E4
Ketzin 49 D4
Keukenhof 16 B2
Keurusselkä 103 D3
Keuruu 102 C3
Kevelaer 17 D3
Kevo 95 E2
Kevo (Nat Pk) 95 E2
Key, L 12 C3
Keynsham 9 D2
Kežmarok 112 B3
Kiani 81 F1
Kiantajärvi 99 F3
Kiáto 87 D1
Kiberg 95 f1
Kičevo 77 D3
Kidderminster 9 D1
Kidlington 9 E2
Kidsgrove 6 C3
Kidwelly 8 C2
Kiefersfelden 56 B4
Kiekinkoski 99 F4
Kiel 48 A1
Kielce 112 B2
Kielder Reservoir 5 E3
Kieler Bucht 48 A1
Kiental 27 F3
Kierinki 99 D1
Kietz 49 F4
Kifissiá 87 F1
Kifissós 83 F4
Kifjord 95 E1
Kihlanki 95 D4
Kihniö 102 C3
Kihti Skiftet 107 D3
Kiihtelysvaara 103 F2
Kiikala 107 E2
Kiikka 107 D2
Kiikoinen 107 D1
Kiimanen 99 E4
Kiiminginjoki 99 D3
Kiiminki 99 D3
Kiiskilä 102 C1
Kiistala 95 E4
Kijev 113 E2
Kijevo (Hrvatska) 75 D1
Kijevo (Kosovo) 77 D2
Kijevskoje Vodochranilišče 113 E2
Kikinda 72 C1
Kikládes 88 B2
Kil 105 E3
Kila 79 D3
Kiláda (Makedonía) 79 E3
Kiláda (Pelopónissos) 87 E2
Kilafors 101 F4
Kilbaha 12 A4
Kilbeggan 12 C4
Kilbirnie 4 C2
Kilboghamn 97 E2
Kilbotn 94 B3
Kilbrannan Sd 4 B2
Kilchoan 2 B4
Kilcock 13 D4
Kilcormac 12 C4
Kilcreggan 4 C2
Kilcullen 13 D4
Kildare 13 D4
Kildare (Co) 13 D4
Kildorrery 14 C3
Kilfenora 12 B4
Kilgarvan 14 B4
Kilija 113 E4
Kilingi-Nõmme 110 C2
Kilíni 86 B1
Kilíni, Óros 87 D1
Kilkee 12 A4
Kilkeel 13 E3
Kilkenny 15 D3
Kilkenny (Co) 15 D3
Kilkhampton 8 B3
Kilkieran B 12 A3
Kilkís 79 F2
Kilkís (Nomos) 79 F2
Killadysert 12 B4
Killala B 12 B2
Killaloe 12 B4
Killarney 14 B4
Killary Harbour 12 A3
Killashandra 12 C3
Killenaule 14 C3
Killimer 12 B4
Killin 4 C1
Killinkoski 102 C3
Killorglin 14 A3
Killybegs 12 C2
Killyleagh 13 E2
Kilmaing 12 B3
Kilmallock 14 B3
Kilmarnock 4 C2
Kilmartin 4 B2
Kilmore Quay 15 D4
Kilmurry 12 B4
Kilninver 4 B1
Kilnsea 7 E2
Kilpisjärvi 94 C3
Kilpisjärvi *L* 94 C3
Kilrea 13 D1
Kilronan 12 B4
Kilrush 12 B4
Kilsyth 4 C2
Kiltamagh 12 B3
Kiltealy 15 D3
Kilwinning 4 C2
Kilyos 115 F3
Kimássi 84 A3
Kiméria 81 D2
Kími 84 B3
Kímina 79 F3
Kímis, Órmos 84 B4
Kimísseos Theotókou 87 D2
Kimito 107 D3
Kímolos 88 B4
Kímolos, N 88 B4
Kimólou Sífnou, Stenó 88 B3
Kimry 111 F2
Kimstad 105 F4
Kínaros, N 89 D3
Kinbrace 3 D2
Kincardine 5 D2
Kindberg 57 E3
Kindelbrück 52 C2
Kinéta 87 E1
Kingisepp 111 D1
Kingissepp 110 B2
Kingsbridge 8 C4
Kingscourt 13 D3
King's Lynn 7 E3
Kingston 9 F2
Kingston-upon-Hull 7 E2
Kingswear 8 C4
Kington 9 D1
Kingussie 3 D4
Kínira 81 D3
Kinlochbervie 2 C2
Kinlochewe 2 C3
Kinloch Rannoch 4 C1
Kinna 108 C1
Kinnairds Head 3 E3
Kinnasniemi 103 F2
Kinnegad 13 D3
Kinnitty 12 C4
Kinnula 103 D2
Kinross 5 D2
Kinsale 14 B4
Kinsarvik 104 B2
Kintaus 103 D3
Kintore 3 E4
Kintyre 4 B2
Kinvarra 12 B4
Kinzig 54 C3
Kióni 82 B4
Kiparissi 87 E3
Kiparissía 86 C3
Kiparissiakós Kólpos 86 B2
Kiparissías, Óri 86 C3
Kipárissos 83 E2
Kípi (Ípiros) 78 C4
Kípi (Thráki) 81 F2
Kipinä 99 D3
Kípos, Akr 81 E3
Kipourío 79 D4
Kippure 13 D4
Kipséli 83 E2
Kir 76 C3
Kirá Panagiá, N 84 B2
Kirchbach 57 E4
Kirchberg (D) 54 B1
Kirchberg (DDR) 53 D3
Kirchberg (Nieder österreich) 57 E2
Kirchberg (Tirol) 59 E1
Kirchberg an der Pielach 57 E3
Kirchdorf 57 D3
Kirchenlamitz 53 D4
Kirchenthumbach 53 D4
Kirchhain 52 A3
Kirchheim (Baden-Württemberg) 55 D2
Kirchheim (Hessen) 52 B3
Kirchheimbolanden 54 C1
Kirchheim unter Teck 55 D2
Kirchhundem 17 F4
Kirchlengern 17 F2
Kirchmöser 49 D4
Kirchschlag 57 F3
Kiriakí 81 F1
Kiriáki 83 F4
Kiriši 111 E1
Kırkağaç 115 E4
Kirkby Lonsdale 6 C1
Kirkby Stephen 5 E4
Kirkcaldy 5 D2
Kirkcolm 4 B3
Kirkcudbright 4 C3
Kirkenær 105 D2
Kirkenes 95 F2
Kirkeøy 105 D4
Kirkestinden 94 B3
Kirkham 6 B2
Kírki 81 E2
Kirkintilloch 4 C2
Kirkjubøur 96 A4
Kirkkonummi 107 E3
Kırklareli 115 E3
Kirkonmaanselkä 103 F4
Kirkwall 3 E1
Kirn 54 B1
Kirov 111 F3
Kirovograd 113 F2
Kirovsk 111 D1
Kirriemuir 5 D1
Kirtorf 52 A3
Kiruna 94 C4
Kisa 109 E1
Kisac 72 C2
Kiseljak (Loznica) 72 B3
Kiseljak (Sarajevo) 75 F1
Kiseljak (Tuzla) 71 F3
Kišin'ov 113 E3
Kisko 107 E3
Kiskőrös 112 B4
Kiskunfélegyháza 112 B4
Kiskunhalas 114 B1
Kißlegg 55 E4

Kissámou, Kólpos	90	B3	Kíta	87	D4	Kíthnos, N	88	A2	Kittilä	95	E4	Kiuruvesi	103	D1	Kivijärvi	L	103	D2	Kivotós	79	D4
Kissoú Kámbos	90	C4	Kitee	103	F3	Kíthnou, Stenó	88	A2	Kittsee	57	F2	Kiutaköngäs	99	E2	Kivijärvi	L	103	D2	Kizário	81	E2
Kistanje	75	D1	Kíthira	90	A2	Kitinen	95	E4	Kitzbühel	59	D3	Kivalo	99	D3	Kivijärvi	L	103	E4	Kjellerup	108	A2
Kisújszállás	112	B4	Kíthira, N	90	A2	Kitka	99	E2	Kitzingen	55	E1	Kivéri	87	D2	Kivilahti	103	F2	Kjerringøy	97	E1
Kisvárda	112	C3	Kíthnos	88	A2	Kitriés, Akr	86	C3	Kiukainen	107	D2	Kívi	88	B2	Kivitaipale	99	D2	Kjerringvåg	100	C1

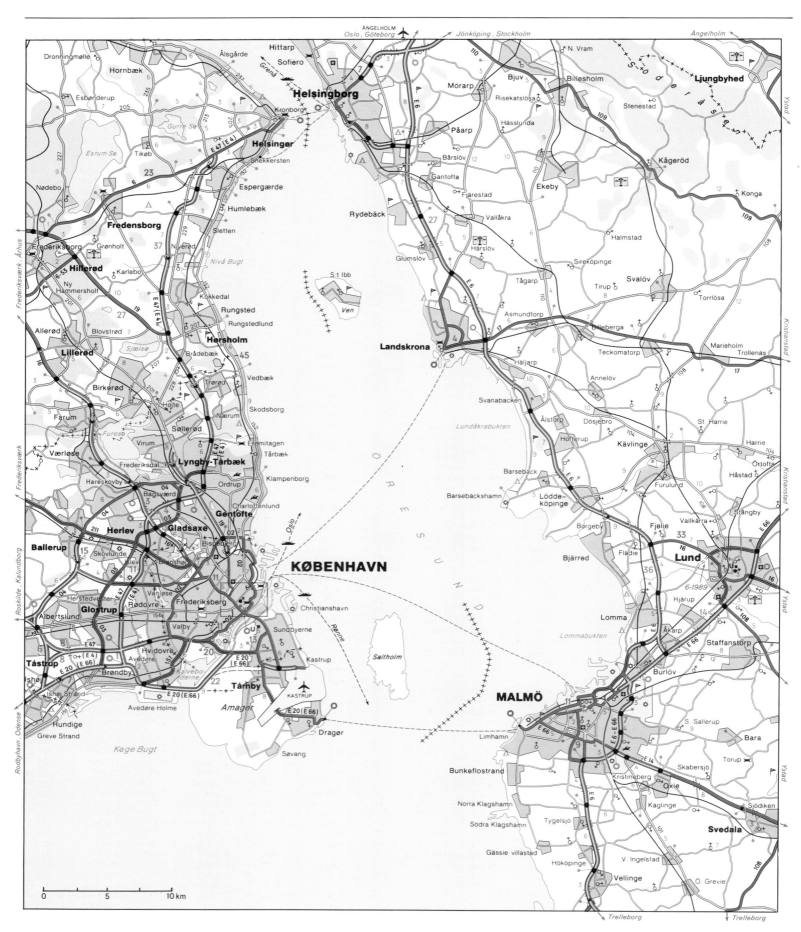

Kjerringvik	101 D1	Knittelfeld	57 D4
Kjølifjell	101 D2	Knivskjellodden	95 D1
Kjøllefjord	95 E1	Knivsta	106 B3
Kjøpsvik	94 B4	Knjaževac	73 F4
Kjustendil	114 C3	Knockmealdown	
Klæbu	100 C2	Mts	14 C3
Kladanj	72 B4	Knokke-Heist	50 A3
Kladnica	76 C1	Knole House	10 C3
Kladnice	75 D1	Knossós	91 D3
Kladno	53 F4	Knutsford	6 C2
Kladovo	73 F2	Koarvikodds	95 E3
Klagenfurt	70 A1	Kobarid	70 A2
Klaipēda	110 B3	Kobbfjorden	95 D1
Klaksvík	96 A3	Kobel'aki	113 F2
Klana	70 B3	København	108 C3
Klanac	70 C4	Kobern-Gondorf	51 E4
Klanxbüll	47 F1	Kobišnica	73 F3
Klarälven	105 E2	Koblenz	51 E4
Klašnice	71 E3	Kobrin	112 C1
Klässbol	105 E3	Koca D	115 F3
Klašterec	53 E3	Kočani	77 F2
Klasvík	96 A3	Koceljevo	72 C3
Klatovy	56 C1	Kočerin	75 E2
Klaukkala	107 E2	Kočevje	70 B2
Klausen	59 D2	Kočevski rog	70 B2
Klausenpass	58 A2	Kochel	56 A4
Klazienaveen	17 E2	ocher	55 E2
Kleinhaugsdorf	57 E2	Kodiksami	107 D2
Kleinheubach	55 D1	Kodisjoki	107 D2
Kleinwalsertal	55 E4	Köflach	57 E4
Klekovača	71 D4	Køge	108 C3
Klenike	77 E2	Køge Bugt	108 C3
Klenovica	70 B3	Kohtla-Järve	110 C1
Kleppe	104 A3	Koikkala	103 E3
Kleppestø	104 A2	Koirakoski	103 E1
Kleve	17 D3	Koitajoki	103 F2
Kličevac	73 D2	Koitelainen	95 E4
Klimoviči	111 E4	Koitere	103 F2
Klimpfjäll	97 E4	Koivujärvi	103 D1
Klin	111 F2	Koi vusuo	103 F2
Klina	76 C2	Kokála	87 D4
Klinča Selo	70 C2	Kökar	106 C3
Klincy	111 E4	Kokári	89 E1
Klingenbach	57 F3	Kökarsfjärden	106 C3
Klingenthal	53 D3	Kokemäenjoki	107 D1
Klinovec	53 E3	Kokemäki	107 D2
Klintehamn	109 F4	Kokin Brod	76 B1
Klippan	108 C3	Kókino Neró	83 F1
Klippen	97 E3	Kokkola	102 C1
Klippitztörl	57 D4	Kokotí	83 F3
Klis	75 D1	Koksijde-Bad	50 A3
Klissoúra	79 D3	Kola	71 E3
Klisura (Makedonija)	77 F3	Koláka	83 F4
Klisura (Srbija)	77 E1	Kolari (SF)	98 C1
Klitoría	86 C1	Kolari (YU)	73 D3
Klitten	53 F2	Kolåsen	101 D1
Klixbüll	47 F1	Kolašin	76 B2
Kljajićevo	72 B2	Kolbäck	105 F3
Ključ	71 D4	Kołbacz	49 F2
Kłodzko	112 A2	Kołbaskowo	49 E2
Kløfta	105 D3	Kolbermoor	56 B3
Klokkarvik	104 A2	Kolby Kås	108 B3
Klokočevac	73 F3	Kolding	108 A3
Klos	76 C4	Kolho	103 D3
Kloštar	71 D2	Koli	103 F2
Kloštar Ivanić	71 D2	Kolima	103 D2
Klösterle	58 B2	Kolimvári	90 B3
Klosterneuburg	57 F2	Kolín	112 A3
Klosters	58 B2	Kolindrós	79 F3
Kloten	58 A2	Kolínes	87 D3
Klötze	48 C4	Kolka	110 B2
Klöverträsk	98 B3	Kolkanlahti	103 D2
Klövsjö	101 E3	Kolkasrags	110 B2
Kluczbork	112 A2	Kólleda	52 C2
Klupe	71 E3	Kolmården	106 A4
Klütz	48 B2	Köln	17 E4
Knapdale	14 B3	Koło	112 B1
Knappogue Castle	12 B4	Kołobrzeg	49 F1
Knåred	109 D2	Koločep	75 F2
Knaresborough	6 C1	Kolomyja	113 D3
Knarvik	104 A2	Koloveč	56 B1
Kneginec	71 D1	Kolovrat	76 B1
Kneža	115 D2	Kolpino	111 D1
Kněžak	56 B3	Kolsva	105 F3
Kneževi Vinogradi	71 F2	Kolubara	72 C3
Kneževo	71 F2	Kolvereid	97 D4
Knežica	71 D3	Komagfjord	95 D2
Knežina	72 B4	Kómanos	79 D3
Knić	73 D4	Komar	71 E4
Knidi	79 D4	Komara	81 F1
Knighton	9 D1	Komárno	112 B4
Knight's Town	14 A4	Koméno	82 C3
Knin	75 D1	Kómi (Kikládes)	88 B2

Kómi (Híos)	89 D1
Komílio	82 B3
Komin	70 C2
Kómito	88 B1
Komiža	75 D2
Komló	114 B1
Komnináda	78 C3
Komniná (Makedonía)	79 D3
Komniná (Thráki)	81 D2
Komorane	77 D2
Komotiní	81 E2
Komovi	76 B2
Komrat	113 E4
Komulanköngäs	99 E4
Konak	73 D2
Konakovo	111 F2
Končanica	71 D2
Kondiás	85 D1
Kondopoúli	85 D1
Kondós, Akr	88 B3
Kondovázena	86 C1
Kondrić	71 F2
Konečka pl	77 E3
Køng	108 C4
Köngernheim	54 C1
Konginkangas	103 D2
Kongsberg	104 C3
Kongselva	94 A3
Kongsfjord	95 F1
Kongsvinger	105 D3
Kœnigsbourg	27 E1
Königsbrück	53 E2
Königsbrunn	55 F3
Königsee	52 C3
Königsfeld	54 C3
Königslutter	52 B1
Königsschlösser	55 F4
Königssee	56 C4
Königssee L	56 C4
Königstein (D)	51 F4
Königstein (DDR)	53 F2
Königswiesen	57 D2
Königswinter	51 E3
Königs-Wusterhausen	49 E4
Konin	112 A1
Koniskós	83 D1
Konístres	84 B4
Kónitsa	78 C4
Konj	75 E1
Konjevrate	75 D1
Konjic	75 F1
Konjsko	76 A2
Konjuh	71 F4
Konkämäälven	94 C3
Könnern	52 C2
Konnevesi	103 D2
Konnevesi L	103 D2
Könönpelto	103 E3
Konopište	77 E3
Konotop	113 F1
Konsko	77 F4
Konsmo	104 B4
Konstantinovy Lázně	53 E4
Konstanz	55 D4
Kontich	50 B3
Kontiolahti	103 F2
Kontiomäki	99 E4
Konttajärvi	98 C2
Konz	54 A1
Kopaída	83 F4
Kopáni	82 C2
Kopanós	79 E3
Kopaonik	77 D1
Koparnes	100 A2
Kópasker	96 C1
Kopavogur	96 A2
Köpenick	49 E4
Koper	70 A3
Kopervik	104 A3
Köping	105 F3
Köpingsvik	109 E2
Koplik	76 B3
Köpmanholmen	102 A2
Koporiče	77 D1
Koppang	100 C3
Kopparberg	105 F3
Kopparbergs Län	105 E2
Kopparleden	101 E2
Kopperby	48 A1
Kopperveien	100 D3
K ornati	74 C1
Koprivna	71 F3

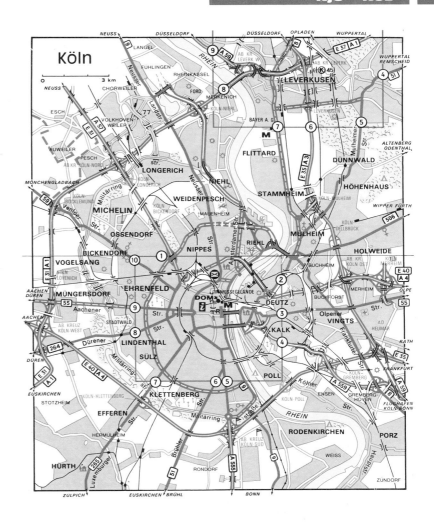

Koprivnica (Bosna i Hercegovina)	71 D1	Kornofoléa	81 F2	Koška	71 F2	Kotorsko	71 F3
Koprivnica (Srbija)	73 F3	Kornwestheim	55 D2	Koskenkorva	102 B2	Kotor Varoš	71 E4
Korab	77 D3	Koromacno	70 B4	Koskenpää	103 D3	Kotovsk (Moldavija)	113 E4
Kórakas, Akr	88 C3	Koróna	79 F2	Koski (Hameen Lääni)	107 D2	Kotovsk (Ukraina)	113 E3
Koralpe	70 B1	Koróni	86 C4	Koski (Turun ja Porin Läani)	107 D2	Kotraža	73 D4
Korana	70 C3	Korónia	83 F4	Kóskina	84 B4	Kótronas	87 D4
Korbach	52 A2	Korónia, L	80 A3	Koskue	102 C3	Kotroniá	81 F2
Korbevac	77 E2	Koroníssia	82 C3	Kosmaj	73 D3	Kötschach-Mauthen	59 E2
Korbovo	73 F2	Kóronos	88 C3	Kosmás	87 D3	Köttsjön	101 F2
Korçë	114 C3	Koronoúda	80 A2	Kosmós	81 E2	Kötzting	56 B1
Korčula	75 E2	Koropí	87 F1	Kos, N	89 F2	Koufália	79 F3
Korčula I	75 E2	Körös	112 B4	Kosovo	77 D2	Koufoníssi (Kikládes)	88 C3
Korčulanski kan	75 E2	Korosten'	113 E2	Kosovo Polje	77 D2	Koufoníssi (Kríti)	91 F4
Korensko sedlo	70 A1	Korostyšev	113 E2	Kosovska Kamenica	77 D2	Koufós	80 B4
Kórfos	87 E2	Korouoma	99 E2	Kössen	59 E1	Kouklií	82 B1
Korgåsen	95 F2	Korpilahti	103 D3	Kósta	87 E3	Koukounariés	84 A2
Korgen	97 E3	Korpilombolo	98 C2	Kostajnica	71 D3	Koúla	81 D1
Koria	107 F2	Korpo	107 D3	Kostanjevac	70 C2	Kouméika	89 E2
Korifássi	86 C3	Korppoo	107 D3	Kostanjevica	70 C2	Koúndouros	88 A2
Koríkio Ándro	83 E4	Korsberga	109 E2	Kostenec	115 D3	Kounoupéli	86 B1
Kórimvos	81 F1	Korsfjorden	104 A2	Koster	105 D4	Koura	102 C2
Korini	83 F4	Korsholm	102 B2	Kostolac	73 D3	Koúrenda	82 B1
Korinós	79 F4	Korsnäs	102 B2	Kostonjärvi	99 E3	Kourkoulí	84 A3
Korinthia	87 D1	Korsør	108 B4	Kostopol'	113 D2	Kournás	90 C3
Korinthiakós Kólpos	87 D1	Korsun-Ševčenkovskij	113 F2	Kostrzyn	49 F4	Kouroúta	86 B2
Kórinthos	87 E1	Kortesjärvi	102 C2	Kosturino	77 F3	Koutselió	82 B1
Korissía	88 A2	Korthio	88 B2	Kosula	103 E2	Koutsó	81 D2
Korissós	79 D3	Kortrijk	50 A3	Koszalin	110 A4	Koutsóhero	83 E1
Korita (Bosna i Hercegovina)	76 A2	Kortteenperä	99 D2	Kőszeg	112 A4	Kouvola	107 F2
Korita (Crna Gora)	76 B2	Korvala	99 D2	Kotala (Keski-Suomen Lääni)	102 C3	Kovačica	72 C2
Korita (Mljet)	75 F2	Korvaluoma	102 C3	Kotala (Lapin Lääni)	99 E1	Kovel'	112 C2
Korithi	86 A1	Korvatunturi	95 F3	Kótas	79 D3	Kovero	103 F2
Koritnik	76 C1	Kos	89 F3	Kotel	115 E2	Kovin	73 D2
Koritnik, M.	77 D2	Kosančić	77 D1	Köthen	53 D1	Köyliö	107 D2
Korkeakangas	103 F3	Kosanica	76 B1	Kotka	103 F4	Kozáni	79 D3
Korkeakoski	103 D2	Kościan	112 A2	Kotor	76 B3	Kozáni	79 D3
Körmend	112 A4	Kościerzyna	110 A4	Kotoriba	71 D1	Kozáni	79 D3
Kornat	74 C1	Kosel	79 D4			Kozarac (Bosna i Hercegovina)	71 D3
Korneuburg	57 F2	Koserow	49 E1			Kozarac (Hrvatska)	71 F2
		Košice	112 C3				
		Kosjerić	72 C4				

154 Koz – La M

Koželʹsk 111 F3
Kozica 75 E2
Kozina 70 A3
Kozjak 77 E4
Kozluk 72 B3
Kožuf 77 F4
Kragenæs 108 B4
Kragerø 104 C4
Kragujevac 73 D4
Krajišnik 73 D2
Krajkovac 77 D1
Krajn 76 C3
Krajnik Dln 49 E3
Krakhella 104 A1
Krakow 48 C2
Kraków 112 B2
Kraljeva Sutjeska 71 F4
Kraljevica 70 B3
Kraljevo 73 D4
Kralovice 53 E4
Kralupy 53 F3
Kramfors 101 F2
Kranenburg 17 D3
Krani 77 E4
Kraniá Elassónas 79 E4
Kraniá
(Makedonía) 79 D4
Kraniá (Thessalía) 82 C1
Kranichfeld 52 C3
Kranídi 87 E2
Kranj 70 A2
Kranjska Gora 70 A1
Krapina 70 C2
Krapinske Toplice 70 C2
Krašić 70 C2
Krâslava 111 D3
Kraslice 53 D3
Krasná Lípa 53 F2
Kraśnik 112 C2
Krasno Polje 70 C4
Krasnyj Cholm 111 F1
Krasnystaw 112 C2
Kráthio 87 D1
Krátigos 85 F3
Kratovo 77 E2
Kratovska-Stena 72 C4
Krauchenwies 55 D3
Krautheim 55 D1
Kravarsko 70 C2
Krefeld 17 D4
Kremastí
(Pelopónissos) 87 E3
Kremastí (Ródos) 93 F1
Kremastón, Teh L 83 D3
Kremenčug 113 F2
Kremenčugskoje
Vodochranilišče 113 F2
Kremenec 113 D2
Kremidi, Akr 87 E4
Kremmen 49 D3
Kremna 72 C4
Kremnica 112 B3
Krems 57 E2
Kremsmünster 57 D3
Krepoljin 73 E3
Kreševo 75 F1
Krestcy 111 E1
Kréstena 86 B2
Kreuth 56 A4
Kreuzbergpass 59 E2
Kreuzlingen 58 A1
Kreuztal 17 F4
Kría Vrissi (Évia) 84 A3
Kría Vrissi
(Makedonía) 79 E3
Kričev 111 E4
Krieglach 57 E3
Kriens 27 F2
Krikelo 83 D3
Krikelos 82 C3
Krikelos, Akr 89 F4
Krimml 59 D2
Krimmler
Wasserfälle 59 D2
Krimpen 16 C3
Krinídes 80 C2
Krionéri
(Makedonía) 80 A2
Krionéri
(Pelopónissos) 86 C3
Krionéri
(Pelopónissos) 87 D1
Kriopigí 80 B4
Kriós, Akr 90 B4
Kristalopigí 78 C3
Kristdala 109 E2
Kristiansand 104 B4
Kristianstad 109 D3
Kristianstads Län 109 D3
Kristiansund 100 B2
Kristiinankaupunki 102 B3
Kristineberg 98 A4
Kristinehamn 105 E4
Kristinehov 109 D3
Kristinestad 102 B3
Krithéa 79 F2
Krithína, Óros 87 E4
Kritikó Pélagos 90 B2
Kriti, N 91 E3
Kritinía 93 E1
Kritsá 91 E4
Kriva Feja 77 E2
Krivaja (Bosna i
Hercegovina) 71 F4
Krivaja (Vojvodina) 72 B1
Kriva Palanka 77 E2
Kriva reka 77 E2
Krivogaštani 77 E4
Krivoj Rog 113 F3
Krivolak 77 E3
Křižanov 57 E1
Križevci 71 D2
Krk 70 B3
Krk *I* 70 B3
Krka 70 B2
Krka *R* 75 D1
Krkonoše 112 A2
Krmčine 74 C1
Krn 70 A2
Krnjača 72 C3
Krnjak 70 C3
Krnjeuša 71 D4
Krnjevo 73 D3
Krnov 112 A3
Krnovo 76 B2
Krøderen 104 C2
Krokeés 87 D3
Krokeide 104 A2
Krokek 106 A4
Krokílio 83 D4
Krokom 101 E2
Krókos 79 E4
Kroksjö 98 A4
Krolevec 113 F1
Kröller Müller 17 D3
Kroměříž 112 A3
Kronach 52 C4
Kronobergs Län 109 D2
Kronoby 102 C1
Kronshagen 48 A1
Kronštadt 111 D1
Kröpelin 48 C2
Kropp 48 A1
Kroppenstedt 52 C1
Krosno 112 C3
Krosno
Odrzańskie 53 F1
Krotoszyn 112 A2
Kroussónas 91 D4
Krovili, Pal 81 E2
Krrabe, M 76 C3
Krško 70 C2
Krstac 76 A2
Krstača 76 C2
Krstinja 70 C3
Kruë i Fushës 76 C3
Kruiningen 16 B4
Krujë 76 C4
Krumbach 55 E3
Krumpendorf 70 A1
Krün 55 F4
Krupà 53 E4
Krupac (Bosna i
Hercegovina) 75 F1
Krupac (Crna Gora) 76 B2
Krupac (Srbija) 77 E1
Krupaja 73 E3
Krupa na Vrbasu 71 E4
Krupanj 72 C3
Krupište 77 E3
Krupka 53 E3
Kruså 108 A4
Kruščica 71 E4
Kruščica, Jezero 70 C4
Krušedol Selo 72 C2
Kruševac 73 E4
Kruševica 73 D3
Kruševo 77 E4
Krute 76 B3
Kruunupyy 102 C1
Krvavec 70 B2
Krynica 112 B3
Krzeszyce 49 F4
Kteniás, Óros 87 D2
Ktismata 82 B1
Kubitzer Bodden 49 D1
Küblis 58 B2
Kučaj 73 E4
Kučevište 77 D2
Kučevo 73 E3
Kuchl 59 E1
Kučina Kosa 71 D4
Kućište 75 E2
Kućište 76 C2
Kudowa-Zdrój 112 A2
Kufstein 59 D1
Kühlungsborn 48 C2
Kuhmalahti 103 D3
Kuhmo 99 F4
Kuhmoinen 103 D3
Kuivajärvi 99 F4
Kuivajoki 99 D3
Kuivalahti 107 D2
Kuivaniemi 99 D3
Kuivasjärvi 102 C3
Kuivi 95 E2
Kuk 70 C4
Kukavica 77 E1
Kukës 76 C3
Kukkia 107 E1
Kukko 102 C2
Kukujevci 72 B2
Kukulje 71 E3
Kula (BG) 114 C2
Kula (TR) 115 F4
Kula (YU) 72 B2
Kuldīga 110 B3
Kulennoinen 103 F3
Kulen Vakuf 71 D4
Kulina 73 E4
Kulju 107 E1
Kulkjica 74 C1
Kullaa 107 D1
Kulm 27 F2
Kulmbach 52 C4
Kuloharju 99 E2
Külsheim 55 D1
Kultakero 99 E1
Kultsjön 97 E4
Kum 70 B2
Kumane 72 C2
Kumanovo 77 E2
Kumla 105 F4
Kumlinge 106 C3
Kummavuopio 94 C3
Kummerower See 49 D2
Kumputunturi 95 E4
Kumrovec 70 C2
Kungälv 108 C1
Kungsbacka 108 C1
Kungshamn 105 D4
Kungsör 105 F3
Kunoy 96 A3
Kunrau 48 B4
Kunszentmárton 112 B4
Künzelsau 55 D2
Kuolimo 103 E4
Kuolio 99 E3
Kuopio 103 E2
Kuopion Lääni 103 E2
Kuorboaivi 95 E2
Kuorevesi 103 D3
Kuortane 102 C2
Kuortovare 94 C4
Kuortti 103 D3
Kupa 70 B3
Kupa 70 C3
Kupferzell 55 D2
Kupinova Glava 73 E3
Kupinovo 72 C3
Kupres 75 E1
Kupreška vrata 75 E1
Kurfar 59 D3
Kurikka 102 B2
Kuřim 57 F1
Kuršėnai 110 C3
Kuršskij Zaliv 110 B3
Kursu 99 E2
Kuršumlija 77 D1
Kuršumlijska
Banja 77 D1
Kurtakko 95 D4
Kuru 102 C3
Kusadak 73 D3
Kuşadasi 115 E4
Kusel 54 B1
Küsnacht 58 A2
Küssnacht 58 A2
Kustavi 107 D2
Küstenkanal 17 E1
Kütahya 115 F3
Kutina 71 D2
Kutjevo 71 E2
Kutná-Hora 112 A3
Kutno 112 B1
Kuttanen 95 D3
Kuttura 95 E3
Kúty 57 F2
Kuumu 99 F4
Kuusamo 99 E2
Kuusamojärvi 99 F2
Kuusankoski 107 F2
Kuusjärvi 103 E2
Kuusjoki 107 E2
Kuvšinovo 111 E2
Kuzma 70 C1
Kuzmin 72 B3
Kvæfjord 94 A3
Kvaløy 94 B2
Kvaløya 95 D1
Kvalsund 95 D1
Kvalvåg 100 B2
Kvam 100 C3
Kvænangen 94 C2
Kvænangsbotn 95 D2
Kvanndal 104 B2
Kvanne 100 B2
Kværndrup 108 B4
Kvarner 70 B4
Kvarnerič 70 B4
Kvernes 100 B2
Kvevlax 102 B2
Kvikkjokk 98 A2
Kvikne 100 C2
Kvina 104 B4
Kvinesdal 104 B4
Kvinesdal *V* 104 B4
Kvisvik 100 B2
Kviteseid 104 B3
Kvitnes 100 B2
Kvitsøy 104 A3
Kwidzyn 110 B4
Kyjov 57 F1
Kyläinpää 102 B2
Kylänlahti 103 F1
Kyleakin 2 B3
Kyle of Lochalsh 2 B3
Kyle of Tongue 2 C2
Kylerhea 2 B3
Kylestrome 2 C2
Kyll 51 D4
Kyllburg 51 D4
Kylmäkoski 107 E2
Kylmälä 99 D4
Kymen Lääni 103 F4
Kynsivesi 103 D3
Kyritz 49 D3
Kyrksæterøra 100 C2
Kyrkslätt 107 E3
Kyrönjoki 102 C2
Kyrösjärvi 102 C3
Kyselka 53 E3
Kyšice 53 F4
Kyyjärvi 102 C2
Kyyvesi 103 E3

L

Laa an der Thaya 57 F2
La Adrada 39 F2
Laage 48 C2
Laakajärvi 103 E1
La Alberca 39 E2
La Alberca de
Záncara 40 C3
La Alberguería de
Argañán 39 D2
La Albuera 38 C4
La Albufera 41 E4
La Alcarria 40 C2
La Algaba 43 D2
La Almarcha 40 C3
La Almunia de Doña
Godina 36 C4
La Antillas 42 C3
La Azohía 45 D3
Labacolla 34 A2
La Baells, Emb de 32 A3
Labajos 40 A1
La Bañeza 35 D3
La Barca de la
Florida 43 D3
Labasheeda 12 B4
Labastida 36 B2
Labastide-
Clairence 28 A4
Labastide-Murat 29 D2
Labastide-
Rouairoux 32 B1
Labe 53 F3
Labin 70 A3
Labinot Fushë 76 C4
La Bisbal de Falset 37 E4
La Bisbal
d'Empordà 32 B3
Laboe 48 A1
Labouheyre 28 A3
Labouret, Col du 31 D3
La Bóveda de Toro 35 D4
La Brède 28 B2
Labrit 28 B3
Labruguière 32 B1
Labudnjača 72 B2
Laç 76 C4
La Cabrera 40 B1
Lacalahorra 44 B3
La Campana 43 E2
Lacanau 28 A2
Lacanau-Océan 28 A2
Lacapelle-Marival 29 D2
Laćarak 72 B3
La Carlota 43 E2
La Carolina 44 A1
Lacaune 32 B1
Lacaune, Mts de 32 B1
La Cava 41 F2
La Cazada de
Oropesa 39 E3
Lacedonia 64 C3
Läckö 105 E4
Lac Léman 27 E3
La Codosera 38 C3
Laconi 66 B3
La Coronada 39 E4
La Coruña 34 B1
Lacq 28 B4
La Cumbre 39 E3
La Espina 35 D1
Ladbergen 17 E2
Ládi 81 F1
Ladispoli 63 E2
Ladoeiro 38 C3
Ladožskoje
Ozero 111 D1
Láerma 93 E2
La Felguera 35 D1
Laferté 27 D1
Laffrey 30 C2
Láfka 87 D1
Láfkos 83 F2
Lafnitz 57 F4
La Franca, 35 E1
Lafrançaise 29 D3
La Fregeneda 39 D1
La Frontera 40 C2
La Fuente de San
Esteban 39 D1
Lagan 109 D2
Lagan *R* 109 D2
Laganá, Kólpos 86 A2
Laganás 86 A2
Lagarfljót 96 C2
La Garganta 34 C1
La Garriga 32 B4
Lagartera 39 E3
Lagastrello, Pso di 60 B3
Lage 17 F3
Lagen 100 C3
Lågen
(Buskerud) 104 C3
Lågen
(Oppland) 100 C3
Laggan 2 C4
Laggan, L 2 C4
Laginá
(Makedonía) 79 F3
Laginá (Thráki) 81 F2
La Gineta 40 C4
Lagnieu 26 C4
Lagny 19 F4
Lago 67 E3
Lagoa 42 A2
Lagoaça 34 C4
Lagonegro 65 D4
Lagonissi 87 F2
Lagos 42 A2
Lágos 81 D2
Łagów 49 F4
La Granjuela 43 E1
Lagrasse 32 B2
Laguardia 36 B2
La Guardia 40 B3
La Guardia de Jaén 44 A2
Laguarres 37 E3
Laguarta 37 E2
Laguiole 29 E2
Laguna de Duero 35 E4
Lahanás 80 A2
La Hermida 35 E2
La Herradura 44 A4
Lahinch 12 B4
Lahn 17 F4
Lahnstein 51 E4
Laholm 108 C2
Laholmsbukten 108 C2
La Horcajada 39 E2
La Horra 35 F4
Lahr 54 C3
Lahti 107 F2
Laichingen 55 D3
Laide 2 B3
La Iglesuela del Cid 41 E2
Laignes 26 B1
Laigueglia 31 F3
Laihia 102 B2
Laïliás 80 B2
Laimbach 57 D2
Laimoluokta 94 C3
Lainate 60 A1
Lainioälven 95 D4
Lairg 2 C2
Laissac 29 E3
Laïsta 78 C4
Laisvall 97 F3
Laitikkala 107 E2
Laitila 107 D2
La Jana 41 F2
Lajkovac 72 C3
La Jonquera 32 B3
Laká 82 A2
Lakavica 77 E3
Lake District
Nat Pk 5 D4
Laki 89 E3
Láki 90 B3
Lákmos, Óri 82 C1
Lákoma 81 E3
Lákones 82 A1
Lakonía 87 D3
Lakonikós Kólpos 87 D4
Lakópetra 86 B1
Laksefjorden 95 E1
Lakselv 95 D2
Laktaši 71 E3
La Laguna 42 B4
La Lantejuela 43 E3
Lálas 86 C2
Lalbenque 29 D3
L'Alcudia 41 E4
L'Aldea 41 F2
Lalín 34 B2
Lalinac 73 F4
Lalinde 28 C2
La Línea de la
Concepción 43 E4
Laliótis 87 D1
Lalm 100 C3
La Losa 44 B2
Lalouvesc 30 B1
Lalueza 37 E3
La Luisiana 43 E2
Lalzit, Gjiri i 76 C4
Lam 56 B1
Lama dei Peligni 64 A2
La Magdalena 35 D2
Lamalou 30 A4
La Manche 10 A4
La Manga del
Mar Menor 45 D2
Lamarche 27 D1
La Marmora, P 66 B3
Lamarque 28 B2
Lamastre 30 B2
Lambach 56 C3
Lamballe 22 C3
Lambesc 30 C4
Lámbia 86 C1
Lambiri 83 D4
Lámbou Míli 85 F2
Lambrecht 54 C2
Lamego 34 B4
La Mesa Roldán 44 C3
Lamía 83 E3
Lamlash 4 B2
Lammermuir Hills 5 D2
Lammhult 109 D2
Lammi 107 E2
La Molina 32 A3
Lamotte-Beuvron 25 E2
Lampaul 22 A2
Lampedusa 68 A4
Lampedusa, I di 68 A4
Lampertheim 54 C1
Lampeter 8 C1
L'Ampolla 41 F2
Lamstedt 47 F3
La Mudarra 35 E4

La Muela 37 D4
Lamure 26 B4
Lana 58 C3
Lanaja 37 D3
Lanaken 51 D3
Lanark 4 C2
La Nava de Ricomalillo 39 F3
La Nava de Santiago 39 D4
Lancashire 6 B2
Lancaster 6 B1
Lanchester 5 E4
Lanciano 64 A2
Landau (Bayern) 56 B2
Landau (Rheinland-Pfalz) 54 C2
Landeck 58 C2
Landerneau 22 B2
Landes 28 B3
Landes de Lanvaux 22 C3
Landete 41 D3
Landévennec 22 A3
Landivisiau 22 B2
Landivy 18 C4
Landmannalaugar 96 B2
Landquart 58 B2
Landrecies 20 A2
Landriano 60 A1
Landsberg 53 D2
Landsberg 56 A3
Land's End 8 A4
Landshut 56 B2
Landskapet Åland 106 C2
Landskrona 108 C3
Landstuhl 54 B2
Landverk 101 D2
Lanersbach 59 D2
Lanesborough 12 C3
Langáda (Híos) 85 F4
Langáda (Pelopónnissos) 87 D4
Langadás 79 F3
Langádas 87 D3
Langa de Duero 36 A3
Langádia 86 C2
Langadíkia 80 A3
Langangen 104 C4
Langeac 29 F2
Langeais 25 D2
Langeland 108 B4
Langelandsbælt 108 B4
Langelmäki 103 D3
Langelmävesi 103 D3
Langelsheim 52 B1
Langenargen 55 D4
Langenau 55 E3
Langenberg 53 D3
Langenbruck 55 F2
Langenburg 55 D2
Langeneß 47 F1
Langenfeld 17 E4
Längenfeld 58 C2
Langenhagen 48 A4
Langenhahn 51 F3
Langen (Hessen) 52 A4
Langen (Niedersachsen) 47 F3
Langenlois 57 E2
Langenthal 27 F2
Langenwang 57 E3
Langenzenn 55 E1
Langeoog 47 E3
Långeserud 105 E3
Langeskov 108 B3
Langesund 104 C4
Langevåg 100 A2
Langevåg 104 A3
Långfjället 101 D3
Langfjord 95 D2
Langfjorden 95 E1
Langfjordjøkelen 94 C2
Langforden 100 B2
Langhirano 60 B2
Langholm 5 D3
Langjökull 96 B2
Langnau 27 F2
Langogne 29 F2
Langon 28 B2
Langøya 94 A3
Langport 9 D3
Langres 26 C1

Langrune 18 C3
Långsele 101 F2
Långshyttan 105 F2
Långträsk 98 B3
Lanjarón 44 A3
Lanke 49 E3
Länkipohja 103 D3
Lanmeur 22 B2
Lannemezan 37 E1
Lannilis 22 A2
Lannion 22 B2
Lanouaille 29 D1
Lans-en-Vercors 30 C1
Lanslebourg 31 E1
Lanta 29 D4
Lantosque 31 E3
La Nuez de Arriba 35 F3
Lanusei 66 C3
Lanvollon 22 C2
Lanzahita 39 F2
Lanzarote 42 C3
Lanzo Tonnese 31 E1
Laois 12 C4
La Oliva (Is Canarias) 42 C4
La Oliva (Navarra) 36 C2
Laon 20 A3
La Orotava 42 B4
La Paca 44 C2
Lapalisse 26 B4
La Palma 42 A4
La Palma del Condado 42 C2
La Panadella 37 F4
Lápas 86 B1
Lapa, Sa da 38 C1
Laperdiguera 37 E3
La Pinilla 36 A4
Lapinjärvi 107 F2
Lapin Lääni 95 E4
Lapinlahti 103 E1
La Platja d'Aro 32 B4
La Plaza 35 D2
Lapleau 29 E1
Laplume 28 C3
La Pobla 41 E4
La Pobla de Lillet 32 A3
La Pobla de Massaluca 37 E4
La Pobla de Segur 37 F3
La Pobla de Vallbona 41 E3
Lapoutroie 27 E1
Lapovo 73 D3
Lappajärvi 102 C2
Lappajärvi L 102 C2
Lappalaisten-Kesätuvat 95 D3
Lappea 98 C2
Lappeenranta 103 F4
Lappfjärd 102 B3
Lappfors 102 C2
Lappi 107 D2
Lappoå 102 C2
Lappohja 107 E3
Lappträsk 98 C3
Lappträsk 107 F2
Lappvesi 106 C3
Lapua 102 C2
Lapuanjoki 102 C2
La Puebla de Almoradiel 40 B3
La Puebla de Cazalla 43 E3
La Puebla de Híjar 37 D4
La Puebla de los Infantes 43 E2
La Puebla del Río 43 D3
La Puebla de Montalbán 39 F3
La Puebla de Valverde 41 D2
La Pueblanueva 39 F3
La Puerta de Segura 44 B1
Lapväärtti 102 B3
L'Aquila 63 F2
La Rábida 42 C3
La Rábita 44 B4
Laracha 34 A1
Laragh 13 D4
Laragne-Montéglin 30 C3
La Rambla 43 F2

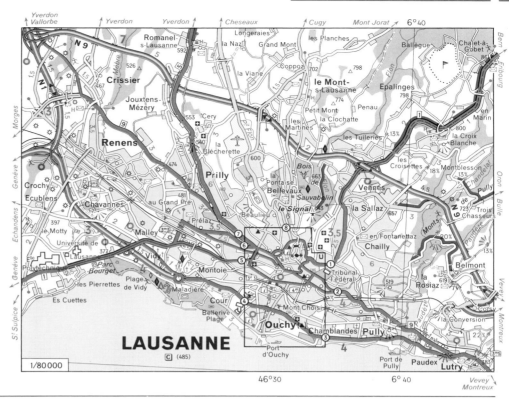

Lärbro 109 F3
Larche (Alpes-de-Haute-Provence) 31 E2
Larche (Corrèze) 29 D2
Larche, Col de 31 E2
Lærdalsøyri 104 B1
Lardarello 60 C4
Lárdos 93 F2
Lárdos, Akr 93 F2
Laredo 36 A1
Laren 16 C2
Largentière 30 B2
Largs 4 C2
Lárimna 84 A4
La Rinconada 43 D2
Larino 64 B2
La Rioja 36 B2
Lárissa 83 E1
Lárissa (Nomos) 83 E2
Larmor 22 B4
Larne 13 E2
La Robla 35 D2
La Roca 32 B4
La Roca de la Sierra 39 D4
Larochette 21 D2
La Roda (Andalucía) 43 E3
La Roda (Castilla-la-Mancha) 40 C4
Laroles 44 B3
Laroquebrou 29 E2
Laroque-d'Olmes 32 A2
Laroque-Timbaut 28 C3
Larouco 34 B3
Larraga 36 C2
Larrau, Pto de 37 D2
Larseng 94 B2
Larsmo 102 C1
Laruns 37 D2
Larv 109 D1
Larvik 104 C4
Lasalle 29 F3
Las Alpujarras 44 A3
Las Arenas 36 B1
Lasarte 36 C1
Las Batuecas 39 E2
Las Cabezas de San Juan 43 D3
Las Cabrillas, Pto de 41 E2
Las Caldas de Besaya 35 F2
Las Campanas
Lascaux, Grotte de 29 D2
La Seca 35 E4

La Selva del Camp 37 F4
La Sénia 41 F2
La Seu d'Urgell 32 A3
Las Huelgas Reales 35 F3
Lasinjski Sjeničak 70 C3
Laško 70 B2
Las Mesas 40 B4
Las Mestas 39 E2
Las Minas 44 C1
Las Navas de la Concepción 43 E2
Las Navas del Marqués 40 A2
Las Negras 44 C4
Læsø 108 B2
La Solana 40 B4
Las Pajanosas 43 D2
Las Palmas de Gran Canaria 42 B4
Las Pedroñeras 40 C4
Las Pedrosas 37 D3
La Spezia 60 B3
Las Portas, Emb de 34 B3
Las Rozas 40 A2
Lassan 49 E2
Lassay 23 E3
Lassigny 19 F3
Lassíthi 91 E4
Lassíthi (Nomos) 91 F4
Lastovo 75 E3
Lastovo I 75 E3
Lastovski kan 75 E2
Lastra a Signa 60 C3
Lastres 35 E1
Lastrup 17 E1
Lastva 76 A2
Lašva 71 E4
Las Veguillas 39 E1
Las Ventas con Peña Aguilera 40 A3
Las Vertientes 44 B3
Las Viñas 43 F2
Lätäseno 95 D3
Laterza 65 D4
Lathen 17 E1
Latheron 3 D2
Latiano 65 E3
Latikberg 97 F4
Latina 63 F3
Latisana 59 E3
Lató 91 E4
Latour-de-France 32 B2
Latronico 65 D4

Latronquière 29 E2
Latvija 110 C3
Lauchhammer 53 E2
Lauder 5 D2
Lauenau 52 A1
Lauenburg 48 B3
Lauenstein 53 E3
Lauf 55 F1
Laufen (CH) 27 E2
Laufen (D) 56 B3
Laufenburg 54 C4
Lauffen 55 D2
Laugarvatn 96 B2
Lauhanvuori 102 B3
Lauingen 55 E2
Laujar de Andarax 44 B3
Laukaa 103 D3
Lauksundskaret
Launceston 8 B3
La Unión 45 D3
Laupheim 55 E3
Lauragh 14 A4
Laureana di Borrello 67 E4
Laurencekirk 3 E4
Laurenzana 65 D4
Lauria 67 E1
Laurière 25 E4
Lausanne 27 D3
Lauta 53 E2
Lautaret, Col du 31 D2
Lautenthal 52 B1
Lauter 54 C2
Lauterbach 52 A3
Lauterbourg 21 F3
Lauterbrunnen 27 F3
Lauterecken 54 B1
Lautrec 32 A1
Lauttakylä 107 D2
Lauvstad 100 A2
Lauvvik 104 A3
Lauzerte 29 D3
Lauzet-Ubaye, le 31 D2
Lauzun 28 C2
Lávara 81 F2
Lavardac 28 C3
La Vecilla 35 E2
La Torre del Valle 35 D3
La Vellés 39 E1
Lavello 64 C3

Lavelsloh 17 F2
Lavenham 11 D1
Laveno 58 A4
Lavéra 30 C4
La Verna 61 D3
Lavia 102 C3
Laviano 64 C4
Lavik 104 A1
La Villa de Don Fadrique 40 B3
Lavinio Lido di Enea 63 E3
La Virgen del Camino 35 D2
Lavis 59 D3
Lavit 28 C3
Låvong 97 E3
Lavour 29 D4
Lavoûte-Chilhac 29 F2
Lavre 38 B4
Lávrio 88 A2
Lavuuoai'vi 95 D3
Laxå 105 E4
Laxe 34 A1
Laxford Bridge 2 C2
Laxo 3 F1
Lay 24 B3
Layos 40 A3
Laza 34 B3
Lazarevac 72 C3
Lazarev Krst 76 B2
Lazarevo 72 C2
Lazaropole 77 D3
Lazio 63 E2
Lazise 60 C1
Láznè Kynžvart 53 D4
Laznica 73 E3
Leadenham 7 D3
Leamington Spa, Royal 9 E1
Leane, L 14 B4
Łeba 110 A4
Lebach 54 B2
Lebane 77 E1
Lebedin 95 E1
Lebesby 95 D1
Lębork 110 A4
Lebrija 43 D3
Lebus 49 F4
Lecce 65 E4
Lecco 58 B4

Léchère, la 31 D1
Lechlade 9 E2
Leciñena 37 D3
Leck 47 F1
Lecques, les 30 C4
Lectoure 28 C3
Lecumberri 36 C1
Ledaña 41 D4
Ledanca 40 B1
Ledbury 9 D1
Ledesma 39 E1
Lédignan 30 B3
Ledmore 2 C2
Lee 14 B4
Leeds 6 C2
Leek 6 C3
Leenane 12 B3
Leer 47 E3
Leerdam 16 C3
Leese 48 A4
Leeuwarden 16 C1
Lefkáda 82 B3
Lefkáda, N 82 B3
Lefkádia 79 E3
Lefkaditi 83 E3
Lefkandí 84 B4
Lefká Óri 90 B3
Léfkara 79 E4
Léfkes 88 C3
Lefkími 81 F2
Lefkími, Akr 82 A2
Lefkógia 80 B1
Lefkopigí 79 D4
Léfktra 83 F4
Legan 48 A2
Leganés 40 A2
Legé 24 B3
Legnago 60 C1
Legnano 60 A1
Legnica 112 A2
Legrad 71 C1
Legrená 87 F2
Léguevin 29 D4
Legutiano 36 B1
Le Havre 19 D3
Lehená 86 B1
Lehnin 49 D4
Léhovo 79 D3
Lehrberg 55 E1
Lehre 52 B1
Lehrte 52 B1
Lehtimäki 102 C2
Lehtovaara (Lapin Lääni) 99 D1
Lehtovaara (Oulun Lääni) 103 E1

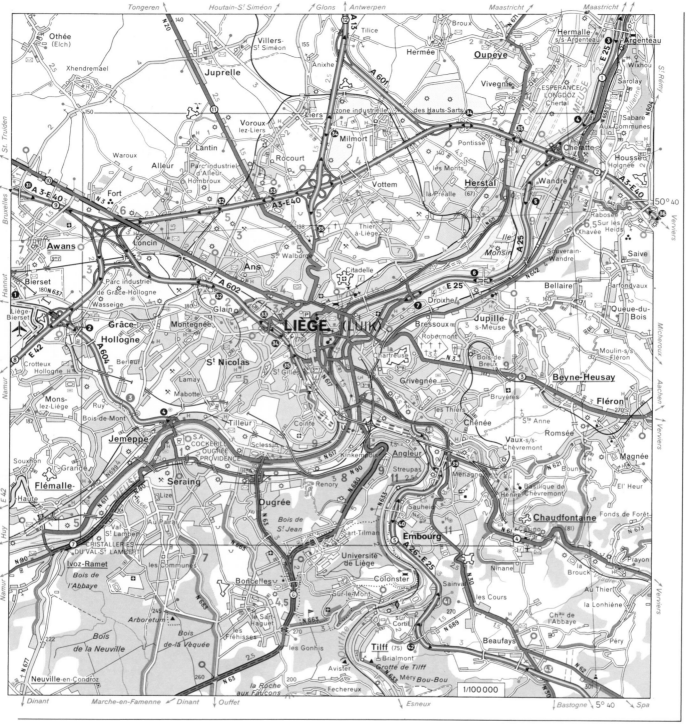

Leptokariá (Thráki)	81	E2
Lercara Friddi	68	B3
Léré	26	A2
Lerici	60	B3
Lérida	37	E4
Lerin	36	C2
Lérins	31	E4
Lerma	35	F3
Lermoos	58	C1
Lérni	87	D2
Léros, N	89	E3
Lerum	108	C1
Lerwick	3	F2
Les	37	F2
Lešak	76	C1
Lešani	77	D4
Les Borges Blanques	37	F4
L'Escala	32	C3
Lescar	28	B4
Lesce	70	A2
Lešće	70	C3
Lescun	37	D2
Leshnicë	77	D4
Lesima, Mte	60	A2
Lesina	64	C2
Lesina, L di	64	C2
Lesja	100	B3
Lesjöfors	105	E3
Leskovac	77	E1
Les Llosses	32	A3
Lesneven	22	B2
Lešnica	72	B3
Lesparre-Médoc	28	A1
L'Espina	41	F2
L'Espluga de Francolí	37	F4
Les Portes de Fer	73	E3
L'Espunyola	32	A3
Lessay	18	B3
Lessebo	109	E2
Lessines	50	B3
Lessini	82	C4
L'Estartit	32	C3
Lestelle-Bétharram	37	E1
Lestijärvi	102	C2
Lestijoki	102	C1
Lestkov	53	E4
Lésvos, N	85	F2
Leszno	112	A2
Letchworth	9	F2
Letenye	114	A1
Letino	64	A3
Letmathe	17	E4
Letterfrack	12	A3
Letterkenny	12	C1
Lettermullan	12	A3
Letur	44	C1
Letuš	70	B1
Letzlingen	48	C4
Leuca	65	F4
Leuchars	5	D1
Leuk	27	F3
Leukerbad	27	F3
Leuna	53	D2
Leutenberg	52	C3
Leutershausen	55	E1
Leutkirch	55	E4
Leutschach	70	B1
Leuven	50	C3
Leuze	50	B4
Levajok	95	E2
Levanger	101	D1
Levanjska Varoš	71	F2
Levant, I du	31	D4
Levanto	60	B3
Levanzo, I di	68	A3
Levásjoki	102	B3
Levene	108	C1
Leven (England)	7	D2
Leven (Scotland)	5	D2
Levens	31	E3
Leverano	65	F4
Leverburgh	2	A3
Leverkusen	17	E4
Levet	25	F3
Levi	95	E4
Levice	112	B3
Levico Terme	59	D3
Levídi	87	D2
Levie	33	F4
Levier	27	D3
Levítha, N	89	E3

Leibnitz	70	B1	Leirvik (Hordaland)	104	A3	Leknes (Nordland)	97	E1	Lemmer	16	C1
Leicester	9	F1	Łeknica	53	F1	Lemonodássos	87	F2
Leicestershire	9	E1	Leirvik (Sogn og Fjordane)	104	A1	Leksand	101	E4	Lempäälä	107	E1
Leiden	16	B3	Leksvik	100	C1	Lempdes	29	F1
Leie	50	B4	Leisnig	53	E2	Leland	97	D3	Lemvig	108	A2
Leighton Buzzard	9	F2	Leiston	11	E1	Lelång	105	D4	Lenart	70	C1
Leikanger	100	A3	Leitáriegos, Pto de	34	C2	Lelija	76	A1	Lencloître	25	D3
Leiknes	97	F1	Leith	5	D2	Lelystad	16	C2	Lend	59	E1
Leine	48	A4	Leitha	57	F2	Lelystad-Haven	16	C2	Léndas	91	D4
Leinefelde	52	B2	Leitir Ceanainn	12	C1	Léman, Lac	27	E3	Lendava	71	D1
Leini	31	E1	Leitrim	12	C3	Le Mans	23	F3	Lendava R	70	C1
Leipheim	55	E3	Leitzkau	52	C1	Lembach	21	E3	Lendinara	61	D2
Leipzig	53	D2	Leivonmäki	103	D3	Lembeye	28	B4	Lengefeld	53	E3
Leira (Møre og Romsdal)	100	B2	Lek	16	C3	Lemförde	17	F2	Lengenfeld	53	D3
Leira (Oppland)	104	C2	Léka	89	E1	Lemgo	17	F2	Lengerich	17	E2
Leirbotn	95	D2	Leka	97	D3	Lemgow	48	C3	Lenggries	56	A4
Leiria	38	B2	Lekáni	80	C2	Lemi	103	E4	Lenhovda	109	E2
Leiro	34	B2	Lekeitio	36	B1	Lemland	106	C3	Leningrad	111	D1
Leirpollskogen	95	F1	Lekenik	71	D2	Lemmenjoki	95	E3	Lenk	27	E3
Leirvåg	104	A1	Leknes (Møre og Romsdal)	100	A2	Lemmenjoki (Nat Pk)	95	E3	Lenne	17	F4
Leirvik (Færøerne)	96	A3	Lemmenjoki R	95	E3	Lennestadt	17	F4

Lemmer	16	C1	Lentföhrden	48	A2	Leondári (Thessalía)	83	E2
Lenti	114	A1	Leóndio	87	D2
Lentiira	99	F4	Leonessa	63	E1
Lenting	55	F2	Leonforte	68	C3
Lentini	69	D3	Leonídio	87	E3
Lentua	99	F4	León, Pto del	43	F3
Lenzburg	27	F2	Leopoldsburg	50	C3
Lenzen	48	C3	Leopoldsdorf	57	F2
Lenzerheide Valbella	58	B3	Leopoldsteinersee	57	D3
Lenzkirch	54	C4	Leovo	113	E4
Leoben	57	E4	Lepel'	111	D3
Leobersdorf	57	F3	Lepenoú	80	C3
Leogang	59	E1	Lepenski vir	73	E3
Leominster	9	D1	Lepetane	76	B3
Leon	28	A3	Lepoglava	70	C1
León	35	D2	Leposavić	77	D1
León, Mtes de	35	D2	Lépoura	84	B4
Leonberg	55	D2	Leppäjärvi	95	D3
Léoncel	30	C2	Leppävirta	103	E2
Leondári (Pelopónnisos)	86	C2	Leptokariá (Makedonía)	79	F4

Levoča	112	B3
Levroux	25	E3
Lévy, Cap	18	B2
Lewes	10	C3
Lewis	2	B2
Leyburn	6	C1
Leyland	6	B2
Leyre	37	D2
Leysdown-on-Sea	11	D2
Leysin	27	E3
Lézardrieux	22	C2
Lézat	37	F1
Lezay	24	C4
Lezhë	76	C3
Lézignan-Corbières	32	B2
Ležimir	72	C2
Lezoux	29	F1
Lezuza	40	C4
L'gov	111	F4
L'Hospitalet de l'Infant	37	F4
Liabygda	100	B2
Liákoura	83	E4
Lianokládi	83	E3
Liathach	2	C3
Liberec	112	A2
Libochovice	53	F3
Libourne	28	B2
Librazhd	77	D4
Librilla	45	D2
Licata	68	C4
Licciana Nardi	60	B3
Lich	52	A4
Lichfield	9	E1
Lichoslavl'	111	F2
Lichtenberg	53	D3
Lichtenfels	52	C4
Lichtenstein	53	D3
Lichtenvoorde	17	D3
Lička Jesenica	70	C3
Lički Osik	70	C4
Ličko Lešće	70	C4
Lida	110	C4
Liddel Water	5	D3
Liden	101	F2
Lidhult	109	D2
Lidingö	106	B4
Lidköping	105	E4
Lido degli Estensi	61	D2
Lido delle Nazioni	61	D2
Lido di Camaiore	60	B3
Lido di Classe	61	E3
Lido di Jesolo	59	E4
Lido di Metaponto	65	E4
Lido di Ostia	63	E3
Lido di Savio	61	E3
Lido di Spina	61	D2
Lido di Venezia	61	D1
Lidoríki	83	E4
Lido Silvana	65	E4
Lidzbark Warmiński	110	B4
Liebenwalde	49	D3
Lieberose	53	F1
Liège	51	D4
Liège (Prov)	51	D4
Lieksa	103	F1
Lienz	59	E2
Liepāja	110	B3
Lier	50	C3
Liérganes	35	F2
Liernais	26	B2
Lieser	59	F2
Liesjärvi	107	E2
Liestal	27	E2
Lieto	107	D2
Liétor	44	C1
Lieurey	19	D3
Lievestuore	103	D3
Liévin	19	F1
Liezen	57	D3
Liffey	13	D4
Liffol-le-Grand	20	C4
Lifford	13	D1
Liffré	23	D3
Lifjell	104	C3
Ligiá	86	B1
Lignano Sabbiadoro	59	F4
Ligné	23	D4
Lignières	25	E3
Ligny-en-Barrois	20	C4

Ligny-le-Châtel	26	B1
Ligourió	87	E2
Ligueil	25	D3
Liguria	60	A3
Liháda	83	F3
Liikasenvaara	99	E2
Lijeva Rijeka	76	B2
Lijevi Dubravčak	71	D2
Lika	70	C4

Limáni Hersoníssou	91	E3
Limáni Litohórou	79	F4
Lima, R	34	A3
Limavady	13	D1
Limbach	53	D3
Limbara, M	66	B2
Limburg (B)	50	C3
Limburg (D)	51	F4

Linas, M	66	B4
Lincoln	7	D3
Lincolnshire	7	D3
Lindås	104	A2
Lindau	55	D4
Linden	52	C4
Lindenberg	55	E4
Linderhof	55	F4
Lindesberg	105	F3

Lille

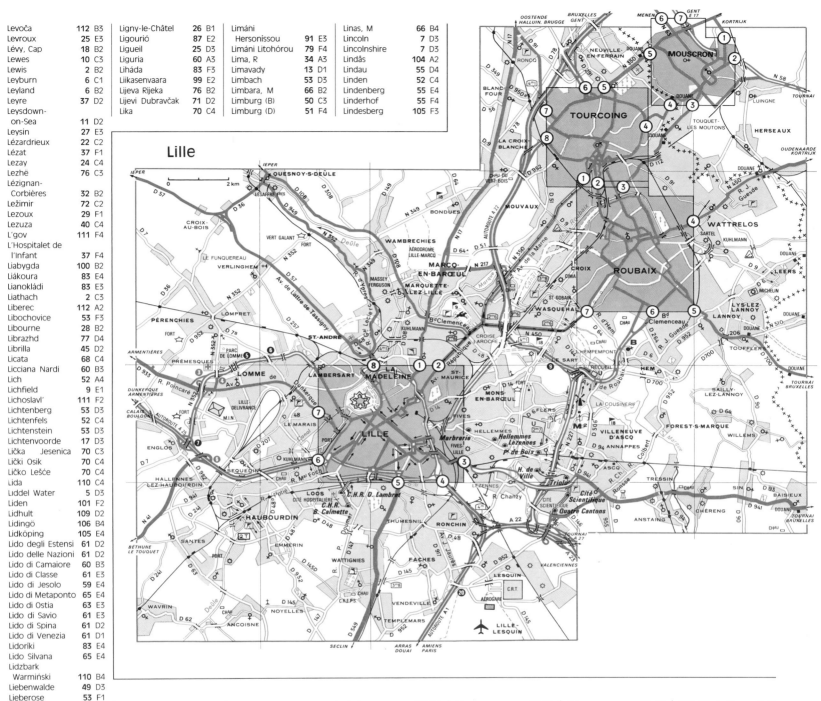

Likenäs	105	E2
Líkeo, Óri	86	C2
Likódimo, Óros	86	C3
Likófos	81	F2
Likoporiá	87	D1
Likórahi	78	C4
Likóstomo	80	C2
Likouría	86	C1
Liland	94	B3
Lilea	83	E3
Lilienfeld	57	E3
Liljendal	107	F2
Lilla Edet	108	C1
Lillby	102	C2
Lille	19	F1
Lille Bælt	108	A3
Lillebonne	19	D3
Lillehammer	105	D2
Lillerød	108	C1
Lillers	19	F1
Lillesand	104	B4
Lillestrøm	105	D3
Lillhärdal	101	E3
Lillo	40	B3
Lillögda	102	A1
Lillholmsjön	101	E1
Lim	76	B1
Lima	101	D4

Limburg (NL)	17	D4
Limenária	80	C3
Limerick	14	B3
Limerick (Co)	14	B3
Limfjorden	108	A2
Limia, R	34	B3
Limingen	97	E4
Liminka	99	D4
Liminpuro	99	E4
Limljani	76	B3
Límnes	87	E2
Límni	84	A3
Limniá	80	C2
Limnítsa	83	D4
Límnos, N	80	C2
Limoges	29	D1
Limogne	29	D3
Limone Piemonte	31	E3
Limonest	26	C4
Limours	19	E4
Limoux	32	B2
Lin	77	D4
Linares	44	A2
Linares del Arroyo, Emb de	36	A3
Linares de Mora	41	E2
Linares de Riofrio	39	E2
Linariá	84	C3

Lindesnes	104	B4
Lindhem	106	A4
Lindö	106	A4
Lindos	93	F2
Lindoso	34	B3
Lindow	49	D3
Lindsdal	109	E2
Lingbo	106	A2
Linge	100	B2
Lingen	17	E2
Linguaglossa	69	D3
Linken	49	E2
Linköping	106	A4
Linlithgow	5	D2
Linnansaari	103	E3
Linnhe, L	4	B1
Linosa, I di	68	A4
Linsell	101	E3
Linslade	9	F2
Linthal	58	A2
Linyola	37	F3
Linz	51	E4
Linz	57	D2
Lion	18	C3
Lion-d'Angers, le	23	E4
Lioni	64	C4
Lióprasso	83	D1
Lioran, le	29	E2

Lipar	72	B2
Lipari	69	D2
Lipari, I	69	D2
Lipenská přehr nádrž	56	C2
Liperi	103	F2
Lipiany	49	F3
Lipica	70	A3
Lipik	71	D2
Lipkovo	77	E2
Lipljan	77	D2
Lipno	57	D2
Lipova	112	C4
Lipovac	72	B3
Lippe	17	E3
Lippstadt	17	E2
Lipsí	89	E2
Lipsí, N	89	E2
Liptovský Mikuláš	112	B3
Liqenas	77	D4
Lírkia	87	D2
Lis	76	C3
Lisac	71	E4
Lisboa	38	A4
Lisburn	13	E2
Lisdoonvarna	12	B4
Lisieux	19	D3

Lisina	71	E4
Liskeard	8	B4
Lisková	56	B1
Lisle	29	D3
Lismore (GB)	4	B1
Lismore (IRL)	14	C4
Lisnaskea	13	D2
Lisovići	71	F3
Lisse	16	C2
List	47	F1
Listafjorden	104	A4
Lištica	75	E2
Listowel	14	B3
Lit	101	E2
Lit-et-Mixe	28	A3
Lithakiá	86	A2
Lithári, Akr	84	C3
Líthines	91	F4
Líthino, Akr	91	D4
Lithio	85	E4
Litija	70	B2
Litóhoro	79	F4
Litoměřice	53	F3
Litomyšl	112	A3
Litschau	57	D1
Littlehampton	10	C3

Little Minch, The	2	A3
Little Moreton Hall	6	C3
Littleport	10	C1
Litva	110	C3
Litvínov	53	E3
Livaara	99	F3
Liváda, Akr	88	C2
Livade	70	A3
Livaderó (Dráma)	80	C2
Livaderó (Kozáni)	79	E4
Livádi (Kithira)	90	A2
Livádi (Makedonía)	80	A3
Livádi (Sérifos)	88	A3
Livádi (Thessalía)	79	E4
Livadiá (Makedonía)	80	A2
Livadiá (Stereá Eláda)	83	F4
Livádia (Tílos)	89	F4
Livadítis	80	C1
Livadohóri	85	D1
Livanátes	83	F3
Livarot	19	D4
Livenza	59	E4

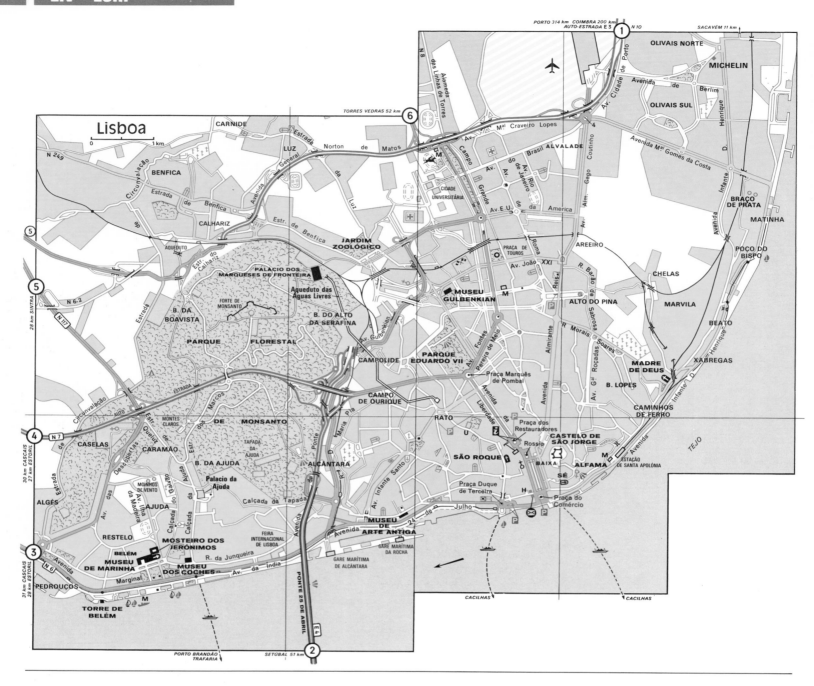

Lisboa
0   1 km

Liverá	79 D3	Ljubišnja	76 B1	Llandysul	8 C1	Lloret de Mar	32 B4	Lochranza	4 B2	Lofthus	104 B2	Loire (Dépt)	29 F1
Liverdun	21 D4	Ljubljana	70 B2	Llanelli	8 C2	Llucmajor	45 F3	Lochvica	113 F2	Loftus	5 F4	Loire-Atlantique	23 D4
Livernon	29 D2	Ljubno	70 B1	Llanerchymedd	6 A2	Llynclys	6 B3	Lochy, L	2 C4	Log	70 A2	Loir-et-Cher	25 E2
Liverpool	6 B2	Ljubojno	77 E4	Llanes	35 E1	Lnáre	56 C1	Lockenhaus	57 F3	Logarska dolina	70 B1	Loiret	25 E1
Liverpool B	6 B2	Ljubostinja	73 D4	Llanfairfechan	6 A2	Loanhead	5 D2	Lockerbie	5 D3	Logatec, D.	70 A2	Loiri	66 B1
Livigno	58 C3	Ljuboten	77 D2	Llanfair-ym-Muallt	9 D1	Loano	31 F3	Löcknitz	49 E2	Logroño	36 B2	Loiron	23 E3
Livingston	5 D2	Ljubovija	72 C4	Llanfyllin	6 B3	Löbau	53 F2	Locle, le	27 E2	Logrosán	39 E3	Loitz	49 D2
Livno	75 E1	Ljubuša	75 E1	Llangadog	8 C2	Löbejún	53 D2	Locmariaquer	22 C4	Løgstør	108 A2	Loja	43 F3
Livo	99 E3	Ljubuški	75 E2	Llangefni	6 A2	Lobenstein	52 C3	Locminé	22 C3	Løgten	108 B3	Lojsta	109 F4
Livojärvi	99 E2	Ljugarn	109 F4	Llangollen	6 B3	Łobez	49 F2	Locorotondo	65 E3	Løgumkloster	108 A4	Lokalahti	107 D2
Livojoki	99 E3	Ljungan	101 F3	Llangurig	8 C1	Löbnitz	49 D1	Locquirec	22 B2	Lohals	108 B4	Lokan Tekojärvi	95 F4
Livold	70 B3	Ljungby	109 D2	Llanidloes	8 C1	Lobo	36 A4	Locri	67 F4	Lohberg	56 B1	Løken	105 D3
Livorno	60 C4	Ljungbyhed	109 D3	Llano, Pto	39 E3	Lobón	39 D4	Locronan	22 B3	Lohilahti	103 E3	Lokeren	50 B3
Livorno Ferraris	31 F1	Ljungdalen	101 F3	Llanrhystud	8 C1	Loburg	53 D1	Loctudy	22 B3	Lohiniva	99 D1	Loket	53 E4
Livron	30 B2	Ljungsbro	105 F4	Llanrwst	6 A3	Locana	31 E1	Lodè	66 C2	Lohja	107 E3	Lokka	95 F4
Lixoúri	82 B4	Ljungskile	108 C1	Llanwrtyd-Wells	8 C1	Locarno	58 A3	Lodève	30 A4	Lohjanjärvi	107 E2	Løkken (N)	100 C2
Lizard	8 B4	Ljusdal	101 F3	Llanymyddfri	8 C1	Lochaline	4 B1	Lodi	60 B1	Lohne	17 F2	Løkken (S)	108 B1
Lizard Pt	8 B4	Ljusnan	101 E3	Llarga	41 E4	Lochboisdale	2 A3	Løding	97 E1	Löhne	17 F2	Lokn'a	111 D2
Lizy	19 F3	Ljusne	101 F4	Llavorsi	37 F2	Lochcarron	2 B3	Lødingen	94 A3	Lohr	52 B4	Lokrum	76 A2
Lizzano in		Ljutići	76 B1	Lleida	37 E4	Lochearnhead	4 C1	Lodosa	36 C2	Lohtaja	102 C1	Lokve (Hrvatska)	70 B3
Belvedere	60 C3	Ljutoglav	77 D2	Llera	43 D1	Lochem	17 D2	Łódź	112 B2	Loiano		Lokve (Slovenija)	70 A2
Ljeskove Vode	71 E3	Ljutomer	70 C1	Llerena	43 D1	Loches	25 D3	Loeches	40 B2	Rioveggio	60 C3	Lokve (Vojvodina)	73 D2
Ljig	72 C3	Llagostera	32 B3	Lles	32 A3	Loch Garman	15 D3	Loen	100 A3	Loibltunnel	70 A1	Lolland	108 B4
Ljubaništa	77 D4	Llanberis	6 A3	Llessui	37 F2	Lochgelly	5 D2	Løfallstrand	104 A2	Loimaa	107 E2	L'Olleria	45 E1
Ljubata, D.	77 E2	Llanca	32 C3	Lleyn Pen	6 A3	Lochgilphead	4 B2	Lofário	81 E2	Loimaan kunta	107 D2	Lom (BG)	115 D2
Ljubelj	70 A1	Llandeilo	8 C2	Lliria	41 E3	Lochinver	2 C2	Lofer	59 E1	Loimijoki	107 D2	Lom (CS)	53 E3
Ljubija	71 D3	Llandovery	8 C1	Llívia	32 A3	Lochmaben	5 D3	Löffingen	54 C4	Loing	26 A2	Lom (N)	100 B3
Ljubinje	75 F2	Llandrindod Wells	9 D1	Llobregat, R	32 A3	Lochmaddy	2 A3	Lofoten	97 E1	Loir	25 E1	Loma Negra	36 C3
Ljubiš	72 C4	Llandudno	6 A2	Llodio	36 B1	Loch Ness	2 C3	Lofsdalen	101 D3	Loire	23 E4	Lomazzo	60 A1

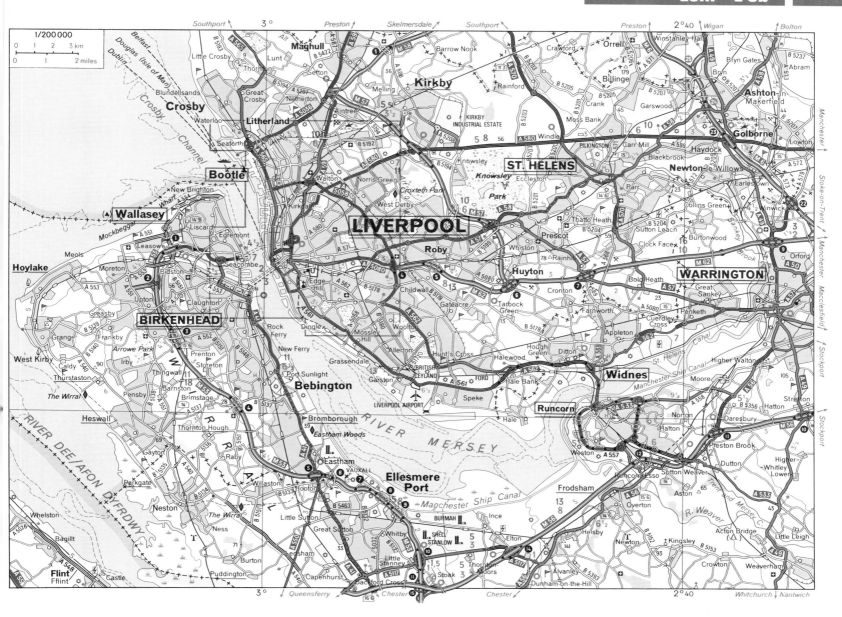

Lombarda,		Longós	82 A2	Lorch (Baden-		Los Dolores	45 D2	Loudías	79 F3	Loutrá Edipsoú	83 F3	Lovag	76 B1
Colle della	31 E3	Long Preston	6 C1	Württemberg)	55 D2	Losenstein	57 D3	Loudías R	79 F3	Loutrá Eleftherón	80 C3	Lövånger	102 B1
Lombardia	60 A1	Long Sutton	7 E3	Lorch (Hessen)	51 F4	Los Gallardos	44 C3	Loudun	25 D3	Loutrá Ipátis	83 E3	Lövberga	101 F1
Lombez	28 C4	Longtown	5 D3	Loreley	51 F4	Losheim	54 B1	Loué	23 E3	Loutrá Kaítsas	83 E2	Lovćen	76 B3
Lomello	60 A2	Longué	23 E4	Loreo	61 D1	Los Hinojosos	40 B3	Loue	26 C2	Loutrá (Kikládes)	88 A2	Loveč	115 D2
Lomen	104 C1	Longueville-sur-		Loreto	61 F4	Lošinj	70 B4	Loughborough	7 D3	Loutráki		Lovere	58 B4
Lomma	108 C3	Scie	19 E2	Loreto Aprutino	64 A1	Los Llanos de		Loughrea	12 B4	(Pelopónnisos)	87 E1	Loviisa	107 F2
Lommatzsch	53 E2	Longuyon	20 C3	Lorgues	31 D4	Aridane	42 A4	Louhans	26 C3	Loutráki		Lovisa	107 F2
Lommel	50 C3	Longwy	20 C3	Lorica	67 F3	Los Lobos	44 C3	Louhisaari	107 D2	(Skópelos)	84 B2	Lovosice	53 F3
Lomond, L	4 C2	Lonigo	60 C1	Lorient	22 B4	Los Navalmorales	39 F3	Louisburgh	12 B3	Loutráki (Stereá		Lovran	70 B3
Lomonosov	111 D1	Löningen	17 E2	Loriga	38 C2	Los Navalucillos	39 F3	Loukinen	95 E4	Eláda)	82 C3	Lovrenc na	
Lomont, Mts du	27 E2	Lonja	71 D3	Loriguilla, Emb de	41 D3	Lößnitz	53 D3	Loukíssia	84 A4	Loutrá Kilínis	86 B1	Pohorju	70 B1
Lompolo	95 E4	Lonja R	71 D2	Loriol	30 B2	Los Palacios y		Loulay	24 C4	Loutrá Langadá	80 A3	Lövstabruk	106 B2
Łomża	112 B1	Lönsboda	109 D3	Lormes	26 B2	Villafranca	43 D3	Loulé	42 B3	Loutrá (Lésvos)	85 F3	Lövstabukten	106 B2
Lonato	60 B1	Lønsdal	97 E2	Lorn, Firth of	4 B1	Los Santos	39 E2	Louny	53 E3	Loutrá		Lovund	97 D2
Lončari	71 F3	Lønset	100 B2	Loro Ciuffenna	61 D4	Los Santos de		Loupe, la	19 E4	(Makedonía)	80 B4	Löwenberg	49 D3
Lončarica	71 E4	Lons-le-Saunier	26 C3	Loroux-Botterreau,		Maimona	43 D1	Loup, Gorge du (L)	21 D2	Loutrá		Lower L Erne	12 C2
Londinières	19 E2	Looe	8 B4	le	24 B2	Los Sauces	42 A4	Loup, Gorges du		(Pelopónnisos)	86 C2	Lowestoft	11 E1
London	9 F2	Loop Head	12 A4	Lorquin	21 E4	Lossiemouth	3 D3	(F)	31 E3	Loutrá Smokóvou	83 D2	Łowicz	112 B1
Londonderry	13 D1	Loosdorf	57 E2	Lörrach	54 C4	Lossnen	101 D3	Lourdes	37 E1	Loutrá Vólvis	80 A3	Low Street	7 F3
Londonderry (Co)	13 D1	Lopar	70 B4	Lorrez-le-Bocage	25 F1	Lostwithiel	8 B4	Loures	38 A4	Loutró Elénis	87 E1	Lož	70 B2
Longa	86 C3	Lopare	72 B3	Lorris	25 F1	Los Villares	44 A2	Lourical	38 B2	Loutropigi	83 D2	Lozère	29 F2
Longádes	82 C1	Lopcombe		Los	101 E3	Los Yébenes	40 A3	Lourinhã	38 A3	Loutrópirgos	87 E1	Lozère, Mt	29 F3
Longanikos	87 D3	Corner	9 E3	Los Alcázares	45 D2	Lot	29 E2	Louros	82 B2	Loutrós	81 F2	Lozna	73 D4
Longares	36 C4	Lopera	43 E2	Losar	39 E2	Lot (Dépt)	29 D3	Loúros R	82 C2	Loútsa (Ípiros)	82 B2	Loznica	72 B3
Longarone	59 E3	Lopes, Mal i	76 C4	Los Arcos	36 B2	Lote	100 A3	Louroux, le	23 E4	Loútsa (Stereá		Lozovac	75 D1
Long Eaton	7 D3	Loppa	94 C2	Los Barreros	40 C4	Lot-et-Garonne	28 C3	Lousa	38 A4	Eláda)	88 A1	Lozovik	73 D3
Longeau	26 C1	Loppi	107 E2	Los Barrios	43 D4	Lothian	5 D2	Lousã	38 B2	Louvain	50 C3	Lozoyuela	40 B1
Longford	12 C3	Lopud	75 F2	Loßburg	54 C3	Lötschbergtunnel	27 F3	Lousada	34 A4	Louvain-la-Neuve	50 C4	Luanco	35 D1
Longford (Co)	12 C3	Lopud I	75 F2	Los Corrales de		Löttorp	109 E2	Lousã, Sa da	38 B2	Louvière, La	50 B4	Luarca	35 D1
Longleat House	9 D3	Lora del Río	43 E2	Buelna	35 F2	Louth	7 E2	Louth	13 D3	Louviers	19 E3	Lubań	112 A2
Longny	19 D4	Lorca	44 C2	Los Cortijos	40 A4	Loučná	53 E3	Louth	13 D3	Louvigné-du-		Lübars	53 D1
Longobucco	67 F2	Lorcé	51 D4	Los Cristianos	42 B4	Loudéac	22 C3	Loutrá Aridéas	79 E2	Désert	18 B4	L'ubaševka	113 E3

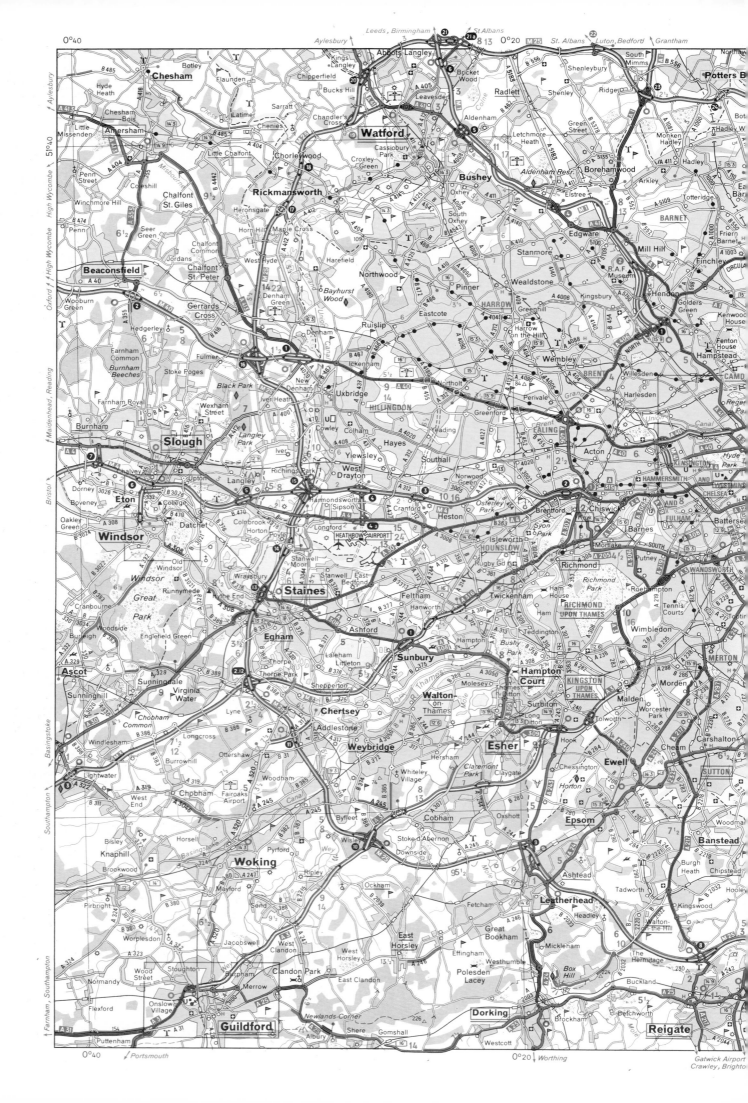

London

1/200 000

0 1 2 3 4 5 6 km

0 1 2 3 4 miles

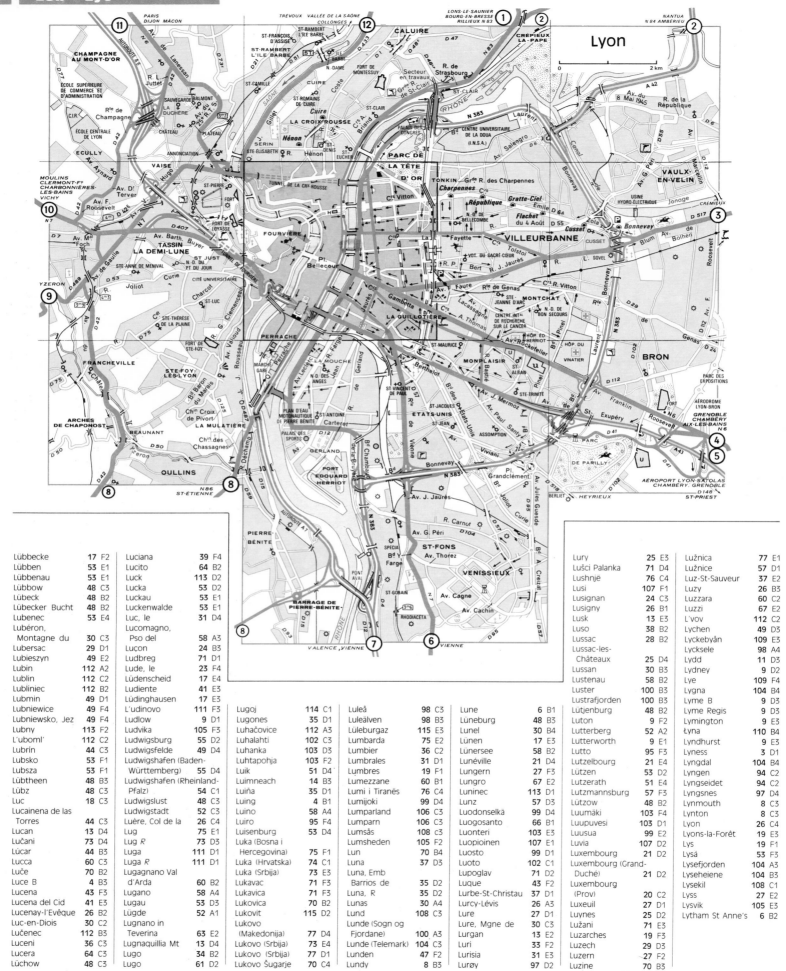

Lyon

Lübbecke	17 F2	Luciana	39 F4	Lugoj	114 C1
Lübben	53 E1	Lucito	64 B2	Lugones	35 D1
Lübbenau	53 E1	Luck	113 D2	Luhačovice	112 A3
Lübbow	48 C3	Lucka	53 D2	Luhalahti	102 C3
Lübeck	48 B2	Luckau	53 E1	Luhanka	103 D3
Lübecker Bucht	48 B2	Luckenwalde	53 E1	Luhtapohja	103 F2
Lubenec	53 E4	Luc, le	31 D4	Luik	51 D4
Lubéron,		Lucomagno,		Luimneach	14 B3
Montagne du	30 C3	Pso del	58 A3	Luiña	35 D1
Lubersac	29 D1	Luçon	24 B3	Luing	4 B1
Lubieszyn	49 E2	Ludbreg	71 D1	Luino	58 A4
Lubin	112 A2	Lude, le	23 F4	Luiro	95 F4
Lublin	112 C2	Lüdenscheid	17 E4	Luisenburg	53 D4
Lubliniec	112 B2	Ludiente	41 E3	Luka (Bosna i	
Lubmin	49 D1	Lüdinghausen	17 E3	Hercegovina)	75 F1
Lubniewice	49 F4	L'udinovo	111 F3	Luka (Hrvatska)	74 C1
Lubniewsko, Jez	49 F4	Ludlow	9 D1	Luka (Srbija)	73 E3
Lubny	113 F2	Ludvika	105 F3	Lukavac	71 F3
L'uboml'	112 C2	Ludwigsburg	55 D2	Lukavica	71 F3
Lubrín	44 C3	Ludwigsfelde	49 D4	Lukovica	70 B2
Lubsko	53 F1	Ludwigshafen (Baden-		Lukovit	115 D2
Lubsza	53 F1	Württemberg)	55 D4	Lukovo	
Lübtheen	48 B3	Ludwigshafen (Rheinland-		(Makedonija)	77 D4
Lübz	48 C3	Pfalz)	54 C1	Lukovo (Srbija)	73 E4
Luc	18 C3	Ludwigslust	48 C3	Lukovo (Srbija)	77 D4
Lucainena de las		Ludwigstadt	52 C3	Lukovo Šugarje	70 C4
Torres	44 C3	Luère, Col de la	26 C4		
Lucan	13 D4	Lug	75 E1		
Lučani	73 D4	Lug R	73 D3		
Lúcar	44 B3	Luga	111 D1		
Lucca	60 C3	Luga R	111 D1		
Luče	70 B2	Lugagnano Val			
Luce B	4 B3	d'Arda	60 B2		
Lucena	43 F3	Lugano	58 A4		
Lucena del Cid	41 E3	Lugau	53 D3		
Lucenay-l'Evêque	26 B2	Lügde	52 A1		
Luc-en-Diois	30 C2	Lugnano in			
Lučenec	112 B3	Teverina	63 E2		
Luceni	36 C3	Lugnaquillia Mt	13 D4		
Lucera	64 C3	Lugo	34 B2		
Lüchow	48 C3	Lugo	61 D2		

Luleå	98 C3	Lune	6 B1
Luleälven	98 B3	Lüneburg	48 B3
Lüleburgaz	115 E3	Lunel	30 B4
Lumbarda	75 E2	Lünen	17 E3
Lumbier	36 C2	Lünersee	58 B2
Lumbrales	31 D1	Lunéville	21 D4
Lumbres	19 F1	Lungern	27 F3
Lumezzane	60 B1	Lungro	67 E2
Lumi i Tiranës	76 C4	Luninec	113 D1
Lumijoki	99 D4	Lunz	57 D3
Lumparland	106 C3	Luodonselkä	99 D4
Lumparn	106 C3	Luogosanto	66 B1
Lumsås	108 C3	Luonteri	103 E3
Lumsheden	105 F2	Luopioinen	107 E1
Lun	70 B4	Luosto	99 D3
Luna	37 D3	Luoto	102 C1
Luna, Emb		Lupoglav	71 D2
Barrios de	35 D2	Luque	43 F2
Luna, R	35 D2	Lurbe-St-Christau	37 D1
Lunas	30 A4	Lurcy-Lévis	26 A3
Lund	108 C2	Lure	27 D1
Lunde (Sogn og		Lure, Mgne de	30 C3
Fjordane)	100 A3	Lurgan	13 E2
Lunde (Telemark)	104 C3	Luri	33 F2
Lunden	47 F2	Lurisia	31 E3
Lundy	8 B3	Lurøy	97 D2

Lury	25 E3	Lužnica	77 E1
Lušci Palanka	71 D4	Lužnice	57 D1
Lushnjë	76 C4	Luz-St-Sauveur	37 E2
Lusi	107 F1	Luzy	26 B3
Lusignan	24 C3	Luzzara	60 C2
Lusigny	26 B1	Luzzi	67 E2
Lusk	13 E3	L'vov	112 C2
Luso	38 B2	Lychen	49 D3
Lussac	28 B2	Lyckebyån	109 E3
Lussac-les-		Lycksele	98 A4
Châteaux	25 D4	Lydd	11 D3
Lussan	30 B3	Lydney	9 D2
Lustenau	58 B2	Lye	109 F4
Luster	100 B3	Lygna	104 B4
Lustrafjorden	100 B3	Lyme B	9 D3
Lütjenburg	48 B2	Lyme Regis	9 D3
Luton	9 F2	Lymington	9 E3
Lutterberg	52 A2	Łyna	110 B4
Lutterworth	9 E1	Lyndhurst	9 E3
Lutto	95 F3	Lyness	3 D1
Lutzelbourg	21 E4	Lyngdal	104 B4
Lützen	53 D2	Lyngen	94 C2
Lutzerath	51 E4	Lyngseidet	94 C2
Lutzmannsburg	57 F3	Lyngsnes	97 D4
Lützow	48 B2	Lynmouth	8 C3
Luumäki	103 F4	Lynton	8 C3
Luupuvesi	103 D1	Lyon	26 C4
Luusua	99 E2	Lyons-la-Forêt	19 E3
Luvia	107 D2	Lys	19 F1
Luxembourg	21 D2	Lysá	53 E2
Luxembourg (Grand-		Lysefjorden	104 A3
Duché)	21 D2	Lyseheiene	104 B3
Luxembourg		Lysekil	108 C1
(Prov)	20 C2	Lyss	27 E2
Luxeuil	27 D1	Lysvik	105 E3
Luynes	25 D2	Lytham St Anne's	6 B2
Lužani	71 E2		
Luzarches	19 F3		
Luzech	29 D3		
Luzern	27 F2		
Luzine	70 B3		

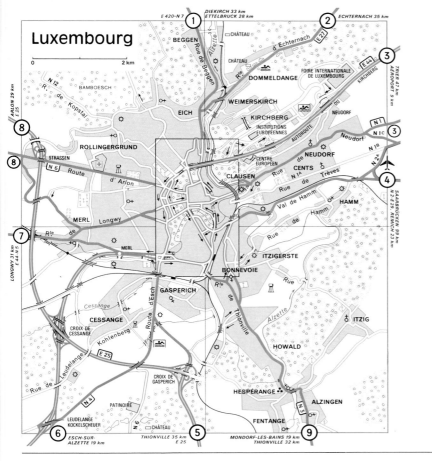

Malax	102	B2	Mamry, Jez	110	B4	Maranhão,		
Malbork	110	B4	Manacor	45	F2	Bgem do	38	B4
Malbuisson	27	D3	Manacore	64	C2	Marano	59	F3
Malcata, Sa de	39	D2	Manamansalo	99	E4	Marano di Napoli	64	B4
Malcesine	58	C4	Manasija	73	E3	Marano, L di	59	F4
Malchin	49	D2	Mancha Real	44	A2	Marans	24	B4
Malchiner See	49	D2	Manche	18	B3	Marão, Sa do	34	A4
Malchow	49	D2	Manchester	6	C2	Marássia	81	F1
Maldegem	50	B3	Manching	55	F2	Maratea	67	E2
Maldon	11	D2	Manciano	63	D2	Marateca	38	A4
Malè	58	C3	Mandal	104	B4	Marathéa	83	D2
Maléas, Akr	87	E4	Mandal selva	104	B4	Marathiá, Akr	86	A2
Máleme	90	B3	Mandamádos	85	F2	Marathiás	83	D4
Malène, la	29	F3	Mandas	66	B3	Marathókambos	89	E1
Malente			Mandela	63	F2	Marathónas	87	F1
Gremsmühlen	48	B2	Mandelieu	31	E4	Marathópoli	86	B3
Male Pijace	72	C1	Manderscheid	51	E4	Márathos	83	D2
Máles	91	E4	Mandínia	87	D2	Marbach	55	D2
Malesherbes	25	F1	Mandoúdi	84	A3	Mårbacka	105	E3
Malessina	83	F3	Mandráki	89	F4	Marbella	43	E4
Malestroit	22	C3	Mándra (Stereá			Marburg	17	
Malgomaj	97	F4	Eláda)	87	F1	Marby	101	E2
Malgrat de Mar	32	B4	Mándra (Thráki)	81	F2	Marčana	70	A4
Mália	91	E3	Mandre	70	B4	March (A)	57	F2
Malicorne	23	E4	Mandrikó	93	E1	March (GB)	10	C1
Mali Haian	70	C4	Mandrioli, Pso dei	61	D3	Marchamalo	40	B2
Mali Iđoš	72	B2	Manduria	65	E4	Marchaux	27	D2
Mali kanal	72	B2	Måne	104	C3	Marche	61	E4
Mali Lošinj	70	B4	Manerbio	60	B1	Marche-en-		
Malin	113	E2	Manětín	53	E4	Famenne	50	C4
Malines	50	B3	Manfredonia	64	C2	Marchegg	57	F2
Malin Head	13	D1	Manfredonia, G di	64	C2	Marchena	43	E3
Malinska	70	B3	Mangalia	115	E2	Marchenoir	25	E1
Mali Požerevac	73	D3	Mángana	81	D2	Marchiennes	20	A1
Mališevo	77	D2	Manganári	88	C4	Marciac	28	C4
Maliskylä	103	D1	Manger	104	A2	Marciana Marina	62	C1
Malit, Maj'e	76	C3	Mangerton Mt	14	B4	Marcianise	64	B3
Mali Zvornik	72	B4	Mangrt, Planica	59	F2	Marcigny	26	B4
Maljen	72	C4	Mangualde	38	C1	Marcilla	36	C2
Malko Târnovo	115	E2	Maniago	59	E3	Marcillac-Vallon	29	E3
Mallaig	2	B4	Manilva	43	E4	Marcillat-en-		
Mållejus	95	D2	Man, I of	6	A1	Combraille	25	F4
Mallén	36	C3	Máni			Marcilly-le-Hayer	20	B4
Mallersdorf-			(Pelopónnissos)	87	D4	Marckolsheim	27	E1
Pfaffenberg	56	B2	Máni (Thráki)	81	F1	Marco de		
Malles Venosta	58	C2	Manisa	115	E4	Canaveses	34	A4
Mallnitz	59	E2	Mánises	41	E4	Marcoule	30	B3
Mallorca	45	E2	Manjača	71	E4	Mære	101	D1
Mallow	14	B4	Mank	57	E3	Maree, L	2	C3
Mallwyd	6	A3	Månkarbo	106	B3	Mare Ligure	60	A4
Malm	101	D1	Manlleu	32	B3	Marene	31	E2
Malmberget	98	B2	Mannersdorf	57	F3	Marennes	28	A1
Malmédy	51	D4	Mannheim	54	C1	Marentes	34	C2
Malmesbury	9	E2	Mannu	66	B4	Maréttimo, I-	68	A3
Malmköping	106	A4	Manojlovac slap	75	D1	Mareuil		
Malmö	108	C3	Manojlovce	77	E1	(Dordogne)	28	C1
Malmslätt	106	A4	Manoppello	64	A2	Mareuil (Vendée)	24	B3
Malo	59	D4	Manorhamilton	12	C2	Margarites	91	D3
Maloja	58	B3	Manosque	30	C3	Margaríti	82	B2
Malojaroslavec	111	F3	Manresa	32	A4	Margate	11	D2
Malo Konjari	77	E4	Manschnow	49	F4	Margherita di		
Malo-les-Bains	19	F1	Mansfeld	52	C2	Savoia	65	D3
Malónas	93	F1	Mansfield	7	D3	Marguerittes	30	B3
Malori	64	B4	Mansilla de las			María	44	C2
Måløy	100	A3	Mulas	35	E3	María Cristina,		
Malpartida de			Mansilla, Emb de	36	B3	Emb de	41	E3
Cáceres	39	D3	Mansle	25	D4	Mariannelund	109	E1
Malpartida de			Manteigas	38	C2	Mariánské Lázně	53	E4
Plasencia	39	E2	Mantes	19	E4	Maria Saal	70	A1
Malpica (E)	34	A1	Mantiel	40	C2	Maria Taferl	57	E2
Malpica (P)	38	C3	Mäntlahti	103	F4	Mariazell	57	E3
Mals	58	C2	Mantorp	109	E1	Maribo	108	B4
Målselv	94	B3	Mantova	60	C2	Maribor	70	C1
Målselva	94	B3	Mänttä	103	D3	Mariborsko		
Målsnes	94	B3	Mäntyharju	103	E3	Pohorje	70	C1
Malsta	101	F3	Mäntyluoto	102	B3	Marica	115	D3
Malta	59	F2	Manzanal, Pto del	35	D2	Mariefred	106	B4
Malta/	68	B4	Manzanares	40	B4	Mariehamn	106	C3
Maltby	7	D2	Manzanares el			Marienberg	53	E3
Maltiotunturi	95	F4	Real	40	A2	Marienborn	52	C1
Malton	7	D1	Manzaneda	34	C3	Marienburg	51	E4
Maluenda	36	C4	Manzanera	41	E3	Marienstedt	48	B3
Malung	105	E2	Manzat	26	A4	Mariestad	105	E4
Malungsfors	101	D4	Manziana	63	D2	Marignane	30	C4
Malveira	38	A4	Maó	45	F2	Marigny	18	B3
Malvik	100	C2	Magellarè	77	D3	Marigny-le-Châtel	20	B4
Malzieu-Ville, le	29	F2	Maqueda	40	A2	Marija Bistrica	70	C2
Mamaia	115	E1	Maramures	112	C3	Marikirk	3	E4
Mamarrosa	38	B1	Maranchón	40	C1	Marín	34	A2
Mamers	23	F3	Maranchón,			Marina	75	D2
Mamonovo	110	B4	Pto de	40	C1	Marina di		
Mampodre	35	E2	Maranello	60	C2	Camerota	67	D2

M

			Madara	115	E2	Mágina	44	A2
			Maddalena, Arc			Magione	61	E4
Maakalla	102	C1	della	66	B1	Maglaj	71	F3
Maalanti	102	B2	Maddalena, Colle			Magliano di Marsi	63	F2
Maam Cross	12	B3	della	31	E2	Magliano in		
Maaninka	103	E2	Maddalena, I	66	B1	Toscana	63	D2
Maaninkavaara	99	E2	Maddalena La	66	B1	Magliano Sabina	63	E2
Maanselkä	103	E1	Maddaloni	64	B3	Maglić	73	D4
Maarestatunturit	95	E3	Madeira,			Maglić Mt	76	A1
Maarianhamina	106	C3	Arquipélago da	42	A3	Maglie	65	F4
Maarianvaara	103	E2	Madeira, I da	42	A3	Magnac-Laval	25	E4
Maas	16	C3	M'adèl'	111	D3	Magnissia	83	E2
Maaseik	51	D3	Madeleine,			Magnor	105	D3
Maasmechelen	51	D3	Col de la	31	D1	Magny-en-Vexin	19	E3
Maassluis	16	B3	Madero, Pto del	36	C3	Magoúla	86	B2
Maastricht	51	D3	Maderuelo	36	A3	Magra	77	D2
Määttälänvaara	99	F2	Madesimo	58	B3	Magreglio	81	E2
Mablethorpe	7	E2	Madine, Lac de	20	C3	Mahaerádo	86	A1
Macael	44	C3	Madon	21	D4	Mahlu	103	D2
Mação	38	B3	Madona	110	C2	Mahón	45	F2
Macclesfield	6	C3	Madonie Nebrodi	68	C3	Mahora	41	D4
Macduff	3	E3	Madonna di			Mahovo	71	D2
Maceda	34	B3	Campiglio	58	C3	Mähring	53	D4
Macedo de			Madrid	40	A2	Maia	34	A4
Cavaleiros	34	C4	Madrid (Prov)	40	A2	Maials	37	E4
Macelj	70	C1	Madridejos	40	B3	Maîche	27	E2
Macerata	61	F4	Madrigal de las Altas			Maida	67	F3
Macerata Feltria	61	E3	Torres	39	F1	Maidenhead	9	F2
Macgillycuddy's			Madrigal de la			Maidstone	11	D3
Reeks	14	A4	Vera	39	E2	Maiella, la	64	A2
Machault	20	B3	Madrigalejo	39	E4	Maienfeld	58	B2
Machecoul	24	B3	Madrona	40	A1	Maignelay	19	F3
Machero	39	F4	Madrona, Sa	44	A1	Maigue	14	B3
Machichaco, C	36	B1	Madroñera	39	E3	Maillezais	24	C4
Machine, la	26	A3	Maël-Carhaix	22	B3	Mailly-le-Camp	20	B4
Máchovo jez	53	F3	Maella	37	E4	Main	55	D1
Machrihanish	4	B3	Maesteg	8	C2	Mainar	36	C4
Machynlleth	6	A3	Mafra	38	A3	Mainburg	55	F2
Mackendorf	52	C1	Magacela	39	E4	Maine-et-Loire	23	E4
Mackenrode	52	B2	Magallón	36	C3	Mainistir na Búille	12	C3
Mačkovci	70	C1	Magaña	36	B3	Mainland (Orkney)	3	D1
Macocha	57	F1	Magaz	35	F3	Mainland (Shetland)	3	F2
Macomer	66	B2	Magdalena,			Maintenon	19	E4
Mâcon	26	C4	Pto de la	35	D2	Mainz	51	F4
Macotera	39	F1	Magdeburg	52	C1	Maira	31	E2
Macroom	14	B4	Magenta	60	A1	Mairena del Alcor	43	D2
Macugnaga	27	F4	Magerøya	95	E1	Maisach	55	F3
Mačvanska			Maggia	58	A3	Maison-Neuve	26	B1
Mitrovica	72	C3	Maggiore, L	58	A4	Maisons-Blanches,		
Mačvanski			Maghera	13	D1	les	25	D4
Pričinović	72	C3	Magherafelt	13	D2	Maissau	57	E2

Maizières	21	D3	Malax			
Maja	70	C3				
Majales, Pto de los	40	A4				
Majdanpek	73	E3				
Majevica	72	B3				
Majšperk	70	C1				
Makarska	75	E2				
Makce	73	E3				
Makedonia	79	F2				
Makedonija	77	E3				
Makedonija	77	F3				
Makedonski Brod	77	D3				
Makljen	75	E1				
Makó	114	B1				
Makovo	77	E4				
Makrakómi	83	E3				
Mákri	81	E2				
Makríamos	80	C3				
Makrígialos	79	F3				
Makrígialos	91	F4				
Makrihóri						
(Makedonía)	80	C2				
Makrihóri						
(Thessalía)	83	E1				
Makrinítsa	83	F2				
Makrinóros	82	C3				
Makriplágio	80	C2				
Makriráhi	83	E3				
Makrivrahos, Akr	81	E3				
Makrohóri	79	E3				
Makronissi	88	A2				
Maksniemi	99	D3				
Mala	14	B4				
Malå	98	A4				
Mala Bosna	72	B1				
Malacky	57	F2				
Maladeta	37	E2				
Malaga	43	F4				
Malagón	40	A4				
Malahide	13	E4				
Malaja Višera	111	E1				
Malaja Viska	113	F2				
Mala Kapela	70	C3				
Mala Krsna	73	D3				
Malalbergo	61	D2				
Malámata	83	D4				
Malandríno	83	E4				
Malangen	94	B2				
Mälären	106	B3				
Mala Subotica	71	D1				
Malaucène	30	C3				

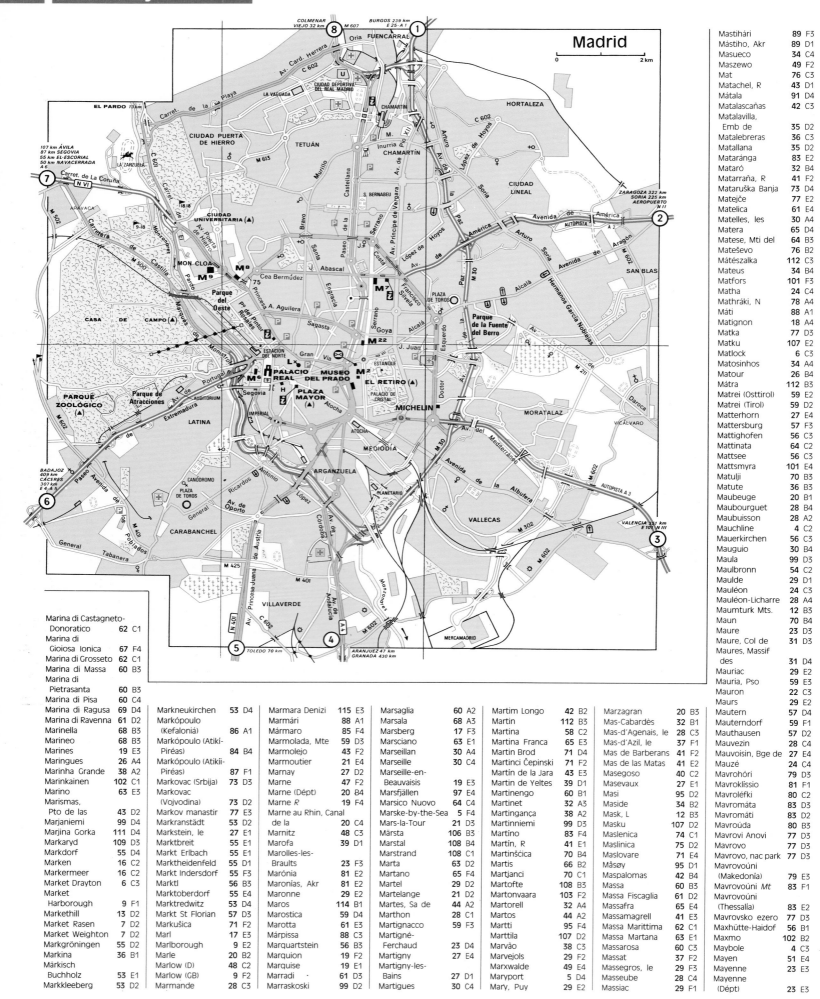

Mastihári	89	F3	
Mástiho, Akr	89	D1	
Masueco	34	C4	
Maszewo	49	F2	
Mat	76	C3	
Matachel, R	43	D1	
Mátala	91	D4	
Matalascañas	42	C3	
Matalavilla, Emb de	35	D2	
Matalebreras	36	C3	
Matallana	35	D2	
Mataránga	83	E2	
Mataró	32	B4	
Matarraña, R	41	F2	
Mataruška Banja	73	D4	
Matejče	77	E2	
Matelica	61	E4	
Matelles, les	30	A4	
Matera	65	D4	
Matese, Mti del	64	B3	
Mateševo	76	B2	
Mátészalka	112	C3	
Mateus	34	B4	
Matfors	101	F3	
Matha	24	C4	
Mathráki, N	78	A4	
Máti	88	A1	
Matignon	18	A4	
Matka	77	D3	
Matku	107	E2	
Matlock	6	C3	
Matosinhos	34	A4	
Matour	26	B4	
Mátra	112	B3	
Matrei (Osttirol)	59	E2	
Matrei (Tirol)	59	D2	
Matterhorn	27	E4	
Mattersburg	57	F3	
Mattighofen	56	C3	
Mattinata	64	C2	
Mattsee	56	C3	
Mattsmyra	101	E4	
Matulji	70	B3	
Matute	36	B3	
Maubeuge	20	B1	
Maubourguet	28	B4	
Maubuisson	28	A2	
Mauchline	4	C2	
Mauerkirchen	56	C3	
Mauguio	30	B4	
Maula	99	D3	
Maulbronn	54	C2	
Maulde	29	D1	
Mauléon	24	C3	
Mauléon-Licharre	28	A4	
Maumturk Mts.	12	B3	
Maun	70	B4	
Maure	23	D3	
Maure, Col de	31	D3	
Maures, Massif des	31	D4	
Mauriac	29	E2	
Mauria, Pso	59	E3	
Mauron	22	C3	
Maurs	29	E2	
Mautern	57	D4	
Mauterndorf	59	F1	
Mauthausen	57	D2	
Mauvezin	28	C4	
Mauvoisin, Bge de	27	E4	
Mauzé	24	C4	
Mavrohóri	79	D3	
Mavroklíssio	81	F1	
Mavroléfki	80	C2	
Mavromáta	83	D3	
Mavromáti	83	D2	
Mavroúda	80	B3	
Mavrovi Anovi	77	D3	
Mavrovo	77	D3	
Mavrovo, nac park	77	D3	
Mavrovoúni (Makedonía)	79	E3	
Mavrovoúni *Mt*	83	F1	
Mavrovoúni (Thessalía)	83	E2	
Mavrovsko ezero	77	D3	
Maxhütte-Haidof	56	B1	
Maxmo	102	B2	
Maybole	4	C3	
Mayen	51	E4	
Mayenne	23	E3	
Mayenne (Dépt)	23	E3	

Marina di Castagneto-Donoratico	62	C1	
Marina di Gioiosa Ionica	67	F4	
Marina di Grosseto	62	C1	
Marina di Massa	60	B3	
Marina di Pietrasanta	60	B3	
Marina di Pisa	60	C4	
Marina di Ragusa	69	D4	
Marina di Ravenna	61	D2	
Marinella	68	B3	
Marineo	68	B3	
Marines	19	E3	
Maringues	26	A4	
Marinha Grande	38	A2	
Marinkainen	102	C1	
Marino	63	E3	
Marismas, Pto de las	43	D2	
Marjaniemi	99	D4	
Marjina Gorka	111	D4	
Markaryd	109	D3	
Markdorf	55	D4	
Marken	16	B3	
Markermeer	16	C2	
Market Drayton	6	C3	
Market Harborough	9	F1	
Markethill	13	D2	
Market Rasen	7	E1	
Market Weighton	7	E1	
Markgröningen	55	D2	
Markina	36	B1	
Märkisch Buchholz	53	E1	
Markkleeberg	53	D2	

Markneukirchen	53	D4	
Markópoulo (Kefaloniá)	86	A1	
Markópoulo (Atikí-Piréas)	84	B4	
Markópoulo (Atikí-Piréas)	87	F1	
Markovac (Srbija)	73	D3	
Markovac (Vojvodina)	73	D2	
Markov manastir	77	E3	
Markranstädt	53	D2	
Markstein, le	27	E1	
Marktbreit	55	E1	
Markt Erlbach	55	E1	
Marktheidenfeld	55	D1	
Markt Indersdorf	55	F3	
Marktl	56	B3	
Marktoberdorf	55	E4	
Marktredwitz	53	D4	
Markt St Florian	57	D3	
Markušica	71	F2	
Marl	17	E3	
Marlborough	9	E2	
Marle	20	B2	
Marlow (D)	48	C2	
Marlow (GB)	9	F2	
Marmande	28	C3	

Marmara Denizi	115	E3	
Marmári	88	A1	
Mármaro	85	F4	
Marmolada, Mte	59	D3	
Marmolejo	43	F2	
Marmoutier	21	E4	
Marnay	27	D2	
Marne	47	F2	
Marne (Dépt)	20	B4	
Marne *R*	19	F4	
Marne au Rhin, Canal de la	20	C4	
Marnitz	48	C3	
Marofa	39	D1	
Marólia	81	E2	
Marónias, Akr	81	E2	
Maronne	29	E2	
Maros	114	B1	
Marostica	59	D4	
Marotta	61	E3	
Marolles-les-Braults	23	F3	
Márpissa	88	C3	
Marquartstein	56	B3	
Marquion	19	F2	
Marquise	19	E1	
Marradi	61	D3	
Marraskoski	99	D2	

Marsaglia	60	A2	
Marsala	68	A3	
Marsberg	17	F3	
Marsciano	63	E1	
Marseillan	30	A4	
Marseille	30	C4	
Marseille-en-Beauvaisis	19	E3	
Marsfjället	97	E4	
Marsico Nuovo	64	C4	
Marske-by-the-Sea	5	F4	
Mars-la-Tour	21	D3	
Märsta	106	B3	
Marstal	108	B4	
Marstrand	108	C1	
Marta	63	D2	
Martano	65	F4	
Martel	29	D2	
Martelange	21	D2	
Martes, Sa de	44	A2	
Marthon	28	C1	
Martignacco	59	F3	
Martigné-Ferchaud	23	D4	
Martigny	27	E4	
Martigny-les-Bains	27	D1	
Martigues	30	C4	

Martim Longo	42	B2	
Martin	112	B3	
Martina	58	C2	
Martina Franca	65	E3	
Martin Brod	71	D4	
Martinci Čepinski	71	F2	
Martín de la Jara	43	E3	
Martin de Yeltes	39	D1	
Martinengo	60	B1	
Martinet	32	A3	
Martingança	38	A2	
Martinniemi	99	D3	
Martino	83	F4	
Martín, R	41	E1	
Martinšćica	70	B4	
Martis	66	B2	
Martjanci	70	C1	
Martofte	108	B3	
Martonvaara	103	F2	
Martorell	32	A4	
Martos	44	A2	
Martti	95	F4	
Marttila	107	D2	
Marvão	38	C3	
Marvejols	29	F2	
Marxwalde	49	E4	
Maryport	5	D4	
Mary, Puy	29	E2	

Marzagran	20	B3	
Mas-Cabardès	32	B1	
Mas-d'Agenais, le	28	C3	
Mas-d'Azil, le	37	F1	
Mas de Barberans	41	F2	
Mas de las Matas	41	E2	
Masegoso	40	C2	
Masevaux	27	E1	
Masi	95	D2	
Maside	34	B2	
Mask, L	12	B3	
Masku	107	D2	
Maslenica	74	C1	
Maslinica	75	D2	
Maslovare	71	E4	
Måsøy	95	D1	
Maspalomas	42	B4	
Massa	60	B3	
Massa Fiscaglia	61	D2	
Massafra	65	E4	
Massamagrell	41	E3	
Massa Marittima	62	C1	
Massa Martana	63	E1	
Massarosa	60	C3	
Massat	37	F2	
Massegros, le	29	F2	
Masseube	28	C4	
Massiac	29	F1	

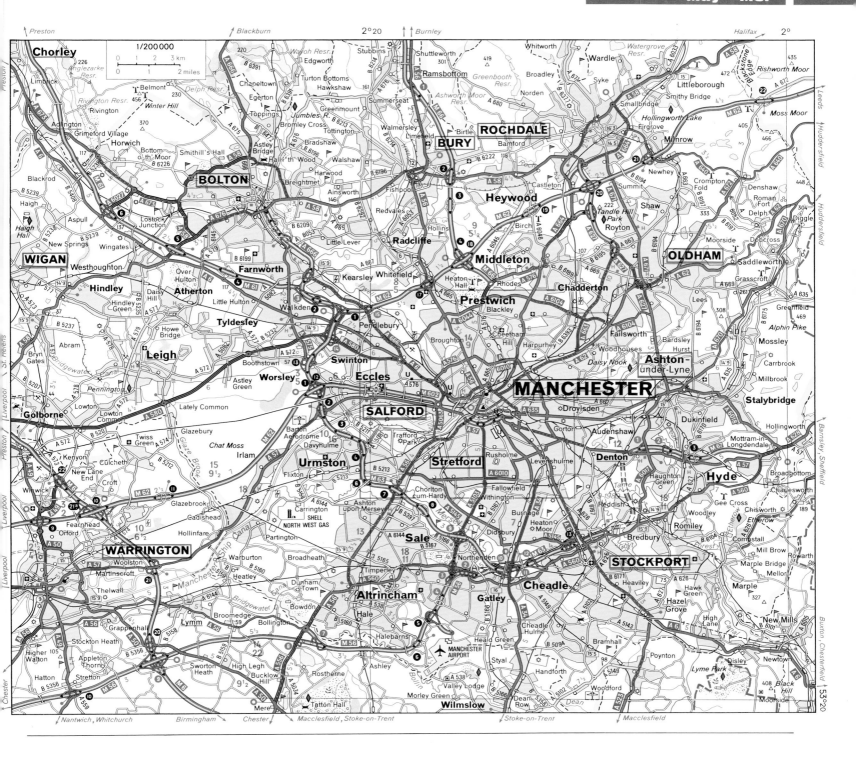

Mayenne *R*	23 E3	Mazières-en-		Medena Selišta	71 E4	Medvednica	70 C2	Megaló Horió		Meiningen	52 B3	Melfi	64 C3
Mayerling	57 E3	Gâtine	24 C3	Mediano, Emb de	37 E2	Medveja	70 B3	(Agathoníssi)	89 F2	Meira	34 C1	Melfjorden	97 E2
Mayet	23 F4	Mazorra, Pto de la	36 A2	Mediaș	113 D4	Medvida	74 C1	Megaló Horió		Meira, Sa de	34 C1	Melgaço	34 B3
Mayet-de-Montagne,		Mazury	110 B4	Medicina	61 D2	Medvode	70 B2	(Tílos)	89 F4	Meiringen	27 F3	Melgar de Abajo	35 E3
le	26 B4	Mazzarino	68 C4	Medina Azahara	43 E2	Medyn'	111 F3	Megísti	93 F2	Meißen	53 E2	Melgar de
Maynooth	13 D4	Mazzarò	69 D3	Medinaceli	36 B4	Medžitlija	77 E4	Megísti, N	93 F2	Meisenheim	54 B1	Fernamental	35 F3
Mayo	12 B2	Mealhada	38 B2	Medina del		Meerane	53 D3	Megístis Lávras	80 C4	Meitingen	55 E3	Melhus	100 C2
Mayor, *C*	35 F1	Meath	13 D3	Campo	35 E4	Meersburg	55 D4	Meg. Livádi	88 A3	Mel	59 E3	Melía	83 E2
Mayorga	35 E3	Meaux	19 F4	Medina de Pomar	36 A1	Mées, les	31 D3	Meg. Panagía	80 B3	Melalahti	99 E4	Melide	34 B2
Mayrhofen	59 D2	Mechelen	50 B3	Medina de		Mefjordbotn	94 B2	Meg. Vólvi	80 B3	Mélambes	91 D4	Melides	42 A1
Maza, Barrié		Meckenbeuren	55 D4	Ríoseco	35 E4	Mefjordvær	94 B2	Mehamn	95 E1	Melaniós	85 E4	Melidóni	91 D3
Emb de la	34 A2	Mecklenburger B	48 C1	Medina-Sidonia	43 D4	Méga Dério	81 F2	Mehedeby	106 B2	Melánthio	78 C3	Meligalás	86 C3
Mazagón	42 C3	Meda	38 C1	Médous,		Mega Horió (Stereá		Mehov Krš	76 C2	Melátes	82 C2	Meliki	79 E3
Mazamet	32 B1	Medđa	73 D2	Grotte de	37 E1	Eláda)	83 D3	Mehun	25 F2	Melbeck	48 B3	Melilli	69 D4
Mazara d. Vallo	68 B4	Medak	70 C4	Médoussa	81 D1	Megalohóri	83 D1	Meigle	5 D1	Melbu	94 A3	Mélisey	27 D1
Mazarakiá	82 B2	Mede	60 A2	Medugorje	75 F2	Megalópoli	86 C2	Meijel	17 D4	Meldal	100 C2	Mélissa	81 D2
Mazarete	40 C1	Medebach	17 F4	Medulin	70 A4	Meganíssi	82 B3	Meije, la	31 D2	Meldola	61 D3	Melissáni	82 B4
Mazarrón	45 D3	Medđeđđa	76 B1	Medđumajdan	71 D3	Megaplátanos	83 F3	Meilen	58 A2	Meldorf	47 F2	Melíssi	87 D1
Mazarrón, G de	45 D3	Medelim	38 C2	Meduna	59 E3	Mégara	87 E1	Meillant	25 F3	Melegnano	60 A1	Melissohóri	84 A4
Mažeikiai	110 B3	Medellín	39 E4	Meduno	59 E3	Megárhi	83 D1	Mêle, le	19 D4	Melenci	72 C2	Melissópetra	78 C4
Mazères	32 A1	Medel, Piz	58 A3	Medđureče	76 C1	Méga Spíleo	86 C1	Meina	58 A4	Melendugno	65 F4	Melissourgós	80 B3
Mázi	78 C4	Medemblik	16 C2	Medvedđa	77 D1	Megève	27 E4	Meinerzhagen	17 E4			

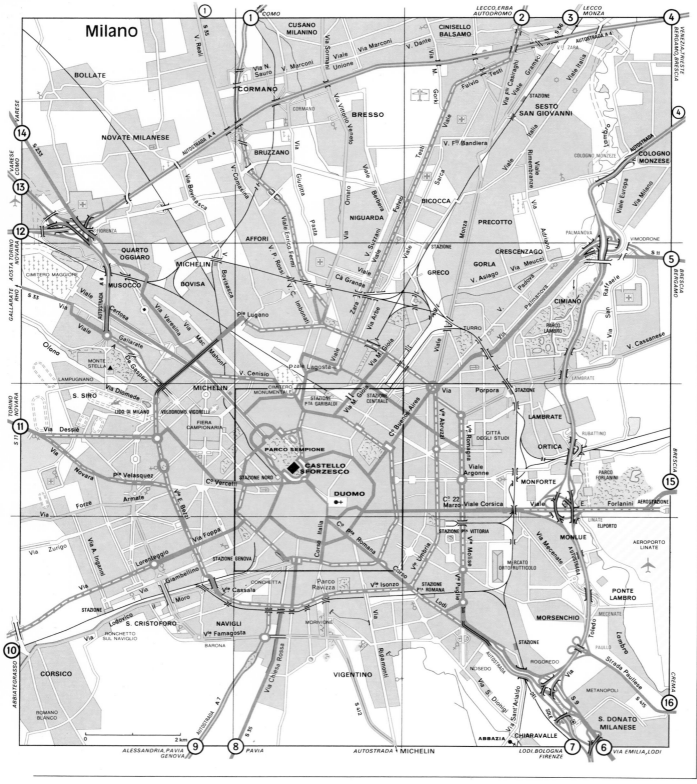

Milano

Méréville	25	F1
Mergozzo	58	A4
Méribel	31	D1
Mérida	39	D4
Mérignac	28	B2
Mérihas	88	A2
Merijärvi	99	D4
Merikarvia	102	B3
Mering	55	F3
Merkendorf	55	E2
Merklingen	55	D3
Merlerault, le	19	D4
Mer Noir	115	F1
Merošina	77	D1
Merrenkurkku	102	B2
Merrick	4	C3
Mers	19	D4
Mersch	21	D2
Merseburg	53	D2
Merthyr Tydfil	8	C2
Mértola	42	B2
Méru	19	F3
Méry	20	B4
Merville (Calvados)	18	C3
Merville (Pas-de-Calais)	19	F1
Merzig	54	A2
Mesagne	65	F3
Mesão Frio	34	B4
Meschede	17	F3
Mescherin	49	E3
Meschers	28	A1
Meßdorf	48	C4
Mešeišta	77	D4
Mesići	76	A1
Mesihovina	75	E1
Meßkirch	55	D3
Meslay	23	E3
Mesocco	58	B3
Mesola	61	D2
Mesón do Vento	34	B1
Mesoraca	67	F3
Mespelbrunn	52	A4
Messanagrós	93	E2
Messarás, Órmos	91	D4
Messariá	88	B1
Messei	18	C4
Méssi	81	D2
Messiméri	79	F3
Messimvría	81	E2
Messina	69	D2
Messíni	86	C3
Messinía	86	C3
Messiniakós Kólpos	86	C4
Messlingen	101	D2
Messohóra	82	C2
Messohóri (Kárpathos)	93	D3
Messohóri (Thessalía)	83	E1
Messolóngi	82	C4
Messongí	82	A2
Messopótamo	82	B2
Messótopos	85	E2
Meßstetten	55	D3
Mestá	85	E4
Mesta	115	D3
Mestanza	44	A1
Mésti	81	E2
Mestlin	48	C2
Mestre	61	D1
Mesvres	26	B3
Metajna	70	C4
Meta, la	64	A2
Metalika	76	B1
Metalikó	79	F2
Metalió	83	E3
Metamórfossi (Halkidikí)	80	B4
Metamórfossi (Kilkís)	79	F2
Metangitsi	80	B4
Metanopoli	60	A1
Metauro	61	E3
Metaxádes	81	F1
Metéora	83	D1
Méthana	87	E2
Methil	5	D2
Methóni (Makedonía)	79	F3
Methóni (Pelopónnissos)	86	C3
Metković	75	F2

Melíti	279	D2	Mellrichstadt	52	B4	Membrilla	40	B4	Mendrisio	58	A4	Menor, Mar	45	D2
Melito di Porto Salvo	67	E4	Mellum	47	F3	Membrio	38	C3	Menée, Col de	30	C2	Mens	30	C2
Melívia (Thessalía)	83	F1	Melnica	73	E3	Memmingen	55	E3	Menen	50	A3	Mentana	63	E2
Melívia (Thráki)	81	D1	Melnice	70	B3	Mena	113	F1	Menesjärvi	95	E3	Menthon	27	D4
Melk	57	E2	Mělník	53	F3	Menaggio	58	B3	Menetés	93	D3	Menton	31	E3
Melksham	9	E2	Mělník	53	F4	Menai Bridge	6	A2	Ménez-Hom	22	B3	Méntrida	40	A2
Mellan Fryken	105	E3	Melogno, Colle di	31	F3	Ménalo, Óros	86	C2	Menfi	68	B3	Menuires, les	31	D1
Mellansel	102	A2	Meløy	97	E2	Menasalbas	40	A3	Mengamuñoz	39	F2	Meppel	17	D2
Melle (D)	17	F2	Meløyfjorden	97	E2	Menat	26	A4	Menga, Pto de	39	F2	Meppen	17	E2
Melle (F)	24	C4	Melpers	52	B3	Mencal	44	B3	Mengara	61	E4	Mequinenza	37	E4
Mellerstair	5	D2	Melrose	5	D2	Mendavia	36	B2	Mengen	55	D3	Mequinenza, Emb de	37	E4
Mellerud	105	D4	Melsungen	52	A3	Mende	29	F3	Mengeš	70	B2	Mercatale (Marche)	61	E3
Mellieha	68	B4	Meltaus	99	D2	Mendelpass	59	D3	Mengíbar	44	A2	Mercatale (Toscana)	61	D4
Mellifont Abbey	13	D3	Melton Mowbray	7	D3	Menden	17	E3	Menídi	82	C2	Mercatino Conca	61	E3
Mellilä	107	D2	Meltosjärvi	99	D2	Mendenítsa	83	E3	Ménigoute	24	C3	Mercato Saraceno	61	D3
Mellin	48	B4	Melun	19	F4	Menderes, B	115	F4	Meníkio, Óros	80	B2	Mercatale (Marche)	61	E3
Mellingen	52	C3	Melvich	3	D2	Mendola, Pso della	59	D3	Mennetou	25	E2	Mer de Crète	90	C2

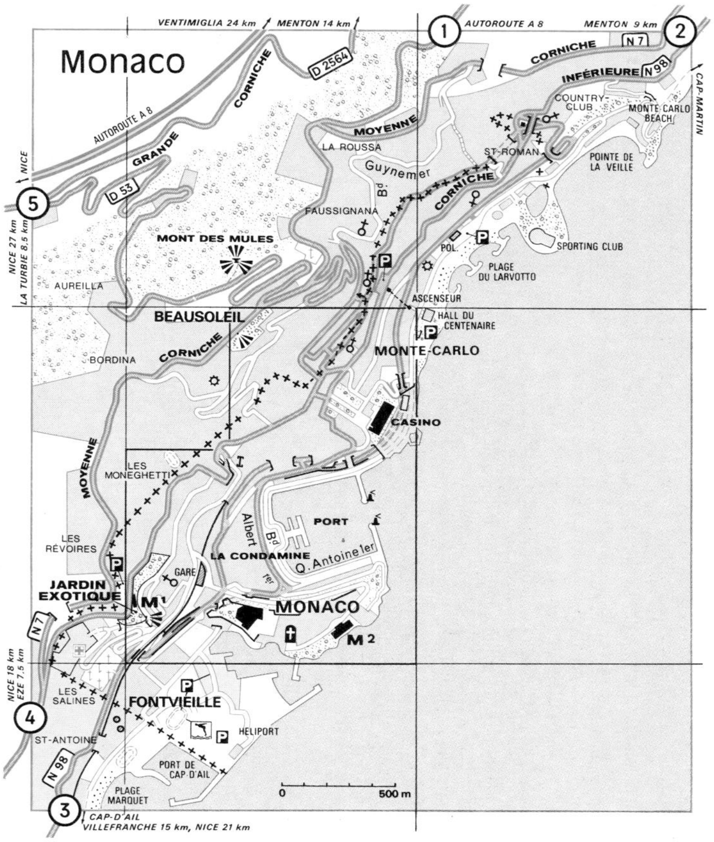
Monaco
VENTIMIGLIA 24 km
MENTON 14 km
AUTOROUTE A 8
MENTON 9 km
1
2
3
4
5
N7
N98
D 2564
D 53
CORNICHE
INFÉRIEURE
MOYENNE
GRANDE
CAP-MARTIN
COUNTRY-CLUB
MONTE CARLO BEACH
POINTE DE LA VEILLE
LA ROUSSA
Guynemer
ST-ROMAN
FAUSSIGNANA
MONT DES MULES
SPORTING CLUB
PLAGE DU LARVOTTO
AUREILLA
ASCENSEUR
HALL DU CENTENAIRE
BEAUSOLEIL
BORDINA
MONTE-CARLO
CASINO
LES MONEGHETTI
PORT
LES REVOIRES
LA CONDAMINE
Q. Antoine 1er
GARE
JARDIN EXOTIQUE
MONACO
M1
M2
LES SALINES
FONTVIEILLE
ST-ANTOINE
HELIPORT
PORT DE CAP D'AIL
PLAGE MARQUET
CAP-D'AIL
VILLEFRANCHE 15 km, NICE 21 km
NICE 27 km
LA TURBIE 8,5 km
NICE 18 km
EZE 7,5 km
NICE
0
500 m

Metlika 70 C2
Metnitz 57 D4
Metóhi (Ahaïa) 86 B1
Metóhi (Argolída) 87 E2
Metóhi (Évia) 84 B3
Metóhi (Thessalía) 83 F2
Metsäkyla 99 E3
Metsäkylä 103 F4
Metsämaa 107 E2
Métsovo 82 C1
Mettingen 17 E2
Mettlach 54 A1
Mettmann 17 E4
Metz 21 D3
Metzervisse 21 D3
Metzingen 55 D3
Meulan 19 E3
Meung 25 E2
Meursault 26 C3
Meurthe-et-Moselle 21 D4
Meuse 20 C3
Meuse (Dépt) 20 C3
Meuselwitz 53 D2
Mevagissey 8 B4
Meximieux 26 C4
Meyenburg 48 C3
Meymac 29 E1
Meyrand, Col de 30 B2
Meyrueis 29 F3
Meyzieu 26 C4
Mezas 39 D2
Mezdra 115 D2
Mèze 30 A4
Mézel 31 D3
Mézenc, Mt 30 B2
Mežgorje 112 C3
Mežica 70 B1
Mézidon 18 C3
Mézières 25 D4
Mezières-en-Brenne 25 E3
Mézin 28 C3
Mezőberény 112 C4
Mezőkövesd 112 B4
Mezőtúr 112 B4
Mezquita de Jarque 41 E2
Mezzano 59 D3
Mezzolombardo 58 C3
Mgarr 68 B4
Miajadas 39 E4
Miastko 110 A4
Michalovce 112 C3
Micheldorf 57 D3
Michelstadt 55 D1
Michendorf 49 D4
Mičurin 115 E2
Middelburg 16 B3
Middelfart 108 B3
Middelharnis 16 B3
Middelkerke-Bad 50 A3
Middlesbrough 5 F4
Middleton-in-Teesdale 5 E4
Middlewich 6 C3
Midhurst 9 F3
Midi, Canal du 32 B1
Midi de Bigorre, Pic du 37 E2
Midi d'Ossau, Pic du 37 D2
Midleton 14 C4
Midouze 28 B3
Midsund 100 B2
Mid Yell 3 F1
Miedes 36 C4
Miedwie, Jez 49 F3
Międzychód 112 A1
Międzylesie 112 A2
Międzyrzec Podlaski 112 C1
Międzyzdroje 49 E2
Miehikkälä 103 F4
Miekojärvi 98 C2
Miélan 28 C4
Mielec 112 B2
Mielno 49 F1
Mieluskylä 103 D1
Miera, R 35 F2
Miercurea-Ciuc 113 D4
Mieres 35 D2
Miesbach 56 B3
Mieszkowice 49 E3
Mietoinen 107 D2
Miettila 103 F3
Migennes 26 A1
Migliarino 61 D2
Miglionico 65 D4
Miguel Esteban 40 B3
Miguelturra 40 A4
Mihajlovac (Srbija) 73 D3
Mihajlovac (Srbija) 73 F3
Mihajlovgrad 115 D2
Mihas 86 C1
Mihóï 86 B1
Mijas 43 E4
Mijoux 27 D3
Miki 81 D2
Mikínes 87 D2
Mikkeli 103 E3
Mikkelin Läär 103 E3
Mikkelvik 94 B2
Mikleuš 71 E2
Míkonos 88 C2
Míkonos, N 88 C2
Mikrí Mandínia 86 C3
Mikrí Préspa, L 78 C3
Mikró Horió 83 D3
Mikrókambos 79 F2
Mikroklissoúra 80 B1
Mikrolímni 78 C3
Mikromiliá 80 C1
Mikrón Dério 81 F1
Mikron Eleftherohóri 79 E4
Mikrópoli 80 B2
Mikulov 57 F1
Milagro 36 C2
Milano 60 A1
Milano Marittimo 61 E3
Milatos 91 E3
Milazzo 69 D2
Mileševo (Srbija) 76 B1
Mileševo (Vojvodina) 72 C1
Milestone 14 C3
Miletići 70 C4
Mileto 67 E3
Miletto, Mte 64 B3
Milevsko 57 D1
Milford (GB) 9 F3
Milford (IRL) 13 D1
Milford Haven 8 B2
Milhão 34 C3
Mili 87 D2
Miliá (Makedonía) 79 D4
Miliá (Pelopónissos) 87 D2
Miliá (Thráki) 81 F1
Milići 72 B4
Miliés 83 F2
Milin 53 F4
Milína 83 F2
Milis 66 B3
Militello in Val di C. 69 D3
Miljevina 76 A1
Millas 32 B2
Millau 29 F3
Millesimo 31 F2
Millevaches, Plateau de 29 D1
Millom 6 B1
Millport 4 C2
Millstatt 59 F2
Millstreet 14 B4
Milltown Malbay 12 B4
Milly 19 F4
Milmarcos 36 C4
Milmersdorf 49 E3
Milna 75 D2
Miločer 76 B3
Milohnić 70 B3
Milopótamos 90 A1
Mílos 88 A4
Miloševa Kula 73 E3
Mílos, N 88 A4
Miltach 56 B1
Miltenberg 55 D1
Milton Keynes 9 F2
Milutinovac 73 F2
Mimizan 28 A3
Mimizan-Plage 28 A3
Mimoň 53 F3
Mina 87 D4
Mina de São Domingos 42 B2
Minas de Riotinto 42 C2
Minaya 40 C4
Minch, The 2 B2
Mincio 60 C1
Mindelheim 55 E3
Minden 17 F2
Mindin 24 A2
Minehead 8 C3
Minerbe 60 C1
Minerbio 61 D2
Minervino Murge 65 D3
Minglanilla 41 D3
Mingorria 39 F1
Minguez, Pto 41 D2
Mingulay 2 A4
Minho 34 A3
Minićevo 73 F4
Minilla, Emb de la 43 D2
Ministra, Sierra 36 B4
Minkiö 107 E2
Miño, R 34 B2
Minsk 111 D4
Mińsk Mazowiecki 112 B1
Minsterley 9 D1
Minthi, Óros 86 C2
Mintlaw 3 E3
Miokovićevo 71 E2
Mionica 72 C3
Mionnay 26 C4
Mira (E) 41 D3
Mira (I) 61 D1
Mira (P) 38 B1
Mirabella Imbaccari 68 C4
Mira de Aire 38 B3
Mirador de Coto Rondo 34 A2
Mirador del Fito 35 E1
Miraflores 35 F3
Miraflores de la Sierra 40 A1
Miramar (F) 31 E4
Miramar (P) 34 A4
Miramare 61 E3
Miramas 30 C4
Mirambeau 28 B1
Mirambélou, Kólpos 91 F3
Miramont-de-Guyenne 28 C2
Miranda de Ebro 36 B2
Miranda del Castañar 39 E2
Miranda do Corvo 38 B2
Miranda do Douro 34 C4
Mirande 28 C4
Mirandela 34 C4
Mirandola 60 C2
Mirano 61 D1
Mira, R 42 A2
Mirador de Llesba 35 E2
Miravalles 34 C2
Miravci 77 F3
Miravete, Pto de 39 E3
Mirditë 76 C3
Mirebeau (Côte-d'Or) 26 C2
Mirebeau (Vienne) 25 D3
Mirecourt 27 D1
Mirepoix 32 A2
Míres 91 D4
Mirgorod 113 F2
Miribel 26 C4
Mirina 85 D1
Mirna 70 B2
Mirna *R* 70 A3
Miroč 73 E3
Mironovka 113 E2
Miroševce 77 E1
Mirotice 56 C1
Mirovice 56 C1
Mirow 49 D3
Mirsíni 87 D4
Mirtiés 89 E3
Mirtóo Pélagos 87 E3
Mírtos 91 E4
Mírtos, Akr 93 E2
Mírtou, Kólpos 82 B4
Mirueña 39 F1
Mišar 72 C3
Misi 99 D2
Misilmeri 68 B3
Miskolc 112 B3
Mislinja 70 B1
Mistelbach 57 F2
Misterbianco 69 D3
Mistrás 87 D3
Mistretta 68 C3
Místros 84 B4
Misurina 59 E2
Mitchelstown 14 C3
Mittelland-Kanal 17 F2
Míthimna 85 F2
Mítikas 82 C3
Mítikas *Mt* 79 E4
Mitilíni 85 F2
Mitilinii 89 E1
Mitrašinci 77 F3
Mitrópoli 83 D2
Mitsikéli, Óros 82 B1
Mittelberg (Tirol) 58 C2
Mittelberg (Vorarlberg) 58 B2
Mittenwald 55 F4
Mittenwalde 49 E4
Mittersill 59 E1
Mitterteich 53 D4
Mittweida 53 E2
Mizen Head 14 A4
Mjällån 101 F2
Mjällom 102 A2
Mjöbäck 108 C2
Mjölby 109 E1
Mjøndalen 104 C3
Mjøsa 105 D2
Mladá Boleslav 112 A2
Mladá Vožice 57 D1
Mladenovac 73 D3
Mlado Nagoričane 77 E2
Mladost, Ez 77 E3
Mlava 73 E3
Mława 112 B1
Mlini 76 A2
Mlinište 71 D4
Mljet 75 E2
Mljetski Kanal 75 F2
Mnichovo Hradiště 53 F3
Moälven 102 A2
Moaña 34 A3
Moate 12 C3
Mocejón 40 A3
Möckern 52 C1
Möckmühl 55 D2
Moclin 44 A3
Modane 31 D1
Modbury 8 C4
Modena 60 C2
Módi 83 E3
Modica 69 D4
Modigliana 61 D3
Mödling 57 F2
Modračko jez 71 F3
Modran 71 E3
Modřany 53 F4
Modrava 56 C1
Modriča 71 F3
Modrište 77 D3
Modugno 65 D3
Moëlan 22 B3
Moelv 105 D2
Moen 94 B3
Moena 59 D3
Moers 17 D3
Moesa 58 B3
Moffat 5 D3
Mogadouro 34 C4
Mogadouro, Sa do 34 C4
Mogente 45 D1
Mogila 77 E4
Mogil'ov 111 E4
Mogil'ov-Podol'skij 113 E3
Moglia 60 C2
Mogliano Veneto 59 E4
Mogón 44 B2
Mogorrit 41 D2
Moguer 42 C2
Mohács 114 B1
Moher, Cliffs of 12 B4
Mohill 12 C3
Möhkö 103 F2
Móhlos 91 F4
Möhne 17 F3
Moholm 105 E4
Moi 104 A4
Moià 32 A4
Moie 61 E4
Moimenta 34 C3
Moimenta da Beira 38 C1
Mo i Rana 97 E2
Moirans 30 C1
Moirans-en-Montagne 27 D3
Moisdon 23 D4
Moisiovaara 99 F4
Moisling 48 B2
Moissac 29 D3
Moita 38 A4
Mojácar 44 C3
Mojados 35 E4
Mojkovac 76 B2
Mojón Pardo, Pto de 36 B3
Mojstrana 70 A1
Mokra Gora 72 C4
Mokra Gora *Mts* 76 C2
Mokrin 72 C1
Mokronog 70 B2
Mokro Polje 75 D1
Mol (B) 50 C3
Mol (YU) 72 C1
Mola di Bari 65 E3
Molái 87 D4
Molat 74 B1
Molat *I* 74 B1
Molatón 41 D4
Mold 6 B3
Moldavija 113 E3
Molde 100 B2
Moldefjorden 100 B2
Moldova Nouă 114 C1
Moldoveanu 113 D4
Møldrup 108 B2
Moledo do Minho 34 A3
Molène 22 A2
Molfetta 65 D3
Molières 29 D3
Molina de Aragón 40 C2
Molina de Segura 45 D2
Molinella 61 D2
Molinicos 44 C1
Molins de Rei 32 A4
Molise 64 B2
Moliterno 65 D4
Molitg-les-Bains 32 B2
Mólivos, Akr 85 F2
Molkom 105 E3
Möllbrücke 59 F2
Mollerussa 37 F3
Molliens-Vidame 19 E2
Mollina 43 F3
Mölln 48 B2
Mollösund 108 C1
Mölnlycke 108 C1
Molodečno 111 D4
Mologa 111 F1
Mólos 83 E3
Molpe 102 B2
Mols 108 B3
Molsheim 21 E4
Molve 71 D1
Molveno 58 C3
Mombeltrán 39 F2
Mombuey 35 D3
Mommark 108 B4
Momo 60 A1
Møn 108 C4
Monach, Sd of 2 A3
Monadhliath Mts 2 C4
Monå fjärd 102 B2
Monaghan 13 D2
Monaghan (Co) 13 D2
Monasterace Marina 67 F4
Monasterboice 13 D3
Monasterevin 13 D4
Monasterio de Rodilla 36 A2
Monastier, le 30 B2
Monastir 66 B4
Monastiráki (Stereá Eláda) 82 C3
Monastiráki (Thráki) 81 F2
Monastíri Doukáto 81 E2
Monastíri, N 83 E2
Monbazillac 28 C2
Moncalieri 31 E2
Moncalvo 31 F1
Monção 34 A3
Moncarapacho 42 B3
Moncayo, Sa de 36 C3
Mönchdorf 57 D2
Mönchengladbach 17 D4
Monchique 42 A2
Monchique, Sa de 42 A2
Monclar-de-Quercy 29 D3
Moncófar 41 E3
Moncontour (Côtes-du-Nord) 22 C3
Moncontour (Vienne) 24 C3
Moncoutant 24 C3
Monda 43 E4
Mondariz 34 A3
Mondavio 61 E3
Mondego, Cabo 38 A2
Mondego, R 38 B2
Mondéjar 40 B2
Mondello 68 B2
Mondim 34 B4
Mondolfo 61 E3
Mondoñedo 34 C1
Mondorf 21 D3
Mondoubleau 23 F3
Mondovi 31 F2
Mondragon 30 B3
Mondragone 64 A3
Mondsee 56 C3
Monein 28 B4
Monemvassía 87 E4
Monesi 31 E3
Monesterio 43 D1
Monestier-de-Clermont 30 C2
Monestiés 29 E3
Monêtier, le 31 D2
Moneygall 12 C4
Moneymore 13 D2
Monfalcone 59 F3
Monflanquin 28 C2
Monforte 38 C4
Monforte de Lemos 34 B2
Mongie, la 37 E2
Mongó 45 E1
Monguelfo 59 D2

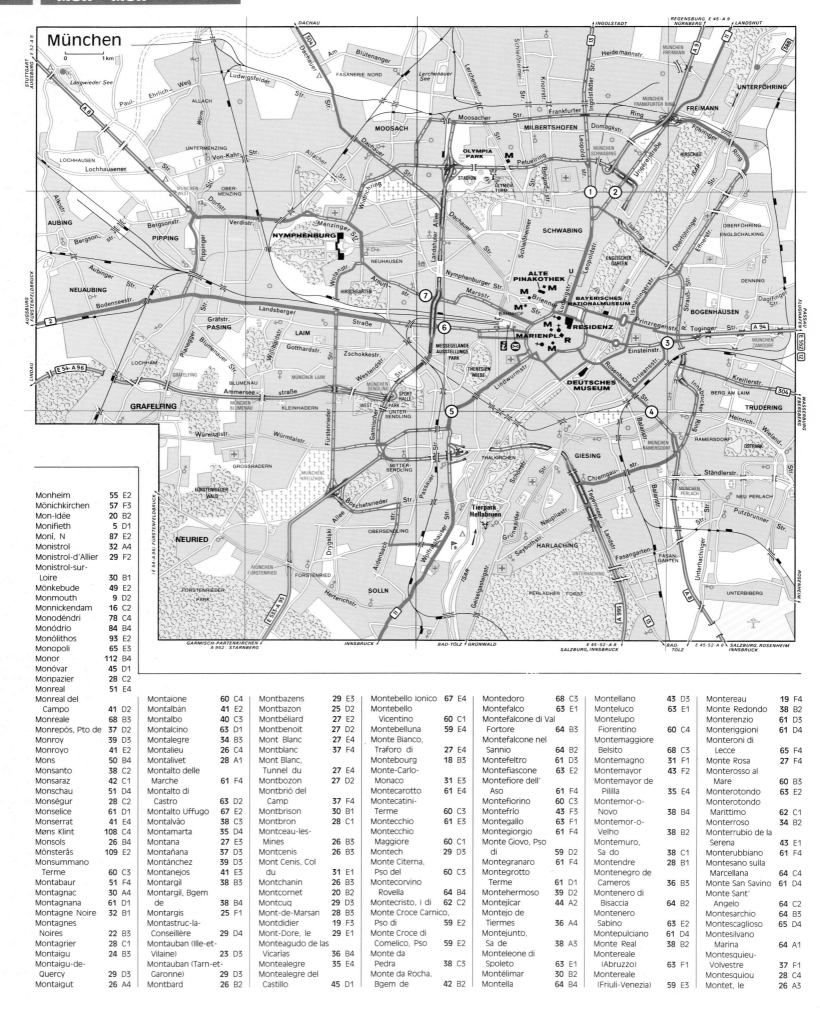

München

Monheim	55	E2
Mönichkirchen	57	F3
Mon-Idée	20	B2
Monifieth	5	D1
Moní, N	87	E2
Monistrol	32	A4
Monistrol-d'Allier	29	F2
Monistrol-sur-Loire	30	B1
Mönkebude	49	E2
Monmouth	9	D2
Monnickendam	16	C2
Monodéndri	78	C4
Monódrio	84	B4
Monólithos	93	E2
Monopoli	65	E3
Monor	112	B4
Monóvar	45	D1
Monpazier	28	C2
Monreal	51	E4
Monreal del Campo	41	D2
Monreale	68	B3
Monrepós, Pto de	37	D2
Monroy	39	D3
Monroyo	41	E2
Mons	50	B4
Monsanto	38	C2
Monsaraz	42	C1
Monschau	51	D4
Monségur	28	C2
Monselice	61	D1
Monserrat	41	E4
Møns Klint	108	C4
Monsols	26	B4
Mönsterås	109	E2
Monsummano Terme	60	C3
Montabaur	51	F4
Montagnac	30	A4
Montagnana	61	D1
Montagne Noire	32	B1
Montagnes Noires	22	B3
Montagrier	28	C1
Montaigu	24	B3
Montaigu-de-Quercy	29	D3
Montaigut	26	A4

Montaione	60	C4
Montalbán	41	E2
Montalbo	40	C3
Montalcino	63	D1
Montalegre	34	B3
Montalieu	26	C4
Montalivet	28	A1
Montalto delle Marche	61	F4
Montalto di Castro	63	D2
Montalto Uffugo	67	E2
Montalvão	38	C3
Montamarta	35	D4
Montana	27	E3
Montañana	37	D3
Montánchez	39	D3
Montanejos	41	E3
Montargil	38	B3
Montargil, Bgem de	38	B4
Montargis	25	F1
Montastruc-la-Conseillère	29	D4
Montauban (Ille-et-Vilaine)	23	D3
Montauban (Tarn-et-Garonne)	29	D3
Montbard	26	B2

Montbazens	29	E3
Montbazon	25	D2
Montbéliard	27	E2
Montbenoit	27	D2
Mont Blanc	27	E4
Montblanc	37	F4
Mont Blanc, Tunnel du	27	E4
Montbozon	27	D2
Montbrió del Camp	37	F4
Montbrison	30	B1
Montbron	28	C1
Montceau-les-Mines	26	B3
Montcenis	26	B3
Montchanin	26	B3
Montcornet	20	B2
Montcuq	29	D3
Mont-de-Marsan	28	B3
Montdidier	19	F3
Mont-Dore, le	29	E1
Monteagudo de las Vicarías	36	B4
Montealegre	35	E4
Montealegre del Castillo	45	D1

Montebello Ionico	67	E4
Montebello Vicentino	60	C1
Montebelluna	59	E4
Monte Bianco, Traforo di	27	E4
Montebourg	18	B3
Monte-Carlo-Monaco	31	E3
Montecarotto	61	E4
Montecatini-Terme	60	C3
Montecchio	61	E3
Montecchio Maggiore	60	C1
Montech	29	D3
Monte Citerna, Pso del	60	C3
Montecorvino Rovella	64	B4
Montecristo, I di	62	C2
Monte Croce Carnico, Pso di	59	E2
Monte Croce di Comelico, Pso	59	E2
Monte da Pedra	38	C3
Monte da Rocha, Bgem de	42	B2

Montedoro	68	C3
Montefalco	63	E1
Montefalcone di Val Fortore	64	B3
Montefalcone nel Sannio	64	B2
Montefeltro	61	D3
Montefiascone	63	E2
Montefiore dell' Aso	61	F4
Montefiorino	60	C3
Montefrío	43	F3
Montegallo	63	F1
Montegiorgio	61	F4
Monte Giovo, Pso di	59	D2
Montegranaro	61	F4
Montegrotto Terme	61	D1
Montehermoso	39	D2
Montejicar	44	A2
Montejo de Tiermes	36	A4
Montejunto, Sa de	38	A3
Montélimar	30	B2
Montella	64	B4

Montellano	43	D3
Monteluco	63	E1
Montelupo Fiorentino	60	C4
Montemaggiore Belsito	68	C3
Montemagno	31	F1
Montemayor	43	F2
Montemayor de Pililla	35	E4
Montemor-o-Novo	38	B4
Montemor-o-Velho	38	B2
Montemuro, Sa do	38	C1
Montendre	28	B1
Montenegro de Cameros	36	B3
Montenero di Bisaccia	64	B2
Montenero Sabino	63	E2
Montepulciano	61	D4
Monte Real	38	B2
Montereale (Abruzzo)	63	F1
Montereale (Friuli-Venezia	59	E3

Montereau	19	F4
Monte Redondo	38	B2
Monterenzio	61	D3
Monteriggioni	61	D4
Monteroni di Lecce	65	F4
Monte Rosa	27	F4
Monterosso al Mare	60	B3
Monterotondo	63	E2
Monterotondo Marittimo	62	C1
Monterroso	34	B2
Monterrubio de la Serena	43	E1
Monterubbiano	61	F4
Montesano sulla Marcellana	64	C4
Monte San Savino	61	D4
Monte Sant' Angelo	64	C2
Montesarchio	64	B3
Montescaglioso	65	D4
Montesilvano Marina	64	A1
Montesquieu-Volvestre	37	F1
Montesquiou	28	C4
Montet, le	26	A3

Montets, Col des 27 E4
Montevarchi 61 D4
Monteviejo, Pto de 35 E2
Montfaucon-en-Velay 30 B1
Montfaucon (Maine-et-Loire) 24 B2
Montfaucon (Meuse) 20 C3
Montfort 23 D3
Montfort-en-Chalosse 28 B4
Montfort-l'Amaury 19 E4
Montfort-sur-Risle 19 D3
Montgaillard 32 A2
Montgenèvre 31 D2
Montgenèvre, Col de 31 D2
Montgiscard 29 D4
Montgomery 9 D1
Montguyon 28 B1
Monthermé 20 C2
Monthey 27 E4
Monthois 20 C3
Monthureux 27 D1
Monti 66 B2
Montichiari 60 B1
Monticiano 61 D4
Montiel 44 B1
Montier-en-Der 20 C4
Montignac 29 D2
Montigny-le-Roi 26 C1
Montigny-sur-Aube 26 C1
Montijo (E) 39 D4
Montijo (P) 38 A4
Montilla 43 F2
Montioni 62 C1
Montivilliers 19 D3
Montjean 23 E4
Montlhéry 19 f4
Montlieu 28 B1
Montlouis 25 D2
Mont-Louis 32 A3
Montluçon 25 F4
Montluel 26 C4
Montmarault 26 A4
Montmartin 18 B3
Montmédy 20 C3
Montmélian 31 D1
Montmirail (Marne) 20 A4
Montmirail (Sarthe) 23 F3
Montmirey-le-Château 26 C2
Montmoreau 28 C1
Montmorillon 25 D4
Montmort 20 B3
Montoggio 60 A3
Montoire 23 F4
Montoito 38 C4
Montone 61 D3
Montorio al Vomano 63 F1
Montoro 43 F2
Montòro, Emb de 43 F1
Montpellier 30 A4
Montpellier-le-Vieux, Chaos de 29 F3
Montpezat-de-Quercy 29 D3
Montpezat-sous-Bauzon 30 B2
Montpon-Ménestérol 28 C2
Montpont 26 C3
Montréal (Aude) 32 A2
Montréal (Gers) 28 C3
Montréal-la-Cluse 26 C4
Montredon-Labessonnie 32 B1
Montréjeau 37 E1
Montrésor 25 E2
Montresta 66 A2
Montreuil 19 E1
Montreuil-Bellay 24 C2
Montreux 27 E3
Montrevault 24 B2
Montrevel 26 C3
Montrichard 25 E2
Mont-roig del Camp 37 F4
Montrond-les-Bains 30 B1
Montrose 5 E1
Mont-St-Michel, le 18 B4
Mont-St-Vincent 26 B3
Montsalvy 29 E2
Montsant, Sa del 37 F4
Montsauche 26 B2
Montsec, Serra de 37 F3
Montseny 32 B4
Montseny, Sa de 32 B4
Montserrat 32 A4
Mont-sous-Vaudrey 26 C3
Monts-sur-Guesnes 25 D3
Montsûrs 23 E3
Montuenga 39 F1
Montuiri 45 F3
Monviso 31 E2
Monza 60 A1
Monzón 37 E3
Monzón de Campos 35 F3
Moordorf 47 E3
Moorfoot Hills 5 D2
Moosburg 56 B2
Mór 112 B4
Mora (E) 40 A3
Mora (P) 38 B4
Mora (S) 101 E4
Morača 76 B2
Morača R 76 B2
Morača klisura 76 B2
Móra d'Ebre 37 E4
Mora de Rubielos 41 E2
Moraira 45 E1
Moraira, Pta de 45 E1
Morais 34 C4
Moraïtika 82 A2
Morakovo, G. 76 B2
Móra la Nova 41 F1
Moral de Calatrava 40 A4
Moraleda de Zafayona 44 A3
Moraleja 39 D2
Moraleja de Sayago 39 E1
Morales de Rey 35 D3
Morales de Toro 35 E4
Morano Calabro 67 E2
Mora, Pto de la 44 A3
Morar, L 2 B4
Mörarp 108 C3
Morasverdes 39 D2
Morata de Jalón 36 C4
Morata de Tajuña 40 B2
Moratalla 44 C2
Morata, Pto de 36 C4
Morava 57 E1
Morava R 112 A3
Moravče 70 B2
Moravci 70 C1
Moravica 73 D4
Moravské Budějovice 57 E1
Moravske Toplice 70 C1
Moravský Krumlov 57 E1
Moray Firth 3 D3
Morbach 54 B1
Morbegno 58 B3
Morbihan 22 C3
Mörbisch 57 F3
Mörbylånga 109 E3
Morcenx 28 A3
Morciano di Romagna 61 E3
Morcone 64 B3
Morcote 58 A4
Morcuera, Pto de la 40 A1
Mordelles 23 D3
Morecambe 6 B1
Morecambe Bay 6 B1
Moreda 44 A3
Morée 25 E1
Moreleja del Vino 35 D4
Morella 41 E2
Møre og Romsdal 100 B2
Mores 66 B2
Morestel 30 C1
Moret 19 F4
Moreton 9 E2
Moretonhampstead 8 C3
Moreuil 19 F2
Morez 27 D3
Morfasso 60 B2
Mórfio 82 B2
Morgat 22 A3
Morges 27 D3
Morgex 27 E4
Morgins, Pas de 27 E4
Morhange 21 D3
Mori 58 C4
Morina 76 C2
Moritzburg 53 E2
Morjärv 98 C3
Morlaàs 37 E1
Morlaix 22 B2
Mormanno 67 E2
Mormant 19 F4
Mormoiron 30 C3
Mornant 30 B1
Mórnou, Teh L 83 E4
Morón de Almazán 36 B4
Morón de la Frontera 43 E3
Morosaglia 33 F3
Morović 72 B3
Morpeth 5 E3
Morrón 44 B3
Mörrum 109 D3
Mors 108 A2
Morsbach 17 E4
Mörsil 101 E2
Morsleben 52 C1
Mortagne 28 B1
Mortagne-au-Perche 19 D4
Mortagne-sur-Sèvre 24 C3
Mortágua 38 B2
Mortain 18 C4
Mortara 60 A2
Morteau 27 D2
Mortrée 19 D4
Morven 3 D2
Moryń 49 E3
Morzine 27 E4
Morzyczyn 49 F2
Mosbach 55 D2
Mosby 104 B4
Mošćenice 70 B3
Mošćenička Draga 70 B3
Moschendorf 57 F4
Mosel 51 E4
Moselle (Dépt) 21 D3
Moselle R 27 D4
Moshokariá 83 E3
Moshopótamos 79 E3
Mosjøen 97 E3
Moskenesøya 97 E1
Moskenstraumen 97 E1
Mosko 76 A2
Moskosel 98 B3
Moskva 111 F2
Moskva R 111 F2
Moslavačka gora 71 D2
Mosonmagyaróvár 112 A4
Mosor 75 E2
Mosqueruela 41 E2
Moss 105 D3
Mossala 107 D3
Mossat 3 D4
Mosses, Col des 27 E3
Mössingen 55 D3
Most (CS) 53 E3
Most (YU) 70 A2
Mosta 68 B4
Mostar 75 F2
Mosteiro 34 A2
Mosterhamn 104 A3
Mostiska 112 C2
Móstoles 40 A2
Mostonga 72 B2
Mostrim 12 C3
Mosty 110 C4
Møsvatn 104 B3
Mosvik 101 D1
Mota del Cuervo 40 B3
Mota del Marqués 35 E4
Motajica 71 E3
Motala 105 F4
Motala S 106 A4
Mothe-Achard, la 24 B3
Motherwell 4 C2
Mothe-St-Héray, la 24 C4
Motilla del Palancar 40 C3
Motovun 70 A3
Motril 44 A4
Motta di Livenza 59 E4
Motta S.A. 69 D3
Motta Visconti 60 A1
Motte-Chalancon, la 30 C2
Motte, la 31 D3
Mottola 65 E4
Mouchard 27 D3
Moudon 27 E3
Moúdros 85 D1
Mougins 31 E4
Mouhijärvi 107 D1
Mouilleron-en-Pareds 24 C3
Moulins 26 A3
Moulins-Engilbert 26 B3
Moulins-la-Marche 19 D4
Moult 18 C3
Moúnda, Akr 86 A1
Mountain Ash 8 C2
Mount Bellew 12 C3
Mountmellick 13 D4
Mountrath 12 C4
Mount's B 8 B4
Mountsoúna 88 C3
Moura 42 B1
Mourão 42 C1
Moúrdzeflos, Akr 85 D1
Mourenx 28 B4
Mouríki 84 A4
Mourmelon-le-Grand 20 B3
Mourne 13 D2
Mourne Mts 13 E3
Mourniés 90 B3
Mourujärvi 99 E2
Mouscron 50 A3
Moustiers-Ste-Marie 31 D3
Mouthe 27 D3
Mouthier 27 D2
Mouthoumet 32 B2
Moutier 27 E2
Moûtiers 31 D1
Moutiers-les-Mauxfaits 24 B3
Mouy 19 F3
Mouzakéi 82 C1
Mouzáki 83 D2
Mouzon 20 C2
Moville 13 D1
Moy 12 B2
Moyenneville 19 E2
Moyeuvre 21 D3
Moyuela 37 D4
Možajsk 111 F2
Mozirje 70 B1
Mozyr' 113 E1
Mrągowo 110 B4
Mrakovica 71 D3
Mramorak 73 D2
Mratinje 76 A1
Mrazovac 70 C3
Mrčajevci 73 D4
Mrežičko 77 E4
Mrkonjić Grad 71 E4
Mrkopalj 70 B3
Mrzeżyno 49 F1
Mšeno 53 F3
Msta 111 E1
Mstislavl' 111 E3
Mú 42 B2
Muć 75 D1
Muccia 61 E4
Much 17 E4
Mücheln 52 C2
Much Wenlock 9 D1
Mucientes 35 E4
Muck 2 B4
Muckle Roe 3 F1
Muckross House 14 B4
Mudanya 115 F3
Mudau 55 D1
Muddus 98 B2
Muel 37 D4
Muelas del Pan 35 D4
Muff 13 D1
Muge 38 B3
Mügeln 53 E2
Muggia 59 F4
Mugron 28 B4
Mugueimes 34 B3
Mühlbach 59 E1
Mühlberg 53 E2
Mühldorf 56 B3
Mühlen-Eichsen 48 B2
Mühlhausen 52 B2
Mühltroff 53 D3
Muhniemi 107 F2
Muhos 99 D4
Muhu 110 B2
Muineachán 13 D2
Muine Bheag 15 D3
Muirkirk 4 C3
Muir of Ord 2 C3
Mukačevo 112 C3
Mukos 77 E3
Mula 45 D2
Mülacker 54 C2
Mula, R 45 D2
Mulargia, L 66 B3
Mulhacén 44 A3
Mülheim 17 E3
Mulhouse 27 E1
Mull 4 B1
Müllheim 54 C4
Mullingar 13 D3
Mull of Galloway 4 B4
Mull of Kintyre 4 B3
Mull of Oa 4 A2
Müllrose 49 F4
Mull, Sd of 4 B1
Mullsjö 109 D1
Mulrany 12 B2
Multia 103 D3
Mumbles, The 8 C2
Muñana 39 F2
Münchberg 53 D4
Müncheberg 49 E4
München 56 A3
Münchhausen 17 F4
Münden 52 B2
Mundesley 7 F3
Mundford 11 D1
Mundo, R 44 C1
Munera 40 C4
Mungia 36 B1
Muñico 39 F2
Muniesa 37 D4
Munkebo 108 B3
Munkedal 105 D4
Munkfors 105 E3
Münnerstadt 52 B4
Muñogalindo 39 F2
Munsala 102 B2
Munsfjället 101 E1
Münsingen (CH) 27 E3
Münsingen (D) 55 D3
Munster (F) 27 E1
Münster (CH) 27 F3
Münster (Niedersachsen) 48 B3
Münster (Nordrhein-Westfalen) 17 E3
Münstertal 54 C4
Münzenberg 52 A4
Münzkirchen 56 C2
Muodoslompolo 95 D4
Muojärvi 99 F2
Muonio 95 D4
Muonioälven 95 D4
Muotkatonturit 95 E2
Mur 57 E4
Mura 70 C1
Muraglione, Pso del 61 D3
Murano 61 D1
Murat 29 E2
Murato 33 F3
Murat-sur-Vèbre 32 B1
Murau 57 D4
Muravera 66 C4
Murça 34 B4
Murchante 36 C3
Murcia 45 D2
Murcia (Reg) 44 C2
Mur-de-Barrez 29 E2
Mur-de-Bretagne 22 C3
Mureck 57 E4
Mure, la 30 C2
Mureș 112 C4
Muret 29 D4
Murg 54 C2
Murguia 36 B1
Muri 27 F2
Murias de Paredes 35 D2
Murino 76 C2
Muriqan 76 B3
Müritz See 49 D3
Murjek 98 B2
Murnau 56 A4
Muro 33 F3
Muro de Alcoy 45 E1
Murol 29 E1
Murole 102 C3
Muro Lucano 64 C4
Muros 34 A2
Mürren 27 F3
Murrhardt 55 D2
Murska Sobota 70 C1
Mursko Središče 70 C1
Murten 27 E3
Murter 74 C1
Murter I 74 C1
Murtosa 38 B1
Murtovaara 99 F3
Murvica 74 C1
Murviel 30 A4
Mürz 57 E3
Mürzsteg 57 E3
Mürzzuschlag 57 E3
Musala 115 D3
Mussalo 103 F4
Musselburgh 5 D2
Musselkanaal 17 E1
Mussidan 28 C2
Mussomeli 68 C3
Mussy 26 B1
Mustair 58 C3
Mustasaari 102 B2
Mustèr 58 A3
Mustion as 107 E3
Mustvee 110 C1
Muta 70 B1
Mutala 102 C3
Mutterstadt 54 C1
Mutzschen 53 E2
Muurame 103 D3
Muurasjärvi 103 D1
Muuratjärvi 103 D3
Muurla 107 E2
Muurola 99 D2
Muuruvesi 103 E2
Muxía 34 A1
Muy, le 31 D4
Muzillac 22 C4
Muzzana del Turgnano 59 F3
Mweelrea Mts. 12 B3
Myckegensjö 101 F2
Mykines 96 A3
Myllykoski 107 F2
Myllykylä 102 C3
Myllymäki 102 C2
Mynämäki 107 D2
Mýrdalsjökull 96 B3
Myre 94 A3
Myrlandshaugen 94 B3
Myrskylä 107 F2
Myrviken 101 E2
Mysen 105 D3
Mysingen 106 B4
Myśla 49 F3
Myślibórskie, Jez 49 F3
Myślibórz 49 F3
Mývatn 96 B1
Mže 53 E4

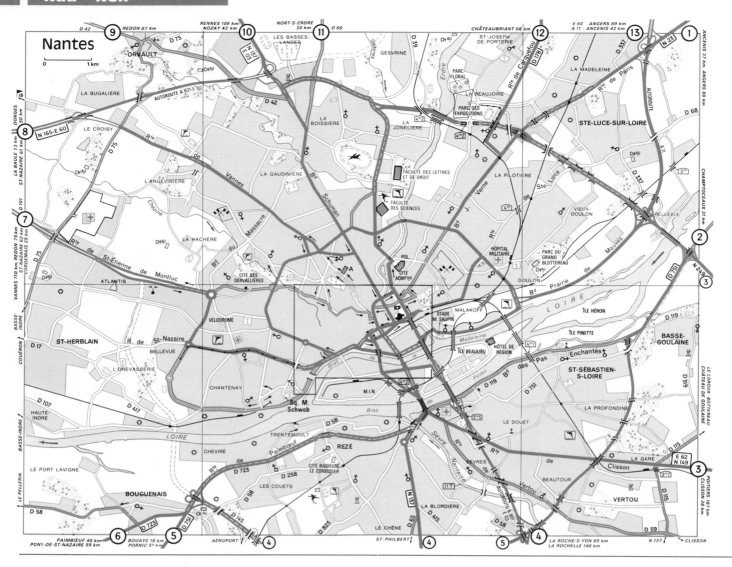

Nantes

N

Naab	55 F1	Nakskov	108 B4	Narcea, R	35 D1	Naustdal	100 A3
Naamijoki	98 C2	Näljänkä	99 E3	Nardò	65 F4	Nauvo	107 D3
Naantali	107 D2	Na Logu	70 A2	Narew	112 C1	Nava	35 E1
Naarajärvi	103 E3	Nalón, R	35 E2	Narila	103 E3	Nava, Colle di	31 F3
Naarva	103 F2	Naltijärvi	95 D3	Narkaus	99 D2	Navacelles, Cirque	
Naas	13 D4	Namdalseid	97 D4	Narni	63 E2	de	29 F3
Näätämöjoki	95 F2	Nämdöfjärden	106 B4	Naro	68 C4	Navacepeda	39 E2
Nabburg	56 B1	Náměšt	57 E1	Naro-Fominsk	111 F2	Navacerrada	40 A2
Načeradec	57 D1	Namsen	97 D4	Nærøy	97 D4	Navacerrada, Pto	
Náchod	112 A2	Namsos	97 D4	Närpes	102 B3	de	40 A1
Naddvik	104 B1	Namsskogan	97 D4	Narta	71 D2	Navachica	44 A3
Nadela	34 B2	Namur	50 C4	Nartháki	83 E2	Navaconcejo	39 E2
Nădlac	114 C1	Namur (Prov)	50 C4	Nartháki, Óros	83 E2	Nava de la	
Nadur	68 B4	Nancy	21 D4	Narva	111 E1	Asunción	40 A1
Nadvornaja	113 D3	Nangis	19 F4	Narvik	94 B3	Nava del Rey	39 E2
Näfels	58 A2	Nannestad	105 D2	Nås	105 E2	Navafria, Pto de	40 A1
Nafpaktías, Óri	83 D4	Nant	29 F3	Näsåker	101 F2	Navahermosa	39 F3
Náfpaktos	83 D4	Nanterre	19 F4	Năsăud	113 D4	Navalcán	39 F2
Náfplio	87 D2	Nantes	24 B2	Nasbinals	29 F2	Navalcarnero	40 A2
Naggen	101 F3	Nantes, Canal		Naßfeld-Paß	59 F2	Navaleno	36 B3
Nagold	54 C3	de	22 C3	Našice	71 E2	Navalmanzano	40 A1
Nagu	107 D3	Nanteuil-le-		Näsijärvi	102 C3	Navalmoral de la	
Nagyatád	114 A1	Haudouin	19 F3	Naso	69 D2	Mata	39 E3
Nagykálló	112 C3	Nantiat	25 E4	Nassau	51 F4	Navalperal de	
Nagykanizsa	114 A1	Nantua	26 C4	Nassereith	58 C2	Pinares	40 A2
Nagykőrös	112 B4	Nantwich	6 C3	Nässjö	109 D1	Navaluenga	39 F2
Nahe	48 A2	Nao, C de la	45 F1	Nastola	107 F2	Navalvillar de Pela	39 E4
Nahe R	54 B1	Náoussa (Kikládes)	88 C3	Næstved	108 C4	Navamorcuende	39 F2
Naila	53 D4	Náoussa		Natalinci	73 D3	Navan	13 D3
Nailloux	32 A1	(Makedonía)	79 E3	Nattaset	95 F3	Navarra	36 C2
Nailsworth	9 D2	Napapiiri	99 D2	Nattavaara	98 B2	Navarredonda de la	
Nairn	3 D3	Napoli	64 B4	Nättraby	109 E3	Sierra	39 F2
Najac	29 D3	Napoli, G di	64 A4	Naucelle	29 E3	Navarrenx	28 B4
Nájera	36 B2	Napoule, la	31 E4	Nauders	58 C2	Navarrés	41 E4
Najerilla, R	36 B2	Narberth	8 B2	Nauen	49 D4	Navarrete	36 B2
Nakkila	107 D1	Nærbø	104 A4	Naul	13 D3	Navascués	37 D2
Nakło	112 A1	Narbolia	66 B3	Naumburg	52 C2	Navas de	
Nakovo	72 C1	Narbonne	32 B1	Naunhof	53 D2	Madroño	39 D3
		Narbonne-Plage	30 A4	Naussac, Bge de	29 F2	Navas de Oro	40 A1
		Narcao	66 B4			Navas de San Juan	44 B2

Navasfrías	39 D2	Néa Mihanióna	79 F3	Nedelišće	70 C1
Navatalgordo	39 F2	Néa Moní	85 E4	Nedervetil	102 C1
Nave	60 B1	Néa Moudaniá	80 A4	Nedstrand	104 A3
Nävekvarn	106 A4	Néa Péla	79 F3	Neede	17 D2
Navelli	63 E2	Néa Péramos (Stereá-		Needles, The	9 E3
Naver, L	2 C2	Eláda)	87 E1	Neermoor	47 E3
Naveros	43 D4	Néa Péramos		Nefyn	6 A3
Navia	34 C1	(Makedonía)	80 C2	Negoiu	113 D4
Navia de Suarna	34 C2	Neápoli (Kríti)	91 E4	Negorci	77 E3
Navia, R	34 C1	Neápoli		Negotin	73 F3
Navl'a	111 F2	(Makedonía)	79 D3	Negotino	77 E3
Náxos	88 C3	Neápoli		Negra de Urbión,	
Náxos Días	88 C3	(Pelopónissos)	87 E4	L	36 B3
Náxos, N	88 C3	Néa Róda	80 B3	Negrar	60 C1
Nay	37 E1	Néa Sánda		Negratín, Emb del	44 B2
Nazaré	38 A3	(Makedonía)	79 F2	Negreira	34 A2
Naze, The	11 D2	Néa Sánda		Nègrepelisse	29 D3
Nazilli	115 F4	(Thráki)	81 E2	Negru Vodă	115 E2
Ndrejaj	76 C2	Néa Silata	80 A3	Neheim-Hüsten	17 F3
Ndroq	76 C4	Néa Skióni	80 B4	Neiden	95 F2
Nea	101 D2	Néa Stíra	84 B4	Neige, Crêt de la	27 D3
Néa Agathoúpoli	79 F3	Néa Tríglia	80 A4	Neila	36 B3
Néa		Néa Víssa	81 F1	Neiße	53 F1
Alikarnassés	91 D3	Néa Zoí	79 E2	Nejdek	53 E3
Néa Anhíalos	83 F2	Néa Zíhni	80 B2	Nekromandío	
Néa Éfessos	79 F4	Nebel	47 F1	Efíras	82 B2
Néa Epídavros	87 E2	Nebljusi	70 C4	Neksø	109 D4
Néa Fókaia	80 A4	Nebra	52 C2	Nela, R	36 A1
Neagh, L	13 E2	Nechranická		Nelas	38 C1
Néa Hilí	81 E2	přehr nádrž	53 E3	Nelidovo	111 E2
Néa Iraklítsa	80 C2	Neckar	55 D1	Nellim	95 F2
Néa Kalikrátia	79 F4	Neckarelz	55 D2	Nelson	6 C2
Néa Kariá	81 D2	Neckargemünd	54 C1	Neman	110 B3
Néa Karváli	80 C2	Neckarsteinach	54 C1	Neméa	87 D1
Néa Kerassoús	82 C2	Neckarsulm	55 D2	Nemirov	113 E3
Néa Kíos	87 D2	Nečujam	75 D2	Nemours	25 F1
Néa Koróni	86 C3	Neda	34 B1	Nemunas	110 C3
Néa Mákri	88 A1	Nédas	86 C2	Nenagh	12 C4
Néa Messángala	83 F1			Nene	10 C1
				Nénita	85 F4

Nenzing	58	B2
Neohoráki	84	A4
Neohóri (Etolía-Akarnanía)	82	C4
Neohóri (Évia)	84	B4
Neohóri (Fthiótida)	83	E3
Neohóri (Ípiros)	82	C2
Neohóri (Kardítsa)	83	D2
Neohóri (Magnisía)	84	A2
Neohóri (Pelopónissos)	86	C2
Neohóri (Thráki)	81	F1
Neohóri (Tríkala)	83	D1
Néo Monastíri	83	E2
Néon Petrítsi	80	A2
Néos Marmarás	80	B4
Néos Skopós	80	B2
Néouvielle, Pic de	37	E2
Nephin	12	B2
Nephin Beg Range	12	B2
Nepomuk	56	C1
Nera	63	E1
Nérac	28	C3
Neráïda (Amárandóos)	83	D2
Neráïda (Neohóri)	83	D2
Neratovice	53	F3

Nesle	19	F2
Nesoddtangen	105	D3
Nesseby	95	F1
Nesselwang	55	E4
Ness, L	2	C3
Nestáni	87	D2
Nesterov	112	C2
Nestório	78	C3
Néstos	81	D2
Nesvik	104	A3
Nesviž	111	D4
Neto	67	F3
Netolice	56	C1
Netretić	70	C3
Nettetal	17	D4
Nettuno	63	E3
Neuastenberg	17	F4
Neubeckum	17	F3
Neubourg, le	19	D3
Neubrandenburg	49	D2
Neubukow	48	C2
Neuburg	55	F2
Neuchâtel	27	E2
Neu Darchau	48	B3
Neuenburg	47	E3
Neuenbürg	54	C2
Neuendorf	49	D1
Neuenhaus	17	E2
Neuenkirchen	48	A3
Neuenstadt	55	D2
Neuerburg	54	A1
Neufahrn	56	B2

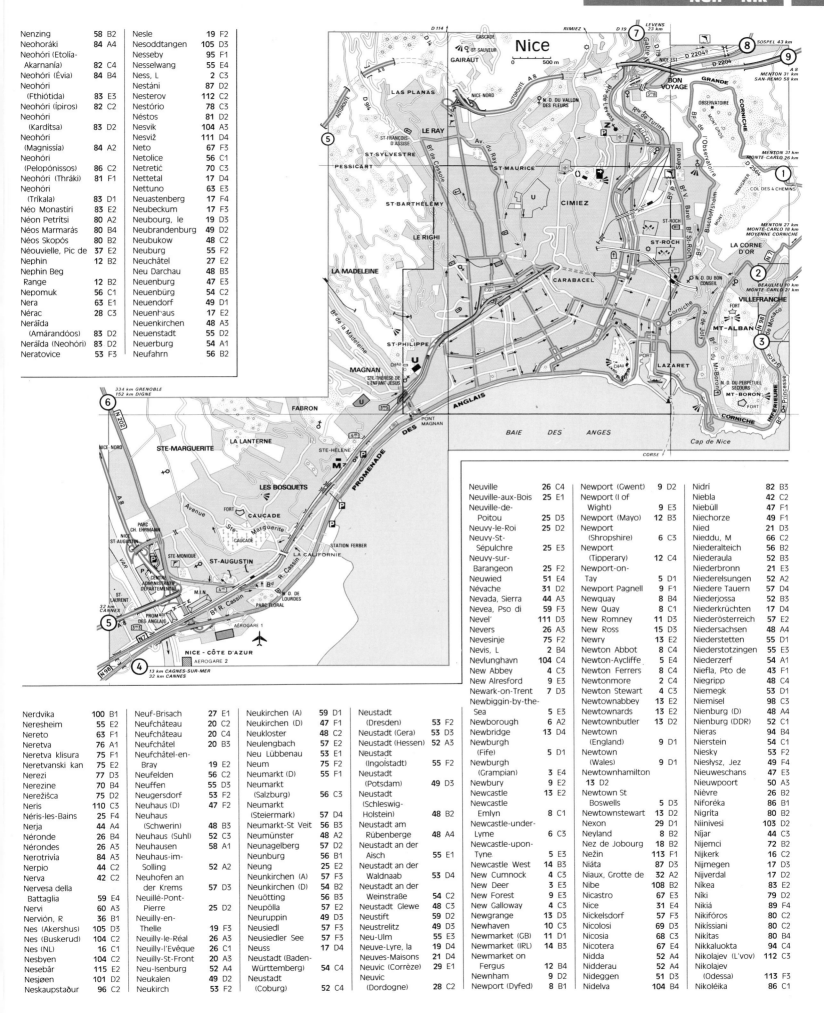

Nice

Neuville	26	C4	Newport (Gwent)	9	D2	Nidri	82	B3
Neuville-aux-Bois	25	E1	Newport (I of Wight)	9	E3	Niebla	42	C2
Neuville-de-Poitou	25	D3	Newport (Mayo)	12	B3	Niebüll	47	F1
Neuvy-le-Roi	25	D2	Newport (Shropshire)	6	C3	Niechorze	49	F1
Neuvy-St-Sépulchre	25	E3	Newport (Tipperary)	12	C4	Nied	21	D3
Neuvy-sur-Barangeon	25	F2	Newport-on-Tay	5	D1	Nieddu, M	66	C2
Neuwied	51	E4	Newport Pagnell	9	F1	Niederalteich	56	B2
Névache	31	D2	Newquay	8	B4	Niederaula	52	B3
Nevada, Sierra	44	A3	New Quay	8	C1	Niederbronn	21	E3
Nevea, Pso di	59	F3	New Romney	11	D3	Niederelsungen	52	A2
Nevel'	111	D3	New Ross	15	D3	Niedere Tauern	57	D4
Nevers	26	A3	Newry	13	E2	Niederjossa	52	B3
Nevesinje	75	F2	Newton Abbot	8	C4	Niederkrüchten	17	D4
Nevis, L	2	B4	Newton-Aycliffe	5	E4	Niederösterreich	57	E2
Nevlunghavn	104	C4	Newton Ferrers	8	C4	Niedersachsen	48	A4
New Abbey	4	C3	Newtonmore	2	C4	Niederstetten	55	D1
New Alresford	9	E3	Newton Stewart	4	C3	Niederstotzingen	55	E3
Newark-on-Trent	7	D3	Newtownabbey	13	E2	Niederzerf	54	A1
Newbiggin-by-the-Sea	5	E3	Newtownards	13	E2	Niefla, Pto de	43	F1
Newborough	6	A2	Newtownbutler	13	D2	Niegripp	48	C4
Newbridge	13	D4	Newtown (England)	9	D1	Niemegk	53	D1
Newburgh (Fife)	5	D1	Newtown (Wales)	9	D1	Niemisel	98	C3
Newburgh (Grampian)	3	E4	Newtownhamilton	13	D2	Nienburg (D)	48	A4
Newbury	9	E2	Newtown St Boswells	5	D3	Nienburg (DDR)	52	C1
Newcastle	13	E2	Newtonstewart	13	D2	Nieras	94	B4
Newcastle Emlyn	8	C1	Nexon	29	D1	Nierstein	54	C1
Newcastle-under-Lyme	6	C3	Neyland	8	B2	Niesky	53	F2
Newcastle-upon-Tyne	5	E3	Nez de Jobourg	18	B2	Nieslysz, Jez	49	F4
Newcastle West	14	B3	Nežin	113	F1	Nieuweschans	47	E3
New Cumnock	4	C3	Niaux, Grotte de	32	A2	Nieuwpoort	50	A3
New Deer	3	E3	Nibe	108	D2	Nièvre	26	B2
New Forest	9	E3	Nicastro	67	E3	Niforéka	86	B1
New Galloway	4	C3	Nice	31	E4	Nigrita	80	B2
Newgrange	13	D3	Nickelsdorf	57	F3	Niinivesi	103	D2
Newhaven	10	C3	Nicolosi	69	D3	Níjar	44	C3
Newmarket (GB)	11	D1	Nicosia	68	C3	Nijemci	72	B2
Newmarket (IRL)	14	B3	Nicotera	67	E4	Nijkerk	16	C2
Newmarket on Fergus	12	B4	Nidda	52	A4	Nijmegen	17	D3
Newnham	9	D2	Nidderau	52	A4	Nijverdal	17	D2
Newport (Dyfed)	8	B1	Nideggen	51	D3	Níkea	83	E2
			Nidelva	104	B4	Níki	79	D2
						Nikiá	89	F4
						Nikifóros	80	C2
						Nikíssiani	80	C2
						Nikitas	80	B4
						Nikkaluokta	94	C4
						Nikolajev (L'vov)	112	C3
						Nikolajev (Odessa)	113	F3
						Nikoléika	86	C1

Nerdvika	100	B1	Neuf-Brisach	27	E1	Neukirchen (A)	59	D1	Neustadt (Dresden)	53	F2
Neresheim	55	E2	Neufchâteau	20	C2	Neukirchen (D)	47	F1	Neustadt (Gera)	53	D3
Nereto	63	F1	Neufchâteau	20	C4	Neukloster	48	C2	Neustadt (Hessen)	52	A3
Neretva	76	A1	Neufchâtel	20	B3	Neulengbach	57	E2	Neustadt (Ingolstadt)	55	F2
Neretva klisura	75	F1	Neufchâtel-en-Bray	19	E2	Neu Lübbenau	53	E1	Neustadt (Potsdam)	49	D3
Neretvanski kan	75	E2	Neufelden	56	C2	Neum	75	F2	Neustadt (Schleswig-Holstein)	48	B2
Nerezi	77	D3	Neuffen	55	D3	Neumarkt (D)	55	F1	Neustadt am Rübenberge	48	A4
Nerezine	70	B4	Neugersdorf	53	F2	Neumarkt (Salzburg)	56	C3	Neustadt an der Aisch	55	E1
Nerežišca	75	D2	Neuhaus (D)	47	F2	Neumarkt (Steiermark)	57	D4	Neustadt an der Waldnaab	53	D4
Neris	110	C3	Neuhaus (Schwerin)	48	B3	Neumarkt-St Veit	56	B3	Neustadt an der Weinstraße	54	C2
Néris-les-Bains	25	F4	Neuhaus (Suhl)	52	C3	Neumünster	48	A2	Neustadt Glewe	48	C3
Nerja	44	A4	Neuhausen	58	A1	Neunagelberg	57	D2	Neustift	59	D2
Néronde	26	B4	Neuhaus-im-Solling	52	A2	Neunburg	56	B1	Neustrelitz	49	D3
Nérondes	26	A3	Neuhofen an der Krems	57	D3	Neung	25	E2	Neu-Ulm	55	E3
Nerotrivia	84	A3	Neuillé-Pont-Pierre	25	D2	Neunkirchen (A)	57	F3	Neuve-Lyre, la	19	D4
Nerpio	44	C2	Neuilly-en-Thelle	19	F3	Neunkirchen (D)	54	B2	Neuves-Maisons	21	D4
Nerva	42	C2	Neuilly-le-Réal	26	A3	Neupölla	57	E2	Neuvic (Corrèze)	29	E1
Nervesa della Battaglia	59	E4	Neuilly-l'Evêque	26	C1	Neuruppin	49	D3	Neuvic (Dordogne)	28	C2
Nervi	60	A3	Neuilly-St-Front	20	A3	Neusiedl	57	F3			
Nervión, R	36	B1	Neu-Isenburg	52	A4	Neusiedler See	57	F3			
Nes (Akershus)	105	D3	Neukalen	49	D2	Neuss	17	D4			
Nes (Buskerud)	104	C2	Neukirch	53	F2	Neustadt (Baden-Württemberg)	54	C2			
Nes (NL)	16	C1				Neustadt (Coburg)	52	C4			
Nesbyen	104	C2									
Nesebăr	115	E2									
Nesjøen	101	D2									
Neskaupstaður	96	C2									

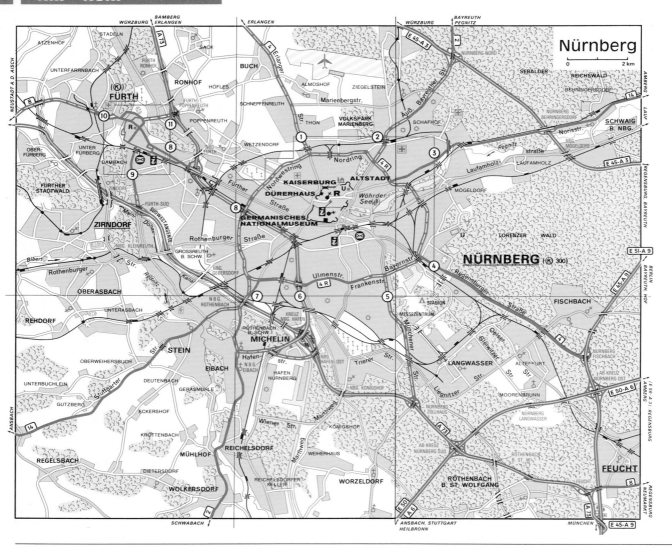

Nürnberg
0   2 km

Novales	37	D3	
Nova Levante	59	D3	
Novalja	70	B4	
Nova Pazova	72	C2	
Novara	60	A1	
Novara di Sicilia	69	D2	
Nova Siri	65	D4	
Nova Topola	71	E3	
Nova Vas	70	B2	
Nova Vavos	76	B1	
Nova Zagora	115	E2	
Novelda	45	D1	
Novellara	60	C2	
Nove Mĕsto nad Váhom	112	A3	
Noventa Vicentino	61	D1	
Noves	30	C3	
Nové Zámky	112	B4	
Novgorod	111	D1	
Novgorod-Severskij	111	F4	
Novi Bečej	72	C2	
Novi di Modena	60	C2	
Novi Dojran	77	F3	
Novigrad (Poreč)	70	A3	
Novigrad (Zadar)	74	C1	
Novi Grad	71	F3	
Novigrad Podravski	71	D2	
Novigradsko more	74	C1	
Novi Karlovci	72	C2	
Novi Kneževac	72	C1	
Novi Ligure	60	A2	
Novi Marof	70	C1	
Novion-Porcien	20	B2	
Novi Pazar	76	C1	
Novi Pazar	115	E2	
Novi Sad	72	C2	
Novi Šeher	71	F4	
Novi Senkovac	71	E2	
Novi Slankamen	72	C2	
Novi Travnik	71	E4	
Novi Vinodolski	70	B3	
Novo Brdo	77	D2	
Novograd-Volynskij	113	D2	
Novogrudok	111	D4	
Novo Hopovo	72	C2	
Novo Mesto	70	B2	
Novo Mi lošeno	72	C1	
Novomirgorod	113	F2	
Novoržev	111	D2	
Novoselica	113	D3	
Novo Selo (Bosna i Hercegovina)	71	E3	
Novo Selo (Makedonija)	77	F3	
Novoukrainka	113	F3	
Novovolynsk	112	C2	
Novo Zvečevo	71	E2	
Novozybkov	111	E4	
Novska	71	D3	
Nový Bor	53	F3	
Novyj Bug	113	F3	
Nový Jičín	112	B3	
Nowa Sól	112	A2	
Nowe Warpno	49	E2	
Nowogard	49	F2	
Nowy Sącz	112	B3	
Nowy Targ	112	B3	
Noyant	23	F4	
Noyers	26	B1	
Noyers-sur-Jabron	30	C3	
Noyon	19	F3	
Nozay	23	D4	
Nuasjärvi	99	E4	
Nueva	35	E1	
Nueva Carteya	43	F2	
Nuévalos Monasterio de Piedra	36	C4	
Nuevo Baztán	40	B2	
Nufenenpass	58	A3	
Nuhppir	95	E2	
Nuijamaa	103	F4	
Nuits-St-Georges	26	C2	
Nules	41	E3	
Nulvi	66	B2	
Numana	61	F4	
Numancia	36	B3	
Numedal	104	C2	
Nummela	107	E2	

Nikopol	115	D2	Niwica	53	F1	Nomeny	21	D3	Nordhorn	17	E2	Norrby	98	A4	North York Moors			
Nikópoli	82	B3	Nizke Beskydy	112	C3	Nomexy	21	D4	Nordingrå	102	A2	Nørre Åby	108	B3	Nat Pk	7	D1	
Nikópolis, Órmos	82	B2	Nizza Monferrato	31	F2	Nómia	87	E4	Nordkapp	95	E1	Nørre Alslev	108	C4	North Yorkshire	6	C1	
Nikšić	76	B2	Njegoš	76	A2	Nonancourt	19	E4	Nordkinnhalvøya	95	E1	Nørre Nebel	108	A3	Norton	7	D1	
Nilakka	103	D2	Njivice	70	B3	Nonant-le-Pin	19	D4	Nordkjosbotn	94	C3	Nørre Snede	108	A3	Nortort	48	A2	
Nilivaara	98	B2	Njunis	94	C3	Nonaspe	37	E3	Nordkvaløy	94	B2	Nørre Vorupør	108	A2	Norwich	11	D1	
Nilsiä	103	E2	Njupeskär	101	D3	None	31	E2	Nordland	97	E2	Norrfjärden	101	F3	Nosovka	113	E1	
Nîmes	30	B3	Noailles	19	F3	Nonio	58	A4	Nord-Lenangen	94	C2	Norrköping	106	A4	Nossebro	108	C1	
Nimféa	81	E2	Noáin	36	C2	Nontron	28	C1	Nordli	97	E4	Norrnäs	102	B3	Nossen	53	E2	
Nimféo	79	D3	Noarvaš	95	D3	Nónza	33	F2	Nördlingen	55	E2	Norrsunda	106	B2	Noss Head	3	C2	
Nímos, N	93	E1	Noblejas	40	B3	Noord-Brabant	16	C3	Nordmaling	102	A2	Norrsundet	106	B2	Noteć	112	A1	
Nin	74	C1	Nocera	64	B4	Noord-Holland	16	C2	Nordmark	105	E3	Norrtälje	106	B3	Nótia	79	E2	
Ninove	50	B3	Nocera Tirinese	67	E3	Noord-Oost-Polder	16	C2	Nord-Ostsee-Kanal	47	F2	Norrviken	108	C3	Nótia Pindos	82	C1	
Niort	24	C4	Nocera Umbra	61	E4	Noordwijk aan Zee	16	B2	Nordøyane	100	A2	Norsjö	98	B4	Nótios Evoikós Kólpos	84	B4	
Nipfjället	101	D3	Noceto	60	B2	Noordzee	46	B3	Nordøyar	96	A3	Norsjø	104	C3	Nótio Stenó Kerkíras	82	B2	
Nípsa	81	F2	Noci	65	E3	Noormarkku	102	B3	Nordrana	97	E2	Norskehavet	96	B4	Noto	69	D4	
Niš	77	E1	Nodeland	104	B4	Nora	105	F3	Nordreisa	94	C2	Nort	23	D4	Notodden	104	C3	
Nisa	38	C3	Nogara	60	C1	Norberg	105	F3	Nordrhein-Westfalen	17	E3	Nörten-Hardenberg	52	B2	Notre-Dame-de-Bellecombe	27	E4	
Nisa, Rib de	38	C3	Nogaro	28	B4	Norcia	63	F1	Nordsee	47	B2	Northallerton	7	D1	Nottingham	7	D3	
Nišava	73	F4	Nogent-le-Roi	19	E4	Nord	20	A1	Nordseter	105	D2	Northam	8	C3	Nottinghamshire	7	D3	
Niscemi	68	C4	Nogent-le-Rotrou	23	F3	Nord Beveland	16	B3	Nordstrand	47	F1	Northampton	9	F1	Nouan-le-Fuzelier	25	E2	
Niška Banja	77	E1	Nogent-sur-Seine	20	A4	Nordborg	108	A4	Nord Trøndelag	101	D1	Northamptonshire	9	F1	Nousiainen	107	D2	
Nissáki	82	A1	Nogueira de Ramuin	34	B2	Nordby (Fanø)	108	A3	Norðurfjörður	96	A1	North Berwick	5	D2	Nouvion	19	E2	
Nissan	109	D2	Nogueira, Sa de	34	C4	Nordby (Samsø)	108	B3	Nore (IRL)	12	C4	North Chan	13	E1	Nouvion-en-Thiérache, le	20	B2	
Nisser	104	B3	Noguera Pallaresa, R	37	F2	Norddeich	47	E3	Nore (N)	104	C2	North Downs	10	C3	Nŏux	19	F1	
Nissilä	103	D1	Noguera Ribagorçana, R	37	F3	Nordeide	100	A3	Norefjell	104	C2	Northeim	52	B2	Nouzonville	20	C2	
Níssiros, N	89	F4	Noguera			Norden	47	E3	Nore, R	15	D3	Northern Ireland	13	D2	Nova Breznica	77	D3	
Nissum Bredning	108	A2	Nohfelden	54	B1	Nordenau	17	F4	Noresund	104	C2	North Esk	3	D4	Nová Bystřice	57	D1	
Nissum Fjord	108	A2	Noia	34	A1	Nordenham	47	F3	Norfolk	7	F3	North Foreland	11	D2	Novaci (Makedonija)	77	E4	
Nith	4	C3	Noirétable	26	B4	Norderney	47	E3	Norg	17	D1	North Leach	9	E2	Novaci (Srbija)	72	C3	
Niton	9	E4	Noirmoutier	56	B1	Norderstedt	48	A2	Norheimsund	104	A2	North Ronaldsay	3	E1	Nova Crnja	72	C1	
Nitra	112	B3	Noirmoutier, I de	24	A3	Nordfjord	100	A3	Norra Bergnäs	98	A2	North Sound, The	3	E1	Novafeltria	61	E3	
Nitry	26	B2	Noja	36	A1	Nordfjordeid	100	A3	Norra Gloppet	102	B2	North Tyne	5	E3	Nova Gorica (I)	59	F3	
Nittedal	105	D3	Nokia	107	E1	Nordfold	97	E1	Norråker	101	F1	North Uist	2	A3	Nova Gorica (YU)	70	A2	
Nittenau	56	B1	Nola	64	B4	Nordfolda	97	E1	Norra Kvarken	102	B2	Northumberland	5	E3	Nova Gradiška	71	E3	
Nittendorf	55	F2	Nolay	26	B3	Nordfriesische Inseln	47	E1	Norra Kvill	109	E1	Northumberland Nat Pk	5	E3	Nova Kasaba	72	B4	
Nivala	102	C1	Noli	60	A3	Nordhalben	52	C3	Norra Råda	105	E3	North Walsham	7	F3				
Nive	28	A4	Noja	36	A1	Nordhausen	52	C2	Norra Storfjället	97	E3	Northwich	6	C3				
Nivelles	50	B4							Norrbottens Län	98	B1	Northwich	6	C3				
Nivernais	26	B3																
Nivolet, Colle del	31	E1																

Nummi 107 E2
Nuneaton 9 E1
Nunnanen 95 D3
Nuñomoral 39 D2
Nunspeet 17 D2
Nuorajärvi 103 F2
Nuorgam 95 E2
Nuoro 66 B2
Nurallao 66 B3
Nürburg 51 E4
Núria 32 B3
Nurmes 103 E1
Nurmijärvi (Pohjois-Karjalan Lääni) 103 F1
Nurmijärvi (Uudenmaan Lääni) 107 E2
Nurmo 102 C2
Nürnberg 55 F1
Nürtingen 55 D3
Nus 27 E4
Nusse 48 B2
Nuštar 71 F2
Nuthe 49 D4
Nuttlar 17 F3
Nuttupera 103 D1
Nuutajärvi 107 E2
Nuvvos-Ailigas 95 E2
Nyåker 102 A1
Nybergsund 105 E2
Nyborg 108 B4
Nybro 109 E2
Nyírbátor 112 C3
Nyíregyháza 112 C3
Nykarleby 102 B2
Nykøbing F (Storstrøm) 108 C4
Nykøbing M (Viborg) 108 A2
Nykøbing S (Vestsjælland) 108 C3
Nyköping 106 B4
Nykvarn 106 B4
Nynäshamn 106 B4
Nyon 27 D3
Nyons 30 C3
Nýřany 53 E4
Nýrdalur 96 B2
Nýrsko 56 B1
Nyrud 95 F2
Nysa 112 A2
Nysa Łużycka 53 F1
Nysäter 105 E3
Nyseter 100 B3
Nysted 108 C4
Nyvoll 95 D2

O

Oadby 9 F1
Oakham 9 F1
Oanes 104 A3
Oassi 87 D1
Oban 4 B1
O Barco 34 C3
Obbola 102 B1
Obdach 57 D4
Obdacher Sattel 57 D4
Obedska bara 72 C3
Obejo 43 F2
Oberalppass 58 A3
Oberammergau 55 F4
Oberau 56 A4
Oberaudorf 56 B4
Oberdrauburg 59 E2
Oberessfeld 52 C4
Obergeis 52 B3
Obergrafendorf 57 E2
Obergrünzburg 55 E4
Obergurgl 58 C2
Oberhaslach 21 E4
Oberhausen 17 E3
Oberhof 52 C3
OberjochPaß 58 C1
Oberkirch 54 C3
Oberkirchen 17 F4
Oberkochen 55 E2
Obermarchtal 55 D3
Obernai 21 E4
Obernberg 56 C3
Obernburg 55 D1
Oberndorf (A) 56 C3
Oberndorf (D) 54 C3
Obernzell 56 C2
Oberölsbach 55 F1
Oberösterreich 56 C2
Oberprechtal 54 C3
Oberpullendorf 57 F3
Oberseebach 21 F3
Obersontheim 55 E2
Oberstaufen 55 E4
Oberstdorf 55 E4
Oberstein 54 B1
Obertauern 59 F1
Obertraun 59 F1
Oberursel 51 F4
Obervellach 59 E2
Oberviechtach 56 B1
Oberwart 57 F4
Oberwesel 51 E4
Oberwiesenthal 53 E3
Oberwölz 57 D4
Oberzeiring 57 D4
Óbidos 38 A3
Obilić 77 D2
Obing 56 B3
Obiou, l' 30 C2
Objat 29 D1
Obninsk 111 F3
O Bolo 34 C3
Obón 41 E1
Oborniki 112 A1
Obornjača 72 C1
Oborovo 70 C2
Obrenovac 72 C3
Obrež 72 C3
Obrov 70 A3
Obrovac (Split) 75 D1
Obrovac (Zadar) 74 C1
Obršani 77 E4
Obsteig 58 C2
Obudovac 71 F3
Obzor 115 E2
Obzova 70 B3
Očakov 113 F3
Oca, Mtes de 36 A2
Ocaña 40 B3
Oca, R 36 A2
Očauš 71 E4
Occhiobello 61 D2
Occhito, L di 64 B3
Očevlje 71 F4
Ochagavia 37 D2
Ochil Hills 5 D1
Ochsenfurt 55 E1
Ochsenhausen 55 E3
Ochtrup 17 E2
Ockelbo 106 A2
Öckerö 108 C1
Ocreza, R 38 C3
Ocrkavlje 76 A1
Ödåkra 108 C3
Odda 104 B2
Odden Færgehavn 108 B3
Odder 108 B3
Oddesund 108 A2
Odeceixe 42 A2
Odeleite 42 B2
Odelzhausen 55 F3
Odemira 42 A2
Ödemiş 115 F4
Odense 108 B3
Odenthal 17 E4
Oder 49 E3
Oderberg 49 E3
Oderbruch 49 E3
Oderbucht 49 E1
Oderhaff 49 E2
Oderzo 59 E4
Ödeshög 109 D1
Odessa 113 F4
Odet 22 B3
Odiel, R 42 C2
Odivelas 42 B1
Odivelas, Bgem de 42 B1
Odolo 60 B1
Odorheiu Secuiesc 113 D4
Odra 112 A2
Odžaci 72 B2
Odžak (Bosna i Hercegovina) 71 F3
Odžak (Crna Gora) 76 B1
Oebisfelde 48 B4
Oebro 105 F4
Oederan 53 E3
Oeiras 38 A4
Oelde 17 F3
Oelsnitz (Plauen) 53 D3
Oelsnitz (Zwickau) 53 D3
Oettingen 55 E2
Oetz 58 C2
Ofanto 64 C3
Ofenpass 58 C3
Offaly 12 C4
Offenbach 52 A4
Offenburg 54 C3
Offida 63 F1
Offranville 19 E2
Ofir 34 A4
Ofotfjorden 94 B3
Oggiono 60 A1
Ogliastro Cilento 67 D1
Oglio 58 C4
Ognon 27 D2
Ogošte 77 E2
Ograđden 77 F3
Ogre 110 C2
Ogulin 70 C3
Ohanes 44 B3
Óhi, Óros 88 A1
Ohiró 80 B1
Ohlstadt 56 A4
Ohorn 53 F2
Ohrdruf 52 C3
Ohre 48 B4
Ohře 53 E3
Ohrid 77 D4
Ohridsko Ez 77 D4
Ohringen 55 D2
Ohrit, Liq i 77 D4
Óhthia 82 C3
Ohthoniá 84 B4
Oijärvi 99 D3
Oijärvi L 99 D3
Oikarainen 99 D2
Oirschot 16 C3
Oise 20 B2
Oise (Dépt) 19 F3
Oisemont 19 E2
Oisterwijk 16 C3
Oitti 107 E2
Oituz 113 D4
Ojakylä 99 D4
Öje 101 E4
Öjebyn 98 B3
Ojën 43 E4
Ojos Negros 41 D2
Ojuelos Altos 43 E1
Öjung 101 E4
Okehampton 8 C3
Oker 48 B4
Oklaj 75 D1
Oknö 109 E2
Okol 76 C2
Oksbøl 108 A3
Oksby 108 A3
Øksfjord 95 D2
Øksfjorden 94 A3
Øksfjordjøkelen 94 C2
Øksnes 94 A3
Okstindan 97 E3
Okučani 71 E3
Okulovka 111 E1
Olafsfjörður 96 B1
Olafsvík 96 A2
Öland 109 E2
Olan, Pic d' 31 D2
Olargues 32 B1
Olazagutía 36 B2
Olbernhau 53 E3
Olbia 66 B1
Oldcastle 13 D3
Oldebroek 17 D2
Oldeide 100 A3
Olden 100 A3
Oldenburg (Niedersachsen) 47 F3
Oldenburg (Schleswig Holstein) 48 B1
Oldenzaal 17 E2
Olderdalen 94 C2
Oldervik 94 C2
Oldfjällen 101 E1
Oldham 6 C2
Old Head of Kinsale 14 B4
Oldmeldrum 3 E4
Oldsum 47 F1
Oleggio 60 A1
Oleiros 34 B1
Oleiros 38 C2
Ølen 104 A3
Oléron, Ile d' 24 B4
Olesa 32 A4
Oleśnica 112 A2
Oletta 33 F2
Olette 32 B2
Olevsk 113 D2
Ølgod 108 A3
Olhão 42 B3
Olhava 99 D3
Oliana 32 A3
Oliana, Emb d' 32 A3
Olib 70 B4
Olib I 70 B4
Oliena 66 B2
Oliete 37 D4
Olimbia 86 C2
Olimbiáda (Makedonía) 80 B3
Olimbiáda (Thessalía) 79 E4
Ólimbos 93 D2
Ólimbos, Óros (Évia) 84 B4
Ólimbos, Óros (Pieriá) 79 E4
Ólinthos 80 A4
Olite 36 C2
Oliva 45 E1
Oliva de la Frontera 42 C1
Oliva de Mérida 39 D4
Olivares 40 C3
Oliveira de Azeméis 38 B1
Oliveira de Frades 38 B1
Oliveira do Bairro 38 B1
Oliveira do Douro 34 B4
Oliveira do Hospital 38 C2
Olivenza 38 C4
Olivenza, R de 38 C4
Olivet 25 E1
Olivone 58 A3
Olleria, Pto de l' 41 E4
Ollerton 7 D3
Ollières, les 30 B2
Olliergues 29 F1
Ollioules 31 D4
Ollöla 103 F2
Olmedillo de Roa 35 F4
Olmedo (E) 35 E4
Olmedo (I) 66 A2
Olmeto 33 F4
Olocau del Rey 41 E2
Olofström 109 D3
Olombrada 35 F4
Olomouc 112 A3
Olonzac 32 B1
Oloron Ste Marie 37 D1
Olost 32 A3
Olot 32 B3
Olovo 71 F4
Olpe 17 F4
Olsberg 17 F3
Olshammar 105 F4
Olst 17 D2
Ølstykke 108 C3
Olsztyn 110 B4
Olszyna 53 F1
Olt 115 D2
Oltedal 104 A3
Olten 27 F2
Oltenia 115 D1
Oltenița 115 E1
Olula del Río 44 C3
Olvega 36 C3
Olvera 43 E3
Omagh 13 D2
Omali 79 D4
Omalós 90 B3
Omarska 71 D3
Ombrone 63 D1
Omegna 58 A4
Omiš 75 E2
Omišalj 70 B3
Omme Å 108 A3
Ommen 17 D2
Omodeo, L 66 B3
Omoljica 73 D3
Omorfohóri 83 E1
Ömossa 102 B3
Oña 36 A2
Oñati 36 B1
Oncala, Pto de 36 B3
Onda 41 E3
Ondara 45 E1
Ondárroa 36 B1
Oneglia 31 F3
OnesseetLaharie 28 A3
Onich 2 C4
Onkamo (Lapin Lääni) 99 E2
Onkamo (Pohjois Karjalan Lääni) 103 F2
Onkivesi 103 E2
Ons, I de 34 A2
Ontaneda 35 F2
Ontiñena 37 E3
Ontinyent 45 E1
Ontojärvi 99 F4
Ontur 45 D1
Onzain 25 E2
Oostburg 16 B4
OostelijkFlevoland 16 C2
Oostende 50 A3
Oosterbeek 17 D3
Oosterend 16 C1
Oosterhout 16 C3
Oostkamp 50 A3
Oostmalle 50 C3
OostVlaanderen 50 B3
OostVlieland 16 C1
Ootmarsum 17 E2
Opatija 70 B3
Opatovac 72 B2
Opava 112 A3
Opladen 17 E4
Oplenac 73 D3
Opočka 111 D2
Opole 112 A2
Opovo 72 C2
Oppach 53 F2
Oppdal 100 C2
Oppenau 54 C3
Oppenheim 54 C1
Opphaug 100 C1
Oppido Lucano 64 C4
Oppido Mamertina 67 E4
Oppland 104 C1
Oputten 16 C2
Opuzen 75 F2
Ora 59 D3
Oradea 112 C4
Oradour-sur-Glane 25 D4
Oradour-sur-Vayres 28 C1
Orahova 71 D3
Orahovac 77 D2
Orahovica 71 E2
Oraison 31 D3
Orajärvi 98 C2
Orange 30 B3
Orani 66 B2
Oranienbaum 53 D1
Oranienburg 49 D3
Oranmore 12 B3
Orašac (Hrvatska) 75 F2
Orašac (Srbija) 73 D3
Orasi 76 B3
Orašje 71 F3
Orăștie 114 C1
Oravainen 102 B2
Oravais 102 B2
Oravikoski 103 E2
Oravița 114 C1
Orb 30 A4
Orba 45 E1
Ørbæk 108 B4
Orbassano 31 E2
Orbe 27 D3
Orbec 19 D3
Orbetello 63 D2
Orbey 27 E1
Orbigo, R 35 D2
Orce 44 B2
Orce, R 44 B2
Orcera 44 B1
Orchies 20 A1
Orcières 31 D2
Orcival 29 E1
Orco 31 E1
Ordes 34 A1
Ordesa, Parque Nac. de 37 E2
Ordino 32 A2
Ordizia 36 C1
Orduña 36 B1
Orduña, Pto de 36 B1
Ore 101 E4
Orea 41 D2
Öreälven 102 A1
Orebić 75 E2
Örebro Län 105 F3
Öregrund 106 B3
Öregrundsgrepen 106 B2
Orei 83 F3
Orellana de la Sierra 39 E4
Orellana, Emb de 39 E4
Orellana la Vieja 39 E4
Orense 34 B3
Oréo 81 D2
Oreókastro 79 F3
Orestiáda 81 F1
Oresund 108 C3
Orfós, Akr 89 F4
Orgáni 81 E2
Organyà 32 A3
Orgañyà 37 F3
Orgaz 40 A3
Orgejev 113 E3
Orgelet 26 C3
Orgères-en-Beauce 25 E1
Orgon 30 C3
Orgosolo 66 B2
Orhi, Pic d' 37 D1
Orhomenós 83 F4
Oria 44 C3
Oria 65 E4
Oria, R 36 C1
Origny-Sainte-Benoîte 20 A2
Orihuela 45 D2
Orihuela del Tremedal 41 D2
Orimattila 107 F2
Orini 80 B2
Oriolo 65 D4
Oripää 187 D2
Orissaare 110 B2
Oristano 66 B3
Oristano, G di 66 A3
Orivesi 102 C3
Orivesi L 103 F2
Orjahovo 115 D2
Ørjavik 100 B2
Ørje 105 D3
Orjen 76 A2
Orjiva 44 A3
Orkanger 100 C2
Örkelljunga 109 D3
Orkla 100 C2
Orkney Is 3 E1
Ørlandet 100 C1
Orlando, C d' 69 D2
Orlane 77 D1
Orlate 77 D2
Orléans 25 E1
Orlická přehr nádrž 56 C1
Orlovat 72 C2
Orly 19 F4
Orménio 81 F1
Ormília 80 B4
Órmos 79 F3
Órmos Korthíou 88 B1
Órmos Panagías 80 B4
Órmos Prínou 80 C3
Ormož 70 C1
Ormsjö 97 F4
Ormsjön 101 F1
Ormskirk 6 B2
Ormtjernkampen 104 C1
Ornain 20 C4
Ornans 27 D2
Orne (Calvados) 18 C4
Orne (Dépt) 20 B3
Orne (Meuse) 21 D3
Ørnes 97 E2
Ornós 88 C2
Örnsköldsvik 102 A2
Or'ol 111 F4
Orolik 72 B2
Orom 72 B1
Oron-la-Ville 27 E3
Oropesa (Castilla la Mancha) 39 F3
Oropesa (Valencia) 41 F3
Orosei 66 C2
Orosei, G di 66 C2
Orosháza 112 B4
Orpierre 30 C3
Orpington 10 C2
Orra 100 C3
Orsa 101 E4
Orša 111 E3
Orsajön 101 E4
Orsay 19 F4
Orsières 27 E4
Orsogna 64 A2
Orșova 114 C1
Ørsta 100 A2
Örsundsbro 106 B3
Orta Nova 64 C3
Orta San Giulio 58 A4
Orte 63 E2
Ortegal, C 34 B1
Orth 57 F2
Orthez 28 B4
Ortigueira 34 B1
Ortisei 59 D3
Ortles 58 C3
Ortnevik 104 B1
Orton 5 D4
Ortona 64 A2
Ortrand 53 E2
Örträsk 102 A1
Orubica 71 E3
Orune 66 B2
Orusco 40 B2
Orvalho 38 C2
Orvieto 63 E1
Órvilos, Óros 80 B1
Orvinio 63 F2
Orzinuovi 60 B1
Os 100 D3

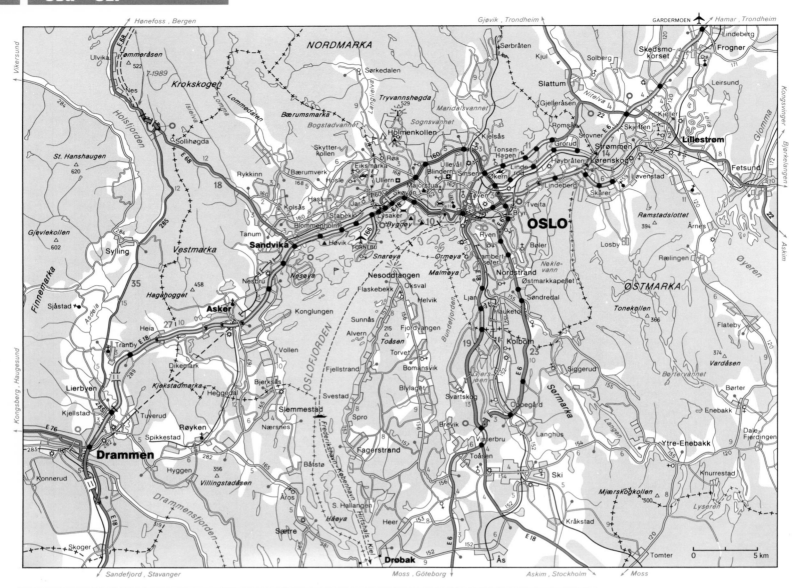

Osa de la Vega	40 B3	Óssa	80 A2	Ostfriesische		Oświęcim	112 B2	Ottobrunn	56 A3	Ourique	42 B2	Øvre Fryken	105 E3
Osâm	115 D2	Ossa de Montiel	40 B4	Inseln	47 D3	Otanmäki	103 D1	Ottsjö	101 D2	Ourol	34 B1	Øvre Pasvik	95 F2
Osby	109 D3	Óssa, Óros	83 F1	Östhammar	106 B3	Otava (CS)	56 C1	Ottweiler	54 B2	Ourthe	20 C1	Øvre Soppero	95 D4
Oschatz	53 E2	Ossa, Sa de	38 C4	Ostheim	52 B4	Otava (SF)	103 E3	Otwock	112 B1	Ourville	19 D2	Ovruč	113 E1
Oschersleben	52 C1	Ossiach	59 F2	Ostia Antica	63 E3	Oteren	94 C3	Otziás	88 A2	Ouse, R.	7 D2	Owel, L	13 D3
Oschiri	66 B2	Ossiacher See	59 F2	Ostiglia	60 C2	Oteševo	77 D4	Ötztal	58 C2	Oust	37 F2	Oxelösund	106 B4
Osečina	72 C3	Óssios Loukás	83 F4	Östmark	105 E3	Othem	109 F4	Ötztaleralpen	58 C2	Outes, Sa de	34 A2	Oxford	9 E2
Oseja de Sajambre	35 E2	Ossun	37 E1	Ost'or	113 E1	Othery	9 D3	Ouchy	27 D3	Outokumpu	103 E2	Oxfordshire	9 E2
Osen	96 C4	Ostaškov	111 E2	Ostra	61 E3	Othoní, N	78 A4	Oucques	25 E1	Outomuro	34 B3	Oxiá, N	82 C4
Osera de Ebro	37 D4	Østbirk	108 B3	Ostrach	55 D4	Óthris, Óros	83 E3	Oud Beijerland	16 B3	Outwell	10 C1	Oxiá (Stereá Eláda)	83 D3
Osijek	71 F2	Østby	105 E2	Östra Gloppet	102 B2	Otívar	44 A3	Ouddorp	16 B3	Ouvèze	30 C3	Oxiá (Thessalia)	83 D2
Osilo	66 B2	Oste	47 F3	Östra Silen	105 D4	Otley	6 C2	Oude Maas	16 B3	Ouzouer	25 F2	Oxie	108 C3
Osimo	61 F4	Osted	108 C3	Ostrava	112 B3	Otnes	100 C3	Oudenaarde	50 B3	Ouzouer-le-Marché	25 E1	Oxilithos	84 B4
Osinja	71 E3	Osterburg	48 C4	Oštrelj	71 D4	Otočac	70 C4	Oudenbosch	16 C3	Ovada	60 A2	Ox Mts, The	12 B2
Osipaonica	73 D3	Osterburken	55 D1	Ostritz	53 F2	Otočec	70 B2	OudePekela	47 E3	Ovanåker	101 F4	Oyarzun	36 C1
Osipoviči	111 D4	Österbybruk	106 B3	Ostróda	110 B4	Otok	72 B2	Ouessant, Ile d'	22 A2	Ovar	38 B1	Oybin	53 F2
Osječenica	71 D4	Østerby Havn	108 B2	Ostrog	113 D2	Otoka	71 D3	Oughterard	12 B3	Ovčar Banja	73 D4	Øye	104 C1
Oskarshamn	109 E2	Österbymo	109 E1	Ostrołęka	112 B1	Otra	104 B4	Ouistreham	18 C3	Ovedskloster	109 D3	Øyer	104 C1
Oskarström	108 C2	Österdalälven	101 D3	Ostrov (CS)	53 E3	Otranto	65 F4	Oul	51 D4	Overath	17 E4	Øyeren	105 D3
Oslava	57 E1	Österdalen	100 C3	Ostrov (RO)	115 E1	Otsamo	95 E3	Oulainen	99 D4	Øverbygd	94 C3	OyMittelberg	55 E4
Oslo	105 D3	Österfärnebo	106 A3	Ostrov (SU)	111 D2	Otta	100 C3	Oulanka	99 E2	Overflakkee	16 B3	Oyntdartfjørdur	96 A3
Oslo (Fylke)	105 D3	Osterfeld	53 D2	Ostrowiec		Ottana	66 B2	Oulankajoki	99 E2	Overhalla	97 D4	Oyón	36 B2
Oslofjorden	104 C3	Östergötlands		Świętokrzyski	112 B2	Ottaviano	64 B4	Oulchy-le-Château	20 A3	Overhörnäs	102 A2	Oyonnax	27 D4
Ösmo	106 B4	Län	109 E1	Ostrów		Ottenschlag	57 E2	Oulu	99 D3	Overijssel	17 D2	Øystese	104 B2
Osnabrück	17 F2	Osterhofen	56 B2	Mazowiecki	112 B1	Ottensheim	57 D2	Oulujärvi	99 E4	Overijse	50 C3	Oyten	47 F3
Ošno Lubuskie	49 F4	Osterholz		Ostrów		Otterburn	5 E3	Oulujoki	99 D4	Överkalix	98 C2	Ozalj	70 C2
Osogovija	77 F2	Scharmbeck	47 F3	Wielkopolski	112 A2	Otter Ferry	4 B2	Oulun Lääni	99 E4	Övermark	102 B2	Ožbalt	70 B1
Osogovske		Osteria del Gatto	61 E4	Ostrožac (Bosna i		Otterlo	17 D3	Oulunsalo	99 D4	Översjuktan	97 F3	Ózd	112 B3
planine	77 E2	Osterode	52 B2	Hercegovina)	70 C3	Otterndorf	47 F3	Oulx	31 D2	Övertornea	98 C2	Ozeblin	70 C4
Osoppo	59 E3	Osterøya	104 A2	Ostrožac (Bosna i		Otterøy	97 D4	Ounasjoki	99 D2	Överum	109 E1	Ozieri	66 B2
Osor	70 B4	Östersund	101 E2	Hercegovina)	75 F1	Ottersberg	47 F3	Oundle	9 F1	Överuman	97 E3	Ozren	71 F3
Osorno	35 F3	Östersundom	107 F2	Ostsee	48 C1	Otterup	108 B3	Our	54 A1	Oviedo	35 D1	Ozren Devica	73 E4
Osøyri	104 A2	Östervåla	106 B3	Osttirol	59 E2	Ottery St Mary	9 D3	Ouranópoli	80 B4	Ovindoli	63 F2		
Ospedaletti	31 E3	Øster Vrå	108 B2	Ostuni	65 E3	Ottmarsheim	27 E1	Ource	26 C1	Øvre Anarjokka	95 D3		
Ospitaletto	60 B1	Osterwieck	52 B1	Osuna	43 E3	Ottnang	56 C3	Ourcq	20 A3	Øvre Årdal	100 B3		
Oss	16 C3	Østfold	105 D3	Oswestry	6 B3	Ottobeuren	55 E3	Ourense	34 B3	Øvre Dividalen	94 C3		

P

Paakkila 103 E2
Paalasmaa 103 E1
Páamo de Masa,
  Pto de 35 F3
Paar 55 F3
Paasselkä 103 F3
Paavola 99 D4
Pabianice 112 B2
Pacaudière, la 26 B4
Paceco 68 A3
Pachino 69 D4
Packsattel 57 E4
Paço de Sousa 34 A4
Paços de Ferreira 34 A4
Pacov 57 D1
Pacy 19 E4
Padasjoki 107 E1
Padej 72 C1
Paddene 75 D1
Paderborn 17 F3
Paderne 42 B2
Padiham 6 C2
Padina 72 C2
Padinska Skela 72 C2
Padirac, Gouffre
  de 29 E2
Padjelanta 97 F1
Padornelo 34 C3
Padova 61 D1
Padrela, Sa da 34 B4
Padrón 34 A2
Padru 66 B2
Padstow 8 B3
Padul 44 A3
Paesana 31 E2
Paestum 64 B4
Pag 70 C4
Pag I 70 B4
Paganico 63 D1
Pagassés, N 83 F2
Pagassitikós
  Kólpos 83 F2
Paglia 63 D1
Pagny 21 D3
Pagóndas (Évia) 84 A3
Pagóndas (Sámos) 89 E2
Pagoúria 81 D2
Paguera 45 E3
Páhi 87 E1
Pahiá Ámos 91 F4
Pahís, Akr 80 C3
Paide 110 C1
Paignton 8 C4
Päijänne 103 D3
Páïko, Óros 79 E2
Paimbœuf 23 D4
Paimio 107 D2
Paimpol 22 C2
Painswick 9 E2
Paisley 4 C2
Paistunturit 95 E2
País Vasco 36 B1
Paittasjärvi 94 C4
Paiva, R 38 B1
Pajala 98 C1
Pájara 42 C4
Pajares, Pto de 35 D2
Paklenica Nac
  Park 70 C4
Pakoštane 74 C1
Pakrac 71 E2
Pakračka Poljana 71 D2
Paks 112 B4
Palacios de la
  Sierra 36 A3
Palacios del Sil 34 C2
Palacios de
  Sanabria 34 C3
Palade, Pso del 58 C3
Paládio 81 D2
Paladru 30 C1
Palafrugell 32 C3
Palagía 81 E2
Palagiano 65 E4
Palagonia 69 D3
Palagruža 75 D3
Palaía 60 C4
Palaiseau 19 F4
Palais, le 22 C4
Palamás 83 E2
Palamós 32 C3
Palancia, R 41 E3

Palanga 110 B3
Pala, Pto del 34 C1
Palas de Rei 34 B2
Palata 64 B2
Palatitsia 79 E3
Palatna 77 D1
Palau 66 B1
Palavas 30 B4
Palazzo del Pero 61 D4
Palazzolo Acreide 69 D4
Palazzolo sull'
  Oglio 60 B1
Palazzo San
  Gervasio 64 C3
Palazzuolo sul
  Senio 61 D3
Paldiski 110 C1
Pale 76 A1
Paléa Epídavros 87 E2
Palékastro 91 F4
Palena 64 A2
Palencia 35 E3
Paleohóra (Égina) 87 F2
Paleohóra (Kríti) 90 B4
Paleohóri
  (Grevená) 79 D4
Paleohóri
  (Halkidikí) 80 B3
Paleohóri (Ípiros) 82 B2
Paleohóri (Lésvos) 85 F3
Paleohóri
  (Pelopónissos) 87 D3
Paleohóri
  (Thessalía) 83 D1
Paleokastrítsa 82 A1
Paleókastro
  (Halkidikí) 80 A3
Paleókastro
  (Kozáni) 79 D4
Paleókastro
  (Sámos) 89 F2
Paleókastro
  (Séres) 80 B2
Paleókastro (Stereá
  Eláda) 83 D3
Paleokómi 80 B2
Paleópirgos (Stereá
  Eláda) 83 D4
Paleópirgos
  (Thessalía) 83 F1
Paleópoli
  (Ándros) 88 B1
Paleópoli
  (Samothráki) 81 E3
Paleós Kavála 80 C2
Paleós Xánthis 81 D2
Palermo 68 B3
Páleros 82 C3
Palérou, Órm 82 B3
Palestrina 63 F2
Palež 72 B4
Páli 89 F4
Paliano 63 F3
Palić 72 B1
Palidoro 63 E2
Palinges 26 B3
Palinuro 67 D2
Palioúri 80 B4
Paliouriá 79 D4
Paliseul 20 C2
Pälkäne 107 E1
Pälkem 98 B2
Pallas
  Ounastunturi 95 D3
Pallastunturi 95 D4
Pallice, la 24 B4
Palluau 24 B3
Palma 45 E3
Palmaces,
  Emb de 36 B4
Palma del Río 43 E2
Palma di
  Montechiaro 68 C4
Palmadula 66 A2
Palmanova 59 F3
Palmela 38 A4
Palmi 67 E4
Palo del Colle 65 D3
Palojoensuu 95 D3
Palojoki 95 D3
Palokki 103 E2
Palomäki 103 E1
Palomares del
  Campo 40 C3

Palomas 39 D4
Palomas, Pto de
  las 44 B2
Palombara Sabina 63 E2
Palombera, Pto de 35 F2
Palomera 41 D2
Pálos, Akr 88 B2
Palos, C de 45 D3
Palos de la
  Frontera 42 C3
Pals 32 C3
Pålsboda 105 F4
Paltamo 99 E4
Paltaselkä 99 E4
Paluzza 59 E2
Pámfila 85 F2
Pamhagen 57 F3
Pamiers 32 A2
Pampilhosa 38 B2
Pampilhosa da
  Serra 38 C2
Pampliega 35 F3
Pamplona 36 C2
Pamporovo 115 D3
Pamukkale 115 F4
Panagía (Ípiros) 82 C2
Panagía (Límnos) 85 D1
Panagía
  (Makedonía) 79 D4
Panagía (Thássos) 81 D3
Panagía (Thessalía) 82 C1
Panagjurište 115 D2
Panahaïkó, Óros 83 D4
Panarea, I 69 D2
Panaro 60 C3
Pancalieri 31 E2
Pančevo 73 D2
Pančičev vrh 77 D1
Pancorbo 36 A2
Pandánassa 87 E4
Pandeleimónas 79 F4
Pandino 60 B1
Pandokrátor 82 A1
Pandrup 108 B2
Panes 35 F2
Panetolikó, Óros 83 D3
Panetólio 82 C4
Panevėžys 110 C3
Pangbourne 9 E2
Pangéo, Óros 80 B2
Paniza, Pto de 36 C4
Pankajärvi 103 F1
Pankakoski 103 F1
Pankow 49 E4
Panórama
  (Dráma) 80 B2
Panórama
  (Thessaloníki) 80 A3
Panormítis 93 E1
Pánormos
  (Kikládes) 88 B2
Pánormos (Kríti) 91 D3
Pántane 102 B3
Pantelleria 68 A4
Pantelleria, I di 68 A4
Paola 67 E2
Pápa 112 A4
Papádes 84 A3
Papádos 85 F3
Pápas, Akr 89 D2
Papasidero 67 E2
Papa Stour 3 F1
Papenburg 47 E3
Papenheim 55 F2
Papíkio 81 D2
Pápingo 78 C4
Pappenheim 55 F2
Papuk Mt 71 E2
Papuk (Reg) 71 E2
Parabita 65 F4
Paracin 73 E4
Paracuellos de
  Jiloca 36 C4
Parada de Cunhos 34 B4
Paradas 43 E3
Paradela 34 B3
Paradíssia 86 C2
Parádissos 81 D2
Parainen 107 D3
Parajes 34 C1
Parakálamos 78 C4
Parálía (Aháïa) 86 C1
Paralía (Lakonía) 87 E3

Paralía
  (Makedonía) 79 F4
Paralía (Stereá
  Eláda) 83 F4
Paralía Akrátas 87 D1
Parália Ástros 87 D2
Paralía Kímis 84 B3
Paralía Kotsikiás 84 A3
Parália Skotínas 79 F4
Paralía Tiroú 87 E3
Paralímni 84 A4
Paralovo 77 D2
Paramé 18 B4
Paramera, Pto de 39 F2
Paramithiá 82 B2
Páramo del Sil 34 C2
Paranésti 80 C2
Parapanda 43 F3
Parapótamos 82 B1
Paraspóri, Akr 93 D2
Paray-le-Monial 26 B3
Parchim 48 C3
Pardubice 112 A3
Paredes 34 A4
Paredes de Coura 34 A3
Paredes de Nava 35 E3
Pareja 40 C2
Pareloup, Lac de 29 E3
Parentis-en-Born 28 A3
Párga 82 B2
Pargas 107 D3
Parikkala 103 F3
Parîngului, M 114 C1
Paris 19 F4
Parkalompolo 95 D4
Parkano 102 C3
Parla 40 A2
Parlavà 32 B3
Parma 60 B2
Parnassós, Óros 83 E4
Parndorf 57 F2
Párnitha, Óros 87 F1
Párnonas, Óros 87 D3
Pärnu 110 C2
Parola 107 E2
Páros 88 C3
Páros, N 88 B3
Parrett 9 D3
Parsberg 55 F2
Parsdorf 56 A3
Parseierspitze 58 C2
Parseta 49 F1
Parsteiner See 49 E3
Partakko 95 F2
Partanna 68 B3
Partenen 58 B2
Partenkirchen 55 F4
Parthenay 24 C3
Parthéni 89 E3
Partille 108 C1
Partinico 68 B3
Partizani 73 D3
Partizanske Vode 72 C4
Partney 7 E3
Partry Mountains 12 B3
Pasaia-Pasajes 36 C1
Pas de la Case 11 E3
Pas-de-Calais
  (Dépt) 19 E1
Pas-de-Calais 19 F2
Pasewalk 49 E2
Pashalítsa 83 E2
Pasikovci 71 E2
Pašman 74 C1
Pašman I 74 C1
Passais 18 C4
Passá-Limáni 85 E4
Passás, N 85 F4
Passau 56 C2
Passvaas 87 D4
Passero, C 69 D4
Passignano sul
  Trasimeno 61 D4
Passwang 27 E2
Pastrana 40 B2
Pastwang 27 E2
Paštrik 76 C3
Pásztó 112 B4
Patay 25 E1
Pateley Bridge 6 C1
Patéras, Óros 87 E1
Paterna del
  Campo 43 D2
Paterna de Rivera 43 D4

Paternion 59 F2
Paternò 69 D3
Paternopoli 64 B3
Patersdorf 56 B2
Paterswald 5 D4
P'atichatki 113 F2
Patiópoulo 82 C2
Patitíri 84 B2
Pátmos 89 E2
Pátmos, N 89 E2
Pátra 83 D4
Patraïkós Kólpos 82 C4
Patreksfjörður 96 A1
Patrington 7
Pattada 66 B2
Patterdale 5 D4
Patti 69 D2
Pattijoki 99 D4
Patvinsuo 103 F2
Pau 37 D1
Paularo 59 F2
Paulhaguet 29 F2
Paullo 60 A1
Pavia (I) 60 A2
Pavia (P) 38 B4
Pavilly 19 D3
Pavino Polje 76 B1
Pávliani 83 E3
Pávlos 83 F4
Pavullo nel
  Frignano 60 C3
Paxí 82 A2
Paymogo 42 C2
Payerne 27 E3
Paymogo 42 C2
Payrac 29 D2
Pazardžik 115 D3
Pazin 70 A3
Pčinja 77 E2
Peč 76 C2
Peča 70 B1
Peccioli 60 C4
Pecekelsheim 52 A2
Pech-Merle,
  Grotte du 29 D3
Pečigrad 70 C3
Pečinci 72 C3
Pecka 72 C4
Peckelsheim 52 A2
Pécs 114 B1
Pecsa Banja 76 C2
Pečurice 76 B3
Pedaso 61 F4
Pedersker 109 D4
Pedersöre 102 C2
Pédi 93 E1
Pedrafita do
  Cebreiro 34 C2
Pedrafita do Cebreiro,
  Pto de 34 C2
Pedrajas de San
  Esteban 35 E4
Pedralba
  (Castilla-León) 34 C3
Pedralba
  (Valencia) 41 E3
Pedras Salgadas 34 B4
Pedraza de la
  Sierra 40 A1
Pedrera 43 E3
Pedrizas, Pto de
  las 43 F3
Pedro Abad 43 F2
Pedro Bernardo 39 F2
Pedrógão
  (Alentejo) 42 B1
Pedrógão
  (Estremadura) 38 A2
Pedrógão Grande 38 B2
Pedro 36 C3
Pedro Muñoz 40 B4
Peebles 5 D2
Peel 6 A1
Peene 49 D2
Peenemünde 49 E1
Peer Gynt veien 100 C3

Pefkári 80 C3
Pefki 83 F3
Péfkos 78 C3
Pega 38 C2
Pegalajar 44 A2
Pegau 53 D2
Pegli 60 A3
Pegnitz 55 F1
Pego 45 E1
Pego do Altar,
  Bgem de 38 B4
Pegognaga 60 C2
Pegolotte 61 D1
Pehčevo 77 F3
Peine 52 B1
Peio Terme 58 C3
Peïra-Cava 31 E3
Peißenberg 56 A4
Peiting 56 A4
Peitz 53 F1
Pek 73 D3
Péla 79 E2
Péla (Nomos) 79 F3
Pelado 41 D3
Pelagie, Is 68 A4
Pelasgía 83 F3
Pelat, Mt 31 D3
Pelcyce 49 F3
Pelekános 79 D3
Pelekas 82 A1
Peletá 87 E3
Pelhřimov 57 D1
Pelinéo 85 E4
Pelister 77 E4
Peljesac 75 E2
Pelkosenniemi 99 E1
Pellegrino, M 68 B2
Pellerin, le 24 B2
Pellesmäki 103 E2
Pello 98 C2
Pellworm 47 F1
Pelopónnissos 86 C2
Peloritani, M 69 D2
Peltosalmi 103 E1
Peltovuoma 95 D3
Pélussin 30 B1
Pelvoux, Mt 31 D2
Pembroke 8 B2
Pembroke Dock 8 B2
Pembrokeshire Coast
  Nat Pk 8 B1
Penacova 38 B2
Peña de Francia 39 D2
Peña, de Francia,
  Sade 39 D2
Peña de Oroel 37 D2
Penafiel 34 A4
Peñafiel 35 F4
Peñaflor 43 E2
Peñagolosa 41 E3
Peña Gorbea 36 B1
Peñalara 40 A1
Penalva do
  Castelo 38 C1
Penamacor 38 C2
Peña Mira 34 C3
Peña Nofre 34 B3
Peña Prieta 35 E2
Peñaranda de
  Bracamonte 39 F1
Peñaranda de
  Duero 36 A3
Peñarroya 41 E2
Peñarroya, Emb
  de 40 B4
Peñarroya-
  Pueblonuevo 43 E1
Peña, Sa de la 37 D2
Peña Sagra 35 F2
Peñas, C de 35 D1
Peñascosa 44 C1
Peñas de Cervera 36 A3
Peñas de San
  Pedro 44 C1
Peña Trevinca 34 C3
Peña Ubiña 35 D2
Peñausende 35 D4
Pendagii 83 D4
Pendálofo 82 C4
Pendálofos 78 C4

Pendéli 87 F1
Pendéli Mt 87 F1
Pendeória 83 E4
Pénde Vrísses 80 A2
Pendine 8 B2
Peneda-Gerês, Pque
  Nac da 34 A3
Peneda, Sa da 34 A3
Penedono 38 C1
Penela 38 B2
Pénestin 22 C4
Penha 34 A4
Penhas da Saude 38 C2
Penhas Juntas 34 C4
Penhir, Pte de 22 A3
Penice, Pso del 60 A2
Peniche 38 A3
Penicuik 5 D2
Penig 53 D3
Peñíscola 41 F2
Penkun 49 E3
Penmaenmawr 6 A2
Penmarch, Pte de 22 A3
Pennabilli 61 E3
Penne 63 F1
Penne-d'Agenais 28 C3
Pennes, Pso di 59 D2
Pennines, The 6 C1
Peñón de Ifach 45 E1
Penrhyndeudraeth 6 A3
Penrith 5 D4
Penryn 8 B4
Penserjoch 59 D2
Pentland Firth 3 D2
Pentland Hills 5 D2
Pentrefoelas 6 B3
Pen-y-bont 8 C2
Penzance 8 A4
Penzberg 56 A4
Penzlin 49 D2
Peqin 76 C4
Perahóra 87 E1
Peraleda de
  Zaucejo 43 E1
Peralejos de
  las Truchas 40 C2
Perales del
  Alfambra 41 D2
Perales del Puerto 39 D2
Perales de Tajuña 40 B2
Perales, Pto de 39 D2
Peralta 36 C2
Peralta de Alcofea 37 E3
Peralva 42 B2
Pérama (Ípiros) 82 C1
Pérama (Kérkira) 82 A1
Pérama (Kríti) 91 D3
Pérama (Lésvos) 85 F3
Pérama (Stereá
  Eláda) 87 F1
Peraméri 98 C3
Perá-Posio 99 E2
Peräseinäjoki 102 C2
Perast 76 B3
Peratáta 86 A1
Percy 18 B4
Perdido, M 37 E2
Pérdika (Égina) 87 F2
Pérdika
  (Ioánina) 82 C2
Pérdika
  (Thesprotía) 82 B2
Perdikáki 82 C3
Perdikas 79 D3
Peréa (Péla) 79 E3
Peréa
  (Thessaloníki) 79 F3
Perejaslav-
  Chmel'nickij 113 F2
Pereruela 35 D4
Pereval
  Jablonickij 113 D3
Pereval
  Srednij Vereckij 112 C3
Pereval Užoskij 112 C3
Perg 57 D2
Pergine
  Valsugana 59 D3
Pergola 61 E4
Perho 102 C2
Perhonjoki 102 C1
Periana 43 F3
Périers 18 B3
Périgueux 28 C2

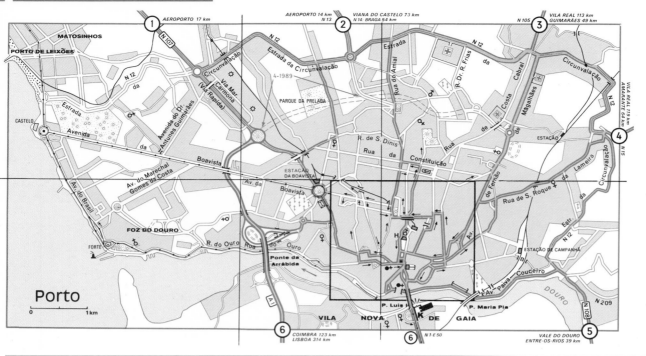

Porto

0 — 1km

Pírgos (Makedonía)	79	F3
Pírgos (Pelopónissos)	86	B2
Pírgos (Sámos)	89	E2
Pírgos (Stereá Eláda)	83	F4
Pírgos Diroú	87	D4
Pírgos Gerakíou	87	D3
Piriac	22	C4
Pirin	115	D3
Pirkkala	107	E1
Pirmasens	54	B2
Pirna	53	F2
Pirok	77	D3
Pirot	77	E1
Pirovac	74	C1
Pirsógiani	78	C4
Pirttikoski	99	E2
Pisa	60	C4
Pisciotta	67	D1
Pisek	56	C1
Piškorevci	71	F1
Pisogne	58	C4
Písses	88	A2
Pissodéri	79	D3
Pissónas	84	B4
Pissos	28	B3
Pisticci	65	D4
Pistoia	60	C3
Pisuerga, R	35	E4
Piteå	98	B3
Piteälven	98	B3
Pitești	115	D1
Pithagório	89	E2
Píthio (Thessalía)	79	E4
Píthio (Thráki)	81	F1
Pithiviers	25	F1
Pitigliano	63	D2
Pitlochry	3	D4
Pitomača	71	D2
Pittenweem	5	D2
Piva	76	B2
Pivka	70	A3
Pivnica	71	E2
Pivnice	72	B2
Pizarra	43	F3
Piz Buin	58	B2
Pizzighettone	60	B2
Pizzo	67	E3
Pizzoli	63	F2
Pjórsá	96	B2
Plabennec	22	A2
Plačenska pl	77	D4
Plačkovica	77	F3
Plagiá (Makedonía)	79	F2
Plagiá (Thráki)	81	E2
Plagne, la	31	D1
Plaisance	28	B4
Pláka (Límnos)	85	D1
Pláka (Pelopónissos)	87	E3
Pláka (Thráki)	81	E2
Pláka, Akr	85	D1
Pláka Litohórou	79	E4
Plakiás	90	C4
Planá	53	E4
Plana	76	A2
Planches-en-Montagne, les	27	D3
Plancoët	22	C3
Plandište	73	D2
Planica Mangrt	70	A1
Plánice	56	C1
Planina (Celje)	70	C2
Planina (Jesenice)	70	A1
Planina (Postojna)	70	A2
Planinica	73	E4
Planitz	53	D3
Plános	86	A1
Plansee	58	C1
Plasencia	39	D2
Plaški	70	C3
Plasy	53	E4
Platamona Lido	66	A2
Platamónas (Kavalá)	80	C2
Platamónas (Piería)	79	F4
Platanákia	79	F2
Platanés	90	C3
Platani	68	B3

Períklia	79	E2	Pescolanciano	64	A2	Pétrola	45	D1	Pianello	61	E4	Pierre-de-Bresse	26	C3	Pílio	89	F3
Perino	60	B2	Pescopagano	64	C4	Petróná	82	C3	Pianoro	61	D3	Pierrefitte	20	C3	Pílio, Óros	83	F2
Veríssa	91	E1	Pescorocchiano	63	F2	Petrosani	114	C1	Pianosa, I (Mare Adriatico)	64	C1	Pierrefitte-Nestaias	37	E2	Pillon, Col du	27	C4
Perísta	83	D3	Peshkopi	77	D3	Petrotá	81	F1	Pianosa, I (Mare Tirreno)	62	B2	Pierrefonds	19	F3	Pilorí	79	D4
Peristerá	80	A3	Pesiökylä	99	E3	Petrothálassa	87	E2	Piansano	63	D2	Pierrefontaine-les-Varans	27	D2	Pílos	86	C3
Peristéra, N	84	B4	Pesmes	26	C2	Petroússa	80	B2	Piapaxaro, P	34	C2	Pierrefort	29	E2	Pilštanj	70	C2
Perithório	80	B1	Pesočani	77	D4	Petrovac (Bosna i Hercegovina)	70	C3	Pias	42	B1	Pierrelatte	30	B3	Pina	37	D2
Perívlepto	83	F2	Pêso da Régua	34	B4	Petrovac (Crna Gora)	76	B3	Piatra-Neamț	113	D4	Pieskehaure	97	F2	Piña de Campos	35	E3
Perivóli	78	C4	Pesoz	34	C1	Petrovac (Srbija)	73	E3	Piave	59	E4	Piešťany	112	A3	Pinar	43	E3
Perivóli, N.	83	E2	Pessáni	81	E2	Petrovaradin	72	C2	Piazza al Serchio	60	B3	Pietersaaren mlk	102	C2	Pineda de la Sierra	36	A2
Perivólio	83	D3	Peštani	77	D4	Petrovčić	72	C3	Piazza Armerina	68	C3	Pietersaari	102	C1	Pineda de Mar	32	B4
Perjasica	70	C3	Pešter	76	C2	Petrovec	77	E3	Piazza Brembana	58	B4	Pietra Ligure	31	F3	Pinerolo	31	E2
Perković	75	D1	Pestovo	111	F1	Petrovice	53	F4	Piazzola sul Brenta	59	D4	Pietralunga	61	E4	Pineto	64	A1
Perleberg	48	C3	Pešurići	72	B4	Petrovići	72	B4	Piber	57	E4	Pietraperzia	68	C3	Piney	20	B1
Perlez	72	C2	Petačinci	77	E1	Pettenbach	56	C3	Pibeste, P de	37	E1	Pietrasanta	60	B3	Pinhal de Leiria	38	A2
Përmet	114	C4	Petäjäskoski	99	D2	Pettigoe	12	C2	Pićan	70	A3	Pietra Spada, Pso di	67	F4	Pinhal Novo	38	A4
Pernå	107	F2	Petäjäves	103	D3	Petworth	9	F3	Picassent	41	E4	Pietrosu	113	D3	Pinhão	34	B4
Pernaja	107	F2	Petalax	102	B2	Peuerbach	56	C3	Piccolo San Bernardo, Colle del	27	E4	Pieux, les	18	B3	Pinheiro	34	A4
Pernarec	53	E4	Petalída, Akr	88	B3	Peura	99	D2	Picerno	64	C4	Pieve de' Burgondi del Cairo	60	A2	Pinhel	39	D1
Pernes	30	C3	Petalídi	86	C3	Pewsey	9	E2	Pickering	7	D1	Pieve di Bono	58	C4	Piniós (Pelopónissos)	86	C1
Pernik	114	C2	Petalií, Nissí	88	A1	Peyrat-le-Château	29	D1	Pico	64	A3	Pieve di Cadore	59	E3	Piniós (Thessalía)	83	E1
Perniö	107	E3	Petalión, Kólpos	88	A1	Peyrehorade	28	A4	Pico, Pto del	39	F2	Pieve di Soligo	59	E3	Pinkafeld	57	F3
Pernitz	57	E3	Petaloúdes	93	F1	Peyresourde, C de	37	E2	Pico Ruivo	42	A3	Pieve di Teco	31	F3	Pinneberg	48	A3
Pernštejn	57	E1	Pétange	21	D3	Peyriac-Minervois	32	B1	Picos de Europa	35	E2	Pievepelago	60	C3	Pino	33	F2
Péronne	19	F2	Pétas	82	C2	Peyrolles	30	C4	Picote, Bgem de	34	C4	Pieve Santo Stefano	61	D4	Pinofranqueado	39	D2
Perosa Argentina	31	E2	Petehovac	70	B3	Peyrol, Pas de	29	E2	Picquigny	19	F2	Pinols	29	F2	Pinoso	45	D1
Pérouges	26	C4	Peterborough	9	F1	Peyruis	31	D3	Pidna	79	F3	Pigádi	83	F3	Pinos Puente	44	A3
Perpignan	32	B2	Peterhead	3	E3	Pézenas	30	A4	Piedicavallo	27	F4	Pigés	82	C2	Pinsk	113	D1
Perrero	31	E2	Peterlee	5	E4	Pezinok	112	A3	Piedicroce	33	F3	Pigí	83	D4	Pintado, Emb de	43	D2
Perreux	26	B4	Petersfield	9	F3	Pezoúla	81	D2	Piediluco	63	E1	Pigna	31	E3	Pintamo	99	E3
Perros-Guirec	22	B2	Petershagen	17	F2	Pfaffenhofen	55	F2	Piedimonte d'A.	64	B3	Pigón, L	82	C1	Pinto	40	A2
Persenbeug	57	D2	Pethelinós	80	B2	Pfäffikon	58	A2	Piedrabuena	40	A4	Pihlajaveden as	102	C3	Pinzano al Tagliamento	59	E3
Pershore	9	E1	Petilia Policastro	67	F3	Pfalzgrafenweiler	54	C3	Piedrafita	35	D2	Pihlajavesi	102	C3	Pinzolo	58	C3
Perstorp	109	D3	Petina	64	C4	Pfarrkirchen	56	B2	Piedrahita	39	E2	Pihlajavesi L	103	F3	Piobbico	61	E4
Perth	5	D1	Petite-Pierre, la	21	E3	Pfeffenhausen	56	B2	Piedralaves	39	F2	Pihlava	102	B3	Piombino	62	C1
Perthus, le	32	B3	Petit Morin	20	A4	Pforzheim	54	C2	Piedra, R	36	C4	Pihtipudas	103	D2	Pione	60	B2
Pertisau	59	D1	Petit St-Bernard, Col du	27	E4	Pfreimd	56	B1	Piedras Albas	39	D3	Piikkiö	107	D2	Pionsat	26	A4
Pertoča	70	C1	Petkula	95	E4	Pfronten	55	E4	Piedras, Emb de	42	C2	Piippola	103	D1	Piotrków Trybunalski	112	B2
Pertoúli	83	D1	Petlovača	72	C3	Pfullendorf	55	D4	Piedra San Martín, Collado de la	37	D2	Piispajärvi	99	F3	Piove di Sacco	61	D1
Pertteli	107	E2	Petlovača	72	C3	Pfullingen	55	D3	Piedras, Emb de	42	C2	Pikal'ovo	111	E1	Piovene Rocchette	59	D4
Pertuis	30	C3	Petoússio	82	B2	Pfunds	58	C2	Piedrasluengas, Pto de	35	F2	Pikérmi	87	F1	Pipéri, N	84	C2
Pertunmaa	103	D3	Petra (E)	45	F3	Pfungstadt	54	C1	Piedratajada	37	D3	Piła	112	A1	Pipriac	23	D3
Pertusa	37	E3	Pétra (Lésvos)	85	F2	Phalsbourg	21	E4	Pieksämäki	103	E3	Pilat-Plage	28	A2	Piqueras, Pto de	36	B3
Perućac Vrelo	72	C4	Pétra (Makedonía)	79	E4	Philippeville	50	C4	Pielavesi	103	D2	Pilas	43	D3	Piran	70	A3
Peručko jez	75	D1	Petralia	68	C3	Philippsreut	56	C2	Pielavesi L	103	D2	Pila, Sa de la	45	D2	Pir'atin	113	F2
Perugia	61	E4	Petrálona	80	A3	Piacenza	60	B2	Piemonte	31	E2	Pilat, Mt	30	B1	Pireás	87	F1
Perušić	70	C4	Petraná	79	E4	Piadena	60	B2	Piennes	20	C3	Pilatus	27	F2	Pirgadíkia	80	B3
Péruwelz	50	B4	Petrčane	74	C1	Piana	33	E3	Pienza	61	D4	Piléa	81	F2	Pirgetós	83	E1
Pervenchères	23	F3	Petrel	45	D1	Piana d. Albanesi	68	B3	Pieriá	79	E3	Piles	41	E4	Pilés	93	D3
Pervomajsk	113	F3	Petrella, Mte	64	A3	Piancastagnaio	63	D1	Piéria, Óri	79	E4	Pilés	93	D3	Pírgi (Dráma)	80	B2
Pesaro	61	E3	Pétres	79	D3	Piancavallo	59	E3	Pierowall	3	E1	Pili (Makedonía)	78	C2	Pírgi (Híos)	85	E4
Pescara	64	A1	Petreto-Bicchisano	33	F4	Piandelagotti	60	C3	Pierre-Buffière	29	D1	Pili (Stereá Eláda)	83	D2	Pírgi (Kérkira)	82	A1
Pescasseroli	64	A2	Petrič	115	D3	Pian delle Fugazze, Pso	59	D4				Pili (Thessalía)	83	D2	Pírgi (Kozáni)	79	E3
Peschici	64	C2	Petrijevki	71	F2	Pian del Voglio	60	C3				Pílio	84	A3	Pírgos (Íos)	88	C4
Peschiera del Garda	60	C1	Petrína	86	C3	Pianella	64	A1							Pírgos (Kríti)	91	D4
Pescia	60	C3	Petrinja	71	D3												
Pescina	63	F2	Petrodvorec	111	D1												
Pescocostanzo	64	A2	Petrohóri	83	D4												

Name	Ref
Plataniá (Makedonía)	80 C2
Platánia (Pelopónnissos)	86 C2
Plataniá (Thessalía)	84 A2
Platanistós	88 A1
Platanítis	83 D4
Plátanos (Kríti)	90 B3
Plátanos (Pelopónnissos)	87 D3
Plátanos (Thessalía)	83 F2
Platariá	82 B2
Plateau-d'Assy	27 E4
Plateés	87 E1
Pláti	81 F1
Platiána	86 C2
Platičevo	72 C3
Platikambos	83 E1
Platís Gialós (Kefaloniá)	86 A1
Platís Gialós (Míkonos)	88 C2
Platís Gialós (Sífnos)	88 B3
Platístomo	83 E3
Plattling	56 B2
Plau	48 C3
Plaue	49 D4
Plauen	53 D3
Plauer See (Potsdam)	49 D4
Plauer See (Schwerin)	48 C3
Plav	76 C2
Plavča	70 C3
Plavna	73 E3
Plavnica	76 B3
Plavnik I	70 B4
Plavnik Mt	70 B3
Playa de Gandía	41 E4
Playa de San Juan	45 E1
Pleaux	29 E2
Pleine-Fougères	18 B4
Pleinfeld	55 F2
Pleiße	53 D2
Plélan-le-Grand	23 D3
Piélan-le-Petit	22 C3
Pléneuf	22 C2
Plentzia	36 B1
Plépi	87 E2
Plešin	76 C1
Plestin	22 B2
Pleternica	71 E2
Plettenberg	17 F4
Pletvar	77 E3
Pleumartin	25 D3
Pleumeur-Bodou	22 B2
Pleven	115 D2
Pleyben	22 B3
Pliego	44 C2
Plítra	87 D4
Plitvice	70 C3
Plitvička jezera	70 C3
Plitvički Ljeskovac	70 C4
Pljesevica	70 C4
Pljevlja	76 B1
Ploaghe	66 B2
Ploče	75 E2
Plochingen	55 D2
Płock	112 B1
Plöckenpaß	59 E2
Plöckenstein	56 C2
Pločno	75 E1
Ploërmel	22 C3
Ploiești	115 D1
Plomári	85 F3
Plomb du Cantal	29 E2
Plombières	27 D1
Plomin	70 B3
Plön	48 B2
Plonéour-Lanvern	22 A3
Płoń, Jez	49 F3
Płońsk	112 B1
Płoty	49 F2
Plouagat	22 C2
Plouaret	22 B2
Plouay	22 B3
Ploubalay	18 A4
Plœuc	22 C3
Ploudalmézeau	22 A2
Plouescat	22 B2
Plougasnou	22 B2
Plougastel-Daoulas	22 A3
Plougonven	22 B2
Plouguenast	22 C3
Plouha	22 C2
Plouigneau	22 B2
Ploumanach	22 B2
Plouzévédé	22 B2
Plovdiv	115 D3
Plumbridge	13 D2
Plunge	110 B3
Pl'ussa	111 D1
Pluvigner	22 C3
Plužine	76 A1
Plympton	8 C4
Plymstock	8 C4
Plzeň	53 E4
Po	60 C2
Poarta de Fier	114 C1
Pobierowo	49 F1
Poblet	37 F4
Pobrdđe	76 C1
Počep	111 F4
Pöchlarn	57 E2
Počinok	111 E3
Počitelj	75 F2
Pocking	56 C2
Poćuta	72 C4
Pódareš	77 F3
Podbořany	53 E3
Podčetrtek	70 C2
Podensac	28 B2
Podersdorf	57 F3
Podgajci Posavski	72 B3
Podgarič	71 D2
Podgora	75 E2
Podgorač (Hrvatska)	71 F2
Podgorac (Srbija)	73 E3
Podgrad	70 A3
Podhum	75 E1
Podjuchy	49 E2
Podkoren	70 A1
Podlugovi	71 F4
Podnovlje	71 F3
Podogorá	82 C3
Podohóri	80 B2
Podol'sk	111 F2
Podol'skaja Vozvyšennost'	113 D3
Podpec	70 B2
Podrašnica	71 E4
Podravska Slatina	71 E2
Podromanija	72 B4
Podsreda	70 C2
Podsused	70 C2
Podturen	71 D1
Podujevo	77 D1
Podunavci	73 D4
Poel	48 C2
Poganovo	77 E1
Poggibonsi	60 C4
Poggio Imperiale	64 C2
Poggio Mirteto	63 E2
Poggio Renatico	61 D2
Poggio Rusco	60 C2
Pöggstall	57 E2
Pogoniani	78 B4
Pogradec	77 D4
Pohja	107 E3
Pohja-Lankila	103 F3
Pohjaslahti (Keski-Suomen Lääni)	102 C3
Pohjaslahti (Lapin Lääni)	99 D2
Pohjois-Karjalan Lääni	103 F2
Pohořelice	57 F1
Pohorje	70 B1
Poiana Brașov	113 D4
Poio	34 A2
Poiré, le	24 B3
Poirino	31 F2
Poissons	20 C4
Poitiers	25 D3
Pöitsamaa	110 C2
Poix	19 E2
Poix-Terron	20 B2
Pojate	73 E4
Pojo	107 E3
Pokka	95 E3
Poklečani	75 E1
Pokljuka	70 A2
Pokupsko	70 C3
Polače	75 E2
Polacra, Pta de la	44 C4
Pola de Allande	34 C1
Pola de Gordón, la	35 D2
Pola de Laviana	35 D2
Pola de Lena	35 D2
Pola de Siero	35 D1
Polán	40 A3
Polcenigo	59 E3
Połczyn-Zdrój	110 A4
Polegate	10 C3
Poles	113 D1
Polesella	61 D2
Polessk	110 B4
Polhov Gradec	70 A2
Policastro	67 D1
Policastro, Golfo di	67 D2
Police	49 E2
Poličnik	74 C1
Policoro	65 D4
Polidéndri	84 B4
Polídrossos	83 E3
Poliégos, N	88 B4
Poliégou Folegándrou, Stenó	88 B4
Polígiros	80 A3
Polignano a Mare	65 E3
Poligny	27 D3
Polihnítos	85 F3
Polikárpi	79 E2
Polikástano	78 C3
Polikastro	79 F2
Polímilos	79 E3
Polinéri (Makedonía)	79 D4
Polinéri (Thessalía)	82 C2
Polipótamo	79 D3
Polipótamos	84 C4
Políraho	79 E4
Polirinía	90 B3
Polis, M	77 D4
Políssito	81 D2
Polistena	67 E4
Polithéa	82 C1
Politiká	84 A4
Poljana (Slovenija)	70 B1
Poljana (Srbija)	73 D3
Poljčane	70 C1
Polje	71 E3
Poljica	75 E2
Poljice	71 F4
Polla	64 C4
Pölläkkä	103 E2
Pöllau	57 E4
Polle	52 A1
Pollença	45 F2
Pollfoss	100 B3
Pollino, Mte	67 E2
Pollos	35 E4
Polmak	95 E2
Polock	111 D3
Polonnoje	113 D2
Polperro	8 B4
Poltava	113 F2
Polvijärvi	103 F2
Polzela	70 B2
Pont-à-Mousson	21 D3
Pontão	38 B2
Pontardawe	8 C2
Pontarddulais	8 C2
Pontarion	25 E4
Pontarlier	27 D3
Pontassieve	61 D3
Pontaubault	18 B4
Pont-Audemer	19 D3
Pontaumur	26 A4
Pont-Aven	22 B3
Pont Canavese	31 E1
Pontcharra	31 D1
Pontchartrain	19 E4
Pontchâteau	23 D4
Pont-Croix	22 A3
Pont-d'Ain	26 C4
Pont-de-Beauvoisin, le	30 C1
Pont-de-Chéruy	26 C4
Pont-de-Claix, le	30 C2
Pont-de-Dore	26 A4
Pont-de-l'Arche	19 E3
Pont-de-Montvert, le	29 F3
Pont-de-Roide	27 E2
Pont-de-Salars	29 E3
Pont-d'Espagne	37 E2
Pont de Suert	37 F2
Pont-de-Vaux	26 C3
Pont-de-Veyle	26 C4
Pont-d'Oléron	28 A1
Pont-d'Ouilly	18 C4
Pont-du-Château	26 A4
Pont-du-Gard	30 B3
Ponte Arche	58 C3
Ponteareas	34 A3
Pontebba	59 F2
Pontecagnano	64 B4
Ponte Caldelas	34 A2
Ponteceno	60 B2
Ponte Ceso	34 A1
Pontecorvo	64 A3
Ponte da Barca	34 A3
Pontedecimo	60 A3
Ponte de Lima	34 A3
Pontedera	60 C4
Ponte de Sor	38 B3
Pontedeume	34 B1
Ponte di Legno	58 C3
Ponte di Piave	59 E4
Pontefract	7 D2
Pontelandolfo	64 B3
Ponte-Leccia	33 F3
Pontenelle Alpi	59 E3
Pont-en-Royans	30 C1
Ponte San Pietro	60 B1
Pontet, le	30 C4
Ponte Tresa	58 A4
Pontevico	60 B1
Pontfaverger-Moronvilliers	20 B3
Pontgibaud	29 E1
Pontigny	26 B1
Pontinia	63 F3
Pontinvrea	31 F2
Pontivy	22 C3
Pont-l'Abbé	22 A3
Pont-l'Evêque	19 D3
Pontlevoy	25 E2
Pontoise	19 E3
Pontones	44 B2
Pontón, Pto del	35 E2
Pontoon	12 B2
Pontorson	18 B4
Pontremoli	60 B3
Pontresina	58 B3
Pontrieux	22 C2
Pontrilas	9 D2
Ponts	37 F3
Pont-Ste-Maxence	19 F3
Pont-St-Esprit	30 B3
Pont St-Martin	31 E1
Pont-St-Vincent	21 D4
Pont-Scorff	22 A3
Ponts-de-Cé, les	23 E4
Pontsenni	8 C1
Pont-sur-Yonne	26 A1
Pontvallain	23 F4
Pontypool	9 D2
Pontypridd	8 C2
Ponza, I	63 F4
Ponziane, I	63 F4
Poole	9 E3
Poperinge	50 A3
Popinci	72 C3
Popoli	64 A2
Popovac	73 E4
Popovača	71 D2
Popova Šapka	77 D3
Popov Most	76 A1
Popovo	115 E2
Poppenhausen	52 B4
Poppi	61 D3
Poprad	112 B3
Porcari	60 C3
Porcuna	43 F2
Pordenone	59 E3
Poreč	70 A3
Pori	107 D1
Porjus	98 B2
Porkkalanselkä	107 E3
Porma, Emb del	35 E2
Porma, R	35 E2
Pornainen	107 F2
Pörnbach	55 F2
Pornic	24 A2
Pornichet	24 A2
Póros (Kefaloniá)	86 A1
Póros (Lefkáda)	82 B3
Póros (Póros)	87 F2
Póros, N	87 F2
Porozina	70 B3
Pörpi	81 D2
Porquerolles	31 D4
Porrentruy	27 E2
Porretta Terme	60 C3
Porriño	34 A3
Porsangen	95 E1
Porsangerhalvøya	95 D1
Porsgrunn	104 C3
Pörshöfn	96 C1
Portadown	13 D2
Portaferry	13 E2
Portaje, Emb de	39 D3
Porta, la	33 F3
Portalegre	38 C3
Portalé, Pto del	37 D2
Portalrubio	41 D2
Portariá	83 F2
Portarlington	13 D4
Port Askaig	4 B2
Portavogie	13 E2
Port-Bacarès	32 B2
Portbail	18 B3
Portbou	32 C3
Port Charlotte	4 A2
Port, Col du	37 F2
Port-Cros	31 D4
Port-de-Bouc	30 C4
Porte, Col de	30 C1
Port-Einon	8 C2
Portella Femmina Morta	69 D3
Port Ellen	4 A2
Portelo	34 C3
Port-en-Bessin	18 C3
Port Erin	6 A1
Pórtes	87 F2
Portet-d'Aspet, Col de	37 F2
Portezuelo	39 D3
Port Glasgow	4 C2
Portglenone	13 E1
Porthcawl	8 C2
Porthmadog	6 A3
Porthmós Elafoníssou	90 A1
Portici	64 B4
Portile de Fier	114 C1
Portilla de la Reina	35 E2
Portillo	35 E4
Portillo de la Canda	34 C3
Portillo de Padornelo	34 C3
Portillo, Pto del	39 E2
Portimão	42 A2
Portimo	99 D2
Portinatx, Cala de	45 D3
Portishead	9 D2
Port-Joinville	24 A3
Port Láirge	15 D4
Portland, Bill of	9 D4
Port-la-Nouvelle	32 B2
Portlaoise	13 D4
Port-Leucate	32 B2
Port-Louis	22 B4
Portman	45 D3
Port-Manech	22 B3
Portmarnock	13 E4
Portnacroish	4 B1
Portnaguran	2 B2
Portnahaven	4 A2
Port-Navalo	22 C4
Porto (F)	33 E3
Porto (P)	34 A4
Porto Azzuro	62 C1
Pórto Carrás	80 B4
Porto Ceresio	58 A4
Porto Cervo	66 B1
Porto Cesareo	65 F4
Porto Cristo	45 F3
Porto de Envalira	32 A2
Porto de Lagos	42 A2
Porto de Mós	38 A3
Portodemouros, Emb de	34 B2
Porto do Barqueiro	34 B1
Porto do Son	34 A2
Porto Empedocle	68 B4
Portoferraio	62 C1
Portofino	60 A3
Porto Garibaldi	61 D2
Porto, G de	33 E3
Pórto Germenó	87 E1
Portogruaro	59 E4
Portohéli	87 E2
Pórto Kágio	87 D4
Pörtom	102 B2
Portomaggiore	61 D2
Portomarin	34 B2
Porto-Maurizio	31 F3
Porto Moniz	42 A3
Portomouro	34 B2
Portonovo	34 A2
Porto Petro	45 F3
Porto Pino	66 B4
Porto Recanati	61 F4
Porto Rotondo	66 C1
Portorož	70 A3
Porto San Giorgio	61 F4
Porto Sant' Elpidio	61 F4
Porto Santo	42 A3
Porto Santo, I de	42 A3
Porto Santo Stefano	63 D2
Portoscuso	66 A4
Porto Tolle	61 D2
Porto Torres	66 A2
Porto-Vecchio	33 F4
Portovenere	60 B3
Portpatrick	4 B3
Portree	2 B3
Portrush	13 D1
Port-Ste-Marie	28 C3
Port-St-Louis	30 B4
Port St Mary	6 A1
Portsalon	13 D1
Pörtschach	70 A1
Portsmouth	9 F3
Portstewart	13 D1
Port-sur-Saône	27 D1
Port Talbot	8 C2
Porttipahdan tekojärvi	95 E4
Portugalete	36 B1
Portumna	12 C4
Port-Vendres	32 B2
Port William	4 C4
Porvoo	107 F2
Porvoonjoki	107 F2
Porzuna	40 A4
Posada	66 C2
Posadas	43 E2
Pöschenhöhe	56 C3
Pošechonje-Volodarsk	111 F1
Posedarje	74 C1
Posets, Pico	37 E2
Posio	99 E2
Positano	64 B4
Poßneck	52 C3
Possídi	80 A4
Possidonia	88 B2
Posta	63 F1
Postavy	111 D3
Postira	75 D2
Postojna	70 B2
Postojnska jama	70 A2
Poštorná	57 F1
Posušje	75 E1
Potamí	80 C1
Potamiá	87 D3
Potamiés	91 E4
Potamós (Andikíthira)	90 A2
Potamós (Kíthira)	90 A1
Potamoúla	82 C3
Potenza	64 C4
Potenza R	61 E4
Potenza Picenza	61 F4
Potes	35 E2
Potídea, N.	80 A4
Potigny	18 C3
Potoci	75 F1
Potok	71 D2
Potós	80 C3
Potpećko jez	76 B1
Potsdam	49 D4
Pottenstein	57 E3
Potters Bar	9 F2
Pöttmes	55 F2
Potton	9 F1
Pouancé	23 D4
Pougues-les-Eaux	26 A2
Pouilly (Nièvre)	26 A2
Pouilly (Rhône)	26 B4
Pouilly-en-Auxois	26 C2
Poulaphouca Reservoir	13 D4
Poúlari, Akr	92 C1
Pouldu, le	22 B3
Pouliguen, le	24 A2
Poúlithra	87 E3
Poúnda	88 C3
Poúnda, Akr	84 B4
Pournári	83 E2
Pournári, Teh L	82 C2
Pourniás, Kólpos	85 D1
Pourri, Mt	31 D1
Poussu	99 F3
Pouyastruc	37 E1
Pouzauges	24 C3
Pouzin, le	30 B2
Považská Bystrica	112 B3
Poveda	40 C2
Povlja	75 E2
Povljana	70 C4
Povljen	72 C4
Povoa de Lanhoso	34 A4
Póvoa de Varzim	34 A4
Powerscourt	13 D4
Powys	9 D1
Poysdorf	57 F2
Pöytyä	107 D2
Poza de la Sal	36 A2
Požarevac	73 D3
Požega	72 C4
Požeranje	77 D2
Poznań	112 A1
Pozo Alcón	44 B2
Pozoblanco	43 F1
Pozo Cañada	44 C1
Pozo de Guadalajara	40 B2
Pozo Higuera	44 C3
Pozohondo	44 C1
Pozondón	41 D2
Pozal, Pto	35 F2
Pozuelo (Castilla-la-Mancha)	44 C1
Pozuelo (Extremadura)	39 D2
Pozuelo de Calatrava	40 A4
Pozzallo	69 D4
Pozzomaggiore	66 B2
Pozzuoli	64 A4
Pozzuolo	59 F3
Prábichl	57 D3
Prača	76 A1
Prachatice	56 C1
Prada, Emb de	34 C3
Pradarena, Pso di	60 B3
Pradelles	29 F2
Prádena	36 A4

Prades (E) 37 F4
Prades (F) 32 B2
Prado del Rey 43 D3
Pradoluengo 36 A2
Prägraten 59 E2
Praha 53 F4
Prahecq 24 C4
Prahova 115 D1
Prahovo 73 F3
Praia a Mare 67 E2
Praia da Barra 38 B1
Praia da Rocha 42 A2
Praia da Vieira 38 A2
Praia de Mira 38 B1
Praia de Santa
Cruz 38 A3
Praia de Tocha 38 B2
Prali 31 E2
Pralognan 31 D1
Pra-Loup 31 E2
Prámanda 82 C2
Pramollo, Pso di 59 F2
Prangío 81 F1
Pranjani 72 C4
Prapatnica 75 D1
Prassiá 83 D2
Prassiés 90 C3
Præstø 108 C4
Prat de Compte 41 F1
Pratella 64 A3
Prati di Tivo 63 F1
Prato (Toscana) 60 C3
Prato (Umbria) 63 E1
Pratola Peligna 64 A2
Pratomagno 61 D4
Prato-Sornico 58 A3
Prats-de-Mollo 32 B3
Pravdinsk 110 B4
Pravia 35 D1
Praz 27 E4
Prebold 70 B2
Précy-sous-Thil 26 B2
Predappio 61 D3
Predazzo 59 D3
Preddvor 70 B2
Predeal 113 D4
Predejane 77 E1
Predel 70 A2
Predela 115 D3
Predil, Pso di 59 F2
Predjama 70 A2
Predoi 59 D2
Predošćica 70 B3
Pré-en-Pail 23 E3
Preetz 48 B2
Pregarten 57 D2
Preiner Gscheid 57 E3
Prekaja 71 D4
Prekestolen 104 A3

Preko 74 C1
Preljina 73 D4
Prelog 71 D1
Preločica 71 D2
Premantura 70 A4
Prémery 26 A2
Premià de Mar 32 B4
Premilcuore 61 D3
Premnitz 49 D4
Premuda 74 B1
Premuda I 74 B1
Prenj 75 F1
Prenjas 77 D4
Prenzlau 49 E3
Prepolac 77 D1
Přerov 112 A3
Prerow 48 C1
Pré-St-Didier 27 E4
Preševo 77 E2
Presjeka 76 B2
Preslav 115 E2
Presolana, Pso
della 58 B4
Prešov 112 B3
Prespansko Ez 77 D4
Pressath 53 D4
Pressbaum 57 E2
Prestatyn 6 B2
Presteigne 9 D1
Preste, la 32 B3
Prestfoss 104 C3
Přeštice 56 C1
Preston 6 B2
Prestonpans 5 D2
Prestwick 4 C2
Pretoro 64 A2
Prettau 59 D2
Prettin 53 D1
Pretzsch 53 D1
Preuilly 25 D3
Préveli 90 C4
Préveza 82 B2
Préveza (Nomos) 82 B2
Prevršac 71 D3
Prezid 70 B3
Pribini 71 E4
Priboj (Bosna i
Hercegovina) 72 B3
Priboj (Srbija) 76 B1
Příbram 53 F4
Priego 40 C2
Priego de
Córdoba 43 F3
Prien 56 B3
Prienai 110 C4
Prievidza 112 B3
Prigradica 75 E2
Priboj 70 C3
Prijedor 71 D3

Prijepolje 76 B1
Prilep 77 E3
Prilike 73 D4
Priluka 75 E1
Priluki 113 F1
Primaube, la 29 E3
Primel-Trégastel 22 B2
Primišlje 70 C3
Primolano 59 D3
Primorsk 111 D1
Primošten 75 D2
Primstal 54 B1
Princetown 8 C3
Prinés 90 C3
Prinos 80 C3
Prior, C 34 B1
Prip' at' 112 C1
Prisad 77 E3
Prislop 113 D3
Prisoje 75 E1
Priština 77 D2
Pritzerbe 49 D4
Pritzier 48 B3
Pritzwalk 48 C3
Privas 30 B2
Priverno 63 F3
Privlaka (Vincovci) 71 F2
Privlaka (Zadar) 70 C4
Prizren 77 D2
Prizzi 68 B3
Prnjavor (Bosna i
Hercegovina) 71 E3
Prnjavor (Srbija) 72 B3
Proaza 35 D1
Probištip 77 E2
Probstzella 52 C3
Procida 64 A4
Pródromos 83 F4
Proença-a-Nova 38 B3
Proevska Banja 77 E2
Profitis Ilías 93 E1
Profondeville 50 C4
Próhoma 79 F3
Prokletije 76 C2
Prokópi 84 A3
Prokuplje 77 D1
Prolom 77 D1
Prómahi 79 E2
Promahónas 80 A1
Promina, V. 75 D1
Promíri 84 A2
Pronsfeld 51 D4
Propriano 33 F4
Proskinás 83 F4
Prosna 112 A2
Prossedi 63 F3
Prossílio 81 D2
Prossotsáni 80 B2
Prostějov 112 A3

Próti 80 B2
Próti, N 86 B3
Protoklíssio 81 F1
Prötzel 49 E4
Proussós 83 D3
Provatónas 81 F2
Provence, Canal
de 30 C4
Provenchères 21 E4
Provins 20 A4
Prozor 75 E1
Prudhoe 5 E3
Prukljansko jezero 75 D1
Prüm 51 D4
Pruna 43 E3
Prunetta 60 C3
Prut 113 D3
Prut 113 E4
Pružany 112 C1
Prvić 70 B4
Przasnysz 112 B1
Przełęcz
Dukielska 112 C3
Przemyśl 112 C2
Przybiernów 49 F2
Psaca 77 E2
Psahná 84 B4
Psáka 82 B2
Psális, Akr 88 A4
Psará 85 E4
Psarádes 78 C2
Psará, N 85 E4
Psári (Arkadía) 86 C2
Psári (Korinthía) 87 D1
Psári (Mt) 80 C3
Psáthi 88 B4
Psathópirgos 83 D4
Psathotópi 82 C2
Psérimos, N 89 F3
Psihikó 83 E2
Psihró 91 E4
Psínthos 93 F1
Pskov 111 D2
Pskovskoje
Ozero 111 D2
Ps'ol 113 F2
Pšov 53 E3
Psunj 71 E2
Ptéléa 80 C2
Ptéri 83 D2
Ptolemaïda 79 D3
Ptóo 84 A4
Ptuj 70 C1
Puchberg 57 E3
Pučišća 75 E2
Puckeridge 9 F2
Puçol 41 E3
Pudasjärvi 99 E3
Puebla de Alcocer 39 E4

Puebla de
Almenara 40 B3
Puebla de Beleña 40 B1
Puebla de
Benifasar 41 F2
Puebla de Don
Fadrique 44 B2
Puebla de D.
Rodrigo 39 F4
Puebla de
Guzmán 42 C2
Puebla de la
Calzada 39 D4
Puebla de la Reina 39 D4
Puebla del
Caramiñal 34 A2
Puebla de Lillo 35 E2
Puebla de Obando 39 D3
Puebla de
Sanabria 34 C3
Puebla de Trives 34 C3
Puebla Tornesa 41 F3
Pueblica de V. 35 D3
Puente de Domingo
Flórez 34 C3
Puente de Génave 44 B1
Puente de los
Fierros 35 D2
Puente Genil 43 F3
Puente la Reina 36 C2
Puente la Reina
de Jaca 37 D2
Puente Nuevo,
Emb de 43 E1
Puentes, Emb de 44 C2
Puentes Viejas,
Emb de 40 B1
Puente Viesgo 35 F2
Puerto Castilla 39 E2
Puerto de Alcudia 45 F2
Puerto de Andratx 45 E3
Puerto de la Cruz 42 B4
Puerto de la
Encina 43 E3
Puerto del Rosario 42 C4
Puerto de
Mazarrón 45 D3
Puerto de
Pollenca 45 F2
Puerto de
San Vicente 39 F3
Puerto de Sóller 45 E2
Puerto Lápice 40 B4
Puertollano 44 A1
Puerto Lumbreras 44 C3
Puerto Real 43 D4
Puerto Serrano 43 E3
Pugets-Théniers 31 E3

Puglia 65 D3
Puhos (Oulun
Lääni) 99 E3
Puhos (Pohjois-
Karjalan Lääni) 103 F3
Puhosjärvi 99 E3
Puhovac 271 F4
Puigcerda 32 A3
Puig Major 45 E2
Puignal 32 A2
Puig-reig 32 A3
Puigsacalm 32 B3
Puiseaux 25 F1
Puisserguier 30 A4
Pujols 28 B2
Pukë 76 C3
Pukiš 72 B3
Pukkila 107 F2
Pula (I) 66 B4
Pula (YU) 70 A4
Pulaj 76 B3
Puławy 112 C2
Pulborough 10 C3
Pulkau 57 E2
Pulkkila 99 D4
Pulpi 44 C3
Pulsnitz 53 E2
Pultusk 112 B1
Punat 70 B3
Punkaharju 103 F3
Punkalaidun 107 E2
Punta Ala 62 C1
Puntagorda 42 A4
Punta Križa 70 B4
Punta Raisi 68 B2
Punta Umbria 42 C3
Puokio 99 E4
Puolanka 99 E4
Purbach 57 F3
Purchena 44 B3
Purgstall 57 E3
Purkersdorf 57 E2
Purmerend 16 C2
Purnu 103 D3
Purullena 44 B3
Puruvesi 103 F3
Puškin 111 D1
Püspökladány 112 C4
Pustoška 111 D2
Pusula 107 E2
Puszcza 112 C1
Putanges 18 C4
Putbus 49 D1
Putgarten 49 D1
Putignano 65 E3
Putinci 72 C2
Putivl' 113 F1
Putlitz 48 C3
Puttelange 21 E3

Puttgarden 48 B1
Puula 103 D3
Puumala 103 E3
Puy de Dôme 29 E1
Puy-de-Dôme
(Dépt) 29 E1
Puy de Sancy 29 E1
Puy-en-Velay, le 30 A2
Puy-Guillaume 26 A4
Puylaurens 29 D4
Puy-l'Evêque 29 D3
Puymirol 28 C3
Puymorens, Col
de 32 A2
Pwllheli 6 A3
Pyhä-Häkki 103 D2
Pyhäjärvi
(Hameen Lääni) 107 E1
Pyäjärvi (Oulun
Lääni) 103 D1
Pyhäjärvi (Pohjois-
Karjalan Lääni) 103 F3
Pyhäjärvi (Turun ja
Porin Lääni) 107 D2
Pyhäjärvi L 103 D1
Pyhäjoki (Oulun
Lääni) 99 D4
Pyhäjoki (Turun ja
Porin Lääni) 107 D2
Pyhäjoki R 99 D4
Pyhälto 103 F4
Pyhäntä
(Piipola) 103 D1
Pyhäntä (Ristijärvi) 99 E4
Pyhäranta 107 D2
Pyhäsalmi 103 D1
Pyhäselkä 107 F2
Pyhäselkä L 103 F2
Pyhätunturi 99 D2
Pyhatunturi 99 E2
Pyhävuori 102 C2
Pyhityvaara 99 E3
Pyhrnpaß 57 D3
Pyhtää 107 F2
Pyla 28 A2
Pylkönmäki 103 D2
Pyrénées 37 E2
Pyrénées-
Atlantiques 28 A4
Pyrénées-
Orientales 32 B2
Pyrénées, Parc
Nat des 37 E2
Pyrzyce 49 F3
Pyttis 107 F2

Q

Qaf'e Shllahut 76 C3
Qaf'e Shtamës 76 C4
Quakenbrück 17 E2
Quarré-les-
Tombes 26 B2
Quarteira 42 B3
Quarto d'Altino 61 D1
Quartu San Elena 66 B4

Quatre Chemins 24 B3
Quatretonda 41 E4
Quedlinburg 52 C2
Queenborough 11 D2
Queen Elizabeth
Forest Park 4 C2
Queensferry 6 B2
Quejigares, Pto de 40 A4
Queluz 38 A4
Queralbs 32 B3

Querfurt 52 C2
Quérigut 32 A2
Quero 40 B3
Quesada 44 B2
Quesnoy, le 20 A2
Questembert 22 C4
Quettehou 18 B3
Quiberon 22 C4
Quickborn 48 A2
Quiévrain 50 B4

Quigley's Point 13 D1
Quillan 32 B2
Quillane, Col de la 32 A2
Quillebeuf 19 D3
Quimper 22 B3
Quimperlé 22 B3
Quincinetto 31 E1
Quincoces de
Yuso 36 A1
Quingey 27 D2

Quintana
(Andalucía) 43 E2
Quintana
(Extremadura) 39 E4
Quintana del
Puente 35 F3
Quintana Martín
Galíndez 36 A2
Quintanar de la
Orden 40 B3

Quintanar de la
Sierra 36 B3
Quintanar del Rey 40 C4
Quintana
Redonda 36 B3
Quintanilha 34 C4
Quintanilla de
Onésimo 35 F4
Quintin 22 C3
Quinto 37 D4

Quinzano d'Oglio 60 B1
Quipar, R 44 C2
Quiroga 34 C2
Quissac 30 B3
Qukës 77 D4
Quoich, L 2 C4

R

Raab 56 C2
Raab *R* 57 E4
Raabs 57 E1
Raahe 99 D4
Raajärvi 99 D2
Rääkkylä 103 F2
Raalte 17 D2
Raanujärvi 99 D2
Raasay 2 B3
Raasay, Sd of 2 B3
Raattama 95 D4
Rab 70 B4
Rab 70 B4
Rába 112 A4
Rabac 70 B3
Rábade 34 B1
Rabastens 29 D4
Rabastens-de-
 Bigorre 37 E1
Rabat 68 B4
Rabe 72 C1
Rabka 112 B3
Rabrovo
 (Makedonija) 77 F3
Rabrovo (Srbija) 73 E3
Rača (Kragujevac) 73 D3
Rača (Radan) 77 D1
Racconigi 31 E2
Rače 70 C1
Rachov 112 C3
Racibórz 112 A2
Račinovci 72 B3
Račišće 75 E2
Radalj 72 B3
Radan 77 D1
Rădăuti 113 D3
Radbuza 56 B1
Rade 48 A3
Råde 105 D3
Radeberg 53 E2
Radebeul 53 E2
Radeburg 53 E2
Radeče 70 B2
Radechov 112 C2
Radenci 70 C1
Radenthein 59 F2
Radevowald 17 E4
Radici, Pso delle 60 C3
Radicondoli 60 C4
Radika 77 D3
Radimlje 75 F2
Radiovce 77 D3
Radlje 70 B1
Radljevo 72 C3
Radnice 53 E4
Radohinës, Maj'e 76 C2
Radojevo 73 D1
Radom 112 B2
Radomsko 112 B2
Radomyšl' 113 E2
Radotin 53 F4
Radovče 76 B2
Radovici 76 B3
Radoviš 77 F3
Radovljica 70 A2
Radovnica 77 E2
Radøy 104 A2
Radstadt 59 F1
Radstädter
 Tauernpaß 59 F1
Radstock 9 D2
Raduša 75 E1
Radusa 77 D3
Radviliškis 110 C3
Radzyn' Podlaski 112 C2
Raesfeld 17 E3
Raffadali 68 B4
Rafina 88 A1
Ragama 39 F1
Raglan 9 D2
Rago 57 E4
Ragua, Pto de la 44 B3
Raguhn 53 D1
Ragunda 101 F2
Ragusa 69 D4
Rahden 17 F2
Ráhes 83 F3
Rahlstedt 48 B3
Raia, Rib de 38 B4
Rain 55 F2
Räisälä 99 E2
Raisduoddarhal'di 94 C2

Raisio 107 D2
Raittijärvi 94 C3
Rajac 73 F3
Raja-Jooseppi 95 F3
Rajamäki 107 E2
Rajince 77 E2
Raka 70 C2
Rakalj 70 A4
Rakitna 70 B2
Rakitnica 71 D2
Rakkestad 105 D3
Rakova Bara 73 E3
Rakovac 71 E3
Rakovica 70 C3
Rakovnik 53 E4
Rakvere 110 C1
Ralja 73 D3
Ram 73 D2
Ramacca 69 D3
Ramales de la
 Victoria 36 A1
Ramallosa 34 A2
Ramberg 97 E1
Rambervillers 21 D4
Rambouillet 19 E4
Rambucourt 20 C4
Ramno 77 D2
Ramnoús 84 B4
Ramor, L 13 D3
Ramsau 56 B4
Ramsau 59 F1
Ramsele 101 F2
Ramsey
 (Cambridge) 9 F1
Ramsey (I of Man) 6 A1
Ramsgate 11 D3
Ramsjö 101 E3
Ramstein 54 B1
Ramsund 94 B3
Ramundberget 101 D2
Ramvik 101 F2
Rana 97 D3
Ranalt 59 D2
Rance 22 C3
Randaberg 104 A3
Randak 104 B3
Randalstown 13 E2
Randan 26 A4
Randanne 29 E1
Randazzo 69 D3
Randers 108 B2
Randijaure 98 A2
Randow 49 E2
Randsfjorden 105 D2
Råneå 98 C3
Råneälven 98 B2
Rangsdorf 49 E4
Rankweil 58 B2
Rannoch, L 4 C1
Ranovac 73 E3
Rantasalmi 103 E3
Rantsila 99 D4
Ranua 99 D3
Raon-l'Etape 21 E4
Rapallo 60 A3
Rapolano Terme 61 D4
Rapolla 64 C3
Rapperswil 58 A2
Rapsáni 83 E1
Raptópoulo 86 C3
Raša 70 A3
Räsälä 103 E2
Raša *R* 70 A3
Rasbo 106 B3
Rascafría 40 A1
Rasdorf 52 B3
Raseiniai 110 C3
Rasimbegov Most 77 E4
Rasina 73 E4
Raška 76 C1
Rasno 75 E2
Raso, C 38 A4
Rasquera 41 F1
Rastatt 54 C2
Rastede 47 F3
Rastegai'sa 95 E2
Rastenberg 52 C2
Rastenfeld 57 E2
Rasueros 39 F1
Rätan 101 E3
Rateče 70 A1
Ratekau 48 B2
Rates 34 A4
Rathdowney 12 C4

Rathdrum 13 D4
Rathenow 49 D4
Rathfriland 13 E2
Rathkeale 14 B3
Rathlin I 13 E1
Rath Luirc 14 B3
Rathmelton 13 D1
Rathmore 14 B4
Rathmullan 13 D1
Raticosa, Pso della 61 D3
Ratingen 17 E4
Ratkovac 76 C2
Ratkovo 72 B2
Ratten 57 E3
Rattenberg 59 D1
Rattersdorf 57 F3
Rattray 5 D1
Rattray Head 3 E3
Rättvik 101 E4
Ratzeburg 48 B2
Raubling 56 B3
Raucourt-et-Flaba 20 C2
Raudanjoki 99 D2
Raudaskylä 102 C1
Raufarhöfn 96 C1
Raufoss 105 D2
Rauha 103 E4
Rauhamäki 103 D3
Rauland 104 B3
Rauma (N) 100 B3
Rauma (SF) 107 D2
Rauris 59 E1
Rautalampi 103 D2
Rautas 94 C4
Rautavaara 103 E1
Rautio 102 C1
Rautjärvi 103 F3
Ravan 71 F4
Ravanica 73 E4
Ravanjska 70 C4
Ravanusa 68 C4
Ravello 64 B4
Raven 71 D2
Ravenna 61 D2
Ravensbrück 49 D3
Ravensburg 55 D4
Ravna Dubrava 77 E1
Ravna Gora 70 B3
Ravna Reka 73 E3
Ravne na
 Koroškem 70 B1
Ravnište 77 D1
Ravnje 72 B3
Ravno 75 F2
Ravno Bučje 73 F4
Ravno, G. 75 E1
Rawicz 112 A2
Rawtenstall 6 C2
Rayleigh 11 D2
Rayol 31 D4
Räyrinki 102 C2
Ražana 72 C4
Ražanac 70 C4
Raždaginja 76 C1
Razelm 113 E4
Razgrad 115 E2
Razbojna 77 D1
Razlog 115 D3
Razlovci 77 F2
Raz, Pte du 22 A3
Reading 9 F2
Reales 43 E4
Réalmont 32 B1
Rebais 20 A4
Rebbenesøy 94 B2
Rebordelo 34 C4
Reç 76 C3
Recanati 61 F4
Recco 60 A3
Recey 26 C1
Rechnitz 57 F4
Rečica (SU) 111 E4
Rečica (YU) 70 C3
Recke 17 E2
Recklinghausen 17 E3
Recknitz 48 C2
Recoaro Terme 59 D4
Recuerda 36 A4
Recz 49 F2
Redange 21 D2
Red B 13 E1
Redcar 5 F4
Redditch 9 E1

Redhill 10 C3
Redon 23 D4
Redondela 34 A3
Redondo 38 C4
Redruth 8 B4
Ree, L 12 C3
Rees 17 D3
Reeth 6 C1
Refsnes 94 A3
Reftele 109 D2
Rega 49 F2
Regalbuto 69 D3
Regen 56 B2
Regensburg 56 B2
Regenstauf 56 B2
Reggello 61 D4
Reggio di Calabria 67 E4
Reggiolo 60 C2
Reggio nell' Emilia 60 C2
Reghin 113 D4
Regnitz 55 E1
Reguengos de
 Monsaraz 42 B1
Rehau 53 D4
Rehburg-
 Loccum 48 A4
Rehden 17 F2
Rehna 48 B2
Reichenau (A) 57 E3
Reichenau (CH) 58 B2
Reichenbach
 (Dresden) 53 F2
Reichenbach
 (Karl-Marx-Stadt) 53 D3
Reichertshofen 55 F2
Reichshoffen 21 E3
Reigate 10 C3
Reignier 27 D4
Ré, Ile de 24 B4
Reillanne 30 C3
Reims 20 B3
Reinach 27 F2
Reinbek 48 B3
Reinberg 49 D1
Reine 97 E1
Reinfeld 48 B2
Reinheim 54 C1
Reinli 104 C2
Reinosa 35 F2
Reinøy 94 C2
Reisaelva 94 C3
Reischenhart 56 B3
Reisjärvi 103 D1
Reit im Winkl 56 B4
Reitzenhain 53 E3
Reka 70 A3
Rekovac 73 E4
Rekvanlahti 99 D4
Remagen 51 E4
Rémalard 23 F3
Remeskylä 103 D1
Remich 21 D2
Remiremont 27 D1
Remolinos 36 C3
Remouchamps 51 D4
Remoulins 30 B3
Rempstone 7 D3
Remscheid 17 E4
Rémuzat 30 C2
Rena 105 D2
Renaix 50 B3
Renazé 23 E4
Renchen 54 C3
Rende 67 E2
Rendina
 (Makedonía) 80 B3
Rendina
 (Thessalía) 83 D3
Rendsburg 48 A2
Renginio 83 F3
Rengsdorf 51 E4
Reni 113 E4
Renish Pt 2 A3
Renko 107 E2
Renkum 17 D3
Rennebu 100 C2
Rennerod 51 F3
Rennes 23 D3
Rennes-les-Bains 32 B2
Rennesøy 104 A3
Rennweg 59 F2
Reno 61 D2
Rensjön 94 C4
Renwez 20 B2

Réole, la 28 B2
Replot 102 B2
Replotfjärden 102 B2
Repojoki 95 E3
Reposaari 102 B3
République, Col de
 la 30 B1
Repvag 95 E1
Requena 41 D4
Réquista 29 E3
Rerik 48 C2
Resanovci 71 D4
Resavica 73 E3
Reschenpaß 58 C2
Resen
 (Makedonija) 77 D4
Resen (Srbija) 77 E2
Resende 34 B4
Resia, Pso di 58 C2
Resita 114 C1
Resko 49 F2
Resmo 109 E3
Resna 76 B3
Resnik 73 D3
Ressons 19 F3
Restafjorden 94 C2
Restelica 77 D3
Resuttano 68 C3
Retezatului, M 114 C1
Rethel 20 B3
Rethem 48 A4
Rethen 52 B1
Réthimno 90 C3
Réthimno
 (Nomos) 90 C3
Retiers 23 D3
Retortillo, Emb de 43 E2
Retuerta 41 D1
Retuerta del
 Bullaque 39 F3
Retuerta, Emb de 36 A3
Retz 57 E2
Reuilly 25 E3
Reus 37 F4
Reusel 16 C4
Reuss 27 F2
Reuterstadt-
 Stavenhagen 49 D2
Reutlingen 55 D3
Reutte 58 C1
Revard, Mt 27 D4
Revel 29 D4
Revesbotn 95 D1
Revigny 20 C4
Revin 20 B2
Řevničov 53 F3
Revolcadores 44 C2
Revonlahti 99 D4
Revsnes 104 B1
Rewal 49 F1
Reyðarfjörður 96 C2
Reykjavik 96 A2
Rēzekne 111 D2
Rezzato 60 B1
Rezzoaglio 60 A3
Rgotina 73 F3
Rhaeadr 8 C1
Rhayader 8 C1
Rheda-
 Wiedenbrück 17 F3
Rhede 17 D3
Rhein 17 D3
Rheinbach 51 E4
Rheinberg 17 D3
Rheinböllen 54 B1
Rheine 17 E2
Rheinfelden (CH) 27 F2
Rheinfelden (D) 54 C4
Rheinhausen 17 D3
Rheinland-Pfalz 51 E4
Rheinsberg 49 D3
Rheinwaldhorn 58 B3
Rhêmes N.D. 31 E1
Rhenen 16 C3
Rheydt 17 D4
Rhinau 21 E4
Rhinow 49 D4
Rho 60 A1
Rhondda 8 C2
Rhône (Dépt) 26 B4
Rhône à Sète,
 Canal du 30 B3
Rhosneigr 6 A2

Rhossili 8 C2
Rhüden 52 B1
Rhum 2 B4
Rhum, Sd of 2 B4
Rhune, la 28 A4
Rhuthun 6 B3
Rhyl 6 B2
Rhynern 17 E3
Rhynie 3 E4
Riaillé 23 D4
Riákia 79 E3
Rial 34 A2
Riaño 35 E2
Riaño, Emb de 35 E2
Rians 30 C4
Riansares R 40 B3
Rianxo 34 A2
Riaza 36 A4
Riba de Saelices 40 C1
Riba de Santiuste 36 B4
Ribadavia 34 B3
Ribadelago 34 C3
Ribadesella 35 E1
Ribarci 77 E2
Ribariće 76 C1
Ribarska Banja 73 E4
Ribas de Campos 35 E3
Ribas de Sil 34 B2
Ribatejo 38 B3
Ribble 6 C2
Ribe 108 A3
Ribeauvillé 27 E1
Ribécourt 19 F3
Ribeira de Pena 34 B4
Ribeira, Emb de la 34 B1
Ribemont 20 A2
Ribera 68 B3
Ribérac 28 C1
Ribera de Cardós 32 A2
Ribera del Fresno 43 D1
Ribes de Freser 32 B3
Ribiers 30 C3
Ribnica (Bosna i
 Hercegovina) 71 F4
Ribnica (Kočevje) 70 B2
Ribnica (Postojna) 70 A3
Ribnica na
 Pohorju 70 B1
Ribnik 70 C2
Ribnitz-
 Damgarten 48 C1
Ribolla 62 C1
Říčany 53 F4
Riccia 64 B3
Riccione 61 E3
Riceys, les 26 B1
Richelieu 25 D3
Richmond
 (London) 9 F2
Richmond (Yorks) 6 C1
Richtenberg 49 D1
Rickling 48 A2
Ricla 36 C4
Ricobayo, Emb de 35 D4
Riddica 72 B1
Riec 22 B3
Ried
 (Oberösterreich) 56 C3
Ried (Tirol) 58 C2
Riedenburg 55 F2
Riedlingen 55 D3
Riegel 54 C3
Riegersburg 57 F4
Riego de la Vega 35 D3
Riesa 53 E2
Riesi 68 C4
Riestedt 52 C2
Rietberg 17 F3
Rieti 63 E2
Rieumes 29 D4
Rieupeyroux 29 E3
Rieux 37 F1
Riez 31 D3
Riezlern 58 B2
Rīga 110 C2
Rigáni 83 D4
Rigeo 83 E2
Rigi 58 A2
Rignac 29 E3
Rignano Flaminio 63 E2
Rihéa 87 E3
Riihimäki 107 E2

Riisitunturi 99 E2
Riistavesi 103 E2
Riječa 72 B4
Rijeka 70 B3
Rijeka Crnojevića 76 B3
Rijssen 17 D2
Rila 115 D3
Rila *Mts* 115 D3
Rillo 41 D2
Rillo de Gallo 40 C1
Rimavská-
 Sobota 112 B3
Rimbo 106 B3
Rimini 61 E3
Rîmnicu Sărat 113 E4
Rîmnicu Vîlcea 115 D1
Rîmnio 79 E4
Rimske Toplice 70 B2
Rincón de la
 Victoria 43 F4
Rincón de Soto 36 C2
Rindal 100 C2
Ringaskiddy 14 C4
Ringe 108 B4
Ringebu 100 C3
Ringford 4 C3
Ringkøbing 108 A3
Ringkøbing
 Fjord 108 A3
Ring of Kerry 14 A4
Ringsaker 105 D2
Ringstad 104 A1
Ringsted 108 C3
Ringvassøy 94 B2
Ringwood 9 E3
Rinia, N 88 C2
Rinkaby 109 D3
Rinns Pt 4 A2
Rinteln 52 A1
Rinvyle Pt 12 A3
Río 83 D4
Riocavado de la
 Sierra 36 A3
Riogordo 43 F3
Riola Sardo 66 A3
Riolo Terme 61 D3
Riom 26 A4
Riomaggiore 60 B3
Rio Maior 38 A3
Rio Marina 62 C1
Riom-ès-
 Montagnes 29 E1
Rionero in Vulture 64 C3
Río, Punta del 44 B4
Rioseco de Tapia 35 D2
Rioz 27 D2
Ripač 70 C4
Ripanj 73 D3
Riparbella 60 C4
Ripatransone 61 F4
Ripley 7 D3
Ripoli 32 A3
Ripollet 32 A4
Ripon 6 C1
Riquewihr 27 E1
Risan 76 B2
Risbäck 97 E4
Risca 9 D2
Riscle 28 B4
Risle 19 D4
Risnes 104 B4
Risnjak 70 B3
Risør 104 C4
Risøyhamn 94 A3
Risøysundet 94 A3
Rissa 100 C1
Ristiina 103 E3
Ristijärvi 99 E4
Ristilampi 99 D2
Ristovac 77 E2
Risum-Lindholm 47 F1
Ritíni 79 E4
Ritoniemi 103 E2
Ritsóna 84 A4
Rittmannshausen 52 B3
Riudoms 37 F4
Riva 58 C4
Rivarolo Canavese 31 E1
Rive-de-Gier 30 B1
Rives 30 C1
Rivesaltes 32 B2
Rivière-Thibouville,
 la 19 D3

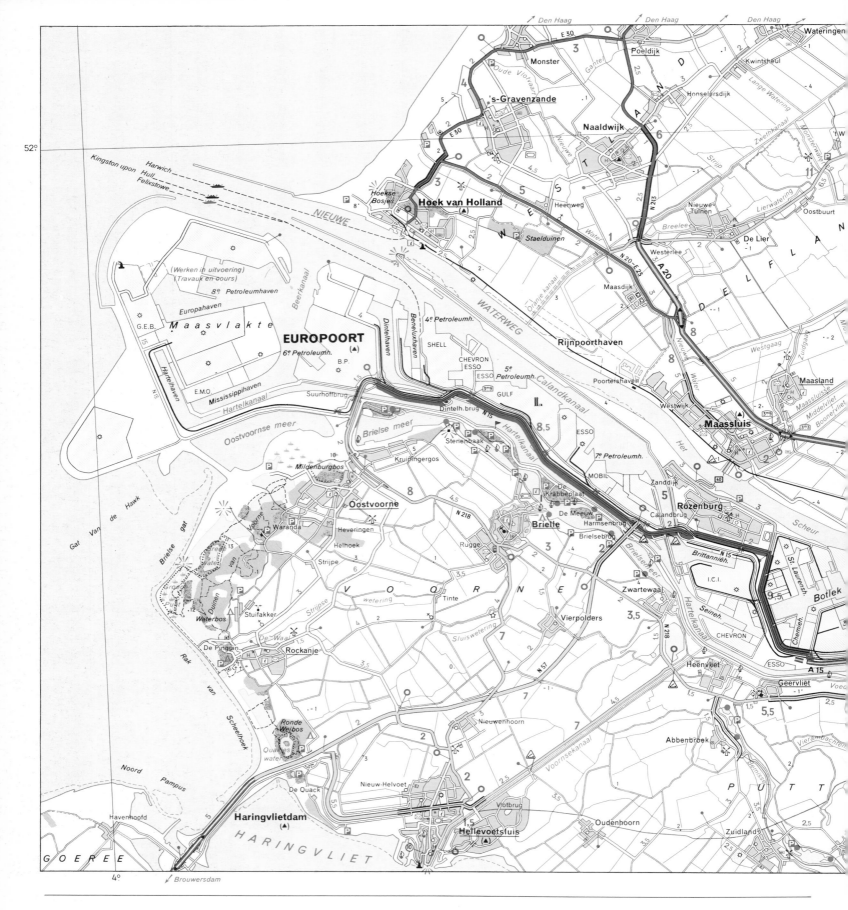

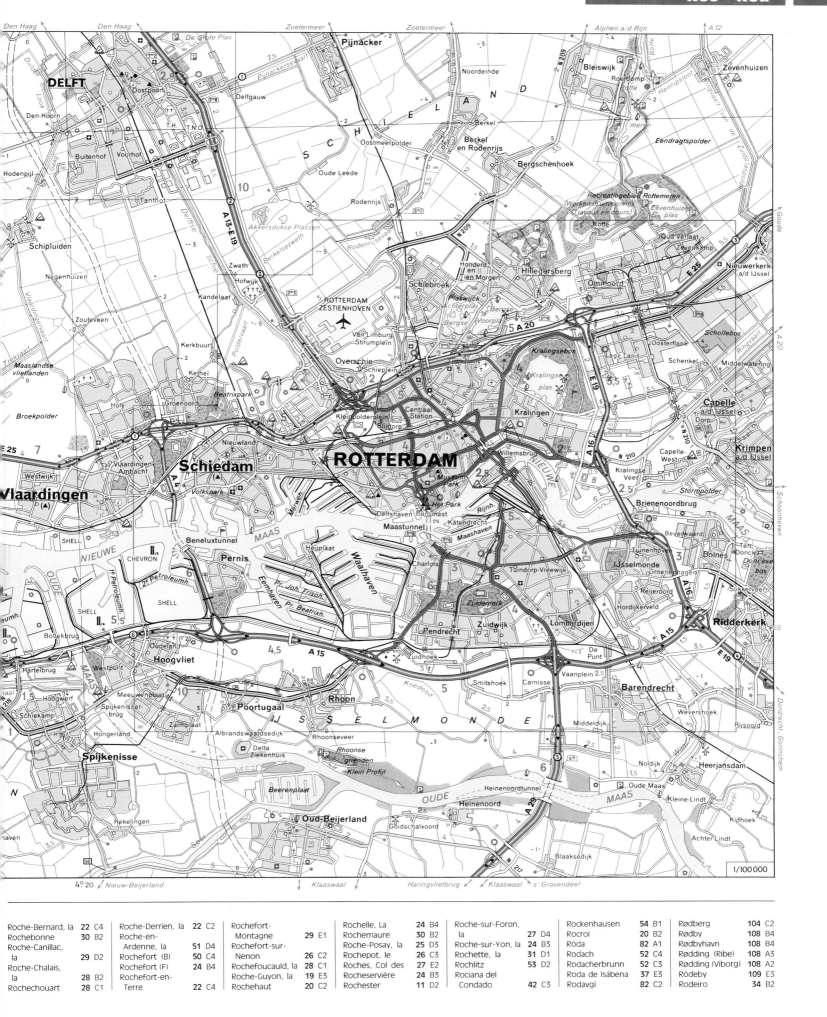

Roche-Bernard, la	22 C4	Roche-Derrien, la	22 C2	Rochefort-Montagne	29 E1	Rochelle, La	24 B4	Roche-sur-Foron, la	27 D4	Rockenhausen	54 B1	Rødberg	104 C2
Rochebonne	30 B2	Roche-en-Ardenne, la	51 D4	Rochefort-sur-Nenon	50 C4	Rochemaure	30 B2	Roche-sur-Yon, la	24 B3	Rocroi	20 B2	Rødby	108 B4
Roche-Canillac, la	29 D2	Rochefort (B)	50 C4	Rochepot, le	26 C3	Rochette, la	31 D1	Róda	82 A1	Rødbyhavn	108 B4
Roche-Chalais, la	28 B2	Rochefort (F)	24 B4	Rochefoucauld, la	28 C1	Roches, Col des	27 E2	Rochlitz	53 D2	Rodach	52 C4	Rødding (Ribe)	108 A3
Rochechouart	28 C1	Rochefort-en-Terre	22 C4	Roche-Guyon, la	19 E3	Rocheservière	24 B3	Rociana del Condado	42 C3	Rodacherbrunn	52 C3	Rødding (Viborg)	108 A2
				Rochehaut	20 C2	Rochester	11 D2			Roda de Isábena	37 E3	Rödeby	109 E3
										Rodavgí	82 C2	Rodeiro	34 B2

Name	Pg	Grid
Rødekro	108	A4
Rodel	2	A3
Rodellar	37	E3
Roden	47	D3
Ródenas	41	D2
Rödermark	52	A4
Rodewisch	53	D3
Rodez	29	E3
Rodiezmo	35	D2
Rodi Garganico	64	C2
Roding	56	B1
Rodítis	81	E2
Rodnei, M	113	D3
Rododáfni	83	D4
Rodohóri	79	E3
Rodolivos	80	B2
Rödön	101	E2
Rodonit, Gjiri i	76	C4
Rodópi (Nomos)	81	E2
Rodopi Mts	115	D3
Rodópoli	79	F2
Rodopós	90	B3
Ródos	93	F1
Ródos, N	93	F2
Rodováni	90	B3
Rodvattnet	102	A1
Rødven	100	B2
Rødvig	108	C4
Roermond	17	D4
Roeselare	50	A3
Rogač	75	D2
Rogača	73	D3
Rogačica (Kosovo)	77	E2
Rogačica (Srbija)	72	C4
Rogačov	111	E4
Rogaland	104	A3
Rogaška Slatina	70	C1
Rogatec	70	C2
Rogatica	76	A1
Rogatin	113	D3
Rogätz	48	C4
Rogen	101	D3
Rogen L	101	D3
Roggendorf	48	B2
Roggiano Gravina	67	E2
Roggosen	53	F1
Rogliano (F)	33	F2
Rogliano (I)	67	E3
Rognan	97	E2
Rogozna	76	C1
Rogoznica	75	D2
Rohan	22	C3
Rohr	52	B3
Rohrbach (A)	56	C2
Rohrbach (F)	21	E3
Rohrbrunn	52	A4
Rohrer Sattel	57	E3
Roignais	27	E4
Roine Mallasvesi	107	E1
Roisel	19	F2
Roissy	19	F4
Rojales	45	D2
Rök	109	D1
Rokiškis	110	C3
Røkland	97	F2
Rokovci	71	F2
Rokua	99	E4
Rokycany	53	E4
Røldal	104	B3
Rolfstorp	108	C2
Rolla	94	B3
Rollag	104	C3
Rolle	27	D3
Rolle, Pso di	59	D3
Rolvsøya	95	D1
Roma	63	E2
Romagnano Sesia	31	F1
Roman	113	D4
Romana	66	B2
Romanche	31	D1
Romangordo	39	E3
România	73	D1
Romanija	71	F4
Romans	30	C2
Romanshorn	58	B1
Romantische straße	55	E3
Rombas	21	D3
Rombo, Pso del	58	C2
Römhild	52	B4
Romilly	20	B4
Romny	113	F1
Rømø	108	A3
Romont	27	E3
Romorantin	25	E2
Romsdalen	100	B2
Romsdalsfjorden	100	B2
Romsey	9	E3
Rona	2	B3
Ronaldsway	6	A1
Roncade	59	E4
Roncal	37	D2
Ronce	28	A1
Roncegno	59	D3
Roncesvalles	36	C1
Ronchamp	27	D1
Ronchi	59	F3
Ronciglione	63	E2
Roncobilaccio	60	C3
Ronda	43	E3
Rondane	100	C3
Ronda, Serr de	43	E4
Rønde	108	B3
Rondeslottet	100	C3
Rondissone	31	F1
Rondvassbu	100	C3
Rönnäng	108	C1
Rønne	109	D4
Ronneburg	53	D3
Ronneby	109	E3
Ronnebyån	109	E3
Rønnede	108	C4
Rönnöfors	101	E1
Ronse	50	B3
Roosendaal	16	B3
Roperuelos del Páramo	35	D3
Ropi	94	C3
Ropinsalmi	94	C3
Ropotovo	77	E3
Roquebillière	31	E3
Roquebrun	30	A4
Roquebrune-Cap-Martin	31	E3
Roquebrussanne, la	31	D4
Roquecourbe	32	B1
Roquefort	28	B3
Roquefort-sur-Soulzon	29	F3
Roque-Gageac, la	29	D2
Roquemaure	30	B3
Roquesteron	31	E3
Roquetas de Mar	44	B4
Roquevaire	30	C4
Rora Head	3	D1
Rore	71	D4
Røros	101	D2
Rørøy	97	D3
Rorschach	58	B1
Rørvig	108	C3
Rørvik (Nord Trøndelag)	97	D4
Rørvik (Sør Trøndelag)	100	C1
Ros'	113	E2
Rosà	59	D4
Rosal de la Frontera	42	C1
Rosans	30	C2
Rosarito, Emb de	39	E2
Rosarno	67	E4
Roscoff	22	B2
Ros Comáin	12	C3
Roscommon	12	C3
Roscommon (Co)	12	C3
Roscrea	12	C4
Rose (I)	67	E2
Rose (YU)	76	A3
Rosegg	70	A1
Roselend, Cormet de	27	E4
Rosell	41	F2
Rosendal	104	A2
Rosenheim	56	B3
Rosenhof	56	B2
Rosenthal	53	F3
Roses	32	C3
Roses, Golfo de	32	C3
Roseto degli Abruzzi	64	A1
Roßhaupten	55	E4
Rosheim	21	E4
Rosice	57	F1
Rosières	19	F2
Rosiers, les	24	C2
Rosignano Marittimo	60	C4
Roşiori de Vede	115	D2
Roskilde	108	C3
Roški slap	75	D1
Roßlau	53	D1
Roslavl'	111	E3
Rosmaninhal	38	C3
Røsnæs	108	B3
Rosolina Mare	61	D1
Rosolini	69	D4
Rosoman	77	E3
Rosova dolina	115	D2
Rosporden	22	B3
Rossano	67	F2
Rossan Pt	12	C1
Rosscarbery	14	B4
Rosses Point	12	C2
Rossija	111	E2
Rossio	38	B3
Rosskreppfjorden	104	B3
Rosslare	15	D4
Rosslare Harbour	15	D4
Rosslea	13	D2
Rossön	101	F1
Ross-on-Wye	9	D2
Røssvatnet	97	E3
Rosthwaite	5	D4
Røstlandet	97	D1
Rostock	48	C2
Rostrenen	22	B3
Rostrevor	13	E3
Rostujávri	94	C3
Røsvik	94	A4
Rosvik	98	C3
Roßwein	53	E2
Rota	43	D3
Rotenburg (Hessen)	52	B3
Rotenburg (Niedersachsen)	48	A3
Roth	55	F1
Rötha	53	D2
Rothbury	5	E3
Röthenbach	55	F1
Rothenburg	53	F2
Rothenburg ob der Tauber	55	E1
Rothéneuf	18	B4
Rotherham	7	D2
Rothes	3	D3
Rothesay	4	B2
Rothwell	9	F1
Rotja, Pta	45	D4
Rotonda	67	E2
Rotondella	65	D4
Rotondo, M	33	F3
Rott (Bayern)	56	A3
Rott (Bayern)	56	B3
Rott R	56	B2
Rottach-Egern	56	A4
Rotten	27	F3
Rottenbach	52	C4
Rottenburg (Baden-Württemberg)	55	D3
Rottenburg (Bayern)	56	B2
Rottenmann	57	D4
Rottenmanner Tauern	57	D4
Rotterdam	16	B3
Rottne	109	D2
Rottneros	105	E3
Rottweil	54	C3
Rötz	56	B1
Roubaix	20	A1
Roudnice	53	F3
Rouen	19	E3
Rouffach	27	E1
Rougé	23	D4
Roßdorf	54	C1
Rougemont	27	D2
Rougemont-le-Château	27	E1
Rouillac	28	B1
Roujan	30	A4
Roulans	27	D2
Roulers	50	A3
Roundstone	12	A3
Rousay	3	C1
Roússa	81	E1
Rousses, les	27	D3
Rousset, Col de	30	C2
Rovaniemi	99	D2
Rovato	60	B1
Rovereto	59	D4
Roverud	105	D3
Roviés	83	F3
Rovigo	61	D2
Rovinj	70	A3
Roviśće	71	D2
Rovno	113	D2
Roxen	106	A4
Roxo, Bgem do	42	B1
Royal Canal	12	C3
Royal Leamington Spa	9	E1
Royal Tunbridge Wells	10	C3
Royan	28	A1
Royat	29	E1
Roybon	30	C1
Roye	19	F3
Royère-de-Vassivière	25	E4
Røyrvik	97	E4
Royston	9	F2
Röyttä	98	C3
Rožaje	76	C2
Rožanstvo	72	C4
Rozay-en-Brie	19	F4
Rozier, le	29	F3
Rožmberk	57	D1
Rožmitál	53	F4
Rožňava	112	B3
Rozoy	20	B2
Roztocze	112	C2
Roztoky	53	F2
Rozvadov	56	B1
Rrasë	76	C3
Rrëshen	76	C3
Rrogozhinë	76	C4
Rtanj	73	E4
Rtanj (Reg)	73	E4
Ruabon	6	B3
Rubbestadneset	104	A2
Rubena	35	F3
Rubeži	76	B2
Rubha a'Mhail	4	B2
Rubha Còigeach	2	C2
Rubha Réidh	2	B3
Rubí	32	A4
Rubiães	34	A3
Rubi de Bracamonte	39	F1
Rubielos de Mora	41	E3
Rubiera	60	C2
Rubio	35	F4
Rudare	77	D1
Rüdersdorf	49	E4
Rüdesheim	51	F4
Rudkøbing	108	B4
Rudn'a	111	E3
Rudna Glava	73	E3
Rudnica (Crna Gora)	76	B1
Rudnica (Srbija)	76	C1
Rudnik (Kosovo)	76	C2
Rudnik (Reg)	73	D4
Rudnik (Srbija)	73	D4
Rudo	76	B1
Rudolstadt	52	C3
Rue	19	E2
Ruecas, R	39	E4
Rueda	35	E4
Rueda de Jalón	36	C3
Ruelle	28	C1
Ruffec	25	D4
Ruffieux	27	D4
Rugby	9	E1
Rugeley	6	C3
Rügen	49	D1
Rugles	19	D4
Rugovska klisura	76	C2
Ruhla	52	B3
Ruhland	53	E2
Ruhner Berge	48	C3
Ruhpolding	56	B3
Ruhr	17	E3
Ruidera	40	B4
Rüjiena	110	C2
Ruka	99	E2
Rukatunturi	99	E2
Ruma	72	C2
Rumblar, Emb del	44	A2
Rumboci	75	E1
Rumburk	53	F2
Rumengol	22	B3
Rumenka	72	C2
Rumigny	20	B2
Rumija	76	B3
Rumilly	27	D4
Runcorn	6	B2
Runde	100	A2
Rundvik	102	A2
Runn	105	F2
Runni	103	D1
Runtuna	106	B4
Ruohtir	95	E2
Ruokojärvi	103	F3
Ruokolahti	103	F3
Ruokovesi	103	E2
Ruokto	98	B1
Ruoms	30	B2
Ruotsinpyhtää	107	F2
Ruovesi	102	C3
Rupa	70	B3
Rupea	113	D4
Ruppiner See	49	D3
Rupt	27	D1
Rur	17	D4
Ruše	70	C1
Ruse	115	D2
Ruševo	71	E2
Rush	13	E3
Rushden	9	F1
Ruski Krstur	72	B2
Rusko	107	D2
Rusko Selo	72	C1
Ruskele	98	A4
Rüsselsheim	51	F4
Russenes	95	D1
Russey, le	27	E2
Russi	61	D3
Rust	57	F3
Rustefjelbma	95	E1
Ruswil	27	F2
Rute	43	F3
Rüthen	17	F3
Ruthin	6	B3
Rúti	58	A2
Rutigliano	65	E3
Rutledal	104	A1
Ruuhitunturi	99	E2
Ruukki	99	D4
Ruuponsaari	103	D2
Ruurlo	17	D3
Ruvo di Puglia	65	D3
Ruwer	54	A1
Ruynes-en-Margeride	29	F2
Ružomberok	112	B3
Ry	108	B3
Rybinsk	111	F1
Rybinskoje Vodochranilišče	111	F1
Rybnica	113	E3
Rybnik	112	B3
Rychnov nad Kněžnou	112	A3
Ryd	109	D3
Ryde	9	E3
Rye	11	D3
Ryfylke	104	A3
Rygge	105	D3
Rykene	104	B4
Ryl'sk	113	F1
Rymań	49	F1
Rymättylä	107	D2
Rypefjord	95	D1
Rysjedalsvika	104	A1
Ryttylä	107	E2
Rzepin	49	F4
Rzeszów	112	C2
Ržev	111	F2

S

Name	Pg	Grid
Sääksjärvi	102	C2
Saal	55	F2
Saalach	59	E1
Saalbach	59	E1
Saale	52	C1
Saaler Bodden	48	C1
Saales	21	E4
Saalfeld	52	C3
Saalfelden	59	E1
Saane	27	E3
Saanen	27	E3
Saar	54	A1
Saarbrücken	54	B2
Saarburg	54	A1
Saaremaa	110	B2
Saarenkylä	99	D2
Saari	103	F3
Saariharju	99	E3
Saarijärvi	103	D2
Saarikoski	94	C3
Saariselkä	95	F3
Saariselkä (Reg)	95	F3
Saaristomeri	107	D3
Saarland	54	A2
Saarlouis	54	B2
Saas- Fee	27	F4
Šabac	72	C3
Sabadell	32	A4
Sabaudia	63	F3
Sabbioneta	60	C2
Sabero	35	E2
Sabiñánigo	37	D2
Sabini, Mti	63	E3
Sabiote	44	B2
Sablé	23	E4
Sables-d'Olonne, les	24	B3
Sables-d'Or	22	C2
Sæbo	100	A2
Sabóia	42	A2
Sabôr, R	34	C4
Sabres	28	B3
Sabrosa	34	B4
Sabugal	39	D2
Sæby	108	B2
Sa Calobra	45	E2
Sacavém	38	A4
Sacedon	40	C2
Saceruela	39	F4
Sacile	59	E3
Sacra di San Michele	31	E1
Sacramenia	35	F4
Sacratif, C	44	A4
Sada	34	B1
Sádaba	36	C2
Sado, R	38	A4
Sadurniño	34	B1
Saelices	40	B3
Safara	42	C1
Säffle	105	E4
Saffron Walden	10	C2
Safonovo	111	E3
Sagard	49	D1
S'Agaró	32	B4
Sagéika	86	B1
Sagfjorden	94	A4
Sagiáda	82	B1
Sagra, Sa de la	44	B2
Sagres	42	A3
Sagres, Pta de	42	A3
Sagunto	41	E3
Sagvåg	104	A3
Sahagún	35	E3
Sahalahti	107	E1
Šahinovići	71	E3
Sahl	108	A2
Sahloinen	103	D3
Saidus	110	B3
Saignelégier	27	E2
Saija	95	F4
Saillagouse	32	A3
Saillans	30	C2
Saimaa	103	E3
Saimaanranta	103	E4
Sains-du-Nord	20	B2
Sains-Richaumont	20	B2
St Abb's Head	5	E2
St Aegyd	57	E3
St-Affrique	29	E3
St-Agnant	24	B4
St-Agrève	30	B2
St-Aignan	25	E2
St-Aignan-sur-Roë	23	E3
St Alban	29	F2
St Albans	9	F2
St Alban's Head	9	E4
St-Amand-en-Puisaye	26	A2
St-Amand-les-Eaux	20	A1

Place	Ref
St-Amand-Longpré	25 D2
St-Amand-Montrond	25 F3
St-Amans-des-Cots	29 E2
St-Amans	29 F2
St-Amans-Soult	32 B1
St-Amant	29 F1
St-Amant-Roche-Savine	29 F1
St-Amarin	27 E1
St-Ambroix	30 B3
St-Amé	27 D1
St-Amour	26 C3
St Andrä	70 B1
St Andreasberg	52 B2
St-André-de-Cubzac	28 B2
St-André-de-l'Eure	19 E4
St-André-de-Vézines	29 F3
St-André-les-Alpes	31 D3
St Andrews	5 D1
St-Anthème	30 B1
St-Antonin-Noble-Val	29 D3
St Anton	58 C2
St-Arnoult	19 E4
St Asaph	6 B2
St-Astier	28 C2
St-Auban	31 D3
St-Aubin-d'Aubigné	23 D3
St-Aubin-du-Cormier	23 D3
St-Aubin	18 C3
St-Aulaye	28 C2
St Austell	8 B4
St-Avold	21 D3
St-Aygulf	31 D4
St-Beauzély	29 E3
St Bees Head	4 C4
St-Benoît-du-Sault	25 E3
St-Benoît	25 F2
St-Bertrand-de-Comminges	37 E1
St-Béat	37 F2
St-Bénin-d'Azy	26 A3
St Blasien	54 C4
St-Blin	26 C1
St-Bonnet	31 D2
St-Bonnet-de-Joux	26 B3
St-Bonnet-le-Château	30 B1
St-Brévin	24 A2
St-Briac	18 A4
St-Brice-en-Coglès	18 B4
St Brides B	8 B2
St-Brieuc	22 C2
St-Calais	23 F3
St-Cast	18 A4
St Catherine's Pt	9 E4
St-Cergue	27 D3
St-Cernin	29 E2
St-Céré	29 D2
St-Chamas	30 C4
St-Chamond	30 B1
St-Chély-d'Apcher	29 F2
St-Chély-d'Aubrac	29 E2
St-Chinian	32 B1
St Christophen	57 E2
St-Ciers	28 B1
St-Cirq-Lapopie	29 D3
St-Clair-sur-l'Elle	18 C3
St-Clar	28 C3
St-Claud	25 D4
St-Claude	27 D3
St Clears	8 C2
St-Cyprien	29 D2
St-Cyprien-Plage	32 B2
St David's	8 B1
St David's Head	8 B1
St-Denis (Charente-Maritime)	24 B4
St-Denis-d'Orques	23 E3
St-Denis (Seine-St-Denis)	19 F4
St-Didier-en-Velay	30 B1
St-Dié	21 E4
St-Dier-d'Auvergne	29 F1
St-Dizier	20 C4
St-Donat-sur-l'Herbasse	30 C1
St-Eloy-les-Mines	26 A4
St-Emilion	28 B2
St-Etienne (Alpes-de-Haute-Provence)	30 C3
St-Etienne-Cantalès, Bge de	29 E2
St-Etienne-de-Baïgorry	28 A4
St-Etienne-de-Lugdarès	29 F2
St-Etienne-de-Montluc	24 B2
St-Etienne-de-St-Geoirs	30 C1
St-Etienne-de-Tinée	31 E3
St-Etienne-en-Dévoluy	31 D2
St-Etienne (Loire)	30 B1
St-Fargeau	26 A2
St-Félicien	30 B2
St Finan's B	14 A4
St-Firmin	31 D2
St-Florent (Cher)	25 F3
St-Florent (Corse)	33 F2
St-Florentin	26 B1
St-Flour	29 F2
St-François-Longchamp	31 D1
St-Fulgent	24 B3
St Gallen (A)	57 D3
St Gallen (CH)	58 B2
St Gallenkirch	58 B2
St-Galmier	30 B1
St-Gaudens	37 F1
St-Gaultier	25 E3
St-Genest-Malifaux	30 B1
St-Gengoux-le-National	26 C3
St-Geniez-d'Olt	29 E3
St-Genis-de-Stonge	28 B1
St-Genis-Laval	30 B1
St-Genix	30 C1
St-Geoire	30 C1
St Georgen (A)	56 C3
St Georgen am Langsee	70 B1
St Georgen (D)	54 C3
St-Georges	23 E4
St Georges Channel	8 A1
St-Georges-de-Didonne	28 A1
St-Georges-en-Couzan	29 F1
St-Germain-de-Calberte	29 F3
St-Germain-des-Fossés	26 A4
St-Germain-du-Bois	26 C3
St-Germain-du-Plain	26 C3
St-Germain-du-Teil	29 F3
St-Germain	19 F4
St-Germain-Laval	26 B4
St-Germain-Lembron	29 F1
St-Germain-les-Belles	29 D1
St-Germain-l'Herm	29 F1
St-Gertraud	58 C3
St-Gervais-d'Auvergne	26 A4
St-Gervais	27 E4
St-Gervais-sur-Mare	30 A4
St-Géry	29 D3
St-Gildas-de-Rhuys	22 C4
St-Gildas-des-Bois	23 D4
St-Gildas, Pte de	24 A2
St Gilgen	56 C3
St-Gilles-Croix-de-Vie	24 A3
St-Gilles	30 B4
St-Gingolph	27 E3
St-Girons	37 F2
St-Girons-Plage	28 A3
St Goar	51 E4
St Goarshausen	51 E4
St-Gobain	20 A3
St Govan's Head	8 B2
St-Guénolé	22 A3
St-Guilhem-le-Désert	29 F4
St-Haon-le-Châtel	26 B4
St Helens	6 B2
St-Hélier	18 B3
St-Hilaire-des-Loges	24 C3
St-Hilaire-de-Villefranche	28 B1
St-Hilaire-du-Harcouet	18 B4
St-Hilaire	32 B1
St-Hippolyte-du-Fort	29 F3
St-Hippolyte	27 E2
St-Honoré	26 B3
St-Hubert	20 C2
St-Imier	27 E2
St Ingbert	54 B2
St Ives (Cambs)	9 F1
St Ives (Cornwall)	8 A4
St-Jacques	23 D3
St-Jacut	18 A4
St Jakob	59 D2
St Jakob im Rosental	70 A1
St James	18 B4
St-Jean-Brévelay	22 C3
St-Jean-Cap-Ferrat	31 E3
St-Jean-d'Angély	24 C4
St-Jean-de-Bournay	30 C1
St-Jean-de-Daye	18 B3
St-Jean-de-Losne	26 C2
St-Jean-de-Luz	28 A4
St-Jean-de-Maurienne	31 D1
St-Jean-de-Monts	24 A3
St-Jean-du-Bruel	29 F3
St-Jean-du-Gard	30 A3
St-Jean-en-Royans	30 C2
St-Jean-Pied-de-Port	28 A4
St-Jeoire	27 D4
St Johann im Pongau	59 E1
St Johann in Tirol	59 E1
St John's Pt	13 E2
St-Jouin-de-Marnes	24 C3
St-Juéry	29 E3
St-Julien-Chapteuil	30 B2
St-Julien-de-Vouvantes	23 D4
St-Julien-du-Sault	26 A1
St-Julien-en-Genevois	27 D4
St-Julien	26 C3
St-Julien-l'Ars	25 D3
St-Junien	25 D4
St Just	8 A4
St-Just-en-Chaussée	19 F3
St-Just-en-Chevalet	26 B4
St-Justin	28 B3
St Keverne	8 B4
St Lambrecht	57 D4
St-Lary-Soulan	37 E2
St-Laurent (Calvados)	18 C3
St-Laurent-de-la-Salanque	32 B2
St-Laurent-du-Pont	30 C1
St-Laurent-en-Grandvaux	27 D3
St-Laurent-les-Bains	29 F2
St-Laurent-Médoc	28 B2
St-Laurent (Vendée)	24 C3
St-Laurent (Vienne)	28 C1
St-Léger	26 B3
St Leonhard (I)	59 D2
St Leonhard (Niederösterreich)	57 E3
St Leonhard (Tirol)	58 C2
St-Léonard-de-Noblat	25 E4
St Lorenzen	59 E2
St-Lô	18 C3
St-Louis	27 E2
St-Loup-Lamairé	24 C3
St-Loup-sur-Semouse	27 D1
St-Luc	27 F3
St-Lunaire	18 B4
St-Lys	29 D4
St-Macaire	28 B2
St Magnus B	3 F1
St-Maixent-l'Ecole	24 C3
St-Malo-de-la-Lande	18 B3
St-Malo	18 B4
St-Mamet-la-Salvetat	29 E2
St-Mandrier	31 D4
St-Marcellin	30 C1
St Margarethen	48 A2
St Margaret's Hope	3 E1
St-Mars-la-Jaille	23 D4
St-Martin (Charente-Maritime)	24 B4
St-Martin-d'Auxigny	25 F2
St-Martin-de-Belleville	31 D1
St-Martin-de-Londres	29 F4
St-Martin-de-Seignan	28 A4
St-Martin-de-Valamas	30 B2
St-Martin-en-Bresse	26 C3
St-Martin (Pyrénées-Orientales)	32 B2
St Martin's	8 A4
St-Martin-Vésubie	31 E3
St-Martory	37 F1
St Mary's	8 A4
St Märgen	54 C4
St-Mathieu	28 C1
St-Mathieu, Pte de	22 A3
St-Maurice	27 E4
St Mawes	8 B4
St-Maximin-la-Ste-Baume	31 D4
St-Médard-en-Jalles	28 B2
St-Méen	22 C3
St Michaelisdonn	48 A2
St Michael (Salzburg)	59 F2
St Michael's Mount	8 A4
St Michael (Steiermark)	57 E4
St-Michel-de-Maurienne	31 D1
St-Michel-en-Grève	22 B2
St-Michel-en-l'Herm	24 B4
St-Michel	20 B3
St-Michel-Mont-Mercure	24 C3
St-Mihiel	20 C3
St Monance	5 D2
St-Moritz	58 B3
St-Nazaire	24 A2
St-Nectaire	29 E1
St Neots	9 F1
St-Nicolas-d'Aliermont	19 E2
St-Nicolas-de-la-Grave	28 C3
St-Nicolas-de-Port	21 D4
St-Nicolas-du-Pélem	22 C3
St-Niklaas	50 B3
St Niklaus	27 F4
St-Oedenrode	16 C3
St-Omer	19 F1
St Oswald	59 F2
St-Pair	18 B4
St-Palais (Charente-Maritime)	28 A1
St-Palais (Pyrénées-Atlantiques)	28 A4
St-Pardoux-la-Rivière	28 C1
St Paul (A)	70 B1
St-Paul (Alpes-de-Haute-Provence)	31 D2
St-Paul (Alpes-Maritimes)	31 E3
St-Paul-Cap-de-Joux	29 D4
St-Paul-de-Fenouillet	32 B2
St-Paulien	29 F2
St-Paul-Trois-Châteaux	30 B3
St-Père-en-Retz	24 A2
St-Pé-de-Bigorre	37 E1
St-Pée	28 A4
St-Péray	30 B2
St Peter in der Au	57 D3
St-Peter-Ording	47 F2
St Peter Port	18 A3
St-Philbert	24 B3
St-Pierre (Charente-Maritime)	24 B4
St-Pierre-d'Albigny	31 D1
St-Pierre-de-Chartreuse	30 C1
St-Pierre-de-Chignac	28 C2
St-Pierre-Eglise	18 B2
St-Pierre-le-Moûtier	26 A3
St-Pierre (Morbihan)	22 C4
St-Pierre-sur-Dives	18 C3
St-Pois	18 C4
St-Pol-de-Léon	22 B2
St-Pol-sur-Ternoise	19 F2
St-Pons-de-Thomières	32 B1
St-Porchaire	28 B1
St Pölten	57 E2
St-Pourçain	26 A4
St-Privat	29 E2
St-Quay-Portrieux	22 C2
St-Quentin	20 A2
St-Rambert	30 B1
St-Rambert-d'Albon	30 B1
St-Rambert-en-Bugey	26 C4
St-Raphaël	31 E4
St-Renan	22 A2
St-Rémy-de-Provence	30 B3
St-Rémy-sur-Durolle	26 B4
St-Riquier	19 E2
St-Romain-de-Colbosc	19 D3
St-Rome-de-Tarn	29 E3
St-Saëns	19 E3
St-Satur	26 A2
St-Saulge	26 A2
St-Sauveur-en-Puisaye	26 A2
St-Sauveur-Lendelin	18 B3
St-Sauveur-le-Vicomte	18 B3
St-Sauveur-sur-Tinée	31 E3
St-Savin (Gironde)	28 B2
St-Savin (Vienne)	25 D3
St-Seine-l'Abbaye	26 C2
St-Sernin-sur-Rance	29 E3
St-Sever (Calvados)	18 C4
St-Sever (Landes)	28 B4
St-Sulpice-les-Feuilles	25 E4
St-Symphorien-de-Lay	26 B4
St-Symphorien-d'Ozon	30 B1
St-Symphorien	28 B3
St-Symphorien-sur-Coise	30 B1
St-Trivier-de-Courtes	26 C3
St-Trivier-sur-Moignans	26 C4
St-Trojan	28 A1
St-Tropez	31 D4
St-Truiden	50 C3
St Ulrich	59 D3
St-Vaast-la-Hougue	18 B3
St Valentin an der Haide	58 C2
St Valentin	57 D3
St-Valery	19 E2
St-Valery-en-Caux	19 D2
St-Valier	30 B1
St-Vallier-de-Thiey	31 D3
St-Varent	24 C3
St-Vaury	25 E4
St Veit	70 A1
St-Véran	31 E2
St-Vincent	27 F4
St-Vincent-de-Tyrosse	28 A4
St-Vivien-de-Médoc	28 A1
St-Wandrille	19 D3
St Wendel	54 B1
St Wolfgang	56 C3
St-Yorre	26 A4
St-Yrieix-la-Perche	29 D1
Ste-Adresse	19 D3
Ste-Anne-d'Auray	22 C4
Ste-Baume, la	31 D4
Ste-Croix-du-Mont	28 B2
Ste-Croix	27 D3
Ste-Croix, Lac de	31 D3
Ste-Croix-Volvestre	37 F1
Ste-Enimie	29 F3
Ste-Foy-la-Grande	28 C2
Ste-Foy-l'Argentière	30 B1
Ste-Geneviève-sur-Argence	29 E2
Ste-Hélène	28 B2
Ste-Hermine	24 B3
Ste-Livrade	28 C3
Ste-Lucie-de-Tallano	33 F4
Ste-Marie-aux-Mines	21 E4
Ste-Maure-de-Touraine	25 D2
Ste-Maxime	31 D4
Ste-Menehould	20 C3
Ste-Mère-Eglise	18 B3
Ste-Odile, Mt	21 E4
Ste-Sévère	25 F3
Ste-Suzanne	23 E3
Ste-Tulle	30 C3
Saintes	28 B1
Stes-Maries-de-la-Mer	30 B4
Saissac	32 B1
Sakarya	115 F3
Sakskøbing	108 B4
Sakule	72 C2
Säkylä	107 D2
Sala	106 A3
Salacgrîva	110 C2
Salada	41 E3
Salakovac	73 D3
Salamajärvi	102 C2
Salamajärvi L	103 D2
Salamanca	39 E1
Salamína	87 F1
Salamína, N	87 E1
Salándi	87 E2
Salangen	94 B3
Salar	43 F3
Salardú	37 F2
Salas	35 D1
Salaš	73 F3
Salas de los Infantes	36 A3
Salazar, R	37 D2
Salbohed	105 F3
Salbris	25 E3
Salcombe	8 C4
Saldaña	35 E3
Sale	60 A2
Sålekinna	100 D3
Salem	55 D4
Salemi	68 A3
Sälen	101 D4
Salen (Highland)	2 B4
Salen (Mull)	4 B1
Salernes	31 D4
Salerno	64 B4
Salerno, Golfo di	64 B4
Salers	29 E2
Salève, Mt	27 D4
Salgótarján	112 B3
Salgueiro do Campo	38 C2
Sali	74 C1
Salice Terme	60 A2
Salies-de-Béarn	28 A4
Salies-du-Salat	37 F1
Salignac-Eyvigues	29 D2
Salihli	115 F4
Salime, Emb de	34 C1
Salina, I	69 D2
Salinas (Andalucía)	43 F3
Salinas (Asturias)	35 D1
Salinas, C	45 F3
Salindres	30 B3
Sälinkää	107 F2
Salins	27 D3
Salisbury	9 E3
Salla	99 E2
Sallanches	27 E4
Sallent	32 A4
Sallent-de-Gállego	37 D2
Salles	32 A1
Salles-Curan	29 E3
Salling	108 A2
Salling Sund	108 A2
Salmerón	40 C2
Salmoral	39 F1
Salò	60 B1
Salo	107 E2
Salobreña	44 A4
Salona	75 D1
Salon-de-Provence	30 C4
Salonta	112 C4
Salorino	38 C3
Salor, R	39 D3
Salou	37 F4
Salou, C de	37 F4
Salpausselkä	107 F2
Salsbruket	97 D4
Salses-le-Château	32 B2
Salso	68 C3
Salsomaggiore Terme	60 B2
Salsta	106 B3
Saltash	8 C4
Saltburn-by-the-Sea	5 F4
Saltcoats	4 C2
Saltee Is	15 D4
Saltfjellet	97 E2
Saltfjorden	97 E2
Salto	34 B4
Saltoluokta	94 B4
Saltvik	106 C3
Saluggia	31 F1
Saluzzo	31 E2
Salvacañete	41 D3
Salvagnac	29 D3
Salvan	27 E4
Salvaterra de Magos	38 A3
Salvatierra-Aguráin	36 B2
Salvatierra de los Barros	42 C1
Salvatierra de Miño	34 A3
Salvetat-Peyralès, la	29 E3

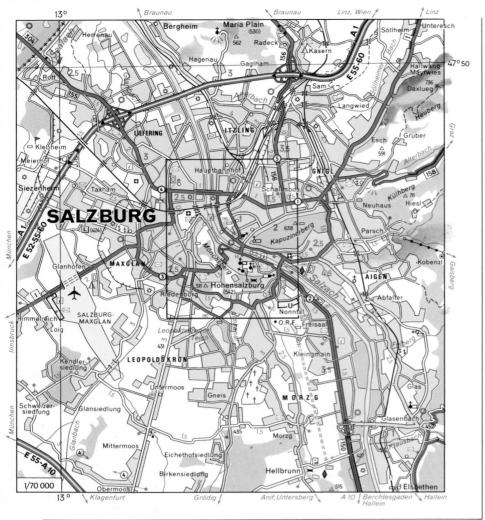

San Giovanni in
Fiore 67 F2
San Giovanni in
Persiceto 60 C2
San Giovanni
Lupatoto 60 C1
San Giovanni
Rotondo 64 C2
San Giovanni
Suergiu 66 B4
San Giovanni
Valdarno 61 D4
San Giuliano
Terme 60 C4
San Giustino 61 D4
San Gloria, Pto de 35 E2
San Gottardo, Pso
del 58 A3
San Ildefonso o la
Granja 40 A1
San Isidro 44 C3
San Isidro, Pto de 35 E2
San Javier 45 D2
San José
(Andalucía) 44 C4
San José (Ibiza) 45 D4
San Juan Bautista 45 D3
San Juan de
Alicante 45 E1
San Juan de
Aznalfarache 43 D2
San Juan de la
Peña 37 D2
San Juan del
Olmo 39 F2
San Juan de los
Terreros 44 C3
San Juan del
Puerto 42 C2
San Juan, Emb de 40 A2
San Just Desvern 32 A4
San Just, Sa de 41 E3
San Lazzaro di
Savena 61 D2
San Leo 61 E3
San Leonardo de
Yagüe 36 A3
San Leonardo 59 D2
San Leonardo, Pso 64 A2
San Lorenzo (E) 36 B2
San Lorenzo (I) 63 D1
San Lorenzo de
Calatrava 44 A1
San Lorenzo de la
Parrilla 40 C3
San Lucido 67 E3
San Luis de
Sabanillas 43 E4
San Luis 45 F2
San Marcello 61 F4
San Marcello
Pistoiese 60 C3
San Marco
Argentano 67 E2
San Marco dei
Cavoti 64 B3
San Marco in
Lamis 64 C2
San Marino 61 E3
San Martino di
Castrozza 59 D3
San Martín de
Castañeda 34 C3
San Martín de la
Vega 40 B2
San Martín de
Mondoñedo 34 C1
San Martín de
Montalbán 39 F3
San Martín de
Valdeiglesias 40 A2
San Mateo 41 F2
San Mateo de
Gállego 37 D3
San Mauro Forte 65 D4
San Michele all'
Adige 59 D3
San Miguel 45 D3
San Miguel de
Escalada 35 E3
San Miguel del
Arroyo 35 E4
San Miguel de
Salinas 45 D2

San Millán 36 A2
San Millán de la
Cogolla 36 B2
San Millán de Lara 36 A3
San Miniato 60 C4
San Nicolás del
Puerto 43 E2
San Nicolás de
Tolentino 42 B4
San Nicolò
Ferrarese 61 D2
San Nicolò Gerrei 66 B3
San Ninfa 68 B3
San Pancrazio
Salentino 65 F4
San Pedro 44 C1
San Pedro de
Alcántara 43 E4
San Pedro del
Arroyo 39 F1
San Pedro de
Latarce 35 E4
San Pedro del
Pinatar 45 D2
San Pedro de
Mérida 39 D4
San Pedro
Manrique 36 B3
San Pedro, Sa de 39 D3
San Pellegrino,
Pso 59 D3
San Pellegrino
Terme 58 B4
San Piero a Sieve 61 D3
San Pietro, I di 66 A4
San Pietro in
Casale 60 C2
San Pietro
Vernotico 65 F4
San Polo d'Enza 60 C2
San Quirico
d'Orcia 63 D1
San Rafael de Navallana,
Emb de 43 F2
San Rafael 40 A2
San Remo 31 F3
San Roque
(Andalucía) 43 E4
San Roque
(Galicia) 34 A1
San Rufo 64 C4
San Salvador de
Cantamuda 35 F2
San Salvador 45 F3
San Salvo 64 B2
San Sebastiano
Curone 60 A2
San Sebastián,
Emb de 34 C3
San Sebastián 42 A4
San Severino
Marche 61 F4
San Severo 64 C2
San Silvestre de
Guzmán 42 C2
San Sperate 66 B4
San Stefano di
Camastra 68 C3
San Stefano
Quisquina 68 B3
San Telmo 42 C2
San Valentino alla
Muta 58 C2
San Vicente de
Alcántara 38 C3
San Vicente de la
Barquera 35 F1
San Vicente de la
Cabeza 35 D3
San Vicente del
Raspeig 45 E1
San Vicenzo 62 C1
San Vigilio di
Marebbe 59 D2
San Vigilio, Pso di 60 C1
San Vitero 34 C4
San Vito al
Tagliamento 59 E3
San Vito Chietino 64 A2
San Vito dei
Normanni 65 E3
San Vito di C. 59 E3
San Vito 66 C4
San Vito lo Capo 68 A3

San Vito sullo
Ionio 67 F3
San Vittore del
Lazio 64 A3
Sana 71 D4
Saná 80 A3
Sanabria, L de 34 C3
Sanary 30 C4
Sancergues 26 A2
Sancerre 26 A2
Sanchidrián 39 F1
Sancho, Emb de 42 C2
Sanclêr 8 C2
Sancoins 26 A3
Sancti Petri 43 D4
Sancti Spíritus 39 D1
Sand (Hedmark) 105 D2
Sand (Rogaland) 104 A3
Sandane 100 A3
Sandanski 115 D3
Sandarne 101 F4
Sandau 48 C3
Sanday 3 E1
Sandbach 6 C3
Sanddøla 97 D4
Sande (D) 47 E3
Sande (Møre og
Romsdal) 100 A2
Sande (P) 34 A4
Sande (Vestfold) 104 C3
Sandefjord 104 C3
Sandeid 104 A3
Sandfjellet 95 E1
Sandgerði 96 A2
Sand in Taufers 59 D2
Sandnes 104 A3
Sandness 3 F1
Sandnessjøen 97 D3
Sando 39 E1
Sandoméri 86 B1
Sandomierz 112 C2
Sandown 9 E3
Sandoy 96 A4
Sandøy 100 A2
Sandrigo 59 D4
Sandringham
House 7 E3
Sandstad 100 C1
Sandur 96 A4
Sandviken 106 B2
Sandvikvåg 104 A2
Sandwich 11 D3
Sandy 9 F1
Sånfjället 101 E3
Sangarcia 40 A1
Sangerhausen 52 C2
Sangis 98 C3
Sangonera, R 45 D2
Sangro 64 A2
Sangüesa 36 C2
Sanguinaires, Iles 33 E4
Sanguinet 28 A3
Sani 80 A4
Sanitz 48 C2
Sankt Olof 109 D3
Sanlúcar de
Barrameda 43 D3
Sanlúcar de
Guadiana 42 B2
Sanlúcar la
Mayor 43 D2
Sanluri 66 B3
Sannainen 107 F2
Sannazzaro 60 A2
Sannicandro di
Bari 65 D3
Sannicandro
Garganico 64 C2
Sanok 112 C3
Sanquhar 4 C3
Sansepolcro 61 D3
Sanski Most 71 D3
Sant' Agata di
Puglia 64 C3
Sant Agusti de
Llucanès 32 A3
Sant Andreu de
Llavaneres 32 B4
Sant' Angelo de'
Lombardi 64 C3
Sant' Angelo in
Vado 61 E4
Sant' Angelo
Lodigiano 60 A2

Salvetat-sur-Agout,
la 32 B1
Salviac 29 D2
Sælvig 108 B3
Sálvora, I de 34 A2
Salza 57 E3
Salzach 56 B3
Salzburg 56 C3
Salzburg (Prov) 59 E1
Salzgitter-Bad 52 B1
Salzgitter-
Lebenstedt 52 B1
Salzhausen 48 B3
Salzkammergut 56 C3
Salzkotten 17 F3
Salzwedel 48 C4
Šamac Slavonski 71 F3
Sama de Langreo 35 D1
Samarina 78 C4
Samatan 28 C4
Sambatiki 87 E3
Sambiase 67 E3
Samboal 40 A1
Sambor 112 C3
Sambre 50 B4
Sambuca di Sicilia 68 B3
Samedan 58 B3
Sameiro, Mte 34 A4
Samer 19 E1
Sámi 82 B4
Samikó 86 B2
Sammatti 107 E2
Sammichele 65 E3
Samnanger 104 A2
Samobor 70 C2
Samodreža 77 D2
Samoëns 27 E4
Samokov (BG) 115 D3
Samokov (YU) 77 D3
Samora Correia 38 A4
Samos 34 C2
Samoš 73 D2

Sámos 89 F1
Sámos, N 89 E1
Samothráki 81 E3
Samothráki, N 81 E3
Samper de
Calanda 37 D4
Sampeyre 31 E2
Samsø 108 B3
Samsø Bælt 108 B3
Samsun 109 E2
Samtens 49 D1
Samugheo 66 B3
San 112 C2
San Adrián 36 C2
San Adrián, C de 34 A1
San Agata de
Goti 64 B3
San Agata di
Militello 69 D2
San Agustín 40 B2
San Amaro 34 B2
San Andrea Frius 66 B3
San Andrés del
Rabanedo 35 D2
San Antioco, I di 66 A4
San Antioco 66 B4
San Antonio 66 B1
San Antonio Abad 45 D3
San Antonio, C de 45 F1
San Bartolomé de las
Abiertas 39 F3
San Bartolomé de la
Torre 42 C2
San Bartolomeo in
Galdo 64 B3
San Benedetto del
Tronto 61 F4
San Benedetto in
Alpe 61 D3
San Benedetto Po 60 C2
San Bernardino 58 B3
San Bernardino,
Psodel 58 B3

San Biagio
Platani 68 B3
San Bonifacio 60 C1
San Candido 59 E2
San Carlos de la
Rápita 41 F2
San Carlos del
Valle 40 B4
San Casciano in Val di
Pesa 60 C4
San Cataldo
(Puglia) 65 F4
San Cataldo
(Sicilia) 68 C3
San Cipirello 68 B3
San Clemente,
Emb de 44 B2
San Clemente 40 C4
San Colombano al
Lambro 60 B2
San Cosme 34 C1
San Cristóbal 42 C1
San Cristóbal de
Entreviñas 35 D3
San Cristóbal de la
Polantera 35 D3
San Cristóbal de la
Vega 39 F1
San Damiano
d'Asti 31 F2
San Daniele del
Friuli 59 E3
San Daniele Po 60 B2
San Demetrio
Corone 67 E2
San Donaci 65 F4
San Donà di Piave 59 E4
San Emiliano 35 D2
San Esteban de
Gormaz 36 A3
San Esteban del
Molar 35 D3

San Esteban del
Valle 39 F2
San Esteban de
Pravia 35 D1
San Fele 64 C4
San Felice a
Cancello 64 B3
San Felice Circeo 63 F3
San Felices de Los
Gallegos 39 D1
San Felice sul
Panaro 60 C2
San Felipe 40 C2
San Feliu de
Guíxols 32 B4
San Ferdinando di
Puglia 64 C3
San Fernando di
Puglia 64 C3
San Fernando 43 D4
San Francisco
Javier 45 D4
San Fratello 69 D2
San Gavino
Monreale 66 B3
San Gemini 63 E1
San Giacomo 59 D2
San Gimignano 60 C4
San Ginesio 61 F4
San Giorgio del
Sannio 64 B3
San Giorgio di
Nogaro 59 F3
San Giorgio
Ionico 65 E4
San Giorgio 31 E1
San Giorgio
Piacentino 60 B2
San Giovanni a
Piro 67 D2
San Giovanni di
Sinis 66 A3

Sant Antoni de C. 32 B3
Sant Antoni, Emb de 37 F3
Sant' Apollinare in Classe 61 D3
Sant' Arcangelo di Romagna 61 E3
Sant Boi de Lluçanès 32 A3
Sant Celoni 32 B4
Sant Cugat 32 A4
Sant' Elia a Pianisi 64 B2
Sant' Elpidio a Mare 61 F4
Sant Esteve d'en Bas 32 B3
Sant'Eufemia, Golfodi 67 E3
Sant'Eufemia Lamezia 67 E3
Sant Gervàs 37 F3
Sant Hilari Sacalm 32 B3
Sant Hipòlit de Voltregà 32 A3
Sant Joan de les Abadesses 32 B3
Sant Julià de Lòria 32 A3
Sant Llorenc de Morunys 32 A3
Sant'Onofrio 67 E3
Sant Pau de Seguries 32 B3
Sant Pere de Roda 32 C3
Sant Pol de Mar 32 B4
Sant Ponç, Emb de 32 A3
Sant Quirze de Besora 32 B3
Sant Quirze Safaja 32 A4
Sant Ramon 37 F3
Sant Sadurní d'Anoia 32 A4
Santa Amalia 39 D4
Santa Ana 40 C4
Santa Anna, Emb de 37 E3
Santa Bàrbara (Catalunya) 41 F2
Santa Bárbara (Andalucía) 42 C2
Santa Bárbara Mt 44 B3
Santa Catarina 42 B3
Santa Caterina Pittinuri 66 A3
Santa Caterina Valfurva 58 C3
Santa Caterina Villarmosa 68 C3
Santa Cesarea Terme 65 F4
Santa Clara-a-Velha 42 A2
Santa Clara, Bgem de 42 A2
Santa Coloma de Farners 32 B3
Santa Coloma de Queralt 37 F4
Santa Colombo de Somoza 35 D3
Santa Comba Dào 38 B2
Santa Comba de Rossas 34 C4
Santa Comba 34 A1
Santa Cristina de Lena 35 D2
Santa Croce di Magliano 64 B2
Santa Cruz de Campezo 36 B2
Santa Cruz de la Palma 42 A4
Santa Cruz de la Sierra 39 E3
Santa Cruz de la Zarza 40 B3
Santa Cruz del Retamar 40 A2
Santa Cruz de Moya 41 D3
Santa Cruz de Mudela 44 A1
Santa Cruz de Tenerife 42 B4

Santa Cruz 36 C4
Santa Elena 44 A1
Santa Eufemia 43 E1
Santa Eugenia 34 A2
Santa Eulalia del Río 45 D3
Santa Eulalia de Oscos 34 C1
Santa Eulalia 41 D2
Santa Eulália 38 C4
Santa Fe 44 A3
Santa Fé 32 B4
Santa Fiora 63 D1
Santa Galdana, Cala 45 F2
Santa Gertrude 58 C3
Santa Giusta 66 B3
Santa Inés, Pto de 36 B3
Santa Liestra y San Quilez 37 E3
Santa Lucia d. Mela 69 D2
Santa Luz 34 C4
Santa Luzia 42 A2
Santa Magdalena de Pulpis 41 F2
Santa Margarida do Sádào 42 B1
Santa Margarida i Els Monjos 32 A4
Santa Margarita 45 F2
Santa Margherita 66 B4
Santa Margherita di Belice 68 B3
Santa Margherita Ligure 60 A3
Santa Maria Capua Vetere 64 B3
Santa Maria, C de 42 B3
Santa Maria da Feira 38 B1
Santa Maria d'Angeli 63 E1
Santa Maria del Campo Rus 40 C3
Santa Maria della Versa 60 A2
Santa Maria di Leuca,C 65 F4
Santa Maria la Real de Nieva 40 A1
Santa Maria la Real de Oseira 34 B2
Santa Maria Maggiore 58 A3
Santa Marina 35 E2
Santa Marina del Rey 35 D3
Santa Marinella 63 D2
Santa María de Huerta 36 B4
Santa María del Campo 35 F3
Santa María del Páramo 35 D3
Santa María de Nieva 44 C3
Santa María de Valverde 35 D3
Santa-Maria-Siché 33 F4
Santa Marta 39 D4
Santa Marta de Penaguião 34 B4
Santa Marta de Tormes 39 E1
Santa Olalla del Cala 43 D2
Santa Olalla 39 F3
Santa Pau 32 B3
Santa Pola 45 E2
Santa sa 45 E3
Santa Sofia 61 D3
Santa Sofia d'Epiro 67 E2
Santa Susanna 32 B4
Santa Tecla 34 A3
Santa Teresa di Riva 69 D2
Santa Teresa, Emb de 39 E2
Santa Teresa Gallura 66 B1
Santaella 43 E2

Santana (Estremadura) 38 A4
Santana (Madeira) 42 A3
Santana de Serra 42 A2
Santander 35 F1
Santanyí 45 F3
Santarém 38 B3
Santas Martas 35 E3
Santeramo in Colle 65 D3
Santes Creus 37 F4
Santesteban 36 C1
Santhià 31 F1
Santiago de Alcántara 38 C3
Santiago de Compostela 34 A2
Santiago de la Espada 44 B2
Santiago de la Ribera 45 D2
Santiago do Cacém 42 A1
Santiago do Escoural 38 B4
Santibáñez de Béjar 39 E2
Santibáñez de la Peña 35 E2
Santibáñez de la Sierra 39 E2
Santibáñez de Vidriales 35 D3
Santillana del Mar 35 F1
Santiponce 43 D2
Säntis 58 B2
Santisteban del Puerto 44 B1
Santo Domingo de la Calzada 36 B2
Santo Domingo de Silos 36 A3
Santo Domingo, Ptode 43 D1
Santo Estêvão (Beira Baixa) 38 C2
Santo Estêvão (Estremadura) 38 A4
Santo Estêvão, Rib de 38 A4
Santo Pedro da Torre 34 A3
Santo Severa 63 D2
Santo Stefano di Cadore 59 E2
Santo Stefano d'Aveto 60 B2
Santo Stino di Livenza 59 E4
Santo Tirso 34 A4
Santo Tomé 44 B2
Santok 49 F3
Santolea, Emb de 41 E2
Santomera, Emb de 45 D2
Santoña 36 A1
Santo-Pietro-di-Tenda 33 F2
Santorini, N 91 E1
Santuario de San Ignacio de Loyola 36 B1
Santuario d'Oropa 27 F4
Santu Lussurgiu 66 B3
Santurtzi 36 B1
Sanxenxo 34 A2
Sanza 67 D1
São Bartolomeu de Messines 42 A2
São Brás de Alportel 42 B3
São Cristóvão 38 B4
São Domingos 42 A1
São Gregório 34 B3
São Jacinto 38 B1
São João da Pesqueira 34 B4
São João de Madeira 38 B1
São João de Tarouca 38 C1
São João dos Caldeireiros 42 B2
São José da Lamarosa 38 B3

São Leonardo 42 C1
São Mamede, Sa de 38 C3
São Manços 42 B1
São Marcos da Serra 42 A2
São Marcos do Campo 42 B1
São Martinho das Amoreiras 42 A2
São Martinho do Porto 38 A3
São Matias 42 B1
São Miguel de Machede 38 B4
São Pedro de Açor 38 C2
São Pedro de Moel 38 A2
São Pedro do Sul 38 C1
São Romão 38 C2
São Teotónio 42 A2
São Vicente, C de 42 A2
São Vicente da Beira 38 C2
Saône 26 C3
Saône-et-Loire 26 B3
Saorge 31 E3
Sapanca 115 F3
Sapataria 38 A3
Sápes 81 E2
Sapiéndza, N 86 C4
Sa Pobla 45 F2
Sappada 59 E2
Sappee 107 E2
Sapri 67 D1
Säräisniemi 99 E4
Sarajärvi 99 E3
Sarajevo 76 A1
Sarakiní 79 E2
Sarakiniko 84 B3
Saramon 28 C4
Sarandáporo 79 E4
Sarandáporos 78 C4
Sarandë 114 C4
Saraváli 86 C1
Saray 115 E3
Sarayköy 115 F4
Šarbanovac 73 E3
Sarbinowo (Gorzów Wlkp) 49 F3
Sarbinowo (Koszalin) 49 F1
Sárbogárd 112 B4
Sarca 58 C3
Sardara 66 B3
Sardegna 66 A2
Sardínia 82 C3
Sardoal 38 B3
Sardona, Piz 58 B2
Sarek 98 A1
Šarengrad 72 B2
Sarentino 59 D2
Särfjället 101 D2
Sargans 58 B2
Sariá, N 93 D2
Sari-d'Orcino 33 F3
Sarine 27 E3
Sariñena 37 E3
Sark 18 A3
Särkisalmi 103 F3
Särkisalo 107 D3
Sarlat-la-Canéda 29 D2
Sarmitunturi 95 F3
Särna 101 D3
Sarnano 61 F4
Sarnen 27 F2
Sarnico 60 B1
Sarno 64 B4
Sarnthein 59 D2
Sarny 113 D2
Sarö 108 C1
Sarón 35 F2
Sarone 59 E3
Saronída 87 F2
Saronikós Kólpos 87 F1
Saronno 60 A1
Sárospatak 112 C3
Sar Planina 77 D3
Sarpsborg 105 D3
Sarracín 35 F3
Sarral 37 F4
Sarralbe 21 E3
Sarrans, Bge de 29 E2

Sarre 21 E3
Sarrebourg 21 E4
Sarreguemines 21 E3
Sarre-Union 21 E3
Sarriá 34 B2
Sarrión 41 E3
Sarroch 66 B4
Sarsina 61 D3
Sars-Poteries 20 B2
Sarstedt 52 B1
Sarteano 63 D1
Sartène 33 F4
Sarthe 23 E4
Sarthe (Dépt) 23 F3
Sárti 80 B4
Sartilly 18 A4
Sarule 66 B2
Sárvár 112 A4
Sarvsjö 101 D2
Sarzana 60 B3
Sarzeau 22 C4
Sarzedas 38 C2
Sasa 77 F2
Saßnitz 49 D1
Sassari 66 A2
Sassello 60 A3
Sassenage 30 C1
Sassenberg 17 F3
Sassenheim 16 B2
Sassetta 62 C1
Sasso 63 E2
Sassoferrato 61 E4
Sassoleone 61 D3
Sasso Marconi 60 C3
Sassuolo 60 C2
Sástago 37 D4
Sasyk, Ozero 113 E4
Sátão 38 C1
Säter 105 F3
Satillieu 30 B1
Satolas 30 C1
Šator 75 D1
Sátoraljaújhely 112 C3
Šatorina 70 B4
Satov 57 E1
Satow 48 C2
Sátres 81 D2
Satrup 48 A1
Sattel 58 A2
Sattledt 57 D3
Satu Mare 112 C3
Saualpe 70 B1
Saucelle, Emb de 39 D1
Sauda 104 A3
Saudárkrókur 96 B1
Sauerlach 56 A3
Sauerland 17 F4
Saugues 29 F2
Saujon 28 B1
Saukkovaara 99 E4
Sauland 104 C3
Sauldre 26 A2
Saulgau 55 D3
Saulieu 26 B2
Sault 30 C3
Saulx 27 D1
Saulxures 27 E1
Saumur 24 C2
Saundersfoot 8 B2
Sauris 59 E3
Saut du Doubs 27 E2
Sautet, Bge du 30 C2
Sautusjärvi 94 C4
Sauve 30 B3
Sauveterre-de-Béarn 28 A4
Sauveterre-de-Guyenne 28 B2
Sauveterre-de-Rouergue 29 E3
Sauvo 107 D2
Sauxillanges 29 F1
Sauze d'Oulx 31 E2
Sauze, le 31 D2
Sauze-Vaussais 24 C4
Sauzon 22 B4
Sava (I) 65 E4
Sava (YU) 71 E3
Savália 86 B1
Sävar 102 B1
Savelli 67 F2
Savenay 23 D4

Saverdun 32 A1
Saverne 21 E4
Savigliano 31 E2
Savignac-les-Eglises 28 C1
Savignano Irpino 64 C3
Savignano sul Rubicone 61 E3
Savigny-sur-Braye 23 F4
Saviñán 36 C4
Savine, Col de la 27 D3
Savines-le-Lac 31 D2
Savinja 70 B1
Savino Selo 72 B2
Savitaipale 103 E4
Sävja 106 B3
Šavnik 76 B2
Savognin 58 B3
Savona 60 A3
Savonlinna 103 E3
Savonranta 103 F3
Sævråsvåg 104 A2
Savudrija 70 A3
Savukoski 95 F4
Sawbridgeworth 10 C2
Sawel Mt 13 D1
Sax 45 D1
Saxmundham 11 E1
Saxnäs 97 E4
Sayatón 40 B2
Säynätsalo 103 D3
Säyneinen 103 E2
Sazadón, Pto de 35 D3
Sázava 112 A3
Scaër 22 B3
Scafa 64 A2
Scafati 64 B4
Scafell Pikes 5 D4
Scala di Santa Regina 33 F3
Scalasaig 4 B2
Scalby 7 D1
Scalea 67 E2
Scalloway 3 F2
Scalpay 2 B3
Scandiano 60 C2
Scanno 64 A2
Scansano 63 D1
Scanzano 65 D4
Scapa Flow 3 D1
Scarba 4 B1
Scarborough 7 D1
Scardovari 61 E2
Scarinish 2 A4
Ščedro 75 E2
Scarriff 12 B4
Scey-sur-Saône 27 D2
Schaalsee 48 B2
Schachendorf 57 F4
Schafberg 56 C3
Schaffhausen 58 A1
Schafstädt 52 C2
Schagen 16 C2
Schaprode 49 D1
Scharbeutz 48 B2
Schärding 56 C2
Scharhörn 47 F2
Scharmützelsee 49 E4
Scharnitz 59 D1
Schauinsland Feldberg 54 C4
Scheeßel 48 A3
Scheggia 61 E4
Scheibbs 57 E3
Scheifling 57 D4
Scheinfeld 55 E1
Schelde 50 B3
Schenefeld (Hamburg) 48 A3
Schenefeld (Itzehoe) 48 A2
Scherfede 52 A2
Schermbeck 17 E3
Scheßlitz 52 C4
Scheveningen 16 B3
Schia 60 B3
Schieder-Schwalenberg 52 A1
Schiedam 16 B3
Schiehallion 4 C1

Schierling 56 B2
Schiermonnikoog 47 D3
Schiermonnikoog / 47 D3
Schiers 58 B2
Schifferstadt 54 C2
Schildau 53 D2
Schilpario 58 C4
Schiltach 54 C3
Schio 59 D4
Schirmeck 21 E4
Schirnding 53 D4
Schkeuditz 53 D2
Schkölen 53 D3
Schladming 59 F1
Schlagsdorf 48 B2
Schlanders 58 C3
Schlangenbad 51 F4
Schleching 56 B3
Schlei 48 A1
Schleiden 51 D4
Schleiz 53 D3
Schleswig 48 A1
Schleswig-Holstein 48 A1
Schleusingen 52 C3
Schließen 53 E1
Schliersee 56 B4
Schlitz 52 B3
Schlotheim 52 B2
Schluchsee 54 C4
Schlucht, Col de la 27 E1
Schlüchtern 52 B4
Schluderbach 59 E2
Schluderns 58 C3
Schlüsselfeld 55 E1
Schlutup 48 B2
Schmalkalden 52 B3
Schmallenberg 17 F4
Schmidmühlen 55 F1
Schmilka 53 F2
Schmölln (Leipzig) 53 D3
Schmölln (Neu-brandenburg) 49 E3
Schnackenburg 48 C3
Schnaittenbach 55 F1
Schneeberg (A) 57 E3
Schneeberg (D) 53 D4
Schneeberg (DDR) 53 D3
Schneverdingen 48 A3
Schoberpaß 57 D4
Schöckl 57 E4
Schönau 54 C4
Schönberg (A) 59 D2
Schönberg (Bayern) 56 C2
Schönberg (Karl-Marx-Stadt) 53 D4
Schönberg (Rostock) 48 B2
Schönberg (Schleswig-Holstein) 48 B1
Schönbrunn 57 F2
Schönebeck 52 C1
Schöneck 53 D3
Schönecken 51 D4
Schönefeld 49 E4
Schönewalde 53 E1
Schongau 55 F4
Schöningen 52 C1
Schönmünzach 54 C3
Schönsee 56 B1
Schönthal 56 B1
Schönwald 54 C3
Schönwalde 48 B2
Schoonhoven 16 C3
Schopfheim 54 C4
Schöppenstedt 52 B1
Schoppernau 58 B2
Schorndorf 55 D2
Schortens 47 E3
Schotten 52 A4
Schouwen Duiveland 16 B3
Schramberg 54 C3
Schrems 57 D2
Schrobenhausen 55 F2
Schröcken 58 B2
Schrozberg 55 E1
Schruns 58 B2
Schuls 58 C2
Schüttorf 17 E2
Schwaan 48 C2

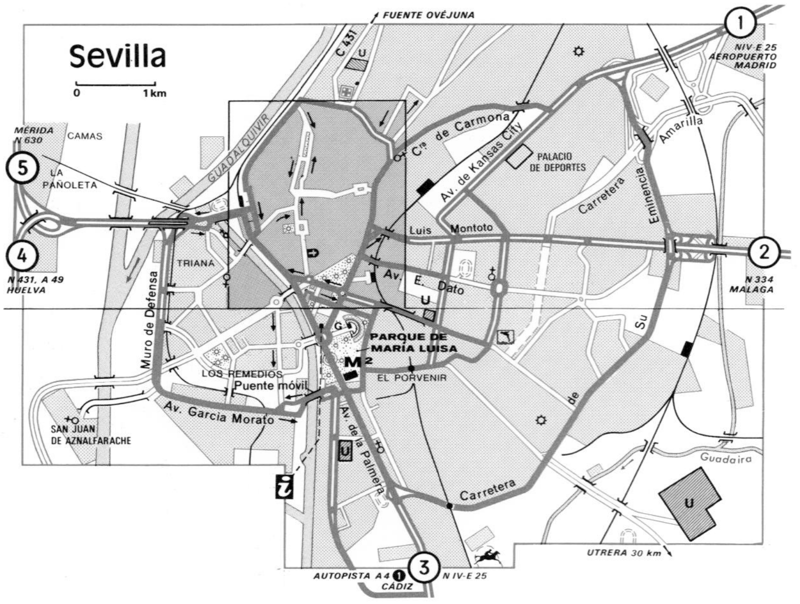
Sevilla
0
1 km
FUENTE OVÉJUNA
N IV-E 25
AEROPUERTO
MADRID
MÉRIDA
N 630
CAMAS
LA PAÑOLETA
N 431, A 49
HUELVA
TRIANA
GUADALQUIVIR
C 431
Cª de Carmona
Av. de Kansas City
PALACIO DE DEPORTES
Amarilla
Carretera
Eminencia
Luis Montoto
N 334
MALAGA
Av. E. Dato
Su
de
PARQUE DE MARIA LUISA
EL PORVENIR
LOS REMEDIOS
Puente móvil
Av. García Morato
Muro de Defensa
SAN JUAN DE AZNALFARACHE
Av. de la Palmera
Carretera
Guadaira
UTRERA 30 km
AUTOPISTA A4
CÁDIZ
N IV-E 25
1
2
3
4
5

Schwabach 55 E1
Schwäbisch Gmünd 55 D2
Schwäbisch Hall 55 D2
Schwabmünchen 55 E3
Schwaigern 55 D2
Schwalmstadt-Treysa 52 A3
Schwalmstadt-Ziegenhain 52 A3
Schwandorf 56 B1
Schwanebeck 52 C1
Schwanenstadt 56 C3
Schwanewede 47 F3
Schwarmstedt 48 A4
Schwarza (A) 57 E3
Schwarza (DDR) 52 C3
Schwarzach 59 E1
Schwarze Elster 53 E1
Schwarzenbach 53 D4
Schwarzenbek 48 B3
Schwarzenberg 53 E3
Schwarzenburg 27 E3
Schwarzenfeld 56 B1
Schwarzheide 53 E2
Schwarzsee 27 E3
Schwarzwald 54 C3
Schwaz 59 D1
Schwechat 57 F2
Schwedt 49 E3
Schweich 54 A1
Schweinfurt 52 B4
Schweinitz 53 E1
Schwelm 17 E4
Schwendi 55 E3
Schwenningen 54 C3
Schwerin 48 C2
Schweriner See 48 C2
Schwerte 17 E3
Schwetzingen 54 C1
Schwielochsee 53 F1
Schwyz 58 A2
Sciacca 68 B3
Scicli 69 D4
Scilla 67 E4
Scilly, Is of 8 A4
Scole 11 D1
Sconser 2 B3
Scopello 58 A4
Scordia 69 D3
Scorff 22 B3
Ščors 113 E1
Scorzè 59 E4
Scotch Corner 6 C1
Scotland 2 C4
Scourie 2 C2
Scrabster 3 D2
Scridain, L 4 B1
Scrivia 60 A2
Ščučin 110 C4
Scunthorpe 7 D2
Scuol 58 C2
Seaford 10 C3
Seaham 5 E4
Seaton 9 D3
Seaton Delaval 5 E3
Sebečevo 76 C1
Sebeş 114 C1
Sebež 111 D3
Sebnitz 53 F2
Sečanj 73 D2
Secchia 60 C2
Seckau 57 D4
Seclin 19 F1
Secondigny 24 C3
Sedan 20 C2
Sedano 35 F2
Seda, Rib de 38 C3
Sedbergh 6 C1
Séderon 30 C3
Sedgefield 5 E4
Sedičany 53 F4
Sedico 59 E3
Sedilo 66 B2
Sedini 66 B2
Sedlare 77 D2
Sedlec-Prčice 53 F4
Sée 18 C4
Seebenau 48 B4
Seebergsattel 70 B1
Seeboden 59 F2
Seebruck 56 B3
Seefeld 58 C1
Seehaus 56 C3
Seehausen (Magdeburg) 52 C1
Seehausen (Stendal) 48 C3
Seeheim 54 C1
Seelisberg 58 A2
Seelow 49 E4
Sées 19 D4
Seesen 52 B1
Seevetal 48 A3
Seewalchen 56 C3
Seewiesen 57 E3
Sefkerin 72 C2
Segesta 68 A3
Segl 58 B3
Segni 63 F3
Segonzac 28 B1
Segorbe 41 E3
Segovia 40 A1
Segré 23 E4
Segre 37 E3
Segre, R 32 A3
Segura 38 C3
Segura de la Sierra 44 B1
Segura de León 43 D1
Segura de los Baños 41 D1
Segura, R 45 D2
Segura, Sa de 44 B2
Sehnde 52 B1
Seia 38 C2
Seiches 23 E4
Seifhennersdorf 53 F2
Seignelay 26 B1
Seil 4 B1
Seiland 95 D1
Seilandsjøkelen 95 D1
Seilhac 29 D1
Seille (Meurthe-et-Moselle) 21 D4
Seille (Saône-et-Loire) 26 C3
Seinäjoki 102 C2
Seine 19 E3
Seine-et-Marne 19 F4
Seine-Maritime 19 D3
Sein, I de 22 A3
Seitenstetten 57 D3
Seitsemisen 102 C3
Seixal 38 A4
Seixo 34 B3
Sejerø 108 B3
Sejerø Bugt 108 B3
Sejm 113 F1
Sékoulas 86 C2
Šekovići 72 B4
Selargius 66 B4
Selassia 87 D3
Selb 53 D4
Selbekken 100 C1
Selbu 101 D2
Selbusjøen 100 C2
Selby 7 D2
Selce 70 B3
Selçuk 115 E4
Sele 64 C4
Selečka pl 77 E4
Selenter See 48 B1
Sélero 81 D2
Sélestat 21 E4
Selevac 73 D3
Selfoss 96 A2
Séli 79 E3
Selia 90 C4
Selianítika 83 D4
Seligenstadt 52 A4
Selinia 87 F1
Selinunte 68 A3
Selishtë 76 C3
Selište 73 E3
Selje 100 A3
Seljord 104 C3
Selkämeri 102 B3
Selkirk 5 D3
Sellajoch 59 D3
Sella Nevea 59 F3
Sella, Pso di 59 D3
Selles 25 E2
Sellières 26 C3
Sellin 49 D1
Selm 17 E3
Selmsdorf 48 B2
Selna 71 F3
Selommes 25 E2
Selongey 26 C2
Seløy 97 D3
Selsey 9 F3
Selsey Bill 9 F3
Selters 52 A4
Seltz 21 F3
Sélune 18 C4
Selva 59 D3
Selvino 58 B4
Seman 114 B3
Semeljci 71 F2
Semič 70 B2
Seminara 67 E4
Semizovac 71 F4
Semmering 57 E3
Semmering -Paß 57 E3
Semois 20 C2
Semproniano 63 D1
Semur-en-Auxois 26 B2
Semur-en-Brionnais 26 B4
Sena 37 E3
Sénas 30 C3
Sendim 34 C4
Senez 31 D3
Senftenberg 53 E2
Sengsengeb 57 D3
Senigallia 61 F3
Senise 65 D4
Senj 70 B3
Senja Ånderdalen 94 B3
Senje 73 E4
Senlis 19 F3
Sennecey-le-Grand 26 C3
Sennen 8 A4
Sennestadt 17 F3
Sennori 66 A2
Senonches 19 E4
Senones 21 E4
Senorbì 66 B3
Senožeče 70 A2
Sens 26 A1
Senta 72 C1
Šentilj 70 C1
Šentjernej 70 C2
Šentjur 70 C2
Šentvid na Šlemenu 70 B1
Sépeaux 26 A1
Šepetovka 113 D2
Sepino 64 B3
Sepúlveda 36 A4
Sequeros 39 E2
Sequillo, R 35 E4
Seraing 50 C4
Seravezza 60 B3
Seregno 60 A1
Serein 26 B2
Séres 80 B2
Séres (Nomos) 80 A2
Serfaus 58 C2
Serfopoúla, N 88 B3
Seriate 60 B1
Sérifos 88 A3
Sérifos, N 88 A3
Serifou, Stenó 88 A3
Sermaize-les-Bains 20 C4
Sermide 60 C2
Sermoneta 63 F3
Sernancelhe 38 C1
Serón 44 B3
Serón de Nágima 36 B4
Serós 37 E4
Serpa 42 B1
Serpeddì, P 66 B4
Serpis, R 45 E1
Serra 41 E3
Serracapriola 64 B2
Serrada 35 E4
Serradifalco 68 C3
Serradilla 39 D3
Serramanna 66 B4
Serrana, Pto de la 39 E3
Serra San Bruno 67 F3
Serravalle Scrivia 60 A2
Serre Chevalier 31 D2
Serre-Ponçon, Bge de 31 D2
Serres 30 C2
Serrières 30 B1
Serrota 39 F2
Sersale 67 F3
Sertã 38 B2
Servan 18 B4
Sérvia 79 E4
Servian 30 A4
Servigliano 61 F4
Servol, R 41 F2
Sesa 37 D3
Sesena 40 A2
Sesia 27 F4
Sesimbra 38 A4
Sesklío, N 93 E1
Sesma 36 C2
Sessa Aurunca 64 A3
Sesta Godano 60 B3
Šestanovac 75 E2
Sestino 61 E3
Sesto 59 E2
Sesto Calende 60 A1
Sesto Fiorentino 60 C3
Sesto San Giovanni 60 A1
Sestola 60 C3
Sestriere 31 E2
Sestri Levante 60 B3
Sestrunj 74 C1
Sestrunj *I* 74 C1
Sestu 66 B4
Sesvete 70 C2
Séta 84 B4
Setcases 32 B3
Sète 30 A4
Setenil 43 E3
Setermoen 94 B3
Setesdalen 104 B3
Setesdalsheiene 104 B3
Settebagni 63 E2
Settimo Torinese 31 E1
Settle 6 C1
Settons, les 26 B2
Setúbal 38 A4
Seudre 28 B1
Seui 66 B3
Seulo 66 B3
Seurre 26 C2
Sevastianá 79 E3
Sevenoaks 10 C3
Sévérac-le-Château 29 F3
Sever do Vouga 38 B1
Severn Bridge 9 D2
Severn, Mouth of the 9 D2
Severn,R 9 D2
Sever, R 38 C3
Seveso 60 A1
Sevettijärvi 95 F2
Sevilla 43 D2
Sevilleja de la Jara 39 F3
Sevlievo 115 D2
Sevnica 70 C2
Sevojno 72 C4
Sèvre Nantaise 24 C3
Sèvre Niortaise 24 C4
Sévrier 27 D4
Sevsk 111 F4
Sexten 59 E2
Seyches 28 C2
Seyda 53 D1
Seydisfjörður 96 C2
Seyne 31 D3
Seyne, la 31 D4
Seyssel 27 D4
Sežana 70 A2
Sézanne 20 B4
Sezimovo-Ústí 57 D1
Sezze 63 F3
Sfáka 91 F4
Sfakiá 90 C4
Sfaktiria, N 86 C3
Sferracavallo 68 B2
Sfikiá, L 79 E3
Sfîntu Gheorghe 113 D4
Sforzacosta 61 F4
's Gravendeel 16 C3
's Gravenhage 16 B3
Sgùrr Mór 2 C3
Sgùrr na Ciche 2 B4
Shaftesbury 9 D3
Shanklin 9 E4
Shannon 12 B4
Shannon, Mouth of the 12 A4
Shannon, R 12 B4
Shap 5 D4
Shapinsay 3 E1
Shebenik, Mal i 77 D4
Sheelin, L 13 D3
Sheep Haven 12 C1
Sheep's Head 14 A4
's Heerenberg 17 D3
Sheerness 11 D2
Sheffield 6 C2
Shefford 9 F2
Shëmri (Shkodër) 76 C3
Shëmri (Tiranë) 76 C4
Shëngjin 76 C3
Sheppey, I of 11 D2
Shepshed 7 D3
Shepton Mallet 9 D3
Sherborne 9 D3
Shercock 13 D3
Sheringham 7 F3
's Hertogenbosch 16 C3
Shetland Is 3 E2
Shiel Bridge 2 C4
Shieldaig 2 B3
Shiel, L 2 B4
Shijak 76 C4
Shinás 79 E3
Shiniás 88 A1
Shin, L 2 C2
Shínos 83 D3
Shinoússa, N 88 C3
Shipston-on-Stour 9 E1
Shíza, N 86 C4
Shkodër 76 B3
Shkodrës, Liq i 76 B3
Shkumbin 76 C4
Sholári 80 A3
Shoreham 10 C3
Shpat, Mal i 77 D4
Shrewsbury 6 B3
Shrewton 9 E3
Shropshire 9 D1
Shupenzë 77 D4
Sía, Pto de la 36 A1
Siátista 79 D4
Šiauliai 110 C3
Sibari 67 E2
Sibbhult 109 D3
Sibbo 107 F2
Sibbofjärden 107 F2
Šibenik 75 D1
Šibenik *Mt* 75 E2
Sibinj 71 E3
Sibiu 113 D4
Sićevo 73 F4
Sichar, Emb de 41 E3
Sicié, Cap 31 D4
Sicignano degli Alburni 64 C4
Sicilia 68 B2
Sicó 38 B2
Šid 72 B2
Sidári 82 A1
Sideby 102 B3
Sidensjö 102 A2
Siderno 67 F4
Síderos, Akr 91 F3
Sidiró 81 F2
Sidirókastro 80 A2
Sidirónero 80 C1
Sidlaw Hills 5 D1
Sidmouth 9 D3
Siebenlehn 53 E2
Siedlce 112 C1
Sieg 51 E3
Siegburg 51 E3
Siegen 17 F4
Siegsdorf 56 B3
Siekierki 49 E3
Siena 61 D4
Sieppijärvi 98 C1
Sieradz 112 B2
Sierck 21 D3
Sierentz 27 E1
Sierninghofen 57 D3
Sierpc 112 B1
Sierra Boyera, Emb de 43 E1
Sierra de Fuentes 39 D3
Sierra de Yeguas 43 E3
Sierre 27 E3
Sievi 102 C1
Sievin as 102 C1
Sífnos, N 88 B3
Sífnou, Stenó 88 B3
Sigean 32 B2
Sigerfjord 94 A3
Siggjarvåg 104 A3
Sighetu Marmaţiei 112 C3
Sighişoara 113 D4
Siglufjörður 96 B1
Sigmaringen 55 D3
Signy-l'Abbaye 20 B2
Sígri 85 E2
Sigtuna 106 B3
Sigüenza 36 B4
Sigulda 110 C2
Siiddasjávri 94 B4
Siikainen 102 B3
Siikajoki 99 D4
Siikajoki *R* 99 D4
Siilinjärvi 103 E2
Sijarinska Banja 77 D1
Sikaminiá 85 F2
Sikås 101 E2
Sikí 84 A2
Sikiá (Makedonía) 80 B4
Sikiá (Pelopónissos) 87 E4
Síkinos 88 C4
Síkinos, N 88 C4
Sikióna 87 D1
Sikoráhi 81 E2
Sikoúrio 83 E1
Sikovuono 95 E3
Sila, La 67 F3
Silandro 58 C3
Silba 70 B4
Silba *I* 70 B4
Silbaš 72 B2
Sildegapet 100 A2
Şile 115 F3
Siles 44 B1
Siliqua 66 B4
Silistra 115 E1
Silivri 115 E3
Siljan (N) 104 C3
Siljan (S) 101 E4
Siljansnäs 101 E4
Silkeborg 108 A3
Silla 41 E4
Silleda 34 B2
Silleiro, C 34 A3
Sillé-le-Guillaume 23 E3
Sillian 59 E2

Name	Page	Grid
Silloth	5	D4
Šilo	70	B3
Silo	81	E2
Sil, R	34	C2
Sils	32	B4
Sils im Engadin	58	B3
Siltakylä	107	F2
Šilutė	110	B3
Silvalen	97	D3
Silvaplana	58	B3
Silvares	38	C2
Silves	42	A2
Silvi Marina	64	A1
Silvrettagruppe	58	B2
Silz	58	C2
Simancas	35	E4
Símandra	80	A3
Šimanovci	72	C3
Simav	115	F4
Simaxis	66	B3
Simbach (Inn)	56	B3
Simbach (Isar)	56	B2
Simbruini, Mti	63	F2
Simeto	69	D3
Sími	93	E1
Šimići	71	E3
Šími, N	60	A1
Simlångsdalen	108	C2
Simmerath	51	D4
Simmern	54	B1
Simo	99	D3
Simojärvi	99	E2
Simojoki	99	D3
Simola	103	F4
Símonos Pétras	80	C4
Simonsbath	8	C3
Simonswald	54	C3
Simópoulo	86	B3
Simplonpass	27	F3
Simrishamn	109	D3
Sinaia	113	D4
Sinalunga	61	D4
Sinarádes	82	A1
Sinarcas	41	D3
Sindelfingen	55	D2
Sindirgi	115	F4
Síndos	79	F3
Sines	42	A1
Sines, C de	42	A1
Sinettä	99	D2
Sineu	45	F3
Singen	55	D4
Singöfjärden	106	B3
Singra, Pto de	41	D2
Siniscola	66	C2
Sinj	75	D1
Sinjajevina	76	B2
Sinni	65	D4
Sinnicolau Mare	114	C1
Sinopoli	67	E4
Sinsheim	55	D2
Sintra	38	A4
Sinzig	51	E4
Siófok	112	B4
Sion	27	E3
Sioule	26	A4
Šipan	75	F2
Šipanska Luka	75	F2
Šipka	115	D2
Sipoo	107	F2
Sipoonselkä	107	F2
Šipovo	71	E4
Sippola	107	F2
Šiprage	71	E4
Sira	104	A4
Sira R	104	B4
Siracusa	69	D4
Sirdalen	104	B4
Sirdalvatn	104	A4
Siret	113	D3
Siret R	113	E4
Sirevåg	104	A4
Sirig	72	C2
Sirino, Mte	65	D4
Širitovci	75	D1
Sirkka	95	E4
Sirma	95	E2
Sirmione	60	C1
Sírna, N	92	C1
Široko Polje	71	F2
Sirolo	61	F4
Síros, N	88	B2
Siruela	39	F4
Sisak	71	D2
Šišan	70	A4
Sisante	40	C4
Šišljavić	70	C3
Sissa	60	B2
Sissach	27	F2
Sissonne	20	B3
Sisteron	31	D3
Sistiana	59	F3
Sistranda	100	C1
Sitges	32	A4
Sithonía	80	B4
Sitía	91	F4
Sitnica	77	D2
Sittard	17	D4
Sittensen	48	A3
Sittingbourne	11	D3
Siuntio	107	E3
Siuro	107	E1
Siurua	99	D3
Siuruanjoki	99	D3
Siusi	59	D3
Sivac	72	B2
Sivaslı	115	F4
Siviri	80	A4
Sívota	82	B2
Sívros	82	B3
Siziano	60	A1
Sizun	22	B3
Sjælland	108	C3
Sjællands Odde	108	B3
Sjenica	76	C1
Sjeništa	76	A1
Sjøåsen	97	D4
Sjöbo	109	D3
Sjøholt	100	B2
Sjona	97	E2
Sjötorp	105	E4
Sjoutnäset	97	E4
Sjøvegan	94	B3
Sjulsmark	102	B1
Sjundea	107	E3
Sjusjøen	104	D2
Skåbu	100	C3
Skäckerfjällen	101	D1
Skadarsko jez	76	B3
Skadovsk	113	F4
Skafidiá	86	B2
Skaftá	96	B2
Skagafjörður	96	B1
Skage	97	D4
Skagen	108	B1
Skagern	105	E4
Skagerrak	108	A1
Skaill	3	E1
Skajálfandi	96	B1
Skála (Kefaloniá)	86	A1
Skála (Lésvos)	85	F2
Skála (Pátmos)	89	E2
Skála (Pelopónnisos)	87	D3
Skála (Stereá Eláda)	83	F3
Skála Eressoú	85	E2
Skála Kaliráhis	80	C3
Skaland	94	B2
Skála Oropoú	84	B4
Skála Potamiás	81	D3
Skála Rahoníou	80	C3
Skalavik	96	A4
Skála Volissoú	85	E4
Skälderviken	108	C3
Skålevik	104	B4
Skálfandafljót	96	B2
Skalka	98	A2
Skalohóri (Lésvos)	85	E2
Skalohóri (Makedonía)	79	D3
Skaloti	80	C1
Skælskør	108	B4
Skamnéli	78	C4
Skandáli	85	D1
Skandári, Akr	89	F3
Skanderborg	108	B3
Skandzoúra, N	84	B3
Skåne	109	D3
Skånevik	104	A3
Skåningsbukt	94	C2
Skånland	94	B3
Skänninge	106	A4
Skanör Falsterbo	108	C4
Skara	109	D1
Skaraborgs Län	109	D1
Skaramangás	87	F1
Skærbæk	108	A4
Skarberget	94	B4
Škarda	74	B1
Skåre	105	E3
Skárfia	83	F3
Skärgårdshavet	107	D3
Skärhamn	108	C1
Skarnes	105	D3
Skarplinge	106	B2
Skarsvåg	95	E1
Skärvången	101	E1
Skarżysko-Kamienna	112	B2
Skattungbyn	101	E4
Skatval	100	C2
Skaulo	94	C4
Skaun	100	C2
Skee	105	D4
Skegness	7	E3
Skei (Møre og Romsdal)	100	B2
Skei (Sogn og Fjordane)	100	A3
Skeiðarársandur	96	B2
Skela	72	C3
Skellefteå	98	B4
Skellefteälven	98	B4
Skelleftehamn	98	B4
Skellig	14	A4
Skelmersdale	6	B2
Skenderbeut, M i	76	C4
Skender Vakuf	71	E4
Skepastó	80	B2
Skerries	13	E3
Ski	105	D3
Skíathos	84	A2
Skíathos, N	84	A2
Skibbereen	14	B4
Skibby	108	C3
Skibotn	94	C2
Skiddaw	5	D4
Skídra	79	E3
Skien	104	C3
Skierniewice	112	B2
Skillingaryd	109	D2
Skiloundía	86	C2
Skinári, Akr	86	A1
Skiniás	91	E4
Skinnarbu	104	B3
Skinnskatteberg	105	F3
Skipagurra	95	F1
Skipton	6	C2
Skíros	84	C3
Skíros, N	84	C3
Skíti	83	F1
Skive	108	A2
Skivjane	76	C2
Skjeberg	105	D3
Skjern	108	A3
Skjersholmane	104	A3
Skjerstad	97	E2
Skjerstadfjorden	97	E2
Skjervøy	94	C2
Skjønhaug	105	D3
Sklavopoúla	90	B3
Sklithro	83	F1
Šklov	111	E3
Skočivir	77	E4
Škocjanske jame	70	A3
Skodje	100	B2
Škofja Loka	70	A2
Škofljica	70	B2
Skog (Gävleborgs Län)	101	F4
Skog (Västernorrlands Län)	102	A2
Skógafoss	96	B3
Skogerøya	95	F2
Skoghall	105	E3
Skogstorp	105	F4
Skokloster	106	B3
Skólis	86	B1
Skópelos (Lésvos)	85	F3
Skópelos (Skópelos)	84	B2
Skópelos, N	84	B3
Skopí	91	F4
Skopiá	83	E2
Skopje	77	E3
Skopós	79	D2
Skopun	96	A4
Skorenovac	73	D3
Skorovatn	97	E4
Skorped	101	F2
Skotina	79	F4
Skotterud	105	D3
Skoulikariá	82	C2
Skoúra	87	D3
Skoúrta	87	F1
Skoútari (Makedonía)	80	B2
Skoútari (Pelopónnissos)	87	D4
Skoutáros	85	E2
Skövde	109	D1
Skrá	79	E2
Skrad	70	B3
Skradin	75	D1
Skradinski buk	75	D1
Skreia	105	D2
Skrim	104	C3
Skrolsvik	94	B3
Skrydstrup	108	A4
Skudeneshavn	104	A3
Skuleskogen	102	A2
Skull	14	A4
Skultuna	106	A3
Skuodas	110	B3
Skuov'gilraš'ša	95	D2
Skurup	109	D3
Skutskär	106	B2
Skutvik	94	A4
Skvira	113	E2
Skye	2	B3
Slagelse	108	B3
Slagnäs	98	A3
Slânčev Brjag	115	E2
Slancy	111	D1
Slane	13	D3
Slaney	15	D3
Slangerup	108	C3
Slano	75	F2
Slany	53	F3
Šlapanice	57	F1
Slapská přehr nádrž	53	F4
Šlask	112	A2
Slatina (Bor)	73	E3
Slatina (Bosna i Hercegovina)	71	E3
Slatina (Kraljevo)	73	D4
Slatina (Makedonija)	77	D3
Slatina (RO)	115	D1
Slatine	75	D2
Slatinski Drenovac	71	E2
Slavgorod	111	E4
Slavinja	77	F1
Slavkovica	72	C4
Slavkov u Brna	57	F1
Slavnik	70	A3
Slavonice	57	E1
Slavonska Požega	71	E2
Slavonski Brod	71	E3
Slavonski Kobaš	71	E3
Slavuta	113	D2
Sławno	110	A4
Sławoborze	49	F2
Sleaford	7	D3
Slea Head	14	A3
Sleat, Sd of	2	B3
Slettfjellet	94	C2
Sliedrecht	16	C3
Sliema	68	B4
Slieve Bloom Mts	12	C4
Slieve Donard	13	E3
Slieve Mish Mts	14	A3
Slievenamon	14	C3
Slieve Snaght	13	D1
Sligachan	2	B3
Sligeach	12	C2
Sligo	12	C2
Sligo (Co)	12	B3
Sligo B	12	C2
Slišane	77	D1
Slite	109	F4
Sliven	115	E2
Sljeme	70	C2
Šljivovica	72	C4
Slobozia	115	E1
Slonim	112	C1
Sloten	16	C1
Slough	9	F2
Slovac	72	C3
Slovenska Bistrica	70	C1
Slovenija	70	A2
Slovenj Gradec	70	B1
Slovenske Konjice	70	C1
Slovenské Rudohorie	112	B3
Slovinci	71	D3
Słubice	49	F4
Sluck	111	D4
Sluderno	58	C3
Sluis	16	A4
Sluknov	53	F2
Slunj	70	C3
Słupsk	110	A4
Slyne Head	12	A3
Småland	109	D2
Smålandsfarvandet	108	B4
Smålands-stenar	109	D2
Šmarje	70	C2
Šmarješke Toplice	70	B2
Šmartin	70	B2
Smedby	109	E2
Smědeč	56	C2
Smederevo	73	D3
Smederevska Palanka	73	D3
Smedjebacken	105	F3
Smela	113	F2
Smigáda	81	E2
Smilčić	74	C1
Smilde	17	D1
Smiltene	110	C2
Smojmirovo	77	F3
Smokovljan	75	F2
Smøla	100	B1
Smolensk	111	E3
Smoleviči	111	D4
Smólikas, Óros	78	C4
Smoljan	115	D3
Smorgon	111	D4
Smørhamn	104	A1
Smygehamn	109	D4
Snaefell	6	A1
Snæfellsnes	96	A2
Snaith	7	D2
Snåsa	101	D1
Snasahögarna	101	D2
Snåsavatnet	101	D1
Sneek	16	C1
Sneem	14	A4
Snežnik	70	B3
Sniardwy, Jez	110	B4
Snigir'ovka	113	F3
Snillfjord	100	C2
Snizort, L	2	B3
Šnjegotina Velika	71	E3
Snøfjord	95	D1
Snøhefta	100	C3
Snøtinden	97	E2
Snowdon	6	A3
Snowdonia Forest and Nat Pk	6	A3
Soave	60	C1
Sobeslav	57	D1
Sobra	75	F2
Sobrado	34	B2
Sobral da Adiça	42	C1
Sobrón, Emb de	36	B2
Sobreira Formosa	38	C2
Sobral de Monte Agraço	38	A3
Søby	108	B4
Soča	70	A2
Soča R	70	A2
Sočanica	77	D1
Soccia	33	F3
Sochaczew	112	B1
Sochaux	27	E2
Socol	73	D2
Socovos	44	C1
Socuéllamos	40	B4
Sodankylä	95	E4
Soderåkra	109	E3
Söderbärke	105	F3
Söderfors	106	B3
Söderhamn	101	F4
Söderköping	106	A4
Södermanlands Län	106	A4
Söderskog	109	D3
Södertälje	106	B4
Sodražica	70	B2
Sodupe	36	B1
Soest (D)	17	F3
Soest (NL)	16	C2
Soestdijk	16	C2
Sofádes	83	E2
Sofia	115	D2
Sofiero	108	C3
Sofikó	87	E1
Sofó	83	E2
Sögel	17	E1
Sogliano al Rubicone	61	E3
Soglio	58	B3
Sogndal	100	B3
Søgne	104	B4
Sognefjell	100	B3
Sognefjorden	104	A1
Sognesjøen	104	A1
Sogn og Fjordane	100	A3
Soham	11	D1
Sohós	80	A2
Soignies	50	B4
Soini	102	C2
Soinlahti	103	D1
Soissons	20	B3
Söke	115	E4
Sokna	104	C2
Soko Banja	73	E4
Sokolac	72	B4
Sokolov	53	D4
Sokołów Podlaski	112	C1
Sokosti	95	F3
Sola (Rogaland)	104	A3
Sola (Sogn og Fjordane)	104	A1
Solana de los Barros	39	D4
Solana del Pino	43	F1
Solares	35	F2
Solberg	101	F1
Solbergfjorden	94	B3
Solčava	70	B1
Sol'cy	111	D2
Solda	58	C3
Sölden	58	C2
Solenzara	33	F4
Solesmes (Nord)	20	A2
Solesmes (Sarthe)	23	E3
Solevåg	100	A2
Solf	102	B2
Solferino	60	C1
Solholmen	100	B2
Solignac (Haute-Loire)	29	F2
Solignac (Haute-Vienne)	29	D1
Soligorsk	111	D4
Solihull	9	E1
Solin	75	D1
Soline	74	B1
Solingen	17	E4
Sölkerpaß	57	D4
Sollana	41	E4
Sollefteå	101	F2
Sollenau	57	F3
Sollentuna	106	B3
Söller	45	E2
Sollerön	101	E4
Søllested	108	B4
Solliès-Pont	31	D4
Solnečnogorsk	111	F2
Solofra	64	B4
Solosancho	39	F2
Solothurn	27	E2
Solre-le-Château	20	B2
Solsona	32	A3
Soltau	48	A3
Solunska Glava	77	E3
Solunto	68	B3
Solvay	60	C4
Sölvesborg	109	D3
Solvorn	100	B3
Solway Firth	4	C4
Solynieve	44	A3
Soma	115	E4
Sombernon	26	C2
Sombor	72	B2
Someren	17	D4
Somero	107	E2
Somerset	9	D3
Somes	112	C4
Somiedo, Pto de	35	D2
Sommarøy	94	B2
Sommatino	68	C4
Somme	19	E2
Somme (Dépt)	19	F2
Sommen	109	E1
Sömmerda	52	C2
Sommesous	20	B4
Sommières	30	B3
Sømna	97	D3
Somolinos	36	A4
Somosierra, Pto de	36	A4
Sompio	95	F3
Somport, Pto de	37	D2
Šomrda	73	E3
Soncillo	35	F2
Soncino	60	B1
Søndeled	104	C4
Sønderborg	108	B4
Sønderby	108	B4
Sønder Felding	108	A3
Sondershausen	52	C2
Søndersø	108	B3
Sondrio	58	B3
Songeons	19	E3
Sonkajärvi	103	E1
Sonnblick	59	E2
Sonneberg	52	C4
Sonnewalde	53	E1
Sonogno	58	A3
Sonsbeck	17	D3
Sonseca	40	A3
Son Servera	45	F3
Sonta	72	B2
Sonthofen	55	E4
Sontra	52	B3
Sopeira	37	F3
Sopilja	76	A1
Sopište	77	D3
Sopoćani	76	C1
Sopot (PL)	110	A4
Sopot (YU)	73	D3
Sopotnica	77	D4
Sopron	112	A4
Sora	64	A3
Soragna	60	B2
Söraker	101	F3
Sørarnøy	97	E2
Sorbas	44	C3
Sorbe, R	40	B1
Sore	28	B3
Soresina	60	B1
Sørfjorden	104	B2
Sør-Flatanger	96	C4
Sørfolda	94	A4
Sörfors	102	A1
Sorga	52	B3
Sorgono	66	B3
Sorgues	30	B3
Sørgutvik	97	D4
Soria	36	B3
Soriano nel Cimino	63	E2
Sørkjosen	94	C2
Sørø	108	B3
Soroki	113	E3
Soro, M	69	D3
Soroni	93	E1
Sørøya	95	D1
Sørøysundet	95	D1
Sorraia, R	38	A4
Sørreisa	94	B3
Sorrento	64	B4
Sor, Rib de	38	B3
Sørrollnes	94	B3
Sorsakoski	103	E2
Sorsele	98	A3
Sorso	66	A2
Sort	37	F2
Sortino	69	D4
Sortland	94	A3
Sortlandsundet	94	A3
Sør Trøndelag	100	C2
Sorunda	106	B4
Sørvågen	97	E1
Sørvågur	96	A4
Sørvær	94	C1
Sørværøy	97	E1
Sörvattnet	101	D3
Sos del Rey Católico	37	D2
Soses	37	E4
Sosnovyj Bor	111	D1
Sosnowiec	112	B2
Sospel	31	E3

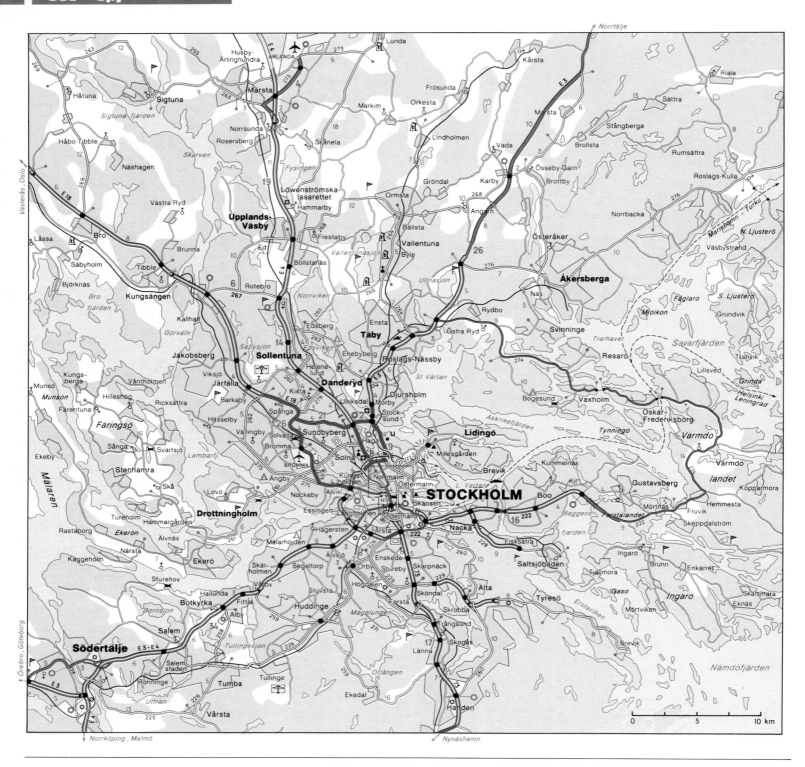

Šoštanj	70 B1	Souesmes	25 F2	Soure	38 B2	South	
Sóstis	81 D2	Soufflenheim	21 F3	Sournia	32 B2	Queensferry	5 D2
Šostka	111 F4	Soufli	81 F2	Souroti	80 A3	South Ronaldsay	3 E1
Sotaseter	100 B3	Soúgia	90 B4	Soúrpi	83 F2	Southsea	9 F3
Sotillo de la		Souillac	29 D2	Sousceyrac	29 D2	South Shields	5 E3
Adrada	39 F2	Souilly	20 C3	Sousel	38 C4	South Tyne	5 D3
Sotin	72 B2	Soulac	28 A1	Soustons	28 A4	South Uist	2 A3
Sotíra	79 E2	Soulaines-Dhuys	20 C4	Soutelo	34 B2	Southwell	7 D3
Sotkamo	99 E4	Soulinári	86 C3	Souterraine, la	25 E4	Southwold	11 E1
Soto del Barco	35 D1	Soulíou, Óri	82 B2	Southam	9 E1	Souvála	87 F2
Soto de los		Soulópoulo	82 B1	Southampton	9 E3	Souvigny	26 A3
Infantes	35 D1	Soultz (Bas-Rhin)	21 E3	Southborough	10 C3	Sovata	113 D4
Soto de Luiña	35 D1	Soultz (Haut-Rhin)	27 E1	South Downs	9 F3	Sövdeborg	109 D3
Soto de Sajambre	35 E2	Soúnio	88 A2	Southend	4 B3	Soverato	67 F3
Sotogrande	43 E4	Soúnio, Akr	88 A2	Southend-on-Sea	11 D2	Soveria Mannelli	67 F3
Sotopalacios	35 D3	Souppes	25 F1	Southern Uplands	4 C3	Sovetsk	110 B3
Sottomarina	61 D1	Source de la Loue	27 D2	South Esk	3 D4	Søvik	100 A2
Sottunga	106 C3	Source du		South Foreland	11 D3	Sož	111 E4
Sotuélamos	40 C4	Lison	27 D3	South Molten	8 C3	Sozopol	115 E2
Soúda	90 C3	Sourdeval	18 C4	Southport	6 B2	Spa	51 D4

Spaichingen	55 D3	Spathí, Akr		Spiddle	12 B3
Spakenburg	16 C2	(Pelopónissos)	87 F2	Spiekeroog	47 E2
Spalding	7 E3	Spodnji Brnik	70 B2	Spielfeld	70 C1
Spánda, Akr	90 B3	Spean Bridge	2 C4	Spiez	27 F3
Spandau	49 D4	Speikkogel	57 E4	Spijkenisse	16 B3
Spangenberg	52 B3	Spello	63 E1	Spílea Diroú	87 D4
Spanish Pt	12 B4	Spennymoor	5 E4	Spíli	90 C4
Sparlösa	108 C1	Sperhiáda	83 E3	Spiliá	83 E1
Spárta	87 E1	Sperhiós	83 E3	Spilimbergo	59 E3
Spárti	87 D3	Sperillen	104 C2	Spilsby	7 E3
Spartivento, C		Sperlonga	63 E3	Spinalónga	91 E3
(Calabria)	67 E4	Sperrin Mts	13 D1	Spinazzola	65 D3
Spartivento, C		Spétses	87 E3	Spincourt	20 C3
(Sardegna)	66 B4	Spétses, N	87 E3	Spišić Bukovica	71 E2
Spárto	82 C3	Spetsopoúla, N	87 E3	Špišská-Nová Ves	112 B3
Spas-Demensk	111 F3	Speyer	54 C2	Spital	57 D3
Spáta	87 F1	Spey, R	3 D3	Spittal	59 F2
Spatharéi	89 E2	Spezzano		Spitz	57 E2
Spathí, Akr		Albanese	67 E2	Spjelkavik	100 A2
(Kíthira)	90 A1	Spezzano della Sila	67 E2		

Split	75 D2	Stansted	10 C2	Steine	104 A1		
Spluga, Pso dello	58 B3	Stapar	72 B2	Steinestø	104 A2		
Splügen	58 B3	Starachowice	112 B2	Steinfeld	17 F2		
Splügenpass	58 B3	Stara Gradina	71 E2	Steinfeld	59 F2		
Spodsbjerg	108 B4	Staraja Russa	111 E2	Steinfurt	17 E2		
Špola	113 F2	Stara Moravica	72 B1	Steingaden	55 F4		
Spoleto	63 E1	Stara Novalja	70 B4	Steinhaus	59 D2		
Spornitz	48 C3	Stara Pazova	72 C2	Steinhausen	55 D3		
Spotorno	60 A3	Stara Pl (BG)	115 D2	Steinheim (Baden-			
Spreča	71 F3	Stara Pl (YU)	73 F4	Württemberg)	55 E2		
Spree	49 E4	Stará Role	53 E4	Steinheim			
Spreewald	53 E1	Staravina	77 E4	(Bayern)	55 E3		
Spremberg	53 F1	Stara Vrata	70 C4	Steinheim (Nordrhein-			
Spresiano	59 E4	Stara Zagora	115 D2	Westfalen)	52 A2		
Springe	52 A1	Staretina	75 D1	Steinkjer	101 D1		
Sprogø	108 B4	Stargard		Steinnuder Meer	48 A1		
Spurn Head	7 E2	Szczeciński	49 F2	Steinpaß	59 E1		
Spuž	76 B2	Stårheim	100 A3	Steinshamn	100 A2		
Squillace, Golfo di	67 F3	Stari	77 F3	Steinsland	104 A2		
Squinzano	65 F4	Stari Bar	76 B3	Stekene	50 B3		
Srb	71 D4	Stari Begej	72 C2	Stelvio, Parco Naz			
Srbac	71 E3	Starica	111 F2	della	58 C3		
Srbica	77 D2	Starigrad (Hvar)	75 D2	Stelvio, Pso dello	58 C3		
Srbija	73 D4	Starigrad		Stená Klissoúras	79 D3		
Srbobran	72 C2	(Velebit)	70 B4	Stenay	20 C3		
Srdđevići	75 E1	Stari Gradac	71 E2	Stendal	48 C4		
Srebrenica	72 C4	Starigrad		Steni	84 B4		
Središče	70 C1	Paklenica	70 C4	Stenlille	108 B3		
Sredna Gora	115 D2	Stari Jankovci	72 B2	Stenløse	108 C3		
Srednje	71 F4	Stari Log	70 B2	Stenness	3 D1		
Srednji kanal	74 C1	Stari Majdan	71 D3	Stenó	87 D2		
Srednogorie	115 D2	Stari Mikanovci	71 F2	Stenó, Akr	88 B2		
Sredska	77 D3	Starnberg	56 A3	Stenó Ithákis	82 B4		
Sremska		Starnberger See	56 A3	Sténoma	83 D3		
Kamenica	72 C2	Starodub	111 F4	Stenudden	98 A2		
Sremska Mitrovica	72 C3	Starogard		Stenungsund	108 C1		
Sremska Rača	72 B3	Gdański	110 A4	Stepanci	77 E3		
Sremski Karlovci	72 C2	Starokonstantinov		Stepnica	49 E2		
Srnetica	71 D4		113 D2	Stepojevac	72 C3		
Srnice Donje	71 F3	Staro Nagoričane	77 E2	Stereá Eláda	83 D3		
Środa		Staro Petrovo Selo	71 E3	Sterkrade	17 E3		
Wielkopolska	112 A1	Staro Slano	76 A2	Stérna			
Srpska Crnja	72 C1	Start Pt	8 C4	(Makedonía)	80 C2		
Srpske Moravice	70 B3	Starý Smokovec	112 B3	Stérna			
Srpski Itebej	73 D1	Staßfurt	52 C1	(Pelopónissos)	87 D2		
Srpski Miletić	72 B2	Statland	97 D4	Stérna (Thráki)	81 F1		
Stabbursdalen	95 D2	Staußfurt	52 C2	Sternberg	48 C2		
Stade	48 A3	Stavanger	104 A3	Stérnes	90 C3		
Stádio	87 D2	Staveley	7 F3	Sterup	48 A1		
Stadskanaal	17 E1	Stavelot	51 D4	Sterza, la	60 C4		
Stadthagen	52 A1	Stavenisse	16 B3	Sterzing	59 D2		
Stadtilm	52 C3	Staveren	16 C1	Stevenage	9 F2		
Stadtkyll	51 D4	Stavern	104 C4	Stevns	108 C4		
Stadtlohn	17 E3	Stavrí, Akr	88 C3	Stevns Klint	108 C4		
Stadtoldendorf	52 A2	Stavrodrómi	86 C1	Stewarton	4 C2		
Stadtroda	52 C3	Stavrohóri	91 F4	Steyr	57 D3		
Stadtsteinach	52 C4	Stavrós (Évia)	84 B3	Steyrermühl	56 C3		
Stadt Wehlen	53 F2	Stavrós (Imathía)	79 E3	Stia	61 D3		
Staffa	4 A1	Stavrós (Itháki)	82 B4	Stigliano	65 D4		
Staffanstorp	108 C3	Stavrós (Kríti)	90 C3	Stigtomta	106 A2		
Staffelsee	56 A4	Stavrós (Thessalía)	83 E2	Stilfserjoch	58 C3		
Staffelstein	52 C4	Stavrós		Stilida	83 E3		
Staffin	2 B3	(Thessaloníki)	80 B3	Stilo	67 F4		
Stafford	6 C3	Stavrós, Akr (Kríti)	91 D3	Stimánga	87 D1		
Staffordshire	6 C3	Stavrós, Akr		Stimfalía, L	87 D1		
Stágira	80 B3	(Thássos)	81 D3	Štimlje	77 D2		
Stahle	52 A2	Stavroúpoli	80 C2	Stintino	66 A1		
Stahovica	70 B2	Steblevë	77 D4	Štip	77 E3		
Staines	9 F2	Štěchovice	53 F4	Stípsi	85 F2		
Stainz	57 E4	Steckborn	58 A1	Stíra	84 C4		
Stajovce	77 E2	Steeg	58 C2	Stirling	4 C2		
Stalać	73 E4	Steenbergen	16 B3	Stirovača	70 C4		
Štalcerji	70 B3	Steenvoorde	19 F1	Štitar	72 C3		
Stalida	91 E3	Steenwijk	17 D2	Štivan	70 B4		
Stall	59 E2	Stefáni (Ípiros)	82 B2	Stjärnhov	106 B4		
Stalle, Pso di	59 E2	Stefáni (Stereá		Stjärnsund	105 F4		
Stallersattel	59 E2	Eláda)	87 F1	Stjernøya	95 D2		
Stalowa Wola	112 C2	Stefaniná	80 B3	Stjernsund	95 D2		
Stamford	9 F1	Stefanovíkio	83 F2	Stjørdal	100 C2		
Stamnes	104 A2	Stege	108 C4	Stjørdalselva	101 D2		
Stams	58 C2	Stegersbach	57 F4	Stjørnfjorden	100 C1		
Stamsund	94 A4	Steibis	55 E4	Stobi	77 E3		
Stange	105 D2	Steiermark	57 D4	Stockach	55 D4		
Stanišić	72 B1	Steigen	97 E1	Stockbridge	9 E3		
Staništinci	73 D4	Stein (A)	57 E2	Stockelsdorf	48 B2		
Štanjel	70 A2	Stein (N)	105 D2	Stockerau	57 F2		
Stanke Dimitrov	115 D3	Steinach (A)	59 D2	Stockholm	106 B4		
Staňkov	56 B1	Steinach (DDR)	52 C3	Stockholms Län	106 B3		
Stankovci	74 C1	Steinau	52 A4	Stockport	6 C2		
Stanley	5 E4	Steinbach-		Stocksbridge	6 C2		
Stanós	80 B3	Hallenberg	52 B3	Stockton-on-Tees	5 E4		
Stános	82 C3	Stein (Baden-		Stod	53 E4		
Stans	27 F2	Württemberg)	55 D4	Stöde	101 F3		
Stansstad	27 F2	Stein (Bayern)	55 E1	Stogovo	77 D4		

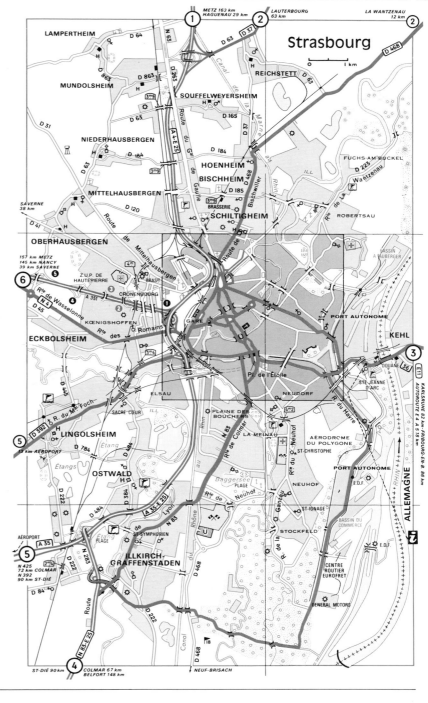

Strasbourg

Stoke-on-Trent	6 C3	Stora Alvaret	109 E3	Stormi	107 D2	Stournaréika	83 D2
Stokke	104 C3	Stora Blåsjón	97 E4	Stornoway	2 B2	Stourport	9 D1
Stokkvågen	97 D2	Stora Lulevatten	98 A2	Storo	58 C4	Støvring	108 B2
Stokmarknes	94 A3	Stora Sjöfallet	94 B4	Storožinec	113 D3	Stowmarket	11 D1
Stol	73 E3	Stora Sjöfallet		Storr, The	2 B3	Stow-on-the-Wold	9 E2
Stolac	75 F2	(National park)	94 B4	Storsjö	101 D2	Strà	61 D1
Stolac Mt	72 C4	Stora Skedvi	105 F2	Storsjøen	105 D1	Strabane	13 D1
Stolbcy	111 D4	Stora Sundby	105 F4	Storsjön (Gävleborgs		Stracin	77 E2
Stolberg (D)	51 D3	Storavan	98 A3	Län)	106 B2	Stradella	60 A2
Stolberg (DDR)	52 C2	Storby	106 C3	Storsjön		Stradsett	11 D1
Stolice	72 B3	Stord	104 A2	(Ljungdalen)	101 D2	Straelen	17 D3
Stolice Mt	73 E4	Stordal	100 B2	Storsjön		Stragari	73 D4
Stolin	113 D1	Store Bælt	108 B3	(Östersund)	101 E2	Strakonice	56 C1
Stollberg	53 E3	Storebø	104 A2	Storsjouten	97 E4	Stralsund	49 D1
Stöllet	105 E2	Storebro	109 E2	Storskarven	101 D2	Stranda	100 B2
Stolpen	53 F2	Store Heddinge	108 C4	Storslett	94 C2	Strandebarm	104 A2
Stølsheimen	104 B2	Store Molvik	95 F1	Storsteinnes	94 C3	Strandhill	12 C2
Stolzenau	48 A4	Store Mosse	109 D2	Storströmmen	108 C4	Strangford	13 E2
Stómio	83 F1	Støren	100 C2	Storuman	97 F4	Strangford L	13 E2
Ston	75 F2	Storfjället	97 F2	Storuman L	97 F3	Strängnäs	106 B3
Stone	6 C3	Storfjorden	100 B2	Storvik (N)	95 D2	Stranice	70 B1
Stonehaven	3 E4	Storfors	105 E2	Storvik (S)	106 A2	Stranorlar	12 C1
Stonehenge	9 E3	Storforsen	98 B3	Storvindeln	97 F3	Stranraer	4 B3
Stonglandet	94 B3	Storforshei	97 E2	Stotel	47 F2	Strasbourg	21 E4
Stopanja	73 E4	Storglomvatnet	97 E2	Stoúpa	86 C3	Strasburg	49 E2
Stör	48 A2	Storkow	49 E4	Stour	11 D2	Straßburg	70 A1
Storå	105 F3	Storlien	101 D2	Stourbridge	9 E1	Straßwalchen	56 C3

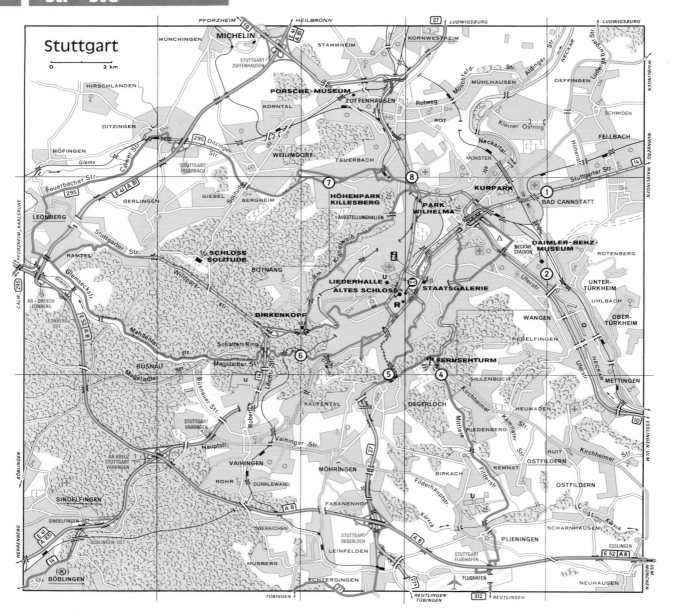

Stuttgart

Suolijärvet	99	E2
Suolijoki	99	D2
Suomenlinna	107	E3
Suomenniemi	103	E3
Suomusjärvi	107	E2
Suomussalmi	99	F3
Suomutunturi	99	E2
Suonenjoki	103	E2
Suontee	103	D3
Suopelto (Kuopion Lääni)	103	D2
Suopelto Mikkelin Lääni)	103	D3
Super-Besse	29	E1
Super-Molina	32	A3
Supetar	75	D2
Supetarska Draga	70	B4
Supino	63	F3
Šuplja-Stijena	76	B1
Surahammar	105	F3
Suraž	111	E4
Surbo	65	F4
Surčin	72	C3
Surduc	114	C1
Surdulica	77	E1
Surdup	76	B2
Šúre	21	D2
Surgères	24	C4
Súria	32	A3
Surnadalsøra	100	C2
Surrey	10	C3
Sursee	27	F2
Survilliers	19	F3
Susa	31	E1
Suså	108	C4
Sušac	75	E3
Susak	70	B4
Susak I	70	B4
Susch	58	B2
Susek	72	B2
Süßen	55	D2
Sušice	56	C1
Suspiro del Moro, Ptodel	44	A3
Susqueda, Emb de	32	B3
Sustenpass	58	A3
Susurluk	115	F3
Sutinjske Toplice	70	C2
Sutivan	75	D2
Sutjeska	73	D2
Sutjeska nac park	76	A1
Sutomore	76	B3
Sutri	63	E2
Sutterton	7	E3
Sutton	9	F2
Sutton Coldfield	9	E1
Sutton-in-Ashfield	7	D3
Sutton-on-Sea	7	E3
Suva gora	77	D3
Suva pl	77	E1
Suva Reka	77	D2
Suvasvesi	103	E2
Suvereto	62	C1
Suvobor	72	C4
Suvodol	77	E3
Suwałki	110	C4
Suze, la	23	F4
Suzzara	60	C2
Sval'ava	112	C3
Svalöv	108	C3
Svaneke	109	D4
Svanstein	98	C2
Svanvik	95	F2
Svappavaara	94	C4
Svärdsjö	105	F2
Svarstad	104	C3
Svarta	105	E4
Svartevatn	104	B3
Svartevatn L	104	B3
Svartisen	97	E3
Sværvolthalvøya	95	E1
Svattälven	105	F3
Svedala	108	C3
Sveg	101	E3
Svelgen	100	A3
Svelvik	104	C3
Svendborg	108	B4
Svenljunga	108	C2
Svensby	94	C2
Svenstavik	101	E3
Švermov	53	F3
Svetac	75	D2
Sveti Andrija	77	D3

Stratford-upon-Avon	9	E1	Streitberg	52	C4	Strovlés	90	B3	Sturup	108	C3	Šuica	75	E1	Sumburgh Head	3	F2
Strathaven	4	C2	Strengberg	57	D3	Strub, Paß	59	E1	Stuttgart	55	D2	Suinula	102	C3	Sümeg	112	A4
Strathclyde	4	C2	Stresa	58	A4	Struer	108	A2	Stykkishólmur	96	A2	Suippes	20	B3	Šumen	115	E2
Strathy Pt	3	D2	Streymoy	96	A3	Struga	77	D4	Styr'	113	D1	Suir, R	14	C3	Sumiainen	103	D2
Stratóni	80	B3	Strezimirovci	77	E1	Struge	70	B2	Suances	35	F1	Sukeva	103	E1	Sumiswald	27	F2
Stratoníki	80	B3	Strezovce	77	D2	Struma	115	D3	Subbiano	61	D4	Sukobin	76	B3	Šumperk	112	A3
Strátos	82	C3	Stříbro	53	E4	Strumble Head	8	B1	Subiaco	63	F3	Sukošan	74	C1	Sumy	113	F1
Stratton	8	B3	Strimónas	80	B2	Strumica	77	F3	Subijana	36	B2	Sukovo	77	E1	Sunart, L	2	B4
Straubing	56	B2	Strimonikó	80	A2	Strumica R	77	F3	Subotica	72	B1	Sukth	76	C4	Sund	106	C3
Straumen (Bodø)	97	E2	Strimonikós Kólpos	80	B3	Stryj	112	C3	Subotište	72	C3	Sula	113	F2	Sunde (Hordaland)	104	A2
Straumen (Fauske)	97	F1	Strmac	71	E2	Stryn	100	A3	Suc-au-May	29	D1	Suldal	104	B3	Sunde (Sør Trøndelag)	100	C1
Straumen (Møre og Romsdal)	100	B2	Strmica	75	D1	Strzelce Krajeńskie	49	F3	Sučevici	71	D4	Suldalsvatn	104	B3	Sunderland	5	E4
Straumen (Nord Trøndelag)	101	D1	Strobl	56	C3	Stubalpe	57	D4	Suceava	113	D3	Sulden	58	C3	Sundern	17	F4
Straumsjøen	94	A3	Strofiliá	84	A3	Stubbekøbing	108	C4	Suceviţa	113	D3	Sulęcin	49	F4	Sundini	96	A3
Straumsnes (Nordland)	97	E1	Strojkovce	77	E1	Stubbenkammer	49	D1	Suchań	49	F2	Sulina	113	F4	Sundom	102	B2
Straumsnes (Troms)	94	B2	Strokestown	12	C3	Štubej	73	E3	Suchiniči	111	F3	Sulingen	17	F2	Sundsvall	101	F3
Straupitz	53	E1	Stromberg	54	B1	Štubik	73	F3	Süchteln	17	D4	Sulitjelma	97	F2	Sundsvallsbukten	101	F3
Strausberg	49	E4	Stromboli, I	69	D1	Stubline	72	C3	Sucina	45	D2	Sulitjelma Mt	97	F2	Suni	66	B2
Straža (Srbija)	73	E4	Stromeferry	2	B3	Stučka	110	C3	Sućuraj	75	E2	Sulkava	103	E3	Sunja	71	D3
Straža (Vojvodina)	73	D2	Strömfors	107	F2	Stuckenborstel	48	A3	Sudbury (Derbys)	6	C3	Sully	25	C2	Sunnansjö	105	F3
Straža, G.	70	B2	Stromness	3	D1	Studena	77	E1	Sudbury (Suffolk)	11	D2	Sulmona	64	A2	Sunndalen	100	C2
Stražbenica	76	B1	Strömsbruk	101	F3	Studenci	75	E1	Suddesjaur	98	A3	Sultanhisar	115	F4	Sunndalsøra	100	C2
Strážný	56	C2	Strömsnäsbruk	109	D2	Studenica	76	C1	Sude	48	B3	Sulz	54	C3	Sunne (Jämtlands Län)	101	E3
Streatley	9	E2	Strömstad	105	D4	Stugun	101	F2	Sulzbach (Baden-Württemberg)	55	D2	Sunne (Värmlands Län)	105	E3
Street	9	D3	Strömsund	101	F1	Stühlingen	54	C4	Suðuroy	96	A4	Sulzbach (Saarland)	54	B2	Sunnemo	105	E3
Strehaia	114	C1	Ströms vattudal	101	E1	Stuhr-Brinkum	17	F1	Suðuroyarfjørdur	96	A4	Sulzbach-Rosenberg	55	F1	Sunnylvsfjorden	100	B3
Strehla	53	E2	Strongoli	67	F2	Stupnik	70	C2	Sueca	41	E4	Sulzemoos	55	F3	Suodenniemi	107	D1
			Stronsay	3	E1	Stura di Demonte	31	E3	Sueros	35	D2	Suffolk	11	D1	Sumartin	75	E2	Suolahti	103	D2
			Stronsay Firth	3	E1	Sturehov	106	B4	Suhl	52	C3	Sumba	96	A4	
			Strontian	2	B4	Sturminster Newton	9	D3	Suhopolje	71	E2	Sumburgh	3	F2	
			Stroud	9	D2				Suho Polje	72	B3				

Sveti Ilija	75 E2	Svetlogorsk		Svištov	115 D2	Swanage	9 E4	Świnoujscie	49 E2
Sveti Janez	70 A2	(Rossija)	110 B4	Svitavy	112 A3	Swanley	10 C2	Swords	13 D3
Sveti Jovan		Svetlovodsk	113 F2	Svodđe	77 E1	Swanlinbar	12 C2	Sybil Head	14 A3
Bigorski	77 D3	Svetozarevo	73 D4	Svolvær	94 A4	Swansea	8 C2	Syčovka	111 F2
Sveti Naum	77 D4	Svetozar Miletić	72 B1	Svor	53 F3	Świdnica	112 A2	Syke	17 F1
Sveti Nikita	77 D2	Svidník	112 C3	Svorkmo	100 C2	Świdwin	49 F2	Sykkylven	100 A2
Sveti Nikola	76 B3	Švihov	56 B1	Svoronáta	86 A1	Świebodzin	112 A2	Sylene	101 D2
Sveti Nikole	77 E3	Svilaja	75 D1	Svorónos	79 F4	Świecie	112 A1	Sylling	104 C3
Sveti Pantelejmon	77 D3	Svilajnac	73 E3	Svrljig	73 F4	Świecko	49 F4	Sylt	47 F1
Sveti Rok	70 C4	Svilengrad	115 E3	Swadlincote	6 C3	Świerzno	49 F1	Sylt Ost	47 F1
Sveti Stefan	76 B3	Svingvoll	104 C1	Swaffham	11 D1	Swilly, L	13 D1	Sylvenstein-	
Svetlogorsk		Svinjar	71 E3	Swale	6 C1	Swindon	9 E2	Stausee	56 A4
(Belorussija)	111 E4	Svinoy	96 A3	Swalmen	17 D4	Swinford	12 B3	Szczecin	49 E2

Synod Inn	8 C1	Szczeciński, Zalew	49 E2						
Syötekylä	99 E3	Szczytno	110 B4						
Syre	3 D2	Szécsény	112 B3						
Sysmä	103 D3	Szeged	114 B1						
Sysslebäck	101 D4	Székesfehérvár	112 B4						
Syväjärvi	99 D1	Szekszárd	114 B1						
Syväri	103 E2	Szentendre	112 B4						
Syvde	100 A3	Szentes	112 B4						
Syvdsnes	100 A2	Szigetvár	114 B1						
Syyspohja	103 E3	Szolnok	112 B4						
Szarvas	112 B4	Szombathely	112 A4						
Szczecinek	110 A4								

T

		Tamames	39 E1	Tarbert (IRL)	14 B3	Taunus	51 F4	Tejeda, Sa de	43 F3
Tabanovce	77 E2	Tamar	8 B3	Tarbert		Taunusstein	51 F4	Tejo, R	38 A3
Tábara	35 D4	Támara	35 F3	(Strathclyde)	4 B2	Tauplitz	57 D4	Tekija	73 E2
Tabarca, I de	45 E2	Tamarite de Litera	37 E3	Tarbert (Western Is)	2 B2	Tauragė	110 B3	Tekirdağ	115 E3
Taberg	109 D1	Tamási	112 B4	Tarbes	37 E1	Taurianova	67 E4	Tekirdağ	115 E3
Tabernas	44 B3	Tambre, R	34 A2	Tarbet	4 C1	Taurion	25 E4	Telč	57 E1
Tabernes de		Támega, R	34 A4	Tarcento	59 F3	Tauste	36 C3	Telde	42 B4
Valldigna	41 E4	Támelos, Akr	88 A2	Tarčin	75 F1	Tauves	29 E1	Telemark	104 C3
Taboada	34 B2	Tamiš	72 C2	Tardets-Sorholus	37 D1	Tavankut	72 B1	Télendos, N	89 E3
Tábor	57 D1	Tammela	107 E2	Tardienta	37 D3	Tavannes	27 E2	Teleno	34 C3
Tábua	38 B2	Tammisaari	107 E3	Tärendo	98 C2	Tavarnelle Val di		Telese	64 B3
Tabuaço	34 B4	Tamnava	72 C3	Tärendöälven	98 C1	Pesa	60 C4	Telford	6 C3
Tabuenca	36 C3	Tampere	107 E1	Targon	28 B2	Tavastila	103 F4	Telfs	58 C2
Täby	106 B3	Tamsweg	56 C4	Târgovište	115 E2	Tavaux	26 C2	Telgte	17 E3
Tachov	53 E4	Tamworth	9 E1	Tarifa	43 D4	Taverna	67 F3	Tellingstedt	48 A2
Tadcaster	7 D2	Tana	95 E1	Tarm	108 A3	Tavernelle	63 E1	Telti	66 B1
Tafalla	36 C2	Tana R	95 E1	Tarmstedt	47 F3	Tavernes	31 D4	Teltow	49 D4
Tafjord	100 B3	Tanafjorden	95 E1	Tarn	29 D3	Tavignano	33 F3	Témbi	83 E1
Taganheira	42 A1	Tanágra	84 A4	Tarn (Dépt)	29 E3	Tavira	42 B3	Tembleque	40 B3
Taggia	31 F3	Tanagro	64 C4	Tärnaby	97 E3	Tavistock	8 C3	Temerin	72 C2
Tagliacozzo	63 F2	Tanamea, Pso di	59 F3	Tarna, Pto de	35 E2	Tavolara, I	66 C1	Temmes	99 D4
Tagliamento	59 E3	Tanaro	31 F2	Tärnäsjön	97 E3	Tavropós	83 D2	Tempelhof	49 E4
Taglio di Po	61 D2	Tancarville, Pont		Tarn-et-Garonne	29 D3	Tavropoú, Teh L	83 D2	Tempio	
Tahal	44 C3	de	19 D3	Tarn, Gges du	29 F3	Tavşanli	115 F3	Pausania	66 B1
Tahkvuori	103 E2	Tandådalen	101 D4	Tarnobrzeg	112 C2	Taw	8 C3	Templemore	12 C4
Taibilla, Sa de	44 C2	Tandragee	13 D2	Tarnos	28 A4	Taxenbach	59 E1	Templin	49 D3
Taígetos, Óros	87 D3	Tandsbyn	101 E2	Tarnów	112 B2	Taxiárhis	80 B3	Temse	50 B3
Tain	3 D3	Tandsjöborg	101 E3	Taro	60 B2	Tay	5 D1	Temska	73 F4
Tain-l'Hermitage	30 B2	Tangerhütte	48 C4	Tarouca	38 C1	Tayinloan	4 B2	Tenala	107 E3
Taipadas	38 A4	Tangermünde	48 C4	Tarp	48 A1	Tay, L	4 C1	Ténaro, Akr	87 D4
Taipalsaari	103 E4	Tanhua	95 F4	Tarporley	6 B3	Taynuilt	4 B1	Tenbury Wells	9 D1
Taivalkoski	99 E3	Taninges	27 E4	Tarquinia	63 D2	Tayport	5 D1	Tenby	8 B2
Taivassalo	107 D2	Tanlay	26 B1	Tarragona	37 F4	Tayside	3 D4	Tence	30 B2
Tajera, Emb de la	40 C1	Tann	52 B3	Tarrasa	32 A4	Tazones	35 E1	Tende	31 E3
Tajo, R	40 B2	Tännäs	101 D3	Tàrrega	37 F4	Tczew	110 A4	Tende, Col de	31 E3
Tajuña, R	40 B2	Tanndalen	101 D3	Tarrekaise	98 A2	Teano	64 A3	Tende, Colle di	31 E3
Takovo	73 D4	Tannheim	58 C1	Tårs	108 B4	Teba	43 E3	Tendilla	40 B2
Taktikoúpoli	87 E2	Tannila	99 D3	Tarsia	67 E2	Tebay	5 D4	Tenerife	42 A4
Tálanda	87 E4	Tanumshede	105 D4	Tartas	28 B3	Tech	32 B3	Tenhola	107 E3
Talarrubias	39 E4	Taormina	69 D3	Tartu	110 C2	Techendorf	59 F2	Tenja	71 F2
Talaván	39 D3	Tapa	110 C1	Tarvasjoki	107 D2	Tecklenburg	17 E2	Tennes	94 B3
Talave, Emb de	44 C1	Tapia de		Tarvisio	59 F2	Tecuci	113 E4	Tenniöjoki	95 F4
Talavera de la		Casariego	34 C1	Täsch	27 F4	Tees	5 E4	Teno	95 E2
Reina	39 F3	Tar	70 A3	Tåsinge	108 B4	Teesside	5 E4	Tensta	106 B3
Talavera la Real	39 D4	Tara	72 C4	Tåsjo	101 F1	Teféli	91 D4	Tenterden	11 D3
Talayuela	39 E2	Tara R	76 B1	Tåsjön	101 F1	Tegéa	87 D2	Tentudia	43 D1
Talayuelas	41 D3	Taracena	40 B2	Tassin	26 C4	Tegel	49 E4	Teolo	61 D1
Taldom	111 F2	Tara klisura	76 B2	Tåstrup	108 C3	Tegelen	17 D4	Teovo	77 E3
Talgarth	9 D1	Tarancón	40 B3	Tata	112 B4	Tegernsee	56 A4	Tepelenë	114 C4
Talkkunapää	95 F3	Taranto	65 E4	Tatabánya	112 B4	Teggiano	64 C4	Teplá	53 E4
Talla	61 D4	Taranto, Golfo di	65 E4	Tatarbunary	113 E4	Teguise	42 C3	Teplice	53 E3
Tallante	45 D3	Tarare	26 B4	Tatry	112 B3	Teide	42 B4	Tepsa	95 E4
Tallard	31 D2	Taraš	72 C2	Tau	104 A3	Teide Mt	42 A4	Teramo	63 F1
Tällberg	101 E4	Tarašča	113 E2	Tauber	55 D1	Teide, Pque Nac		Ter Apel	17 E1
Tallinn	110 C1	Tarascon (Ariège)	32 A2	Tauberbischofsheim		del	42 B4	Tera, R	35 D3
Talloires	27 D4	Tarascon			55 D1	Teignmouth	8 C4	Terebovl'a	113 D3
Tallow	14 C4	(Vaucluse)	30 B3	Taucha	53 D2	Teijo	107 D3	Terena	38 C4
Talluskylä	103 D2	Taravo	33 F3	Tauerntal	59 E2	Teil, le	30 B2	Terespol	112 C1
Talmont	24 B3	Tarayuela	41 E2	Tauerntunnel	59 E2	Teilleul, le	18 C4	Terezino Polje	71 E2
Tal'noje	113 E2	Tarazona	36 C3	Taufers i. M.	58 C3	Teisendorf	56 B3	Terges, Rib de	42 B2
Talsi	110 B2	Tarazona de la		Taufkirchen	56 B3	Teisko	102 C3	Tergnier	20 A2
Tållberg	101 E4	Mancha	40 C4	Taulé	22 B2	Teisnach	56 B2	Terjärv	102 C2
Talvik	95 D2	Tarbat Ness	3 D3	Taunton	9 D3	Teixeiro	34 B1	Terlizzi	65 D3

Termas de		Thalfang	54 B1			
Monfortinho	39 D2	Thalgau	56 C3			
Terme Luigiane	67 E2	Thalheim	53 E3			
Termini Imerese	68 B3	Thalmässing	55 F2			
Terminillo	63 F2	Thalwil	58 A2			
Terminillo, Mte	63 F2	Thame	9 F2			
Terneuzen	16 B4	Thames, R	11 D2			
Terni	63 E2	Thanes, K e	76 C4			
Ternitz	57 E3	Thann	27 E1			
Ternopol'	113 D2	Thannhausen	55 E3			
Térovo	82 C2	Thaon	27 D1			
Térpilos	80 A2	Tharandt	53 E2			
Terpní	80 B2	Tharsis	42 C2			
Terpsithéa	83 D4	Thássos	80 C3			
Ter, R	32 B3	Thássos, N	81 D3			
Terracina	63 F3	Thatë, Mal i	77 D4			
Terra de Basto	34 B4	Thau, Bessin de	30 A4			
Terradets, Emb		Thaya	57 F1			
dels	37 F3	Thégonnec	22 B2			
Terralba	66 B3	Theil, le	23 F3			
Terranova di		Themar	52 C3			
Pollino	67 E2	Thenon	29 D2			
Terranuova Braccio		Theológos (Stereá				
lini	61 D4	Eláda)	83 F3			
Terras de Bouro	34 A3	Theológos				
Terrassa	32 A4	(Thássos)	80 C3			
Terrasson-la-		Théoule	31 E4			
Villedieu	29 D2	Thérain	19 F3			
Terrenoire	30 B1	Thérma (Ikaría)	89 D2			
Terriente	41 D2	Thermá				
Terschelling	16 C1	(Makedonía)	80 B2			
Teruel	41 D2	Thérma				
Tervakoski	107 E2	(Samothráki)	81 E3			
Tervo	103 D2	Thermaïkós				
Tervola	99 D2	Kólpos	80 A4			
Tervuren	50 C3	Thérma Lefkádas	89 D2			
Terzaga	40 C2	Thérmi	79 F3			
Tešanj	71 F3	Thérmi	85 F2			
Teslić	71 E3	Thermissía	87 E2			
Tessin	48 C2	Thérmo	83 D4			
Tessy	18 C3	Thermopíles	83 E3			
Teste, la	28 A2	Thérouanne	19 F1			
Tetbury	9 E2	Thespiés	83 F4			
Teterev	113 E2	Thesprotía	82 B2			
Teterow	49 D2	Thesprotikó	82 B2			
Tetica	44 B3	Thessalía	83 E2			
Tetijev	113 E2	Thessaloníki	79 F3			
Tetovo	77 D3	Thessaloníki				
Tetrákomo	82 C2	(Nomos)	80 A3			
Tettnang	55 D4	Thetford	11 D1			
Teuchern	53 D2	Theux	51 D4			
Teufen	58 B2	The Wash	7 E3			
Teulada	66 B4	Thèze	28 B4			
Teupitz	53 E1	Thézenay	24 C3			
Teuva	102 B3	Thiamis	82 B1			
Tevere	63 E2	Thiaucourt	21 D3			
Teviot	5 D3	Thiberville	19 D3			
Tewkesbury	9 E2	Thiéblemont-				
Texel	16 C1	Farémont	20 C4			
Thabor, Mt	31 D1	Thiendorf	53 E2			
Thale	52 C2	Thiene	59 D4			
		Thiers	26 B4			
		Thiesi	66 B2			

Torino

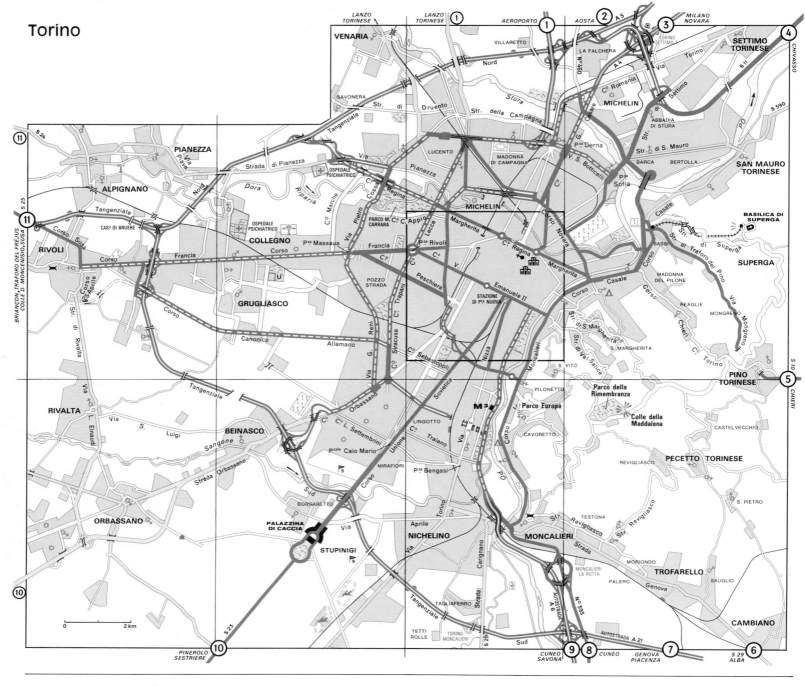

Thiessow	49 D1	Thornhill	4 C3	Tibro	109 D1	Tíjola	44 B3	Tinchebray	18 C4	Tiree	2 A4	Titaríssios	83 E1
Thillot, le	27 E1	Thouarcé	24 C2	Tichvin	111 E1	Tikkakoski	103 D3	Tindari	69 D2	Tirgo-Neamt	113 D4	Titel	72 C2
Thimariá	81 F2	Thouars	24 C3	Ticino	60 A1	Tikkala	103 F2	Tineo	35 D1	Tírgoviste	115 D1	Titisee	54 C4
Thímena	89 E2	Thouet	24 C2	Ticino R	58 A3	Tikveš, Ez	77 E3	Tinée	31 E3	Tírgu Frumos	113 E3	Titlis	58 A3
Thímena, N	89 E2	Thouría	86 C3	Tidaholm	109 D1	Tilburg	16 C3	Tingáki	89 F3	Tírgu Jiu	114 C1	Tito	64 C4
Thiní, Akr	87 E2	Thoúrio	81 F1	Tidö	106 A3	Tilbury	10 C2	Tinglev	108 A4	Tírgu Mures	113 D4	Titograd	76 B3
Thionville	21 D3	Thráki	81 E2	Tiefenbronn	54 C2	Tílissos	91 D3	Tingsryd	109 E2	Tírgu Secuiesc	113 D4	Titova Korenica	70 C4
Thíra	91 E1	Thrakikó		Tiefencastel	58 B3	Tillberga	106 A3	Tingvoll	100 B2	Tirig	41 F2	Titova Mitrovica	77 D1
Thíra, N	91 E1	Pélagos	81 D3	Tiefensee	49 E4	Tillières	19 E4	Tingvollfjorden	100 B2	Tírintha	87 D2	Titov Drvar	71 D4
Thirassía, N	91 E1	Thrapston	9 F1	Tiel	16 C3	Tilly-sur-Seulles	18 C3	Tinja	71 F3	Tiriolo	67 F3	Titovo Užice	72 C4
Thirsk	7 D1	Threshfield	6 C1	Tielt	50 A3	Tílos, N	89 F4	Tinn	104 C3	Tírnavos	83 E1	Titov Veles	77 E3
Thisted	108 A2	Thueyts	30 B2	Tienen	50 C3	Timanfaya, Parque		Tinnsjø	104 C3	Tirol	58 C2	Titov vrh	77 D3
Thíva	84 A4	Thuile, la	27 E4	Tiengen	54 C4	Nac. de	42 C3	Tínos	88 C3	Tirós	87 D3	Titran	100 B1
Thiviers	28 C1	Thuin	50 B4	Tierbmesvarri	94 C3	Timbáki	91 D4	Tiñosillos	39 F1	Tirrenia	60 C4	Tittmoning	56 B3
Thizy	26 B4	Thuir	32 B2	Tiercé	23 E4	Timbano	81 D2	Tínos, N	88 C3	Tirreno, Mare	68 B2	Tiumpan Head	2 B2
Thoissey	26 C4	Thum	53 E3	Tierga	36 C3	Timfi, Óros	78 C4	Tiñoso, C	45 D3	Tirschenreuth	53 D4	Tivat	76 B3
Tholen	16 B3	Thun	27 E3	Tierp	106 B3	Timfristós	83 D3	Tintagel	8 B3	Tirso	66 B2	Tiveden	105 E4
Tholey	54 B1	Thur	58 A1	Tiétar, R	39 E2	Timfristós Mt	83 D3	Tinténiac	23 D3	Tirstrup	108 B3	Tivenys	41 F2
Thollon	27 E3	Thüringen	58 B2	Tigharry	2 A3	Timiş	114 C1	Tinto, R	42 C2	Tirteafuera, R	39 F4	Tiverton	8 C3
Tholó	86 C2	Thüringer Wald	52 B3	Tighnabruaich	4 B2	Timişoara	114 C1	Tiobraid Árann	14 C3	Tisa	72 C2	Tivissa	41 F1
Tholopotámi	85 E4	Thurles	14 C3	Tignes	31 D1	Timmelsjoch	58 C2	Tione di Trento	58 C3	Tiscar, Pto de	44 B2	Tivoli	63 E2
Tholós	80 B2	Thurn, Paß	59 E1	Tignes, Bge de	31 E1	Timmendorfer		Tipasoja	103 E1	Tisnaren	105 F4	Tjaktjajaure	98 A2
Thomastown	15 D3	Thursby	5 D4	Tiheró	81 F2	Strand	48 B2	Tipperary	14 C3	Tišnov	57 E1	Tjällmo	105 F4
Thônes	27 D4	Thurso	3 D2	Tihío	79 D3	Timok	73 F3	Tipperary (Co)	12 C3	Tisvildeleje	108 C3	Tjeggelvas	98 A2
Thonon	27 D3	Thury-Harcourt	18 C3	Tihuţa	113 D4	Timoleague	14 B4	Tiranë	76 C4	Tisza	112 B4	Tjeldøya	94 B3
Thorens-Glières	27 D4	Thusis	58 B3	Tiilikkajärvi	103 E1	Timrå	101 F3	Tirano	58 C3	Tiszafüred	112 B4	Tjeldstø	104 A2
Thorikó	88 A2	Thy	108 A2	Tiistenjoki	102 C2	Timv. Peristéria	86 C3	Tiraspol'	113 E3	Tiszavasvári	112 C3	Tjentište	76 A1
Thorne	7 D2	Thyborøn	108 A2	Tijesno	74 C1	Tinahely	13 D4	Tire	115 F4	Titaguas	41 D3	Tjøme	104 C4

- Tjong 97 E2
- Tjørnuvik 96 A3
- Tjøtta 97 D3
- Tkon 74 C1
- Tobarra 44 C1
- Tobercurry 12 B2
- Tobermore 13 D2
- Tobermory 2 B4
- Toberonochy 4 B1
- Toblach 59 E2
- Toce 58 A3
- Tocha 38 B2
- Tocina 43 D2
- Todi 63 E1
- Todmorden 6 C2
- Todorići 71 E4
- Todtmoos 54 C4
- Todtnau 54 C4
- Toe Head (GB) 2 A2
- Toe Head (IRL) 14 B4
- Töfsingdalen 101 D3
- Toft 3 F1
- Tofte 104 C3
- Toftir 96 A4
- Toftlund 108 A4
- Tohmajärvi 103 F2
- Toholampi 102 C1
- Toijala 107 E2
- Toivakka 103 D3
- Toivala 103 E3
- Tojšici 72 B3
- Tok 53 F4
- Tokaj 112 C3
- Tolbuhin 115 E2
- Toledo 40 A3
- Toledo, Mts de 40 A3
- Tolentino 61 F4
- Tolfa 63 D2
- Tolga 100 C3
- Tollarp 109 D3
- Tollense 49 D2
- Tølløse 108 C3.
- Tolmezzo 59 E3
- Tolmin 70 A2
- Toló 87 D2
- Tolosa (E) 36 C1
- Tolosa (P) 38 C3
- Tolox 43 E4
- Tolva 99 E2
- Tolve 65 D4
- Tomar 38 B3
- Tomaševac 73 D2
- Tomaševo 76 B2
- Tomašica 71 D3
- Tomaszów Lubelski 112 C2
- Tomaszów Mazowiecki 112 B2
- Tombebœuf 28 C3
- Tomelilla 109 D3
- Tomelloso 40 B4
- Tomiño 34 A3
- Tomintoul 3 D4
- Tomma 97 D2
- Tømmervåg 100 B2
- Tomra 100 B2
- Tomtabacken 109 D2
- Tona 32 B3
- Tonale, Pso del 58 C3
- Tonara 66 B3
- Tonbridge 10 C3
- Tondela 38 B1
- Tønder 108 A4
- Tongeren 50 C2
- Tongue 2 C2
- Tonnay-Boutonne 24 C4
- Tonnay-Charente 24 C4
- Tonneins 28 C3
- Tonnerre 26 B1
- Tönning 47 F2
- Tønsberg 104 C3
- Tonstad 104 B4
- Töpen 53 D3
- Topeno 107 E2
- Topla 70 B1
- Toplica 77 D1
- Topli Do 73 E3
- Toplița 113 D4
- Toplou 91 F4
- Topola 73 D3
- Topolčani 77 E4
- Topol'čany 112 B3
- Topólia 90 B3

- Topolovnik 73 E3
- Topusko 70 C3
- Torà de Riubregòs 32 A3
- Torano Castello 67 E2
- Torbay 8 C4
- Torbole 58 C4
- Torcello 61 D1
- Torchiarolo 65 F3
- Tordera 32 B4
- Tordesillas 35 E4
- Tordesilos 41 D2
- Tore 2 C3
- Töre 98 C3
- Töreboda 105 E4
- Torella d. Sannio 64 B3
- Toreno 34 C2
- Torgau 53 E2
- Torgelow 49 E2
- Torhout 50 A3
- Torigni 18 C3
- Torija 40 B2
- Torino 31 E1
- Torio, R 35 D2
- Torla 37 E2
- Törmänen 95 F3
- Törmänmäki 99 E4
- Tormes, R 39 E1
- Tormos 37 D3
- Tornavacas 39 E2
- Tornavacas, Pto de 39 E2
- Torneälven 94 C3
- Torneträsk 94 C3
- Tornik 76 B1
- Tornio 98 C3
- Tornionjoki 98 C2
- Tornjoš 72 C1
- Toro 35 D4
- Törökszentmiklós 112 B4
- Toro, Monte 45 F1
- Toróni 80 B4
- Toropec 111 E2
- Torpo 104 C2
- Torpoint 8 C4
- Torpshammar 101 F3
- Torquay 8 C4
- Torquemada 35 F3
- Torralba de Calatrava 40 A4
- Torrão 42 B1
- Torre 38 C2
- Torre Annunziata 64 B4
- Torre Baja 41 D3
- Torre Beretti 60 A2
- Torreblanca 41 F3
- Torrecaballeros 40 A1
- Torrecampo 43 F1
- Torre Canne 65 E3
- Torrecilla 43 E4
- Torrecilla en Cameros 36 B2
- Torrecillas de la Tiesa 39 E3
- Torre de Abraham, Emb de 40 A3
- Torre de D. Chama 34 C4
- Torre de Embesora 41 E2
- Torre de Juan Abad 44 B1
- Torre del Aguila, Emb de 43 D3
- Torre de la Higuera 42 C3
- Torre del Bierzo 35 D2
- Torre del Campo 44 A2
- Torre del Greco 64 B4
- Torre del Mar 43 F4
- Torredembarra 37 F4
- Torre de Moncorvo 34 C4
- Torre de Passeri 64 A2
- Torre d. Impiso 68 A3
- Torredonjimeno 43 F2
- Torre Faro 69 E2
- Torre Grande 66 A3
- Torregrossa 37 F4
- Torreira 38 B1
- Torrejoncillo 39 D2
- Torrejoncillo del Rey 40 C3
- Torrejón de Ardoz 40 B2

- Torrejón de la Calzada 40 A2
- Torrejón el Rubio 39 E3
- Torrejón-Tajo, Emb de 39 E3
- Torre la Carcel 41 D2
- Torrelaguna 40 B1
- Torrelapaja 36 C3
- Torrelavega 35 F2
- Torrellano 45 E2
- Torrelobatón 35 E4
- Torrelodones 40 A2
- Torremaggiore 64 B2
- Torremegía 39 D4
- Torre Mileto 64 C2
- Torre Miró, Pto de 41 E2
- Torremocha 39 D3
- Torremolinos 43 F4
- Torrent 41 E4
- Torrente de Cinca 37 E4
- Torrenueva 44 B1
- Torre-Pacheco 45 D2
- Torre Pellice 31 E2
- Torreperogil 44 B2
- Torres del Río 36 B2
- Torres Novas 38 B3
- Torres Vedras 38 A3
- Torrevieja 45 D2
- Torrico de San Pedro 38 C3
- Torri del Benaco 60 C1
- Torridon 2 B3
- Torridon, L 2 B3
- Torriglia 60 A3
- Torrijas 41 D3
- Torrijo 36 C4
- Torrijos 40 A3
- Tørring 108 A3
- Torrita di Siena 61 D4
- Torroella de Montgrí 32 C3
- Torröjen 101 D1
- Torrox 43 F4
- Torsås 109 E3
- Torsby 105 E3
- Torshälla 106 A3
- Tórshavn 96 A4
- Torsken 94 B2
- Torsminde 108 A2
- Törtoles de Esgueva 35 F4
- Tortoli 66 C3
- Tortona 60 A2
- Tortorici 69 D2
- Tortosa 41 F2
- Tortosendo 38 C2
- Toruń 112 B1
- Torup 108 C2
- Tørvikbygd 104 B2
- Tory I 12 C1
- Toržok 111 F2
- Torzym 49 F4

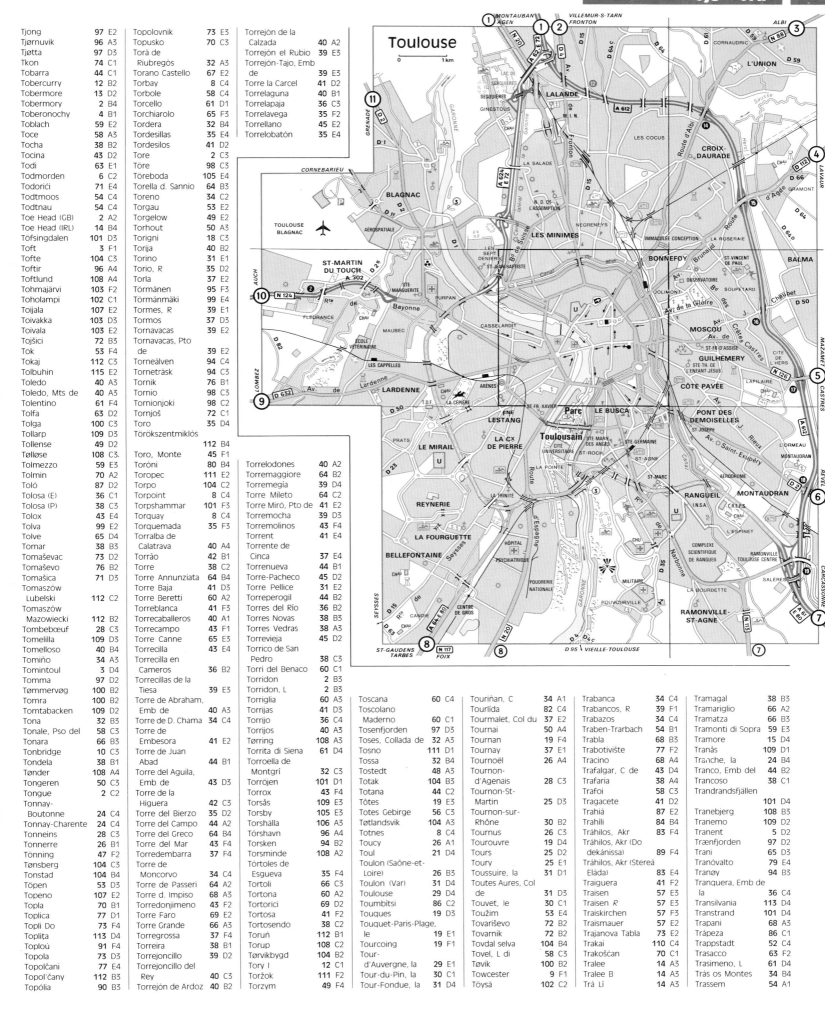

Toulouse (map, 0 – 1 km)

- Toscana 60 C4
- Toscolano Maderno 60 C1
- Tosenfjorden 97 D3
- Toses, Collada de 32 A3
- Tosno 111 D1
- Tossa 32 B4
- Tostedt 48 A3
- Totak 104 B3
- Totana 44 C2
- Tôtes 19 E3
- Totes Gebirge 56 C3
- Tøtlandsvik 104 A3
- Totnes 8 C4
- Toucy 26 A1
- Toul 21 D4
- Toulon (Saône-et-Loire) 26 B3
- Toulon (Var) 31 D4
- Toulouse 29 D4
- Toumbítsi 86 C2
- Touquet-Paris-Plage, le 19 E1
- Tourcoing 19 F1
- Tour-d'Auvergne, la 29 E1
- Tour-du-Pin, la 30 C1
- Tour-Fondue, la 31 D4

- Touriñan, C 34 A1
- Tourlída 82 C4
- Tourmalet, Col du 37 E2
- Tournai 50 A4
- Tournan 19 E4
- Tournay 37 E1
- Tournoël 26 A4
- Tournon-d'Agenais 28 C3
- Tournon-St-Martin 25 D3
- Tournon-sur-Rhône 30 B2
- Tournus 26 C3
- Toutes Aures, Col de 31 D3
- Touvet, le 30 C1
- Toužim 53 E4
- Tovariševo 72 B2
- Tovarnik 72 B2
- Tovdal selva 104 B4
- Tovel, L di 58 C3
- Tøvik 100 B2
- Towcester 9 F1
- Töysä 102 C2

- Trabanca 34 C4
- Trabancos, R 39 F1
- Trabazos 34 C4
- Traben-Trarbach 54 B1
- Trabla 68 B3
- Trabotivište 77 F2
- Tracino 68 A4
- Trafalgar, C de 43 D4
- Trafaria 38 A4
- Trafoi 58 C3
- Tragacete 41 D2
- Trahiá 87 E2
- Trahíli 84 B4
- Tráhilos, Akr 83 F4
- Tráhilos, Akr (Do dekánissa) 89 F4
- Tráhilos, Akr (Stereá Eláda) 83 E4
- Traiguera 41 F2
- Traisen 57 E3
- Traisen R 57 E3
- Traiskirchen 57 E3
- Traismauer 57 E3
- Trajanova Tabla 73 E2
- Trakai 110 C4
- Trakošćan 70 C1
- Tralee 14 A3
- Tralee B 14 A3
- Trá Lí 14 A3

- Tramagal 38 B3
- Tramariglio 66 A2
- Tramatza 66 B3
- Tramonti di Sopra 59 E3
- Tramore 15 D4
- Tranås 109 D1
- Tranche, la 24 B4
- Tranco, Emb del 44 B2
- Trancoso 38 C1
- Trandrandsfjällen 101 D4
- Tranebjerg 108 B3
- Tranemo 109 D2
- Tranent 5 D2
- Trænfjorden 97 D2
- Trani 65 D3
- Tranóvalto 79 E4
- Tranøy 94 B3
- Tranquera, Emb de la 36 C4
- Transilvania 113 D4
- Transtrand 101 D4
- Trapani 68 A3
- Trápeza 86 C1
- Trappstadt 52 C4
- Trasacco 63 F2
- Trasimeno, L 61 D4
- Trás os Montes 34 B4
- Trassem 54 A1

Name	Pg	Grid	Name	Pg	Grid	Name	Pg	Grid	Name	Pg	Grid
Trasvase Tajo Segura, Canal de	40	C4	Tremezzo	58	B4	Tricarico	65	D4	Trizina	87	E2
Traun	57	D3	Tremiti, I	64	C2	Tricase	65	F4	Trlica	76	B1
Traun R	56	C3	Tremp	37	F3	Tricesimo	59	F3	Trnava	112	A3
Traunkirchen	56	C3	Trenčín	112	B3	Trichiana	59	E3	Trnovo (Bosna i Hercegov ina)	75	F1
Traunreut	56	B3	Trendelburg	52	A2	Trie	37	E1	Trnovo (Slovenija)	70	A2
Traunsee	56	C3	Trentino-Alto Adige	58	C3	Trieben	57	D4	Trnova Poljana	75	D1
Traunstein	56	B3	Trento	59	D3	Trier	54	A1	Troarn	18	C3
Travemünde	48	B2	Trent, R	7	D2	Trieste	59	F4	Trofa	34	A4
Travnik	71	E4	Trepča (Crna Gora)	76	C2	Trieste, G di	59	F4	Trofaiach	57	E4
Trayas, le	31	E4	Trepča (Kosovo)	77	D1	Trifels	54	C2	Trofors	97	E3
Trbovlje	70	B2	Tréport, le	19	E2	Trifili	81	F2	Trogir	75	D2
Trbuk	71	F3	Trepuzzi	65	F4	Triglav	70	A2	Troglav, V.	75	D1
Trbušani	73	D4	Tresco	8	A4	Trigóna	82	C1	Tróhalos	83	E1
Trdinov Vrh	70	C2	Trescore Balneario	60	B1	Trigueros	42	C2	Troia	64	C3
Trebbia	60	B1	Tresenda	58	B3	Trihonída, L	83	D4	Tróia, Pen de	38	A4
Trebbin	49	D4	Tresfjord	100	B2	Trijueque	40	B2	Troina	68	C3
Trébeurden	22	B2	Tresjuncos	40	B3	Tríkala (Makedonía)	79	F3	Trois Epis, les	27	E1
Trebević nac park	76	A1	Treska	77	D3	Tríkala (Nomos)	82	C1	Trois-Moutiers, les	24	C3
Třebíč	57	E1	Treskavica	75	F1	Tríkala (Pelopónissos)	87	D1	Trois-Ponts	51	D4
Trebinje	76	A2	Tres Mares, Pico de	35	F2	Tríkala (Thessalía)	83	D1	Trojan	115	D2
Trebisacce	67	F2	Trešnjevica	73	E4	Tríkeri	83	F2	Trojane	70	B2
Trebišnjica	75	F2	Trešnjevik	76	B2	Trilj	75	E1	Trollhättan	108	C1
Trebišov	112	C3	Trespaderne	36	A2	Trillevallen	101	D2	Trollheimen	100	C2
Trebnje	70	B2	Třešť	57	E1	Trillo	40	C2	Troms	94	C3
Třeboň	57	D1	Trets	30	C4	Trílofo	83	E3	Tromsdalen	94	B2
Tréboul	22	A3	Tretten	104	C1	Trim	13	D3	Tromsø	94	B2
Trebsen	53	D2	Treuchtlingen	55	E2	Trimouille, la	25	D3	Trondheim	100	C2
Trebujena	43	D3	Treuen	53	D3	Trindade	34	C4	Trondheimsfjorden	100	C1
Trecastagni	69	D3	Treuenbrietzen	53	D1	Třinec	112	B3	Trondsheimsleia	100	B1
Trecate	60	A1	Treungen	104	B4	Tring	9	F2	Tronö	101	F4
Tre Croci, Pso	59	D2	Trevélez	44	A3	Tringia	82	C1	Tronto	63	F1
Tredegar	9	D2	Trèves	29	F3	Trinità d'Agultu e V.	66	B1	Troo	23	F4
Tredozio	61	D3	Trevi	63	E1	Trinitapoli	64	C3	Troon	4	C2
Treene	48	A1	Trévières	18	C3	Trinité, la	22	C4	Tropea	67	E3
Treffort	26	C4	Treviglio	60	B1	Trinité-Porhoët, la	22	C3	Trópea	86	C2
Treffurt	52	B3	Trevignano Romano	63	E2	Trino	31	F1	Tropojë	76	C2
Trefynwy	9	D2	Treviño	36	B2	Triora	31	F3	Trosa	106	B4
Tregaron	8	C1	Trevišo	59	E4	Trípi	87	D3	Trossachs, The	4	C1
Trégastel	22	B2	Trévoux	26	C4	Tripití, Akr	85	D2	Trostan	13	E1
Tregnago	60	C1	Trezzo sull' Adda	60	A1	Trípoli	87	D2	Trostberg	56	B3
Tregony	8	B4	Trgovište	77	E2	Triponzo	63	E1	Trouville	19	D3
Tréguier	22	C2	Trhové Sviny	57	D2	Tripótama	86	C1	Trowbridge	9	D2
Trehörningsjö	102	A1	Triánda	93	F1	Triptis	53	D3	Troyes	26	B1
Treia (D)	47	F1	Tría Nissiá	92	C1	Trisanna	58	C2	Trpanj	75	E2
Treia (I)	61	F4	Triaucourt	20	C3	Trischen	47	F2	Trpezi	76	C2
Treignac	29	D1	Tribanj Kruščica	70	C4	Trittau	48	B3	Trpinja	71	F2
Trelleborg (S)	108	C4	Triberg	54	C3	Trittenheim	54	B1	Trsa	76	B2
Trelleborg (SF)	108	B3	Tribsees	49	D2	Trivento	64	B2	Tršić	72	B3
Trélon	20	B2							Trstenik (Kosovo)	77	D2
Tremblade, la	28	A1							Trstenik (Pelješac)	75	E2
Tremestieri	69	D2									

Name	Pg	Grid	Name	Pg	Grid	Name	Pg	Grid
Trstenik (Srbija)	73	D4	Tulla	12	B4	Turtola	98	C2
Trsteno	75	F2	Tullamore	12	C4	Tuscania	63	D2
Trubčevsk	111	F4	Tulle	29	D1	Tuse	108	C3
Trubia	35	D1	Tullgarn	106	B4	Tušilović	70	C3
Trubia, R	35	D1	Tullins	30	C1	Tustna	100	B2
Trubjela	76	B2	Tulln	57	E2	Tutin	76	C1
Truchas	34	C3	Tullow	13	D4	Tutrakan	115	E2
Truchtersheim	21	E4	Tulppio	95	F4	Tuttlingen	55	D3
Trujillo	39	E3	Tulsk	12	C3	Turun ja Porin Lääni	107	D2
Trun	19	D4	Tumba	106	B4	Tuturano	65	F3
Truro	8	B4	Tunbridge Wells, Royal	10	C3	Tutzing	56	A3
Trutnov	112	A2	Tundža	115	E3	Tuulos	107	E2
Truyère, Gorges de la	29	E2	Tunnhovdfjorden	104	C2	Tuupovaara	103	F2
Tryde	109	D3	Tunnsjøen	97	E4	Tuusniemi	103	E2
Trysiselva	100	D3	Tuohikotti	107	F2	Tuusula	107	E2
Tržac	70	C3	Tuoro sul Trasimeno	61	D4	Tuxford	7	D3
Trzcińsko-Zdrój	49	E3	Tupalaki	95	E3	Tuzi	76	B3
Trzebiatów	49	F1	Turalići	72	B4	Tuzla	71	F3
Trzebiez	49	E2	Turballe, la	22	C4	Tvedestrand	104	C4
Tržič Golnik	70	A2	Turbe	71	E4	Tverrfjellet	100	B3
Tsamandás	82	B1	Turbie, la	31	E3	Tvøroyri	96	A4
Tsambíka	93	F1	Turckheim	27	E1	Tweed, R	5	E2
Tsangaráda	83	F2	Turda	112	C4	Twelve Pins, The	12	A3
Tsangário	82	B2	Turégano	40	A1	Twimberg	70	B1
Tsaritsani	83	E1	Turenki	107	E2	Twist	17	E2
Tsarkassiános	82	B4	Turgutlu	115	F4	Twistringen	17	F1
Tsotíli	79	D4	Turi	65	E3	Tydal	101	D2
Tsoukaládes	82	B3	Türi	110	C1	Tyin	104	C1
Tuaim	12	B3	Turija (Bosna i Hercegov ina)	71	F3	Tyin L	100	B3
Tuam	12	B3	Turija (Srbija)	73	E3	Týn	57	D1
Tua, R	34	B4	Turija (Vojvodina)	72	C2	Tyndrum	4	C1
Tuath, L	4	B1	Turinge	106	B4	Tynemouth	5	E3
Tubilla del Agua	35	F2	Turís	41	E4	Tynkä	102	C1
Tübingen	55	D3	Turjak	70	B2	Tynset	100	C3
Tubre	58	C3	Türkheim	55	E3	Tyräjärvi	99	E3
Tučepi	75	E2	Turku	107	D2	Tyresö	106	B4
Tuchan	32	B2	Turmiel	40	C1	Tyrifjorden	104	C3
Tudela	36	C3	Turnberry	4	C3	Tyringe	109	D3
Tudela de Duero	35	E4	Turnhout	50	C3	Tyristrand	104	C3
Tuella, R	34	C3	Türnitz	57	E3	Tyrnävä	99	D4
Tuerto, R	35	D2	Turnov	112	A2	Tyrone	13	D2
Tuffé	23	F3	Turnu Măgurele	115	D2	Tysfjorden	97	F1
Tuheljske Toplice	70	C2	Turnu Roşu	113	D4	Tysnesøy	104	A2
Tuhkakylä	103	E1	Turracherhöhe	59	F2	Tysse	104	A2
Tui	34	A3	Turre	44	C3	Tyssebotn	104	A2
Tuineje	42	C4	Turriff	3	E3	Tyssedal	104	B2
Tukums	110	B2	Tursi	65	D4	Tysvær	104	A3
Tulach Mhór	12	C4				Tywi	8	C2
Tulare	77	D1				Tywyn	6	A3
Tulcea	113	E4						
Tul'čin	113	E3						

U

Name	Pg	Grid	Name	Pg	Grid	Name	Pg	Grid	Name	Pg	Grid	Name	Pg	Grid	Name	Pg	Grid	Name	Pg	Grid
Ub	72	C3	Uebigau	53	E2	Uithoorn	16	C2	Ulm	55	E3	Umeälven	98	A4	Unnukka	103	E2	Urbino	61	E3
Ubaye	31	D2	Uecker	49	E2	Uithuizen	47	D3	Ulmen	51	E4	Umhausen	58	C2	Unquera	35	F1	Urbión, Sa de	36	B3
Úbeda	44	A2	Ueckermünde	49	E2	Ukkola	103	F2	Ulog	75	F1	Umin Dol	77	E2	Unst	3	F1	Urdos	37	D2
Überlingen	55	D4	Uelzen	48	B3	Ukmergė	110	C3	Ulricehamn	109	D1	Umka	72	C3	Unstrut	52	C2	Ure	6	C1
Ubl'a	112	C3	Uetersen	48	A2	Ukonselkä	95	E3	Ulrichsberg	56	C2	Umljanović	75	D1	Unterach	56	C3	Uredakke	97	E4
Ubli (Crna Gora)	76	B2	Uetze	48	B4	Ukraina	113	E2	Ulsberg	100	C2	Una	71	D3	Unterhaching	56	A3	Urepel	36	C1
Ubli (Lastovo)	75	E3	Uffenheim	55	E1	Ukrina	71	E3	Ulsta	3	F1	Unac	71	D4	Unter-Schleissheim	55	F3	Urfahr	57	D2
Ubrique	43	E4	Ugao	76	C1	Ulcinj	76	B3	Ulsteinvik	100	A2	Unari	99	D1	Unterwalden	27	F3	Urfeld	56	A4
Uchte	17	F2	Ugento	65	F4	Uleåborg	99	D3	Uludağ	115	F3	Unari L	99	D1	Unterwasser	58	B2	Urho Kekkonens kansallis puisto	95	F3
Učka	70	B3	Ugijar	44	B3	Ulefoss	104	C3	Ul'ugai'sa	95	E2	Uncastillo	37	D2	Unterweißenbach	57	D2	Uri (CH)	58	A3
Uckange	21	D3	Ugine	27	D4	Uleila del Campo	44	C3	Ulva	4	B1	Unden	105	E4	Upavon	9	E3	Uri (I)	66	A2
Uckfield	10	C3	Uglič	111	F1	Ulëzë	76	C3	Ulverston	6	B1	Undersåker	101	D2	Upinniemi	107	E3	Uriage	30	C1
Uclés	40	B3	Ugljan	74	C1	Ulfborg	108	A2	Ulvik	104	B2	Undredal	104	B2	Upper L Erne	13	D2	Urjala	107	E2
Udbina	70	C4	Ugljan I	74	C1	Uljanik	71	D2	Ulvila	107	D1	Uneča	111	F4	Uppingham	9	F1	Urk	16	C2
Udbyhøj	108	B2	Ugljane	75	E1	Uljanovka	113	E3	Ulvsjö	101	E3	Unešić	75	D1	Upplands-Väsby	106	B3	Urla	115	E4
Uddevalla	108	C1	Ugljevik	72	B3	Uljma	73	D2	Ulzës, Liq i	76	C3	Úněšov	53	E4	Uppsala	106	B3	Urlingford	14	C3
Uddheden	105	E3	Ugra	111	F3	Ullånger	102	A2	Umag	70	A3	Ungeny	113	E3	Uppsala Län	106	B3	Urnäsch	58	B2
Uddjaure	98	A3	Ugrinovci	73	D3	Ullapool	2	C3	Uman'	113	E3	Ungilde	34	C3	Upton	9	E1	Urnes	100	B3
Uden	16	C3	Uherské Hradiště	112	A3	Ulla, R	34	B2	Umbertide	61	E4	Unhais da Serra	38	C2	Uras	66	B3	Uroševac	77	D2
Udine	59	F3	Uhingen	55	D2	Ullared	108	C2	Umbrail, Pass	58	C3	Unhošt	53	F4	Urbania	61	E3	Urovica	73	F3
Udovo	77	F3	Úhlava	56	C1	Ulldecona	41	F2	Umbria	63	E1	Unije	70	B4	Urbasa, Pto de	36	C2	Urquiola, Pto	36	B1
Udvar	72	A1	Uhrsleben	52	C1	Ullsfjorden	94	C2	Umbukta	97	E3	Universales, Mts	41	D2	Urbasa, Sa de	36	C2	Urshult	109	D3
			Uig	2	B3	Ullswater	5	D4	Umčari	73	D3	Unna	17	E3	Urbe	60	A3	Ursprungpaß	59	D1
			Uimaharju	103	F2				Umeå	102	B1	Unnaryd	109	D2						

Urtivaara	95 D3	Usk	9 D2	Ustaritz	28 A4	Utajärvi	99 D4	Utrillas	41 E2	Uukuniemi	103 F3	Užgorod	112 C3
Ururi	64 B2	Usk R	9 D2	Uster	58 A2	Utåker	104 A3	Utsjoki	95 E2	Uurainen	103 D2	Uzin	113 E2
Ury	25 F1	Uskoplie	76 A2	Ustevatn	104 A3	Utbjoa	104 A3	Utsjoki R	95 E2	Uusikaarlepyy	102 B2	Uzunköprü	115 E3
Urziceni	115 E1	Üsküdar	115 F3	Ustibar	76 B1	Utebo	37 D3	Uttendorf		Uusikaupunki	107 D2		
Usagre	43 D1	Uslar	52 B2	Ustica, I di	68 B2	Utelle	31 E3	(Oberösterreich)	56 C3	Uvac	76 B1		
Uşak	115 F4	Ussat-les-Bains	32 A2	Ustikolina	76 A1	Utena	110 C3	Uttendorf		Uvac R	76 B1		
Ušće	73 D4	Ussé	25 D2	Ústi nad Labem	53 F3	Utiel	41 E1	(Salzburg)	59 E1	Uvdal	104 C2		
Usedom	49 E2	Usseglio	31 E1	Ustiprača	76 B1	Utne	104 B2	Utting	56 A3	Uzdin	72 C2		
Usedom I	49 E1	Ussel	29 E1	Ustka	110 A4	Utrecht	16 C3	Uttoxeter	6 C3	Uzel	22 C3		
Useras	41 E3	Usseln	17 F4	Ustronie Morskie	49 F1	Utrecht (Prov)	16 C2	Uudenmaan		Uzerche	29 D1		
Usingen	51 F4	Ustaoset	104 B2	Usťužna	111 F1	Utrera	43 D3	Lääni	107 F2	Uzès	30 B3		

V

Vä	109 D3	Vålberg	105 E3	Valdelinares	41 E2	Valdosa	36 A3	Valenciennes	20 A1	Valkenswaard	16 C4	Vallø	108 C3
Vaajakoski	103 D3	Valbo	106 B2	Valdemarsvik	109 E1	Valdres	104 C2	Valensole	31 D3	Valko	107 F2	Vallo della Lucania	67 D1
Vääkiö	99 E3	Valbondione	58 B3	Valdemeca	41 D2	Valdres Flya	100 B3	Valentano	63 D2	Valladolid	35 E4	Valloire	31 D1
Vaala	99 E4	Valbonë	76 C2	Valdemorillo	40 A2	Vale de Açor	42 B2	Valentigney	27 E2	Vallata	64 C3	Vallombrosa	61 D3
Vaalajärvi	95 E4	Valbonnais	31 D2	Valdemoro	40 A2	Vale de Cambra	38 B1	Valenza	60 A2	Vallbo	101 D2	Vallon-en-Sully	25 F3
Vaalimaa	103 F4	Val Camonica	58 C4	Valdenoceda	36 A2	Vale de Estrela	38 C2	Valeria	40 C3	Våler (Hedmark)	105 D2	Vallon-Pont-d'arc	30 B3
Vaals	51 D3	Valcarlos	36 C1	Valdeobispo, Emb		Vale de Prazeres	38 C2	Valevåg	104 A3	Våler (Østfold)	105 D3	Vallorbe	27 D3
Vaaraslahti	103 D2	Valdagno	59 D4	de	39 D2	Vale, Emb de	37 F2	Valfabbrica	61 E4	Vall d'Alba	41 E3	Vallorcine	27 E4
Vaasa	102 B2	Valdahon	27 D2	Valdepeñas	44 A1	Valença do Minho	34 A3	Valga	110 C2	Valldemossa	45 E2	Valls	37 F4
Vaasan Lääni	102 C2	Valdaj	111 E1	Valdepeñas da		Valençay	25 E2	Val Gardena	59 D3	Vall de Uxó	41 E3	Vallsta	101 F4
Vaassen	17 D2	Val-d'Ajol, le	27 D1	Jaén	44 A2	Valence-		Valgorge	30 B2	Valle	104 B3	Valmiera	110 C2
Vabre	32 B1	Valdajskaja		Valderaduey, R	35 D4	d'Albigeois	29 E3	Valgrisenche	31 E1	Valleberga	109 D4	Valmojado	40 A2
Vác	112 B4	Vozvyšennosť	111 E2	Valderas	35 E3	Valence (Drôme)	30 C2	Valguarnera		Valle Castellana	63 F1	Valmont	19 D2
Vaccarès, Etang		Valdavia, R	35 E3	Val de Reuil	19 E3	Valence (Gers)	28 C3	Caropepe	68 C3	Valle d'Aosta	27 E4	Valmontone	63 F3
de	30 B4	Valdeazogues, R	43 F1	Valderiès	29 E3	Valencia	41 E4	Valhelhas	38 C2	Valle de Abdalajis	43 E3	Valogne	18 B3
Vacha	52 B3	Valdecaballeros	39 E4	Valderøy	100 A2	Valencia (Prov)	41 D4	Valico della		Valle de la Serena	39 E4	Valongo	34 A4
Väddö	106 B3	Valdecabras	40 C3	Valderrepisa, Pto		Valencia de		Forchetta	64 A2	Valle de los Caidos	40 A2	Valoria la Buena	35 E4
Vadehavet	108 A4	Valdecañas, Emb		de	43 F1	Alcántara	38 C3	Valimítika	83 C3	Valle de		Valpaços	34 b4
Vadheim	100 A3	de	39 E3	Valderrobres	41 F2	Valencia de Don		Valíra	86 C3	Matamoros	42 C1	Valpalmas	37 D3
Vado Ligure	60 A3	Valdecarros	39 E1	Valdestillas	35 E4	Juan	35 D3	Valjevo	72 C3	Vallehermoso	42 A4	Val Passiria	59 D2
Vadsø	95 F1	Valdecebollas	35 F2	Valdeverdeja	39 E3	Valencia de las		Valjok	95 E2	Vallejera, Pto de	39 E3	Valpovo	71 F2
Vadstena	109 D1	Valdediós	35 E1	Valdevimbre	35 D3	Torres	43 D1	Valjunquera	41 F1	Valle-Mosso	31 F1	Valprato Soana	31 E1
Vaduz	58 B2	Valdeganga	41 D4	Valdezcaray	36 B2	Valencia del		Valkeakoski	107 E2	Vallentuna	106 B3	Valras-Plage	30 A4
Vadvetjåkka	94 B3	Valdeinfierno, Emb		Valdieri	31 E3	Ventoso	43 D1	Valkeala	107 F2	Valleraugue	29 F3	Valréas	30 C3
Vaféika	81 D2	de	44 C2	Valdihuela	39 F2	Valencia de las		Valkenburg	51 D3	Vallet	24 B2	Valsamónero	91 D4
Vafiohóri	79 F2	Valdelacasa de		Val-d'Isère	31 D1	Valencia I	14 A4			Valletta	68 B4	Valsavarenche	31 E1
Vågaholmen	97 E2	Tajo	39 E3	Valdobbiadene	59 D3					Vallgrund	102 B2	Valserine	27 D4
Vågåmo	100 B3									Valli di Comacchio	61 D2		
Vågan	97 E1												
Vaganj	75 E1												
Vaganski vrh	70 C4												
Vágar	96 A3												
Våge	104 A2												
Væggerløse	108 C4												
Vaggeryd	109 D2												
Vágia	83 F4												
Vagioniá	91 D4												
Vagnhärad	106 B4												
Vagos	38 B1												
Vågsfjorden	94 B3												
Vågsøy	100 A3												
Vágur	96 A4												
Váh	112 B3												
Vähäkyrö	102 B2												
Vahto	107 D2												
Váï	91 F3												
Vaiano	60 C3												
Vaiges	23 E3												
Vaihingen	55 D2												
Vailly (Aisne)	20 A3												
Vailly (Cher)	26 A2												
Vainikkala	103 F4												
Vaisaluokta	94 B4												
Vaison-la-													
Romaine	30 C3												
Vaksdal	104 A2												
Vålådalen	101 D2												
Valadares	34 A4												
Valais	27 E4												
Valalta	70 A3												
Valamen	103 E2												
Valandovo	77 F3												
Val-André, le	22 C2												
Valareña	36 C3												
Valašské Meziříčí	112 B3												
Valax	107 F2												
Valberg	31 E3												

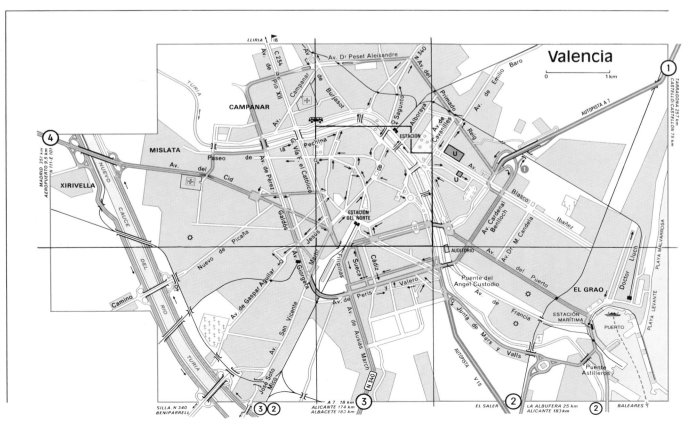

Valencia

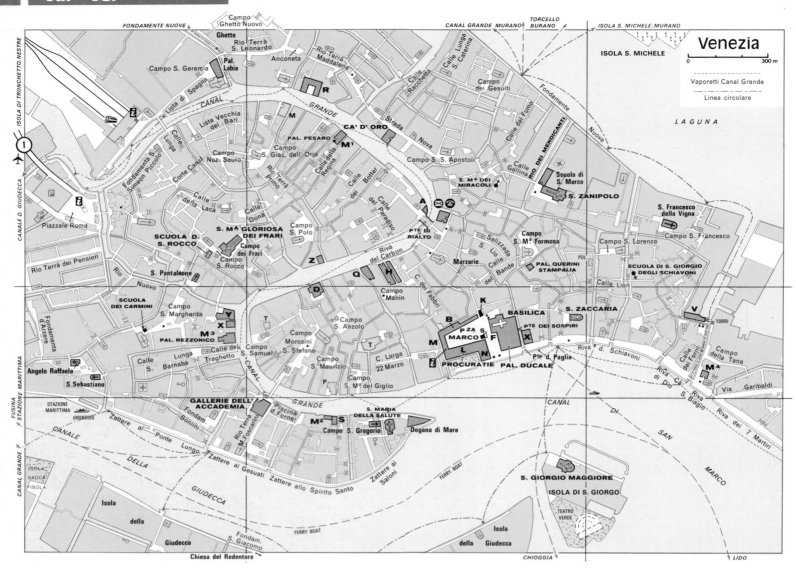

Venezia

Vaporetti Canal Grande
Linea circolare

Name	Page	Grid
Valset	100	C1
Valsjöbyn	101	E1
Vals-les-Bains	30	B2
Valtellina	58	B3
Valtessiníko	86	C2
Val-Thorens	31	D1
Valtierra	36	C3
Valtimo	103	E1
Váltos	81	F1
Valtotópi	80	B2
Váltou, Óri	82	C2
Valtournenche	27	F4
Valun	70	B4
Valvasone	59	E3
Valverde (Is Canarias)	42	A4
Valverde (La Rioja)	36	C3
Valverde del Camino	42	C2
Valverde de Leganés	38	C4
Valverde del Fresno	39	D2
Valverde del Júcar	40	C3
Valøya	97	D4
Våmb	109	D1
Våmhus	101	E4
Vamlingbo	109	F4
Vammala	107	D1
Vampula	107	D2
Vamvakás, Akr	85	F4
Vamvakoú (Pelopónissos)	87	D3
Vamvakoú (Thessalía)	83	E2
Vanajavesi	107	E2
Vanån	101	D4
Vanda	107	E2
Vandellòs	41	F1
Vänern	105	E4
Vangshylla	101	D1
Vangsnes	104	B1
Vangsvik	94	B3
Vanha Vaasa	102	B2
Vanna	94	C2
Vännäs	102	A1
Vannavålen	94	C2
Vannes	22	C4
Vannsjø	105	D3
Vannsundet	94	C2
Vanoise, Massif de la	31	D1
Vanoise, Parc Nat de la	31	D1
Vansbro	105	E2
Vans, les	30	B3
Vantaa	107	E2
Vanttauskoski	99	D2
Vaour	29	D3
Vaqueira	37	F2
Var	31	D1
Vara	108	C1
Varades	23	E4
Varallo	58	A4
Varangerbotn	95	F1
Varangerfjorden	95	F1
Varangerhalvøya	95	F1
Varano de' Melegari	60	B2
Varano, L di	64	C2
Varaždin	70	C1
Varaždinske Toplice	71	D1
Varazze	60	A3
Varberg	108	C2
Vårbica	115	D3
Varda	72	C4
Várda	86	B1
Vardar	77	E3
Varde	108	A3
Vardenik	77	E2
Vardø	95	F1
Vårdö	106	C3
Vardoússia, Óri	83	D3
Varel	47	F3
Vareleii	84	C4
Varengeville	19	D2
Varenna	58	B4
Varennes-en-Argonne	20	C3
Varennes-sur-Allier	26	A4
Varennes-sur-Amance	26	C1
Vareš	71	F4
Varese	58	A4
Varese Ligure	60	B3
Vårgårda	108	C1
Vargas	35	F2
Vargsund	95	D1
Varhaug	104	A4
Vári (Kikládes)	88	B2
Vári (Steréa Eláda)	87	F1
Varilhes	32	A2
Varimbómbi	87	F1
Váris	79	D4
Varkaus	103	E3
Várkiza	87	F2
Värmlands Län	105	E3
Varmo	59	E3
Varna (BG)	115	D3
Varna (YU)	72	C3
Várnamo	109	D2
Varnhem	109	D1
Varnsdorf	53	F2
Värö	108	C2
Varoš Selo	77	D2
Varpaisjärvi	103	E1
Várpalota	112	B4
Värriötunturit	95	F4
Vars	31	D2
Vars, Col de	31	D2
Vartdalsfjorden	100	A2
Vartholomió 20	86	B1
Vartius	99	F4
Värtsilä	103	F2
Varvára	80	B3
Varvarin	73	E4
Varzi	60	A2
Varzy	26	A2
Vasa	102	B2
Vasarapera	99	E2
Vásárosnamény	112	C1
Vascão, Rib do	42	B2
Vasikkaselkä	95	F4
Vasil'kov	113	D2
Vaskijärvi	107	D2
Vaskio	107	D2
Vaskivesi	102	C3
Vaslui	113	E4
Vassarás	87	D3
Vassés	86	C2
Vassieux	30	C2
Vassiliká (Évia)	84	A3
Vassiliká (Lésvos)	85	F2
Vassiliká (Makedonía)	80	A3
Vassilikí (Lefkáda)	82	B3
Vassilikí (Thessalía)	83	D1
Vassilikó	84	B4
Vassilikós	86	A2
Vassilís	83	E2
Vassilítsa	78	C4
Vassy	18	C4
Västanbäck	101	F2
Västanfyärd	107	D3
Vastenjaure	97	F1
Västerås	106	A3
Västerdalälven	101	D4
Väster Haninge	106	B4
Västernorrlands Län	101	F2
Västervik	109	E1
Västmanlands Län	105	F3
Vasto	64	B2
Vatan	25	E3
Väte	109	F4
Vaterá	85	F3
Vateró	79	D4
Váthia	87	D4
Vathí (Dodekánissa)	84	B4
Vathí (Lefkáda)	79	F2
Vathí (Makedonía)	92	C1
Vathí (Steréa Eláda)	82	B3
Vathílakos (Dráma)	80	C2
Vathílakos (Kozáni)	79	E4
Vathílakos (Thessaloníki)	79	F3
Vathípetro	91	D4
Vathís	89	F3
Vatin	73	D2
Vatnajökull	96	B2
Vatne	100	B2
Vatólakos	79	D4
Vatopediou	80	C4
Vatra Dornei	113	D4
Vättern	109	D1
Vattholma	106	B3
Vaucluse	30	C3
Vaucouleurs	20	C4
Vaud	27	D3
Vau i Dejës	76	C3
Vaut të Dejës, Liq i	76	C3
Vauvert	30	B4
Vauvillers	27	D1
Vaux-le-Vicomte	19	F4
Vávdos	80	A3
Växjö	109	D2
Växtorp	108	C3
Vayrac	29	D2
V'az'ma	111	F2
Veberöd	109	D3
Vecht	17	D2
Vechta	17	F1
Vechte	17	E2
Vecinos	39	E1
Vedelago	59	E4
Vedrá, I	45	D4
Vedungfjället	101	D3
Veendam	47	D3
Veenendaal	16	C3
Veere	16	B3
Vefsna	97	E3
Vefsnfjorden	97	E3
Vega	97	D3
Vega de Espinareda	34	C2
Vegadeo	34	C1
Vega de Valcarce	34	C2
Vegafjorden	97	D3
Vegárshei	104	C4
Vegas	35	E2
Vegas del Condado	35	E2
Vegesack	47	F3
Veghel	16	C3
Vegoritida, L	79	E3
Vehkalahti	103	F4
Vehmaa	101	D2
Vehmersalmi	103	E2
Veiðivötn	96	B2
Veidnesklubben	95	E1
Veikkola	107	E2
Veines	95	F1
Veinge	108	C2
Veiros	38	C4
Vejen	108	A3
Vejer de la Frontera	43	D4
Vejle	108	A3
Velada	39	F3
Velagići	71	D4
Vela Luka	75	E2
Velanídia	87	E4

Name	Page	Ref
Velate, Pto de	36	C1
Velayos	39	F1
Velbert	17	E4
Velburg	55	F1
Velde	101	D1
Velden (A)	70	A1
Velden (Nüberg)	55	F1
Velden (München)	56	B3
Veldhoven	16	C4
Velebit	70	C4
Velebitski kanal	70	B4
Velenje	70	B1
Velešta	77	D4
Velestíno	83	F2
Veleta, Pico	44	A3
Velež	75	F2
Vélez Blanco	44	C2
Vélez de Benaudalla	44	A3
Vélez-Málaga	43	F3
Vélez Rubio	44	C2
Velfjorden	97	D3
Veličani	75	F2
Veliés	87	E4
Velika	71	E2
Velika Drenova	73	E4
Velika Gorica	70	C2
Velikaja	111	D2
Velika Jablanica	76	C2
Velika Jamnička	70	C2
Velika Kapela	70	B3
Velika Kladuša	70	C3
Velika Kopanica	71	F3
Velika Kruša	77	D2
Velika Morava	73	D3
Velika Mučna	71	D1
Velika Plana (Morava)	73	D3
Velika Plana (Prokuplje)	77	D1
Velika Tresta	73	E3
Veliki Alan	70	B4
Veliki Bastaji	71	E2
Veliki Gaj	73	D2
Veliki Grđevac	71	D2
Veliki Izvor	73	F3
Veliki Jastrebac	77	D1
Velikije Luki	111	E2
Veliki kanal	72	B2
Veliki Krš	73	E3
Veliki Popović	73	E3
Veliki Prolog	75	E2
Veliki Radinci	72	C2
Veliki Trnovac	77	E2
Veliki Vitao	76	A2
Veliki Zdenci	71	D2
Veliko Gradište	73	D2
Veliko Lašče	70	B2
Veliko Orašje	73	D3
Veliko Târnovo	115	D2
Velilla del R Carrión	35	E2
Veli Lošinj	70	B4
Velimlje	76	A2
Vélines	28	C2
Velingrad	115	D3
Velino	63	F2
Velino, Mte	63	F2
Veliž	111	E3
Veljun	70	C3
Velká Bíteš	57	E1
Velké Meziříčí	57	E1
Velkua	107	D2
Vellahn	48	B3
Velletri	63	E3
Vellinge	108	C3
Velopoúla	87	E3
Vélos	84	B4
Velpke	48	B4
Velten	49	D4
Velvendós	79	E4
Vemdalen	101	E3
Vemdalsskalet	101	E3
Vemhån	101	E3
Véna	81	E2
Venaco	33	F3
Venafro	64	A3
Venarey-les-Laumes	26	B2
Venaria	31	E1
Venčani	73	D3
Vence	31	E3
Venda Nova	34	B4
Vendas Novas	38	B4
Vendée	24	B3
Vendel	106	B3
Vendeuvre	26	B1
Vendôme	25	E2
Vendsyssel	108	B2
Veneheitto	99	D4
Veneta, Laguna	61	D1
Veneto	61	D1
Venezia	61	D1
Vengjaneset	104	A2
Venialbo	35	D4
Venjan	101	E4
Venjansjön	101	E4
Venlo	17	D4
Vennebeck	17	F2
Vennesla	104	B4
Vennesund	97	D3
Venosa	64	C3
Venosta	58	C3
Venray	17	D3
Venta	110	B3
Venta de Cruce	43	D3
Venta de Don Quijote	40	B3
Ventana, Pto de	35	D2
Venta Nueva	34	C2
Ventas de Huelma	44	A3
Veternica	77	E1
Ventimiglia	31	E3
Ventnor	9	E4
Ventotene, I	63	F4
Ventoux, Mt	30	C3
Ventspils	110	B2
Venturina	62	C1
Vera (E)	44	C3
Vera (N)	101	D1
Vera de Bidasoa	36	C1
Verbania-Pallanza	58	A4
Verberie	19	F3
Verbicaro	67	E2
Verbier	27	E4
Vercelli	31	F1
Vercel-Villedieu	27	D2
Verchnedvinsk	111	D3
Verdalsøra	101	D1
Verde, Col de	33	F3
Verden	48	A4
Verdikoússa	83	D1
Verdon	31	D3
Verdon, le	28	A1
Verdun (Meuse)	20	C3
Verdun (Saône-et-Loire)	26	C3
Verdun (Tarn-et-Garonne)	29	D3
Verfeil	29	D4
Vergato	60	C3
Vérgi	80	A2
Vergiate	60	A1
Vergina	79	E3
Vergio, Col de	33	F3
Vergt	28	C2
Véria	79	E3
Verin	34	B3
Verl	17	F3
Vermand	20	A2
Vermenton	26	B2
Vérmio, Óros	79	E3
Verna, Pzo di	69	D2
Vernet-les-Bains	32	B2
Verneuil	19	D4
Vernon	19	E3
Vérno, Óros	79	D3
Vernoux-en-Vivarais	30	B2
Verny	21	D3
Veroli	63	F3
Verona	60	C1
Verpillière	30	C1
Verran	101	D1
Verrès	27	F4
Versailles	19	F4
Versmold	17	F2
Verteillac	28	C1
Vertiskos, Óros	80	A2
Vertus	20	B4
Verucchio	61	E3
Veruela	36	C3
Verviers	51	D4
Vervins	20	B2
Verzuolo	31	E2
Verzy	20	B3
Vesanto	103	D2
Vescovato	33	F3
Veselí	57	D1
Vesijärvi	107	F2
Vesilahti	107	E1
Vesivehmaa	107	F2
Vesjegonsk	111	F1
Veskoniemi	95	F3
Vesle	20	B3
Vesoul	27	D2
Véssa	85	E4
Vest-Agder	104	B4
Vestby	105	D3
Vestbygda	104	A4
Vesterålen	94	A3
Vesterø Havn	108	B2
Vestertana	95	E1
Vestfjorden	97	E1
Vestfold	104	C3
Vestmanna	96	A3
Vestmannaeyjar	96	B3
Vestnes	100	B2
Vestone	58	C4
Vestre Jakobselv	95	F1
Vestvågøy	94	A4
Vésubie, Gorges de la	31	E3
Vesuvio	64	B4
Veszprém	112	B4
Veteli	102	C2
Veternica	77	E1
Vetlanda	109	E2
Vetralla	63	E2
Vetriolo Terme	59	D3
Vetschau	53	E1
Vettore, M	63	F1
Veules-les-Roses	19	D2
Veulettes	19	D2
Veurne	50	A3
Vevey	27	E3
Vévi	79	D3
Veynes	30	C2
Veyre	29	F1
Veyrier	27	D4
Vezdemarbán	35	D4
Vézelay	26	B2
Vézelise	21	D4
Vézénobres	30	B3
Vézère	29	D2
Vézins-de-Lévézou	29	E3
Vezzani	33	F3
Vezzano	58	C3
Via Appia	63	F3
Via Aurelia	60	C4
Via Casilina	63	E2
Via Cassia	63	D1
Viadana	60	C2
Via Emilia	61	D3
Via Flaminia	61	E3
Viana	36	B2
Viana do Bolo	34	C3
Viana do Castelo	34	A3
Vianden	21	D2
Viano do Alentejo	42	B1
Viareggio	60	B3
Viar, R	43	D2
Vias	30	A4
Via Salaria	63	E2
Via Tiburtina Valeria	63	F2
Viaur	29	E3
Viborg	108	A2
Vibo Valentia	67	E3
Vibraye	23	F3
Vič	70	B1
Vic (E)	32	A3
Vic (F)	19	F3
Vicálvaro	40	B2
Vicdessos	37	F2
Vic-en-Bigorre	28	B4
Vicenza	59	D4
Vic-Fézensac	28	C4
Vich	32	A3
Vichy	26	A4
Vic-le-Comte	29	F1
Vico	33	E3
Vico del Gargano	64	C2
Vico Equense	64	B4
Vico, Lago di	63	E2
Vic-sur-Cère	29	E2
Victoria	68	B4
Vidå	108	A4
Vidago	34	B4
Viðareiði	96	A3
Vidauban	31	D4
Viddal	100	A3
Videbæk	108	A3
Vidiáki	86	C1
Vidigueira	42	B1
Vidin	114	C2
Vidio, C	35	D1
Viðoy	96	A3
Vidreres	32	B4
Vidrovan	76	B2
Vidsel	98	B3
Viduša	76	A2
Viechtach	56	B2
Viechtwang	56	C3
Vieira	38	A2
Vieira do Minho	34	B4
Viejo, Pto	39	D2
Viekinjärvi	103	F1
Vielha	37	F2
Vielle-Aure	37	E2
Vielmur	32	A1
Vielsalm	51	D4
Vienenburg	52	B1
Vienne	30	B1
Vienne (Dépt)	25	D3
Vienne R	25	D4
Vieremä	103	D1
Viernheim	54	C1
Vierraden	49	E3
Viersen	17	D4
Vierumäki	107	F2
Vierzehnheiligen	52	C4
Vierzon	25	F2
Vieste	64	C2
Vietas	94	B4
Vietri di Potenza	64	C4
Vietri sul Mare	64	B4
Vieux-Boucau	28	A3
Vieux Chaillol	31	D2
Vif	30	C2
Vig	108	C3
Vigan, le	29	F3
Vigeland	104	B4
Vigeois	29	D1
Vigevano	60	A1
Viggiano	65	D4
Vígla	82	C2
Vígla, Akr	91	D1
Vignale	31	F1
Vignanello	63	E2
Vignemale	37	E2
Vignes, les	29	F3
Vigneulles	20	C3
Vignola	60	C2
Vignole Borbera	60	A2
Vignory	26	C1
Vigo	34	A3
Vigo di Fassa	59	D3
Vigone	31	E2
Vigonza	61	D1
Vigrestad	104	A4
Vihanti	99	D4
Vihiers	24	C2
Vihtavuori	103	D3
Vihteljärvi	102	C3
Vihti	107	E2
Viiala	107	E1
Viinijärvi	103	F2
Viipustunturit	95	E3
Viitasaari	103	D2
Vik (Aust-Agder)	104	B4
Vík (IS)	96	B3
Vik (Nordland)	97	D3
Vik (Sogn og Fjordane)	104	B1
Vika	105	F2
Vikajärvi	99	D2
Vikanes	104	A2
Vikebukt	100	B2
Vikedal	104	A3
Vikersund	104	C3
Vikeså	104	A3
Vikevåg	104	A3
Vikingstad	106	A4
Vikna	97	D4
Vikoč	76	A1
Vikran	94	B2
Viksdalen	100	A3
Viksjö	101	F2
Viksjøfjell	95	F2
Viksta	106	B3
Vila Boim	38	C4
Vilada	32	A3
Viladamat	32	B3
Vila de Cruces	34	B2
Vila de Rei	38	B3
Vila do Bispo	42	A2
Vila do Conde	34	A4
Viladrau	32	B3
Vila Fernando	38	C4
Vila Flor	34	C4
Vila Franca das Naves	38	C1
Vilafranca del Penedès	32	A4
Vila Franca de Xira	38	A4
Vila Fresca de Azeitão	38	A4
Vilagarcia de Arosa	34	A2
Vilaine	22	C4
Vilaller	37	F2
Vilanova	34	C1
Vila Nova da Barquinha	38	B3
Vilanova de Arousa	34	A2
Vila Nova de Cerveira	34	A3
Vila Nova de Famalicão	34	A4
Vila Nova de Foz Côa	39	D1
Vila Nova de Gaia	34	A4
Vila Nova de Milfontes	42	A2
Vila Nova de Ourém	38	B3
Vila Nova de Paiva	38	C1
Vila Nova de Poiares	38	B2
Vilanova de Sau	32	A3
Vilanova i la Geltrú	32	A4
Vila Pouca de Aguiar	34	B4
Vila Praia de Âncora	34	A3
Vilar de Barrio	34	B3
Vila Real	34	B4
Vila-real	41	E3
Vila Real de Santo António	42	B3
Vila-rodona	37	F4
Vila-seca	37	F4
Vila Velha de Ródão	38	C3
Vila Verde	34	A3
Vila Verde de Ficalho	42	C1
Vila Verde de Raia	34	B3
Vila Viçosa	38	C4
Vilches	44	A2
Vilejka	111	D4
Vilhelmina	97	F4
Vília	87	E1
Viljakkala	102	C3
Viljandi	110	C2
Vilkaviškis	110	C3
Vilkovo	113	E4
Villa Adriana	63	E2
Villa Bartolomea	60	C1
Villablanca	42	C2
Villablino	35	D2
Villabona	36	C1
Villabrágima	35	E4
Villacarriedo	35	F2
Villacarrillo	44	B2
Villacastín	40	A1
Villach	59	F2
Villacidro	66	B4
Villada	35	E3
Villa del Prado	40	A2
Villa del Río	43	F2
Villadiego	35	F3
Villadossola	27	F4
Villaescusa de Haro	40	C3
Villafáfila	35	D4
Villafamés	41	E3
Villaflores	39	F1
Villafranca	36	C2
Villafranca del Bierzo	34	C2
Villafranca del Cid	41	E2
Villafranca de los Barros	43	D1
Villafranca de los Caballeros	40	B3
Villafranca di Verona	60	C1
Villafranca in Lunigiana	60	B3
Villafranca-Montes de Oca	36	A2
Villafranca Piemonte	31	E2
Villafranca Tirrena	69	D2
Villafranco del Guadalquivir	43	D3
Villafrati	68	B3
Villafrechos	35	E3
Villafruela	35	F4
Villafuerte	35	F4
Villagarcía del Llano	40	C4
Villager	35	D2
Villaggio Mancuso	67	F3
Villaggio Gonzalo	39	D4
Villaharta	43	E1
Villahermosa	44	B1
Villahoz	35	F3
Villaines-la-Juhel	23	E3
Villajoyosa	45	E1
Villala	103	F3
Villalba	34	B1
Villalba de Guardo	35	E2
Villalba de la Sierra	40	C3
Villalba de los Barros	43	D1
Villalba del Rey	40	C2
Villalcampo, Emb de	35	D4
Villalcázar de Sirga	35	E3
Villalenga	36	C4
Villalón de Campos	35	E3
Villalonga	45	E1
Villalpando	35	E4
Villalpardo	41	D4
Villamañán	35	D3
Villamanrique	44	B1
Villamarchante	41	E3
Villamartín (Andalucía)	43	D3
Villamartín (Castilla-León)	35	E3
Villamassargia	66	B4
Villamayor	37	D3
Villamayor de Campos	35	E3
Villamayor de Santiago	40	B3
Villameca, Emb de	35	D2
Villa Minozzo	60	C3
Villandraut	28	B3
Villandry	25	D2
Villanova Monteleone	66	A2
Villanubla	35	E4
Villanueva de Alcardete	40	B3
Villanueva de Alcolea	41	F3
Villanueva de Alcorón	40	C2
Villanueva de Algaidas	43	F3
Villanueva de Argaño	35	F3
Villanueva de Arzobispo	44	B2
Villanueva de Bogas	40	A3
Villanueva de Cameros	36	B3
Villanueva de Córdoba	43	F1
Villanueva de Franco	40	B4
Villanueva de Gállego	37	D3
Villanueva de la Concepción	43	F3
Villanueva de la Fuente	44	B1
Villanueva de la Jara	40	C4
Villanueva de la Reina	44	A2
Villanueva de la Serena	39	E4
Villanueva de la Sierra	39	D2
Villanueva de las Torres	44	B2
Villanueva de la Vera	39	E2
Villanueva del Campo	35	D3
Villanueva del Duque	43	E1
Villanueva del Fresno	42	C1
Villanueva del Huerva	37	D4
Villanueva de los Castillejos	42	C2
Villanueva de los Infantes	44	B1
Villanueva del Rey	43	E1
Villanueva del Río y Minas	43	D2
Villanueva de San Carlos	44	A1
Villa Opicina	59	F3
Villa Potenza	61	F4
Villaquejida	35	D3
Villaquilambre	35	D2
Villarcayo	36	A1
Villard-de-Lans	30	C2
Villar de Cañas	40	C3
Villardeciervos	35	D3
Villar de Domingo Garcia	40	C2
Villardefrades	35	E4
Villar del Arzobispo	41	E3
Villar del Rey	39	D4
Villar de Peralonso	39	E1
Villarejo de Fuentes	40	C3
Villarejo de Orbigo	35	D3
Villarejo de Salvanés	40	B2
Villarente	35	E3
Villares de la Reina	39	E1
Villares del Saz	40	C3
Villargordo de Cabriel	41	D4
Villaricos	44	C3
Villarín de Campos	35	D4
Villarino	34	C4
Villarquemado	41	D2
Villarramiel	35	E3
Villarrobledo	40	C4
Villarroya	36	C3
Villarroya de la Sierra	36	C4
Villarroya de los Pinares	41	E2
Villarroya, Pto de	41	E2
Villarrubia de Santiago	40	B3
Villars	27	E3
Villars-les-Dombes	26	C4
Villarta de San Juan	40	B4
Villarubia de los Ojos	40	A4
Villasalto	66	C3
Villasana de Mena	36	A1
Villasandino	35	F3
Villa San Giovanni	67	E4
Villa Santa Maria	64	A2
Villasante	36	A1
Villa Santina	59	E3
Villasarracino	35	E3
Villasayas, Pto de	36	B4
Villaseco de los Reyes	39	E1
Villasequilla de Yepes	40	A3
Villasimius	66	C4
Villasor	66	B4
Villatobas	40	C3
Villatoro, Pto de	39	F2
Villatoya	41	D4
Villava	36	C2

Villavaara 95 F2
Villaverde del Río 43 D2
Villaviciosa 35 E1
Villaviciosa de
  Córdoba 43 E2
Villaviciosa de
  Odón 40 A2
Villavieja de Yeltes 39 D1
Villa Vomano 63 F1
Villé 21 E4
Villebois-Lavalette 28 C1
Villedieu, la 25 D3
Villedieu-les-
  Poêles 18 B4
Ville-en-Tardenois 20 B3
Villefagnan 24 C4
Villefort 29 F3
Villefranche-
  d'Albigeois 29 E3
Villefranche-de-
  Lauragais 29 D4
Villefranche-de-
  Lonchat 28 C2
Villefranche-de-
  Rouergue 29 E3
Villefranche-du-
  Périgord 29 D2
Villefranche-sur-
  Cher 25 E2
Villefranche-sur-
  Mer 31 E3
Villefranche-sur-
  Saône 26 C4
Villel 41 D2
Villemur 29 D3
Villena 45 D1
Villenauxe-la-
  Grande 20 A4
Villeneuve 30 B3
Villeneuve-de-
  Berg 30 B2
Villeneuve-de-
  Marsan 28 B3
Villeneuve-
  l'Archevêque 26 A1
Villeneuve-sur-Lot 28 C3
Villeneuve-sur-
  Yonne 26 A1
Villeréal 28 C2
Villers 19 D3
Villers-Bocage
  (Calvados) 18 C3
Villers-Bocage
  (Somme) 19 F2
Villers-
  Bretonneux 19 F2
Villers-Cotterêts 19 F3
Villers-devant-
  Orval 20 C2
Villersexel 27 D2
Villers-Farlay 27 D2
Villers la Ville 50 C4
Villers-le-Lac 27 E2
Villerupt 21 D2
Villerville 19 D3
Ville-sur-Tourbe 20 C3
Villeta Barrea 64 A2
Villiers-St-Georges 20 A4
Villingen-
  Schwenningen 54 C3
Villoldo 35 E3
Villoria 39 E1
Villotta 59 E3
Villuercas 39 E3
Vilnius 110 C3

Vilppula 102 C3
Vils (Bayern) 55 F1
Vils (Bayern) 56 B2
Vilsbiburg 56 B2
Vilseck 55 F1
Vilshofen 56 B2
Vilusi 76 A2
Vilvoorde 50 B3
Vimercate 60 A1
Vimianzo 34 A1
Vimieiro 38 B4
Vimioso 34 C4
Vimmerby 109 E1
Vimoutiers 19 D4
Vimpeli 102 C2
Vimperk 56 C1
Vinac 71 E4
Vinadio 31 E3
Vinaixa 37 F4
Vinalapó, R 45 D2
Vinaròs 41 F2
Vinay 30 C1
Vinça 32 B2
Vinča 73 D3
Vinchiaturo 64 B3
Vinci 60 C3
Vindafjorden 104 A3
Vindelälven 102 A1
Vindelfjällens N.R. 97 E3
Vindeln 102 A1
Vinderup 108 A2
Vindsvik 104 A3
Vingåker 105 F4
Vingelen 100 C3
Vingeveien 100 C3
Vinhais 34 C3
Vinica
  (Makedonija) 77 F3
Vinica (Slovenija) 70 C3
Viničani 77 E3
Vinje 104 B3
Vinkovci 71 F2
Vinnica 113 E2
Vinsternes 100 B2
Vinstra 100 C3
Vinstri 104 C1
Vintilänkaira 95 F4
Viñuelas 40 B2
Vinuesa 36 B3
Viotía 83 F4
Vípava 70 A2
Vipava R 70 A2
Vipiteno 59 E2
Vir (Bosna i
  Hercegovina) 75 E1
Vir (Hrvatska) 70 C4
Vir I 70 C4
Vira 75 D2
Vire 18 C4
Virgen 59 E2
Virgen de la
  Cabeza 43 F2
Virginia 13 D3
Virieu 30 C1
Virieu-le-Grand 27 D4
Virihaure 97 F1
Virkby 107 E3
Virkkala 107 E3
Virkkula 99 E2
Virksund 108 A2
Virmasvesi 103 D2
Virmutjoki 103 F3
Virolahti 103 F4
Virónia 80 A1
Virovitica 71 E2

Virpazar 76 B3
Virrat 102 C3
Virsbo 105 F3
Virserum 109 E2
Virsko more 70 C4
Virtasalmi 103 E3
Virton 20 C3
Virtsu 110 B2
Vis 75 D2
Vis I 75 D2
Visaurin 37 D2
Visby 109 F4
Viségrad 72 C4
Viségradska Banja 72 C4
Viserba 61 E3
Viseu 38 C1
Viševica 70 B3
Viskan 108 C2
Viški kan 75 D2
Višnja Gora 70 B2
Višnjica 73 D3
Visočica 75 F1
Visočica R 73 F4
Viso del Marqués 44 A1
Visoki Dečani 76 C2
Visoko 71 F4
Visovac 75 D1
Visp 27 F3
Víssani 78 B4
Visselhövede 48 A3
Vissenbjerg 108 B3
Vissiniá 79 D3
Visso 63 F1
Vistabella del
  Maestrazgo 41 E2
Vistasvägi 94 B4
Vistheden 98 B3
Vistonída, L 81 D2
Visuvesi 102 C3
Vitaby 109 D3
Vitala 84 B4
Vitanovac 73 D4
Vitebsk 111 E3
Viterbo 63 E2
Vitez 71 E4
Vitigudino 39 D1
Vitina 86 C2
Vitina (Bosna i
  Hercegovina) 75 E2
Vitina (Kosovo) 77 D2
Vitlycke 105 D4
Vito d'Asio 59 E3
Vítoli 83 D3
Vitolište 77 E4
Vitomirica 76 C2
Vitoria-Gasteiz 36 B2
Vitorog 71 E4
Vitovlje 71 E4
Vitré 23 D3
Vitrey 27 D1
Vitry-en-Artois 19 F2
Vitry-le-François 20 B4
Vítsa 78 C4
Vitsand 105 E2
Vittangi 94 C4
Vittangiälven 94 C4
Vitteaux 26 B2
Vittel 27 D1
Vittoria 69 D4
Vittoriosa 68 B4
Vittorio Veneto 59 E3
Vittsjö 109 D3
Vitznau 58 A2

Viù 31 E1
Vivaro 59 E3
Vivel del R Martín 41 E2
Viver 41 E3
Viverio 34 B1
Viverols 29 F1
Viveros 44 B1
Vivier, le 18 B4
Viviers 30 B2
Vivonne 25 D4
Vizille 30 C2
Vižinada 70 A3
Vizitsa 83 F2
Vižnica 113 D3
Vizzavona 33 F3
Vizzavona, Col de 33 F3
Vizzini 69 D4
Vjosë 114 B4
Vlaardingen 16 B3
Vladičin Han 77 E1
Vladevci 77 F3
Vladimirci 72 C3
Vladimirovac 73 D2
Vladimirovo 77 F3
Vladimir-
  Volynskij 112 C2
Vlagtwedde 17 E1
Vlaháva 83 D1
Vlahérna (Ípiros) 82 C2
Vlahérna
  (Pelopónissos) 86 C2
Vlahiótis 87 D3
Vlahokerassiá 87 D2
Vlahomándra 83 D4
Vlahópoulo 86 C2
Vlanen 16 C3
Vlasenica 72 B4
Vlašić (Bosna i
  Hercegovina) 71 E4
Vlašić (Srbija) 72 C3
Vlasina Okruglica 77 E1
Vlasinsko jez 77 E1
Vlasotince 77 E1
Vlássio 83 D2
Vlásti 79 D3
Vlieland 16 C1
Vlihó 82 B3
Vlissingen 16 B4
Vlorë 114 B4
Vlotho 17 F2
Vltava 53 F3
Vobbia 60 A2
Vočin 71 E2
Vöcklabruck 56 C3
Vodice (Rijeka) 70 A3
Vodice (Šibenik) 74 C1
Vodna 73 E3
Vodňany 56 C1
Vodnjan 70 A4
Voe 3 F1
Vogatsikó 79 D3
Vogel 70 A2
Vogelsberg 52 A4
Vogelsdorf 49 E2
Voghera 60 A2
Vogošća 72 B4
Vohenstrauß 56 B1
Vöhringen 55 E3
Void 20 C4
Voikoski 107 F1
Vóïo, Óros 78 C4
Voiron 30 C1
Voiteur 26 C3
Vojens 108 A3

Vojka 72 C3
Vojmsjön 97 F4
Vojnić 70 C3
Vojnik 70 B1
Vojska 73 D3
Vojtanov 53 D4
Vojvodina 72 C2
Vólakas 80 B1
Volary 56 C2
Volchov 111 E1
Volchov R 111 E1
Volda 100 A3
Voldafjorden 100 A2
Volders 59 D2
Volendam 16 C2
Volga 111 F1
Volímes 86 A1
Volissós 85 E4
Volkach 52 B4
Völkermarkt 70 B1
Völklingen 54 B2
Volkmarsen 52 A2
Volkovija 77 D3
Volkovysk 110 C4
Volmunster 21 E3
Voločisk 113 D2
Volokolamsk 111 F2
Volonne 31 D3
Vólos 83 F2
Voložin 111 D4
Volpiano 31 E1
Volta 60 C1
Volterra 60 C4
Voltri 60 A3
Volturara Appula 64 B3
Volturino, Mte 64 C4
Volturno 64 A3
Volvic 26 A4
Vólvi, L 80 B3
Volyn' 113 D2
Volyně 56 C1
Vónitsa 82 C3
Vonnas 26 C4
Voors 17 D2
Voorschoten 16 B3
Voorthuizen 16 C2
Vopnafjörður 96 C1
Vorarlberg 58 B2
Vóras, Óros 79 E2
Vorau 57 E3
Vorchdorf 56 C3
Vorden 17 D3
Vordernberg 57 E3
Vorderrhein 58 A3
Vorderriß 56 A4
Vordingborg 108 C4
Vorë 76 C4
Voreppe 30 C1
Vorey 30 A1
Vóri 91 D4
Vória Píndos 78 C4
Vóries Sporádes 84 C2
Vøringfossen 104 B2
Vórios Evoïkós
  Kólpos 83 F3
Vório Stenó
  Kerkíras 82 A1
Vorma 105 D3
Vormsi 110 B1
Vorna 99 D4
Voroneț 113 D3
Vorsfelde 48 B4
Vorskla 113 F2
Võrtsjärv 110 C2
Võru 110 C2

Vosges (Dépt) 27 D1
Voss 104 B2
Votice 53 F4
Votonóssi 82 C1
Voúdia 88 B4
Vouga, R 38 C1
Vouglans, Lac de 27 D3
Vouhorína 79 D4
Vouillé 25 D3
Voukoliés 90 B3
Voúla 87 F1
Voulgára 83 D2
Voulkariá, L 82 B3
Voúlpi 83 D3
Voulte, la 30 B2
Vouná Goúras 83 E2
Vouraïkós 86 C1
Voúrinos, Óros 79 D4
Vourkári 88 A2
Vourliótes 89 E1
Voúrvoura 87 D2
Vourvouroú 80 B4
Voutás 83 F3
Vouvant 24 C3
Vouvray 25 D2
Voúxa, Akr 90 B3
Vouzela 38 B1
Vouziers 20 B3
Voves 25 E1
Vovoússa 78 C4
Voxnan 101 E4
Vöyri 102 B2
Voz 70 B3
Vozarci 77 E3
Voznesensk 113 F3
Vrå 108 D2
Vraca 115 D2
Vraca pl 77 D3
Vračev Gaj 73 D2
Vračevšnica 73 D4
Vrådal 104 B3
Vraháti 87 D1
Vrahiónas, Óros 86 A2
Vrahnéika 86 C1
Vrams-
  Gunnarstorp 108 C3
Vrana 70 B4
Vrancei, M 113 D3
Vranduk 71 F4
Vranica 71 E4
Vranja 70 A3
Vranjak 75 F2
Vranje 77 E2
Vranjska Banja 77 E2
Vranovská přehr
  nádrž 57 E1
Vran pl 75 E1
Vransko 70 B2
Vransko jezero 74 C1
Vrástama 80 B3
Vratarnica 73 F4
Vratnica 77 D2
Vratnik 70 B3
Vratno 70 C1
Vravróna 88 A1
Vrbanja 72 B3
Vrbanja R 71 E3
Vrbas 72 B2
Vrbas R 71 E3
Vrbaška 71 E3
Vrbas klisura 71 E4
Vrbljani 71 D4
Vrbnica 77 D3

Vrbnik 70 B3
Vrboska 75 E2
Vrbovec 71 D2
Vrbovsko 70 B3
Vrčin 73 D3
Vrdnik 72 C2
Vreden 17 E3
Vrela 76 C2
Vrelo (Hrvatska) 70 C4
Vrelo (Srbija) 73 E4
Vreoci 72 C3
Vresse 20 C2
Vrésthena 87 D3
Vreta Kloster 106 A4
Vrginmost 70 C3
Vrgorac 75 E2
Vrh Kapele 70 C3
Vrhnika 70 A2
Vrhpolje 71 D4
Vría 79 E4
Vrínena 83 F3
Vríssa 85 F3
Vrisses 90 C3
Vrissiá 83 E2
Vrissoúla 82 B2
Vrlika 75 D1
Vrnjačka Banja 73 D4
Vrnograč 70 C3
Vrondádos 85 F4
Vrondamás 87 D3
Vronderó 78 C3
Vrondissí 91 D4
Vrondoú 79 E4
Vrondoús, Óri 80 B2
Vrossína 82 B1
Vrouhás 91 E3
Vrpolje (Osijek) 72 B2
Vrpolje (Šibenik) 75 D1
Vršac 73 D2
Vršani 72 B3
Vrsar 70 A3
Vrsi 70 C4
Vrška Čuka 73 F4
Vrtac 76 B2
Vrtoče 71 D4
Vrutok 77 D3
Vučitrh 77 D2
Vučjak 77 F3
Vučje 77 E1
Vučkovica 73 D4
Vue des Alpes 27 E2
Vuka 71 F2
Vukovar 72 B2
Vulcano, I 69 D2
Vulture, Mte 64 C3
Vuohijärvi 107 F2
Vuohijärvi L 107 F1
Vuokatti 99 E4
Vuokkijärvi 99 F3
Vuokojaure 94 C3
Vuoksenniska 103 F3
Vuolijoki 99 E4
Vuollerim 98 B2
Vuolvojaure 98 A2
Vuonislahti 103 F2
Vuorji 95 D2
Vuosjärvi 103 D2
Vuoskuvarri 95 D3
Vuostimo 99 E2
Vuotso 95 E3
Vyškov 57 F1
Vyšnij Voloček 111 E2

W

Waal	16 C3	Wädenswil	58 A2	Waidring	59 E1	Waldeck	52 A2	Waldmünchen	56 B1	Wallerstein	55 E2	Wandlitz	49 E3
Waalwijk	16 C3	Wagenfeld	17 F2	Waischenfeld	52 C4	Waldenbuch	55 D3	Waldsassen	53 D4	Wallingford	9 E2	Wanfried	52 B2
Waasmunster	50 B3	Wageningen	17 D3	Waizenkirchen	56 C2	Waldenburg	53 D3	Waldshut	54 C4	Walls	3 F2	Wangen	55 E4
Wabern	52 A3	Waging	56 B3	Wakefield	7 D2	Waldfischbach-		Walensee	58 B2	Walsall	9 E1	Wangenbourg	21 E4
Wachau	57 E2	Wagrain	59 E1	Wałbrzych	112 A2	Burgalben	54 B2	Walenstadt	58 B2	Walsrode	48 A4	Wangerland-
Wachow	49 D4	Wągrowiec	112 A1	Walchensee	56 A4	Waldheim	53 E2	Wales	8 C1	Walsum	17 D3	Hooksiel	47 E3
Wächtersbach	52 A4	Wahlstedt	48 A2	Walcheren	16 B3	Waldkappel	52 B3	Wallasey	6 B2	Waltershausen	52 B3	Wangerooge	47 E2
Waddeneilanden	16 C1	Waiblingen	55 D2	Walchsee	59 D1	Waldkirch	54 C3	Walldorf	54 C2	Walton-on-the-		Wängi	58 A1
Wadebridge	8 B3	Waidhaus	56 B1	Wałcz	112 A1	Waldkirchen	56 C2	Walldürn	55 D1	Naze	11 D2	Wanna	47 F2
		Waidhofen (Ybbs)	57 D3	Wald	58 A2	Waldkraiburg	56 B3	Wallenfels	52 C4	Waltrop	17 E3	Wanne-Eickel	17 E3
		Waidhofen (Thaya)	57 E2	Waldbröl	17 E4	Wald-Michelbach	54 C1	Wallersdorf	56 B2	Wanderup	48 A1	Wantage	9 E2

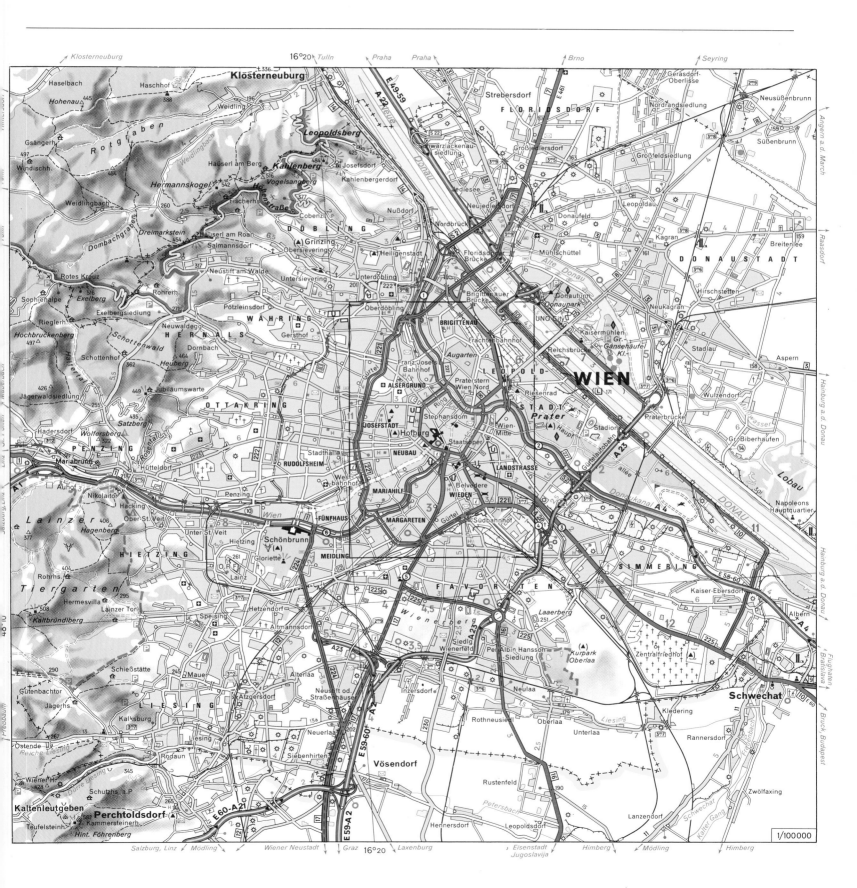

1/100000

Wantzenau, la 21 F4
Wanzleben 52 C1
Warburg 52 A2
Wardenburg 47 F3
Ware 9 F2
Waregem 50 B3
Wareham 9 D3
Waremme 50 C3
Waren 49 D2
Warendorf 17 F3
Warin 48 C2
Warkworth 5 E3
Warmensteinach 53 D4
Warminster 9 E3
Warnemunde 48 C2
Warnow 48 C2
Warrenpoint 13 E3
Warrington 6 B2
Warstein 17 F3
Warszawa 112 B1
Warszów 49 E2
Warta 49 F3
Warth 58 B2
Wartha 52 B3
Warwick 9 E1
Warwickshire 9 E1
Washington 5 E4
Wasselonne 21 E4
Wassen 58 A3
Wassenaar 16 B3
Wassenberg 17 D4
Wasseralfingen 55 E2
Wasserbillig 21 D2
Wasserburg 56 B3
Wasser-Kuppe 52 B3
Wassertrüdingen 55 E2
Wassigny 20 A2
Wassy 20 C4
Wasungen 52 B3
Watchet 8 C3
Waterfoot 13 E1
Waterford 15 D4
Waterford (Co) 14 C4
Waterford Harbour 15 D4
Waterloo 50 B3
Waternish Pt 2 B3
Waterville 14 A4
Watford 9 F2
Wattens 59 D2
Watton 11 D1
Wattwil 58 A2
Watzmann 56 C4
Waulsort 50 C4
Waveney 11 D1
Wavre 50 C3
Waxweiler 51 D4
Wear 5 E4
Wechsel 57 E3
Wedel 48 A3
Wedemark-Mellendorf 48 A4
Weener 47 E3
Weert 17 D4
Weferlingen 48 C4
Wegberg 17 D4
Wegeleben 52 C1
Weggis 27 F2
Węgorzewo 110 B4
Węgorzyno 49 F2
Wegscheid 56 C2
Wehr 54 C4
Weibersbrunn 52 A4
Weichshofen 56 B2
Weida 53 D3
Weiden 56 A1
Weikersheim 55 D1
Weilburg 51 F4
Weil der Stadt 55 D2
Weilheim (Baden-Württemberg) 55 D3
Weilheim (Bayern) 56 A3
Weimar 52 C3
Weinfelden 58 A1
Weingarten 55 D4
Weinheim 54 C1
Weinsberg 55 D2
Weismain 52 C4
Weißbriach 59 F2
Weiße Elster 53 D3
Weißenbach 58 C1
Weißenberg 53 F2
Weißenburg 55 F2
Weißenfels 53 D2
Weißenhorn 55 E3
Weißenkirchen 57 E2
Weißensee 52 C2
Weißensee (L) 59 F2
Weissenstadt 53 D4
Weissenstein 27 E2
Weissfluhgipfel 58 B2
Weißkirchen 57 D4
Weißkugel 58 C2
Weißwasser 53 F1
Weitra 57 D2
Weiz 57 E4
Wejherowo 110 A4
Weldon 9 F1
Welgetschlag 57 D2
Welland 9 F1
Wellin 20 C2
Wellingborough 9 F1
Wellington 9 D3
Wellington Bridge 15 D4
Wells 9 D3
Wells-next-the-Sea 7 E3
Wels 56 C3
Welsberg 59 D2
Welschnofen 59 D3
Welshpool 9 D1
Weltenburg 55 F2
Welwyn Garden City 9 F2
Welzheim 55 D2
Wem 6 B3
Wemding 55 E2
Wemyss Bay 4 C2
Wendelstein 56 B4
Wenden 52 B1
Wengen 27 F3
Wenns 58 C2
Werbellinsee 49 E3
Werben 48 C3
Werdau 53 D3
Werder 49 D4
Werdohl 17 E4
Werfen 59 E1
Werl 17 F3
Werlte 17 E1
Wermelskirchen 17 E4
Wermsdorf 53 E2
Wernberg 56 B1
Werne 17 E3
Werneck 52 B4
Werneuchen 49 E4
Wernigerode 52 C1
Werra 52 B3
Wertach 55 E4
Wertach (R) 55 E3
Wertheim 55 D1
Werther 17 F2
Wertingen 55 E3
Wervik 50 A3
Wesel 17 D3
Wesenberg 49 D3
Wesendorf 48 B4
Weser 47 F3
Weser-Elbe-Kanal 48 C4
Wesselburen 47 F2
Wessobrunn 56 A3
West Auckland 5 E4
West Bridgford 7 D3
Westbury 9 D3
Westendorf 59 D1
Westenholz 48 A4
Westerburg 51 F4
Westerholt 47 E3
Westerland 47 F1
Westerlo 50 C3
Westernbödefeld 17 F4
Western Isles 2 B2
Wester Ross 2 C3
Westerstede 47 E3
Westerwald 51 E3
Westhofen 54 C1
West Kilbride 4 C2
West Linton 5 D2
West Loch Tarbert 2 A2
Westmeath 12 C3
West Mersea 11 D2
Weston-Super-Mare 9 D2
Westport 12 B3
Westray 3 E1
Westray Firth 3 E1
West Sussex 9 F3
West-Terschelling 16 C1
West-Vlaanderen 50 A3
Wetherby 7 D2
Wetter 17 E3
Wetteren 50 B3
Wettin 52 C2
Wettringen 17 E2
Wetwang 7 D1
Wetzikon 58 A2
Wetzlar 51 F3
Wexford 15 D3
Wexford (Co) 15 D3
Weyer-Markt 57 D3
Weyhausen 48 B4
Weyhill 9 E3
Weymouth 9 D3
Weyregg 56 C3
Whaley Bridge 6 C2
Whalsay 3 F1
Wharfe 6 C1
Whernside 6 C1
Whitburn 5 D2
Whitby 5 F4
Whitchurch 6 B3
White Bridge 2 C4
Whitehaven 5 D4
Whitehead 13 E2
Whiteness 3 F2
Whiten Head 2 C2
Whithorn 4 C4
Whitland 8 B2
Whitley Bay 5 E3
Whitstable 11 D3
Whittlesey 9 F1
Wick 3 D2
Wickford 11 D2
Wicklow 13 E4
Wicklow (Co) 13 D4
Wicklow Head 13 E4
Wicklow Mts 13 D4
Widnes 6 B2
Wiehe 52 C2
Wiek 49 D1
Wieliczka 112 B3
Wieluń 112 B2
Wien 57 F2
Wiener-Neudorf 57 F2
Wiener Neustadt 57 F3
Wienerwald 57 E3
Wies (A) 70 B1
Wies (D) 56 A4
Wiesau 53 D4
Wiesbaden 51 F4
Wieselburg 57 E3
Wiesenburg 53 D1
Wiesensteig 55 D3
Wiesentheid 55 E1
Wiesenttal 52 C4
Wiesing 59 D1
Wiesloch 54 C2
Wiesmath 57 F3
Wiesmoor 47 E3
Wigan 6 C2
Wight, I of 9 E4
Wigton 5 D4
Wigtown 4 C3
Wigtown B 4 C4
Wijhe 17 D2
Wil 58 A2
Wildalpen 57 D3
Wildbad 54 C2
Wildeck 52 B3
Wildeshausen 17 F1
Wildon 57 E4
Wildspitze 58 C2
Wildstrubel 27 E3
Wilfersdorf 57 F2
Wilhelmina kan 16 C3
Wilhelm Pieck-Stadt 53 F1
Wilhelmsburg (A) 57 E3
Wilhelmsburg (D) 48 A3
Wilhelmshaven 47 F3
Wilhering 57 D2
Wilkau-Haßlau 53 D3
Willebroek 50 B3
Willemstad 16 B3
Willingen 17 F4
Williton 8 C3
Wilmslow 6 C2
Wilnsdorf 17 F4
Wilsdruff 53 E2
Wilseder Berg 48 A3
Wilster 48 A2
Wilton 9 E3
Wiltshire 9 E3
Wiltz 21 D2
Wimborne Minster 9 E3
Wimereux 19 E1
Wincanton 9 D3
Winchcombe 9 E2
Winchelsea 11 D3
Winchester 9 E3
Windeck 51 E3
Windermere 5 D4
Windischeschenbach 53 D4
Windischgarsten 57 D3
Windsbach 55 E1
Windsor 9 F2
Winkleigh 8 C3
Winklern 59 E2
Winnenden 55 D2
Winnigstedt 52 B1
Winnweiler 54 B1
Winschoten 47 E3
Winsen (Celle) 48 A4
Winsen (Lüneburg) 48 B3
Winsford 6 C3
Winsum 47 D3
Winterberg 17 F4
Winterswijk 17 D3
Winterthur 58 A2
Wintzenheim 27 E1
Wipper 52 C2
Wipperfürth 17 E4
Wisbech 10 C1
Wischhafen 48 A2
Wisełka 49 E2
Wishaw 4 C2
Wisła 110 B4
Wismar 48 C2
Wissant 19 E1
Wissembourg 21 F3
Wissen 51 E3
Witham 7 D3
Witham 11 D2
Withernsea 7 E2
Witney 9 E2
Witnica 49 F3
Wittdün 47 F1
Witte 49 D1
Witten 17 E3
Wittenberg 53 D1
Wittenberge 48 C3
Wittenburg 48 B3
Wittichenau 53 F2
Wittingen 48 B4
Wittlich 51 E4
Wittmund 47 E3
Wittow 49 D1
Wittstock 49 D3
Witzenhausen 52 B2
Władysławowo 110 A4
Włocławek 112 B1
Włodawa 112 C2
Wöbbelin 48 C3
Woburn 9 F2
Woburn Abbey 9 F2
Woensdrecht 16 B4
Woerden 16 C3
Wohlen 27 F2
Woippy 21 D3
Woking 9 F3
Wokingham 9 F2
Wołczenica 49 F2
Woldegk 49 E2
Wolfach 54 C3
Wolfegg 55 E4
Wolfen 53 D2
Wolfenbüttel 52 B1
Wolfhagen 52 A2
Wolfratshausen 56 A3
Wolfsberg 70 B1
Wolfsburg 48 B4
Wolgast 49 E2
Wolin 49 E2
Wolin (Reg) 49 E2
Woliński Park Narodowy 49 E2
Wolkenstein 59 D3
Wolkersdorf 57 F2
Wöllersdorf 57 F3
Wollersheim 51 D3
Wollin 49 D4
Wolmirstedt 48 C4
Wolsingham 5 E4
Wolsztyn 112 A2
Wolvega 17 D1
Wolverhampton 9 E1
Wolverton 9 F1
Wolznach 55 F2
Woodbridge 11 D1
Woodhall Spa 7 E3
Woodstock 9 E2
Wooler 5 E3
Worb 27 E2
Worbis 52 B2
Worcester 9 D1
Wörgl 59 D1
Workington 5 D4
Worksop 7 D2
Workum 16 C1
Wörlitz 53 D1
Wormerveer 16 C2
Wormhout 19 F1
Worms 54 C1
Worms Head 8 C2
Wörnitz 55 E2
Wörrstadt 54 C1
Wœrth 21 E3
Wörth (Donau) 56 B2
Wörth (Main) 55 D1
Wörth (Rheinland-Pfalz) 54 C2
Worther See 70 A1
Worthing 10 C3
Woświn, Jez 49 F2
Wragby 7 D3
Wrath, Cape 2 C2
Wrecsam 6 B3
Wrexham 6 B3
Wriezen 49 E3
Wrocław 112 A2
Wroughton 9 E2
Września 112 A1
Wulfen 17 E3
Wullowitz 57 D2
Wümme 48 A3
Wümme *R* 48 A3
Wünnenberg 17 F3
Wünsdorf 49 E4
Wunsiedel 53 D4
Wunstorf 48 A4
Wuppertal 17 E4
Würzburg 55 D1
Wurzen 53 D2
Wurzen-Paß 59 F2
Wusterhausen 49 D3
Wustrow (Rostock) 48 C1
Wustrow (Wismar) 48 C2
Wuustwezel 50 C2
Wye, R 9 D2
Wyk 47 F1
Wymondham 11 D1

X

Xallas, R 34 A2
Xanten 17 D3
Xánthi 81 D2
Xánthi (Nomos) 81 D2
Xarrama, R 42 B1
Xàtiva 41 E4
Xeresa 41 E4
Xerovoúni 82 C2
Xerta 41 F2
Xertigny 27 D1
Xesta, Pto de la 34 C1
Xifianí 79 E2
Xilagani 81 E2
Xilikí 83 E3
Xilís, Akr 87 D4
Xilókastro 87 D1
Xilopáriko 83 D2
Xilópoli 80 A2
Xilóskalo 90 B3
Xiniáda 83 E3
Xinó Neró 79 D3
Xinzo de Limia 34 B3
Xiró 83 F3
Xirokámbi 87 D3
Xirókambos 89 E3
Xirolímni 79 D3
Xistral 34 B1
Xódoto, Akr 89 D3
Xubia 34 B1
Xunqueira de Ambía 34 B3

Y

Yaiza 42 C4
Yalova 115 F3
Yanguas 36 B3
Yare 7 F4
Yarmouth 9 E3
Yarmouth, Great 7 F4
Ybbs 57 D2
Ybbs *R* 57 D3
Yebra 40 B2
Yecla 45 D1
Yeguas, Emb de 43 F2
Yeguas, R de las 43 F1
Yell 3 F1
Yell Sd 3 F1
Yelmo 44 B2
Yeltes, R 39 D1
Yenne 27 D4
Yeovil 9 D3
Yepes 40 B3
Yerville 19 D3
Yesa 36 C2
Yesa, Emb de 37 D2
Yeşilova 115 F4
Yeste 44 C1
Yeu, I d' 24 A3
Yèvre 26 A2
Y-Fenni 9 D2
Yıldız Dağları 115 E3
Ylämaa 103 F4
Ylämylly 103 F2
Yläne 107 D2
Ylihärmä 102 C2
Yli-Kärppä 99 D3
Ylikiiminki 99 D3
Yli-Kitka 99 E2
Yli-li 99 D3
Yli-Muonio 95 D4
Yli-Nampa 99 D2
Yli-Olhava 99 D3
Ylistaro 102 B2
Ylitornio 98 C2
Ylivieska 102 C1
Ylläs 95 D4
Ylläsjärvi 95 D4
Ylöjärvi 102 C3
Yngaren 106 A4
Yonne 20 A4
Yonne (Dépt) 26 A1
York 7 D2
Yorkshire Dales Nat Pk 6 C1
Youghal 14 C4
Youghal B 14 C4
Yoxford 11 E1
Ypäjä 107 E2
Yport 19 D2
Yppäri 99 D4
Ypres 50 A3
Yr Wyddgrug 6 B3
Yser 19 F1
Yssingeaux 30 B1
Ystad 109 D4
Y Trallwng 9 D1
Ytterhogdal 101 E3
Yttermalung 105 E2
Yuncos 40 A2
Yunquera 43 E4
Yunquera de Henares 40 B2
Yuste 39 E2
Yverdon 27 E3
Yvetot 19 D3
Yvoir 50 C4
Yvoire 27 D3

Z

Zaandam 16 C2
Žabali 72 C2
Žabari 73 D3
Zablaće 75 D1
Žabljak (Durmitor) 76 B1
Žabljak (Titograd) 76 B3
Žabno 71 D2
Zabok 70 C2
Zabrdđe 72 B3
Zadar 70 C1
Zadarski kanal 70 B4
Zadvarje 75 E2
Zafarraya 43 F3
Zafóra, Ni 92 C2
Zafra 43 D1
Žaga 70 A2
Žagań 112 A2
Zaglavak 72 C4
Zagorá 83 F2
Zagória 82 C1
Zagorje 70 B2
Zagreb 70 C2
Žagubica 73 E3
Zagvozd 75 E2
Zahara de los Atunes 43 D4
Zaháro 86 B2
Zahinos 42 C1
Zahna 53 D1
Záhony 112 C3
Zaidín 37 E4
Zajas 77 D3
Zaječar 73 F3
Zákinthos 86 A1
Zákinthos, N 86 A1
Zakopane 112 B3
Zákros 91 F4
Zala 112 A4
Zalaegerszeg 112 A4
Zalamea de la Serena 43 E1
Zalamea la Real 42 C2
Zalău 112 C4
Žalec 70 B2
Zaleščiki 113 D3
Zalew Wiślany 110 B4
Zalla 36 A1
Zálongo 82 B2
Zaltbommel 16 C3
Zalužnica 70 C4
Zambrana 36 B2
Zamora 35 D4
Zamość 112 C2
Záncara, R 40 B4
Zandvoort 16 B2
Zángano, Pto del 39 D4
Zanglivéri 80 A3
Zannone, I 63 F4
Zaorejas 40 C2
Zaostrog 75 E2
Zaovine Vežanja 72 C4
Zapadnaja Dvina 111 E2
Zapadnaja Dvina R 111 E2
Zapadna Morava 73 D4
Zapardiel, R 39 F1
Zapatón, R 39 D3
Zápio 83 E2
Zapponeta 64 C3
Zaprešić 70 C2
Zaragoza 37 D3
Zárakes 84 B4
Zaratán 35 E4
Zarautz 36 C1
Zarcilla de Ramos 44 C2

Zárkos 83 E1
Zarós 91 D4
Zaroúhla 87 D1
Zarrentin 48 B3
Žary 112 A2
Zarza la Mayor 39 D2
Zasieki 53 F1
Žaškov 113 E2
Žatec 53 E3
Zatoka Gdańska 110 B4
Zaton 75 F2
Zavala 75 F2
Zavattarello 60 A2
Zavidovići 71 F4
Zavlaka 72 C3
Zavratnica 70 B4
Zawiercie 112 B2
Žažina 71 D2
Zbaraž 113 D2
Zbraslav 53 F4
Žďár nad Sázavou 112 A3
Zdenac 70 C3
Zdice 53 F4
Ždrelac 74 C1
Ždrelo 73 E3
Zdunje 77 D3
Zduńska Wola 112 B2
Zebë, Maj'e 76 C3
Zebreira 38 C2
Žednik 72 B1
Zeebrugge 50 A3
Zeeland 16 B3
Žegovac 77 D2
Žegra 77 D2
Žegulja 75 F2
Zehdenick 49 D3
Zeist 16 C3
Zeitz 53 D2
Zejtun 68 B4
Žekovec 70 B1
Zele 50 B3
Zelengora 76 A1
Zelengora (Reg) 76 A1
Zelenika 76 A3
Zelenogorsk 111 D1
Železná Ruda 56 C1
Železnik 72 C3
Železniki 70 A2
Železnogorsk 111 F4
Zelina 70 C2
Zélio 83 F3
Željezno Polje 71 F4
Željin 73 D4
Zell (D) 54 B1
Zell (Oberösterreich) 56 C2
Zell (Tirol) 59 D2
Zella-Mehlis 52 C3
Zell am See 59 E1
Zellerrain 57 E3
Zeltweg 57 D4
Zelzate 50 B3
Zemun 72 C3
Zenica 71 F4
Zen'kov 113 F2
Žep 72 B4
Žepče 71 F4
Zerbst 53 D1
Zeri 60 B3
Zermatt 27 F4
Zernez 58 B3
Zerqan 77 D4
Zestoa 36 B1
Zeta 76 B2
Zetel 47 E3

Zeulenroda 53 D3
Zeven 48 A3
Zevenaar 17 D3
Zevgaráki 82 C4
Zevgolatió 86 C3
Zevio 60 C1
Zêzere, R 38 C2
Zicavo 33 F4
Žiča 73 D4
Židlochovice 57 F1
Ziefsdorf 57 E2
Ziegenrück 52 C3
Ziesar 49 D4
Zielona Góra 112 A2
Zierikzee 16 B3
Zierzow 48 C3
Zi, Guri i 77 D4
Zijemlje 75 F1
Žilina 112 B3
Žilindar 76 C1
Ziller 59 D2
Zillertal 59 D1
Zimnicea 115 D2
Zinal 27 F4
Zingst 49 D1
Zinnowitz 49 E1
Zinnwald 53 E3
Zirbitzkogel 57 D4
Zirchow 49 E2
Žiri 70 A2
Žirje 74 C1
Zirl 58 C2
Zirndorf 55 D4
Zirndorf 55 E1
Žiros 91 F4
Zistersdorf 57 F2
Žitište 72 C2
Žitkovac 73 E4
Žitkoviči 113 D1
Žitomir 113 E2
Žitoradđa 77 D1
Zittau 53 F2
Živinice 71 F3
Živogošće 75 E2
Žizdra 111 F3
Zjum 77 D2
Zlarin 75 D1
Zlarin I 75 D1
Zlata 77 D1
Zlatar 76 B1
Zlatar Bistrica 70 C2
Zlatarevo 77 F3
Zlatari 77 D1
Zlatarsko jez 76 B1
Zlatibor 72 C4
Zlatica 72 C4
Zlatni Pjasăci 115 E2
Zlatkop 77 E2
Zletovo 77 E2
Žljebovi 72 B4
Žlobin 111 E4
Zlot 73 E3
Žlutice 53 E4
Zmajevo 72 C2
Žman 74 C1
Žmerinka 113 E3
Žminj 70 A3
Znamenka 113 F2
Znojmo 57 E1
Zöblitz 53 E3
Zoetermeer 16 B3
Zogaj 76 C3
Zollikofen 27 E2
Zoločev 113 D2
Zolotonoša 113 F2
Žoltyje Vody 113 F2

Zonári, Akr 93 F1
Zóni 81 F1
Zoniá 91 D3
Zonza 33 F4
Zoodóhos Pigí (Makedonía) 79 E3
Zoodóhos Pigii (Pelopónissos) 87 F2
Zörbig 53 D2
Zorita 39 E3
Zossen 49 E4
Zoúrvas, Akr 87 F2
Zoutkamp 47 D3
Zoutleeuw 50 C3
Zoúzouli 78 C4
Zrenjanin 72 C2
Zrin 71 D3
Zrinska gora 71 D3
Zrmanja R 74 C1
Zrmanja 75 D1
Žrnovnica 75 D2
Zrze 77 D2
Zschopau 53 E3
Zschopau R 53 E3
Zubcov 111 F2
Zubin Potoku 76 C2

Žuč 77 D1
Zucaina 41 E3
Zuckerhütl 58 C2
Zudar 49 D1
Zuera 37 D3
Zufre 43 D2
Zufre, Emb de 43 D2
Zug 58 A2
Zugspitze 55 F4
Zuid Beveland 16 B4
Zuidelijk-Flevoland 16 C2
Zuid Holland 16 B3
Zuidlaren 17 D1
Žujar, Emb de 39 E4
Žujar, R 43 E1
Žukovka 111 F3
Zuljana 75 E2
Zumaia 36 B1
Zumárraga 36 B1
Zundert 16 C3
Zuoz 58 B3
Županja 71 F3
Zupich 51 D3
Žur 77 D3

Zürich 58 A2
Zurrieq 68 B4
Zürs 58 B2
Zurzach 58 A1
Zusmarshausen 55 E3
Zut 74 C1
Žuta Lokva 70 C3
Zutphen 17 D2
Žužemberk 70 B2
Zvečan 77 D1
Zvenigorodka 113 E2
Zvijezda nac park 72 C4
Zvikovec 53 E4
Zvolen 112 B3
Zvonce 77 E1
Zvorničko jez 72 B4
Zvornik 72 B4
Zweibrücken 54 B2
Zweisimmen 27 E3
Zwenkau 53 D2

Zwiefalten 55 D3
Zwiesel 56 C2
Zwijndrecht 16 C3
Zwolle 17 D2
Žyrardów 112 B1
Żywiec 112 B3

Þ

Þingeyri 96 A1
Þingvallavatn 96 A2
Þistilfjörður 96 C1
Þjórsá 96 B2
Þorlákshöfn 96 A2
Þórshöfn 96 C1
Þórsmörk 96 B3

5/9 6/9
594 674

Notes

Ed - Hull 250 12:15 3:15

∅ 3/9 Edinburgh → Hull 250 12:15 - 5:15
26.56 £ 15 mins @ Mums, 15 mins @ Scotch Corner
587 4/9 Zebrugge-Assmannshausen 337 9:00 - 4.30
30 mins @ grotty snack bar E40 (26)
1 hr @ service stn outside KÖLN
594 5/9 trip to Koblenz 80 45 mins e/u
L 6/9 12:10 Assmannshausen 674
15 mins @ 2 service stations
2 hours @ Regensburg
A 6/9 7:30 Passau 1004
L 7/9 2:30 Passau 1004
333/10.20 a few stops looking for credit card signs, money & food
A 7/9 7:00 Vienna 1192
L 10/9 12:10 Vienna 1192
day trip along danube
A 10/9 6:30 Vienna 1342
L 11/9 12:00 Vienna 1342
302/01.98 A 11/9 6:30 Templitz 1541
L 13/9 2:50
A 5:30 Salzburg 1609
L 14 4:35
A 7:00 Innsbruck 1724
347.03/10.18 L 15 10:00 2037 Bash
A 5:00 Baveno 2037
L 18 11:05

A 5:00 Chamonix 2197
L 21/9 8:15 am 2197
A 8:15 p.m. 2821
L 23/9 4:05 p. 2821
4.30 2831

2108.5 FF / 5.98 FF
Lux 790.- / 22.-